D1825945

1 MONTH OF
FREE
READING

at

www.ForgottenBooks.com

By purchasing this book you are eligible for one month membership to ForgottenBooks.com, giving you unlimited access to our entire collection of over 1,000,000 titles via our web site and mobile apps.

To claim your free month visit:

www.forgottenbooks.com/free651899

ISBN 978-0-656-80661-4
PIBN 10651899

REPORTS

OF

CASES ARGUED AND DETERMINED

IN THE

SUPREME COURT

OF THE

STATE OF WISCONSIN,

WITH

TABLES OF THE CASES AND PRINCIPAL MATTERS.

FREDERIC K. CONOVER,

OFFICIAL REPORTER.

VOLUME 71.

FEBRUARY 28 — MAY 12, 1888.

CHICAGO:

CALLAGHAN & COMPANY,

LAW BOOK PUBLISHERS.

1888.

DAVID ATWOOD,
PRINTER AND STEREOTYPER,
MADISON, WIS.

JUDGES OF THE SUPREME COURT

OF THE

STATE OF WISCONSIN

DURING THE PERIOD COMPRISED IN THIS VOLUME.

ORSAMUS COLE, CHIEF JUSTICE.

WILLIAM P. LYON,

DAVID TAYLOR,

HARLOW S. ORTON, } ASSOCIATE JUSTICES.

JOHN B. CASSODAY,

Attorney General, CHARLES E. ESTABROOK.

Clerk, - - - CLARENCE KELLOGG.

ERRORS NOTED IN THIS AND PREVIOUS VOLUMES.

VOL. XLIIL

Page 583, headnote 3, line 3. For mortgagors, read mortgagees.

VOL. 69.

Page 5, headnote 7, line 6. *Dele* the word contributory.

Pages 564–575, running title. For Life Ins. Co., read Fire Ins. Co.

VOL. 70.

Page 558, line — 11. For sec. 3, read sec. 1.

Page 727, in table. Same correction.

VOL. 71.

Page 413, line — 6. For *Larkin*, read *Lakin*.

TABLE

OF THE

NAMES OF CASES

REPORTED IN THIS VOLUME.

TABLE OF CASES

CITED BY THE COURT.

CASES DETERMINED

AT THE

January Term, 1888.

Schweickhart and another, Respondents, vs. Stuewe, Appellant.

January 31 — February 28, 1888.

Sale of chattels: Delay in delivery: Acceptance: Counterclaim: Pleading: Indefiniteness.

1. In an action for the contract price of building materials, the defendant may counterclaim for damages on account of delay in the delivery and a failure to deliver a part of the quantity contracted for, even though he received and used what was delivered without objection or notice that he would claim damages.

2. In such case. where the counterclaim alleges that the defendant requested and ordered the delivery of the materials under the contract, it need not allege that he was ready and willing to receive and pay for them.

3. Where a counterclaim states the main facts which would constitute an affirmative cause of action, but does not definitely state the nature of the damages sustained, the remedy is by motion and not by demurrer.

APPEAL from the County Court of *Milwaukee* County. The case is stated in the opinion. The defendant appeals from a judgment in favor of the plaintiffs.

For the appellant there was a brief by *Fiebing & Killilea*, and oral argument by *Mr. Killilea*. To the point that even if the appellant by receiving and paying for *some* building stone furnished to him by the respondents had

thereby waived all claims for damages on account of delay, this could not affect that part of the counterclaim in
which damages are claimed for loss of time and expense incurred by him in being compelled to purchase elsewhere a
portion of the stone which the respondents had contracted
to furnish but failed to deliver, they cited Benj. on Sales
(4th Am. ed.), sec. 1032, note 19; *Highlands C. & M. Co. v.
Matthews,* 76 N. Y. 145; *Per Lee v. Beebe,* 13 Hun, 89;
Richards v. Shaw, 67 Ill. 222; *Goodwin v. Merrill,* 13 Wis.
658; *Bowker v. Hoyt,* 18 Pick. 555; *Booth v. Tyson,* 15 Vt.
515; *Fisk v. Tank,* 12 Wis. 306; *Norfolk & W. R. Co. v.
Shippers' Comp. Co.* 2 S. E. Rep. (Va.), 139; *Blood v. Wilson,* 141 Mass. 25; 3 Starkie on Evi. 1769.

For the respondents there was a brief by *Stark & Sutherland,* and oral argument by *Mr. G. E. Sutherland.* They
contended, *inter alia,* that by receiving without objection a
portion of the stone contracted to be delivered, the appellant waived any irregularity in the time of the delivery of
the part accepted. *McKinney v. Jones,* 55 Wis. 39; *Pike
v. Nash,* 3 App. Dec. (N. Y.), 610; *Merrimack Mfg. Co. v.
Quintard,* 107 Mass. 127; *Locke v. Williamson,* 40 Wis. 377;
Morford v. Mastin, 17 Am. Dec. 168, 173. The counterclaim should show a clear breach of the contract, and distinctly allege the definite damages sustained. *Miller v.
Mariners' Church,* 7 Me. 51; *Griffin v. Colver,* 16 N. Y. 489;
Blanchard v. Ely, 21 Wend. 342; *Benton v. Fay,* 64 Ill. 417;
Freeman v. Clute, 3 Barb. 424; *Ward v. N. Y. C. R. Co.*
47 N. Y. 29; *Edwards v. Sanborn,* 6 Mich. 348. It should
allege that the defendant was ready to receive the stone
and ready and willing to pay for it when it ought to have
been delivered. 2 Benj. on Sales, 1119, sec. 1305; *Smith v.
Wright,* 1 Abb. Pr. 243; *Clark v. Dales,* 20 Barb. 42; *Coon-
ley v. Anderson,* 1 Hill, 519; *Vail v. Rice,* 5 N. Y. 155;
Bronson v. Wiman, 8 id. 182; *Boody v. R. & B. R. Co.* 24
Vt. 660; *Beard v. Sloan,* 30 Ind. 279; *Sorrell v. Craig,* 8

Ala. 567. It should show that there was a difference between the market price and the contract price, or that the defendant was unable with reasonable diligence to procure the stone elewhere for use for the particular purpose, of which proposed use the plaintiffs had knowledge. Sedgw. on Dam. (6th ed.), 313, ch. 10; 2 Benj. on Sales, sec. 1305; *Chapman v. Ingram*, 30 Wis. 290; *Richardson v. Chynoweth*, 26 id. 656; *Hammer v. Schœnfelder*, 47 id. 455, 459.

ORTON, J. The respondents were engaged in quarrying and dealing in building-stone. The appellant had contracted to build a county jail for Milwaukee county. The respondents agreed to deliver to the appellant, in the city of Milwaukee, " all the building-stone needed or required by [him] in or about the erection or construction of said jail building, promptly and punctually, whenever [he] might want the same for such purpose, and without any delay on their part," at certain agreed rates. This action is for the recovery of the balance unpaid for the delivery of said stone. The appellant answered, among other things, by way of counterclaim, " that said plaintiffs have neglected and failed to perform said agreement on their part, in that they did not furnish and deliver such stone promptly and punctually when the same was wanted and needed by this defendant for such purpose, as they had agreed and bound themselves to do, but compelled him to wait for such stone for an unreasonably long time after they had been requested and ordered by this defendant to deliver the same; that this defendant, at said times, as the plaintiffs well knew, was at work upon such building with a large number of men, and that by reason of such failure, fault, and neglect on part of said plaintiffs in not delivering such stone promptly and punctually, as they had so bound themselves and agreed to do, this defendant was actually and necessarily hindered and delayed in executing and completing such work, and by reason of said premises suffered and sustained great loss of time, . . . and necessarily incurred an expense of about $400, in that he was compelled to and actually did procure and purchase such stone elsewhere, all of which to the great damage of this defendant, for which he claims the sum of four hundred dollars." The defendant prays that the plaintiffs' complaint be dismissed, and for judgment against the plaintiffs upon his counterclaim for $400 and costs. The plaintiffs replied to said counterclaim that they did deliver such stone as agreed and that the same was received by said defendant without objection. On the trial the respondents objected to any evidence of said counterclaim "because it does not state facts sufficient to constitute a counterclaim," and the court sustained said objection, and directed the jury to render a verdict for the plaintiffs for the amount of their claim. On this appeal the alleged error of sustaining the objection to any evidence of said counterclaim is the main ground urged for the reversal of the judgment, and it is unnecessary to consider any other. Those parts of the answer pertinent to this question have only been quoted. To sustain this ruling of the court, the respondents' counsel contends,—

1. That the counterclaim as to the breach and damages incurred thereby is too indefinite to constitute a substantive cause of action, and that it should allege with distinctness the nature of the damages sustained, and the definite damages sustained. In view of the well-established rule that on a demurrer *ore tenus* the pleading should be liberally construed, we think that this counterclaim states the main facts which would constitute an affirmative cause of action. It states that by the unreasonable delay the defendant suffered damages in the sum of $400, by loss of time and expenses. The building was delayed by it, and the defendant had many hands employed, and that he was compelled to procure stone elsewhere, etc. If, as to these facts, the

counterclaim is too indefinite and uncertain, the remedy is pointed out by the statute. A motion may be made to compel the defendant to make it more definite and certain. Sec. 2683, R. S.

2. That the counterclaim ought to state that the defendant was ready and willing to receive the stone at the proper time and to pay for the same. As to his being ready to receive the same, the defendant alleges that he particularly requested and ordered the delivery of the stone under the contract; and, as to his being ready to pay for the same, his contract is sufficient as to his liability and the plaintiffs' security for payment on delivery.

3. The *third* contention is the main one — that the answer shows that the defendant received the stone without objection, and had used them, so that they could not be returned; and that therefore he could not counterclaim for damages for the delay. That which was recoupment in New York and some other states before the Codes, is now a counterclaim under the statute: (1) " A cause of action arising out of the contract or transaction set forth in the complaint as the foundation of the plaintiff's claim, or connected with the subject of the action." Sec. 2656, R. S. The doctrine of recoupment would seem to be most applicable to just such a case as this. "The right of the defendant in the same action to claim damages from the plaintiff, either because he has not complied with some cross-obligation of the contract upon which he sues, or because he has violated some duty which the law imposed upon him in the making or performance of the contract." *McAllister v. Reab*, 4 Wend. 483; *M'Allister v. Reab*, 8 Wend. 109; *Mayor v. Mabie*, 13 N. Y. 151; *Epperly v. Bailey*, 3 Ind. 72; *Robertson v. Davenport*, 27 Ala. 574; *Wheat v. Dotson*, 12 Ark. 699; *Culver v. Blake*, 6 B. Mon. 528; *Ward v. Fellers*, 3 Mich. 281; *Higgins v. Lee*, 16 Ill. 495. But there was a limitation to recoupment which does not exist in the statutory coun-

terclaim in this class of cases. The damages were limited to defeat the plaintiff's claim, and for no excess, and no action could be brought for the excess. At least it was so held in many of the states. The very nature of recoupment was such that, aside from it, the plaintiff might be entitled to recover; but against such recovery, the defendant might recoup his damages on account of the plaintiff's violation of the contract. It is peculiarly applicable to that class of cases where the plaintiff is bound to deliver certain material necessary to some work or engagement of the defendant, and which he well knows he must receive even long after the time fixed by the contract, or suffer far greater damages than by the mere delay of delivery. In such a case, the plaintiff may be entitled to recover on the ground that the defendant had received and used the material, and the defendant be entitled to recoup his damages suffered by the delay or any other violation of the contract by the plaintiff, to the extent of the plaintiff's claim. The substitution of the statutory counterclaim in such cases does not change its nature in these respects. This doctrine has been so long established in this state, we need not go to other states for authority.

In *Getty v. Rountree*, 2 Pin. 379, the plaintiff, as the manufacturer, contracted to deliver to the defendant a pump designed to exhaust water from a mine, and there was an implied warranty that it would answer the purpose for which it was intended; the defendant received and used the pump, and in an action for its price he was allowed to reduce it by his damages for its failure to work well by reason of its improper construction. The court says: "To return it and resort to an action for the recovery of their money paid, would have been but adding to their losses." The case of *Fisk v. Tank*, 12 Wis. 276, was decided upon the authority of the above case, and is especially applicable to this case. That was an action for breach of a contract to make and set up on a steamboat, engines, etc., suitable for propelling the same, and for damages by delay and defective construction. The engine was received and used. One of the points made by the counsel in that case was that "the machinery was accepted and reduced to use by the plaintiff *without any sufficient notice that he would claim damages.*" That is the main point made by the respondents' counsel in this case. After that case, the doctrine ought to have been treated as settled for this state, for the arguments and opinion are very full and elaborate. This doctrine is equally favorable to the vendor, for where the contract is apportionable, as in this case, and after the delivery of part and on failure to deliver the whole, he may sue for the contract price of that already delivered, and the defendant may counterclaim his damages, against the plaintiffs' claim, for the violation of the contract in not delivering the whole. *Goodwin v. Merrill*, 13 Wis. 659. In *Ketchum v. Wells*, 19 Wis. 34, the contract was to deliver stave bolts to the defendants, to be manufactured into barrels. Those received and used were not of good quality, and the defendant was allowed to counterclaim his damages against the price of those delivered. The cases in this court cited by the learned counsel of the respondents to this point are not applicable to such a case. The plaintiffs knew for what purpose the stone they were to deliver was to be used, and are presumed to have known the consequences of the delay. This case is a strong one for the application of this doctrine. The defendant was compelled to receive the stone, although out of time, or suffer still greater loss. The objection to any evidence under the counterclaim ought to have been overruled, for the counterclaim was clearly sufficient.

By the Court.— The judgment of the county court is reversed, and the cause is remanded to the superior court of Milwaukee county for a new trial.

FALKENBERG, Respondent, vs. GORMAN, Appellant.

January 31 — February 28, 1888.

New trial: Discretion: Negligence of attorney: Stipulation.

1. Before a case had been placed on the day calendar, the defendant's attorney had twice notified her to call at his office respecting the same. On the day of the trial he telephoned twice to her place of abode that it was important that he should see her, and afterwards called twice at such place of abode, finally finding her there in bed, dead drunk. In her absence a verdict was rendered against her. *Held,* that there was no abuse of discretion in denying a motion to set aside such verdict on the ground of the negligence of her attorney.

2. The attorneys in a case stipulated that it should be placed at the foot of the calendar, but with the understanding that if reached in its regular order by a certain day it should then be tried. The stipulation was contrary to the rules of the court. The case was reached on the day mentioned, and in the absence of the defendant a verdict was rendered against her. *Held,* that the making of the stipulation furnished no reason for setting aside the verdict.

APPEAL from the County Court of *Milwaukee* County. The following statement of the case was prepared by Mr. Justice CASSODAY:

This is an action of replevin for certain baggage and effects of the plaintiff, commenced in justice's court. The defendant justified the detention by virtue of a lien as boarding-house keeper. On the trial before the justice, the plaintiff recovered. The defendant appealed to the county court. The cause was noticed for trial in that court, and placed upon the day calendar for September 29, 1886. The cause was reached for trial on the afternoon of that day, and tried in the absence of the defendant. Upon that trial, the plaintiff obtained a verdict in her favor. Up to October 4, 1886, the defendant's attorney in the cause was Mr. Simon. At or about that time, the defendant's attorneys on this appeal were substituted in his place. October 28, 1886, upon the affidavit of the defendant and another, and a certain stipulation between the attorneys, the plaintiff was ordered to show cause October 30, 1886, why said verdict should not be aside and a new trial granted. Upon the hearing of that motion, affidavits were read in opposition; one of which was made by said Simon, another by the defendant's mother, and another by one of the attorneys for the plaintiff. From the order denying said motion the defendant appeals.

For the appellant the cause was submitted on the brief of *Jared Thompson, Jr.*

For the respondent there was a brief by *Fiebing & Killilea*, and oral argument by *Mr. Killilea.*

CASSODAY, J. The limitations upon the discretion vested in trial courts in the matter of opening defaults and allowing a defense have been so often and so recently stated by this court as to require no repetition here. *Whereatt v. Ellis*, 70 Wis. 207, and cases there cited. Upon the rules thus established, we do not feel justified in holding in this case that there was any abuse of such discretion. In some particulars the affidavits were conflicting. Mr. Simon gives in detail his conduct in relation to the case from September 20, 1886, to October 4, 1886, when the case was taken from him. It appears from that affidavit that he notified the defendant by letter to call at his office respecting the case as early as September 20, 1886, but that she did not do so; that on the morning of September 28, 1886, he repeated such notice by letter, but got no response; that at 2 P. M. of that day the next day's calendar was made up, including this case, which was the sixth and last on that day's calendar; that September 29, 1886, at 8:30 A. M., he telephoned the defendant's husband at her place of abode in Milwaukee, and the response came that the defendant

was in bed; that at 9 A. M. the same was repeated, with the
same response; that he then telephoned at her said place
of abode the importance of seeing her; that at 10:30 he
called at her place of abode, and was then informed that
she was not there, and had not been there for a day or so,
but was at her mother's, sick in bed; that he then went to
her mother's house, and was there informed that she was
not there, but was at her aunt's; that he then went to her
aunt's, and was there informed that she had gone home; that
soon after 4 P. M. he again went to the defendant's house,
and was there informed by her mother that she was sick in
bed,— "dead drunk;" that he then went where he could
see into her bedroom, and there saw her in bed in an unconscious condition. The facts are stated in a way to
carry conviction; and in relation to her condition and
some other particulars Mr. Simon was corroborated by the
defendant's mother and the plaintiff's counsel. A party
who is absent under such circumstances is not in a condition to obtain relief from the equity side of the court on
the ground of the negligence of her attorney.

2. It is moreover claimed that the motion should have
been granted, because the stipulation mentioned operated
as a continuance of the cause. It appears that September
30, 1886, was a day to be kept sacred, or as a holiday, in
the belief of Mr. Simon. Fearing that the case might not
be reached for trial on September 29, 1886, he on that day,
and some time before it was in fact reached, and for his
own accommodation, induced the plaintiff's attorneys to
stipulate with him, in effect, that the case be placed at the
foot of the September calendar, and then not to be tried
until reached in its regular order, but with the understanding that the cause should be tried if reached in its order on
the day calendar of the 29th, as it was. The court refused
to receive the stipulation, on the ground that it was contrary to the rules of the court, as appears to have been the

fact. Manifestly, the making of the stipulation, under the circumstances mentioned, furnished no reason for opening the default.

· *By the Court.*— The order of the county court is affirmed.

ENGFER, Respondent, vs. ROEMER, Appellant.

January 31 — February 28, 1888.

Liens: Unauthorized work: Retention of bill: Ratification: Agency:
Evidence.

1. In an action to enforce a mechanic's lien for repairing a house and building a barn, the defendant admitted that she had authorized the repairs, but claimed that the barn was built without her knowledge or consent, and there was no direct proof that she had authorized it to be built. A bill for the whole work had been presented to her, and there was evidence that she then told the plaintiff that he must look to the tenant for his pay for the barn, because she had not authorized it to be built and did not want it. *Held*, that the mere fact that she received the bill and retained it for a long time would not warrant the inference that she assented to it or acknowledged her liability to pay for the barn.

2. *Quære*, whether an agreement by the owner of land to pay for work done thereon without his knowledge or consent would give the right to a lien.

3. Parol agency to charge a principal's realty ought to be express and clearly established.

APPEAL from the County Court of *Milwaukee* County. Action to enforce a lien for labor performed and materials furnished in repairing a dwelling-house and building a barn upon land owned by the defendant. There was a special verdict, by which it was found, among other things, that the labor and materials, exclusive of the barn, were reasonably worth $52; that the building of the barn and furnishing of the materials therefor were reasonably worth $28; and that the plaintiff had been paid $40, which he received in part payment of the total of $80. Other facts are stated in the opinion. From a judgment in favor of the plaintiff for $40 and costs, the defendant appealed.

The cause was submitted for the appellant on the brief of *Charles M. Bice,* and for the respondent on that of *Thompson & Schoof.*

COLE, C. J. There is no serious controversy as to the repairs upon the house. The defendant admits in her answer that through her tenant, Kohlman, she entered into an agreement with the plaintiff to take out the front of the old building and put in place thereof a new front; to take down the partition in the building, and put in place thereof a wooden partition; put up shelves, and make stairs in front; for which she agreed to pay what these repairs were reasonably worth. She further alleged that the plaintiff presented to her a bill of $40 for this work, which she has paid. The payment of the $40 is not disputed, but the plaintiff claims it is not what the work was worth, and the jury found, in answer to the fifth question submitted, that the work done and materials furnished by the plaintiff, exclusive of the barn, were reasonably worth $52. To the extent of the unpaid balance found to be due for this work, if any, the plaintiff's right to a lien would seem to be indisputable. The contract for it was made by the tenant, who was authorized by the defendant to make it, and she is clearly bound by it.

The real controversy in the case is in reference to the barn which plaintiff built upon the lot. This barn the defendant claims was built without her authority, knowledge, or consent, for the convenience of the tenant, and that she is not liable to pay for it. It is true, the defendant owned the lot upon which the barn was built, but it is obvious that that fact alone would not render the premises subject to a lien, ·if the barn was put upon them without her authority, knowledge, or consent.   A person cannot obtain a lien upon the premises of another unless the work was done by the authority, knowledge, or assent of the owner.   This proposition is too plain for argument.   There was no direct authority shown on the part of the defendant for building the barn. The tenant, Kohlman, made the contract with the plaintiff for putting it up, but he does not pretend that he was authorized by the defendant to have the work done.   The question then is, Upon what ground can the premises be subject to a lien for its payment?

In answer to the first question, the jury found, in effect, that the plaintiff built the barn at the defendant's instance and request; also, in answer to the sixth, that the barn was built with her knowledge and assent at the time, or that she accepted and approved of the job when done.   If there were evidence to support these findings, the case would be measurably free from difficulty.   Of course, if the defendant requested the plaintiff to put up the barn, the law would imply a promise to pay for it; or, if she assented to it at the time, and accepted and approved of the work when done, this, perhaps, might be deemed a ratification of the acts of her agent, and would bind her.   But there is really no affirmative evidence that the defendant authorized the barn to be built, or that she even knew of its construction until after it was erected, or that she ever accepted and agreed to pay for it.   We are inclined to think the jury must have reached the conclusions they did upon these points because of certain things in the charge of the learned county court which were well calculated to mislead. There was evidence which tended to prove that the plaintiff, after he completed the repairs upon the house and built the barn, presented to the defendant a bill for the entire work, which bill she retained.   Upon this point the court, in effect, charged that the plaintiff would be entitled to a lien upon the premises for the balance due for repairs on

the house, unless such repairs had been settled and paid
for; but that the defendant would not be liable for the
barn, if she did not know or was not informed of the construction of it until after it was built, unless she thereafter
assumed the payment in the manner which had been stated,
either by receiving the bill and retaining it for so long a
time that the law would infer that she assented to it, or
had agreed to receive it and pay for it.

In our opinion, the fact that the defendant received and
retained the plaintiff's bill for a long time, if such were the
case, was entitled to but little weight.   The bill was partly
for work which the defendant admitted she had authorized.
It also contained charges for work which there is no direct
proof that she ever authorized.   Under some circumstances,
the failure of a party to object to an account rendered raises
a strong presumption of its correctness; but even that presumption may be rebutted by proof tending to establish a
contrary inference.   Where a party receives and retains an
account which has been presented, makes no objection to
items therein charged, after a lapse of time it becomes a
stated account, and a strong proof of its correctness. *Lockwood v. Thorne*, 11 N. Y. 170, and cases cited.   In *Toland
v. Sprague*, 12 Pet. 334, the court say: "We agree that the
mere rendering an account does not make it a stated one;
but that, if the other party receives the account, admits the
correctness of the items, claims the balance or offers to pay
it, as it may be in his favor or against him, then it becomes
a stated account."   See, also, *Lockwood v. Thorne*, 18 N. Y.
285; *Cobb v. Arundell*, 26 Wis. 553; *Hinton v. Coleman*, 45
Wis. 165.   There is considerable evidence that the defendant informed the plaintiff, when he presented the bill in
question, that he must look to the tenant for his pay for the
barn, because she did not authorize it to be built and did
not want it; so that the mere fact that she retained the bill
for a long time would not warrant the inference that she

assented to it, or acknowledged her liability to pay for the barn. Besides, it admits of grave doubt, if she actually agreed to pay the entire bill as the plaintiff claims, whether this would give a lien upon the premises for the expense of the barn. The defendant, upon a sufficient consideration, might become personally liable for the payment of that debt without subjecting her property to a lien for its payment.

We have said that there was no direct proof that the defendant ever authorized her tenant to contract for the building of the barn. Such agency is attempted to be established by mere circumstances. "Parol agency to charge a principal's realty ought to be express and clearly established." RYAN, C. J., in *Lauer v. Bandow*, 43 Wis. 556. There ought certainly to be some satisfactory evidence that the defendant authorized the tenant to make the contract for building the barn in the first instance, or that she subsequently ratified his acts in that regard in some unequivocal manner. The fact that she received and retained the bill for the work, we deem, under the circumstances, insufficient to give the plaintiff a right to a lien upon the premises for that work. *Lauer v. Bandow, supra.* We therefore think the charge above referred to was calculated to prejudice the defendant, and that the judgment of the county court must be reversed, and the cause be remanded to the superior court for a new trial.

By the Court.— It is so ordered.

TURNER and another, Respondents, vs. NACHTSHEIM, Appellant.

January 31 — February 28, 1888.

' REFERENCE: *(1) Vacating order of denial:* Res adjudicata. *(2) " Long account."*

1. Though an order denying a reference is absolute in its terms, the court may at any time during the same term vacate it and grant a reference.
2. An account which contains some twenty charges for different kinds of service, rendered at different times during a period of several months, is a " long account," within the meaning of sec. 2864, R. S.

APPEAL from the Circuit Court for *Milwaukee* County. Action to recover for legal services. A bill of particulars is annexed to the complaint and made a part of it, containing twenty items for services rendered, commencing September 1, 1886, and ending May 2, 1887. The answer, in substance and effect, is a general denial. The plaintiffs applied to the court for a reference of the cause, but the court denied the application. The order denying the motion gives no leave to renew it. Subsequently, at the same term, the plaintiffs moved to vacate such order, and that the cause be referred. The motion was granted, and an order was entered vacating the former order and referring the cause to a court commissioner to hear, try, and determine the same. From this last order the defendant appeals.

For the appellant there was a brief by *Rogers & Mann,* and oral argument by *Mr. Mann.* The issues were not referable, and the account sued upon is not a long account. *Druse v. Horter,* 57 Wis. 648; *Knips v. Stefan,* 50 id. 290. The motion for a reference having been denied unconditionally, and no leave given or asked to renew it, the matter of the motion is *res adjudicata. Webster v. Oconto Co.*

47 Wis. 225; *Cothren v. Connaughton*, 24 id. 138; Herman on Estoppel, sec. 472; *Hoppe v. C., M. & St. P. R. Co.* 61 Wis. 367.

For the respondents the cause was submitted on the brief of *Anthony Koenen*. The account was a "long account." *U. S. Rolling Stock Co. v. Johnston*, 67 Wis. 182; *Dane Co. v. Dunning*, 20 id. 210; *Monitor Iron Works Co. v. Ketchum*, 47 id. 177; *Carpenter v. Shepardson*, 43 id. 413. The order denying the reference might be vacated at the same term, and then could be no bar to another motion. *Servatius v. Pickel*, 30 Wis. 507; *Brown v. Brown*, 53 id. 29.

Lyon, J. 1. It is claimed on behalf of defendant that the first order, which denied the motion to refer the cause, is *res adjudicata* of the question, and that the court had no power to make the second order, from which this appeal is taken. Had the court referred the cause without vacating the first order, the objection would be well taken, because that order is absolute in its terms. This court has frequently so held. But it was entirely competent for the court to vacate that order at any time during the term at which it was made, and when that was done it ceased to be an impediment to a reference of the cause. That the court had power to vacate such order at that term is unquestionable; for this court has often asserted the general rule that the court has entire control over its own orders and judgments, and may modify or vacate them at any time during the term at which they were made or rendered.

2. If the plaintiffs' bill of particulars annexed to the complaint is a "long account," within the meaning of sec. 2864, R. S., the cause was properly referred. We think it does contain a "long account." There are some twenty charges for different kinds of service, rendered at different times during a period of several months. It is claimed that they were all rendered in the same action. Were this true, it is

Thorn vs. Smith.

not perceived that the fact has any significance; but it is not true. As to several of the items, it does not appear in what action the services were rendered. The defendant could have avoided the reference by admitting the correctness of the account; thus narrowing the issue to the question of his liability. Failing to do this, he must submit to the reference.

By the Court.— Order affirmed.

THORN, Respondent, vs. SMITH, Appellant.

January 31 — February 28, 1888.

(1, 2) Pleading: Amendment of answer at trial: Hypothetical form: Payment: Evidence. (3) Interest on note set up as counterclaim. (4) Value of services: Evidence: Account rendered: Reversal of judgment.

1. In an action by an attorney to recover for professional services, the defendant denied that a part of the services were performed for him, and omitted to set up a payment which had been made for them. After introducing evidence of such payment he moved to amend his answer so as to allege that if it should be found that the services in question were performed for him then the said payment therefor had been made to and received by the plaintiff. The motion was denied. *Held,* that the defendant should have been allowed to so amend his answer as to obtain credit for the payment, and that the hypothetical form of the proposed amendment was not objectionable.

2. Upon the evidence in this case (stated in the opinion) it is *held* that a certain payment to the plaintiff, claimed to have been made by check payable to him or bearer, was in fact made.

3. Where a promissory note made by the plaintiff is set up as a counterclaim, interest thereon should be allowed by the referee to the date of his report at the rate specified in the note.

4. In an action to recover the value of services the defendant offered in evidence an account previously rendered by the plaintiff, in which, it was claimed, a smaller sum was fixed as the value of the

services than that claimed in the complaint. The court excluded it. The record does not contain such account. *Held*, that as it does not appear that the defendant was prejudiced thereby, the exclusion of the account is not a sufficient ground for a reversal of the judgment.

APPEAL from the Circuit Court for *Milwaukee* County. The following statement of the case was prepared by Mr. Justice TAYLOR as a part of the opinion:

Action to recover for legal services and for money expended for and on behalf of the defendant. As to the larger part of the alleged services, the defendant denied that he had employed the plaintiff, or that such services were performed for him. He also set up some payments made to the plaintiff, and also three counterclaims upon three promissory notes given by the plaintiff to third persons, and transferred to the defendant before the commencement of the action. These notes drew interest at ten per cent. per annum.

The case was referred to a referee for trial. The action was commenced on the 11th of July, 1878, and the report of the referee was not made until April 5, 1887. The referee, by his report, found that the defendant at the commencement of the action was indebted to the plaintiff in the sum of $2,495.97, less the payments made by the defendant, amounting to the sum of $485.81, and the amount due on the three notes set up by way of counterclaim, $235.35, making, in all, $721.85; leaving a balance due the plaintiff at the commencement of the action, $1,744.12. To that sum he added interest at the rate of seven per cent. from the date of the commencement of the action to the date of the report, $1,084.76; making, in all, $2,858.88, for which judgment was rendered in favor of the plaintiff, against the defendant, with the costs of the action.

The defendant took exceptions to several of the findings of fact and conclusions of law, and made a motion in the court below to set aside the report or some parts thereof. The motion of the defendant was denied, and judgment rendered for the plaintiff in accordance with the report of the referee. The defendant appealed from the judgment.

H. C. Sloan, for the appellant.

For the respondent there was a brief by *Shepard & Shepard*, and oral argument by *Mr. C. E. Shepard*.

TAYLOR, J. We are urged very strongly by the learned counsel for the appellant to reverse the judgment on the ground that the evidence does not sustain the findings of fact as to the value of the services of the plaintiff, as found by the referee and confirmed by the court. Upon a review of the evidence, it is very clear that the value of the services as found by the referee is not only sustained by the testimony in the case, but by a clear preponderance of such testimony. We cannot, therefore, reverse the judgment, as against the clear preponderance of the evidence in the case.

There were two other exceptions taken to the rulings of the referee in the court below which the appellant alleges as error. In the defendant's answer, setting up the several payments made by him, he gave a bill of items, and, as he claims, in said bill of items by mistake left out a payment which was made to the plaintiff by the "Appleton Iron Company" for the services claimed to have been performed by him, and for which he was seeking payment of the defendant in this action, amounting to the sum of $260. On the trial, he gave evidence tending strongly to prove such payment, and then moved to amend his answer so as to set up this payment. The motion was denied, and the defendant duly excepted.

The motion to amend was in the following language: "I move to amend the answer in this case by inserting, immediately preceding the first counterclaim, the following: 'In case it should be found or held that the services performed by the plaintiff in the bankruptcy proceedings and the re-organization of the company, as testified to, were performed for the defendant *A. L. Smith,* then and in that case there has been paid to and received by the plaintiff in payment therefor the sum of $260, paid on the 28th day of November, 1876.' " The motion was opposed in the following language: "Proposed amendment objected to as being hypothetical. It is also objected to because it is not according to the evidence." The motion was denied by the referee without stating any reason therefor, and exception was duly taken.

The pertinency of the form in which the amendment was proposed to be made, arises out of the fact that a very large claim was made by the plaintiff from the defendant for services in conducting a proceeding in bankruptcy for the Appleton Iron Company, and for the organization of the Appleton Furnace Company. For this service the plaintiff was allowed the sum of $1,200 by the referee. The defendant had denied that he was under any obligation to pay the plaintiff for such service. The $260 which he desired to have allowed as a payment in part of these services was claimed by the defendant to have been paid by a check drawn by *A. L. Smith,* president of the Appleton Furnace Company, on the First National Bank of Appleton, payable to the plaintiff or bearer. The check, offered in evidence, was in the following words and figures:

"$260.   APPLETON, WIS., November 28, 1876.

"The First National Bank of Appleton pay to *Gerry Thorn* or bearer two hundred and sixty dollars in currency.

[Signed]   "A. L. SMITH, Pt. Appleton Furnace Co."

The check was stamped: "First National Bank, Appleton, Wis. Paid November 29, 1876."

In regard to this check the defendant, in answer to a question of the plaintiff on cross-examination, testified as follows: "*Question.* This check of $260, did you ever deliver that to me? *Answer*. I delivered that check to you; yes, sir." On the direct examination the defendant testified: "I drew my check for *Mr. Thorn* on behalf of the furnace company for $250. I had the check of the furnace company for it. I saw the check exhibited here this morning. This is the same one; it is in my handwriting. . . . It was a furnace company check; and as soon as I could get the check, or when I found it, I added the word 'President,' so that it would not be charged to my account, but be charged to the furnace company account. . . . Was in the habit of drawing checks for that company. I state positively that addition was made in November, 1876. The payment of the $250 was made on account of the furnace company or iron company to *Col. Thorn* as attorney. Don't know as it was on any identical case. He claimed the amount was due him, and wanted some money; and I presume Mr. Smith [meaning H. D. Smith] was not there for some reason, and I was most accessible to him, and he asked me for it." Although the defendant speaks of the check as one for $250, he evidently refers to the check then in court, and which was offered in evidence and is a check for $260.

II. D. Smith, the secretary and treasurer of the furnace company, testified, on direct examination, "that the company paid *Mr. Thorn* $260 on the 28th of November, 1876, by check." On cross-examination, he testified as follows: "*Question*. Now, you say you paid me a check of $260? *Answer*. I did not say so. I said that you were paid by the company. I have got that check." Witness produced the check, and said: "That check was returned to me through the bank, and I entered it up. The check is an Appleton Iron Company check. It is on the 'Appleton Iron Company' books. I charged it up myself on the 6th of November, 1876. I was secretary and treasurer. I generally signed the checks of the Appleton Furnace Com-

pany. *A. L. Smith*, the president, signed some in my absence. This check is in *A. L. Smith's* handwriting. I have
the bank-books showing that it was charged up to our accounts. I got the check from the First National Bank. It
was returned with my bank-book."

This is substantially the evidence of the defendant in regard to the payment of the $260. Opposed to this is the
testimony of *Mr. Thorn* denying any knowledge of the
check, and denying that he ever received the check or the
money thereon. *Mr. Thorn* was testifying eight years or
more after the alleged transaction, and from mere memory.
He does not show' that he kept any account of the payments made to him by the defendant or by the Appleton
Furnace Company on account of the services he performed
in behalf of said defendant or said company. Upon this
evidence we think it must be held that the $260 was in fact
paid to the plaintiff for his legal services in the matters for
which he claims pay from the defendant in this action; and
the only reasonable doubt about the matter is whether the
payment was made by *A. L. Smith* or by the furnace company. So far, however, as the right to have it allowed as
a payment in part for the services performed, it is immaterial whether the defendant paid or the furnace company.
In either case it was in part payment for the services of the
plaintiff in relation to matters he seeks to recover for in
this action. No objection was made to the evidence when
offered on the trial, and, under a well-established rule of
practice of the courts, it might perhaps have been allowed
as a payment by the referee and court without any formal
amendment of the answer setting up the payment. To this
view of the case it might be objected that the evidence,
when offered and received, was admissible and relevant
upon this issue in the case made by the defendant's denial
that he had employed the plaintiff or agreed to pay him
for his services in the bankruptcy proceedings of the Ap-

pleton Iron Company and in the organization of the "Furnace Company;" and so the failure to object to the evidence
was no waiver on the part of the plaintiff that the evidence
was not admissible under the answer.   Undoubtedly, the
evidence was admissible for the defendant upon the issue
named; but, the evidence being in the case, it seems to us
that it was the .right of the party to have his answer so
amended as to have the payment allowed as against the
claim of the plaintiff for compensation for the same services for which the money was paid.   It was long ago established by this court that a more liberal rule should be
allowed the defendant in the amendment of his answer
than was allowed the plaintiff in the amendment of his
complaint; especially when the defendant would necessarily
lose all benefit of the defense unless allowed in the pending
case.   See note upon this subject by Chief Justice Dixon,
5 Wis. 628, 629.   Unless the defendant can be allowed this
$260 as a part payment of this claim in the present action,
it is clear that both he and the furnace company must lose
all benefit of the payment made.

It is contended by both the defendant and the furnace
company that this money was paid to the plaintiff in part
discharge for his services in the bankruptcy proceedings
and the organization of the furnace company, for which
compensation was claimed by and allowed to the plaintiff
in this action to the amount of $1,200. And, unless allowed
as payment in this action, there would seem to be no way
in which either the company or the defendant could hereafter recover the amount of the plaintiff.   There was no
valid objection to the form of the amendment.   The defendant had the right to contest his liability to pay for the services rendered for the Appleton Iron and Furnace Companies, and, if he failed in that defense, it was certainly just
that he should be allowed to show that the plaintiff had
been paid for his services in respect to these matters, either

Thorn vs. Smith.

in whole or in part. See *Willard v. Giles*, 24 Wis. 319; *Grace v. Newbre*, 31 Wis. 19; *Zeidler v. Johnson*, 38 Wis. 340. We think the referee and court erred in refusing the amendment, and also in not allowing the claim of payment for the sum of $260.

It is also alleged that the court erred in refusing to allow interest on the three notes set up as counterclaims at the rate of ten per cent. per annum up to the·time of the report of the referee. The referee allowed the interest at ten per cent. only to the time of the commencement of the plaintiff's action, and then deducted the amount of the said notes, with interest to that time, from the account found due the plaintiff at the commencement of the action, and allowed the plaintiff interest at seven per cent. upon the balance from the date of the commencement of the action to the date of the report of the referee. We think this was error. The counterclaims upon these notes are nothing more or less than actions by the defendant against the plaintiff. Had not these actions been set up in the action of the plaintiff against him, and a separate action had been brought on them by the defendant against the plaintiff, there could be no doubt that interest must have been computed on the notes at the rate of ten per cent. from their date to the date of the trial of the action; and there is no reason for holding a different rule when they are set up by a defendant by way of counterclaim, which is an action by the defendant against the plaintiff. In this case the rule of the circuit court was favorable to the plaintiff, but, if it be the true rule, then if the plaintiff brought his action upon a note of the defendant bearing interest at ten per cent., and the defendant counterclaimed a note of the plaintiff drawing interest at five per cent., the interest on the plaintiff's note would only draw ten per cent. to the commencement of the action, and the amount of the defendant's five per cent. note would have to be deducted at the date of the commencement of the action. It is said that in this case it is inequitable that the plaintiff should pay ten per cent. on these notes, when the defendant was indebted to him far beyond the amount of the notes. Had not the defendant purchased these notes from the parties to whom the plaintiff had given them, he would have been compelled to pay the ten per cent. to the holders of them. If it was a hardship to pay ten per cent. on these notes for several years, it could have been avoided by paying them at maturity. There is nothing in the case of *Yates v. Shepardson*, 39 Wis. 173, which justifies the rule of the circuit court in this case. In that case the interest on an obligation of the defendant drawing twelve per cent. was computed at only seven per cent. up to the commencement of the trial, but no objection was taken to such compensation by the defendant, and no question was raised in the case as to the right of the defendant to have interest computed at any given rate per cent. up to the date of the trial. The question raised in the case at bar was not considered in that case.

It was also urged by the learned counsel for the appellant that the court erred in refusing to permit the defendant to give in evidence an account rendered by the plaintiff to the defendant, before the action was commenced, in which the defendant claimed the plaintiff had fixed a much smaller sum as the value of his services than was claimed by his complaint in the action. It is a sufficient answer to this objection that the record does not contain such account, and we cannot say that, if it had been received in evidence, it would have benefited the defendant. In any event, it could have had but little weight as evidence on the trial. *Nauman v. Zoerhlaut*, 21 Wis. 466, 469. The record does not disclose that the defendant was prejudiced by the refusal of the court to receive the account in evidence, and it is not therefore a sufficient ground for a reversal of the judgment.

Thorn vs. Smith.

For the errors in not allowing the $260 as part payment
of the plaintiff's claim, and not computing interest on the
three notes set up as counterclaims at ten per cent. interest
to the date of the report, the judgment must be reversed.
In fixing the amount of the judgment to which the plaintiff
is entitled, the $260 should be added to the $485.81, the
amount of the other payments made by the defendant; making, in all, the sum of $745.81. This sum should be deducted
from the sum found due the plaintiff at the time of the commencement of the action, viz., $2,495.97; leaving a balance
of $1,750.16. Interest should be computed on this sum of
$1,750.16 from the date of the commencement of the action,
July 11, 1878, to the date of the report, April 5, 1887, at
seven per cent. per annum, and added to said $1,750.16, and
this would be the amount due the plaintiff at the date of
the report. Interest should be computed on the three notes
mentioned in the counterclaims at ten per cent. from the
respective dates to the date of the report, viz., April 5, 1887,
and the amount of the notes, with the interest added to
such date, should be deducted from the amount found due
the plaintiff on that day; and the plaintiff should have judgment for the balance of his claim against the defendant,
with interest to the date of the judgment.

By the Court.— The judgment of the circuit court is reversed, and the cause remanded with directions to that court
to enter judgment for the plaintiff in accordance with this
opinion.

ORTON, J., took no part.

FLANNIGAN, Appellant, vs. GOGGINS, Respondent.

February 1 — February 28, 1888.

Deed: Delivery: Possession by stranger: Replevin.

1. On the day of the date of a deed the grantor and grantee named
therein, and the defendant and one W. were together in the office
of W. W. drew the deed and also two mortgages, one on other
lands, to secure the purchase money. The instruments were
signed and acknowledged in the presence of W., and then laid by
him on a show-case in his office. A discussion arose as to the description and title of the land covered by one of the mortgages,
and as to how some one in possession of the land deeded might
be removed. Finally the defendant took the papers from the
show-case, without authority or objection from either of the parties thereto, and said that he would examine the title and ascertain whether everything was all right. Afterwards, when the
grantee demanded the deed, the defendant refused to give it to
him, but offered to give him back the mortgages. *Held*, that there
had been no delivery of the deed sufficient to pass the title, and
that the grantee could not maintain replevin therefor.

2. *It seems* that if replevin will lie in any case for a deed in possession
of a stranger, there should be no question as to whether the deed
had been so delivered as to be a valid conveyance. That question
should only be tried in an action to which the grantor is a party,
and, since it involves the title to land, cannot be tried in replevin.

3. In replevin to recover a deed its value must be proved.

APPEAL from the Circuit Court for *Winnebago* County.
Replevin. The facts are stated in the opinion. At the
close of the plaintiff's testimony a motion for a nonsuit
was granted, and from the judgment dismissing the complaint the plaintiff appealed.

For the appellant there was a brief by *Hicks & Phillips*,
and oral argument by *Mr. Hicks.* They contended, *inter
alia*, that assent to the delivery of the deed to the defendant in escrow was given by both parties thereto. If the
deed was so disposed of as to clearly evince that it was the
intention of the parties that the defendant should hold it

upon certain conditions, it is a sufficient delivery in escrow. *Conlan v. Grace*, 36 Minn. 276; *Schmidt v. Deegan*, 69 Wis. 300; *Lindsay v. Lindsay*, 11 Vt. 621. Whether there has been a delivery of a deed is a question of fact rather than of law. *Conlan v. Grace, supra; Lindsay v. Lindsay, supra; Daggett v. Daggett*, 143 Mass. 516. When the plaintiff had complied with the conditions of the escrow, and offered to show that the description in the mortgage was correct, he was entitled to the absolute possession of the deed. *Prutsman v. Baker*, 30 Wis. 644; *Schmidt v. Deegan*, 69 Wis. 300. The party having the absolute right of possession in replevin must prevail. *Martin v. Watson*, 8 Wis. 315.

For the respondent there was a brief by *Weisbrod, Harshaw & Nevitt*, and oral argument by *Mr. Weisbrod*.

ORTON, J. This is an action of replevin to recover the possession or the value of a certain deed made out in statutory form for certain land by one Patrick Morrow and wife to the plaintiff on the 4th day of May, 1886, for the consideration expressed therein of $2,600. The preliminary practice in this case, to say the least of it, was certainly very singular and unusual. There was no affidavit made or bond given, and the property could have been taken by the writ, for the plaintiff obtained an order with his summons to have the deed deposited with the clerk of the court, and it was not taken, and the plaintiff voluntarily allowed it to pass back to the defendant. The case was tried as one in trover and conversion, on proof of demand and refusal to deliver. The object of the action would seem to be to obtain possession of the deed as the evidence of the plaintiff's title to a valuable tract of land which he claims to own as his property, and yet it is allowed to be retained by the defendant, and its value only sought to be recovered, and that value at most would have been merely nominal,

Flannigan vs. Goggins.

as of a mere paper or written instrument. It is very clear that the value of the land conveyed by the deed could not be recovered, for the defendant was a stranger to the deed, and if the deed was a valid conveyance of the land, by delivery and ownership, as the plaintiff claims, the retention of the deed by the defendant would not impair or affect his title to the land. The theory of the case is that the defendant has obtained possession wrongfully of a deed made by Morrow to the plaintiff, as a valid deed of which the plaintiff is the owner, and possession of which, merely as a title paper, he had demanded. The defendant could not if he would affect the plaintiff's title in the least by retaining the deed or otherwise. The plaintiff cannot retain his title to the land and yet recover the value of the land from any one. He is certainly not entitled to recover both the land and its value in any action. The prayer of the complaint is to recover the possession of the deed or the sum of $2,600, the consideration thereof. Aside from the inconsistency and novelty of this practice, in the plain and well-understood action of replevin, it would almost seem that the action ought to have been dismissed as a frivolous trifling with the court. But there are other questions of more importance to be disposed of.

The facts disclosed by the testimony appear to be substantially as follows: On the day said deed bears date the plaintiff and said Morrow, the defendant, Morrow's brother-in-law, and P. M. Wright, Esq., were together in the office of Wright at Omro. Wright made out said deed, together with two mortgages, one on the land deeded and the other on other land, to secure the purchase money of $2,600. They were respectively signed and acknowledged in the presence of Wright, and then laid together on a show-case in said office by Wright. The parties then commenced a discussion as to the description and title of the land in one of the mortgages, and as to how some one in possession of the land deeded might be removed. This conversation lasted about an hour. Then the defendant took the papers from the show-case, and said he would go to Oshkosh and examine the title and ascertain whether everything was all right. Wright testified that there appeared to be something not quite settled. Neither party to the deed made any objection. The plaintiff's counsel offered to prove "that the defendant voluntarily assumed to take possession of the deed without the authority of the grantor or grantee, and that the plaintiff never had the deed." The plaintiff's counsel also said on the trial: "We do not claim that there was an actual manual delivery of the deed itself on the part of Morrow to *Flannigan*, but that it was the intention of the parties that the deed should be delivered, and that the estate passed from Morrow to *Flannigan.*" The defendant retained the papers, and when they were demanded by the plaintiff he said he would give up to him the mortgages, but would not give up the deed, for the mortgages were not right.

It will be seen that the real issue in the case is whether the deed had ever been delivered. The deed in the hands of the defendant was not an escrow, for the plaintiff offered to prove that he took it without authority from either the grantor or grantee, and such was the effect of the evidence given. The question is, Was there *then* and *there* a present delivery of the deed? There is not the slightest evidence that the deed was then delivered, and it has not since been delivered. If the deed was delivered, so were the mortgages, and yet Morrow has never had them in his possession, and it would seem that the plaintiff himself had received them back, for the defendant offered to deliver them back to him, and he offered to introduce them in evidence on the trial. But this is not material. There was certainly no delivery of either the deed or the mortgages. The mortgages were not ready for delivery, and were withheld until the title of the land could be ascertained. The de-

livery of the deed and of the mortgages was to be concurrent, and therefore they were both withheld and not
delivered. It would seem to be the law that if replevin
would lie in any case for a deed in possession of a stranger,
there should be no question about the validity of the deed
as a conveyance, for upon the question of its delivery or
validity the grantor as well as the grantee should be heard
in the action. He has far more interest in the matter than
the nominal defendant. Yet how is he to be made a party
in the action of replevin? That question should only be
tried in some action, legal or equitable, in which he may
be made a party. Replevin is not that action. But if he
could be made a party in this action it is sufficient that he
was not. The court very properly rejected much evidence
in respect to the purchase of the land, and to other matters
in which Morrow only had an interest, and finally dismissed
the action. The plaintiff did not prove, or offer to prove,
the value of the deed, the property which was the subject
of the action, one of the material issues in the case, and
that of itself justified the dismissal of the action. R. S.
sec. 2888; *Wallace v. Hilliard*, 7 Wis. 627; *Rose v. Tolly*,
15 Wis. 443; *Jenkins v. Steanka*, 19 Wis. 126. To recover
in the case on proof of the delivery of the deed, would
have directly involved the title of the land. If it had been
delivered, then the plaintiff held the title; and if it had
not, he did not have title. This cannot be done in replevin.
"The title to land cannot be tried in this action." Wells
on Replevin, sec. 58, and note of cases. The learned counsel of the appellant admitted that the deed had not been
delivered actually and manually, but claimed that he had
an estate in the land, and that it was the intention that the
deed should be delivered. If that is true, the plaintiff has
no legal title to the estate or the deed, and he must therefore go into equity to enforce a mere equity, and that, too,
against Morrow as well as the defendant. In any view

the plaintiff was not entitled to recover in the action, and the circuit court very properly dismissed it. To invent new actions, or change the form of old ones, and try legal experiments, and wander away from the well-worn paths of long-settled legal practice, may show ingenuity, but is not to be encouraged.

By the Court.— The judgment of the circuit court is affirmed.

See note to this case in 86 N. W. Rep. 848.— REP.

THE HOME MUTUAL INSURANCE COMPANY OF CALIFORNIA, Plaintiff in error, vs. ROE, Defendant in error.

February 1 — February 28, 1888.

Insurance against fire: Property covered by policy: "Addition:" Court and jury.

1. A policy covered a "planing-mill building *and addition*" and "machinery, including shafting, gearing, belting, saws, tools, force-pump, and hose therein." The engine-room, from which the entire motive power was furnished, was situated twenty-two feet from the mill building. and was connected therewith by a shaft for the transmission of the power and by a spout through which shavings were forced into the engine-room. A roadway passed between the buildings under the shaft and spout. There was no other addition to the mill building. *Held*, that the policy covered the engine-room and the engine and other machinery therein.

2. Where there is no ambiguity in the language of a contract when applied to the undisputed facts, it is the province of the court to interpret it.

ERROR to the Circuit Court for *Winnebago* County.

Action upon a policy of insurance against fire. The following statement of the case was prepared by Mr. Justice CASSODAY:

January 26, 1885, J. H. Weed, in behalf of *G. W. Roe*,

through one L. D. Harmon, an insurance agent at Oshkosh, and in consideration of $60 paid to the *Home Mutual Insurance Company of California*, obtained from it, by the hands of its agents at Oshkosh, Palmer & McLaren, a written policy of insurance issued by said company, wherein and whereby it insured said " *G. W. Roe* against loss or damage by fire, to the amount of $1,000 in United States .gold coin, viz.: $250 on his one-story frame planing-mill building *and addition*, situate at Antigo, Langlade county, Wis.; $750 on machinery, including shafting, gearing, belting, saws, tools, force-pump, and hose *therein;*" and wherein said company agreed "to make good to the assured, or his legal representatives, all such immediate loss or damage, not exceeding in amount the interest of the assured nor the sum insured as aforesaid, as" should " happen by fire to the property above specified, from the 26th day of January, 1885, at noon, to the 26th day of January, 1886, at noon."

The complaint, among other things, alleged that a fire occurred June 29, 1885, by which the said planing-mill was damaged and destroyed by fire to the amount of $175, and said machinery was destroyed and damaged by fire to the amount of $750; also, the making of proofs of such losses, respectively, and delivering the same to said company. It also negatived the exceptions in the policy; and alleged the failure to pay; and demanded judgment for $925, with interest from November 1, 1885, with costs.

The answer of the company specifically admitted the incorporation of the company; the making and issuing of the policy; that the fire was not caused by any of the negative things alleged; that proofs of loss had been made as stated; that no part thereof had been paid; but otherwise denied each and every allegation of the complaint; and alleged that the property so claimed to have been destroyed by fire was not insured by the defendant, nor contained in, mentioned, described, or referred to in said policy; and that no part of the property insured in and by the policy had at any time been injured, damaged, or destroyed by fire.

The cause was tried by a court and jury; and at the close of the plaintiff's evidence, and on May 11, 1887, the defendant requested the court to direct a verdict in its favor, but the court refused and directed the jury to find for the plaintiff, *G. W. Roe,* and assess his damages at $1,022.12, which they did accordingly. To review the judgment entered upon such verdict, the company has sued out a writ of error.

For the plaintiff in error there was a brief by *Charles W. Felker,* and oral argument by *Mr. Felker* and *Thos. Bates.* They argued that the word "addition" as used in this policy may properly be defined to be an adding or joining to the original structure, and implies an increase or enlargement of the building. Rapalje's Law. Dict. tit. ADDITION; Worcester's Dict., Webster's Dict., and Encyclopedic Dict. tit. ADD and ADDITION. Where the policy is specific as to the subject matter of the risk it cannot be extended by implication. *Arball v. Commerce Ins. Co.* 69 N. Y. 191–3; *Liebenstein v. Baltic Ins. Co.* 45 Ill. 303; *English v. Franklin F. Ins. Co.* 55 Mich. 273; *Bryce v. Lorillard F. Ins. Co.* 55 N. Y. 240; *Sampson v. Security Ins. Co.* 133 Mass. 49; *Annapolis & E. R. Co. v. Baltimore F. Ins. Co.* 32 Md. 37; Wood on Ins. sec. 56; *Hews v. Atlas Ins. Co.* 126 Mass. 389. If the policy was not written in accordance with the intentions of the parties the remedy is in equity. *Hammel v. Queen Ins. Co.* 50 Wis. 240, 243.

For the defendant in error there was a brief by *Weisbrod, Harshaw & Nevitt,* and oral argument by *Mr. A. W. Weisbrod.* They contended, *inter alia,* that the construction and effect of the contract is a matter of law to be determined by the court. *Farnsworth v. Brunquist,* 36 Wis. 202; *Buchanan v. Exchange F. Ins. Co.* 61 N. Y. 26, 33; Wood on Ins.

sec. 57. Policies are to be liberally construed for the insured, and strictly construed with respect to the insurance company. Wood on Ins. secs. 57, 59, and cases cited; · *Prieger v. Exchange M. Ins. Co.* 6 Wis. 89; *Sawyer v. Dodge Co. M. Ins. Co.* 87 id. 503; *Hull v. N. W. M. L. Ins. Co.* 39 id. 397; *Wakefield v. Orient Ins. Co.* 50 id. 532, 540; *Wells Fargo Co. v. Pacific Ins. Co.* 44 Cal. 397; *Insurance Co. v. Wright,* 1 Wall. 468; *Franklin F. Ins. Co. v. Updegraff,* 43 Pa. St. 350; *Franklin F. Ins. Co. v. Brock,* 57 id. 74; *Aurora F. Ins. Co. v. Eddy,* 49 Ill. 106; *Niagara F. Ins. Co. v. Scammon,* 100 id. 644. If possible, effect must be given to every *clause, sentence, or word* of the policy, so as to carry out the true intention of the parties. Wood on Ins. sec. 57; *Stettiner v. Granite Ins. Co.* 5 Duer, 594. A policy of insurance upon a *building* covers every part of it, everything that in any measure forms an essential element of it. Wood on Ins. sec. 83. Where a number of buildings *are used for the same purpose by the same person* in the same enclosure, and together are called "a mill" or "factory," and the term applies to all collectively, a policy that describes the property "as contained in his factory" or "in his mill" will cover the property in *either or all* of the buildings. Wood on Ins. sec. 77; *Liebenstein v. Baltic Ins. Co.* 45 Ill. 301; *Bigler v. N. Y. Cent. Ins. Co.* 20 Barb. 635; *Meadowcraft v. Standard F. Ins. Co.* 61 Pa. St. 91; *Workman v. Ins. Co.* 2 La. (O. S.), 507; *Peoria M. & F. Ins. Co. v. Lewis,* 18 Ill. 553; *Blake v. Exchange Mut. Ins. Co.* 12 Gray, 265; *James River Ins. Co. v. Merritt,* 47 Ala. 387; *Cargill v. Millers' & M. Mut. Ins. Co.* 33 Minn. 90.

CASSODAY, J. The important question presented is whether the engine-room and the machinery therein destroyed by fire were covered by the policy. Much of the parol evidence offered on the part of *Mr. Roe* was excluded on the ground that the contract was in writing and the best evidence.

No evidence was offered on the part of the company.
What little evidence there was admitted in the case is undisputed. It is to the effect that the planing-mill mentioned was on the south side of the mill pond; that, as a
matter of security, the engine-room was twenty-two feet
south of the planing-mill and contained the engine and
machinery that was burned; that there was a three and a
half inch wrought-iron shaft running from the planing-mill
and connected with the engine, which furnished the only
motive power for propelling the machinery in the planing-
mill; that the engine pulley was belted on to this connecting shaft that ran the planing-mill, and this connection was
boxed up and covered in the mill; that there was a spout
or box two and one-half feet square, and ten feet above
the ground or roadway, connected with the machinery in
the planing-mill, through which the shavings produced
therein were drawn by suction or forced by an exhaust fan
into the engine-room; that there was no other connection
between the two buildings; that there was a roadway between the two buildings and under such shaft and spout;
that there were two or three machines connected in the
planing-mill with the main conductor; that the force pump
was run by water; that the engine-room was about twenty-
eight feet long and twenty-five feet wide; that the engine-
room was entirely consumed by the fire, together with the
belting, shafting, pulleys, and pump therein; that the connection between the two buildings was twisted all out of
shape; that the spout through which the shavings were
drawn was burned and was worth about $15; that some
of the belting in the planing-room was cut in the excitement
of the moment at the time of the fire; that the value of the
machinery, pumps, shafting, belting, saws, tools, hose, etc.,
in the engine-room, including the connections, pulleys, engine and boiler, was twelve or fifteen hundred dollars; that
the main building was burned some at the gable end facing

the engine-room, and the damage to it was about $75; that the total value of the machinery in the planing-mill and the belts and other property described in the policy in both buildings was about $6,000; that the fire occurred and caused the damage as stated; that the company was duly notified thereof; that its adjusting agent adjusted the damage to the planing-mill at $75, which the plaintiff refused to accept; that said adjuster refused to adjust the damage to the engine-room and the machinery therein destroyed, on the ground that they were not covered by the policy. There was no evidence of any addition to the planing-mill, other than the engine-room.

Upon these undisputed facts was the court justified in directing a verdict in favor of the plaintiff? Or should a verdict have been directed in favor of the company? Or were there any such conflicting inferences as to whether the policy covered the engine-room and the machinery therein, as required a submission of the case to the jury? Parol evidence was certainly admissible as to the character, nature and situation of the property insured, in order to place the court in the position of the parties at the time of making the contract of insurance. Had there been any dispute in any of these respects, the question would have been properly determinable by a jury. But there was no such dispute. The question therefore recurs whether there is any ambiguity or uncertainty in the language of the policy, when applied to the undisputed facts thus stated. Here the policy was for a certain amount on *Mr. Roe's* "one-story frame *planing-mill building and addition,* situate at Antigo," and for a certain other amount "on machinery, *including* shafting, gearing, belting, saws, tools, force-pump and hose *therein.*" A "mill" is defined to be "(1) An engine or machine for grinding or comminuting any substance; . . . usually having a word prefixed, denoting the particular object to which it is applied. . . . (2) The building, with its machinery, where grinding or *some process of manufact-uring is carried on.*" *Webster.* " The original purpose of mills was to comminute grain for food, but the word mill is extended to engines or machines moved by water, wind, or steam, for carrying on many other operations." *Imperial.* Here, it conclusively appears, that the engine in the engine-room was the only motive power for propelling any of the machinery in either of the buildings. The engine was used for no other purpose. It was, therefore, an essential part of the mill. Without it, there would have been no com-plete mill. The insurance was upon the "*planing-mill building and addition,*" and upon the "machinery, includ-ing shafting, gearing, belting, saws, tools, force-pump and hose *therein.*" It is claimed that the engine-room can-not be construed to mean an " addition " to the " planing-mill building," because it does not join directly upon the same; but, as we have seen, they were both essential to the completion of the mill. The motive power was by means of pulleys, belts, and shafts transmitted from the engine in the engine-room to the machinery in the main building. And the waste shavings, etc., were conveyed from the lat-ter building to the engine-room to generate heat to propel the engine. Thus the two buildings were not only con-nected, but the machinery in each was inseparable, while the whole continued to be a planing-mill. The words " planing-mill building " would seem to be broad enough to include the engine-room. The words of the policy, " plan-ing-mill building *and addition,*" cannot be of less signifi-cance. Especially is this so in the absence of any proof of any other addition. True, *Mr. Roe* did not prove there was no other addition; but he did prove this one, and thereby established, *prima facie,* that the subject matter answered the designation in the policy. The buildings were not only connected as stated, but were both in the same curtilage, constructed for and devoted to the same general purpose

and none other.   The fact that the premium paid was six
per cent. for one year, is a circumstance in favor of this
view rather than against it.   Stress is laid upon the fact
that the engine, which was the principal machine, was not
specifically mentioned in the policy.   But we are inclined
to think that it was covered by the word "machinery," and
that the other things were specifically enumerated for fear
that they might not otherwise be included.   These views,
it is believed, are supported by several adjudications cited by
counsel, which will be reported herewith, and not in conflict with any well considered case.

It seems to us that there was no ambiguity, nor uncer-
·tainty, nor conflicting inferences in the language of the
policy, when applied to the undisputed facts stated.   Had
there been, the question might have been properly submitted to the jury.   *Ganson v. Madigan,* 15 Wis. 144, 82
Am. Dec. 659; *Bedard v. Bonville,* 57 Wis. 274; *Faqin v.
Connoly,* 25 Mo 94, 69 Am. Dec. 450.   In a note to the
last citation it is said by the learned annotator that "it is
a firmly established and universally recognized rule of law
that the construction of a written instrument is a question
of law for the court.   It is the duty of the court, in all
cases where the question is simply the determination of the
meaning of a written document, to declare its legal interpretation; and it is error to leave its construction to the
jury."   69 Am. Dec. 454, where numerous authorities are
cited in support of the rule, which is there said to be applicable to written instruments of every description.   Thus
it has been recently held in New York that "when the
·construction of a contract depends upon the language of
the instrument itself, it is a question of law for the court,
and a submission thereof to the jury is error."   *Dwight v.
G. L. Ins. Co.* 103 N. Y. 341.   RUGER, C. J., there said:
" It would seem from the authorities hereinbefore referred
to that no question affecting the interpretation of contracts

can properly be submitted to a jury, except those arising upon conflicting evidence as to the terms of the agreement, or where extrinsic evidence raises some doubt over the identity of the subject matter or of the claimants thereunder." Page 353. This is deemed to be a correct statement of a rule of law applicable here. See, also, *Farnsworth v. Brunquest*, 36 Wis. 202; *March v. Allabough*, 103 Pa. St. 335; *Emery v. Owings*, 6 Gill, 191. We are forced to the conclusion that the direction of a verdict by the trial court was proper.

By the Court.—The judgment of the circuit court is affirmed.

See note to this case in 36 N. W. Rep. 594.— REP.

McCANDLESS, Respondent, vs. THE CHICAGO & NORTHWESTERN RAILWAY COMPANY, Appellant.

February 1 — February 28, 1888.

Railroads: Failure to restore street to former condition: Proximate cause of injury.

The complaint alleged that the defendant company had unnecessarily constructed its tracks and had for more than ten years operated its road along a certain street, but had never restored the street to its former condition of usefulness; that the tracks rendered the street narrow, unsafe, and insufficient, and at a certain point so obstructed and narrowed it that it was only wide enough for one team: that by reason thereof the plaintiff, while walking along the street at that point, was run into and injured by a team which, though driven by a careful driver, was prancing and sheering out, excited by the passing along the street of a long, noisy freight train; and that the plaintiff was passing along the main traveled part of the street, away from the sidewalk which was impassable because of deep snow-drifts. *Held*, that the failure of the defendant to restore the street to its former condition was not the proximate cause of the injury, and that the complaint did not state a cause of action.

APPEAL from the Circuit Court for *Winnebago* County. The case is stated in the opinion. The defendant appealed from an order overruling a general demurrer to the complaint.

For the appellant there was a brief by *Jenkins, Winkler & Smith,* and oral argument by *H. C. Sloan.* A railroad company is not responsible to a traveler for injuries happening in consequence of horses taking fright at the noise made by a passing train. Wood on Nuisances, sec. 307; *Rex v. Pease,* 4 B. & Ad. 30; *Rex v. Morris,* 1 id. 441; *Bordentown & S. A. Turnpike Co. v. C. & A. R. Co.* 17 N. J. Law, 314; *Favor v. B. & L. R. Corp.* 114 Mass. 350; *Norton v. E. R. Co.* 113 id. 366; *Hall v. Brown,* 54 N. H. 495; *Coy v. U. & S. R. Co.* 23 Barb. 643; *Culp v. A. & N. R. Co.* 17 Kan. 475; *Philadelphia, W. & B. R. Co. v. Stinger,* 78 Pa. St. 219; *Burton v. P., W. & B. R. Co.* 4 Harr. (Del.), 252; *Flint v. N. & W. R. Co.* 110 Mass. 222; *Hudson v. L. & N. R. Co.* 14 Bush, 303; *Whitney v. M. C. R. Co.* 69 Me. 208. Nor would the company be liable for damages caused by the horses of a traveler taking fright at the necessary blowing off of steam from one of its locomotives. *Hahn v. S. P. R. Co.* 51 Cal. 605; *Selleck v. L. S. & M. S. R. Co.* 58 Mich. 195. Nor is the company obliged to erect barriers to prevent horses taking fright. *Coy v. U. & S. R. Co.* 23 Barb. 643; *Hill v. P. & R. R. Co.* 55 Me. 438. The fright of the team, and that alone, was the proximate cause of the injury in this case, and for that the company is not responsible. *Cuff v. N. & N. Y. R. Co.* 35 N. J. Law, 17; *Lewis v. F. & P. M. R. Co.* 54 Mich. 55; *Selleck v. L. S. & M. S. R. Co.* 58 id. 195; *Jackson v. N., C. & St. L. R. Co.* 13 Lea, 491; *Railway Co. v. Staley,* 41 Ohio St. 118; *South Side P. R. Co. v. Trich,* 117 Pa. St. 390.

For the respondent the cause was submitted on the brief of *P. V. Lawson.* He cited *Hamden v. N. H. & N. R. Co.* 27 Conn. 158; *Pittsburg, Ft. W. & C. R. Co. v. Reich,* 101

Ill. 172; *Great Western Railway v. Decatur*, 33 id. 382; *Peterson v. C. & W. M. R. Co.* 31 N. W. Rep. (Mich.), 550; *Young v. D., G. H. & M. R. Co.* 56 Mich. 430; 2 Lacey's Dig. 476, 481; *Kearney v. L., B. & S. C. R. Co.* L. R. 6 Q. B. Cas. 759; *S. C.* 5 id. 411; *Powell v. Deveney,* 3 Cush. 300; *Kellogg v. C. & N. W. R. Co.* 26 Wis. 278, 280; *Mil. & C. R. Co. v. Hunter,* 11 id. 173; *McCall v. Chamberlain,* 13 id. 639–641; *Antisdel v. C. & N. W. R. Co.* 26 id. 149; *Blair v. M. & P. du C. R. Co.* 20 id. 257; *Liston v. C. 1. R. Co.* 70 Iowa, 714; *Young v. St. L., K. C. & N. R. Co.* 44 id. 172; *Kraus v. B., C. R. & N. R. Co.* 55 id. 338; *Dunnigan v. C. & N. W. R. Co.* 18 Wis. 31; *Gear v. C. C. & D. R. Co.* 43 Iowa, 83; *Comm. v. N. & L. R. Corp.* 2 Gray, 54; *Comm. v. B. & L. R. Corp.* 12 Cush. 254; *Comm. v. O. C. & F. R. R. Co.* 14 Gray, 93; *State v. V. C. R. Co.* 27 Vt. 103; *Linsley v. Bushnell,* 15 Conn. 225.

COLE, C. J.   The complaint in this case states no cause of action, and the demurrer to it should have been sustained. The complaint alleges, in substance, that more than ten years ago the defendant company constructed two or more railroad tracks and its roadway along and wholly within River street, in the city of Menasha, together with numerous switches, side tracks, etc., and has ever since maintained and operated its road in such street; that the construction of the tracks thus in the street was entirely unnecessary; that the defendant has never restored the street to its former state of usefulness, but that public travel in the street by carriages, sleighs, and foot travel is impeded and made unsafe, dangerous, and inconvenient by the defendant's tracks and switches; that the street at lots 29, 30, etc., of block 50, is so obstructed and narrowed by the railroad tracks that it is only wide enough for one team drawing a bob-sleigh, and is not wide enough for teams and sleighs to pass and repass each other without going into the ditch on one side, or upon the railroad track on the other side; that before the construction of the railroad the street was level and perfectly safe and passable the whole width thereof for the public travel with teams and carriages and foot travelers, but by the construction of the railroad therein it is made narrow, unsafe, and insufficient, and is a public nuisance; that it was absolutely unnecessary to construct the railroad track along the street at lots 29, 30, etc., because the company could have procured lands on either side of the street for its roadway. The company could also have restored the street to its former usefulness. But, because of its failure and neglect to restore the street to its former state, and because of the narrowness of the street, while the defendant was operating its locomotive and cars on its road in a noisy manner, on the 5th of February, 1887, the plaintiff, while walking along the street, without fault or negligence on her part, was run into, knocked down, and run over by a team drawing an empty bob-sleigh, driven by a careful driver, which team was prancing and sheering out, excited by the passing along the street of a long, noisy freight train. The plaintiff was passing along the main traveled part of the street, away from the sidewalk which was impassable because of the deep snow-drifts, when she was struck by the team and run over.

These are the material facts upon which the cause of action is predicated; and the question is, Do they state sufficient grounds to entitle the plaintiff to recover for the injury which she sustained by being run over by the team driven along the street? It seems to us they do not. The only negligence of the defendant stated is the failure of the company to restore the street to its former state of usefulness. It is conceded that the charter authorized the company to construct its road along the street when necessary, and the general statute also gives the company the same right. Ch. 87, R. S. True, the general law requires the company thus appropriating the street to the use of its road to restore such street to its former state or to such condition as that its usefulness shall not be materially impaired. Sec. 1836. The defendant, then, had the right to construct its road in the street. If it failed to perform its duty by restoring such street to its former usefulness, this failure was a matter for the city authorities to attend to. The plaintiff cannot complain of that omission of duty, because it was not the proximate cause of her injury; for, as we have said, the company had the right to construct its track in the street, and operate its road thereon. It is not charged that there was any negligence in operating the freight train. True, it is alleged that it was a long, noisy freight train; but noise is incident to the moving of such trains. With the present appliances they cannot be moved without making more or less noise. The allegation is that the team was excited by the passing along the street of a long, noisy freight train, then rushing and roaring along on the railroad track. There is no fact stated showing that the freight train was run in a careless or unusual manner. So the case comes to this: It appears that the company was lawfully operating its road along the street, when a team passing along the same took fright at one of its trains, and turned one side, and knocked the plaintiff down and ran over her. The real cause of the injury was the horses' taking fright and running against her. The injury was doubtless attributable less to the neglect of the company to restore the street than to the failure of the city to keep the sidewalk at that place free from snowdrifts. But, assuming that the defendant was at fault for not restoring the street to its former usefulness, still it is obvious that, in the most favorable view of the complaint for the plaintiff, that was but a remote cause of her injury. The direct, immediate, and natural cause was the fright of the horses which ran against her and knocked her down. That was the proximate force which produced the injury complained of. It is idle to attempt to trace this fright back to the failure of the defendant to restore the street to its former state. It is enough to say that that act of negligence was not the proximate cause of the injury; indeed, it is not very clear that it had any connection with it. See, upon this point, *Lewis v. F. & P. M. R. Co.* 54 Mich. 55; *Selleck v. L. S. & M. S. R. Co.* 58 Mich. 195; *Jackson v. N. C. & St. L. R. Co.* 13 Lea, 491; *Railway Co. v. Staley*, 41 Ohio St. 118. For these reasons we think the complaint fails to state a cause of action against the defendant.

By the Court.— The order of the circuit court overruling the demurrer is reversed, and the cause is remanded for further proceedings according to law.

CUTTS, Respondent, vs. THE WESTERN UNION TELEGRAPH COMPANY, Appellant.

February 1 — February 28, 1888.

Telegraph companies: Negligence: Measure of damages.

1. Ch. 171, Laws of 1885, renders telegraph companies liable for the damages resulting directly from their negligence in the matter of transmitting messages, especially where their agents are acquainted with the contents and significance of such messages.
2. In an action to recover damages for the delay in the transmission of a telegram, unless the special injury claimed is shown to have resulted from such delay, only the amount paid for the transmission can be recovered.

APPEAL from the Circuit Court for *Winnebago* County.

The plaintiff resides at Oshkosh. The night of Friday, April 23, 1886, at about midnight, he received from the defendant company a telegram from Hurley, Wisconsin, announcing the death of his son at that place, in the words:

"Will died at 6 P. M. What shall we do?" The plaintiff immediately answered: "Will come on first train," and delivered the answer to the agent of the defendant for transmission to Hurley, paying therefor forty cents. Plaintiff thereupon procured a casket, and, taking with him an undertaker, left Oshkosh on the first train for Hurley; arriving there at 6 P. M. on Saturday evening. He found that a coffin had been procured, and the remains of his son placed in it before his arrival, and that the remains were in a bad condition. He paid the person who furnished the coffin five dollars to take it back. He also had the remains embalmed, which cost him $20 more than it would had they been in good condition. The telegram which he had sent did not reach Hurley until about 11 o'clock A. M. on Sunday,— just as he was about leaving with the remains for Oshkosh. The plaintiff's son was an adult, and had been engaged in business at Hurley on his own account. This action was brought to recover damages for the failure to transmit the message from Oshkosh on Friday night. A trial of the action resulted in a verdict for the plaintiff for $25.40 (being the above items). Motion for a new trial was denied, and judgment entered pursuant to the verdict. The defendant appeals from such judgment.

For the appellant there were briefs by *Finch & Barber*, and oral argument by *Mr. Henry Barber*. To the point that a telegraph company is not liable for a special and contingent injury caused by delay in delivering a message when there is nothing in the message indicating that special damage will result from any neglect, they cited *Candee v. W. U. Tel. Co.* 34 Wis. 471; *Baldwin v. U. S. Tel. Co.* 45 N. Y. 744; *Landsberger v. M. Tel. Co.* 32 Barb. 530; *Leonard v. N. Y., A. & B. E. M. Tel. Co.* 41 N. Y. 544; *British Col. S. M. Co. v. Nettleship*, L. R. 3 C. P. 499; *Horne v. Midland R. Co.* 7 id. 590, 8 id. 131; *Cory v. Thames Iron Works Co.* L. R. 3 Q. B. 190; *Simpson v. L. & N. W. Riv. Co.* 1 Q. B. Div. 274;

Sanders v. Stuart, 17 Eng. (Moak), 286; *Breese v. U. S. Tel. Co.* 45 Barb. 274; *Belger v. Dinsmore,* 51 N. Y. 166; *Smeed v. Foord,* 1 Ell. & Ell. 616.

For the respondent there was a brief by *John W. Hume* and *George Hilton,* and oral argument by *Gabe Bouck.*

LYON, J.   Ch. 171, Laws of 1885, is as follows: "Any person, association, or corporation operating or owning any telegraph lines doing business in this state shall be liable for all damages occasioned by failure or negligence of their operators, servants, or employees in receiving, copying, transmitting, or delivering dispatches or messages." Although this statute was referred to by Mr. Justice TAYLOR in *Thompson v. W. U. Tel. Co.* 64 Wis. 537, yet this is the first case subject to that statute which has reached this court. The case just cited arose before the statute was enacted. It is claimed by counsel for the plaintiff that the above law renders each telegraph company doing business in this state liable for any and all damages sustained through its negligence in respect to the transmission of messages delivered to it for that purpose, and flowing directly and proximately therefrom, even though the import of the telegram is wholly unknown to the company's agents, as in the case of cipher dispatches not translated to the agent. We shall not attempt an interpretation of this statute any further than to hold that it does render telegraph companies liable for the damages resulting directly from their negligence in the matter of transmitting messages, especially where, as in this case, the agent of the telegraph company is acquainted with the contents and significance of the message. It is unnecessary that we should go further in this case.

There is no testimony in the present case showing, or tending to show, when the coffin was procured and the body of the plaintiff's son placed in it, or the cause of the bad condition of the body, or that the circumstances would have been any different had the message been forwarded to Hurley and received there in proper time. In the absence of proof of those facts, it does not appear that the items of expense to which the plaintiff was subjected on account of the coffin and for embalming the body had any connection whatever with the failure of the defendant to transmit the message in time. Such proof is absolutely essential to a re- covery by plaintiff for those expenses. Because of such failure of proof, it was error for the court to submit to the jury the question of the liability of the defendant for those expenses. Under the evidence, the most the plaintiff could recover was the sum he paid the defendant for transmitting the message, which was forty cents. For these reasons the judgment of the county court must be reversed, and the cause will be remanded for a new trial.

By the Court.— It is so ordered.

ADAMS, Respondent, vs. THE CITY OF OSHKOSH, Appellant.

February 2 — February 28, 1888.

Municipal corporations: Defective streets: Notice: Charter construed.

The provision in the charter of the city of Oshkosh (sec. 32, subch. 10, ch. 183, Laws of 1883) that the city shall not be liable for any dam- ages arising out of any street being in a defective or dangerous con- dition, unless it be shown that one of the aldermen of the ward had knowledge thereof, etc., does not apply to an obstruction placed in the street by an employee of the city while repairing such street.

APPEAL from the County Court of *Winnebago* County. The facts will sufficiently appear from the opinion. The plaintiff had a verdict in the court below, and from the judgment entered thereon the defendant appealed.

Wm. H. Casey, for the appellant, contended that the city authorities had no notice of the defective condition of the road so as to charge the city with liability. *Goodnough v. Oshkosh*, 24 Wis. 549; *Ward v. Jefferson*, id. 342; *Brady v. Lowell*, 3 Cush. 121. Persons engaged in repairing streets, not hired for that purpose by the city corporation, are not, when performing such work, servants or agents in the employment of the city, for whose conduct the city can be held liable; and hence the maxim *respondeat superior* has no application. *Hayes v. Oshkosh*, 33 Wis. 314; *Hafford v. New Bedford*, 16 Gray, 297; *Fisher v. Boston*, 104 Mass. 87; *Hill v. Boston*, 122 id. 344; *Walcott v. Swampscott*, 1 Allen, 101.

For the respondent there was a brief by *Finch & Barber*, and oral argument by *Mr. Henry Barber*. They cited, besides cases cited in the opinion, *Kittredge v. Milwaukee*, 26 Wis. 46; *Harper v. Milwaukee*, 30 id. 372, and cases cited; *Orne v. Richmond*, 79 Va. 86; *Logansport v. Dick*, 70 Ind. 65; *Keating v. Cincinnati*, 38 Ohio St. 141; *Circleville v. Neuding*, 41 Ohio St. 465; *Mulcairns v. Janesville*, 67 Wis. 34, and note in 29 N. W. Rep. 516; *Kendall v. Albia*, 34 N. W. Rep. (Ia.). 833.

TAYLOR, J. The respondent brought an action against the city of *Oshkosh* to recover for the value of a horse which was killed in the night-time by running upon a pile of gravel and stones alleged to have been placed in one of the principal streets of said city by the said city, and permitted to remain there without any lights or barriers to warn persons traveling said street of the danger. The evidence satisfactorily shows that the obstruction was placed in the street by an employee of the city on the day the accident happened, and that such employee, with others, was at the time engaged in repairing said street. The only real question arising on this appeal is whether the city of *Oshkosh* is liable for an injury occurring to a citizen traveling such street, by reason of an obstruction placed in said street by an employee of said city while engaged in repairing the same, unless the person injured can show that previous to the injury one of the aldermen of the ward in which the obstruction was placed had actual notice of such obstruction. It is contended by the learned counsel for the appellant that, under the charter of the city of *Oshkosh*, no damages can be recovered of the city caused by an obstruction placed in the street even by an employee of the city engaged in repairing such street, unless actual notice of the obstruction be given to one of the proper ward aldermen, or it be shown that one of such aldermen had actual knowledge of the existence of the obstruction before the accident happened. This contention is based upon the following provision in the charter of said city, viz.: " The city shall not be liable to or for any damages arising or growing out of any sidewalks, streets, drains, sewers, gutters, or ditches, or bridges in said city being in a defective or dangerous condition or out of repair, unless it be shown that, previous to the happening of the same, one of the aldermen of the ward in which the same is located had knowledge thereof; and no knowledge of such condition of the same shall be presumed, unless the defect out of which the same occurred existed three weeks before such damages accrued: provided, however, that nothing herein contained shall be so construed as to mean that knowledge is to be presumed because such three weeks had elapsed."

There is no claim that either of the aldermen of the ward had actual notice of the obstruction in the street, nor that it had existed for three weeks; so that, if the statute applies to an obstruction placed in the street by an employee of the city while engaged in repairing said street, the plaintiff did not make out a case. After a careful consideration of the statute, we think it was not the intent of the legislature to cover a case of this kind. In the case at bar the aldermen of the ward, in discharging a duty imposed upon them

by law, were in fact engaged in repairing the street in question, and one of their employees negligently permitted the
obstruction to be placed in and remain in said street. We
think, in a case of this kind, the act of the employee while
engaged in his employment must be considered as the act
of the alderman of the ward, and that the city, through the
action of its ward officer, permitted the obstruction to be
placed in the street and to remain there. It cannot be supposed that the legislature intended to release the city from
damages caused by the action of its officers in repairing its
streets, when its employees create the obstruction, because
such officers had no actual notice of the obstruction. In
such case the acts of the employees are the acts of the officers, and their knowledge must be construed to be the
knowledge of the employer. This would be the rule in
every other case, and we cannot think the legislature intended to alter so just a rule in favor of the city. It was
long ago held by this court that the city officers had the
power to grade and improve the streets, but that in doing
so " their agents or contractors have not the right to lay
traps or dig pits in the public streets. They are bound,
as all other persons are, to use ordinary care and diligence
in their operations." See *Milwaukee v. Davis*, 6 Wis. 377,
388. It was held in that case that it was " the duty of the
city to see that the work of altering, grading, and improv-
ing streets be so performed that no person be injured by
any negligence, want of care, or omission of duty by any
of its agents or operatives in performing the work." The
rule laid down in this case has been sustained in several
other cases in this court. *Klatt v. Milwaukee*, 53 Wis. 196,
201; *Prideaux v. Mineral Point*, 43 Wis. 513, 523. In all
these cases it was taken for granted that the city had notice
of what it had itself created. It would seem something
near an absurdity to say that the city should have actual
notice of an obstruction in a street which it had caused by

its own act, before it could be made liable for injury resulting from it. That no notice is required in a case where the
obstruction or defect in the street was caused by the direct
act of the officers of the city or by their employees, was expressly decided in *Springfield v. Le Claire*, 49 Ill. 476; *Barton v. Syracuse*, 36 N. Y. 54, 58; *Chicago v. Johnson*, 53 Ill.
91. See, also, 2 Dill. Mun. Corp. § 1024, and notes. The
statute requiring notice was evidently intended to apply to
acts of omission on the part of the city or its officers or
agents, by reason of which a street becomes out of repair or
obstructed; and not to cases where, in the discharge of its
duty, the city is in the act of repairing the street, and
thereby creates an obstruction which endangers the public.
In all such cases the city becomes liable for the injury resulting from such obstruction, unless the public are in some
way warned against the danger by proper signals or guards.
See cases cited above.

    That the city is liable as any other employer for the acts
of those employed by it in the opening, improvement,
or repair of streets, has lately been decided by this court in the
following cases: *Meinzer v. Racine*, 70 Wis. 561, and *Addy
v. Janesville*, 70 Wis. 401. The provision in the charter of
the city of *Oshkosh* above quoted must be construed, not as
extending the law of notice to cases that did not theretofore require any notice, but as defining how the notice
which the law then required should be given must thereafter be proven. This was the construction given to the
provision by this court in *Studley v. Oshkosh*, 45 Wis. 382,
and is undoubtedly the true construction. In that case
Justice LYON, in his opinion, says: "Upon full consideration of the whole section, it seems to us that the legislature
intended thereby to change or qualify the then existing
law only in these two particulars: (1) By designating an
officer who must have notice of the defect before the city
can be held liable for injuries caused by it; and (2) by fix-

ing a time before which no presumption of notice of such defect can arise, and after which such presumption does arise. In all other respects we think the law remains as it was before the section was enacted."

By the Court.— The judgment of the county court is affirmed.

GREEN, Respondent, vs. BATSON, Appellant.

February 2 — February 28, 1888.

Vendor and purchaser of land: Deed: Parol warranty of quality: Recoupment.

Though a deed conveying land contains only the usual covenants, a warranty as to the *quality* of the land, which was a part of the prior or contemporaneous agreement of sale, may be shown by parol; and damages for a breach of such warranty may be recouped in an action by the grantor upon a note given for a part of the purchase price.

APPEAL from the Circuit Court for *Green Lake* County. The facts are stated in the opinion.

For the appellant there was a brief by *Runals & Dunlap,* attorneys, and *Geo. E. Sutherland,* of counsel, and oral argument by *Mr. Sutherland.* Besides the cases referred to in the opinion, they cited *Frey v. Vanderhoof,* 15 Wis. 401; *Thomas v. Hammond,* 47 Tex. 42; *Graves v. Graves,* 45 N. H. 323; *Ballston Spa Bank v. Marine Bank,* 16 Wis. 136.

The cause was submitted for the respondent on the brief of *Waring, Eichstaedt & Niskern.* They contended, *inter alia,* that the circuit court was justified in holding that the contract between the parties was reduced to writing and that the writing must be presumed to contain the whole contract. *Hubbard v. Marshall,* 50 Wis. 322; *Hei v. Heller,*

53 id. 415; *Yenner v. Hammond*, 36 id. 278; *Wiener v. Whipple*, 53 id. 298, and cases cited; *Lowber v. Connit*, 36 id. 180; *Van Ostrand v. Reed*, 1 Wend. 424. The deed contained several covenants of warranty, and it was not competent to add to these by parol. *Merriam v. Field*, 24 Wis. 640; *Frost v. Blanchard*, 97 Mass. 155; *Whitmore v. South Boston Iron Co.* 2 Allen, 52, 58; *Cunningham v. Hall*, 4 id. 268, 272; *Wiener v. Whipple*, 53 Wis. 298, 304; *Shepherd v. Gilroy*, 46 Iowa, 193; *Merriam v. Field*, 24 Wis. 640; *Shultz v. Coon*, 51 id. 416; *Yenner v. Hammond*, 36 id. 277; *Cooper v. Cleghorn*, 50 id. 113; 2 Benj. on Sales, 821; Story on Cont. (5th ed.), 514; 1 Pars. on Cont. 589; Story on Sales, 445; 2 Phillips on Ev. (Cowen & Hill), note 494; *Smith v. Williams*, 1 Murphey (N. C.), 426; *Wren v. Wardlaw*, Minor (Ala.), 363; *Mumford v. M'Pherson*, 1 Johns. 414; *Thompson v. Libby*, 34 Minn. 374; *Hutton v. Maines*, 68 Iowa, 650; *Marsh v. McNair*, 99 N. Y. 180; *Corse v. Peck*, 102 id. 513.

ORTON, J. This action was brought to recover the unpaid balance of a $400 note given by the defendants to the plaintiff as the difference on an exchange or trade of lands. The defense was that the plaintiff, as an inducement to the trade, represented, stated, and warranted to the defendants, immediately before said sale, that part of said land — being about forty acres — was and were good hay meadow; that said lands were then covered with snow, so that they could not be examined so as to ascertain their character in that respect, and the defendant did not know of their character as hay meadow or otherwise, except what the plaintiff had so told, represented, and warranted, and that it was impossible for him then to see or know that the plaintiff's statements, representations, and warranty were false and not true; and that, putting faith, confidence, and reliance in and upon such statements, representation, and warranty, and believing the same to be true, the defendants made the said trade or exchange and gave the said notes as the supposed difference between the value of said tracts of land; that in fact and truth said lands were not as they were so stated, represented, and warranted to be, and that not more than fifteen acres of said land were good hay meadow or would produce or raise good hay, but were nearly or wholly worthless, and of much less value than they would have been if they had been as so stated, represented, and warranted, and were worth $250 less than they would have been had they been as so stated, represented, and warranted; and that the defendants were thereby damaged in said sum of $250, which they recouped against the plaintiff's claim; and no judgment for any excess is demanded. On the trial the defendants made many attempts, and asked many questions, to prove the said false statements, representations, and warranty set forth in their answer; but on objection — (1) that it is parol evidence in regard to the sale of land; and (2) that it appears in the deed there are several warranties, and you cannot add other warranties by parol,— the court ruled out all of such evidence, and, on motion, directed a verdict for the plaintiff for the whole amount of his claim. From the judgment entered upon said verdict this appeal is taken.

If this defense may be proved by parol, then there is no question but what it constitutes recoupment,—"the right of the defendant, in the same action, to claim damages from the plaintiff, either because he has not complied with some cross-obligation of the contract upon which he sues, or because he has violated some duty which the law imposed upon him in the making or performance of that contract." *Schweickhart v. Stuewe, ante,* p. 1. The question, therefore, presented by the numerous exceptions is narrowed down to this: May the damages accruing to the defendants from the breach of the plaintiff's warranty of the *quality* of the land conveyed to the defendants by deed in this exchange of land be proved by *parol* to defeat the plaintiff's claim. The circuit court held that they could not. The ground assumed by the learned counsel of the respondent is that the deed contained all the covenants which could be proved, and, the contract of the parties being in writing, parol evidence could not be given to alter, vary, change, or add to it. As a general rule, when the contract of the parties is reduced to writing and is apparently complete, the written instrument is supposed to contain the whole contract, and it cannot be varied by parol. This perhaps is the universal rule in respect to contracts relating to personal property. But contracts in respect to the sale and conveyance of land form an exception to this general and salutary rule. It might be more proper to say that such contracts do not come within the general rule. Preceding the conveyance, there is, of course, always an agreement of sale. The deed may contain a very small part of such contract. The deed is made only in execution of the contract. It does not attempt to state the entire agreement in respect to the subject matter, but is merely adapted to transfer the title in part execution of the contract, and is manifestly incomplete. Deeds are supposed to contain only the ordinary covenants of title, and seldom, if ever, contain a covenant of warranty in respect to the *quality* of the land. This deed is in the ordinary form, and contains only the ordinary covenants. Therefore an agreement or covenant of warranty as to the *quality* of the land, and as to many other things which were a part of the prior or contemporaneous agreement of sale, may be shown by parol. Such evidence does not affect the deed or change it in any respect.

This court has recognized this exception in respect to deeds of conveyance in *Hahn v. Doolittle*, 18 Wis. 196, and in *Hubbard v. Marshall*, 50 Wis. 326. This is the general doctrine of the courts of this country. Wood, Pr. Ev. 5690;

2 Whart. Ev. § 1026; *Chapin v. Dobson*, 78 N. Y. 74. The doctrine is well expressed in *Miller v. Fichthorn*, 31 Pa. St. 260. " A conveyance of land may be complete for its purpose, which is to declare and prove the fact of conveyance; yet very naturally and *commonly* it is but a part execution of a prior contract, and *parol* evidence is admissible to show the true consideration for which it was given *and all other parts* of the transaction, provided the fact of conveyance *be not affected by it*." *Carr v. Dooley*, 119 Mass. 294; *McCormick v. Cheevers*, 124 Mass. 262. In *Ludeke v. Sutherland*, 87 Ill. 481, the sale and the conveyance were for 140 acres of land; and, as a part of the agreement of sale, if, on a resurvey the tract should contain more than 140 acres, the grantee was to pay for it at the same rate, and if less, the grantor should restore the excess paid or promised. This agreement was allowed to be proved by parol, and such excess was recouped against the note of the grantee in suit. In *Buzzell v. Willard*, 44 Vt. 44, it was part of the contract of sale that the grantor should put a wheel into the mill. It was allowed to be proved by parol. See, also, *Ingersoll v. Truebody*, 40 Cal. 603; *Kingsbury v. Moses*, 45 N. H. 223. It is useless to prolong the citation of authorities beyond the above, which were furnished by the counsel of the appellant. This doctrine is not shaken or even affected by the authorities in the brief of the respondent's counsel. They relate to agreements which are supposed to be wholly reduced to writing, and in respect to personal property and other transactions.

By the Court.— The judgment of the circuit court is reversed, and the cause remanded for a new trial.

VERBECK, Appellant, vs. SCOTT, imp., Respondent.

February 2 — February 28, 1888.

(1) Municipal bonds: Preliminary injunction to restrain disposal by holder: Discretion. (2) Who is bona fide purchaser. (3) Elections: Failure of electors to vote.

1. In this case the refusal of the circuit court to grant a preliminary injunction restraining the holder of municipal bonds from disposing of them pending the action to have them declared void, is *held* not to have been an abuse of discretion, the facts entitling the plaintiff to such relief not being clearly shown.

2. One who buys municipal bonds from a *bona fide* purchaser, is himself a *bona fide* purchaser, notwithstanding any prior knowledge on his part.

3. An election is not vitiated by the mere fact that a considerable number of the electors failed to vote.

APPEAL from the Circuit Court for *Winnebago* County. The following statement of the case was prepared by Mr. Justice CASSODAY:

This action was commenced July 14, 1887, to restrain the town officers of Menasha from collecting a tax to pay certain bonds issued by such officers in 1871 to the Wisconsin Central Railroad Company, and to have said bonds declared void in the hands of the defendant *Scott*, and to restrain him from disposing of the same during the litigation. None of the defendants resisted the application for a temporary injunction except *Scott*, and upon the hearing the court made an order restraining such officers from collecting the tax, but refusing to restrain *Scott* from disposing of the bonds during the litigation. From so much of said order as refused to so restrain *Scott*, the plaintiff appeals.

It appears, from the plaintiff's showing, in effect, that May 10, 1870, the railroad company, pursuant to ch. 126, Laws of 1869, submitted to the voters of the towns of Menasha and Neenah, respectively, the proposition men-

tioned in *Menasha v. Wis. Cent. R. Co.* 65 Wis. 502, for
their aid by each voting to such company $50,000 of its
bonds in consideration of that amount of the capital stock
of such company, and the building of its depot on block 3
on Doty's island, and its road from thence to the Wolf
river, as therein provided; but in the event that Neenah
failed to accept, and the required additional sum of $50,000
should be furnished to the company by individual subscrip-
tion to stock in like amount and satisfactorily secured to be
paid, the depot should be located, and the road constructed
therefrom, in such place in said town of Menasha, and on
such route as might be agreed upon between the company
and the town, under the proposition as thereby qualified;
that Neenah refused to accept the proposition; that Menasha
accepted of it June 4, 1870; that July 15, 1871, Menasha
town bonds to the amount of $50,000 were issued to the
company, bearing date June 1, 1871, each payable to the
company, or bearer, in New York, twenty years from date,
with coupons attached for semi-annual interest at the rate
of seven per cent.; that October 12, 1871, such town officers burned and destroyed all of said bonds, and October
26, 1871, issued similar bonds to the same amount; that the
tax in the tax roll for paying the interest thereon in 1872
was restrained by order of the court February 18, 1873;
that upon the organization of the city of Menasha in 1874,
one fourth of said bonds remained outstanding against
the town; that the company never constructed any railroad
from said block 3 to the Wolf river, or to any other point;
that the town officers knew, when they issued the bonds, that
the company had not complied with their proposition;
that during the time *Scott* was a resident of Menasha, and
knew all the facts stated, and actively participated in procuring the vote; that May 20, 1887, the officers of the
town agreed upon a compromise and settlement with *Scott*,
whereby the town was to pay him $5,750 in full discharge

and satisfaction of said bonds so held by him; and the same was submitted to the qualified electors of the town at a special town meeting therefor June 6, 1887, and ratified and agreed to by 47 of the 83 votes cast thereat; and it is alleged that there were over 150 qualified electors in the town. Bad faith and collusion between *Scott* and such officers in making said settlement is charged, and denied on the part of the defense.

The complaint alleges that *Scott* "is not a *bona fide* holder of said bonds; and that he received the same well knowing all the facts and circumstances aforesaid in relation to the execution and issuing of said bonds; and that the same do not constitute a valid and *bona fide* indebtedness of said town of Menasha *to him*." This is denied in the same language, except the omission of the words "*to him*." The complaint alleges, upon information and belief, that if the $5,750 is not paid, *Scott* threatens and intends to remove the bonds from the state and dispose of the same to non-residents who can enforce payment in the United States courts. This, however, is denied on the part of the defense. The defense denied that the company had not complied with the terms and conditions of its proposition submitted to the town; and, in effect, alleged that all the terms and conditions of said proposition had been complied with; that Neenah never subscribed to such railroad stock or any part thereof, and never issued its bonds to said company, and said company never had any Neenah bonds, whereupon the company made its starting point in Menasha and constructed its road to the Wolf river, as it had a lawful right to do; that the railroad runs nearer said block 3, and has a depot in Menasha and also in Neenah, giving both of said cities and the present town of Menasha better and nearer facilities for railroad purposes than if the station or starting point had been upon said block 3; that the city and town of Menasha several years ago settled and took up all said bonds except the sixteen owned by *Scott*, and in such settlement used and enjoyed $50,000 of stock issued and given by the railroad company; that *Scott* had always been advised that the bonds were issued by authority of law; that he received them in good faith, and knew the owner thereof paid a full and valuable consideration therefor, having no knowledge whatever of any injunction or restraining order or any other fact or circumstance tending to invalidate the same; that *Scott's* entire connection with said bonds was *bona fide*, without any knowledge or information of any unlawfulness or irregularity in the issue or delivery thereof or since, and he denies that he had owned and held the bonds since about the time they were issued; that the railroad was constructed from a point in Menasha to the Wolf river; that the injunction mentioned in the complaint, and which was issued July 31, 1871, was answered and never prosecuted to final judgment; that the plaintiff therein had died, and the suit never revived; that the tax-warrant to collect such taxes was issued under ch. 216, Laws of 1887, returnable in forty days; that all the bonds had been paid, except the sixteen owned by Scott, and for one fourth of which the town was liable. There were other affidavits in support of the allegations on the part of the defense, and asserting the good faith of the settlement between the town officers and *Scott* and the vote thereon by the qualified electors of the town.

For the appellant there was a brief by *Gary & Forward*, attorneys, and *Moses Hooper*, of counsel, and oral argument by *Mr. Gary.*

For the respondent there was a brief by *Gabe Bouck*, *Henry Fitzgibbon*, and *Smith & Schoetz*, and the cause was argued orally by *Mr. Bouck*. They argued, *inter alia*, that when the material facts are denied an injunction should not issue. *Menasha v. M. & N. R. Co.* 52 Wis. 414. It should issue only when the right of the plaintiff is evident, *prima facie,* free from doubt. Extreme caution should be exercised. Willard's Eq. Jur. 343; *Muir v. Howell,* 37 N. J. Eq. 39. If the respondent bought the bonds from a *bona fide* holder, he has a good title, and can transmit it to a person having full knowledge of the illegality, if any, in their inception. 1 Daniel on Neg. Inst. sec. 803; Burroughs on Pub. Sec. 361; *Comm'rs v. Clark,* 94 U. S. 286; *Cromwell v. Sac,* 96 id. 59; *Bailey v. Bidwell,* 13 Mees. & W. 73; *Mitchell v. Catchings,* 23 Fed. Rep. 710; *Patterson v. Wright,* 64 Wis. 289; *Pringle v. Dunn,* 37 id. 449; *Kinney v. Kruse,* 28 id. 184.

CASSODAY, J. The application for this preliminary injunction was undoubtedly addressed to the sound discretion of the trial court under the facts and circumstances alleged in the complaint and supported by affidavits. Upon such hearing the defendant *Scott* controverted, and in fact disproved, many of such allegations; and alleged others as stated. The court, in the exercise of such discretion, refused to restrain *Scott* from disposing of his bonds; and we are now asked upon the whole record, a brief summary of which is given above, to reverse that part of the order. After a careful examination of the record we are unable to say that such discretion has been abused. The plaintiff brings this suit as a resident freeholder and tax-payer of the town issuing the bonds. The burden was upon him to allege facts calling for equitable interference to prevent irreparable injury. It seems to us that the complaint, with the allegations therein disproved, as stated, does not come up to this requirement. It does not clearly appear that the railroad company did not comply with the proposition submitted in 1870, so far as Menasha was concerned. It does not clearly appear that the particular bonds in question were issued in violation of any injunction. It does pretty clearly appear that the railroad stock received in consideration for such bonds was used by the town and city of Menasha, or one of them with the consent of the other, many years ago, in taking up and settling all of the bonds so issued, except those owned by *Scott.* It does not clearly appear that the sixteen bonds in question were never owned by a *bona fide* purchaser for a full and valuable consideration paid therefor. If they were ever owned by such purchaser, and subsequently were transferred to *Scott,* then he would be such *bona fide* purchaser, notwithstanding any prior knowledge on his part. It does not clearly appear that the compromise and settlement agreed upon by *Scott* and the officers of the town in May, 1887, was not honestly made and in good faith submitted to the qualified electors of the town at a special town meeting therefor, June 6, 1887, and in good faith ratified and agreed to by a majority of the votes cast at that election. The mere fact that a considerable number of such qualified electors failed to vote thereon did not vitiate the election. Under the circumstances stated we are unwilling to disturb the action of the trial court.

By the Court.— That part of the order of the circuit court appealed from is affirmed.

ABBOT, Trustee, etc., Plaintiff in error, vs. TOLLIVER, Defendant in error.

February 2 — February 28, 1888.

Excessive damages: Personal injuries: Unchastity.

1. The railroad car in which the plaintiff was riding was derailed, and she was thrown upon the floor and, while attempting to rise, was again thrown backwards in a sitting position. She was a large woman, weighing about 200 pounds. The evidence tended to show that she was rendered unconscious for a long time; that for several months she was quite helpless, could not be moved without mak-

ing her scream, and had frequent fainting spells; that she suffered from pain in her spine and womb, and at times from pain and numbness in her left arm and limb; and that up to the time of the trial, about thirteen months after the accident, she had been confined to her bed most of the time. The physicians who examined her found a displacement and laceration of the womb, but agreed that these were not caused by the shock or fall in the car. It did not satisfactorily appear that there was any permanent injury to the spine. There was evidence that the plaintiff was of unchaste character. *Held*, that a verdict awarding $7,000 should have been set aside on the ground that the damages were excessive.

2. The fact that the plaintiff is of unchaste character may be considered by the jury in assessing compensatory damages for personal injuries caused by negligence.

ERROR to the Circuit Court for *Winnebago* County.

The action was brought against *Edwin H. Abbot* and John A. Stewart, as trustees of the Wisconsin Central Railroad Company, to recover damages for personal injuries alleged to have been sustained by the plaintiff by reason of the negligence of the said trustees and their servants in the construction, maintenance, and care of the railroad and its equipments. The facts will sufficiently appear from the opinion. The trial took place in May, 1887. The plaintiff had a verdict for $7,000. The defendant *Abbot* sued out a writ of error to review the judgment entered thereon.

For the plaintiff in error there was a brief by *Charles W. Felker*, and oral argument by *Mr. Felker* and *D. S. Wegg*. In the following cases, where the injuries received were much more severe, the probable injury much more certain, the capacity to earn much greater, and the pecuniary loss growing out of the disability to attend to business far more apparent, it has been held that a less amount of damages was excessive: *Baker v. Madison*, 62 Wis. 137; *Goodno v. Oshkosh*, 28 id. 300; *Sioux City & P. R. Co. v. Finlayson*, 18 Am. & Eng. R. Cas. 68, 76; *McIntyre v. N. Y. C. R. Co.* 47 Barb. 515; *Chicago & R. I. R. Co. v. McKean*, 40 Ill. 218, 238, 242; *Chicago, R. I. & P. R. Co.*

v. McAra, 52 id. 296; *Chicago, R. I. & P. R. Co. v. McKit-trick*, 78 id. 619; *Spicer v. C. & N. W. R. Co.* 29 Wis. 580; *Murray v. H. R. R. Co.* 47 Barb. 196, 204.

For the defendant in error there was a brief by *Gabe Bouck*, attorney, and *Geo. P. Rossman*, of counsel, and oral argument by *Mr. Bouck*. To the point that the damages were not excessive, they cited *Groves v. Rochester*, 39 Hun, 5; *International & G. N. R. Co. v. Gilbert*, 64 Tex. 536; *Cummings v. Nat. F. Co.* 60 Wis. 617; *Draper v. Baker*, 61 id. 450; *Funston v. C., R. I. & P. R. Co.* 61 Iowa, 452; *Harrold v. N. Y. Ele. R. Co.* 24 Hun, 184; *Ferguson v. W. C. R. Co.* 63 Wis. 145; 3 Suth. on Dam. 289; *Johnson v. C. & N. W. R. Co.* 64 Wis. 425.

COLE, C. J. Some objections are taken to the rulings of the circuit court in admitting or excluding evidence on the trial, but as we have concluded that the judgment must be reversed on another ground it is not necessary to determine whether these rulings were erroneous or not. Whether the court erred in not permitting the witness Jones to testify to the matters concerning which he was interrogated, depended upon the fact whether Jones was the plaintiff's husband or not. The plaintiff testified on the trial that she was never married to him, though she had stated in her deposition previously taken that she was married to Jones after she was divorced from Miller. Jones was called by the defendant, and testified that he was married to the plaintiff in 1877, at Hancock, Wisconsin, by a justice of the peace by the name of Moore, and the justice himself testified that he performed the marriage ceremony between Jones and the plaintiff on the 25th or 26th of February, 1877, at the town of Hancock, where he then lived and held the office of justice of the peace. On this state of the evidence there was good ground for holding that Jones was not a competent witness. The defendant ought not to discredit his own witness, but assume that he told the truth in the matter. This is the only remark we feel called upon to make upon this point.

The plaintiff was injured while traveling as a passenger on the Wisconsin Central Railway, in April, 1886, between Dorchester and Stetsonville. The parlor car in which she was riding got partially off the track, made a lurch, and threw the plaintiff, as she was rising from her chair, down on the floor in the center of the car; and while she was attempting to rise she was again thrown backwards in a sitting position. The accident doubtless happened in consequence of ·the track being in a defective state; the ties were badly decayed, and this caused the rail to spread and the car getting off the track or becoming derailed. The negligence of the defendant in failing to keep the road-bed in a reasonably safe condition is not seriously denied, nor could it well be upon the proofs. The plaintiff was rendered unconscious by the fall, and had no recollection of anything which occurred on her journey home to Ashland. She was entirely helpless, and says it was quite a number of days before she became conscious, and when she did she could not even move her fingers without crying out. Her left arm and limb were numb; "she was in sinking spells most of the time, and was in pain all over," as she describes her condition. She suffered from pain in her spine and womb. Dr. Hosmer, who was called to attend her the night she reached home, says she complained of her womb, and he found she was sore up and down the back; he saw no black and blue spots on her body anywhere, but her spine was sensitive or tender. When he made an examination, as he did some weeks after the accident, he found a displacement and laceration of the womb, and he thought there was more or less concussion of the spinal column. He says she was troubled with fainting spells, something like epileptic fits. He attended upon her for some months.

At times, he says, she got along very well, and was recovering, but a little indiscretion on her part, in attempting to sit up, would bring her back just as she was at first. Dr. Madden also called to see the plaintiff, in consultation with Dr. Hosmer, three or four days after she was injured, and he saw her several times afterwards. He made an examination, and found a soreness or tenderness along the spinal column, and an enlargement and laceration of the womb. He agreed with Dr. Hosmer as to her condition, but thought she was suffering from no organic trouble except the displacement or inflammation of the womb. He discovered no symptoms of any organic disease of the spine, except the statements of the plaintiff. The nurses who had the care of the plaintiff for several months say she complained of pain, was quite helpless, could not be moved without making her scream, and that she had frequent fainting spells. The plaintiff says she has not walked nor stood upon her feet since the injury, and that at times she suffered from pain and numbness in her left arm and limb. It appears that she has been confined to her bed most of the time up to the trial, and has suffered considerable pain. The jury gave a verdict for $7,000 damages, which, it is claimed on the part of the defendant below, is disproportionate to any injury proven, and should be set aside as excessive. We are inclined to sustain this position as sound.

We have stated the material testimony given on the part of the plaintiff as to the nature and extent of her injury. To our minds it fails to show that she sustained any permanent injury by the fall. She is a large woman, weighing about 200 pounds, and doubtless received a severe shock or jar when thrown upon the floor of the car. But the medical testimony offered on her side does not satisfactorily show that she suffered any permanent injury to the spine by the fall. The probability that she did sustain any such injury is greatly weakened, if not fully disproved, by the medical testimony given on the part of the defendant. These physicians were of the opinion that, if there had been any concussion of the spine, there would be some indications of paralysis resulting from it, and none such was shown. They thought all the real pain which the plaintiff suffered was caused by the disease and laceration of the womb; and all the physicians agreed that this womb difficulty was not produced by the shock or fall in the car. Dr. Hosmer says the plaintiff was getting better of her nervous symptoms, and Dr. Madden thought there was probably no organic trouble of the nervous system. The physicians on the part of the defense were of the opinion that her pains were largely imaginary or feigned. But the evidence is so unsatisfactory and inconclusive as to whether there was any injury to the spine resulting from the fall, that it does not warrant giving damages on that ground; for, unless we are prepared to say that the whole matter of damages, in a case of personal injury by a railroad company, rests entirely in the judgment and discretion of the jury, it is obvious there should be some basis for damages in the proof offered. The learned circuit judge charged the jury that if they found the plaintiff had an injury to or disease of the womb prior to the accident, they ought to take into consideration the nature and extent of that injury or disease, and whether any or all the pains which she claims to have suffered proceeded from, or were caused by, this injury or disease of the womb. If so, the plaintiff was not entitled to recover damages for such pain and suffering. Notwithstanding this direction, we are unable to account for the verdict, except upon the theory that damages were actually given for a supposed permanent injury or disability of the spine, of which there was no satisfactory proof. We have, in a number of cases, set aside verdicts where the damages awarded exceeded all fair compensation for injuries proven. In the present case we think the jury must have been misled, or were influenced by some improper bias, in giving so large a verdict, which is quite disproportionate to any injury proven.

The judge likewise charged that the defendant, if liable, was liable for all the direct injuries resulting from its negligent acts; that the fact that the plaintiff is an unchaste woman, or has more than one husband, has nothing to do with the damages, if any, she is entitled to recover for injuries received; that an unchaste woman, or a woman who has several husbands, if injured on a railroad train, is entitled to recover the same damages for injuries received as a chaste woman, or a woman who has only one husband. This charge was excepted to, and we think it had a tendency to mislead the jury on the question of damages. We do not wish to intimate that an unchaste woman who is maimed and disabled by an accident on the railroad may not suffer as much pain of body or anxiety of mind as a virtuous woman would from a like injury; but still, when it comes to a question of awarding damages, it may be that a jury would not give — perhaps ought not to give — the *same damages* for injuries to an unchaste woman that they would allow a virtuous, intelligent, and industrious woman, who could command good wages or take care of a family. The fact of chastity, as well as other personal virtues and business qualifications, would be proper matters for a jury to consider in making up their verdict as to what damages should be given as a compensation for the injury received, in view of all the facts.

We think the court erred in refusing a new trial on the ground that the damages were excessive. For this reason the judgment of the circuit court is reversed and a new trial awarded.

By the Court.— Ordered accordingly.

See note to this case in 86 N. W. Rep. 622.— REP.

WALTER A. WOOD REAPING AND MOWING MACHINE COMPANY, Appellant, vs. STENEL, Respondent.

February 2 — February 28, 1888.

Sale of chattels: Statute of frauds: Acceptance: Instructions to jury: New trial.

> In an action to recover $200, the price of a harvester, there was evidence of a parol contract that defendant would accept the machine if, in a field trial, the judges should decide in its favor. The court instructed the jury that this evidence was of no consequence, except as it might aid them in determining whether defendant did accept the machine, and that they had a right to take it into consideration only for the purpose of determining that question. *Held,* that an order granting a new trial because the court failed to instruct the jury that such promise did not constitute an acceptance and that defendant could refuse to take the machine notwithstanding the promise, must be reversed because the charge given covered the ground.

APPEAL from the Circuit Court for *Calumet* County. The case is stated in the opinion.

For the appellant there was a brief by *Nash & Nash,* and oral argument by *Mr. L. J. Nash.*

Gabe Bouck, for the respondent.

LYON, J. This is an appeal from an order of the circuit court granting a new trial for errors which the court deemed it had committed by refusing to give the jury certain instructions proposed on behalf of the defendant.

The action is for the price of a harvester and binder alleged to have been sold by the plaintiff to the defendant. The answer is a general denial. The price of the machine was $200. The contract of sale was by parol, and hence within the statute of frauds. The question litigated was whether the defendant had accepted the machine. He had received it upon trial, and, before accepting it, arranged with the agent of the plaintiff for a competitive trial with another machine. This is referred to as a field trial. It was claimed on the part of the plaintiff that the defendant agreed that if a committee which had been agreed upon should decide in favor of the plaintiff's machine he (the defendant) would keep it. The testimony tended to prove such agreement. The committee so decided.

It was stated in the order granting a new trial that the same was granted for the sole and only reason that the court refused to give the following instructions asked by the defendant, to wit: "If the defendant, on the day of the trial or before the trial, said to the agent or agents or employee of the plaintiff that he would keep the machine the committee decided in favor of, and, after the trial, refused to take the Wood machine, this did not constitute an acceptance. Such promise was not valid, unless followed by an acceptance. Unless followed by an acceptance, a void contract. He was not, by reason of such promise and the decision of the committee, obliged to accept the machine. He could refuse to accept the machine, even if he so said he would take the machine if the committee decided in favor of it." Such being the order of the court, no question of discretion is presented. If it was error to refuse the above instructions, a new trial was properly granted; otherwise, not. *Bushnell v. Scott*, 21 Wis. 451; *Jones v. Evans*, 28 Wis. 168; *Duffy v. C. & N. W. R. Co.* 34 Wis. 188.

Probably, the propositions which the court refused to give were correct statements of the law, but we think they were substantially given in the general charge. If so, it was not error to refuse to give them. In the general charge we find the following instructions:

"The principal question with which you have got to deal is to determine, from all the evidence in the case, whether or not the defendant did accept the machine. Now, there has been a good deal of talk, gentlemen, and

Walter A. Wood Reaping and Mowing Machine Co. vs. Stenel.

considerable proof *pro* and *con*, as to the trial of this machine,—the first trial which was had the first day, and as to the field trial; and what was done at that time, and what the judges said, and the decision they rendered about it. Now, so far as the present issue is concerned,—so far as you are concerned in dealing with this case,—all that is of no consequence, except as it may bear upon the question whether or not the defendant accepted this machine. It is all of no consequence, except as it may aid you, if it does aid you, in determining the question whether or not the defendant did accept this machine; and for that purpose only you have a right to take into consideration all that evidence."

By this instruction the jury were emphatically told that the defendant's agreement to take the machine in favor of which the committee should decide did not bind the defendant, and was of no importance in the case, except they might consider the circumstance as bearing upon the question of acceptance. The charge covers the whole ground of the proposed instructions, and the defendant has no cause for complaint because such instructions were not repeated.

By the Court.—The order of the circuit court is reversed, and the cause will be remanded with directions to that court to deny the motion for a new trial.

HINER, Administrator, etc., Respondent, vs. THE CITY OF
FOND DU LAC, Appellant.

February 3 — February 28, 1888.

*(1-3) Municipal corporations: Injury from defective sidewalk: Fond
du Lac charter: Notice of injury: Exhausting remedy against lot-
owner: Burden of proof: Pleading: Notice of defect: Nonsuit.
(4) Survival of actions. (5) Taxation of costs in supreme court:
Printed case.*

1. Sec. 204 of the Fond du Lac city charter (ch. 240, Laws of 1879), relating to the notice to be given before an action in tort can be
   maintained against the city, being at variance with sec. 1339, R. S.,
   supersedes that section, and in an action of that nature against
   said city the complaint must allege the giving of the notice required by the charter. *Plum v. Fond du Lac,* 51 Wis. 393, distinguished.

2. Sec. 206 of said charter provides that in case of injury from the
   defective or dangerous condition of a sidewalk caused by the negligence of any person, such person shall be primarily liable, and
   the city shall not be liable until all legal remedies against him have
   been exhausted. Sec. 207 makes the obligation of lot-owners to
   keep the sidewalks in repair an absolute one, not dependent on
   any notice from the city authorities. *Held,* that in an action
   against the city where the plaintiff has proved the facts which
   show the primary liability of a lot-owner, the burden is upon him
   to show further that he has exhausted his legal remedies against
   such owner. [Whether the latter fact is a condition precedent to
   the right to maintain the action, performance of which must be
   averred in the complaint, not determined.] *Amos v. Fond du Lac,*
   46 Wis. 695, distinguished.

3. A sidewalk had been defective for several weeks. On the day of
   the injury it had been repaired and new planks laid, but the work
   of spiking the planks down had not been completed. The plaintiff
   was injured, in the evening, by stepping upon the end of one of
   such loose planks. The case was tried on the theory that the previous defective condition of the sidewalk was the proximate cause
   of the injury, and on that theory the jury found that the injury
   was caused by the negligence of the city. There being no claim
   or pretense that any city official had anything to do with leaving
   the new planks loose, or had actual or constructive notice that they
   were so left, it is *held* that a nonsuit should have been granted.

[4. Whether the words "or other damage to the person " in sec. 4253, R. S., as amended by ch. 280, Laws of 1887 (relating to the survival of actions), should be construed to mean damage resulting from force, not determined.]

5. The printed case herein consists of 222 pages, and contains about 200 pages of testimony, which should have been condensed into one third of that space. The clerk is directed, in the taxation of costs, to allow for the printing of 100 pages only.

APPEAL from the Circuit Court for *Winnebago* County. This action was originally brought by the plaintiff's intestate, Bridget Cuff, together with her husband, to recover damages alleged to have been received by the said Bridget on April 11, 1879, by reason of a defective sidewalk on Rose street in the defendant city. The complaint was afterwards dismissed as to the husband, and the action proceeded in the name of the said Bridget as the sole plaintiff.

It is alleged in the complaint that the sidewalk in question adjoined lots 93 and 94. The complaint also states the condition of the sidewalk and the circumstances of the injury with reasonable particularity, and the duty of the city to keep the same in repair. It also alleges that notice in writing, signed by the plaintiff, "describing generally the insufficiency or want of repair of said sidewalk, and describing the place where the injury occurred, and claiming satisfaction for such injury from said city, was duly served on the city clerk of the city of *Fond du Lac* within ninety days after the happening of the accident."

The answer is substantially a general denial. It also alleges that said lots 93 and 94 were owned by some person unknown to the defendant; that it was the duty of such owner to keep the same in repair; and that the plaintiff has not exhausted all her legal remedies against such owner or the occupant of the premises.

The evidence given on the trial showed conclusively that the sidewalk at the place of the injury had been greatly damaged and partly destroyed by a freshet some weeks before the plaintiff was injured, portions of it having been washed away; and that it became thereby practically impassable, and remained in that condition until the day the plaintiff was injured. On that day, and before the injury, the sidewalk was repaired by and under the direction of the agent of the owner of the lot. Mrs. Cuff lived near the place, and frequently passed there, always going in the street after the destruction of the sidewalk. She passed the place on the afternoon of April 11th while the sidewalk was being repaired, going in the street at that point. On her return home, in the evening, she found the planks of the walk all in place, and attempted to pass over them. The planks were laid lengthwise of the walk. She stepped upon a plank that had not been spiked, one end of which did not rest upon the stringer. The plank was displaced by her weight, and she fell through the sidewalk, receiving the injuries complained of.

At the close of the plaintiff's testimony a motion for a nonsuit was made on behalf of the defendant and denied by the court. The jury returned a special verdict as follows: "(1) Was the sidewalk on the north side of Rose street, in the city of *Fond du Lac*, defendant, on the 11th day of April, 1879, at or about the place described in this action, out of repair and unsafe to pass over? Yes. (2) Had such defect existed for a period of four weeks or more before said 11th day of April? Yes. (3) Were there suitable barriers erected or placed across said sidewalk on both sides of the place out of repair on or about 7 o'clock in the evening of April 11th, 1879, to remain there for the night, by persons engaged in repairing said walk, to warn off and give notice to all persons passing over the same that said walk was out of repair and unsafe to pass over? No. (4) Was the defendant guilty of negligence in failing to repair said sidewalk or in leaving it in the condition it was on said evening? Yes. (5) Did the plaintiff use ordinary care and prudence by choosing to pass over said sidewalk, so out of repair, on her return home on the evening of said 11th day of April? Yes. (6) Did the plaintiff fall into said sidewalk on the evening of April 11, 1879, and receive an injury therefrom? Yes. (7) Was such injury, if any, caused by the negligence of the city? Yes. (8) What amount of damages, if any, did the plaintiff sustain from the injury received in falling into said sidewalk at the time and place aforesaid? $4,500."

At the same term, and before judgment, a motion was made on behalf of the defendant city for a new trial. Several reasons were assigned therefor, among them that the verdict was not supported by the evidence, and that the damages were excessive. The court ordered that a new trial be granted, unless the plaintiff remit $1,000 of the verdict. The plaintiff thereupon remitted $1,000 therefrom, and the motion for a new trial was denied. Judgment was thereupon entered for the plaintiff for $3,500, and costs. The defendant appeals from such judgment.

. After the appeal was taken, probably in the early part of 1887, the plaintiff Mrs. Cuff died, and July 11th of that year the action was revived in this court in the name of her administrator, the present plaintiff.

For the appellant there was a brief by *P. H. Martin*, City Attorney, and oral argument by *Edw. S. Bragg* and *Mr. Martin*.

For the respondent there was a brief by *J. H. McCrory*, and oral argument by *F. F. Duffy* and *Mr. McCrory*.

LYON, J. This record develops at least three material errors, any one of which is necessarily fatal to the judgment. These will be stated and considered in their order.

1. At the commencement of the trial the defendant objected to the admission of any evidence under the complaint, for the reason that it does not state facts sufficient

to constitute a cause of action. The point of the objection was that the complaint does not aver the giving of any sufficient notice of the injury to the city authorities. The objection was overruled. If the giving of the notice required by law is not averred in the complaint, the pleading is fatally defective, and the objection should have been sustained. *Susenguth v. Rantoul,* 48 Wis. 334; *Benware v. Pine Valley,* 53 Wis. 527; *C. & N. W. R. Co. v. Langlade,* 55 Wis. 116. The notice alleged in the complaint would probably be sufficient under sec. 1339, R. S., but that statute is not in force in the city of *Fond du Lac.* Sec. 204, tit. 17, of the charter of that city, enacted in 1879, is as follows: "No action in tort shall lie or be maintained against the city of *Fond du Lac*, unless a statement in writing, signed by the person injured or claiming to be injured, of the wrong and circumstances thereof, and amount of damages claimed, shall be presented to the common council within ninety days after the occurring or happening of the tort alleged." Laws of 1879, ch. 240, p. 443. It will be seen by comparing them that the charter provision is at variance with sec. 1339, R. S., in that it requires the notice to be given to the common council instead of the mayor or city clerk, and requires the amount of damages claimed to be stated in the notice, which sec. 1339 does not, and also requires the wrong and circumstances thereof to be stated, instead of stating the place where such damages occurred and the insufficiency or want of repair which occasioned it. Some of these variances are material, and render the two acts inconsistent with each other. They cannot both stand. Hence, under sec. 4086, R. S., the charter provision prevails, and sec. 1339 is not in force in the city of *Fond du Lac.*

It is quite true that the testimony (received under objection) shows a substantial compliance with the requirements of sec. 204. But, without an amendment of the complaint, the testimony should not have been received. No offer to amend the complaint was made. It is clear that the complaint avers no sufficient notice of the injury, as required by sec. 204; and, inasmuch as such averment is essential to the validity of the complaint, the demurrer *ore tenus* thereto should have been sustained.

Before leaving this branch of the case, it should be observed that the case of *Plum v. Fond du Lac*, 51 Wis. 393, arose before the enactment of the charter of 1879, and it was there held that the notice required by sec. 1339, R. S., should have been averred. At that time the charter of *Fond du Lac* contained no provision corresponding with sec. 204 of the present charter, so far as we are advised.

2. The next error is the failure of the plaintiff to exhaust her legal remedies against the owner of lots 93 and 94 before bringing this action. The charter provision on that subject is found in sec. 206 of the charter of 1879. The section reads as follows: "In case of injury or damage by reason of insufficient, defective, or dangerous condition of streets, sidewalks, drains, sewers, gutters, ditches, or bridges, produced or caused by the wrong, neglect of duty, default, or negligence of any person or corporation, such person or corporation shall be primarily liable for all damages for such injury, in suit for the recovery thereof by the person sustaining such damages, and the city shall not be liable therefor until all legal remedies shall have been exhausted to collect such damages from such person or corporation."

It was held in *Amos v. Fond du Lac*, 46 Wis. 695, that under the city charter of 1868 (P. & L. Laws of 1868, ch. 59, subch. 13, sec. 11) the obligation of the owner or occupant of the adjoining lot to repair a sidewalk did not arise until he had notice from the city authorities to do so. But the charter of 1879 makes such obligation absolute and not dependent upon any action of the city or the city authorities. Sec. 207 is as follows: "The duty of always keeping the sidewalks, gutters, drains, and ditches on or adjacent to the lots and premises of any person, in safe condition and good repair, is hereby expressly enjoined and imposed upon all owners or occupants of said lots and premises." Laws of 1879, ch. 240, p. 443. Hence the owner of lots 93 and 94 was under legal obligation to repair the sidewalk in question from the time it was first washed away or injured until it was repaired, and was in default for not doing so, without regard to the action of the city authorities.

On the trial, the plaintiff proved that lots 93 and 94 belonged to one Drury, and that the sidewalk was rebuilt under the direction of Drury's agent on the day the plaintiff was injured, and was left by him in the condition it was when she was injured.

It was held in *Amos v. Fond du Lac,* that under the charter of 1868 the failure to exhaust legal remedies against the owner was matter of defense. Such failure was so pleaded in this action. But after the plaintiff had proved the facts which showed the primary liability of the owner of the lots, it was incumbent upon her to go further, and prove that she had exhausted her legal remedies against such owner; failing in this, she failed to prove a cause of action.

One of the grounds upon which the motion for a nonsuit was predicated was that, under the complaint and proof, the plaintiff had not made a case entitling her to recover. The motion should have been granted or a new trial awarded for that reason. The rule of pleading established in *Amos v. Fond du Lac* was based upon the provisions of the charter of 1868, under which no duty was imposed upon the lot-owner to repair or build the sidewalk on his lot until after due notice. There was no presumption that he had received such notice; hence the necessity of stating the fact as a defense in order to show his duty in the premises and consequent liability for injuries caused by the defective walk. But the charter of 1879 makes such duty and liability absolute. Hence there is great force in the position maintained by counsel for defendant, that the exhausting of all legal remedies against the lot-owner is a condition precedent to the right to maintain this action. If so, the performance of such condition should be averred in the complaint. Such would be the safer practice; but we do not here determine the point.

3. The third and most vital error is that the case was tried and the verdict and judgment rendered upon the hypothesis that the defective condition of the sidewalk for the four weeks or more before Mrs. Cuff was injured was the direct and proximate cause of her injury. Nothing could be further from the real fact. The broken and defective sidewalk, during all that time, was practically impassable; at least, the plaintiff never attempted to pass over it. It was inconvenient, no doubt, to travelers who otherwise would have used it, but was perfectly harmless so far as exposing any one to peril is concerned. It was the same as though there had been no sidewalk there. The proximate cause of the injury complained of was the loose plank, the end of which did not rest upon the stringer. That, and that alone, was the defect in the walk which was the direct cause of the injury. That defect had existed but a few hours before Mrs. Cuff was hurt, and there is no claim or pretense that any city official had anything to do with leaving the plank in that condition, or had the slightest knowledge of the existence of the defect. As a matter of course, there is nothing in the case to charge those officials with constructive notice of the defect. Hence the finding that the injury was caused by the negligence of the city is entirely unsupported by evidence. For these reasons the nonsuit should have been granted. That being denied, a new trial should have been ordered.

4. At the common law the cause of action would not have survived the death of the plaintiff, and a reversal of the

judgment would end the case. *Randall v. N. W. Tel. Co.* 54 Wis. 140; R. S. sec. 4253. But by ch. 280, Laws of 1887, it is enacted that actions "for assault and battery or false imprisonment, or other damage to the person," shall survive. This is an amendment to sec. 4253, R. S., the amendment consisting, in part, in adding to that section the words "or other damage to the person." Whether or not this act extends to damages to the person occasioned by negligence, or is confined to damages resulting from force, like assault and battery or false imprisonment, we do not here determine. It might be claimed, however, with some plausibility, that because the amendatory words are used in connection with personal injuries committed with force, the maxim *noscitur a sociis* should be applied, and the words " other damage to the person " construed to mean damage resulting from force. Neither do we determine whether, in any event, the amendatory act is properly applicable to this case. These questions have not been argued, and they probably are not important in this case, as our judgment goes upon grounds which seem to be fatal to the action; and it is not probable that a new trial will be desired. If one is demanded, we leave it to the learned circuit judge to determine, in the first instance, whether to grant the same or dismiss the complaint.

5. The printed case contains about 200 pages of printed testimony. The reporter's minutes of the testimony is signed as the bill of exceptions, and nearly the whole of it is inserted in the printed case. A very large proportion of it is entirely useless for the purposes of this appeal. It is mere chaff, and confuses, rather than aids, the investigation of the case. This is a gross violation of the rules of this court in that behalf. [In the original opinion a statement as to who is responsible for this violation of the rule was here inserted, but having been found erroneous it is omitted by direction of Mr. Justice Lyon.] The testimony could

easily have been condensed into one third the space it now occupies without detriment to either party and greatly to the advantage of the court. It only remains to apply the usual remedy in such cases. The printed case contains 222 pages. In the taxation of costs the clerk will allow for the printing of 100 pages only. '

By the Court.— The judgment of the circuit court is reversed, and the cause remanded for further proceedings according to law.

WILL OF McCRORY.

February 3 — February 28, 1888.

Change of venue: Prejudice of judges of other circuits.

Though the party applying for a change of venue under sec. 2625, R. S., on the ground of the prejudice of the judge, states in his affidavit that the judges of certain other judicial circuits are also prejudiced, this is not conclusive of that fact, and the place of trial may nevertheless be changed to one of such circuits. *N. W. Iron Co. v. Crane,* 66 Wis. 567, distinguished.

APPEAL from the Circuit Court for *Winnebago* County. The following statement of the case was prepared by Mr. Justice TAYLOR as a part of the opinion:

The last will and testament of Charles McCrory, deceased, was presented to the county court of Fond du Lac county for probate, and the probate thereof was contested by *Mary McCrory,* the appellant. The county court admitted the will to probate, and from the order of that court admitting the same to probate the contestant appealed to the circuit court of Fond du Lac county. After the record had been transmitted to the circuit court of Fond du Lac county, the contestant appeared in that court and moved for a change of the place of trial, upon an affidavit of prejudice of the judge of said circuit; and thereupon the said circuit court made an order changing the place of trial to the circuit court of Winnebago county. To the making of this order the contestant excepted. The record was transmitted to the clerk of the circuit court of Winnebago county, and the action was brought to trial in that court by the proponent of the will. The contestant did not appear in that court, and said court affirmed the order of the county court admitting the will to probate. From the judgment and order of the circuit court the contestant appeals to this court. The only error alleged by the appellant is that the order made by the circuit court of Fond du Lac county was erroneous and void. The following is a copy of the affidavit upon which the contestant moved for a change of the place of trial in the circuit court of Fond du Lac county (after the title of the cause):

" *State of Wisconsin, Fond du Lac County* — *ss.*: *Mary McCrory*, being duly sworn, says that she is the contestant of the above-named last will and testament of said Charles McCrory, deceased, and one of the legatees named in said last will and testament, and as such contestant is one of the parties interested in said matter; that she has good reason to believe, and does believe, that she cannot have a fair trial of said action and matter in the court where the said action is now pending, on account of the prejudice of the Hon. N. S. Gilson, judge of said circuit court. Said *Mary McCrory* also says on oath that she has good reason to believe, and does believe, that she cannot have a fair trial of said matter and action in the 13th judicial circuit of the state of Wisconsin, on account of the prejudice of the Hon. A. Scott Sloan, the presiding judge of said 13th circuit. Said *Mary McCrory* further says, on oath, that she has good reason to believe, and does believe, that she cannot have a fair trial of said action and matter in the 3d judicial circuit of the state of Wisconsin, on account of the prejudice of the Hon. GEORGE W. BURNELL, the presiding judge of said 3d circuit.   MARY McCRORY.

"Subscribed and sworn to before me this 8th day of November, 1886.   MAURICE McKENNA,
            "Notary Public, Fond du Lac Co."

For the appellant the cause was submitted on the brief of *Gerpheide & McKenna.*

For the respondent there was a brief by *Duffy & McCrory,* and oral argument by *Mr. F. F. Duffy.*

TAYLOR, J.   The application to change the place of trial in this case was made under the provisions of sec. 2625, R. S. That section reads as follows: "The court shall change the place of trial of any action upon the application of any party thereto who shall file his affidavit that he has good reason to believe, and does believe, that he cannot have a fair trial of such action on account of the prejudice of the judge, naming him. . . . But one change of the place of trial shall be granted to the same side under the provisions of this section." The right to a change of the place of trial is purely statutory, and is imperative on the court when the proper affidavit is presented by a proper party. Under that section, the only thing the party moving has to do is to allege, in the form prescribed, the prejudice of the presiding judge of the court, and when that is shown in the way prescribed the presiding judge has no discretion except to change the place of trial. The presiding judge has nothing to do in the case except to make an order changing the place of trial.

But it is urged that because sec. 2626 provides that "when the place of trial shall be changed it shall be changed to some county where the causes complained of do not exist," if the party applying includes in the affidavit required to be made in order to obtain an order of removal, a further

statement that some other judges in the state are also prejudiced, the court making the order is absolutely prohibited
from changing the place of trial to any county where such
other alleged prejudiced judges preside, and that the affidavit of the prejudice of the other judges is just as conclusive on the judge making the order as it is as to his own
prejudice.   This we think is clearly erroneous, and would
extend the right to disqualify the judges of the courts to try
actions on the ground of prejudice to an extent never contemplated by the statute.   If the party applying to change
the place of the trial, by his statements under oath that he
believes other judges than the one before whom the action
is pending are prejudiced, can disqualify such judges from
trying his case, then he has the power to disqualify all the
judges in the state, and no trial of the case could be had.
Such a construction of the law would open the door for one
having the hardihood to make the proper affidavit to prevent the case from trial in any court.   A proceeding which
might lead to such absurd results cannot be tolerated.

If the allegations in the affidavit for a change of venue of
the prejudice of any other judge or judges have any place
in the motion to change the place of trial, they can only be
mentioned for the purpose of consideration by the court in
directing the county to which the change shall be made, but
they can have no conclusive effect upon that question.   We
think, however, that under said sec. 2625 such allegations
have no place in the affidavit upon which the motion is
based; and if the party applying for the change thinks some
other judge is prejudiced against him, he should bring that
matter before the court in some other way, for the purpose of
obtaining the order to change the place of trial to some
place where such other supposed prejudiced judge does not
preside.   The statute, which makes it absolutely necessary
for a court of record to order a change of the place of trial
upon the mere affidavit of a party alleging prejudice, is of

.very doubtful propriety, and the legislature has restricted it within pretty narrow limits; and it is neither the policy of courts or of the legislature to extend the right.

It is urged that this court in *Northwestern Iron Co. v. Crane*, 66 Wis. 567, is authority for the practice adopted in this case. The proceeding in that case for a change of the place of trial was taken under a special statute, regulating the change of the place of trial from the county court of Dodge county. The statute regulating the change of venue in that court expressly provides that it shall be changed to the circuit court of the same county, "unless it shall appear that the circuit judge thereof is also prejudiced or disqualified in such action or proceeding; in which case the action shall be removed to some other court." Under this section, this court held that as the statute did not absolutely require the county court to remove the case to the circuit court of the same county when it appeared that the circuit judge was prejudiced or disqualified, the affidavit of the party making the motion to change the place of trial of the prejudice of the circuit judge was conclusive in that case, and it was the duty of the county court to remove the case to some other court. Under the general statute under which the application in this case is made, there is no such provision as to the prejudice of any other judge; and the direction in sec. 2626 that the place of trial shall be changed to some county where the causes complained of do not exist is general and applies to all the causes for a change of place of trial as well as for the one for prejudice. Whether the cause for which the change was made in this case existed in the county of Winnebago was a question to be determined by the circuit judge of Fond du Lac county; and we are not prepared to say that he erred in holding that it did not exist, simply because the appellant made affidavit that she believed it did exist. The mere belief in such case is not evidence of the fact, when such fact is to be established by proof. The fact that the statute declares that, for the purpose of a removal of the case from the court where the action is pending, such affidavit shall be conclusive, is no reason for holding that her belief shall be conclusive upon the question of the prejudice of all the other judges in the state.

We see no reason for charging the costs of this litigation to the estate of the deceased. The record does not disclose that there was any merit in the contest made by the appellant against the probate of the will of the deceased.

By the Court.— The judgment of the circuit court is affirmed. .

THE WISCONSIN CENTRAL RAILROAD COMPANY, Respondent, vs. COMSTOCK, Appellant.

February 4 — February 28, 1888.

(1) Ejectment: Constitutional law: Defendant's defective tax title: Payments by plaintiff, as condition of judgment. (2, 3) Taxation: Railroad lands: Extension of exemption: Equitable title.

1. Sec. 1, ch. 805, Laws of 1880, provides that in ejectment when the plaintiff is entitled to recover by reason of a defect or insufficiency in any tax deed under which the defendant claims, or in the tax proceedings antecedent thereto, unless the plaintiff shall show that the land was not liable to taxation for the tax for which it was sold, or that the tax was paid prior to the sale, or the land was redeemed from such sale, the court shall order that the 'amount for which the land was sold, and the cost of executing and recording the tax deed, and the amount paid by the defendant for taxes subsequently assessed, with interest on all such sums at the rate of twenty-five per cent. per annum, shall be set off against the damages awarded to the plaintiff; and if there be any excess, that the plaintiff, as a condition of judgment, shall pay the same within ninety days, and that in default thereof the defendant shall have judgment. *Held:*

    (1) The act is constitutional.

(2) A judgment entered for the plaintiff, without the making of such order or payment of the sums required, is erroneous and will be reversed.

2. By sec. 1, ch. 21, Laws of 1877, the time during which the lands in question were exempted from taxation was "*extended* three years." *Held,* that the three years began to run from the termination of the original exemption, and not from the date when the act of 1877 took effect.

3. When lands granted to aid in the construction of a railroad have been fully earned, and the company is entitled to a patent therefor, they are taxable by the state although the patent has not in fact been issued.

APPEAL from the Circuit Court for *Winnebago* County. Ejectment. The case is sufficiently stated in the opinion.

W. F. Bailey, for the appellant, to the point that the lands were taxable in 1879, although the patents therefor had not been issued, cited *Wis. Cent. R. Co. v. Price Co.* 64 Wis. 579; *West Wis. R. Co. v. Trempealeau Co.* 35 id. 273; *Van Wyck v. Knevals,* 106 U. S. 360; *Walden v. Knevals,* 114 id. 373; *Price v. Lancaster Co.* 20 Neb. 252; *Kansas P. R. Co. v. Dunmeyer,* 113 U. S. 641; *Gwynne v. Niswanger,* 15 Ohio, 367; *Ross v. Outagamie Co.* 12 Wis. 26, 37; *Wheeler v. Merriman,* 30 Minn. 379; *Witherspoon v. Duncan,* 4 Wall. 210; *Irvine v. Irvine,* 9 Wall. 617; *Grinnell v. Railroad Co.* 103 U. S. 739; *Railway Co. v. Prescott,* 16 Wall. 603; *Railway Co. v. McShane,* 22 id. 444; *White v. B. & M. R. Co.* 5 Neb. 393. Ch. 21, Laws of 1877, merely extended the previous exemption, and did not grant a new exemption. *Wis. Cent. R. Co. v. Taylor Co.* 52 Wis. 37; *Wis. Cent. R. Co. v. Lincoln Co.* 67 id. 478; *St. Louis, I. M. & S. R. Co. v. McGee,* 115 U. S. 475; *Doe v. Larmore,* 116 id. 198; *Kansas P. R. Co. v. A., T. & S. F. R. Co.* 112 id. 417.

For the respondent there was a brief by *Charles W. Felker,* and oral argument by *D. S. Wegg* and *Mr. Felker.* To the point that ch. 305, Laws of 1880, is unconstitutional, they cited Cooley on Taxation, 551; *Conway v. Cable,* 37

Ill. 82; *Lassitter v. Lee*, 68 Ala. 287; *Stoudenmire v. Brown*, 48 id. 699; *Sinclair v. Learned*, 51 Mich. 335–342; *Weller v. St. Paul*, 5 Minn. 95; *Lombard v. Antioch College*, 60 Wis. 459.

ORTON, J.   This is an action of ejectment for lands in the possession of the defendant, which were a part of the grant of the United States to this state made by act of Congress in 1864, and conferred upon the respondent company, and within the main body and place limit of said grant.   The plaintiff proved title.   The defendant introduced a tax deed for said lands, executed by the clerk of Price county to himself on the 4th day of June, 1883, on the tax sale of May 11, 1880, for taxes assessed for the year 1879.   The said tax deed was shown to be void for certain defects in the tax proceedings antecedent thereto, but " not going to the validity of the assessment or affecting the groundwork of such tax."   The plaintiff took judgment without compliance with the provisions of sec. 1, ch. 305, Laws of 1880. The failure of the plaintiff to comply with this section is the error complained of.

I. It is contended by the respondent's counsel that the judgment in such a case is independent of such payment, and that there should have been an order made by the court requiring such payment on the motion of the defendant, and, if the court had denied such motion, he should have appealed from such order, and not from the judgment. It will be observed that such payment is a condition precedent to the entry of judgment.

II. It is contended that the tax deed set up by the defendant is absolutely void for defects in the tax proceedings "going to the validity of the assessment and affecting the groundwork of the tax," and that therefore no such payment could be required as a condition of recovery.

1. Because the lands, as a part of said grant, were ex-

empted from taxation and assessment in the year 1879, when they were assessed as the basis of the tax, by sec. 21, ch. 314, and sec. 22, ch. 362, P. & L. Laws of 1866, exempting them from taxation for ten years from the taking effect of said acts, and by sec. 1, ch. 21, Laws of 1877, extending said time three years. This depends upon the construction of said extension act. Did the three years commence to run from the termination of the original exemption, or from the taking effect of the extension act of 1877? If the latter, then the three years extension had not expired when these lands were assessed in 1879. The language of said act would seem to be so plain as to leave little room for construction. It is as follows: "The time fixed, . . . during which the lands granted to said companies by said acts are exempted, . . . is hereby extended three years." There was a lapse of the exemption between the time it expired and the time of the extension. The word "extended" implies something to be extended, and must necessarily be connected with that something. It is derived from "ex," from or out of, and "tendere," to stretch or stretch out, and signifies to draw forth or stretch or prolong. Webst. Dict. "The *time* is hereby extended," is the language. The time is *stretched out or prolonged* three years. The other construction would not make it an *extension*, but a new exemption independent of any other exemption. If such be not the meaning, what was the use of sec. 4 of the act, which provides that it shall not exempt the lands which had theretofore been assessed? For all the lands were taxable for the year 1876,— those which had been actually assessed, and those not assessed. It appears to me that this question was so settled and decided in *Wis. Cent. R. Co. v. Lincoln Co.* 67 Wis. 478. In that case it was the interest of this same company to contend for this construction, and make the lands exempt in the year 1876, when they were actually assessed. The contention was that such pretended assessment was so absolutely void as to be no assessment, and therefore they did not come within this exception, but were exempt by virtue of this extension act. It was held that they were assessed in that year, and did, therefore, come within the exception, and were not exempt. Mr. Justice LYON said, in the opinion, " that taxes were assessed against the plaintiff's land in 1876, within the meaning of sec. 4, ch. 21, Laws of 1877, and that such assessment was therefore *saved from the exemption of that act.*" There could be nothing plainer than this. The same meaning of similar language was approved in *St. Louis, I. M. & S. R. Co. v. McGee,* 115 U. S. 475. It is unfortunate that it is now the interest of this same company to contend that such extension did not embrace the year 1876, but ran from the taking effect of the act of 1877, three years in the future, so as to embrace the year 1879, when these lands were assessed. But there is no law or rule of professional ethics against inconsistent positions in different cases. We hold, therefore, that in the year 1879 these lands were not exempt from taxation, as the extended time of exemption had already expired.

2. It is contended that these lands were not taxable in 1879 because the legal title was in the United States, and no patent had been issued to the company. It was sufficient that these lands had been fully earned, and that the company was legally entitled to the government patent. The company *owned* the lands, and if they only had an equitable title the lands were equally taxable in this state. This question was so decided in *West. Wis. R. Co. v. Trempealeau Co.* 35 Wis. 257; *Wis. Cent. R. Co. v. Price Co.* 64 Wis. 579.

III. The learned counsel of the respondent contends lastly that sec. 1, ch. 305, Laws of 1880, requiring such payments before the entry of judgment, in respect to the twenty-five per cent. interest per annum is unconstitutional.

There would seem to be scarcely a doubt that this twenty-five per cent., whether as a penalty, or indemnity, or provided on grounds of public policy to discourage delinquency in the payment of taxes, or as an equitable condition precedent to relief against a merely irregular tax proceeding, was clearly within the discretion and power of the legislature. So far as this act affects the sale of these lands for taxes, it was prospective. The act was passed before the sale. If the legislature has the power to impose any condition of recovery in such a case, then what such condition should be must be within the discretion of the legislature. They may require the payment of the purchase money and subsequent taxes, no matter how irregular, and may add to it seven per cent. Why not twenty-five per cent.? The betterment laws, and condition of payment for improvements and for taxes to the recovery of land from one having no legal right, vindicate such legislation. It would not be denied that the legislature might provide that the plaintiff, in such a case as this, should not recover at all, and make the tax deed conclusive, or make such mere irregularities immaterial and all the proceedings of taxation before the sale as merely directory, and far greater injustice be done. On redemption, the statute requires the payment of twenty-five per cent. interest per annum upon the purchase money of the lands sold, and twelve per cent. interest per annum on all taxes and charges paid. Sec. 1165, R. S. It seems to me that this act, imposing such an interest as a condition of recovery, and similar acts, so far as they have prospective effect as in this case, are unquestionably within the power of the legislature. This section was approved by this court in *Pier v. Prouty*, 67 Wis. 218. The authorities cited by the learned counsel do not seem to be in point.

We conclude, therefore, that before the judgment in this case was entered the order should have been made and the plaintiff should have made the payments required to be made by sec. 1, ch. 305, Laws of 1880, and, not having done so, the judgment is erroneous.

By the Court.— The judgment of the circuit court is reversed, and the cause remanded with directions to make the order for the payments required by sec. 1, ch. 305, Laws of 1880, and for further proceedings according to law.

THE WISCONSIN CENTRAL RAILROAD COMPANY, Respondent, vs. THE WISCONSIN RIVER LAND COMPANY and another, Appellants.

February 4 — February 28, 1888.

(1) Trust deed: Mortgage. (2) Ejectment before issuance of patent to plaintiff. (3) When patent from state takes effect: Delivery. (4) Tax sale: Estoppel. (5) Notice of tax sale: Proof of posting. (6, 7) Lis pendens: Purchaser with notice: Statute of limitations: Corporations.

1. A trust deed of lands, given by a railroad company to secure the payment of bonds and providing that if there should be no default the estate, right, title, and interest of the trustees should cease, determine, and become void, is *held* to be in effect a mortgage and to leave the legal title in the company.

2. Lands granted to the state in trust to aid in the construction of a railroad had been fully earned by the plaintiff company and it was entitled to a patent therefor from the United States. It had also the right to the possession of the lands by virtue of a patent or release from the state, made in pursuance of the original grant and evidencing full compliance with the terms thereof. *Held*, that although the patent from the United States had not been issued, the company might maintain ejectment in the courts of this state against persons making an unlawful claim to the lands under a tax deed fair on its face.

3. The patent or release from the state, made in pursuance of the original grant from the United States, took effect from the time it was signed, sealed, and recorded, although it was not delivered until afterward

4. In ejectment for lands which were taxed as the property of the plaintiff company and sold for nonpayment of the taxes, the defendants who claim title under such tax sale are estopped from claiming that the plaintiff cannot recover because the patent from the United States has not yet been issued to it.

5. An affidavit by the county treasurer of the posting of the notices of a tax sale, which states that "he did, in accordance with ch. 1180, R. S., post notices in four public places in said county," etc., but does not state when or where such notices were posted, or that any notice was posted in his office, is insufficient.

6. Where a defendant in ejectment conveys the land in controversy pending the suit to one having full knowledge thereof, although no notice of *lis pendens* was filed, such grantee takes subject to the litigation, and can avail himself of no statute of limitations which was not available to such original defendant.

7. The defendant in ejectment conveyed the land to a corporation organized after the commencement of the action and of which he was an incorporator, a stockholder, and the first president. *Held*, that the corporation must be regarded as having received the conveyance with full knowledge of the pendency of the suit.

APPEAL from the Circuit Court for *Winnebago* County. The following statement of the case was prepared by Mr. Justice Cassoday:

This is an action of ejectment to recover about 29,000 acres of land described, and situated in Price county. The summons and complaint were served on the defendant *Comstock* March 1, 1884, and on the defendant land company, which had succeeded to *Comstock's* interest *pendente lite*, January 4, 1887, and which was then made a defendant by order of the court upon the application of the plaintiff.

The *Wisconsin River Land Company* separately answered to the effect (1) that August 9, 1871 the plaintiff had parted with all its right, title, and interest in the lands described, to George T. Bigelow and John Stewart, by trust deed set forth; and, upon the death of Bigelow, to Edwin H. Abbot, as co-trustee with Stewart, by papers set forth; (2) that May 11, 1880, each parcel of land described had been sold to Price county for taxes lawfully assessed thereon for the

year 1879, and a tax certificate issued to the county thereon;
(3) that the one-year limitation in sec. 3, ch. 309, Laws of
1880, was a bar to any action to set aside the sale or cancel
the certificate; (4) that June 4, 1883, the defendant *Comstock*, being the owner of such certificates, obtained a tax
deed thereon from Price county, duly executed, witnessed,
acknowledged, and on that day recorded; (5) that March
12, 1885, said *Comstock* conveyed all said lands to the defendant land company, which claimed to own the same in
fee; (6) that the plaintiff and said trustees were, before the
commencement of this action, barred from maintaining this
or any action by chapters 305 and 309, Laws of 1880;
(7) that the lands were the same as granted to the plaintiff
for the building of its railroad by the acts of Congress and
the several acts of the legislature, as stated in the report of
Wis. Cent. R. Co. v. Price Co. 64 Wis. 579, and in fact for
the same lands; that the said railroad was completed as
early as June, 1877; that prior to January 1, 1879, said lands
in the indemnity limits were "duly selected as required by
law and the rules and regulations of the general land-office,
and such selections so made, so far as their being proper
lands to be selected, were approved by the secretary of the
interior; that said company had fully and completely, before the 1st day of January, 1879, performed and completed
all the conditions required by said acts and the rules of said
land department to entitle it to a patent to said lands, and
had fully and completely earned the same, and, at such time
last aforesaid, held the equitable title in and to said lands,"
but that the legal title thereof during all said time and since
was in the United States, and hence denied that the plaintiff is or ever was the owner in fee simple of said lands, but
admits that he was the equitable owner up to the time of
the recording of said tax deed; (8) that February 25, 1884,
the governor, under his hand and the great seal of the state,
and the secretary of state executed to the plaintiff a release

or patent of all of said lands, and the same was recorded in said secretary of state's office on the day and year last aforesaid; (9) that the action was barred by the limitations prescribed by ch. 50, R. S.

At the close of the trial, the jury, under the direction of the court, returned this verdict: "We, the jury, find for the plaintiff; that it is now, and was at the time of the commencement of this action, the owner of the premises described in the complaint in fee simple; that the defendant wrongfully withholds the possession thereof from the plaintiff, and we assess the damages for the plaintiff, for the wrongful withholding of said premises by the defendant from the plaintiff, in the sum of six cents." Thereupon it was "ordered by the court that the amount for which such lands were sold, and the cost of executing and recording such tax deed, with interest on all such sums at the rate of twenty-five per cent. per annum from the time they were paid until the date of the verdict herein rendered, be set off against the damages awarded to the plaintiff by the verdict, and that the excess the plaintiff, as a condition of judgment, shall pay the same with interest from the date of the verdict within ninety days, and that in default thereof the defendants herein shall have judgment in the action; it having been stipulated that such sum is the sum of $2,540.28, with interest from the date of the verdict."

From the judgment entered in accordance with such verdict and order the defendants appeal.

W. F. Bailey, for the appellants.

For the respondent there was a brief by *Charles W. Felker*, and oral argument by *D. S. Wegg* and *Mr. Felker*.

CASSODAY, J. This is an action of ejectment. The plaintiff claims title to the lands as the original owner. The defendant land company claims title under the tax deed of June 4, 1883.

1. It is claimed that the plaintiff parted with whatever title it had to the lands by the trust deed given to Stewart and another, August 9, 1871. That deed is a lengthy document. It recites the purpose for which it was given. It was to secure the payment of bonds to be issued, not exceeding a certain amount per mile of the road, and therein severally designated as a "First *Mortgage* Land Grant and Sinking Fund, Seven Per Cent. Gold Bond, Free of United States Tax, Receivable in Payment for Lands." Each bond was for $1,000, which the plaintiff therein promised to pay to the bearer with interest at seven per cent., payable semiannually. The bonds were to be negotiated and used by the plaintiff in procuring loans with which to build its railroad. The plaintiff was to remain in possession of the road and all the property embraced in such trust deed until there should be a breach in the conditions thereof, and was expressly authorized to contract for the sale of any of such lands at prices to be approved by the trustees; but the proceeds of such sales were to be deposited with the trustees. In case of default, the trustees were, after a certain length of time and in a certain manner, authorized to sell and convey such lands to satisfy the amounts payable. But, in case there should be no default, and the plaintiff should fully perform, then "the estate, right, title, and interest" of such trustees and "their successors in trust" thereby created, was to "cease, determine, and become void." It seems to us that such deed of trust was given as mere security for the money thus obtained, and hence was, in legal effect, nothing more than a mortgage. *Hoyt v. Fass*, 64 Wis. 279. In fact, it is characterized in several places therein as a "mortgage." In this state a mortgage upon land is a mere lien or security. The title remains in the mortgagor, and the mortgagee holds the mortgage as such mere security for the debt. So stringent is this rule that it has often been held by this court that a deed in fee simple absolute, given merely to

secure a debt, with a parol defeasance, is nothing more nor less than a mortgage, leaving the title in the grantor and giving to the grantee a mere security for his debt, to be enforced like an ordinary mortgage. *Schriber v. Le Clair*, 66 Wis. 586. We must hold that the trust deed in question was in legal effect a mortgage, and left whatever right, title, or interest the plaintiff had in the lands in question at the time of giving it, still in the plaintiff, subject, of course, to the lien thereby created. *Bernstein v. Humes*, 71 Ala. 265, 266; *Hoyt v. Fass*, 64 Wis. 279.

2. It is claimed that the plaintiff cannot recover in this action of ejectment by reason of its failure to show title under a patent from the secretary of the interior. It has frequently been held that a plaintiff having a mere equitable title cannot recover in ejectment in the federal courts. *Langdon v. Sherwood*, 124 U. S. 74, and cases there cited. The same court has held "that whenever the question in any court, state or federal, is whether a title to land which had once been the property of the United States has passed, that question must be resolved by the laws of the United States; but that whenever, according to those laws, the title shall have passed, then that property, like all other property in the state, is subject to the state legislation, so far as that legislation is consistent with the admission that the title passed and vested according to the laws of the United States." *Wilcox v. Jackson*, 13 Pet. 516, 517; *Paige v. Peters*, 70 Wis. 178.

It was in accordance with "the laws of the United States" granting the lands in question to this state in trust for the purposes of building the railroad, as construed by the supreme court of the United States in *Winona & St. P. R. Co. v. Barney*, 113 U. S. 618, that we held these same lands to be taxable. *Wis. Cent. R. Co. v. Price Co.* 64 Wis. 579, 590. After stating the nature of the grant and what was done under it, it was there said: "From this decision we are forced to the conclusion that each of the learned secretaries of the interior named refused to issue patents for the lands in question solely by reason of a misconception of what the supreme court of the United States had in fact decided some ten years" before in *Leavenworth, L. & G. R. Co. v. U. S.* 92 U. S. 733. The plaintiff, prior to the completion of its road, was there likened to the vendee in an executory contract, and after such completion to a vendee who had fully executed the contract on his part. 64 Wis. 591, 592. It was there said: "There can be no doubt but what the plaintiff, prior to 1880, acquired such complete equitable rights to the eleven forties in the place limits. The same is true in respect to the lands selected from the indemnity limits, and certified and presented to the secretary of the interior as stated, unless the mere refusal of the secretary to issue patents therefor on the ground mentioned prevented such equitable rights from vesting in the plaintiff. . . . True, the act of Congress declared that the selections should be 'subject to the approval of the secretary of the interior.' No objection having been made by that officer to the selections certified and presented to him as stated, except on the ground mentioned, must be regarded as equivalent to an acceptance by him of such selections, since it now appears that the only objection made was unfounded, and that the plaintiff was then legally entitled to the lands." Pages 592, 593. Then after showing that the objects of such selection and approval had in fact been secured, it was said: "We must hold that the secretary of the interior did, in effect, approve by implication of the selections made, certified, and presented to him as stated." It was then held, in effect, that, as the plaintiff had acquired the equitable right to the patents, and hence the equitable title to the lands by operation of law, the lands thereupon became subject to taxation.

It is here stipulated that the facts in this case, respecting the plaintiff's equitable right to the lands, are substantially as they appear in the report of that case. While it is conceded, as there held, that the lands were only taxable by reason of the plaintiff's ownership, it is nevertheless contended that the plaintiff cannot, in this action of ejectment, controvert the tax title in question, by reason of its want of legal ownership. In other words, it is claimed that such tax title cannot be controverted in ejectment in a state court, upon facts which would preclude such controversy in ejectment in the federal courts, upon the rule and authorities already mentioned. But "the distinction between actions at law and suits in equity, and the forms of all such actions and suits have" never "been abolished" in those courts as they have been in this state, where "there is . . . but one form of action for the enforcement or protection of private rights and the redress or prevention of private wrongs, which is denominated a civil action." Sec. 2600, R. S. The objection of the defendants, as admitted upon the argument, does not go to the plaintiff's equitable right to the lands, which is conceded, but merely to the *form* of the action; and it may be that it would have been available had the action been brought in the federal court. This is on the ground that "the remedies in the courts of the United States are to be at common law *or* in equity; not according to the practice in the state courts, but according to the principles of the common law and equity, as distinguished and defined in that country from which we derive our knowledge of those principles." *Fenn v. Holme*, 21 How. 485. But the same court has often recognized the right of a plaintiff in ejectment in certain state courts, to recover on the strength of his equitable title merely. Thus it is said on the page last cited: "In some states in the Union no court of chancery exists to administer equitable relief. In some of those states courts of law recognize and enforce in suits at law all equitable rights and claims which a court of equity would recognize and enforce; in others all relief is denied, and such equitable claims and rights are to be considered as mere nullities at law." *Ibid.* "It is also the settled doctrine of " that " court that no action of ejectment will lie on such an equitable title, notwithstanding a state legislature may have provided otherwise by statute. *The law is only binding on the state courts*, and has no force in the circuit courts of the Union." *Hooper v. Scheimer*, 23 How. 249. This was sanctioned in the recent case of *Langdon v. Sherwood*, 124 U. S. 84. But a mere vendee in an executory contract, entitled to the possession under it, may maintain ejectment even in the federal courts. *Melenthin v. Keith*, 17 Fed. Rep. 583, MILLER, J. In several of the states it has been held, under statutes similar to ours, that an equitable owner, entitled to the immediate possession of the land, could maintain ejectment against a stranger or one unlawfully claiming such right to possession. *Glover v. Stamps*, 73 Ga. 209; *Covert v. Morrison*, 49 Mich. 133; *Pierce v. Felter*, 53 Cal. 18; *Phillips v. Gorham*, 17 N. Y. 270; *Lattin v. McCarty*, 41 N. Y. 107; *Sheehan v. Hamilton*, 4 Abb. Dec. 211; *Murphy v. Loomis*, 26 Hun, 659.

The mere fact that the plaintiff's equitable rights to the lands " must be resolved by the laws of the United States,"— that is to say, were acquired by operation of the law of Congress granting the lands to the state in trust for the building of the plaintiff's railroad,— does not preclude the plaintiff from the remedy given by the state, laws in the state courts for obtaining the possession from one making an unlawful claim to the same under a tax deed fair upon its face. It is by statute that such tax deed operates as a constructive eviction of the land-owner. Sec. 1176, R. S.; *Warren v. Putnam*, 63 Wis. 410–417; *Hewitt v. Week*, 59 Wis. 444; *Hewitt v. Butterfield*, 52 Wis. 384. Since such statute operated as a constructive eviction of the plaintiff in favor of the defendants the plaintiff may certainly have the benefit of the other provision of the statutes to regain the possession which, without legal right, it thus constructively lost.

Under our statutes the complaint in ejectment must "set forth that the plaintiff has an estate or interest in the premises claimed, describing them," and "particularly state the *nature* and extent of such estate or interest, . . . and that he *is entitled to the possession* of such premises, and that the defendant unlawfully withholds the possession thereof from him to his damage," etc.   Sec. 3077, R. S. The statute moreover declares that "it shall not be necessary . . . for the plaintiff to prove an actual entry under title, nor the actual receipt of any profits of the premises demanded, but it shall be sufficient for him to show *a right to the possession of* such premises at the time of the commencement of the action, as heir, devisee, *purchaser, or otherwise.*"   Sec. 3079, R. S.   Here the plaintiff was, in legal contemplation, a "purchaser" of the lands from the state, in consideration of the building and completion of the railroad as required, and the selection and approval of the lands prior to the levy of the taxes in question. 64 Wis. 591, 592.   This court has gone so far as to hold that, under our statutes, the holder of a school-land certificate may maintain ejectment.   Sec. 220, R. S.; *Tobey v. Secor*, 60 Wis. 310.   A person holding a contract or certificate of sale of any real property contracted to be sold by the state but not conveyed, is deemed the owner for the purposes of taxation. 64 Wis. 595; secs. 1034, 1035, 1043, R. S.

Here the plaintiff acquired its right to the possession of the land on the completion of its road, by virtue of a grant from the state made in pursuance of a grant from the United States. 64 Wis. 585–587.   The patent from the governor and secretary of state was *prima facie* evidence that the plaintiff had fully complied with the terms of the grants,

and that, so far as it and the state were concerned, the
trust had been fully executed, and hence extinguished. See
references, 64 Wis. 587; also sec. 4153, R. S., as amended
by ch. 18, Laws of 1880. Such being the nature and purpose of that instrument, it would seem to operate as such
prima facie evidence the moment it was completed and entered of record, which was before the commencement of
this action. It was never intended to operate as the grant
of a title, but only as the evidence of a title previously
granted. The same would be true respecting patents issued
by the secretary of the interior for these lands. 64 Wis.
591, *et seq.* Thus in *U. S. v. Schurz*, 102 U. S. 397, it is said
by the court: "We are of opinion that when, upon the decision of the proper office that the citizen has become entitled to a patent for a portion of the public lands, such a
patent made out in that office is signed by the president,
sealed with the seal of the general land office, countersigned
by the recorder of the land office, and duly recorded in the
record-book kept for that purpose, it becomes a solemn public act of the government of the United States, and needs
no further delivery or other authentication to make it perfect and valid. In such case the title to the land conveyed
passes by matter of record to the grantee, and the delivery
which is required when a deed is made by a private individual is not necessary to give effect to the granting clause
of the instrument." We must hold that the patent from
the governor took effect upon completion, and without delivery, as of February 25, 1884.

3. But there is still another reason why the plaintiff
should be entitled to maintain such an action. The defendants do not claim under any patent or grant from the
United States, but solely under a tax deed issued in pursuance of the statutes of the state. This being so, their
only claim to the lands necessarily presupposed title in the
plaintiff; otherwise, the lands would not have been taxable,

and hence their tax deed would have been a nullity. Their claim, therefore, was not only necessarily dependent upon the plaintiff's title, but also upon a constructive eviction of the plaintiff, or an actual rightful possession under a valid tax deed, or as mere intruders upon the plaintiff's right to possession. That is to say, such claim of title by the defendants is, under our statutes, either derivative from the plaintiff or tortious as against the plaintiff. Such being the relationship of the parties to the lands and hence to each other, it would seem that the defendants are estopped from disclaiming the plaintiff's title and right to possession, except on the theory that such title has been divested and the right to possession acquired by eviction under such tax deed. *Brandirff v. Harrison Co.* 50 Iowa, 164; *Austin v. Bremer Co.* 44 Iowa, 155. This is on the theory that where both parties claim title from a common source, the one having the better claim from that source must prevail. *Hewitt v. Butterfield*, 52 Wis. 384; *McCready v. Lansdale*, 58 Miss. 878; *Hunter v. Starin*, 26 Hun, 529. This rule has recently been applied in California, in a case where the outstanding legal title was in the United States. *Gray v. Dixon*, 16 Pac. Rep. 305. Of course, the plaintiff must recover on the strength of its own title, which was necessarily on trial, but it does not follow that its title is without any strength merely because it is not evidenced by a patent from the general government. Especially is this so as against the defendants, whose only claim of title is based entirely upon a supposed acquisition of the plaintiff's title and right to possession.

4. It is virtually conceded that the tax sales upon which the tax deed in question was issued were void for want of the requisite notice of the same or proof thereof as required by statute. Sec. 1130, R. S., as amended. The only proof or affidavit to be found in the county offices as to the posting of notices was the affidavit of the county treasurer,

sworn to May 15, 1880, to the effect " that he did, in accordance with chapter 1130 of the Revised Statutes, post notices in four public places in said [Price] county, that he would, on the 11th day of May, 1880, sell to the highest bidder so much of each parcel and tract of land on which the taxes of 1879 remain unpaid as would be sufficient to pay the taxes, interest, and charges to the date of sale, a copy of which notice is hereunto attached." When or where such notice was posted does not appear; nor does it appear that any notice thereof was ever posted in the treasurer's office, as required by the statute cited. It is unnecessary to mention other defects. The necessity of record proof of the requisite posting has been too frequently and too recently declared by this court to require repetition. *Ward v. Walters*, 63 Wis. 43; *Ramsay v. Hommel*, 68 Wis. 12; *Morris v. Carmichael*, 68 Wis. 133.

5. The action was commenced, as against *Comstock*, within one year after the execution of the tax deed. There is no claim of any statute of limitations being available as to him. But the defendant land company was not made a party until more than three years after the recording of the tax deed. It answered and pleaded the several statutes of limitation in such cases, and the question arises whether any of them are available in this action. The defect in the tax proceedings mentioned did not go to the validity of the assessment or affect the groundwork of such tax. These things being so, the limitation mentioned in the third section of ch. 309, Laws of 1880, barring an action within one year of the date of the tax sale, has no application to the case. *Urquhart v. Wescott*, 65 Wis. 135; *Pier v. Prouty*, 67 Wis. 218; *Ramsay v. Hommel*, 68 Wis. 12; *Morris v. Carmichael*, 68 Wis. 133.

The question recurs whether the second section of that act, barring the land-owner unless his action is commenced within three years after the recording of such tax deed, is available. No *lis pendens* was filed. The mere failure to file notice of *lis pendens*, however, is not such an irregularity as to work a reversal in this case. The object of such notice is to conclude subsequent *bona fide* purchasers or incumbrancers by constructive notice. Sec. 3187, R. S. Here the action was commenced by the service of the summons and complaint upon *Comstock*, the grantee named in the tax deed, March 1, 1884. Subsequently, the defendant land company was incorporated and organized, and *Comstock* was one of its incorporators and stockholders, and its first president, and has continued such ever since. These things being so, the defendant land company must be regarded as having received the conveyance from *Comstock* in 1885 with full knowledge of the pendency of the suit against him, and hence subject to the result of that suit as it then stood. We must hold that where a defendant in ejectment conveys the land in controversy pending the suit to one having full knowledge thereof, such grantee takes subject to the litigation, and can avail himself of no statute of limitations which was not available to such original defendant. Any other rule would work interminable mischief, without being productive of any substantial good.

We find no statute of limitations available to either of the defendants.

By the Court.—The judgment of the circuit court is affirmed.

CONOVER, Respondent, vs. MANKE and others, Appellants.

February 4 — February 28, 1888.

(1) Sale of chattels: Breach of contract: Damages: Pleading. (2)
Error in excluding evidence, when cured.

1. In an action upon a contract for the sale and delivery of chattels, where the complaint alleges that the defendant refused to deliver the property, to the damage of the plaintiff in a certain sum, it need not further allege the price or value of the property at the time and place of delivery, or that the plaintiff could have resold the same at a profit.

2. Where the court had erroneously sustained objections to a large number of questions asked for the purpose of proving a certain fact, the subsequent withdrawal of a similar question which was not objected to does not cure the error.

APPEAL from the Circuit Court for *Manitowoc* County. Action to recover damages for the breach of a written agreement for the sale and delivery of a quantity of cheese to the plaintiff by the defendants, who were manufacturers of cheese. The facts are sufficiently stated in the opinion. The defendants appealed from the judgment of the circuit court reversing the judgment of the justice.

The cause was submitted for the appellants on briefs by *Schmitz & Kirwan* and *G. A. Forrest*, and for the respondent on the brief of *M. C. Mead* and *Nash & Nash*.

COLE, C. J. This appears to us to be a very plain case. We have not the time nor the patience, nor do we deem it necessary, to go through the elaborate briefs of the counsel for the appellants and notice all the points relied on by them to sustain the judgment of the trial court. They have gone largely into the law relating to pleadings, evidence, agency, and sales of personal property,— a discussion of which is interesting, but which, as we have intimated, it is not necessary to enter upon in the decision of this case.

The action was commenced before the county judge of Manitowoc county, with the jurisdiction of justice of the peace. It was based upon a written contract for the sale of a quantity of cheese. The contract, on the part of the defendants, was signed by one *John Pape*, "salesman." The complaint alleged that *Pape* was duly authorized to make the contract on behalf of the defendants. On the trial before the justice the complaint was dismissed. The cause was then taken to the circuit court, where it was heard on the return of the justice, and the judgment of the justice was reversed. We are now called upon to review the decision of the circuit court, which we deem correct.

It is insisted that the circuit court erred in holding that the complaint stated a cause of action. The objection to the complaint is clearly untenable. After setting forth the substance of the written agreement, it is alleged that the plaintiff, at the time and place appointed, was ready and willing to receive the cheese and pay for it according to the agreement; but that the defendants neglected to perform on their part, and refused to deliver the property, to the damage of the plaintiff $79. The specific objection to the complaint is that it should have alleged the price or value of the cheese at the time and place of delivery, or that the plaintiff could have resold the same at a profit. Of course the plaintiff, to show his damages by reason of the failure of the defendants to perform, would be obliged to prove that the contract price was less than the market price at the place of delivery. In other words, that he had suffered loss by the breach. But it is not necessary that the plaintiff should set forth his evidence in the complaint. We consider the complaint entirely sufficient, and shall spend no further time in considering objections to it.

It is next insisted that the circuit court erred in holding that the evidence given on the part of the plaintiff on the trial before the justice, together with that which was offered and excluded, was sufficient to make out a case. The circuit court doubtless held that proper testimony was offered and excluded by the justice, and that in fact the plaintiff was prevented from proving the cause of action stated in the complaint. In that view we fully concur. Question after question was asked, which had a tendency to prove that *Pape* had original power to make the contract and bind the defendants; that the cheese-maker, *Manke*, who, the answer alleges, only had power to sell, had seen the contract sued on and approved of it, and promised to deliver the cheese; that the committee likewise saw the contract and ratified it; that *Pape* was jointly interested in the manufacture and sale of the cheese, and had made contracts of sale with other parties. These, and in short nearly every question asked, were objected to as immaterial, incompetent, and "out of the order of proof," and were excluded. We are at a loss to know what idea the justice had of the "proper order of proof." We should infer from his ruling that he considered no evidence offered to prove the plaintiff's case was in order. At all events, he excluded much material testimony. Finally, the witness was asked this question: "Do you know if the committee and cheese-maker appointed by the defendants authorized the defendant *Pape* to make sales of cheese for the defendants, and do all things necessary in and about executing contracts?" The defendants did not object to this question, but the plaintiff withdrew it. It is argued that, as the plaintiff had an opportunity to prove his case by this question and failed to do so, all errors in excluding proper testimony were cured. We cannot adopt that view. The justice had already repeatedly excluded specific questions to prove *Pape's* authority, and all questions from which his authority might be inferred; questions as to ratification, etc.; and the plaintiff would not feel at liberty to go into these matters again under the general question. After the plaintiff had attempted to bring before the justice proof of agency, ratification, etc., and the justice had excluded the evidence, the plaintiff was bound by respect to submit to the rulings of the justice. It would have been unseemly for him to persist in going over the same matters to prove his case, or to offer evidence of facts to establish it which had already been held improper. It is said that the plaintiff offered no proof that he was present, ready and willing to perform the contract by accepting and paying for the cheese. Why should he offer such testimony. He was not permitted to show that a contract had been made which bound the defendants. It is very manifest that the cause of justice would have been better subserved if the case had been tried upon its merits, without regard to "tactical maneuvers for position on the record."

By the Court.— The judgment of the circuit court is affirmed.

CARRIER, Respondent, vs. CARRIER and another, Appellants.

February 4—February 28, 1888.

Replevin: Judgment: Recovery of part of property.

1. The verdict and judgment in replevin must determine the right to the possession of all the property involved, even though a part thereof was not taken from the defendant and the answer did not claim a return of the property.
2. Where the judgment in replevin is for the recovery of five of six horses and one of two wagons claimed, a failure sufficiently to identify those not recovered is probably sufficient ground for a reversal.

APPEAL from the Circuit Court for *Fond du Lac* County. The action is replevin brought to recover six horses, three colts, thirty-five cows, thirteen two-year olds, twelve yearlings, nineteen calves, two hogs, fourteen pigs, fifty-three tons of hay, one platform wagon, one sleigh, two lumber wagons, and two sets of double harness, all alleged to be the property of the plaintiff, of the value in all of $2,850. The answer denies the plaintiff's ownership of the property, and alleges the same to be the property of one Emily S. Carrier, and that the defendants hold the same as her bailees. No proceedings were had for an immediate delivery of the property, and the same remained in the possession of the defendants until judgment.

The trial of the action resulted in a verdict for the plaintiff for five horses, three colts, one platform wagon, one double wagon, two sets of harness, fourteen pigs, and two hogs, of the aggregate value of $751. There was no finding in respect to the residue of the property, which consisted of one horse, all of the cows, two-year olds, yearlings, calves, and hay, one lumber wagon, and the sleigh. The verdict is in the form prescribed by the court in case the jury should find the plaintiff entitled to part of the property only. To the instruction in that behalf the plaintiff excepted in due time,— that is to say, before the close of the term at which the action was tried (R. S. sec. 2869); and such exception appears in the bill of exceptions.

Judgment for the plaintiff was entered pursuant to the verdict. The defendants appeal from the judgment.

For the appellants there was a brief by *Kelly & Martin*, and oral argument by *Mr. P. H. Martin*.

For the respondent there was a brief by *Duffy & McCrory*, and oral argument by *Mr. J. H. McCrory*. They contended, *inter alia*, that the verdict sufficiently determined the rights of the parties to this suit under the issues raised. *Walker v. Hunter*, 5 Cranch C. C. 462; *Waldman v. Broder*, 10 Cal. 378; *Dowell v. Richardson*, 10 Ind. 573; *Edwards v. McCurdy*, 13 Ill. 496; *Emmons v. Dowe*, 2 Wis. 322.

LYON, J. The verdict and judgment leave wholly undetermined the issue made by the pleadings as to the right to the possession of the property not included therein. This is an irregularity fatal to the judgment. No rule is better settled than that the verdict and judgment must dispose of all the issues involved in the action, and the right to the possession of the property not included therein is one of those issues. *Ronge v. Dawson*, 9 Wis. 246, and numerous cases there cited.

It was argued on behalf of the plaintiff that, because the omitted property had not been taken from the possession of the defendants, the omission thereof is immaterial. We cannot concur in this view. In replevin both parties are actors, and the defendants may justly insist that their right to the possession of the omitted property be established by the verdict and judgment. *Young v. Lego*, 38 Wis. 206, holds this doctrine. In that case the omitted property had not been replevied, but remained in the hands of the defendant, yet the judgment was reversed because of the omission. The fact that *Young v. Lego* arose in a justice's court is immaterial. The rule above stated extends to all courts having jurisdiction of the action of replevin. In the present case the verdict should have been that the defendants were entitled to the possession of the omitted property, and the judgment should have followed the verdict. An argument is based upon the omission of the defendants to claim in their answer a return of the property. *Timp v. Dockham*, 32 Wis. 146, is authority that such omission has no significance.

There is another defect in the judgment. Six horses were claimed, and the plaintiff recovered only five of them. Also two lumber wagons were claimed, and the plaintiff recovered but one of these. The horse and wagon not so recovered are not sufficiently identified to inform the sheriff serving an execution, or defendants, which of the horses and which

of the wagons were thus omitted. This defect alone is probably a sufficient ground for a reversal of the judgment.

By the Court.— The judgment of the circuit court is reversed, and the cause remanded for a new trial.

COLE, Respondent, vs. THE CHICAGO & NORTHWESTERN RAIL-
WAY COMPANY, Appellant.

February 6 — February 28, 1888.

*Master and servant: Negligence: Temporary work outside of ordinary
employment.*

When an employee of mature years and of ordinary intelligence and
experience is directed to do a temporary work outside of the business he has engaged to do, and consents to do such work, without
objection on account of his want of knowledge, skill, or experience
in doing such work, no negligence of the employer can be predicated upon that state of facts alone. So *held*, where the foreman
of a gang of men engaged in constructing bridges and buildings
for a railroad company was directed to take his engine and men
and do some switching, and undertook such work without objection, and was injured while personally making a coupling, by reason of the negligence of the engineer and a defect in the coupling
apparatus of which the railroad company was not shown to have
had knowledge.

APPEAL from the Circuit Court for *Fond du Lac* County.

The following statement of the case was prepared by Mr.
Justice TAYLOR as a part of the opinion:

This action was brought to recover damages for an injury sustained by the plaintiff while in the employ of
said company. The material allegations of the complaint,
which were put in issue, are as follows, viz.: "That the
plaintiff on the 25th day of November, 1880, at the time
of the grievances hereinafter mentioned, was, and prior

thereto had been, in the employment of the defendant as
foreman in charge of a gang or crew of men constructing
and building bridges and buildings for said defendant railway company along its lines on what was known as the
'Wisconsin Division' of said railway, and was then at
work along the line of what was known as the 'Sheboygan and Western Division' of said company's lines. That
on said day said plaintiff was engaged in the employment
aforesaid, near Peeble station, just out of the city of Fond
du Lac, Wisconsin, upon said road, and while so engaged
he came into the city of Fond du Lac with the engine
hereinafter mentioned, and then received a telegraph dispatch or request from C. X. Smith, who was then train-
master and acting as superintendent of said Sheboygan
and Western Division of the defendant's road and had due
authority in the premises, which dispatch requested the ·
plaintiff to switch certain of said company's cars, and do
certain switch-work, at the depot of said Sheboygan and
Western Division in said city of Fond du Lac. That the
performance of such work was no part of the plaintiff's
employment above set forth, and was not contemplated in
or by the contract made between plaintiff and defendant
pursuant to which plaintiff was employed. That, in obedi-
ence to said request of said superintendent, the plaintiff, in
order to do the said switching, was compelled to couple a
certain car to the said locomotive engine hereinafter mentioned. That in performance of said work the said plaintiff was unversed and inexperienced, which fact was well
known to the train-master and acting superintendent and
said defendant; that, while the plaintiff was so engaged,
the engine or locomotive was managed by the engineer
then in charge of said engine and employed by the defendant for that work, carelessly and with great negligence,
as this plaintiff has been informed and verily believes, so
that when plaintiff signaled said engineer to start said

engine forward it was on the contrary backed with great
force against this plaintiff. That it was the duty of the defendant company to provide a good, careful, and skilful
engineer, and to provide a good, safe, and secure locomotive engine, with good, safe, and secure machinery, appliances, and apparatus; but said defendant did in fact furnish
a careless and unskilful engineer, as the defendant well
knew, and did furnish a locomotive to convey the materials
and perform other work for the gang of men aforesaid in
building bridges, buildings, as above alleged, and in doing
the said switching aforesaid, which was, as the plaintiff
has been informed and verily believes, about twenty-five
years old, had become so worn, broken, and decayed as to
become unfit for any service upon said road; which defective condition was then, and for a long *time prior thereto
had been, known by the defendant company. That said
engine was a passenger engine, and had no coupling appliances fit to couple on any car except a passenger car.
That the coupling apparatus on said engine was of an old
pattern, and of an unsafe and dangerous character, while
on other engines then used by defendant a newer and
safer appliance was in general use. That at the time of
the accident hereinafter mentioned one of the long bolts
which held the draw-castings on the rear of the tender of
said engine, at the place of coupling, was projecting about
two inches beyond the plate, either from having been broken
or having been drawn out through the rotted wood; whereas
it should not have projected at all beyond the face of the
casting. The plaintiff, without carelessness or negligence
on his part, or knowledge of said projecting bolt, attempted to make the said coupling between the said tender
and caboose car, in accordance with the said request of said
acting superintendent; and when said engine and tender
came back upon him, as above alleged, he endeavored to .
withdraw his hand, but by reason of the said defects the

Cole vs. The Chicago & Northwestern R. Co.

same was caught and held fast by the said projecting end of said bolt; his right wrist was pierced by said bolt, and was seriously lacerated, bruised, and injured, so that the same has consequently become and is permanently stiffened and disabled; and at the same time the plaintiff's right hand was wounded and bruised, and the second finger of said hand was so crushed and cut that it had to be at once amputated."

Upon the trial in the circuit court, the plaintiff had a verdict for $2,750 damages; upon which verdict judgment was entered in his favor. From said judgment the railway company appeals to this court. On the trial the jury rendered a special verdict as follows: "(1) Was the injury to the plaintiff caused by catching his glove on the rod from which the jam-nut was gone, which thereby prevented him from withdrawing his hand in time to have escaped injury? *Answer*. Yes. (2) Would the plaintiff have withdrawn his hand in time to have avoided the accident if his glove had not caught on the rod? *A.* Yes. (3) Had there been any change in the original position or condition of the rod, except that the jam-nut was off? If you answer yes then state what the change was. *A.* No. (4) Did the jam-nut come off from the rod at the time of switching out the coal cars on the day the plaintiff was injured? *A.* We believe not. (5) How long had the nut been off from the rod in question? *A.* We do not know; no evidence to show. (6) Had the nut been off from the rod for such a length of time before the accident that the defendant, in the exercise of ordinary care in the inspection of engines and appliances, could have discovered it and put on a new nut? *A.* We do not know; no evidence to show. (7) Did the plaintiff see or know the condition of the rod at the time he attempted to make the coupling? *A.* No. (8) Could the plaintiff, by the exercise of ordinary care, have seen the rod and avoided catching his glove on it? *A.* No. (9) Did the plaintiff use and exercise ordinary care in attempting to couple the engine and car at the time he was injured? *A.* Yes. (10) Did the rod, in the condition it was, materially increase the danger of making the coupling? *A.* Yes. (11) Did the plaintiff, immediately before he went between the car and tender to make the coupling at the time his hand was caught and injured, signal the fireman to back up? *A.* No. (12) Did the plaintiff, immediately before he went between the tender and car, signal the fireman to start up, and did the engine start up, and then without further signal back up, and injure the plaintiff's hand? *A.* Yes. (13) Did the engine back up without any signals from the plaintiff either to go ahead or back up? *A.* Yes. (14) Was the engine backed up against the car with ordinary care and prudence by those servants of the defendant in charge of it? *A.* No. (15) Was it necessary, in order to shove the car back to the place where it was desired to be left, that the coupling should be made? *A.* No. (16) Did the plaintiff have sufficient knowledge, experience, and intelligence to understand and comprehend the dangers incident to the employment of coupling engines with a Miller engine coupler to cars? *A.* No. (17) If the court shall be of the opinion that the plaintiff is entitled to recover, at what sum do you assess his damages? *A.* $2,750."

At the close of the evidence, the defendant moved the court to direct a verdict in its favor, which motion was denied, and exception was duly taken; and on the rendition of the verdict the defendant moved for judgment upon the special verdict, which was also denied, and exception taken. Various other exceptions were taken by the defendant upon the trial, which need not be here stated or considered.

For the appellant there was a brief by *Jenkins, Winkler & Smith*, and oral argument by *Mr. Jenkins.* To the point that if a servant of full age and ordinary intelligence, upon being required by his master to perform other duties more dangerous and complicated than those embraced in his original hiring, undertakes the same, knowing their dangers, although unwillingly and from fear of losing his employment, and is injured by reason of his ignorance and inexperience, he cannot maintain an action against the master for such injury, they cited, besides cases cited in the opinion: *Capper v. L., E. & St. L. R. Co.* 103 Ind. 305; *Cummings v. Collins,* 61 Mo. 520; *Hulett v. St. L., K. C. & N. R. Co.* 67 id. 239; *Brown v. Byroads,* 47 Ind. 435; *McGlynn v. Brodie,* 31 Cal. 376; *Russell v. Tillotson,* 140 Mass. 201; 22 Cent. L. J. 446, note; *Atlas Engine Works v. Randall,* 100 Ind. 293; *Chicago & N. W. R. Co. v. Bayfield,* 37 Mich. 205; *Dowling v. Allen,* 74 Mo. 13; *Buzzell v. Laconia Mfg. Co.* 48 Me. 113; *Kean v. Detroit C. & B. Rolling Mills Co.* 33 N. W. Rep. (Mich.), 395; *Thompson v. C., M. & St. P. R. Co.* 14 Fed. Rep. 564.

Sutherland & Sutherland, for the respondent, to sustain the proposition that when the servant by direction of his master undertakes extra-hazardous work outside of the scope of his employment he does not take upon himself the risks of such work, cited, besides the cases cited in the opinion: *Miller v. U. P. R. Co.* 12 Fed. Rep. 600, 602; *S. C.* 17 id. 67; *Patterson v. P. & C. R. Co.* 76 Pa. St. 389, 393; *Chicago & N. W. R. Co. v. Jackson,* 55 Ill. 496; *Keegan v. Kavanaugh,* 62 Mo. 232; *Stephens v. H. & St. J. R. Co.* 86 id. 221, 230; Cooley on Torts, 555.

TAYLOR, J. Upon the argument of the appeal in this court it was not deemed by the learned counsel for the respondent that there was sufficient evidence in the case to sustain a verdict in favor of the respondent on the ground that the defendant was guilty of negligence in furnishing him unsuitable or unsafe machinery for doing his work, or that the company was guilty of negligence in employing a

careless or incompetent engineer for managing the engine
which was used in the performance of the work in which
he was engaged when the injury was sustained by him. As
to the competency of the engineer in charge of the locomotive, no evidence was given, or, if given, no claim was made
that he was incompetent. As to the dangerous and unsafe
condition of the engine and tender used in doing the switching of the cars to be switched, some evidence was given;
but it is not claimed by the learned counsel for the respondent that, on the findings of the jury upon that question, the
plaintiff would be entitled to recover upon that ground
alone. By an examination of the answers to the first eight
questions submitted to the jury as a part of the special verdict, it is very clear that the defect in the tender which it
is claimed was the proximate cause of the injury was not
shown to have been known to the defendant, nor that it
was of such long standing that, in the exercise of ordinary
care in that respect, the company ought to have known of
such defect.

The only ground for sustaining the verdict in favor of the
plaintiff relied upon by the learned counsel for the respondent is that, at the time the plaintiff was directed to do this
switching by the company, he was not employed by the
company to do such work; that the work of switching in
the yard of the defendant was dangerous work, and that
the plaintiff was not accustomed to do such work, nor was
he acquainted with the danger incident thereto; and that
in such case the defendant is liable for the injury if the injury was caused by the negligence of the engineer in charge
of the engine, or by a defect in the machinery, whether
such defect was known to the defendant company or not.
If this rule be as claimed by the learned counsel for the respondent, the findings of the special verdict are perhaps
sufficient to sustain the verdict, when aided by the undisputed evidence in the case. By an examination of the

findings from the ninth to the sixteenth, inclusive, it will be seen that there is no finding that the defendant company directed the plaintiff to do this work of switching, nor that such work was not such as the plaintiff had been employed to do. These two points are probably supplied by evidence which is not controverted by the defendant, and so the verdict may be aided to that extent. If it be necessary, in order to entitle the plaintiff to recover in this action, to show affirmatively that switching cars in the yard of the company is a more dangerous employment than the employment which the plaintiff had contracted with the defendant to perform, then the verdict would be insufficient for want of any such finding, or, if it be necessary for him to show that the company knew that such employment was more dangerous than the ordinary employment of the plaintiff, then the special verdict would be imperfect in that respect also. The findings upon this part of the case simply show that the plaintiff used ordinary care on his part, and that the injury was either the result of the negligence of the engineer or the defect in the tender, and that the plaintiff had not sufficient experience and intelligence to understand and comprehend the danger incident to the employment of coupling engines with a Miller engine coupler to cars.

The theory of the learned counsel for the plaintiff is that where the master directs his employee temporarily to perform work not contemplated by his contract of employment, and such work is of a dangerous character,— whether more dangerous than his general employment or not is immaterial,— the master becomes liable to protect him while so employed against the carelessness of his employees, and also against any injury he may receive on account of defective machinery, whether the company have any previous knowledge of the defect or not. He claims that the basis of recovery in such case lies in the fact that the master directs the employee to perform a work outside of his usual employment, which is in its nature a dangerous employment; and that the mere direction of the master to perform such temporary and dangerous work is negligence on the part of the master sufficient to sustain the action of the employee so injured in the performance of such work while he is using ordinary care on his part. Stating it in a little different form, the learned counsel says that the ordinary rule that the employee assumes the dangers incident to his employment is not to be applied to the case where the employee, at the direction of the master, does work, temporarily, outside of his contract of employment.

In order to sustain the judgment in favor of the plaintiff in this case, we think it will be necessary to adopt the rule as stated by the learned counsel to its full extent, because the questions as to whether the temporary employment was more or less dangerous than the ordinary employment of the plaintiff, or whether the defendant was guilty of negligence in directing the plaintiff to do the work in the doing of which he was injured, were not submitted to the jury. The negligence of the defendant upon which the action must be sustained if sustained at all, consists in his directing the plaintiff to do the work, and under that rule the question as to the knowledge of the employee of the dangers incident to the work to be done, or his want of knowledge, would be wholly immaterial.

We are very clear that the broad rule contended for by the learned counsel for the respondent is not sustained by the authorities, nor by the general rules of law which define the relations of the employer and employee. Some of the cases cited by the learned counsel for the respondent may have some general statements in the opinions which give some countenance to the rule as stated by counsel, but when the facts of each case are considered it will, we think, be found that no such broad rule was ever intended to be sanctioned by any of the courts. Whether the employer is guilty of negligence such as will entitle his employee to recover for an injury sustained while doing a temporary work outside of his contract of employment, when such injury is the result of the negligence of a co-employee, or of a defect of machinery not known to the employer, or other cause, is in every case a question of fact to be determined by all the circumstances of the case, and cannot be predicated simply on the fact that he directed his employee to do the work.

In order to make the employer responsible for an injury to his employee while in his employ, the evidence must in every case show that the employer has neglected some duty which he owes to the employee; and no case can, we think, be found where it has been held that the mere fact that the employer requested his employee to perform a temporary work, outside of his ordinary employment, was a violation of any duty which he owes to his employee. Whether it be a violation of such duty depends always upon the surrounding circumstances. If the particular work ordered to be done is of a dangerous character, and one which requires peculiar skill in its performance, and the person directed to perform such work has not the requisite knowledge or skill for doing the work with safety, and such want of skill or knowledge is known, or might be reasonably supposed to be known, to the employer, in that case the direction of the employer to do the work might be justly held to be a violation of a duty which he owes to his employee, even though the employee undertook to do the work without objection or protest upon his part. None of the cases go further than this, and we can see no reason for holding a stricter rule. Counsel says it is well settled that "the employee assumes all the ordinary risks within the scope of his employment." To this proposition no exception can be taken, and there is no need of the citation of authorities to sustain it. It is urged that the converse of this proposition is also true, viz., that "the servant, when he enters upon the discharge of his duties, does not assume any risks outside of the scope of his-employment;" and it is also insisted that when the servant undertakes, at the order of his master, to do work outside of his ordinary employment, there is no presumption that he assumes any of the risks attending such employment. To sustain this proposition the learned counsel for the respondent cites the following cases: *Ohio & M. R. Co. v. Hammersley*, 28 Ind. 374; *Lalor v. C., B. & Q. R. Co.* 52 Ill. 401; *Pittsburgh, C. & St. L. R. Co. v. Adams*, 105 Ind. 151; *Jones v. L. S. & M. S. R. Co.* 49 Mich. 573; *Mann v. Oriental Print Works*, 11 R. I. 152; *Chicago & N. W. R. Co. v. Bayfield*, 37 Mich. 205; *Broderick v. Detroit U. D. Co.* 56 Mich. 261; *Cook v. St. P., M. & M. R. Co.* 34 Minn. 45; *Dowling v. Allen*, 74 Mo. 13; *Railroad Co. v. Fort*, 17 Wall. 553; *Benzing v. Steinway*, 101 N. Y. 547; *O'Connor v. Adams*, 120 Mass. 427.

In the case in 28 Ind. 374, the court reversed the trial court on the ground that the employee, a minor, assumed the risk of his employment. In *Pittsburgh, C. & St. L. R. Co. v. Adams*, 105 Ind. 151, the court state the rule as follows: "In all cases the master is bound to disclose to the servant latent defects and dangers of which he has knowledge, or of which he ought to have knowledge by the exercise of reasonable attention, care, and diligence, and of which the servant has no knowledge, and would not discover by the exercise of reasonable care. This is particularly so when the master employs for hazardous and dangerous work a child, young person, or other person without experience and of immature judgment." "In the cases last above mentioned the *gravamen* of the action is the negligence of the master in failing to give the proper warning, and in employing a person of such immature years and judgment that such warning and instructions would furnish no protection. *And hence, in order that the master may be properly charged as being thus negligent, and made liable for resulting injury, it must be made to appear that he knew, or by the exercise of reasonable care and observation might have known, of the inexperience, disqualification, and immature judgment of the servant employed.* When a person of apparently sufficient age, physical ability, and mental caliber to perform the service, seeks an employment at the hands of a railway company or other master, he ought to be held to an implied representation that he is competent to perform the duties of the position he seeks, and competent to apprehend and avoid all dangers that may be discovered by the exercise of ordinary care and prudence. In such case we know of no good reason or rule of law that will compel the master to pass him through a critical examination to discover his competency for the place, or that will convict the master of negligence for not doing so." The court further say: "When, by the orders of the master, the servant is carried beyond his employment, he is carried away from his implied undertaking to assume the risks incident to the employment. Hence it is that when a servant is thus, by the orders of the master, put to work outside of his employment, and is injured by reason of defective machinery, railroad track, etc., without his fault, the master is liable, regardless of the care he may have exercised to keep the machinery, railroad track, etc., in a safe condition. When a servant is thus ordered at work at a particular place, or with particular machinery, etc., outside of his employment, the master impliedly assures him, not only that he has exercised reasonable care to have the place, machinery, etc., in a safe condition, but also that they are in a safe condition and fit for the business for which they are used. This principle or rule of law has been more frequently and more rigorously applied in cases of employees immature in years, judgment, and experi-

ence." " Here, again, it should be observed that the master
will not be liable if the circumstances are such as to show
that the servant is competent to apprehend the danger, and
expressly or impliedly assumes the risk."

We have cited at considerable length from this case, as it
goes as far to uphold the rule as claimed by the learned
counsel for the respondent, if not further than any of the
other cases cited by him on the argument.   And in this case
thé last paragraph qualifies all that is said before, and destroys the rule as contended for by the learned counsel.   It
leaves it, as stated above, a question of fact in all cases
whether the master is guilty of negligence in directing the
servant to do the act outside of his employment.

In *Lalor v. C., B. & Q. R. Co.* 52 Ill. 401, it was found
that the person representing the master knew that the employee whom he directed to couple the cars was unversed
and inexperienced in that business.   The decision is clearly
placed on the ground that the master was guilty of negligence in directing a servant to do an extra-hazardous work
whom he knew to be unskilled and inexperienced in the
business.   In *Jones v. L. S. & M. S. R. Co.* 49 Mich. 573,
the person who was injured while employed in the discharge of work not within the contract of his employment,
showed that he protested against doing the work.   In *Chicago & N. W. R. Co. v. Bayfield,* 37 Mich. 205, the instruction at the trial which was upheld as good law, was as
follows: "If you find that the deceased, at the time he was
employed by the defendant, was a lad of seventeen or eighteen years of age, inexperienced in handling the brakes on a
train of cars such as that in question, and that he was un-
fitted for that work by reason of his unskilfulness, inexperience, and youth, and this was known to Smith, . . .
and was ordered by Smith, the foreman and conductor of
the construction train in question, acting for and as the
agent of said defendant, then if he was killed while endeavor-

ing to perform such work, without negligence on his part, the plaintiff was entitled to recover." In *Broderick v. Detroit U. D. Co.* 56 Mich. 261, it was held that the plaintiff was entitled to recover for a defect in the construction of a ventilator which the employée was directed to open when he received his injury, and no question appears to have been made upon the point that he was doing work outside of his ordinary employment. In *Cook v. St. P., M. & M. R. Co.* 34 Minn. 45, the negligence for which the defendant was held responsible was in not providing a suitable place for the plaintiff to do his work. The plaintiff in this case was also a minor. In *Dowling v. Allen,* 74 Mo. 13, the person injured was a boy seventeen years old, and was working in a dangerous place, and had requested the person directing his work to relieve him from the work and get some other person to perform it. The defendant was held liable, on the ground that he had not performed his duty in sufficiently instructing the servant of the danger incident to the performance of his work. All that was decided in *Mann v. Oriental Print Works,* 11 R. I. 152, was that if the servant "was suddenly called upon to perform a dangerous service, not strictly within the line of his duty, and requiring peculiar skill, there would be no presumption that he knew the risks of it, and, if so, he should not have been directed to do it without information of the nature of the service." In *Benzing v. Steinway,* 101 N. Y. 547, the recovery was sustained, on the ground that the defendant did not furnish a safe place for the performance of the work which the servant was directed to do, and not upon the ground that the service was outside of his usual employment. The rule laid down in *O'Connor v. Adams,* 120 Mass. 431, and *Railroad Co. v. Fort,* 17 Wall. 553, is stated as follows: "If the defendant knew the peril to which the servant would be exposed, and did not give him sufficient and reasonable notice of it, and he, without negligence on his part, through inexperience or reliance on the directions given him, failed to perceive or understand the risk, and was injured, the defendant would be responsible." This rule was laid down in cases where the servant was an inexperienced minor.

We think that it may be safely said that none of the cases cited by the learned counsel for the respondent hold that merely directing a servant to perform a duty outside of his usual employment is such negligence on the part of the employer as will render him liable for any injury the servant may receive while engaged in such employment; but, on the other hand, all the circumstances attending the case, such as the dangerous character of the work directed to be done, the age and experience or inexperience of the servant, and the knowledge of the master as to these attendant circumstances, must be taken into consideration in determining the question of negligence.

In the case at bar the plaintiff was a man of forty years and upwards, an intelligent mechanic. He had been in the employ of the railroad company for over ten years, and for several years had been the foreman of a gang of men employed in building and repairing bridges and other structures for the defendant on its road, and was so engaged at the time the accident happened. In his employment he had an engine and cars under his control, for the purpose of doing his work, and a man or men whose duty it was to couple or uncouple cars as needed in such work. At the time he was requested to do the switching in the defendant's yard, he was requested to take the engine he had in use for doing his ordinary work, and the gang of men under him, and do such work. He made no objection to doing the work on the ground that it was dangerous, or that he had not sufficient knowledge or experience to do the same safely to himself and the men under his charge. Under these circumstances it seems to us that no negligence can be attributed to the company for directing him to do the work.

He undertook the work voluntarily, knowing the general danger of the employment, and the rule applicable to work done in his ordinary employment must be applied to the work done by him under such order. If the finding of the jury that the plaintiff did not comprehend the dangers incident to the work was supported by the evidence, it cannot alter the case. That fact was not made known to the defendant at the time, and there is nothing in the evidence which would tend to show the, defendant that the plaintiff had not sufficient knowledge, experience, and skill to perform the work safely to himself and those in his employ.

That the plaintiff cánnot recover upon the facts proved in this case is well settled by the authorities cited by the learned counsel for the appellant. *McGinnis v. C. S. Bridge Co.* 49 Mich. 466, 8 Am. & Eng. R. Cas. 135; *Wormell v. M. C. R. Co.* 10 Atl. Rep. (Me.), 49; *Rummell v. Dilworth,* 111 Pa. St. 343, 345; *Leary v. B. & A. R. Co.* 139 Mass. 587; *Railroad Co. v. Fort,* 17 Wall. 554, 558; *Cahill v. Hilton,* 106 N. Y. 512, 518; 3 Wood, Ry. Law, 1487; Wood, Mast. & Serv. § 344; *May v. O. & Q. R. Co.* 10 Ont. 70; *Hawk v. Penn. R. Co.* 11 Atl. R. 459.

We are not called upon in this case to determine what the rule would be if the employee, when ordered to do work which his general employment did not require him to do and which was dangerous in its character, objected to doing the work on the ground of want of experience and knowledge sufficient to enable him to perform the work with safety to himself and those under him, and, notwithstanding such declaration on his part, his employer insisted upon his doing it, and thereupon he undertook to do the work after such protest, rather than subject himself to the risk of being discharged from his employment. We do not in this case either affirm or disaffirm the rule stated by the supreme court of Massachusetts in *Leary v. B. & A. R. Co.* 139 Mass. 587, upon that state of the case. All we decide in this case is that when an employee of mature years and of ordinary intelligence and experience is directed to do a temporary work outside of the business he has engaged to do, and consents to do such work, without objection on account of his want of knowledge, skill, or experience in doing such work, no negligence of the employer can be predicated upon that state of facts alone.

There are other reasons why the plaintiff ought not to recover in this action. He was not directed to couple or uncouple cars. He was the foreman of a gang of men, having in charge an engine and some one to do the coupling and uncoupling of cars. He was directed to take the engine and his men and do the switching of some loaded cars in the defendant's yard. The order did not direct him personally to do the coupling of the cars. Again, according to the testimony of the plaintiff himself, he was not injured on account of his inexperience in coupling cars, but by reason of a defect in the car he attempted to couple to the engine. He claims, and we are inclined to think his claim is well founded, that he would not have been injured had it not been for the projecting bolt or rod which caught his glove when he attempted to withdraw his hand from the place of danger.

In no view of the case can the verdict be sustained, except upon the theory advanced by the learned counsel for the respondent, as stated above. We think the rule of liability as claimed by the learned counsel is not sustained either by authority or upon the principles of law applicable to employer and employee. Upon the undisputed evidence in the case, and upon the findings of the jury, judgment should have been rendered in favor of the appellant.

By the Court.— The judgment of the circuit court is reversed, and the cause is remanded with directions to render judgment for the defendant.

See note to this case in 37 N. W. Rep. 84.— REP.

WILKINSON. Guardian, etc., Respondent, vs. BAYLEY, imp.,
Appellant.

February 6 — February 28, 1888.

Jurisdiction: Judgment by default: Proof of service of summons.

Where the proof of service by a person other than the sheriff does not
show that a copy of the summons was *left with,* as well as delivered to, the defendant (sec. 2642, R. S.), the court acquires no jurisdiction to render judgment by default.

APPEAL from the Circuit Court for *Grant* County.

Action to foreclose a mortgage. The affidavits of service were to the effect that the affiants did, at a certain time
and place, duly and personally serve the summons and complaint (or notice of the object of the action) upon the defendants named by delivering to them and each of them a
true copy thereof, and that the affiants personally knew the
persons upon whom they respectively made such service to
be the persons in respect to whom such service was to be
made. The defendants failed to appear, and judgment by
default was rendered against them. The defendant *Bayley,*
appearing specially for that purpose, appealed from the
judgment.

For the appellant there was a brief by *A. W. & W. E.
Bell,* and oral argument by *Mr. A. W. Bell.*

For the respondent the cause was submitted on the brief
of *W. H. Beebe.* He contended that the judgment of a
court of general jurisdiction is *prima facie* proof of the
regularity of the proceedings in obtaining it, and presumptive of the jurisdiction of the court. *Allen v. Huntington,*
16 Am. Dec. 702; *Loomis v. Wheeler,* 18 Wis. 524; *Jarvis
v. Robinson,* 21 id. 523; *Archer v. Romaine,* 14 id. 375.
The *onus* of impeaching a judgment is upon him who seeks
to resist it. *Scott v. Coleman,* 15 Am. Dec. 71. A party
seeking to set aside a judgment for irregularity will be held

to the strictest rules of proceeding. *Ætna L. Ins. Co. v. McCormick*, 20 Wis. 265.

ORTON, J. This is an appeal from a judgment of foreclosure by one of the defendants appearing specially for such purpose. The summonses, with the proof of the pretended service thereof by the affidavit of two private persons on the same, which are a part of the record, show that no service was legally made upon any of the defendants, and that the court therefore did not acquire any jurisdiction to render said judgment. The affidavits do not state that a copy of the summons was left with any of the defendants, as required by sec. 2642, R. S. The judgment is clearly void for such reason. There was no appearance in the circuit court, and judgment was taken by default. The case of *Hall v. Graham*, 49 Wis. 553, is closely in point. In that case, as in this, the defective service appears by the affidavit of the person making the same, indorsed upon the summons, and there was no appearance, and the defect is the same. The judgment was reversed for that reason alone. In that case it was held that due and proper service must appear upon the record before the court was authorized to render judgment by default, which sufficiently answers the argument of the respondent's counsel that it must be presumed that due service was made by the sheriff or other officer. *Matteson v. Smith*, 37 Wis. 333, is equally in point. See, also *Pollard v. Wegener*, 13 Wis. 569; *Rape v. Heaton*, 9 Wis. 328; *Sayles v. Davis*, 20 Wis. 302; *Dundon v. Starin*, 19 Wis. 261, and other cases in this court.

By the Court.— The judgment of the circuit court is reversed, and the cause remanded for further proceedings according to law.

BOWERS, Respondent, vs. EVANS, Assignee, etc., Appellant.

February 6 — February 28, 1888.

Equity: Banks and banking: Voluntary assignment: Trust fund: Paramount right to payment.

> Bonds deposited with a banker for safe-keeping were by him disposed of, and the proceeds went to increase the assets of the bank which were shortly afterwards assigned by him for the benefit of creditors. *Held*, that the owner of the bonds had a paramount right to be first paid in full out of such assets. *McLeod v. Evans*, 66 Wis. 401, and *Francis v. Evans*, 69 id. 115, followed.

APPEAL from the Circuit Court for *Grant* County.

This was an action by *Maggie Bowers* against *Jonathan H. Evans*, assignee of Isaac Hodges, to recover the proceeds of certain bonds sold by said assignor. The court made the following findings of facts and conclusions of law:

" 1· On the —— day of October, 1882, Isaac Hodges, the assignor of the defendant, was a banker and doing business as such at Platteville, Wisconsin, and on that day the plaintiff deposited with him, for safe-keeping and not otherwise, six United States government bonds, each of the denomination of $500, and bearing interest at the rate of four per cent. per annum, which said bonds were negotiable by delivery. 2. That on August 1, 1883, said Hodges, in the course of his regular business, deposited said bonds with the National Bank of Galena, Illinois, as collateral security on his note for $7,000 to said bank, with other collaterals. 3. On January ——, 1884, the plaintiff directed said Hodges to sell said bonds and immediately remit the proceeds thereof to her at San Buena Ventura, California, where she then resided. 4. On February 7, 1884, said Hodges directed said bank to sell said bonds and apply the proceeds thereof on his said note to it, which was not then due; and on February 11, 1884, said bank notified said

Hodges that said bonds were sold for $3,710.90, and the proceeds indorsed on said note. 5. On February 8, 1884, said Hodges closed his doors as a banker, and on February 11, 1884, assigned all his property to the defendant for the benefit of his creditors, and said defendant thereupon immediately accepted of the trust as such assignee, and took possession of the estate assigned to him, and now has money and property in his hands as such assignee to the value of at least $20,000. 6. That on May 6, 1884, the plaintiff made proof of a claim against said I. Hodges, based upon the facts aforesaid, for the sum of $3,710.90, and duly filed the same; and on June 4, 1884, the plaintiff received a six per cent. dividend thereon, amounting to $222.65, from said assignee. 7 That in making such assignment said Hodges stated the value of his property and assets by him so assigned, under oath, at the sum of $226,000, and in like manner stated the amount of his liabilities at $164,554.11, and in like manner listed the plaintiff as one of his creditors in the said sum of $3,710.91, growing out of the facts aforesaid, but that said Hodges was then in fact largely insolvent, as the plaintiff discovered after filing her said claim. 8. And as conclusions of law, the court finds that the plaintiff is entitled to judgment against the defendant for the said sum of $3,710.91, with interest from February 11, 1884, less the said sum of $222.65, paid June 4, 1884, together with the costs of the action, and that the same be paid in out of the estate of said Hodges so in the hands of the defendant; and judgment is ordered accordingly."

From the judgment entered accordingly the defendant appeals.

For the appellant there was a brief by *Carter & Cleary*, and oral argument by *Mr. W. E. Carter*.

For the respondent there was a brief by *J. W. Murphy, A. W. & W. E. Bell,* and *Bushnell & Watkins,* and oral argument by *Mr. A. W. Bell* and *Mr. A. R. Bushnell.*

COLE, C. J. This case is clearly ruled by the decision in *McLeod v. Evans*, 66 Wis. 401, and *Francis v. Evans*, 69 Wis. 115, unless those cases are to be overruled. A majority of the court are not disposed to disturb them or modify the doctrine laid down in them. The equities of the plaintiff to a preference over the general creditors are certainly as strong, if not superior to the equities of the plaintiffs in those cases. Here the plaintiff left her United States bonds with Hodges for *safe-keeping*, in October, 1882. In August, 1883, Hodges, in the course of his regular business as banker, deposited the bonds with a Galena bank, as collateral security for the payment of his note then made, of $7,000. The proceeds of the Hodges note, the cashier, Griswold, says, were put into his general banking business. On February 6th or 7th Hodges directed the Galena bank to sell the bonds and apply the proceeds on his note, which had been renewed and was not then due. The Galena bank informed Hodges that they had sold the bonds and applied the proceeds as directed. The Hodges note is indorsed February 11, 1884, with a payment of $3,710.90, the proceeds of the bonds. Hodges' bank closed on the 8th of February, and he made an assignment of all his property for the benefit of his creditors on the 11th. It appears that some time in January, 1884, the plaintiff directed Hodges to sell her bonds and immediately remit the proceeds to her in California, where she resided. It is not pretended that Hodges assumed to act, in directing the bonds to be sold, under any instructions given him by the plaintiff. He simply misappropriated or wrongfully converted the bonds to his own use, without the least color of right or authority. They were left with him for safe-keeping merely, and he sold or pledged them to raise money to put into his banking business. This is the fair inference from the testimony. It is true, Griswold, on being subsequently called, qualified the statement that the money borrowed of the Galena bank on

the Hodges note was put by Hodges in "his general banking business," but we are inclined to take the first statement
as correct.   It is more probable that the money was thus
used.

The question then is, Must the plaintiff, whose property has
thus been wrongfully misapplied, stand upon the same footing as the general creditors as to the assets assigned?   We
think not.   We say, as we did in the *McLeod Case*, that it
is an irresistible conclusion from the facts that the proceeds
of these bonds found their way into the Hodges estate and
went to increase the assets of the bank which were assigned.
It seems inequitable that the general creditors should profit
by, or have the benefit of, the fraud committed by the assignor in respect to these bonds.   For Hodges never owned
them; they were never a part of his estate by right, but,
by a gross violation of trust, amounting to a crime, he
mixed this trust property with his own, and the assignee
seeks to hold it for the benefit of all the creditors.   The
plaintiff has a paramount right to be first paid out of the
assets.   This is the doctrine of the cases decided by the
court, which we see no sufficient reason for changing.   It
was not my purpose, at this time, to enter upon a discussion of the principles upon which these cases rest.   Enough
is said in the opinions to indicate our views upon that subject.   I shall make but one further remark.   Among the
authorities cited to sustain the decision in the *McLeod Case*
was *People v. City Bank*, 96 N. Y. 32, which, as reported,
would seem to be in point.   In that case the court says that
the object of Sartwell, Hough & Ford, in drawing and de-
positing their checks with the bank, was to provide a fund
for the payment of the specific notes mentioned, and the
engagement of the bank was thus to apply the fund.
"Thus a trust was created, the violation of which constituted a fraud, by which the bank could not profit, and to
the benefit of which the receiver is not entitled. . . .

The checks were impressed with a trust, and no change of them into any other shape could divest it so as to give the bank or its receiver any different or more valid claim in respect to them than the bank had before their conversion." The decision of the same court in *Cavin v. Gleason*, 105 N. Y. 256, would seem to be in direct conflict with that in the *City Bank Case*. The court, however, say, in *Cavin v. Gleason*, that the case of *People v. City Bank* seems to have been misunderstood; that it was not claimed in the latter case that the proceeds of the checks of Sartwell, Hough & Co., the petitioners, had not gone into the general funds of the bank, or that they had not passed in some form to the receiver. In fact, what the case does show upon that point is that these checks were marked paid, and the amounts were deducted from the deposits of the drawers in the bank. But the notes themselves, which the checks were intended to pay, were not owned by the bank, but had been previously sold and the avails used in its business, as we infer. These are the facts, as we understand them. We shall not attempt to reconcile these cases in New York. It is sufficient to say that a majority of this court adhere to the decisions which we have made and which clearly dispose of every point relied on in the case at bar for a reversal of the judgment of the court below.

TAYLOR and CASSODAY, JJ. While approving of the "progressive" or "modern rule" of equity, as affirmed in *Re Hallett's Estate*, 13 Ch. Div. 696, we were forced to dissent from the conclusions of the majority of this court in *McLeod v. Evans*, 66 Wis. 413, for the reasons there given, to the effect that, in our judgment, that decision was a departure from a well-established rule of equity, and not supported by any well-considered adjudication. It is true that some things were said in *People v. City Bank*, 96 N. Y. 32, and *Peak v. Ellicott*, 30 Kan. 156, cited in the majority opinion, which seemed to support such new departure, but the report of those cases left the facts upon which each turned so obscure that we were constrained to believe that the trust fund was still on hand and either capable of identification or traceable into a still present existing fund, and not, as in these *Evans Cases*, previously paid out on such trustees' or agents' indebtedness; but if otherwise, they ought not to be followed. In the case of *Francis v. Evans*, 69 Wis. 115, we attempted to expose what we regarded as a fallacy, in assuming that, if an insolvent debtor used funds which he held in trust, or in any fiduciary capacity, in payment of his debts, he thereby benefited his estate, when, as a matter of fact, the wrongful conversion of the money so held in trust created a new indebtedness of precisely the same amount as the one paid; and hence the result must always be that by such misappropriation the insolvent's volume of indebtedness is not diminished a penny, nor his assets increased a penny. We there stated the equitable rule thus: "That rule, as we understand, was never based upon any supposed right of preference of one creditor over another, as sometimes provided by statute, but upon the supposed equitable right of the person whose property has been wrongfully converted to trace and retake his own property; and, when its identity has been lost by being mixed with other funds, then to retake its equivalent from the property or funds it has so enriched, and to the extent of such enrichment." Soon after the decision in that case, there appeared two decisions of courts of conceded ability upon the very questions here involved, and holding the true rule to be substantially as stated above. One was by the court of appeals of New York, in *Cavin v. Gleason*, 105 N. Y. 256; and the other by the supreme court of Pennsylvania in the *Appeal of Hopkins*, 9 Atl. Rep. (Pa.), 867. In the New York case the authorities are reviewed to some extent by Mr. Justice ANDREWS, and *People v. City Bank* is explained as not involving the question thus assumed to have been decided; and saying, that: "We know of no authority for such a contention." The opinion in that case, as well as the conclusions reached by the several judges in *Re Hallett's Estate, supra,* are so clearly in harmony with our views, that we refrain from adding anything; and we have written this merely to relieve ourselves from the responsibility of the decision in this case.

By the Court.— The judgment of the circuit court is affirmed.

BELL and another, Appellants, vs. THE CITY OF PLATTEVILLE, Respondent.

February 7 — February 28, 1888.

MUNICIPAL CORPORATIONS. *(1) Power to rent city hall for entertainments. (2) Action to enjoin, by whom to be brought.*

1. Where the city authorities are by the charter given " the management and control of the finances and of all property of the city," and are charged with " the government of the city and the exercise of its corporate powers and management of its financial, prudential, and municipal concerns," they may lease a hall owned by the city to be used for concerts, theaters, and other entertainments for which it is adapted.

2. *It seems* that an action to restrain a city from exercising powers alleged to be in excess of its corporate authority cannot be maintained by citizens or tax-payers whose private rights are in no way jeopardized, and that such actions should always be in the name of the state and prosecuted by the public authorities.

APPEAL from the Circuit Court for *Grant* County.

The following statement of the case was prepared by Mr. Justice CASSODAY:

This action was commenced April 20, 1885, by the plaintiffs, as tax-payers of the city, to restrain the defendant from renting or allowing the city hall, then lately completed therein, and worth $25,000, to be used for the purposes of theatcrs, concerts, lectures, shows, dances, and general entertainments. The complaint contained suitable allegations, and among others that such renting and use would increase the danger of the building by fire and avoid the insurance thereon.

The answer alleged, among other things, in effect, that its city hall was built for and with money belonging to the city, and was occupied by it for its municipal uses; that the lower floor and basement thereof was occupied by its fire department, its clerk's office, and its common council meetings; that in the lower floor of said building, above the basement, there was a room built and suitable for use as a court-room in which to hold justice's court, and that it had leased and let the same to the town of Platteville (owning no part of said building), to use for the meetings of the board of supervisors of said town, and for the use of the town clerk of said town, and it proposes to permit the justices of the peace of said town to hold their courts therein, they paying a reasonable compensation therefor; that the whole of the upper floor of said building, being 98 feet long, 48 feet wide, and 28 feet high, with a gallery at one end and a platform suitable for lecture purposes and theatrical representations at the other, had been built and fitted up expressly for a hall or large room in which to hold public meetings and gatherings of the people; that prior to such building there was no hall-room or other place reasonably suitable and safe for such meetings and gatherings in said city; that such room was voted by the people and voters of said city as an absolute necessity for the safety and comfort and well-being of the people therein for amusement and culture, and that the plaintiff, as contractor or agent, took part in the building of said hall; that the defendant has paid nearly the whole cost of the building; that said large room or hall is wholly useless to the defendant for any other purpose than for a place in which to hold public meetings, concerts, lectures, and other entertainments; that for such purposes it will bring a rental to the defendant of at least $500 a year; that the defendant proposed, unless restrained, to continue such use of the hall under proper regulations, and for reasonable rent; that the plaintiffs had not suffered, nor were liable to suffer, any money damage or injury by reason of anything done or threatened by the city. The answer denied that any of the things mentioned would avoid any insurance on the building.

At the close of the trial the court found in effect that the plaintiffs were such tax-payers; that the building was insured in two companies, in the aggregate for $16,000; that the scenery added to the fixtures of such large room known as "Opera Hall" had increased the rate of insurance one per cent. for the period of three years; that said policies were still in full force and in no way affected as to validity by the addition of such scenery; "that the material facts set forth in the answer for the purposes of this case must be taken as true." As a conclusion of law the court found that the complaint should be dismissed, with costs. From the judgment entered thereon, in accordance with such findings and conclusion, the plaintiffs appeal.

For the appellants there was a brief by *Bushnell' & Watkins*, attorneys, and a separate brief by *A. R. Bushnell*, of counsel, and the cause was argued orally by *A. W. Bell*, in person, and by *Mr. Bushnell*. They contended, *inter alia*, that the use of the hall in the manner contemplated by the city should be restrained, because it is unlawful and improper and would result in wear and tear as well as increase the risk of the destruction of the building by fire and the cost of its insurance. *School District v. Arnold*, 21 Wis. 57; *Scofield v. Eighth School Dist.* 27 Conn. 499; *Weir v. Day*, 35 Ohio St. 143; *Spencer v. Joint School Dist.* 15 Kan. 259;

Dorton v. Hearn, 67 Mo. 301; *Cooper v. Alden,* Harr. (Mich.), 72; *Perry v. McEwen,* 22 Ind. 440; *Niebuhr v. Piersdorff,* 24 Wis. 317; *Pope v. Halifax,* 12 Cush. 411. As to the right of property holders to resort to equity to restrain municipal corporations and their officers from transcending their lawful powers or violating their legal duties in any mode which injuriously affects the tax-payers, they cited 2 Dillon on Mun. Corp. (3d ed.), secs. 914, 916, 917, 919, 922; *Crampton v. Zabriskie,* 101 U. S. 601; *Judd v. Fox Lake,* 28 Wis. 583; *State ex rel. Manitowoc v. County Clerk,* 59 id. 17; *Nevil v. Clifford,* 55 id. 171; *Peck v. School District,* 21 id. 516; *Helms v. McFadden,* 18 id. 191; *McLachlan v. Staples,* 13 id. 448.

For the respondent there was a brief by *Carter & Cleary,* and oral argument by *Mr. W. E. Carter.*

CASSODAY, J. It is undoubtedly true that the corporate authorities of a city possess only such powers as are expressly granted by legislative enactment, and such others as are necessarily or fairly implied in or incident to the powers thus expressly granted, or essential to the declared objects and purposes of the corporation. 1 Dill. Mun. Corp. (3d ed.), sec. 89; *Appeal of Whelen,* 108 Pa. St. 197; *Le Couteulx v. Buffalo,* 33 N. Y. 333; *Meinzer v. Racine,* 68 Wis. 245, 246; *Gilman v. Milwaukee,* 61 Wis. 592.

By the charter there was conferred upon the city of *Platteville* the general powers possessed by municipal corporations at common law, and in addition thereto such as are therein "specifically granted." Sec. 1, subch. 1, ch. 83, Laws of 1880. The government of the city and the exercise of its corporate powers and management of its financial, prudential, and municipal concerns, were vested in a mayor and six aldermen, who were denominated the common council, and such other officers as are therein provided for. Sec. 3, Id. To the common council was given "the management

and control of the finances and of all property of the city,"
and "in addition to all other powers" vested in the common council, numerous specific powers were granted to it
by the several subdivisions of sec. 17, subch. 4 of the charter,
among which are the following: "38. To receive, purchase,
and hold for the use of the city any estate, real or personal,
to sell and convey the same, and to insure any property of
the city against loss or damage by fire, lightning, wind, or
hail. . . . 40. To establish a fire department; . . .
to provide protection from fire by the purchase of fire-
engines and all the necessary apparatus for the extinguishment of fires; . . . to erect engine-houses," etc. These
subsections were amended by ch. 94, Laws of 1881, particularly by adding to subsection 38 the following: "*Provided,*
no purchase of any said real estate shall be made to exceed
one thousand dollars in value during any current year, unless the question of such purchase shall have been submitted
to the electors of said city at a general or special election,
upon due notice, and a majority thereof shall vote in favor
of such purchase. Notice of the submission of such question
shall be given at least ten days prior to such election by posting or publication thereof as in other cases." The statutes
provided that any city may borrow money and issue its negotiable bonds for the purchase or erection of public buildings; but such bonds are not to issue until such proposition
to issue shall have been submitted to the people of such
municipality and adopted by the majority voting thereon.
Secs. 942, 943, R. S.

It is said there is no proof of any meeting ever being
called to vote upon the question of the building of a theater. It may be added that the record fails to disclose
whether any proposition for the purchase of the land, or
the construction of the city hall, or the issuing of any bonds
therefor, was ever submitted to the people or voted upon.
The answer to all such suggestions, however, is that this

action is not brought to restrain the purchase of the lots, nor the construction of the building. Its only purpose is to restrain the alleged misuse of certain portions of the building, and hence presupposes its construction and substantial completion. The complaint alleges, in effect, that the city owned the hall; that it was of the value mentioned; that it had been "built by taxes legally voted by the citizens of said city." We must therefore assume, even in the absence of proof, that the city authorities were duly authorized to purchase the lots, construct and complete the building as they did, and put the same in the condition in which it existed at the time the action was commenced. The character of the building, and the several rooms and apartments thereof, and their respective uses, are set out in detail in the verified answer. The trial court, for the purposes of the case, and in the absence of evidence to the contrary, assumed such statements to be true. If they were not true and prejudicial to the plaintiffs, they should have made it so appear, since the burden was upon them to show affirmatively their right to equitable interference. In the absence of such proofs, the plaintiffs occupied the same position in those respects as though they had demurred to the answer.

We start, then, with the city as the lawful owner of the building containing the rooms and apartments mentioned. From what has been said, it will appear, that the question so fully argued by the learned counsel for the plaintiffs as to whether the municipality had any legal authority to build a coliseum, a theater, a circus, a beer-garden, or any structure for mere amusement, recreation, or culture, is not involved in the case nor pertinent to any of the issues raised. So far as this case is concerned, it must be assumed that the city had authority to build a city hall, and built it. Such authority having been given without restriction, included, by necessary implication, the right to determine the plan of the building and the mode in which it should be constructed. *Konrad v. Rogers*, 70 Wis. 492; *Ely v. Rochester*, 26 Barb. 133; 1 Dill. Mun. Corp. sec. 140; *Poillon v. Brooklyn*, 101 N. Y. 132. Human wisdom is not infallible, and it may be that the plan of this building was unwise; that it extended beyond the immediate, or even prospective, *municipal* wants of the city. Nevertheless it was the plan determined upon by the only officials vested with the authority to determine the same. The lower part of the building seems to be adapted to the municipal purposes to which it is devoted. Whether, prior to such construction, the courts had power to confine the city authorities to some plan measured by or limited to the municipal necessities or wants of the city, is a question not here presented. It may be said, however, that courts of high authority have, in effect, held that such questions are largely within the discretion of the municipal authorities, and that courts should not interfere with such discretion except in a plain case of its abuse. *Greeley v. People*, 60 Ill. 20; *Torrent v. Muskegon*, 47 Mich. 115. In this last case such intervention was asked upon the ground that the proposed building was more expensive than needed by the fire department, and that there was no authority for building a city hall. In the language of Lord Chancellor Selborne, "this doctrine [of *ultra vires*] ought to be reasonably and not unreasonably understood and applied, and that whatever may fairly be regarded as incidental to, or consequential upon, those things which the legislature has authorized, ought not, unless expressly prohibited, to be held by judicial construction to be *ultra vires*." *Att'y Gen. v. Great Eastern R. Co.* L. R. 5 App. Cas. 473, 33 Eng. (Moak.) 773. As indicated, the city is the lawful owner of the building with the opera hall in it. This being so, there are really but two questions presented for determination.

1. Have the city authorities the lawful right to let or use

the opera hall for the purposes mentioned? As observed, the charter expressly gives them "the management and control of the finances *and of all property of the city*." They are, moreover, charged with "the government of the city and the exercise of its corporate powers and management of its financial, prudential, and municipal concerns." With the city owning the lots and building, and the city authorities possessing the powers thus expressly granted, it seems to us they have, by necessary implication, and as incident to such ownership, the lawful right to let or use the opera hall for the purposes mentioned. In fact this seems to be the logical result of former decisions of this court. Thus, while it was held in *Att'y Gen. v. Eau Claire*, 37 Wis. 400, that the legislature could not authorize the erection of a dam across the river at the expense of the city, "for the purpose of leasing the water-power for private purposes" *merely*, yet, upon the subsequent amendment of the act, it was in effect held that as the city had lawful authority to erect the dam "for the purpose of water-works for the city," it might, as incident to such authority, lease for private purposes any excess of water power not required for its water-works. *S. C.* 40 Wis. 533. This doctrine was reaffirmed in the recent case of *Green Bay & M. Canal Co. v. Kaukauna W.-P. Co.* 70 Wis. 635. The decisions in other states in cases similar to this confirm the same rule. Thus, in *Spaulding v. Lowell*, 23 Pick. 71, "a town built a market-house two stories high, and appropriated the lower story for a market, which was *bona fide* their principal and leading object in erecting the building," and "it was held that the appropriation of the upper story to other subordinate purposes was not such an excess of authority as to render the erection of the building and the raising of money therefor illegal." In *French v. Quincy*, 3 Allen, 9, it was in effect held that in the erection of a town-house the municipality might "make suitable provision for its prospective wants; and if the building contains rooms not wanted for the time being for municipal business, the town may let them temporarily, or allow them to be used gratuitously." To the same effect, *Camden v. Village Corp.* 77 Me. 530; *S. C.* 33 Alb. L. J. 28; *Worden v. New Bedford*, 131 Mass. 23; *The Maggie P.*, 25 Fed. Rep. 202. The cases relating to powers of school districts and towns cannot be regarded as authority for limiting the powers of cities as claimed, since their powers are very much more restricted, being, at most, *quasi* corporations, or corporations *sub modo* only. *Cathcart v. Comstock*, 56 Wis. 606–608. We must hold that the letting and use mentioned was not unauthorized.

2. There seems to be another insuperable objection to the maintenance of this action by the plaintiffs as mere tax-payers. The case is wholly barren of any action of the municipality tending to cloud the title of any of their property or in any way to increase the burden of taxation upon any property within the municipality. These things being so, the private rights of the plaintiffs are in no way jeopardized. *Gilkey v. Merrill*, 67 Wis. 459. On the contrary, their taxes will apparently be diminished by the revenue derived from the proposed letting or use. The plaintiffs appear in the case, therefore, as mere citizens of the municipality, asking the court to restrain the city officials from exercising powers said to be in excess of their corporate authority. That, however, seems to be a matter wholly between the municipality and the state. 2 Dill. Mun. Corp. sec. 574, and cases there cited; *Camden & A. R. Co. v. M. L. & E. H. C. R. Co.* 48 N. J. Law, 530. Undoubtedly the courts have a supervisory power over municipal corporations as well as others in such cases. Our statute provides that "in an action for that purpose commenced by the *attorney general* in the name of the state, in any circuit court, against a corporation, such court may restrain such corporation by injunction from assuming or exercising

any franchise, liberty, or privilege, or transacting any business, *not authorized by its charter.*" Sec. 3236, R. S. It seems very proper that an action of such public concern should always be in the name of the state, and prosecuted by the public authorities.

By the Court.— The judgment of the circuit court is affirmed.

=========

ANDREW, Administratrix, etc., Appellant, vs. HINDERMAN and another, Respondents.

February 7 —February 28, 1888.

Estates of decedents: Recovery of property fraudulently conveyed

An administrator need not wait until the deficiency of assets is judicially determined by the allowance of claims or otherwise before bringing an action under sec. 3832, R. S., to recover property conveyed by his intestate in fraud of creditors. He should proceed as soon as he is satisfied from the inventory that there will be a deficiency.

APPEAL from the Circuit Court for *Grant* County.

The facts are stated in the opinion. The plaintiff appealed from an order sustaining a demurrer to the complaint.

For the appellant there was a brief by *Bushnell & Watkins,* and oral argument by *Mr. A. R. Bushnell.*

For the respondents there was a brief by *Carter & Cleary,* and oral argument by *Mr. W. E. Carter.*

COLE, C. J. We think the demurrer to the complaint should have been overruled. The action is brought by the plaintiff, as administratrix of Joseph Hinderman, deceased, to cancel and set aside certain deeds, which, it is alleged, Hinderman made in his lifetime with the intent to defraud

his creditors.   It appears to us that the action is clearly
authorized by sec. 3832, R. S., which provides: "When
there shall be a deficiency of assets in the hands of an executor or administrator, and when the deceased shall in his
lifetime have conveyed any real estate, or any right or interest therein, with intent to defraud his creditors, or to
avoid any right, debt, or duty, or shall have so conveyed
such estate that by law the deeds or conveyances are void
as against creditors, the executor or administrator may and
it shall be his duty to commence and prosecute to final
judgment any proper action for the recovery of the same,
and may recover for the benefit of the creditors all such
real estate so fraudulently conveyed." The facts stated in
the complaint show with sufficient certainty that Hinderman made the conveyances in question with intent to defraud his creditors and especially the unpaid beneficiaries
in the bond, and that the subsequent grantees took their
conveyances with notice of this intent.   It likewise appears
that Hinderman died, leaving no visible property, real or
personal, except the lands thus conveyed, to meet the debts
due or to become due on the bond which he had signed as
surety for Schmitt, as principal.   It is objected that it does
not appear that Hinderman signed such bond as surety.   A
copy of the bond is attached to the complaint, from which
it appears that one Joseph Hinderman, with others, signed
the same as surety.   It is a fair presumption from all the
facts stated that it was the deceased who signed as surety,
though that distinct allegation is not made.   It was doubtless a mere clerical mistake in omitting to aver that the deceased executed the bond with the other sureties named.
The bond itself shows that certain sums are due upon it;
and it appears that the principal in the bond is insolvent;
and that the other sureties are likewise insolvent; and that
unless this real estate, thus fraudulently conveyed, can be
recovered, the beneficiaries are remediless.

The real objection to the complaint is that it does not appear that there are any debts against the estate of Joseph Hinderman, deceased; that before this action could be instituted it must be established by some judicial proceeding that there were creditors of such estate. It will be observed, the statute authorizes the administrator to proceed to recover real and personal property fraudulently conveyed by his intestate when there shall be a deficiency of assets in his hands to meet the debts of the deceased. As soon as the administrator is satisfied of the fact that there is a deficiency of assets, it is made his duty to commence and prosecute, for the benefit of creditors, an action to recover any property which may have been fraudulently conveyed. It is not necessary that the deficiency of assets should be ascertained by claims against the deceased allowed by the county court or by commissioners appointed by such court. The administrator can readily ascertain, by the inventory of the property and the claims presented, whether there will probably be a deficiency of assets in his hands or not. If satisfied there will be, he should not wait for the final settlement of his administration, but proceed with reasonable diligence to recover, for the benefit of the creditors, any property which may have been fraudulently conveyed by his intestate. This is the plain requirement of the statute. By delay, he might lose property which should be subject to the debts of his intestate. When the action is brought by the creditors, as it may be under the subsequent sections, to reach real estate not included in the inventory, there being just ground to apprehend that the estate of the deceased, as set forth in the inventory, may be insufficient to pay the debts of the intestate, there it is provided that the action of the creditors shall not be brought to trial until the sufficiency or insufficiency of the estate in the hands of the administrator to pay the debts of the deceased shall be ascertained. Secs. 3835, 3836, R. S. This implies that the debts against the estate shall be judicially determined in some way, by being allowed by the county court, or perhaps by commissioners appointed for that purpose. Some such determination would be essential in order to ascertain the deficiency of the assets. That was the nature of the action of *German Bank v. Leyser*, 50 Wis. 258, and what is there said has reference to such a case. But where the action is brought by the administrator, who is reasonably certain, from the information which the inventory and claims made furnish, that there will be a deficiency of assets in his hands, he should proceed promptly, under sec. 3832, to recover any property conveyed in fraud of creditors. He should not wait until the deficiency is ascertained on the final settlement of his account before the county court; for to wait until that time might, and often would, render valueless the remedy given by this statute. The complaint in this case shows that the Hinderman estate is insolvent; and that there is no other property, except the lands conveyed by the deeds mentioned, to pay the debts against it. These lands, it is alleged, were conveyed without any consideration actually paid by any one of the grantees, and such grantees were privy to the fraudulent intent. The present holder had notice of the fraudulent purpose of the conveyances. Upon these facts, as we have before said, we think the complaint states a cause of action under sec. 3832.

By the Court.— The order of the circuit court sustaining the demurrer is reversed, and the cause remanded for further proceedings according to law.

JONES, Respondent, vs. WARD, Appellant.

February 7 — February 28, 1888.

Principal and surety: Release: Indemnity.

The release of the principal debtor without the consent of the surety and without payment of the debt, does not release the surety if he is fully indemnified against loss by reason of having become such.

APPEAL from the Circuit Court for *Grant* County.

Action on two promissory notes. The facts in the case. as they appear by the testimony and the findings of the court, are as follows:

November 11, 1884, one McArthur and the plaintiff, *Jones.* were the owners, in unequal shares, of a printing establishment consisting of presses and printing materials, from which establishment was issued a weekly newspaper called "The Dodgeville Sun." They also owned a quantity of book-accounts, which had accrued in their business. On that day McArthur sold a portion of his interest in such establishment to one George E. Ward. December 1, 1884, George E. sold a portion of his interest in the property to the plaintiff, giving him a note for $345, which the defendant, his brother, signed as surety. This is one of the notes in suit in this action, but the defendant's liability thereon is not disputed. December 12, 1884, the plaintiff sold his interest in the property to one Cook, for $600, taking therefor three notes of $200 each, signed by Cook and also by the defendant as a surety for Cook. One of these $200 notes is sued upon in this action, and the defendant contests his liability thereon. At the same time, Cook executed to the defendant a chattel mortgage on the property so purchased by him, conditioned for the payment of the three $200 notes, upon which the defendant had thus become liable as surety. January 3, 1885, George E. Ward sold his interest in the property to McArthur. January 8, 1885, Cook sold his interest therein to George E. Ward. One of the considerations of this sale was that the latter should induce the plaintiff to release Cook from liability on the three $200 notes. The plaintiff did so release Cook, without the consent or knowledge of the defendant. No payment was made on the notes as consideration of the release. January 28, 1885, George E. Ward, by the defendant as his agent, sold his interest in the property to McArthur. As one of the considerations of this sale, the defendant assigned to McArthur the mortgage of December 12, 1884, executed to him by Cook. At the date of such assignment, such mortgage interest was worth more than the amount due on the $200 note in suit. Such assignment was made without the consent of the plaintiff, and, after it was made, McArthur withdrew the mortgage from the files of the town clerk's office.

From the above facts the circuit court held that the defendant, being fully indemnified by Cook's chattel mortgage to the extent of the $200 note in suit, is liable to the plaintiff for the amount of such note. Judgment for the plaintiff was entered accordingly for the amount due on both notes in suit, from which judgment the defendant appeals.

For the appellant there was a brief by *Bushnell & Watkins*, and oral argument by *Mr. A. R. Bushnell.* They conceded that if a surety is indemnified by receiving property from his principal to apply on the liability, the creditor is, *in equity*, entitled to the full benefit of such security; but they insisted that a creditor cannot avail himself of personal indemnity against a surety, unless the surety could have done so. Equity would never permit the defendant to enforce the chattel mortgage unless he became liable to pay something as surety. Being released by the release of his principal, he never could become so liable.   Brandt on Suretyship, secs. 284–5.

For the respondent there was a brief by *Clark & Mills*, and oral argument by *Mr. J. T. Mills*.   They cited *Fay v. Tower*, 58 Wis. 286; Brandt on Suretyship, sec. 123; *Moore v. Paine*, 12 Wend. 123; Story's Eq. Jur. sec. 502b; *Smith v. Est. of Steele*, 25 Vt. 427; *Richards v. Yoder*, 10 Neb. 429; *Nat. Bank v. Bigler*, 83 N. Y. 60; *Curtis v. Tyler*, 9 Paige, 432.

LYON, J.   Briefly stated, the case, so far as there is any controversy, is as follows: The defendant became surety for Cook's debt to the plaintiff, and Cook indemnified him by executing to him a chattel mortgage on certain property. The plaintiff released Cook from liability for such debt, without the consent of the defendant.   Afterwards, defendant sold his security to McArthur, without the consent of the plaintiff, for the consideration (as the circuit court found) of $475.

The only question in the case is, Did the release of Cook also release the defendant, his surety?   The general rule undoubtedly is that the release of the principal debtor, without the consent of the surety, releases the surety.   But if the surety is fully indemnified against loss by reason of having become such, a release of the principal without payment of the debt does not release the surety.   This is the rule laid down in *Fay v. Tower*, 58 Wis. 286, as applied to a case in which an unauthorized extension of credit had been given to the principal.   Manifestly, the same rule should be applied where the surety is absolutely released from the debt.   The rule is founded upon a very plain principle of justice.   To illustrate: A. becomes security for B. to C. for the payment of $1,000.   B. puts property into the hands of A., worth $1,000, to indemnify him against loss

Stone vs. The City of Oconomowoc.

because of the obligation thus assumed by him. C. releases B., the principal debtor, from all liability on account of the debt, but receives no payment thereon. A., the surety, then sells the pledged property for $1,000 and retains the proceeds. ·It is entirely reasonable and just that, notwithstanding the release of the principal debtor, C. should have his remedy against the surety for the amount realized by him in the sale of the pledged property. Such, we think, is the law. It seems to us that we have here just such a case.

By the Court.— The judgment of the circuit court is affirmed.

STONE, Appellant, vs. THE CITY OF OCONOMOWOC, Respondent.

February 7 — February 28, 1888.

MUNICIPAL CORPORATIONS: PLEADING. *(1) Power to rent city hall for entertainments. (2) Injury to owner of private hall. (3) Mere conclusions not admitted by demurrer.*

1. The common council of a city had, by the charter, "the control and management of the finances of the city and of all other property thereof," and had power to lease the real estate of the city, and to prevent or license and regulate theatrical performances, etc. *Held*, that it might let or use the auditorium of the city hall for theatrical and other entertainments. *Bell v. Platteville, ante,* p. 139, followed.

2. The fact that such use of the city hall lessens the profits derived by a citizen and tax-payer from his own hall built for similar purposes, gives him no right to have such use restrained.

3. An allegation in a complaint that the authorities of the defendant city intended to use certain property "precisely as if the said city was a private corporation and had erected the same with its private corporate funds," is *held* to be a mere conclusion from the other facts alleged, and not to have been admitted by a demurrer.

APPEAL from the Circuit Court for *Waukesha* County.
The following statement of the case was prepared by
Mr. Justice CASSODAY:

This action was commenced in March, 1887, to restrain
the defendant from letting, leasing, or allowing the main
auditorium of its city hall to be used for theaters, operas,
concerts, lectures, dances, shows, or other entertainments.
for profit or otherwise, and to restrict its use to municipal
purposes. The defendant demurred to the complaint on
the ground that it did not state facts sufficient to constitute a cause of action. From the order sustaining the demurrer the plaintiff appeals.

The complaint is to the effect that the plaintiff is a resident and owner of a large amount of real estate in the
defendant city, assessed at $17,500, upon which he pays
taxes; that in 1886 the defendant purchased certain lots
therein for the purpose of erecting a city hall, lock-up, and
such other buildings as it might desire; that pursuant to a
petition presented to the common council, March 15, 1886,
the said council submitted to the qualified electors of the
city the question of bonding the city for the purpose of raising money to build city buildings for the use of the city;
that said electors thereupon voted to bond the city for
$16,000 at the election thereof in April, 1886; that by aid
of the bonds thus voted, and other moneys raised by taxes
levied, the mayor and common council did erect and build
on said lots a city hall, at a cost, including accrued interest
on the bonds, of $26,379.76; that February 16, 1887, the
mayor and common council did by ordinance create an office of the "custodian of the main auditorium of the city
hall," and thereby gave such officer authority to lease said
hall for such purposes as were lawful when not used for
city purposes; that it is the purpose and intention of the
mayor and common council to rent and lease, to whomso-
ever may desire, the main hall of said building, for profit

and gain, for theaters, operas, concerts, lectures, dances, shows, and all public amusements, and to realize and reap gain and profit thereby, subject to whatever may be the damage of the wear and tear thereof; "that it is their intention and purpose thus to use the said property precisely as if the said city was a private corporation and had erected the same with its private corporate funds;" that the defendant has already used the same for such purposes, and already leased the same at divers and different times for dances and other public amusements, for which it received rent in some instances and in others gave the rent for nothing; that the plaintiff objects to the use of said building for any purpose except such as is strictly municipal and as is necessary to the city and the people in the exercise of its and their municipal functions and duties; that a part of the plaintiff's said real estate consisted of a large and costly block of buildings in which was and is a large and capacious hall expressly fitted and prepared for use for concerts, dances, operas, theaters, public amusements, and gatherings, from which use he derived large and valuable profit from the rent thereof; and that the same materially enhanced the value of his said property; that he purchased that property some six years before in the belief that in a city of that size private capital would not be invested in any building which would seriously come into competition with his; that the erection and use of said city hall for municipal purposes worked no harm to his property, but that such use of the same for such private purposes was and is a serious harm and injury to him and his said property, and materially detracts from both its value and income.

For the appellant there were briefs by *Warham Parks* and *Bushnell & Watkins*, and oral argument by *Mr. Parks* and *Mr. A. R. Bushnell*. They contended, *inter alia*, that the public building in which is this hall was erected solely for city purposes, and could not, under the law, have been built for any other object.   It is the privilege of the plaintiff, as a tax-payer, to insist that its use should be confined to the purpose for which it was erected, and he has properly sought that relief in a court of equity. *Scofield v. Eighth School Dist.* 27 Conn. 499; *Pratt v. Pratt,* 33 id. 455; 2 Dillon on Mun. Corp. (1st ed.), secs. 731–736; *Judd v. Fox Lake,* 28 Wis. 583; *Smith v. Appleton,* 19 id. 471; *Lawson v. Schnellen,* 33 id. 292; *Aurora v. C., B. & Q. R. Co.* 119 Ill. 246.

For the respondent there was a brief by *Jenkins, Winkler & Smith,* and oral argument by *Mr. F. C. Winkler.*

CASSODAY, J. 1. By its charter the city is given "the general powers possessed by municipal corporations at common law, and in addition thereto" such other powers as are therein "specifically granted." Sec. 1, subch. 1, ch. 239, Laws of 1879.   The charter further provides that "the common council shall have the control and management of the finances of the city and of *all other property thereof;* and, in addition to the powers otherwise vested in it, it shall have full power by ordinance, resolution, or by-laws — (1) To receive, purchase, and hold, for the use of the city, any estate, real or personal, and to sell, lease, or convey the same.   (2) To limit and define the duties and powers of officers and agents of the city. . . . (5) To control and protect the public buildings, property, and records, and insure the same. . . . (12) To prevent or license and regulate the exhibitions of . . . theatrical performances or shows of any kind."   Subd. 1, 2, 5, 12, sec. 3, subch. 4, ch. 239, Laws of 1879.   These provisions of the charter, with the general statutes, gave to the mayor and common council of the city substantially the same powers in regard to letting the auditorium of the city hall for theaters, etc., for profit, as were possessed by the city of Platteville, as indicated in the opinion filed herewith in the case of *Bell v. Platteville, ante,*

p. 139. The facts in the two cases are substantially alike so far as they are material to the question presented. For the reasons given in that opinion, we must hold that, with the powers thus possessed by the municipal authorities, and as incident to the city's ownership of the property, they had the lawful right to let or use the auditorium of the hall for the purposes mentioned.

2. Having determined that such letting and use is lawful, there seems to be no ground for holding that the plaintiff may nevertheless restrain such lawful use merely because it lessens the profits which otherwise would accrue to him by the letting and use of his own hall for similar purposes. If the plaintiff is in fact injured by such diminution of customers, such injury is necessarily too remote and consequential to be the basis of an action, and hence *damnum absque injuria.* This is too plain to require the citation of authority.

3. The mere allegation that it was the intention and purpose of the city authorities to use the " property precisely as if the said city was a private corporation and had erected the same with its private corporate funds," imports no new fact into the complaint, but is at most a mere conclusion from the other facts alleged, which was not admitted by the demurrer. *Pratt v. Lincoln Co.* 61 Wis. 66.

By the Court.— The order of the circuit court is affirmed.

LAMAR, Appellant, vs. SCALES, Respondent.

February 8 — February 28, 1888.

Contract: Sale of land: Evidence: Unauthorized offer by vendor's husband.

The plaintiff's husband had offered to sell her interest in certain land to the defendant (her brother) for $4,000 if taken at once, but the defendant had refused to give more than $3,500. The plaintiff denied having authorized such offer, and there was no evidence to show that she even knew of it. Afterwards, having made a contract to sell at a large advance, the defendant obtained a quitclaim deed from the plaintiff, paying her $4,000. The plaintiff claims that when the deed was given the defendant further agreed to pay her whatever he should obtain above $4,000 for her interest. The defendant denies having made such agreement, and claims to have purchased her interest absolutely. It is *held* that, in determining what the terms of the sale were, the trial court gave undue weight to the previous unauthorized offer by the plaintiff's husband, and that, upon the evidence (stated in the opinion), the contract was as claimed by the plaintiff.

APPEAL from the Circuit Court for *La Fayette* County. The following statement of the case was prepared by Mr. Justice TAYLOR as a part of the opinion:

This action was brought by *Elizabeth Lamar* against *Frank Scales* to recover a part of the purchase price of certain real estate sold by her to him. The material facts alleged in the complaint, which were either proved or admitted on the trial, are the following: Samuel H. Scales, the father of the plaintiff and the defendant and four other children, died in September, 1877, leaving a widow, and among other real and personal property a deed of trust in 315 acres of land, situate south of Chicago and near the present city of Pullman, to secure a large sum of money. After his decease, the deed of trust was foreclosed, and the executors of the deceased bid in the property for the benefit of the six children and of the widow. The right of the widow was disputed, and it was afterwards adjudged that she took no interest in the said 315 acres of land, and that said land belonged to the six children as tenants in common, each owning one undivided one-sixth part thereof. [See *Hardy v. Scales*, 54 Wis. 452.] Before the claim of the widow to the land had been settled adversely to her, the plaintiff, on the 17th day of November, 1879, sold and conveyed her entire interest to the defendant, whether an undivided sixth or an undivided seventh, as she alleges in her complaint, upon the following terms: "That said defendant, being desirous of acquiring the entire title to all of said tract in order that he might thereafter make a sale of the same, did, on or about November 17, 1879, procure from the plaintiff a deed of her entire share and portion of said property for and upon the consideration that, upon the sale of said property thereafter by him, he would pay to the plaintiff such a proportionate amount of the sum he should realize from the sale of all said property as it should be determined by the court thereafter that she was by law entitled to, and owned; and as a part payment of said consideration the defendant did then pay to this plaintiff the sum of $4,000 " The plaintiff further alleges that the defendant afterwards procured the title to the whole of said lands, and on or about the 23d day of January, 1880, sold and conveyed the whole thereof to one Amos Cotting for the sum of $60,000; that her proportionate share of said sum is $10,000; that the sum of $6,000 is still unpaid by the defendant; and that upon request he has refused to pay the said $6,000 or any part thereof, etc.

The answer denies each and every allegation of the complaint not therein expressly admitted, and then admits that Samuel H. Scales died, leaving a widow and the six heirs at law as set up in the complaint, and that he died seized of the notes and trust deed upon the lands described in the complaint; that the trust deed was foreclosed, and the land was bid in in the name of the widow and heirs at law of said deceased. And the defendant further admits "that he purchased the interest of the plaintiff in said real estate, but denies that he is indebted to the said plaintiff therefor in the sum of $6,000, or in any other sum, and denies that he is indebted to said plaintiff in any sum on any account."

The case was tried by the court without a jury. After hearing the evidence the learned circuit judge made twenty-five findings of fact. Nineteen of them are matters concerning which there is no dispute. The following are the 20th, 21st, 22d, 23d, 24th, and 25th findings, which are the material ones to be considered upon this appeal, viz.: "(20) That the proof fails to establish the agreement set forth in the complaint; but, on the contrary, the preponderance of the proof is that all the defendant agreed to give the plaintiff for her interest in the land was the $4,000 which he paid her. (21) I am led to this conclusion, notwithstanding the plaintiff and her son testify to such an agreement, that Hardy's testimony somewhat tends to sustain them, and that as against them the only oral testimony is that of the defendant, by the following considerations: (22) *Mrs. Lamar*, her son, and Mr. Hardy all testified from unaided memory as to what the defendant said more than six years ago. All know that it is difficult to recall, even in substance, conversations after such length of time. However, if this case had to be determined upon the recollection of the plaintiff and her two witnesses, and of the defendant alone, it would be my duty to find that the preponderance of evidence confirmed the agreement relied upon. But there are certain uncontroverted facts that in this case stand prominently forth, and which have a controlling influence with me. (23) The letters show beyond question that as late as November 6, 1879, the plaintiff was willing to sell her interest in the land for $4,000. From that time to the execution of the quitclaim deed to the defendant, upon November 17, 1879, she had learned nothing to make her ask more for it. When, therefore, upon that day, the defendant paid her $4,000 for her interest, there was no apparent reason why she should have been unsatisfied and have exacted, as further consideration, the agreement that if, when he sold the land, he got more than that for her interest, he would would pay the surplus to her. If there had been such an agreement, would it not likely have been mentioned in the deed or expressed in some other writing? As far as she or her husband could see, the fulfilment of such an agreement would be for the indefinite future. It is not reasonable to suppose that, if such agreement was made, as prudent a man as his letters show Charles Lamar to have been would have been content to let it rest simply in memory. (24) The agreement claimed to have been made at the time the deed was executed was not such a one as a business man and a lawyer of the defendant's evident capacity would have wittingly made. It was his object to make money by buying *Mrs. Lamar's* interest. The agreement set up cuts him off from making anything. It was a one-sided agreement. All he got for her interest beyond $4,000 was to be paid to her, and if he realized less for it than that, she was under no obligation to pay back any part of the money he had paid to her. (25) There is no question of fraud in this case. This action is not based upon a claim of fraud for the concealment by the defendant from the plaintiff of the Cotting agreement. It is brought upon an alleged express contract, and upon that it must be determined. If it had been founded upon alleged fraud because of the failure to make known to the plaintiff the existence of that agreement before the execution of the deed, it is questionable whether, under the testimony, it would have been maintainable. There is no proof that the defendant did anything to mislead the plaintiff. She did not rely upon his judgment as to the value of the land, and it would seem, under the authorities, that he was under no legal obligation to inform her that he had entered into an agreement with Cotting to sell the land for $60,000."

As a conclusion of law the court found that the complaint should be dismissed upon the merits with costs. From the judgment entered accordingly the plaintiff appealed.

For the appellant there was a brief by *Orton & Osborn*, and oral argument by *Mr. P. A. Orton*.

For the respondent there was a brief by *T. J. Law* and *W. E. Carter*, and oral argument by *Mr. Carter*.

TAYLOR, J.   The learned judge, in the twenty-second finding, states it as his opinion that if the question of contract or no contract is to be determined by the evidence of what was done and said at the time the deed was executed and when the contract was in fact made, the preponderance of the evidence confirms the agreement as claimed by the plaintiff.   Upon this question there does not seem any reasonable doubt.   The plaintiff and her son, an intelligent young man, testify very clearly to the agreement as set up in the plaintiff's complaint, and their evidence is confirmed by the evidence of the brother-in-law of the defendant, Mr. Hardy.   In opposition to this evidence there is nothing except the general denials of the defendant, and his contention that he had no conversation with the plaintiff, at the time of the purchase, as to the price he was to pay or as to any other matter relating to the sale; but that the transaction was in fact between him and the plaintiff's husband. And when they had concluded the trade she signed the deed presented by her husband, and then asked him, " Now, *Frank*, what are you going to do with that land?" and that Mr. Lamar replied, "Why he is going to make money out of it if he can; we have sold it;" and to that remark of the husband she made no reply.   If defendant's version of what took place be the true one, it certainly shows a great want of interest on the part of *Mrs. Lamar* in a business in which she would naturally have the greatest interest.

The learned circuit judge was, as he says, influenced in arriving at the conclusion he did from the fact that certain negotiations were had in regard to the sale of this land between the plaintiff's husband and the defendant previous to the day when the transaction was finally completed. In our view of the previous transactions shown in the evidence they do not, we think, tend to disprove the claim made by the plaintiff as to what in fact took place at the time the sale was made. It is said that the correspondence shows that the plaintiff was willing to sell her interest in the land, unqualifiedly, for the sum of $4,000. If any force is to be given to the correspondence as against the plaintiff, it ought to appear from the evidence that *Mrs. Lamar* knew what the correspondence was, or that she had directed the correspondence. All the correspondence there ever had been was between her husband and the defendant. To make this correspondence weigh against *Mrs. Lamar* it should appear that she expressly authorized it, or, if not, that she knew what it was, and so impliedly, at least, authorized it. Upon this point the plaintiff testified " that her husband, Charles H. Lamar, was present and took part in the conversation at the time the sale was made, and that he had not previous to that time done any business in regard to this Chicago land. There was a letter or two passed between my husband and a Mr. Potwin, a real-estate man in Chicago. I think there were no negotiations for sale with Mr. Potwin. We inquired of him its value. He made no offer for the land that I know of." Again she says, " I was not aware that my husband was corresponding with *Frank* [the respondent] as well as Potwin about this land." Again she testifies, after the letters had been received in evidence: " I have read the letters in evidence purporting to have been written by my husband, and the letters written by *Frank*, the defendant, also in evidence. I had no knowledge that my husband wrote those letters, or either of them, when they were written, nor did I ever know of his ever receiving any of the letters from *Frank* which were in evidence. . . . I never heard, until this trial, anything of *Frank's* letter to Mr. Lamar of the 14th of November, 1879, saying he accepted our offer to sell." "I knew nothing of the existence of any of these letters from Mr. Lamar to *Frank* until the last year in Chicago. I don't remember but one presented to me then. I did not read that. To-day is the first I have known of the contents of either of these letters written by my husband." The son of the plaintiff testified " that on the day the deed for the land was made no allusion was made to any correspondence between *Scales* and father or mother respecting the land in question." There is no evidence in the case tending to show that *Mrs. Lamar* ever authorized her husband to negotiate for a sale of this land on her behalf, except so far as he took part in the negotiations at the time the sale was actually made.

Upon this state of the evidence it is very doubtful whether the letters were competent evidence against the plaintiff, had they been objected to by her, and, having been given in evidence without objection, they should have no influence in determining the question at issue when it clearly appears that she neither authorized the correspondence nor was aware of its nature. The evidence in this case to bind the plaintiff by the acts and correspondence of her husband is no stronger, if as strong as in the case of *Hadfield v. Skelton,* 69 Wis. 460, where it was held that the wife was not bound by the acts of the husband done in her behalf but without her knowledge.

But if this court had the right to consider this correspondence between the husband of the plaintiff and the defendant for the purpose of determining the question as to what the contract of sale was, we do not think they should destroy the case as made by the evidence as to what took place at the day the trade was actually consummated. The facts are that at the time of the sale plaintiff was one of the tenants in common of the land in question, with her brother *Frank* and the other sisters and brother, and, it was claimed by the defendant, with her mother; that *Frank* was a lawyer, and lived in Chicago, near where the land was situated, and could look after the land better than the plaintiff, who was living in the state of Iowa. She had given him a power of attorney in October, 1878, authorizing him to make leases and collect the rents to become due on such land, and to institute suits necessary to perfect the title to said land, and to do all and every act necessary to be done about said premises, etc. There was no power of sale given in this writing. The correspondence opens between the defendant and the husband of the plaintiff by a letter from defendant to Mr. Lamar, dated October 1, 1879, in which he inquires whether he would like to put his interest in the market at $75 per acre. To this a reply was made, October 5th, by Mr. Lamar, saying that he did not know what it was worth, and asking if the other owners would be willing to sell at that price, and intimating that they would trade their interest for a stock of merchandise. To this the defendant replied, October 14, 1879, saying he did not want to advise about the land, but said he thought *he could get* $3,500 for their interest. To this Mr. Lamar replied, October 31, 1879, in which he says he had delayed answering until he had received a letter from Mr. Potwin, who was anxious to buy for some parties in Chicago, and saying he would give $3,500 for their interest. "I said you had offered us that, and if I sold for that you should have' the refusal," and then saying he thought it was worth more, and would not take less than $4,000 cash down. In this letter he also stated that Hardy, his brother-in-law, said the property was worth $150 per acre, and that some real-estate men said it was worth $200 per acre, but said they were not waiting for such prices, and if they could get $4,000 down, he could invest it in cattle and make it pay better, and closed with requesting an early answer, as they wished to close the trade soon with some one if they could. To this the defendant replied November 3, 1879, saying he could not give more than $3,500 for their interest; referred to the taxes on the land, amounting to $800, and after referring to the offer of Potwin he closes by requesting an early reply if they would take $3,500 cash down. To this Lamar replied November 6, 1879, as follows: "Yours of 3d received, and in reply would say we have made up our minds not to sell for $3,500 at present. Will not take less than $4,000, as I wrote you, and do not consider that a standing offer; but if you want it for that at the present time let me know at once, and make out a quitclaim deed and send it to me, and we will sign it and close the matters up. And if you don't want it let me know at once, as I told other parties you had the refusal. I have no doubt it will be worth a great deal more in a year, and we will try and work on without it. As for the taxes, they are large, but I suppose the rent is something; and as for the suit, it is a cloud, but one, from what you told me, is but a small affair. At all events, if I don't sell, I will chance it." To this the defendant made the following reply: "DEAR UNCLE: I have your letter at hand, and want to say that I did not mention the taxes and suit to influence you or *Lizzie* to make the sale, but only to show that a stranger buying would have to have all these matters arranged, and that would take time. I do not think the tax suit amounts to anything. But it costs something; that is all. I shall send you a copy of my argument in the case in a few days. Now, I would like to pay you the amount you ask if I could. Potwin came to see me, and I made up my mind that he wanted to get the selling of the land. Now, I can make a sale as good as anybody. I told him that I had written you that I would give you $3,500 for your interest; that I would not give any more; and I have no doubt he intended to help me get the interest you had, and then thought he might make a sale for me. You know how such things are. If you do not choose to sell for the figures named I shall try to get all I can for you."

These two letters seemed to have closed the correspondence. Lamar had made a final offer at $4,000,— not a standing offer,— and requested a speedy answer. The answer came and the proposition was declined when the defendant wrote the letter of November 10, 1879, declining the offer to purchase at $4,000. Admitting that Lamar had authority from his wife to make the offer, the offer was no longer binding on her, and had it been accepted after the receipt of the letter of November 10th, it is clear the plaintiff would not have been compelled to convey for the $4,000.

It will be noticed that in this letter of the 10th of November the defendant suggests, at least, if he does not expressly request, that they should not put the lands in the hands of any one else for sale. He knew from the correspondence that Lamar had been making inquiries from other parties about the value of the land, and had reason to suppose that after he had refused the final offer they might seek a sale through some other person. So he says: "I can make a sale as good as anybody." "If you do not choose to sell for the figures named I shall try and get all I can for you." Three days after this letter was written, the defendant makes a contract with a responsible party for the absolute conveyance of five sevenths of the land at the rate of $60,000 for the whole interest, and receives $5,000 down in part payment of the five sevenths; $20,000 to be paid in five days after abstract of title to said premises, written down to date, showing said title to be satisfactory in the defendant for five sevenths of said land. This abstract of title was to be furnished within twenty days after the date of contract, and on payment of the $20,000 a warranty deed was to be executed for the five sevenths, and the balance for the five sevenths, viz., $17,857.17, was to be then paid. The balance of the $60,000 was to be paid as soon as the title to the other two sevenths was furnished. The proof shows that this sale was perfected by the defendant, and the title to the whole tract was conveyed to said purchaser, and the consideration of $60,000 was paid to the defendant, less the sum of $10,500 which was paid to Mrs. Hardy for her one-sixth interest in the same, so that for the five-sixths interest which the defendant had acquired he received from said Cotting the sum of $49,500. On the 14th day of November, after making the trade with Cotting, the defendant wrote the following letter to Mr. Lamar: "Dear Uncle: Since writing you I have concluded to accept your offer to sell lands here, and inclose deed, which you and *Lizzie* acknowledge before a notary and send to me, and I will send you draft for $4,000. What I would like to do would be to assume the two $500 notes that Sam. holds, and pay you the difference. That would prevent me borrowing so much money. The amount due on the notes, with interest up to the 20th of this month, is, as Sam. writes me, $1,133.33. That would leave a balance of $2,866.67. If you wish to do this it will accommodate me. If not, I will send you the $4,000. I would not like to have you sell to anybody else." On the same day he started for the home of Mr. Lamar, in Iowa, where he completed the trade. There is no evidence that this letter of the 14th of November was ever received by either Lamar or the plaintiff.

The foregoing facts are stated, not for the purpose of showing that the defendant had assumed a fiduciary relation to the plaintiff in regard to this land, so that in equity he would be held liable to account to her for the money received by him on the contract of sale of her one-sixth interest to Cotting, but for the purpose of showing that when this sale to Cotting was made, and when the plaintiff sold her interest to the defendant, the negotiation for sale

with her husband had been closed, and there was no standing offer ever made on his part to sell the land for $4,000;
and also for the purpose of showing that the relation of
the defendant to this land and to the plaintiff had radi-
cally changed since he had refused to pay more than $3,500
for her interest, and that when he appeared at the plaintiff's residence in Iowa to make the purchase he was in a
position to make almost any reasonable concession to his
sister in order to procure her interest in the land, so as to
enable him to complete the sale to Cotting and reap the
benefits thereof.   That in his contract to make a good title
to Cotting of the five sevenths within twenty days, he
contemplated that, as a part of said five sevenths, he must
obtain the title of the plaintiff to what he supposed was
her one seventh, is evident.   He had, as the evidence shows,
claimed that his mother was entitled to one seventh, his
sister, Mrs. Hardy, was entitled to another seventh, and it
would seem he had become the owner of the other four
sevenths.   He knew he could not purchase of Mrs. Hardy,
except at a very large price.   His only way to furnish the
required title to five sevenths was to buy the interest of
the plaintiff.   The mother's title was disputed, and he could
not make a satisfactory title from her.   Mrs. Hardy was
standing out for a large price, full as much as he sold for.
So it is fair to presume that his contract to sell the five
sevenths was intended to include the interest of the plaintiff.   No injustice is done to either party by holding that the
contract made was as is claimed by the plaintiff; whereas,
to hold that the contract was as claimed by the defendant,
would be, *in foro conscientiæ* if not in law, a fraud upon
her.   Considering the changed situation of the defendant
at the time the sale was actually made, and the fact that
there is no evidence in the case showing that the plaintiff
either directed the correspondence between her husband
and the defendant, or that she had any knowledge of the

character of such correspondence, we think the learned circuit judge gave undue weight to it, in determining the question as to what the terms of the sale in fact were. It being found by the learned circuit judge that if the case must be decided upon the evidence as to what took place at the time the sale was in fact made, it should be decided in favor of the plaintiff, we do not think that the apparently unauthorized negotiations of her husband with the defendant ought to have any influence in changing the result, especially in view of the changed situation of the defendant after such negotiations had ended.

The learned judge says there is no question of fraud in the case, as the action is brought upon an alleged express contract. This is true, and we determine to reverse the decision of the learned judge on the ground that the evidence establishes such express contract. We have, however, very grave doubts, upon all the facts of the case, . whether the relation of the defendant to the plaintiff, and his conduct in procuring her conveyance for this land, would not have been set aside by a court of equity upon proper pleading, if he had in fact procured from her a deed of such land for the consideration of $4,000; or, if the plaintiff did not wish to avoid the sale, would have held the defendant to account to her for the entire consideration received by him on such sale for her interest. See *Laidlaw v. Organ*, 2 Wheat. 178, 195; *Bench v. Sheldon*, 14 Barb. 66, 74; *Turner v. Harvey*, Jac. 178. These cases illustrate the strict rule applied by courts to cases of this character.   .

The evidence shows that in order to complete the sale for the $60,000 the defendant was compelled to pay his sister, Mrs. Hardy, the sum of $10,500 for her share. This sum, deducted from the $60,000, would leave $49,500 as the amount he received for the other five sixths. One fifth of this amount would be what the plaintiff would be entitled to recover for her interest, viz., $9,900. Of this she has received $4,000, leaving unpaid $5,900, and for this amount, less her proportionate share of any taxes ·and other necessary disbursements made by the defendant in making the title good to said land, the plaintiff is entitled to judgment, with interest at the rate prescribed by the laws of Iowa from the 1st of March, 1880, that being the date fixed by the court at which the sale to Cotting was completed and the consideration finally paid.

By the Court.— The judgment of the circuit court is reversed, and the cause remitted to that court to take such further proceedings as may be necessary to ascertain the amount due the plaintiff according to this opinion, and to enter judgment therefor as directed therein.

JAMES, Appellant, vs. THE CITY OF DARLINGTON and another, Respondents.

February 8 — February 28, 1888.

Cities: Vacating streets.

Where the common council of a city is authorized to vacate or discontinue streets it must proceed, if the charter does not otherwise provide, in the manner prescribed by sec. 904, R. S.   R. S. sec. 927.

APPEAL from the Circuit Court for *La Fayette* County. The case is sufficiently stated in the opinion.

For the appellant there was a brief by *Orton & Osborn*, and oral argument by *Mr. P. A. Orton*.

For the respondents there was a brief by *R. J. Wilson*, attorney, and *H. C. Martin*, of counsel, and oral argument by *Mr. Wilson*.

ORTON, J. The plaintiff is the owner of parts of two blocks, contiguous to Louisa street in said city, used for a lumber yard which is accessible to Main street, the principal business street, and other parts of said city, by said Louisa street, and the use of said street is essential to the business of said lumber yard and the profitable use of said premises. The *Chicago, Milwaukee & St. Paul Railway Company*, the other defendant, owns a right of way diagonally across said Louisa street and near said premises. The common council of said city passed an ordinance, without any previous petition or notice, vacating and discontinuing that part of said street occupied by said company's right of way, in order to allow said company to build a depot building therein, and close up and permanently obstruct said street at that point. The plaintiff obtained an injunction restraining said city, its officers, and certain persons, from closing, vacating, or discontinuing said street, and restraining said railroad company from shutting up, closing, or permanently obstructing said street at that point, and from building a depot within the limits of said street. On the motion of the defendants the circuit court vacated said injunction, and this appeal is taken from said order.

The only question in the case is whether said ordinance is valid and effectual to vacate Louisa street at that point. Subd. 26, sec. 1, ch. 6, City Charter, contained in ch. 30, Laws of 1877, gives the common council the following general power: "To make, open, keep in repair, grade, improve, lay out, alter, widen, *vacate*, or *discontinue* streets, avenues," etc. The learned counsel of the respondents contend that this power is general and unlimited, and vests the common council with the fullest discretion as to the manner in which it may be exercised, and that by a mere ordinance is the usual and proper manner of exercising such a power. The contention of the learned counsel of the appellant is that such power is to be exercised in the manner provided by sec. 904, R. S., which reads as follows: "Upon the petition in writing of all the owners of lots or land on any street or alley in such village, *and not otherwise*, the board of trustees may discontinue such street or alley, or any part thereof. At least one week before acting on such petition the board shall cause a written or printed notice to be posted in three public places in such village, stating when the petition will be acted on, and what street or alley or part thereof is proposed to be vacated." This section, by its terms, only refers to villages, and not to cities. The sections preceding it and including section 895 provide that village boards, "whenever they shall intend to lay out, open, change, widen, or extend streets, lanes, alleys, public grounds, square, or other place, to construct and open, alter, enlarge, or extend drains, canals, or sewers, or alter, widen, or straighten watercourses, or to take grounds for the use or improvement of a harbor," shall proceed in a certain manner specfiically pointed out; and then follows sec. 904, providing the manner for *vacating* streets, alleys, etc. This is plain enough,— whenever a village board intends to do any of these things, it must proceed as here directed. It will be observed that among the things specified in sec. 895 vacating streets, alleys, etc., is not mentioned, and that is left to be provided for in sec. 904. Now, the question is, and the only question, Are cities, when not otherwise provided in their charters, to proceed in the same manner to do these same things? Sec. 927 provides that "the trustees of every village and the *common council of every city* may exercise all the powers conferred on village boards by sections 895 to *904 inclusive*, and proceed in the manner therein prescribed" to do the same things specified in sec. 895, and leaves out, the same as that section, the vacation of streets, which is provided for alone in sec. 904. The contention of the learned counsel of the respondents is that because in sec. 927, which extends these provisions to cities, the *vacation* of streets is not mentioned specifically, it was the intention of the legislature not to include the vacation of streets, and that the language "to 904 inclusive," must be a mistake, or have some other meaning. But it might as well be said that because sec. 895 does not include vacating streets, and it is only mentioned and provided for in sec. 904, *that* must be a mistake or mean something else than to give village boards such power. The language and the things to be done are the same in sections 895 and 927. It follows conclusively that the common council of cities, when their charters do not otherwise provide, must proceed to do all of these things, including the vacation or discontinuance of streets, in the same manner as village boards were required to proceed in sections 895 to 904 inclusive. This could not be made plainer by referring to any other sections. But the learned counsel of the appellant has referred to sec. 4986, R. S., as supporting this view. That section provides that the general statutes (Revised Statutes) "shall apply to and be in force in each and every *city* and village in the state, so far as the same are applicable and not inconsistent with the charter of any such city or village." It seems that most of the charters of cities and villages in this state contain directions how to proceed, and prescribe the manner in which it shall be done, to vacate streets, and many of them in the language of sec. 904. The charter of the city of *Darlington* would seem to be peculiar in making no such provision, and leaving the matter to be governed by the general law. It is significant that the same provision as to vacating streets was contained in the charter of the *village* of Darlington. Could there then have been any doubt that it would have to be done in the manner provided in sec. 904? There is as little doubt that the city must proceed in the same way. There must be a petition in writing of all the owners of lots or land on any street or part of street to be vacated presented to the common council before they proceed to do anything about it, and then the proper notice must be posted up of the time when said petition would be acted on.   Such a petition is necessary to give the council any jurisdiction of the matter, and without it their proceedings would be void, as it was in this case.   The injunction should have been continued, and it was obvious error to vacate it.

By the Court.— The order of the circuit court is reversed, and the cause remanded with direction to rescind the order vacating, or to continue said preliminary injunction.

Jacobs, Appellant, vs. Spalding and others, Respondents.

February 9 — February 28, 1888.

(1) Limitation of actions: Contract under seal. (2-4) Contracts: Construction: Forfeiture: Separate contracts in one instrument: Consideration: Conditional agreement: Construction by parties, when shown by delay in bringing action.

1. An action to recover the purchase price of land, etc., based upon a contract under seal executed by private persons, may be brought at any time within twenty years after the cause of action has accrued. R. S. sec. 4220.

2. In construing a contract all of its terms should be considered.

3. When the terms of a contract are indefinite, uncertain, and susceptible of two constructions, and by giving them one construction one of the parties would be subjected to a forfeiture, and by giving them the other no such forfeiture would be incurred and no injustice would be done to the other party, the contract should be so construed as not to create the forfeiture.

4. The first paragraph of a written contract stated that in consideration of $13,000 the plaintiff had sold a steamboat and certain real estate to the defendants, the deeds thereof being executed on the same day as the contract.   The second paragraph stated that the plaintiff had further agreed to sell and convey certain other land for $2,000, to be paid when a deed of said land could be procured under a proper order of court for the sale of the same; that the plaintiff would use due diligence in procuring the guardian of the minor owner to make application for an order for such sale; and

that in the event that such land, at its offer at public sale under such order, should not bring over $2,000, the same should be sold to the defendants for that sum; but in case the plaintiff should fail to make such title good to the defendants he should suffer no other forfeiture than in the contract mentioned. The third paragraph provided for the payment of $12,000, and that the defendants should retain $1,000 until the plaintiff should cause to be executed and delivered to them a conveyance of the land mentioned in the second paragraph, founded upon a proper order of court; and upon delivery of such conveyance the defendants should pay to the plaintiff said $1,000 as well as the $2,000 purchase money of said land; and if the plaintiff should entirely fail to cause said land to be conveyed to the defendants, the said $1,000, part of the $13,000 first aforesaid, should be forfeited to the defendants as liquidated damages for such breach. The land mentioned in the second paragraph sold at the public sale for more than $2,000, and the plaintiff was unable to purchase it for that sum. Nearly twenty years later he brought this action to recover the $1,000 retained by the defendants. *Held*, on demurrer:

(1) The contracts in the first and second paragraphs were separate and distinct contracts, for separate and distinct considerations; and the $1,000 was retained not as a part of the consideration for the land mentioned in the second paragraph, but merely as security for the performance of the contract as to such land.

(2) The contract for the conveyance of the land mentioned in the second paragraph was upon the condition that such land could be purchased for $2,000 at the public sale.

(3) Upon the demurrer the delay in bringing the action should not be considered as showing the construction which the parties themselves put upon the contract.

APPEAL from the Circuit Court for *Brown* County.

The following statement of the case was prepared by Mr. Justice TAYLOR as a part of the opinion:

The plaintiff brought this action, on May 12, 1886, to recover $1,000, and the interest thereon, from the defendants, upon the following contract, viz.:

" This agreement, made by and between *John B. Jacobs*, of the town of Marinette, in the county of Oconto and the state of Wisconsin, of the one part, and *Jesse Spalding*, of the city of Chicago, in the state of Illinois, *Abner Kirby*, of the city of Milwaukee, in the state of Wisconsin, *Isaac Stephenson*, of said town of Marinette, Oconto county, and *Samuel M. Stephenson*, of Menominee, in the county of Menominee in the state of Michigan, of the other part, witnesseth, that the said *John B. Jacobs*, in consideration of the sum of $13,000, hath bargained and sold to the party of the other part that certain property known as the Steamboat Queen City, with her machinery, furniture, and appurtenances, and all those certain tracts of real estate owned by him in the Menominee river, and on the bank of said river, in Oconto county, described as follows: Lot three (3) of section thirty-three (33), containing 1 74–100 acres; lot number five (5) in section thirty-two (32), containing 21–100 acres; lot six (6) of section thirty-two (32), containing 1 25–100 acres,— all in township thirty-one (31) of range twenty-three (23) E.; lot number eight (8), section six (6),in township number thirty (30) N., range twenty-four (24) west [east?], containing 56–100 acres; also lots of land described in warranty deed from party of first part to party of second part, dated May 14, 1866, the deeds for said boat and land being executed this May 14, 1866; also a description of land described in auditor's deed of state of Michigan, dated May 2, 1860.

"And further hath agreed to sell and convey that certain real estate on the bank of the Menominee river, in said town of Marinette, meaning all the land known as the 'Jane Dunnett Land,' and willed by her to her son James Dunnett, for the sum of two thousand dollars, to be paid when a deed of the said land can be procured under a proper order of the court for the sale of the same; it being understood and agreed that said *John B. Jacobs* will use due diligence in procuring the guardian of said minor child of Jane Dunnett to make application for an order of such sale, and to prosecute all proper and legal proceedings therefor with diligence; *and that in the event that said real estate, at its offer at public sale under such order, shall not bring over the* *sum of $2,000, the same shall be sold to said party of the sec-* *ond part for that sum, and they agree to pay said sum of* *money for the same;* but, in case the said *John B. Jacobs* shall fail to make such title good to said parties, he shall suffer no other forfeiture than herein mentioned.

"And it is agreed that the parties of the second part pay party of the first part the sum of $3,000 down, and the sum of $9,000 in equal annual payments, in one, two, and three years from the date, with seven per cent. per annum, an- nually, interest thereon; and that the party of the second part keep and retain the sum of $1,000 until the party of the first part shall cause to be executed and delivered to them a good deed of conveyance of said property so willed by said Jane Dunnett to her son, founded upon and under a proper order of a court of competent jurisdiction for the sale thereof; and, upon delivery of the deed aforesaid, party of the second part shall pay party of the first part the said sum of $1,000, as well, also, as the said sum of $2,000 for the purchase money of said land; and, if said party of the first part shall entirely fail to cause said Dunnett land to be conveyed to party of the second part, the said sum of $1,000, part of the $13,000 first aforesaid, be deemed to be forfeited to party of the second part in payment as and for liquidated damages for his breach in so failing to procure such con- veyance to them.

"Witness the hands of the parties hereto, respectively, this 14th day of May, A. D. 1866.
"JOHN B. JACOBS.   [Seal.]   WELLS & SPALDING.   [Seal.]
"S. M. STEPHENSON. [Seal.]   I. STEPHENSON.   [Seal.]
"ABNER KIRBY.   '[Seal.]
"In the presence of E. S. INGALLS."

The plaintiff, in his complaint, sets out the contract, and alleges full performance on his part, except as to the con- dition upon which the defendants were to be entitled to retain the $1,000 to recover which the action is brought, and, as to such condition, he alleges generally that it became impossible for him to perform it, and then alleges the following facts as an excuse for the nonperformance of said condition on his part, to wit: "And as to the aforesaid condition of said agreement, which it became impossible for the plaintiff to perform, and from the performance of which the plaintiff was excused and discharged, plaintiff alleges that said condition only relates to the lands mentioned in said written agreement as the 'Jane Dunnett Land;' that he used due diligence in procuring the minor child of Jane Dunnett to make application for an order for sale of the land in said agreement referred to as the 'Jane Dunnett Land,' willed by her to her son James Dunnett, and that, upon application duly made on behalf of said minor, an order of license for the sale of said land was duly made by the county court in and for said county of Oconto on the 4th day of September, 1866; and that after due notice, pursuant to said order and the laws of Wisconsin, the said land known as the 'Jane Dunnett Land' was offered for sale at public vendue, on the 8th day of October, 1866, at the place in said town of Marinette designated in the notice of said sale, and was thereupon duly struck off and sold to the highest bidder for more than $2,000, to wit, for the sum of $3,000 or upwards; that plaintiff attended said sale, and endeavored to bid off and purchase the said 'Jane Dunnett Land for $2,000 or less, and did actually bid $2,000 therefor at said sale, but the plaintiff was overbidden by other parties, and was thereby, without any fault on his part, prevented from purchasing said lands for $2,000; that the defendant *Isaac Stephenson,* for himself and the other defendants herein, also attended said sale, and was then and there notified by the plaintiff that, because plaintiff was overbidden, he (the plaintiff) could not buy said 'Jane Dunnett Land' for $2,000, and that if they (said defendants) wanted the land they should bid for it; that, accordingly, the said *Isaac Stephenson* made a bid of about $2,200 for said land, when a higher bid was made by some other person; that the said *Isaac Stephenson*, for himself and by authority of the other defendants, then abandoned all further efforts to purchase said land, and the same was afterwards, at the same sale, duly struck off and sold to this plaintiff for $3,300 or thereabouts, which was the highest sum bidden therefor. And the plaintiff alleges that the aforesaid sum of $1,000, part of said $13,000, by virtue of said agreement and of the facts above stated became, immediately after the date of said public sale, and still is, due and payable from said defendants to said plaintiff, with interest thereon from October 8, 1866; but although then and often afterwards thereunto notified and requested, the said defendants have never paid said sum of $1,000, nor any part thereof, but have refused, and still do refuse, to pay the same, or any part thereof, to the damage of this plaintiff in the sum of $2,500."

To this complaint the defendants demurred, upon two grounds: "(1) That the complaint does not state facts sufficient to constitute a cause of action. (2) That the action was not commenced within the time limited by law; that is to say, the time within which plaintiff could commence his action was limited, by section 4222 of the Revised Statutes, to the term of six years after the cause of action accrued." The circuit court sustained the demurrer, and, as the plaintiff declined to serve an amended complaint within the time fixed in the order sustaining the demurrer, judgment was entered upon such order, dismissing the complaint of the plaintiff, with costs to the defendants; and from such judgment the plaintiff appeals to this court.

For the appellant there were briefs by *Ellis, Greene & Merrill*, and oral argument by *Mr. E. H. Ellis*.

For the respondents there was a brief by *Fairchild & Fairchild*, and oral argument by *Mr. H. O. Fairchild*.

TAYLOR, J.   Whether the learned circuit judge sustained the demurrer on the ground that the complaint did not state facts constituting a cause of action, or upon the ground that the action was barred by the statute, or upon both grounds, does not appear from the records.   From the course of the argument on this appeal, we are led to believe that the circuit judge sustained the demurrer upon the first ground, viz., that the complaint does not state facts sufficient to constitute a cause of action.   We think it too clear for argument that the action was not barred by the six years statute.   The promise of the defendants upon which the action is brought is contained in a sealed written contract, and the action is based solely upon such sealed written contract.   The limitation of such actions is contained in sec. 4220, R. S., instead of sec. 4222, R. S.   Sec. 4220 prescribes a twenty years limitation.   Subd. 2 of said section reads as follows: "An action upon a sealed instrument, when the cause of action accrues within this state, except those mentioned in section four thousand two hundred and twenty-two."   The exception referred to in sec. 4222 is as follows: "An action upon any bond, coupon, interest warrant, or other contract for the payment of money, whether *sealed* or otherwise, made or issued by any town, county, city, or school district in this state."   There can be no pretense that the contract set up in the complaint in this action is a contract of the kind mentioned in said sec. 4222, and so it does not come within the six years limitation prescribed by said section.

If the demurrer can be sustained at all, it must be upon the ground that the complaint does not state facts constituting a cause of action, and whether it does or not depends upon the construction which should be given to the second paragraph of the contract.   The learned counsel for the appellant contends that, by a proper construction of such paragraph, it is evident that the plaintiff's contract to convey the Dunnett land was conditional, and that he only agreed to convey it in case it was sold at the public sale for a sum not exceeding $2,000; and if, at such sale, it was sold for more than $2,000, then he was under no obligation to make a good title to the defendants therefor. On the part of the learned counsel for the respondents it is contended that the contract of the appellant was to convey the land absolutely, without regard to the price at which it might be sold at public sale, and without any regard to the fact whether a judicial sale of this property could or could not be obtained.

In determining what the parties really intended in the second paragraph of the contract, it is important to determine, first, whether the $1,000 retained by the vendees to secure the performance of the contract in the second paragraph thereof was any part of the consideration which was agreed to be paid for the lands described in such second paragraph. The learned counsel for the respondents insist that such $1,000 was part of the consideration agreed to be paid for such lands, or, if not, that it must be held that the agreement in the second paragraph was an inducement to the respondents to make the purchase mentioned in the first paragraph. The counsel for the appellant contends that the two contracts are as much independent of each other as though made by different writings and at different times; and the fact that they are contained in the same writing does not connect or make them dependent upon each other. That the contract in this case is a separate contract, for a separate and specific consideration agreed to be paid for the steamboat and land described in the first paragraph of the contract, and for a separate and specific consideration agreed to be paid for the land described in the second paragraph, can hardly admit of a doubt. The first paragraph asserts that the plaintiff has sold and conveyed to the defendants the steamboat and certain lands therein described, for the consideration of $13,000, and the third paragraph provides how the $13,000 shall be paid; and the $1,000 out of the $13,000 agreed to be paid for the property described in the first paragraph is not retained as a part of the consideration for the Dunnett land, but as security for the performance of the plaintiff's contract for the sale of that land. The second paragraph expressly declares that the consideration to be paid for the Dunnett land is $2,000, and no more.

In the case of *Johnson v. Johnson*, 3 Bos. & P. 162, it was decided that where the two tracts of land were conveyed in the same instrument for the sum of £1,000 and the title failed as to one tract, the grantor could recover the purchase money paid for that tract, without regard to the relative value of the tracts or the value of the lands conveyed as a whole. The recovery was sustained on the ground that, before the conveyance was made, the tracts had been valued separately; the one to which the title failed at £300, and the other at £700. This case is cited with approval by this court in *Sawyer v. C. & N. W. R. Co.* 22 Wis. 411. Parsons, in his work on Contracts, says: "If the part to be performed by one party consists of several distinct and separate items, and the price to be paid by the other is apportioned to each item to be performed, or is left to be implied by law, such a contract will generally be held to be severable. And the same rule holds where the price to be paid is clearly and distinctly apportioned to different parts of what is to be performed, although the latter is in its nature single and entire." See, also, upon this subject, *Goodwin v. Merrill*, 13 Wis. 658; *Robinson v. Green*, 3 Met. 159; *Lucesco Oil Co. v. Brewer*, 66 Pa. St. 351; *Quigley v. De Haas*, 82 Pa. St. 273; *Sickels v. Pattison*, 14 Wend. 257.

It seems quite apparent that the two contracts in the first and second paragraphs of the writing are separate and distinct contracts, for separate and distinct considerations; and that the reservation, in the third paragraph, of the $1,000 due on the first contract which had been executed on the part of the plaintiff, was simply a reservation to secure the performance of the second contract for the sale of the Dunnett land, and not at all as a part consideration for said land.

Treating the contract for the sale of the Dunnett land as an independent contract, it is evident that the only consideration for the promise of the plaintiff to procure a title to those lands and then convey them to the defendants, is the promise of the defendants to pay him $2,000; with an agreement on the part of the plaintiff to forfeit, as liquidated damages, $1,000 in case he failed to perform his contract. We agree with the learned counsel for the respondents that it is not very clear from the language of the contract what was the real intent of the parties, and that the language used is susceptible of different constructions. In that state of the case, it seems to us it is the duty of the court to give such construction to the language used as would make a contract such as a man of ordinary prudence would be likely to make, if the language used is fairly susceptible of such construction. Under the circumstances surrounding the parties at the time this contract was made, is it reasonable to suppose that the plaintiff would contract, without condition, to make a good title to these lands to the defendants for the consideration of $2,000, and, if he did not, that he would forfeit or pay, as liquidated damages, the sum of $1,000?

We think this question must be answered in the negative. At the time the contract was made, both parties knew that the title to said lands was not in the plaintiff, but was owned by a minor; that such title could only be obtained from such minor by a judicial proceeding and by a judicial public sale; and that the law required that at such public sale, if the court directed one, the lands must be sold to the highest bidder. It does not seem that an ordinarily prudent man would make an unconditional promise to procure such title for a consideration not exceeding the real value of the property, and agree to forfeit half such sum if he should fail to procure it. We think the case shows that the $2,000 agreed to be paid by the defendants did not exceed its supposed real value, and was not, at the time, considered by the parties as anything more than a fair value for the land. This is evident from the fact that it was then anticipated by the parties that it might sell for more at the judicial sale. The fact that it might sell for more is anticipated in the contract, and, in the event that it did sell for more, was to have some effect on the contract made. The learned counsel for the plaintiff and appellant contends that, in the event the lands sold for more than $2,000 at the public judicial sale, the plaintiff was released from all further liability on his contract, or, in other words, that his contract to sell the lands to the defendants was a conditional one; the condition being that he would sell the same to the defendants, or procure for them a title to the lands in case the land was sold at the judicial sale for $2,000 or less, and not otherwise. On the other hand, it is contended by the learned counsel for the defendants that the fact that it might sell for more than $2,000 had no effect upon the contract of sale. It seems to us that such a construction of the contract convicts the plaintiff of the want of not only ordinary prudence, but of any prudence. Had he owned the land to be sold, and was to receive for himself the consideration to be paid therefor, and for some reason he could not promptly give a title, and the consideration was paid down by the purchaser, there would be some reason for his assuming the risks of procuring the title, and agreeing to a large forfeiture if he failed to make good the title. But in this case he had no title. He did not receive any of the consideration down. The consideration he was to receive was not more than the fair value of the land and the amount he would probably have to pay for the same; and that consideration was none of it to be paid until such time as he procured a good title for the defendants. Why, then, should he agree to forfeit $1,000 if he failed to procure the title unless he paid more for it than he was to get from the defendants? Such an agreement would be so one-sided and unfair that no man of ordinary prudence would make it, and we may fairly presume that the plaintiff did not intend to make such agreement in this case.

Does the language of the contract clearly show that the plaintiff did make such a contract? If it does, then he must be held to it, unless he can have it reformed so as to express what he intended. We think, as is admitted by the learned counsel for the respondents, that the language used is not so clearly in favor of the construction given to it by the defendants as to compel a court, notwithstanding its injustice, to give it that construction. We think that, standing as an independent contract for the sale of the Dunnett land, as we have said above it must stand, the construction sought to be put upon it by the defendants is not a fair construction of its language. If we construe it as contended for by the defendants, no effect is given to the following words of the contract, viz.: "And that in the event that said real estate, at its offer at public sale under such order, shall not bring over the sum of $2,000, the same shall be sold to said party of the second part for that sum, and they agree to pay said sum for the same." Now, if these words do not limit the right of the respondents to demand a conveyance of the lands only in case they shall not bring over the sum of $2,000 at the public sale contemplated, then they perform no purpose in the contract. The construction claimed by the respondents would have been better expressed if these words had been omitted. If the plaintiff had only been anxious to limit his liability for damages to $1,000, that would have been just as effectually done if the language of the contract above quoted had been wholly omitted. By construing the contract as contended for by the respondents,\one of the fundamental rules of construction is ignored, viz.: "That, in construing a contract, all of its terms must be considered." See 1 Chit. Cont. (11th Am. ed.), 117, and cases cited in note *y*. It is there said: "It is the most important of all the rules of construction that the whole of the agreement is to be considered; for, obviously, it cannot be the intention of the parties to an agreement with stipulations or qualifications, that some of them should be altogether disregarded and part of the agreement magnified into an equality with the whole, but, on the contrary, such a meaning is to be given to particular parts as will, without violence to the words, be consistent with all the rest, and with the evident object and intention of the contracting parties." *Plano Mfg. Co. v. Ellis*, 35 N. W. Rep. (Mich.), 841.

In the contract, previous to the language above quoted, the plaintiff had agreed to sell and convey this land to the defendants for the sum of $2,000, and to proceed with due diligence to procure a judicial sale of said lands, so that he could make such conveyance; and then the language above quoted is inserted, and in the clause quoted the defendants make the only promise anywhere made in the contract to pay the $2,000. Had it not been for the words at the commencement of the paragraph, "And further hath agreed to sell and convey that certain real estate . . . for the sum of $2,000," there would not be the least doubt as to the meaning of the contract. Had the contract read that, in consideration of the sum of $2,000 hereinafter agreed to be paid by the defendants, the plaintiff agrees to proceed with all due diligence to procure a judicial sale of the lands in question, "and that in the event," etc., as above quoted, there would be no doubt that the sale to the defendants would be upon the condition that it did not sell for more than $2,000 at such judicial sale. And in the contract as written the words quoted must be entirely ignored as a part of the contract, or they must be construed to make the sale a conditional one, depending upon the fact that it could be purchased for the sum of $2,000 when publicly sold. We think this the only fair construction, and that it is not a strained construction. We think the language used in the contract may fairly be construed to mean that the plaintiff agrees to sell the land for the sum of $2,000 to the defendants; that he will proceed with due diligence to procure the title by a public sale thereof; and if at such public sale he can purchase the same for $2,000 or less, he will convey the same to the defendants, and not otherwise. This construction gives some effect to all parts of the contract, whereas the construction contended for by the defendants gives no meaning to the clause of the contract above quoted.

When the terms of a contract are indefinite, uncertain, and susceptible of two constructions, and by giving them one construction one of the parties would be subjected to a forfeiture, and by giving them the other no such forfeiture would be incurred and no injustice would be done to the other party, the contract should be so construed as not to create the forfeiture. We think this rule of law is clearly applicable to the contract set out in this case. See the following cases upon this rule: *Helms v. P. L. Ins. Co.* 61 Pa. St. 107; *Appleton Iron Co. v. B. A. Assurance Co.* 46 Wis. 23; *Badger v. Phœnix Ins. Co.* 49 Wis. 396; *Wier v. Simmons,* 55 Wis. 643; *Morse v. B. F. & M. Ins. Co.* 30 Wis. 540; *Clinton v. Hope Ins. Co.* 45 N. Y. 454; *Hoffman v. Ætna F. Ins. Co.* 32 N. Y. 405.

It is urged by the learned counsel for the respondents that the long delay of the plaintiff in bringing his action should be taken into consideration in determining the construction which the parties themselves put upon the contract. Possibly this fact might be considered if there had been a trial of the action upon the merits of the case, and on such trial it had been shown that the plaintiff had never made any claim for the money he now seeks to recover until this action was commenced. In this case there has been no such trial; and it may be, as alleged by the learned counsel for the appellant, that on such trial he would be able to show that he made the claim promptly, and has constantly insisted upon it, and that the delay in bringing the action was attributable to other causes than a want of faith in the justice of his claim.

By the Court.— The judgment of the circuit court is reversed, and the cause is remanded for further proceedings according to law.

CASSODAY, J., took no part.

LEE, Respondent, vs. WAGNER and others, imp., Appellants.

February 9 — February 28, 1888.

Mortgages: Release: Mistake: Estoppel: Reformation.

The plaintiff owned as her separate property a mortgage of land, executed by her husband. Without any consideration, and for the sole purpose of enabling a subsequent mortgagee to acquire a prior lien, she executed a release of her mortgage, acknowledging full payment and satisfaction. The release was not read or explained to her, and she did not understand that it was a full release. *Held,* that such release, though recorded, did not discharge the lien of mortgage as against the heirs of the mortgagor, or estop the plaintiff from showing that the mortgage had not in fact been paid; and that the release might be reformed so as to make it effective as to the subsequent mortgage only.

APPEAL from the Circuit Court for *Iowa* County.

The following statement of the case was prepared by Mr. Justice CASSODAY:

It appears from the record, and is in effect found by the

court, that December 13, 1876, one Robert C. Lee, upon being divorced from his former wife, Christiana C., executed and delivered to her his notes and mortgage for $1,150; that February 16, 1879, the plaintiff, *Jane*, married said Robert C. Lee; that March 2, 1880, the said *Jane Lee* purchased with her own separate estate the said notes and mortgage, then outstanding, and upon which there was then due $1,100, and obtained the title thereof through several assignments, to wit, from said Christiana C. to Strong, and from Strong to Imhoff, and from Imhoff to the plaintiff; that said notes and mortgage were then, and ever since have been, the sole and separate property of the plaintiff; that no part of the principal or interest upon said notes and mortgage has ever been paid to the plaintiff, but the same is still due and owing to her thereon; that March 17, 1885, and without any consideration received by the plaintiff for the same, and for the sole purpose of enabling said Robert C. Lee to give a mortgage of $300 to one Dring, which should take precedence of hers, she executed a release of her said mortgage, but the same was never delivered to said Robert C. Lee, nor to any one for him; that said Dring mortgage had long since been paid and satisfied of record; that November 28, 1885, the said Robert C. Lee, and the plaintiff as his wife, executed and delivered to the defendant Dolan a mortgage upon the same lands as the plaintiff's mortgage, to secure $310 then loaned by said Dolan to said Robert C., with the understanding that it should become a prior lien to the plaintiff's mortgage; that at the same time, upon information and belief that it was necessary in order to put said Dolan mortgage ahead of hers on the record, she, without any consideration, executed a release of her said mortgage, which release was then recorded; that said last-named release was not read to her, nor explained to her, except as stated; and that when she signed said last-named release she did not know that it was a full release of her own mortgage. Robert C. Lee died October 21, 1886. and the defendant Dolan was appointed administrator of his estate, December 7, 1886.

This action is to cancel, set aside, and declare void said last-named release and the record thereof, and to restore the lien of the plaintiff's mortgage, subject, however, and subordinate to the said Dolan mortgage. The other defendants are the children of the said Robert C. Lee by his first wife, Christiana C., and they alone defend the action. As conclusions of law, the court, in effect, found that the plaintiff was entitled to judgment canceling or reforming said last-named release and the record thereof, so as to make the same effective only so far as the Dolan mortgage was concerned, leaving her mortgage standing as though no release thereof had ever been made, except to make the Dolan mortgage prior thereto, as aforesaid; and costs and disbursements to be taxed, except as against Dolan; and ordered judgment accordingly. From the judgment entered thereon the defendants who are children of said Robert C. Lee have appealed.

J. F. Grace, attorney, and *Aldro Jenks,* of counsel, for the appellants, contended, *inter alia,* that the release should not be set aside or reformed except upon clear proof that it did not conform to the agreement of the parties. *Newton v. Holley,* 6 Wis. 592; *Lake v. Meacham,* 13 id. 355; *Kent v. Lasley,* 24 id. 654; *McClellan v. Sanford,* 26 id. 595; *Harter v. Christoph,* 32 id. 245; *Sable v. Maloney,* 48 id. 331; *Smith v. Allis,* 52 id. 347. Courts will not grant relief against mistakes of law. *Hurd v. Hall,* 12 Wis. 137; *Green Bay & M. C. Co. v. Hewitt,* 62 id. 331.

J. P. Smelker, for the respondent, argued, among other things, that a release of a mortgage obtained by fraud or made through mistake may be canceled if other parties, having no notice of the fraud, have not in the meantime acquired an interest in the property. The burden is upon the person who would impeach the release to show that the mortgage`was not actually paid, and that the release was obtained either by fraud practiced upon the holder of the mortgage, or was made by him through some mistake of fact. *Barnes v. Camack*, 1 Barb. 392; *Vannice v. Bergen*, 16 Iowa, 555; *Russell v. Mixer*, 42 Cal. 475; *Dudley v. Bergen*, 23 N. J. Eq. 397; 2 Jones on Mortg. secs. 966, 970, and cases cited. But heirs at law, or judgment creditors, or subsequent mortgagees, whose rights existed at the time of the discharge, are not included within the meaning of the words "other parties." Those words refer only to those who may have purchased the property in good faith *after the release* of the mortgage, or have advanced money upon it upon the faith of a clear record title. 2 Jones on Mortg. sec. 967; *Downer v. Miller*, 15 Wis. 612, 628.

CASSODAY, J. The findings of the court are sustained by the evidence. It is confessed that the plaintiff's notes and mortgage have never been paid nor surrendered. She is not seeking to make her mortgage a prior lien to Dolan's. She concedes that she executed the release at the time his mortgage was given, for the very purpose of making her mortgage subordinate to his; but she insists that it was not intended for any other purpose, and should have no other effect. The transaction seems to have taken that form merely because Dolan and his counsel at the time demanded such release as a condition of making the loan to the husband. Seemingly, they supposed Dolan could in no other way obtain a priority of lien. No one else at the time seems to have desired such release. Its only purpose was to secure such priority. There is no evidence to warrant the belief that the husband exacted such release, or ever expected that it would operate as an absolute discharge of the mortgage as against him. Manifestly, the plaintiff had no such expectation. She executed the release, as she had the

Dring release, because it was exacted for the purpose mentioned, and with no other intent. Neither Dolan nor his counsel represented the mortgagor, and had no authority to make any contract or exact any condition in his behalf. Whether the mortgage should be absolutely discharged of record was a matter in which neither of them had any interest or concern.

The question is whether the effect of the release shall be confined to the object for which it was made, or shall extend to a purpose not in contemplation of any of the persons concerned in its execution. That is, Did it operate as an estoppel against the plaintiff and in favor of the mortgagor and those claiming under him? The defendants are not here insisting upon such estoppel as subsequent *bona fide* purchasers of the mortgaged premises, nor even as creditors. They are here merely as heirs at law of the mortgagor,— mere volunteers. The action is in equity, and yet they are contending, confessedly, without any equity. Their defense is based wholly upon a naked estoppel, without any consideration whatever to support it, and is made in order to secure an unmerited benefit by defeating a meritorious claim. The mortgage would have been a valid lien, as against such heirs, without ever having been recorded. The release or satisfaction was to the effect that such mortgage had been "fully paid, satisfied, and discharged." Since the want of record would not bar the lien as against these defendants, the mere discharge of the mortgage on the record cannot prevent the enforcement of the lien as against them.

The question, however, recurs, whether the acknowledgment of payment and satisfaction, obtained under the circumstances stated, estopped the plaintiff from showing that the mortgage was never paid or satisfied. So far as the mere acknowledgment of payment, it operated as a mere receipt, and of course was open to explanation by parol evidence. *Gilchrist v. Brande*, 58 Wis. 197; *Hubbard v. Marshall*, 50 Wis. 325, 326. It is, moreover, a well-established rule of law, that the payment of a part of an admitted indebtedness, due at the time, upon an agreement that it shall be in full payment and satisfaction of the whole, is *nudum pactum* and not binding upon the party making the same. *Foakes v. Beer*, L. R. 9 App. 605, 24 Am. Law Reg. 21; *Daniels v. Hatch*, 21 N. J. Law, 391, 47 Am. Dec. 169; *Keeler v. Salisbury*, 33 N. Y. 653. For exceptions, see *Goddard v. O'Brien*, 9 Q. B. Div. 37, 21 Am. Law Reg. 637, and notes. For a much stronger reason, such acknowledgment should not be binding where it is given, as here, without any payment or consideration, and under a misapprehension as to its meaning and legal effect.

By the Court.— The judgment of the circuit court is affirmed.

WELLS, Appellant, vs. McGEOCH, Respondent.

September 22, 1887 — March 27, 1888.

(1) Findings of fact: Insufficiency: Review on appeal. (2-5) Illegal contracts: "Corners:" Accounting: Fraudulent representations: Recovery of overpayment in settlement of losses: Release fraudulently obtained: Reliance on partner's statements.

1. A party need not indicate to the trial court in advance the specific facts upon which he desires findings, but may assume that the court will find upon all disputed questions. And it is sufficient to secure a review on appeal if due exception be taken that the findings fail to cover and include certain specified material questions of fact litigated on the trial.

2. The parties had made large profits out of a successful corner of the wheat market, and the plaintiff's share was left with the defendant and afterwards invested by him in a lard deal by direction of the plaintiff. *Held*, that the illegality of the wheat deal would not protect the defendant from accounting for the money.

8. The parties were jointly interested in an unsuccessful attempt to corner the market for lard. In arranging between themselves for a settlement of their losses, the defendant overstated the amount invested by himself in the deal, and understated the amount invested by him for the plaintiff. Relying upon such statements the plaintiff paid more than his share in the settlement of the losses, and also gave the defendant a full release from all claims and demands on account of the deal. *Held:*

(1) The statements by the defendant were fraudulent, whether he knew them to be untrue or made them in ignorance of the real facts.

(2) Notwithstanding the illegality of the attempt to corner the market, the plaintiff may recover from the defendant such a sum as will reduce his payment to the amount he would have been required to pay on an accounting between the parties.

(3) The release, fraudulently obtained, is no obstacle to such recovery.

4. The plaintiff had for a long time had joint transactions of great magnitude with the defendant, in whom he had unbounded confidence and to whom he had trusted their entire management. The business was done by defendant's firm in Chicago, but the accounts were sent to his Milwaukee house, and the plaintiff had free access to them. The plaintiff's share of the profits had been left with the defendant, and were afterwards invested by him in a lard deal by direction of the plaintiff. *Held,* that in arranging for a settlement of the losses by such deal the plaintiff had a right to rely upon the defendant's statement of the amounts invested therein by himself and for the plaintiff.

5. As a result of the unsuccessful deal in lard a firm in which the defendant was a partner failed. It was agreed between the parties that the capital stock of such firm was not to be considered a debt of the firm which the parties were to assume or endeavor to pay. *Held,* that such agreement affected only such capital as remained a liability of the firm, and in an accounting between the parties of their respective investments in the deal the defendant was entitled to be allowed his capital which he had drawn out of the firm and invested in the deal.

APPEAL from the County Court of *Milwaukee* County. The action is to recover a large sum of money which the plaintiff, *Daniel Wells, Jr.,* alleges he was induced to pay by means of certain false and fraudulent representations made to him by the defendant, *Peter McGeoch*, concerning certain large business transactions in which they had been engaged as partners, and which had culminated in heavy losses to them. The complaint sets out such alleged fraudulent statements at considerable length, and prays that a certain settlement and adjustment of their losses between themselves, alleged to have been made and performed by *Wells* on the faith of such statements, be opened, and the amount of the common loss which each party ought to pay ascertained and adjusted. The answer denies the fraud charged in the complaint, and maintains that the settlement was an honest one and should not be disturbed. It is also alleged in the answer that the transactions had by the parties as partners, which they thus settled and adjusted, were illegal, and hence, in respect to them, neither party can have any relief.

A general knowledge of the transactions out of which this action arose can be most readily obtained by a perusal of the findings of the county court herein, and the contract executed by the parties in which they settled and adjusted their respective losses and provided for the payment thereof. Although quite lengthy, those instruments will be here inserted. The findings of fact are supplemented by other facts not found therein, which are stated in the opinion as found by this court. The findings are as follows:

"The defendant, several years prior to June 16th, 1883, was engaged in business in the city of Milwaukee under the name of Peter McGeoch & Co., as a commission merchant, in commodities dealt in upon the floor of the chamber of commerce of this city. In 1881, down to June 16, 1883, he was the leading partner in the firm of McGeoch, Everingham & Co., doing like business on the board of trade of Chicago. During those years the defendant, through his Chicago firm, had extensive dealings upon the Chicago board of trade in various commodities, chiefly in futures, on account of himself and the plaintiff jointly. Such dealings began in January, 1881, and continued until about the middle of February, 1882, when a settlement was had, and on the 23d day of that month the plaintiff received from the defendant full payment of the balance then appearing to be due him for his share of the profits. The total net profits up to February 23, 1882, received by the plaintiff, was a little more than $300,000, including the half share ($278,161.41) of the profits of an extensive deal in pork and ribs. About February 20, 1882, the plaintiff became associated with the defendant and others in a wheat speculation in Chicago, known as the April wheat deal, or corner in April wheat, 1882. The defendant, with George C. Walker, N. K. Fairbank, and S. A. Kent, of Chicago, Illinois, commission merchants and members of the board of trade of that city, though not associated in business generally, in February, 1882, bought, and soon took out of the market, all the No. 2 spring wheat within reach and available to fill contracts for about 3,500,000 bushels, and secured contracts from dealers for the sale and delivery to them in April, 1882, of about 10,000,000 bushels more; and having thus obtained control of the market, compelled those who had contracted to deliver them wheat which they could not get, to settle their contracts by the payment of differences upon fictitious values. The defendant was actively engaged in the management and manipulation of the corner, and the plaintiff advanced moneys to be used in carrying it on, upon the agreement that they should divide equally as partners; the share of the defendant, as member of the combination associated in the deal, being one third. The combination entered into the arrangement with the express purpose of creating a corner in wheat in the market, and the plaintiff well knew such to be the intention when he entered into said agreement with the defendant and furnished him money to assist in accomplishing that end; and the result shows that the combination was entirely successful. The corner ended with the month of April, 1882. An arbitration, under the rules of the board of trade, to fix the just commercial value of the wheat on the last day of April in Chicago, as the basis of difference to be paid by certain defaulting sellers to members of the combination, was had. The accounts of the deal were closed June 30, 1882. The defendant's one-third share of the net profits was ascertained to be $278,705.57, which sum was passed to his credit on the books of McGeoch, Everingham & Co., in Chicago, on that day. The largest proportion of this profit had been realized by a settlement of differences before the rule authorizing arbitration had been invoked by any of the persons involved in the said corner.

"No account was kept with the plaintiff on the books of the Chicago firms. The plaintiff's account was kept on the books of P. McGeoch & Co., in Milwaukee, and it was the practice that the dealings of the plaintiff and defendant on joint account through McGeoch, Everingham & Co., were reported to P. McGeoch & Co. (the defendant), and the plaintiff's share was entered on his account in the books of that commission house in Milwaukee. The plaintiff's share of the profits of the April wheat corner was not credited on his account in Milwaukee at the time the profits were ascertained, but the whole profit realized in the wheat deal was credited to XX account on the books in Milwaukee,— both parties knowing that XX represented the wheat deal,— owing to some pending suit which might affect the amount; and the fact that it was not so credited seems to have been afterwards overlooked or forgotten,— not with a view of concealing the same from the plaintiff, for he had oftentimes been informed that a large profit resulted from the corner and that XX represented such profit. Following this corner, the plaintiff and defendant continued speculative dealings for their joint account through the agency of McGeoch, Everingham & Co., in wheat, oats, pork, lard, and other commodities; making profits and losses, which they shared equally. Their profits were quite large during September and October, 1882. They had operated together several years, and both were well acquainted with the manner of doing business upon the chamber of commerce in Milwaukee and the board of trade in Chicago, and well knew how to operate successfully. Early in 1883, the plaintiff and defendant agreed to make a deal in lard in Chicago, and commenced buying (through defendant's firm in Chicago) futures for April, May, and June, and afterwards for July, 1883. As their purchases matured, they received and paid for the lard, and continued to contract for all they could get, within certain limits as to price, for future delivery, until June 16th, when they found themselves unable to provide money sufficient to keep up payments for lard then due upon their contracts, and margins upon their futures; and, as a consequence, the firm of McGeoch, Everingham & Co. failed. In pursuance of the rules of the board of trade, their pending contracts for purchase or sale were closed out. The price of both cash lard and option lard (so called) fell at once fifteen to twenty per cent.; and the firm who had represented the plaintiff and defendant in operating the deal for them, and under their direction, found themselves insolvent, having lost their capital, their earnings, and all the moneys furnished by the plaintiff and defendant and by other principals as advances upon deals which the firm were carrying for them as their agents or brokers. At the time of the failure, McGeoch, Everingham & Co. held for the parties to this suit about 125,000 tierces of cash lard, which had cost some $5,100,000; and of this amount 119,500 tierces were hypothecated to sundry banks in Chicago to secure loans to the firm, amounting to about $3,981,000. Said firm at the same time had contracted to purchase for account of the plaintiff and defendant about 177,000 tierces of lard to be delivered in June and July, 1883, aggregating not less than $7,000,000; on which contracts they had put up several hundred thousand dollars as margins to secure their performance.

"The plaintiff and defendant had furnished to said firm, for the purpose of the deal during its progress, the proceeds of their notes to the amount of $950,000, which were used in paying for lard, in providing margins on the futures, and in paying interest, insurance, and other expenses of the deal. The balances due from said firm to the defendant and to others, and the capital and accumulated earnings of the firm, were to a great extent invested and employed in paying for the property and contracts taken for the parties to this suit in the working of their said lard deal.

"The firm had some commission for other parties, but much the larger part of their losses by their failure were incurred on lard, and for the account of *Wells* and *McGeoch*. The failure involved many houses and heavy losses. Values were greatly disturbed, both of lard and other commodities. The indebtedness of McGeoch, Everingham & Co. was to a great number of persons. Their transactions were extensive, and the accurate adjustment of all accounts was laborious. The lard held and pledged by banks was not sold until several weeks after the failure of McGeoch, Everingham & Co., which occurred on Saturday, June 16, 1883. On Monday, June 18th, John R. Bensley was appointed receiver of the assets of the firm, in a suit by judgment creditors. He set about ascertaining losses and liabilities. Creditors brought actions against *Wells* and *McGeoch* as principals, and attached their property in Chicago, Milwaukee, and Michigan. It was soon claimed that the creditors of the Chicago firm would accept fifty cents of the amount due them, if paid shortly in cash. The receiver visited Milwaukee before the end of June, and conferred with the defendant and his attorney, and with the plaintiff's attorney. He stated that in his judgment $450,000, in addition to the available assets in his hands, would be required, and would be adequate to effect a settlement at fifty cents on the dollar.

"I further find that the plaintiff authorized the use for the purposes of said deal of the moneys due him from *McGeoch*, or in the hands of McGeoch, Everingham & Co., and derived from or arising out of former transactions in which plaintiff was interested; and under such authority, and with the consent of plaintiff, the $100,455.39 was so used in the lard deal, and also the plaintiff's share of the profits of the wheat corner of 1882, and represented in the XX account, was so used, and both sums were wholly lost in said deal.

"I further find that it clearly appears to me from the evidence, and from the manner in which, and the objects for which, the lard deal was inaugurated and carried on, that it was for the purpose of creating a corner in lard, and so understood by both parties, with the intention of cornering the market by investing large sums in the purchase of lard, and for futures for the months of June and July, and the scheme failed solely for want of funds to carry it through; and an indebtedness remained unpaid amounting to upwards of $1,300,000, as a result of the failure of said parties to sustain or consummate the corner enterprise. Of this indebtedness about $1,000,000 was owing on account of transactions made by the firm for *Wells* and *McGeoch* in the furtherance of their lard corner.

"I further find that prior to July 4, 1883, it was verbally agreed between the parties that they would each furnish one half of $450,000 to enable McGeoch, Everingham & Co. to compromise and settle their liabilities resulting from their inability to corner the market in lard; and that *McGeoch* should assume the payment of $25,000 to the Wisconsin Marine & Fire Ins. Co. Bank for *Wells*. Early in

July a compromise proposition at fifty per cent. was circulated in Chicago among the creditors, and by the middle of July it was accepted by all. Disagreements arose between the parties when it came to making of a contract between them. It was understood that the liabilities of the firm of McGeoch, Everingham & Co. on the board of trade were about $1,300,000 over and above all offsets; that the assets of the firm in the hands of the receiver were a little over $200,000, and that the whole indebtedness could be compromised for about $650,000. The plaintiff insisted that, if he paid the sum of $225,000, he should be fully released from all liabilities to McGeoch, Everingham & Co., or any of their creditors, or to *McGeoch*, and should be fully indemnified against any claims, costs, or damages growing out of the lard deal; and he sought, in addition thereto, to reserve the right to have a subsequent accounting with McGeoch, Everingham & Co., and with *McGeoch*, in respect to the whole business of the lard deal. The defendant insisted that the release should be mutual, and the settlement final and absolute. And for the purpose of compromising their supposed liability, incurred on their failure to successfully corner the market in lard or in their attempt to do so, an agreement to be executed by the parties was prepared, and after delay and discussion, resulting in important modifications of the original draught so as to make it express clearly the intentions of the parties, was signed by them on or about July 18th, in form and substance as set forth in the complaint."

Several extracts from such contract or agreement are then inserted in the findings, but, as that instrument will be copied herein at length, those extracts therefrom are now omitted. The findings proceed as follows:

"By the agreement, *Wells* agreed to assume and pay $675,000, and *McGeoch* $275,000, of their notes to the banks, and each of them agreed to pay forthwith the sum of

$225,000 towards the liquidation and discharge of the said indebtedness of McGeoch, Everingham & Co. under said compromise, and particularly of the indebtedness on which it was claimed that *Wells* was liable, and to the execution of the compromise agreement; and both parties intrusted the making of the payment of such indebtedness to the firm of Finches, Lynde & Miller and John R. Bensley, the receiver.

"I further find that *McGeoch* fully performed the agreement on his part. He furnished $225,000 at once to assist in effecting the compromise. The indebtedness was all discharged; the suits were all discontinued without expense to the plaintiff; and plaintiff has hitherto been fully indemnified against all claims and demands of McGeoch, Everingham & Co., or their creditors, or any one else, arising out of said lard transaction. I further find that from the time of the failure of McGeoch, Everingham & Co., June 16, 1883, up to the time of the execution of the compromise agreement, on July 17, 1883, the parties were under great excitement on account of the failure, the property and credits of each having been attached and garnished; and, while in this condition and situation, several interviews were had between the parties and their several attorneys, and various estimates were made as to the extent of the loss; and it could not be expected that accurate statements of so large a transaction could be made by either of the parties. The business was done through the firm of McGeoch, Everingham & Co., in Chicago, and, although *McGeoch* was the senior member of that firm, yet his business was on the board of trade; the firm employing book-keepers to assist in keeping a record of the various transactions on the board of trade and otherwise. *McGeoch* was no book-keeper, and had no knowledge of the books. Statements were delivered to him as he asked for them, and they were usually

sent to *McGeoch's* book-keeper in Milwaukee, who kept an
entry of such statements. The plaintiff had free access to
those books, both in Milwaukee and Chicago, and almost
daily visited the office in Milwaukee, and was informed by
the book-keeper in Milwaukee of the transactions in lard
many times; as also by *McGeoch*, personally and by letter,
during the lard deal and until the failure; so that the plaintiff probably had nearly, if not quite, as accurate a knowledge of the lard deal as defendant. And what was said by
defendant during the negotiations for a compromise was
not said with a view of cheating and defrauding the plaintiff, but was only an estimate of the probable losses and liabilities, and not relied on by plaintiff; for the settlement
was finally consummated upon the estimate made by Mr.
Bensley, the receiver, who had found from the books as accurate a statement as possible, for everything had to be
done in haste, as to the amount of the liabilities, and the
money necessary to be furnished by each.

"I further find that the moneys furnished by plaintiff and
delivered to defendant, together with the amount due him
on the April wheat corner, and also the amount specified in
the agreement of July 17th, together with the money furnished by defendant individually and through his firm in
Chicago, was all paid and lost. The moneys paid to the
receiver were by him applied on the settlement with the
creditors, and not one penny of it was retained by the defendant, or repaid to him or for his use or benefit; and he
had no money in his hands, possession, or control furnished
by the plaintiff; and, as before found, the amount specified
in the agreement of July 17th, and the credit of plaintiff
resulting from the April wheat corner, was, with the knowledge and consent of plaintiff, used and paid by defendant
towards the furtherance of the lard corner, and all lost
through the failure of McGeoch, Everingham & Co., result-

ing from the failure of plaintiff and defendant to furnish
the money necessary to carry on the lard deal to a successful corner.

"I also find that at the time the several transactions
upon the board of trade in the city of Chicago, Ill., took
place between plaintiff and defendant, the following statute, offered and received in evidence, was in force, to wit:
The Public Statutes of the State of Illinois, Heard's edition
of 1880, sec. 130, ch. 38 of the Revised Statutes of Illinois,
and reads as follows: ' Whoever contracts to have, or to
give to himself or another, an option to sell or buy at a future time any grain or other commodity, stock of any railroad or other company, or gold, or forestalls the market
by spreading false rumors to influence the price of commodities therein, or corners the market, or attempts to do
so, in relation to any such commodities, shall be fined not
less than ten dollars nor more than $1,000, or confined in
the county jail not to exceed one year, or both; and all
contracts made in violation of this section shall be considered gambling contracts, and shall be void.' It seems to
me beyond any doubt, from all the evidence, that the parties to this suit, in their combination and management of
the April wheat deal and securing and obtaining a successful corner in wheat, clearly violated the provisions of the
foregoing statute; and also, in attempting to corner the
market in lard, they violated the same statute. Such contracts, as stated in such statute, ' shall be considered gambling contracts, and shall be void.'

"As a result arising from the failure to successfully create a corner in lard, the contract agreement of July 17,
1883, was entered into by the parties to relieve themselves
from their great liability resulting from the failure to carry
their illegal deal to a successful corner, and the numerous
suits, attachments, and garnishments commenced and pending against them.

"The object of this action is to compel the defendant to account, or, in other words, to surcharge the account, as prayed for in the complaint, for the excess of moneys claimed by plaintiff to have been furnished by him over and above the amount furnished by defendant, and employed and lost in the prosecution of this illegal venture, this effort to corner the market in lard. The question is, the parties having violated the statute above mentioned, will the courts entertain an action asking contribution for losses incurred by the one party against the other, or for excess of moneys paid in carrying out the illegal venture or contract? And as conclusions of law from the foregoing facts, I find it quite doubtful in my mind, taking into consideration the testimony of all the circumstances leading to and surrounding it, whether this contract ought to be disturbed, even if the original ventures entered into by the parties, and upon which it is founded and based, were not illegal, or against the statute, or contrary to public policy. The rule in this state is, as often stated by the court in the language of the court in *Case v. Fish*, 58 Wis. 108, ' that a settlement once deliberately made is not to be opened except upon the clearest and most positive proof of fraud or mistake therein.' And especially is this so when the same has been fully complied with and carried out, but the contracts were contrary to the statute and illegal and void.

" 2. The supreme court of this state has also declared in *Melchoir v. McCarty*, 31 Wis. 254, in the following language: ' The general rule of law is that all contracts which are repugnant to justice, or founded upon an immoral consideration, or which are against the general policy of the common law, or contrary to the provisions of any statute, are void; and that if a party, claiming a right to recover a debt, is obliged to trace his title or right to the debt through any such illegal contract, he cannot recover, because he cannot be allowed to prove the illegal contract as the foundation for his right of recovery. ' It is quite immaterial whether such illegal contract be *malum in se*, or only *malum prohibitum*. In either case the maxim *ex turpi causa non oritur actio* is applicable. And a contract in violation of a statute is void, although the statute fails to provide expressly that contracts made in violation of its provisions shall not be valid. It is sufficient that it is prohibited, and its invalidity follows as a legal consequence.'

"So, also, it is decided by the supreme court of Michigan, in the case of *Raymond v. Leavitt*, 46 Mich. 447, that one who lends or advances money to be used for the purpose of making a corner in wheat, cannot recover it back by any legal measures; and on pages 452 and 453 of the opinion the court used this language: 'There may be difficulties in determining the conduct as to any violation of public policy, when it has not been covered by the statutes or precedents. But in the case before us the conduct of the parties comes within the undisputed censure of the law of the land; and we cannot save the transaction without doing so on the ground that such dealings are so manifestly sanctioned by usage and public approval that it would be absurd to suppose the legislature, if attention were called to them, would not legalize them. We do not think public opinion has become so thoroughly demoralized; and until the law is changed we shall decline enforcing such contracts. If parties see fit to invest money in such ventures, they must get it back by some other than legal means.' It would seem, from the foregoing opinion, that there was no statute in Michigan making such contracts illegal and void; and hence, it appears to me, is a very strong case, and very applicable to this case, in respect to the ventures of the parties to this suit in the so-called April wheat corner and so-called lard corner.

"I have also been referred to the case of *Keene v. Kent*, decided at a general term of the supreme court of the state

of New York, at the October term of said court, 1886 [42
Hun, 659], which also was a case involving lard. In that
case the parties, as in this, entered into an unlawful contract or combination to control the price of lard, and in
the opinion the court say: ' This was an agreement and
combination which the law will not execute. It will not
permit parties receiving property, and contemplating the
purchase and sale of more of it, to combine together to
keep it off the market, and in that manner oblige the public to pay a larger price for the article than it would otherwise secure. Such a combination is an unlawful conspiracy,
punishable as a crime. When it may be successfully carried
out, the effect is to impose upon the public, and to oblige
individuals having occasion to purchase the article dealt in
to pay more for it than its market value. So far as such a
combination or scheme may be rendered successful, it is
little if anything less than respectable robbery, which the
law will not sustain. On the contrary, it will leave the parties precisely where they have placed themselves. It will
not interpose to secure to either that advantage which,
under the terms of the agreement entered into and executed, he had reason to expect would be conceded to him by
the other parties to the unlawful transaction. If persons
devise and enter into schemes or combinations of this character, they must depend for their remedy upon the application of the rule, which may be observed by other confed-
erates, requiring that there shall be honor among certain
classes of persons who violate the laws of the state. They
cannot appeal to the courts for redress, or for any aid or
assistance in endeavoring to enforce the contract, so far
as may be, in favor of one of the parties against the other.'

  " 3. The contracts or combinations of the parties entered
into for the purpose of cornering the market in wheat, and
attempt to create the corner in lard, are by the statutes of
Illinois denominated gambling contracts, and declared to be

void. Such contracts the courts will not enforce, but will leave the parties in the condition in which they have placed themselves. The authorities are all to this effect.

"4. I therefore have come to the conclusion, from the foregoing facts found and the law applicable to them, that the court cannot grant the plaintiff the relief prayed for in his complaint. It is therefore ordered and adjudged that the complaint of the plaintiff be, and the same is, dismissed, with costs. Let judgment be entered accordingly."

The contract above mentioned bears date July 17, 1883, and is as follows:

"Whereas, the firm of McGeoch, Everingham & Co. are indebted to a number of creditors in large sums of money, which indebtedness they have arranged to discharge and settle by a compromise proposition which has been accepted by their creditors; and whereas, it has been claimed that *Daniel Wells, Jr.*, of the city of Milwaukee, Wisconsin, and *Peter McGeoch*, of the same place, are liable upon some ground to pay, or to assist in paying, the whole or some part of such indebtedness on account of transactions which the said *Wells* and *McGeoch* have had or authorized with or through the said firm, of which the said *Peter McGeoch* is senior member; and whereas, the said *Wells* and *McGeoch* have agreed to contribute and pay a sum of money for the purpose of assisting in the compromise, payment, discharge, and satisfaction of all the indebtedness of the said firm, and of their own indebtedness, if any, to said firm, or to the creditors of said firm, and also of their mutual indebtedness towards each other; and whereas, the said *Wells* and *McGeoch* have executed certain notes as makers, or as maker and indorser, to certain banks, for money raised for the benefit of the said *Wells* and *McGeoch*, or of one of them, which notes are to be paid in full, being secured by hypothecation of property pledged, deposited, or mortgaged by the said *Wells* or the said *McGeoch:*

"Now, therefore, for the purpose of a full, final, and complete settlement between the said parties, it is agreed between the said *Daniel Wells, Jr.*, and the said *Peter McGeoch*, that the said *Daniel Wells, Jr.*, shall pay to the National Bank of America, in Chicago, the notes, amounting to $100,000, held by the said bank and signed or indorsed by the said *Wells* and *McGeoch;* and that he shall also pay the note or notes for $100,000 held by the National Exchange Bank of Milwaukee, and the note or notes, amounting to $200,000, held by the First National Bank of Milwaukee, and the note or notes, amounting to $50,000, held by the Milwaukee National Bank of Wisconsin, whether such notes be also signed or indorsed by the said *Peter McGeoch* or not; and that the said *Wells* shall pay to the Wisconsin Marine and Fire Insurance Company Bank the note of $200,000 on which said *Wells* and *McGeoch* are liable to the said bank, and also $25,000 of and to apply upon the note of $300,000 held by the said bank on which the said *Wells* and *McGeoch* are liable, together with all interest accruing on the said notes and the said sums from and after the date hereof. And the said *Wells* shall procure, as soon as practicable, the release of said *Peter McGeoch* from each and all of the said indebtedness which the said *Wells* has so agreed to pay; and also, as soon as practicable, the release and discharge of all liens, mortgages, pledges, or hypothecations of property of the said *Peter McGeoch*, holden as collateral for the indebtedness so to be paid by the said *Daniel Wells, Jr.*

And whereas, there is a balance shown by the books of said McGeoch, Everingham & Co. in favor of the said *Daniel Wells, Jr.*, amounting to $100,455.39, as stated by that firm to said *Daniel Wells, Jr.*, the said *Wells* hereby releases and discharges the said *McGeoch* and the said McGeoch, Everingham & Co. from the said indebtedness, and from all liability to pay him the said sum of $100,455.39, or any part thereof, and from any and all liability whatever except as herein provided. The said *Daniel Wells, Jr.*, further agrees to pay towards the liquidation and discharge of the said indebtedness the sum of $225,000, which amount he will pay, or cause to be paid, to the firm of Finches, Lynde & Miller, of the city of Milwaukee, immediately upon the execution of this agreement, for the purpose only of paying towards the liquidation and compromise of the indebtedness aforesaid, and particularly of the indebtedness upon which it is claimed that the said *Wells* is liable.

"And the said *Peter McGeoch*, on his part, agrees, in consideration of the foregoing, that he will pay to the said Wisconsin Marine and Fire Insurance Company Bank the remaining $275,000 out of the said note of $300,000 owing thereto by him and the said *Daniel Wells, Jr.*, together with all interest accruing thereon from and after this date; and that he will pay, or cause to be paid, forthwith, all indebtedness of the said *Wells* to the said McGeoch, Everingham & Co., and to any and all of the creditors of the said McGeoch, Everingham & Co., by executing promptly and faithfully the terms of the compromise made between the the said McGeoch, Everingham & Co. and their said creditors; and will procure the full and unconditional discharge of all liabilities, claims, and demands of the said McGeoch, Everingham & Co., and of each of the creditors, or persons holding contracts of the said McGeoch, Everingham & Co., against him, the said *Daniel Wells, Jr.*, whether included or not in the said compromise, within the time fixed by said agreement of compromise, to wit, ten days from Saturday last, or as soon thereafter as practicable; and that he will procure, also, as soon as practicable, the discharge of the liability of the said *Daniel Wells, Jr.*, to the said Wisconsin Marine and Fire Insurance Co. Bank for said $275,000; and also, as soon as practicable, the release and discharge of all mortgages, liens, pledges, or hypothecations of property of the said *Daniel Wells, Jr.*, held by the said last-named bank as collateral to the said indebtedness of $275,000. And the said *Peter McGeoch* hereby releases and discharges the said *Daniel Wells, Jr.*, of and from all claims, liabilities, and demands whatever heretofore existing, except those herein agreed to be paid by the said *Wells;* and further agrees that the money so contributed by the said *Daniel Wells, Jr.*, and to be paid to the said firm of Finches, Lynde & Miller, together with an equal or greater sum which he agrees forthwith to contribute for that purpose, and together with the money now in possession of the receiver of the estate of the said firm of McGeoch, Everingham & Co., shall be forthwith applied to the payment and discharge of the indebtedness which the said *McGeoch* is by this agreement bound to cause to be paid or discharged, and particularly to the execution of the compromise agreement aforesaid between the said firm and their creditors; the making of which payment is intrusted by both parties hereto to the said firm of Finches, Lynde & Miller and John R. Bensley.

"It is understood that, by the said agreement of compromise, the creditors have agreed to receive, in full discharge of the said unsecured indebtedness, fifty cents upon the dollar, or one half the amount thereof. It is also understood that the said agreement of compromise does not include the debts owing by the said firm which are secured by the pledge of property or otherwise to the extent of the proceeds of such property, but does include the balances or remainders which may be found due to the said creditors after applying upon their respective indebtedness the amounts of securities so deposited with or pledged to them.

" This agreement is made in full settlement and discharge of all liabilities between the parties hereto; and the said *McGeoch* agrees to hold the said *Wells* harmless, and to indemnify him against all losses, damages, expenses, costs of suits, of whatever nature, which may arise hereafter out of any failure upon the part of said *McGeoch* to perform the stipulations herein contained, and also against all such costs or expenses which have arisen in the suits now pending against the said *Wells* on account of the matters aforesaid, whether as principal or garnishee, except as to counsel fees owing by the said *Wells*, which he undertakes to pay and discharge; which pending suits said *McGeoch* shall cause to be discontinued as soon as practicable."

The terms of the above contract were fully performed by the respective parties. The case is further stated in the opinion. The plaintiff appeals from a judgment dismissing the complaint with costs.

For the appellant there were briefs by *Winfield Smith* and *Wells, Brigham & Upham*, attorneys, and *Winfield Smith* and *Jenkins, Winkler, Fish & Smith*, of counsel, and the cause was argued orally by *Winfield Smith, John T. Fish*, and *F. C. Winkler*. They argued that the *gravamen* of the action is the fraud practiced by the defendant in obtaining from the plaintiff the money assumed and paid on and after July 17, 1883, by reason of the false representations of the defendant as to the amount which the plaintiff should pay to make his contribution equal to that of the defendant. The action is not upon any contract to buy lard or wheat upon the Chicago market. These contracts are set out in the complaint to show the means employed by the defendant in perpetrating the fraud. *Kiewert v. Rindskopf*, 46 Wis. 484; *Western Ass. Co. v. Towle*, 65 id. 258; *Catts v. Phalen*, 2 How. 376. The defendant cannot refuse to account for the plaintiff's share of the profits of the wheat deal, which was left in his hands, on the ground that that transaction was illegal. *Kiewert v. Rindskopf*, 46 Wis. 485; *Heckman v. Swartz*, 50 id. 270; *Lemon v. Grosskopf*, 22 id. 451; *Tenant v. Elliott*, 1 Bos. & P. 4; *Farmer v.*

Russell, id. 296; *Bousfield v. Wilson*, 16 Mees. & W. 185; *Owen v. Davis*, 1 Bailey (S. C.), 316; *Gilliam v. Brown*, 43 Miss. 641; *Anderson v. Moncrieff*, 3 Desaus. (S. C.), 126; *Sharp v. Taylor*, 2 Phill. (22 Eng. Ch.), 801; *McBlair v. Gibbes*, 17 How. 232, 237; *Brooks v. Martin*, 2 Wall. 70; *Planters' Bank v. Union Bank*, 16 id. 483; *Wann v. Kelly*, 5 Fed. Rep. 584; *Cook v. Sherman*, 20 id. 167; *Merritt v. Millard*, 5 Bosw. 645; *S. C.* 4 Keyes, 208; *Berkshire v. Evans*, 4 Leigh, 223; *Blakesley v. Johnson*, 13 Wis. 530; *Clemens v. Clemens*, 28 id. 637. If the defendant had occupied no other relation to the plaintiff than that of agent, he could have been convicted of embezzlement for appropriating this money to his own use. *Woodward v. State*, 103 Ind. 127; *U. S. Exp. Co. v. Lucas*, 36 Ind. 361; *Rothrock v. Perkinson*, 61 id. 39; *State v. Turney*, 81 id. 559; *Carkins v. Anderson*, 21 Neb. 364; *Bell v. Day*, 32 N. Y. 165, 173.

The following cases, as well as many of those above cited, show clearly the distinction drawn by the courts. They point out that while the vendor of wheat or lard may set up the illegality of the contract of sale, yet when he has closed that contract, paying damages for nonfulfilment, that contract is at an end. The proceeds are then in the hands of the recipient lawful money untainted by the preceding transaction, and he must account for it to his principal or partner. *Bronson A. & B. Asso. v. Ramsdell*, 24 Mich. 441; *Willson v. Owen*, 30 id. 474; *Ingram v. Mitchell*, 30 Ga. 547; *Warren v. Hewitt*, 45 id. 507; *Daniels v. Barney*, 22 Ind. 207; *Barney v. Daniels*, 32 id. 19; *Murray v. Vanderbilt*, 39 Barb. 141; *De Leon v. Trevino*, 49 Tex. 89; *Pfeuffer v. Maltby*, 54 id. 454; *Lewis v. Alexander*, 51 id. 578, 590.

Counsel for the appellant also argued, among other things, that both as the agent and partner of the plaintiff the defendant was bound to exercise the utmost good faith and to keep the plaintiff fully informed of all material facts; that the plaintiff's misunderstanding of facts, considered as a mere mistake, is yet sufficient ground for relief; and that the case clearly shows both misrepresentation and concealment by the defendant of facts material to the plaintiff's interest, which he should have disclosed to the plaintiff, but failed to do so with the purpose of gaining an undue advantage.

For the respondent there were briefs by *Joshua Stark* and *Finches, Lynde & Miller,* and oral argument by· *Mr. Stark* and *Mr. Geo. P. Miller.* They contended, *inter alia,* that the combination for cornering the market in relation to wheat in the spring of 1882, was an unlawful conspiracy punishable as a crime. 1 Rapalje & L. Law Dict. 296; *Sampson v. Shaw,* 101 Mass. 145, 3 Am. Rep. 327; 14 Chicago L. News, 37; R. S. of Ill. (1880), p. 38, sec. 130; *Lyon v. Culbertson,* 83 Ill. 33, 25 Am. Rep. 349; *Raymond v. Leavitt,* 46 Mich. 447, 41 Am. Rep. 170; *Morris Run Coal Co. v. Barclay Coal Co.* 68 Pa. St. 173, 8 Am. Rep. 159; *Arnot v. P. & E. Coal Co.* 68 N. Y. 558, 23 Am. Rep. 190; *Ex parte Young,* 6 Biss. 53, 65; Wharton's Cr. Law, sec. 2322; *Comm. v. Carlisle,* Brightly, 40; *People v. Fisher,* 14 Wend. 9, 28 Am. Dec. 501; R. S. sec. 4568; 1 Lindley on Part. 180–192.

The agreement or conspiracy of *Wells, McGeoch,* and others to corner the market in relation to wheat and divide the profits among them being illegal, fraudulent, and void, it follows that no action can be maintained by any party to such conspiracy against his associates, or either of them, to enforce an accounting, contribution, or division of profits, or for any other relief founded upon such agreement. *Mitchell v. Cockburne,* 2 H. Blackst. 379; *Steers v. Lashley,* 6 Term, 61; *Aubert v. Maze,* 2 Bos. & P. 371; *Knowles v. Haughton,* 11 Ves. Jr. 168; *Cousins v. Smith,* 13 id. 542; *Ex parte Bulmer,* id. 313; *Evans v. Richardson,* 3 Meriv. 469;

Battersby v. Smyth, 3 Madd. 110; *Armstrong v. Armstrong*, 3 Mylne & K. 45; *Ewing v. Osbaldiston*, 2 Mylne & C. 53; *Sykes v. Beadon*, L. R. 11 Ch. Div. 170; *Bartle v. Nutt*, 4 Pet. 184; *Wheeler v. Sage*, 1 Wall. 518; *Brown v. Tarkington*, 3 id. 377; *Fletcher v. Watson*, 7 Gratt. 1; *Watson v. Murray*, 23 N. J. Eq. 257; *Gregory v. Wilson*, 36 N. J. Law, 315; *Todd v. Rafferty's Adm'rs*, 30 N. J. Eq. 254; *Root v. Stevenson's Adm'r*, 24 Ind. 115; *Miller v. Davidson*, 8 Ill. 518, 44 Am. Dec. 715; *Skeels v. Phillips*, 54 Ill. 309; *Neustadt v. Hall*, 58 id. 172; *Craft v. McConoughy*, 79 id. 346, 22 Am. Rep. 171; *Lane v. Thomas*, 37 Tex. 157; *Read v. Smith*, 60 id. 379; *Mulhollan v. Voorhies*, 3 Martin (N. S.), 46; *Anderson v. Powell*, 44 Iowa, 20; *Boyd v. Barclay*, 1 Ala. 34, 34 Am. Dec. 762; *Belding v. Pitkin*, 2 Caines R. 147; *Hooker v. Vandewater*, 4 Denio, 349; *Stanton v. Allen*, 5 id. 434; *Atcheson v. Mallon*, 43 N. Y. 147; *Gray v. Hook*, 4 id. 449; *Woodworth v. Bennett*, 43 id. 273; *Arnot v. P. & E. Coal Co.* 68 id. 558, 23 Am. Rep. 190; *Sampson v. Shaw*, 101 Mass. 145, 3 Am. Rep. 327; *Snell v. Dwight*, 120 Mass. 9; *Dunham v. Presby*, id. 285; *Morris Run Coal Co. v. Barclay Coal Co.* 68 Pa. St. 173, 8 Am. Rep. 159; *King v. Winants*, 71 N. C. 469, 17 Am. Rep. 11; *Gould v. Kendall*, 15 Neb. 549; *Hardy v. Stonebraker*, 31 Wis. 640; *Fairbank v. Leary*, 40 id. 637.

There are many well considered cases holding that even in transactions between a principal and his agent or broker, in illegal grain, stock, or other speculations, notes given for losses, advances, or profits are void because of their connection with the illegal adventure. See cases above cited, also *Brown v. Turner*, 7 Term, 630; *Harley v. Stapleton's Adm'r*, 24 Mo. 248; *Whitesides v. Hunt*, 97 Ind. 191, 49 Am. Rep. 441; *Cunningham v. Nat. Bank*, 71 Ga. 400; 51 Am. Rep. 266; *Collins v. Nevin*, 27 Alb. L. J. 354; *Fareira v. Gabell*, 89 Pa. St. 89; *Bell v. Quinn*, 2 Sandf. 146; *Workingmen's B. Co. v. Rautenberg*, 103 Ill. 460; *In re Green*, 7 Biss. 338;

Barnard v. Backhaus, 52 Wis. 593; *Everingham v. Meighan*, 55 id. 354; *Lowry v. Dillman*, 59 id. 197; *Lemon v. Grosskopf*, 22 id. 447.

It is also well settled that no action can be maintained to recover for goods sold and delivered, or for money loaned or advanced for the purpose of aiding any illegal or criminal enterprise. Money loaned to aid in making a corner in wheat: *Raymond v. Leavitt*, 46 Mich. 447, 41 Am. Rep. 170. Money advanced to aid a corner in stocks: *Sampson v. Shaw*, 101 Mass. 145. Money loaned for the settlement of losses in illegal stock-jobbing: *Cannan v. Bryce*, 3 Barn. & Ald. 179. Goods sold to aid a corner in coal: *Arnot v. P. & E. Coal Co.* 68 N. Y. 558. Money lent to be used in gaming: *McKinnell v. Robinson*, 3 Mees. & W. 434; *Cutler v. Welsh*, 43 N. H. 497; *Mordecai v. Dawkins*, 9 Rich. 262. Goods sold to be used by the Confederate States in aid of the rebellion: *Hanauer v. Doane*, 12 Wall. 342; *Oxford Iron Co. v. Spradley*, 51 Ala. 171; *Booker v. Robbins*, 26 Ark. 660. Sale of liquor on Sunday and without license: *Melchoir v. McCarty*, 31 Wis. 252. Services or losses of broker in wagering contracts for grain: *Irwin v. Williar*, 110 U. S. 499; *Higgins v. McCrea*, 116 id. 671. Moneys paid in furtherance of a contract the object of which is to violate the spirit and policy of a public statute, and not expended: *Perkins v. Savage*, 15 Wend. 412. See, also, *De Groot v. Van Duzer*, 20 id. 390; *Hull v. Ruggles*, 56 N. Y. 424; *Tyler v. Carlisle*, 11 East. Rep. (Me.), 242. Cases holding and applying the same doctrine might be cited almost without number.

The rule that a servant or agent receiving money for his principal will not be permitted to withhold it on the ground that it is the fruit of illegal transactions, is not applicable in the present case. The defendant was not the agent of the plaintiff in the wheat deal, in any other sense than as his partner or associate in a joint adventure. Both parties being *in pari delicto*, the defendant cannot be held to account. *Lemon v. Grosskopf*, 22 Wis. 447; *Booth v. Hodgson*, 6 Term, 405; *Kirk v. Morrow*, 6 Heisk. 445; *Chappell v. Wysham*, 4 Har. & J. 560; *Brewer v. Kingsberry*, 69 Ga. 754; *Campbell v. Anderson's Adm'r*, 2 Duv. (Ky.), 384; *Wooten v. Miller*, 7 Smedes & M. 380; *Thorne v. Travelers' Ins. Co.* 80 Pa. St. 15; *Rolfe v. Delmar*, 7 Rob. (N. Y.), 80; *Overby v. Overby*, 21 La. Ann. 493.

The charge of fraud does not affect the defense of illegality. The real object of this action is to surcharge the account or compel a re-accounting between the parties in respect to their transactions in the wheat and lard corner speculations. Fraud or mistake in inducing the agreement of July 17, 1883, and the mutual releases therein, if proved, can have no other effect than to remove an obstacle to the enforcement of an accounting in equity. The real cause of action lies back of that agreement and is quite independent of it. It rests upon the agreement of the parties to share equally losses and profits of their unlawful ventures. In none of the cases cited by plaintiff's counsel on this point did the transaction which was infected with fraud originate in or arise out of antecedent criminal transactions in which the two parties were jointly interested.

As to the effect of illegality upon the rights and remedies of parties to contracts tainted therewith, see, generally, note to *Ex parte Pyke*, 25 Eng. (Moak), 650–659; 1 Story's Eq. Jur. secs. 263–296; 1 Lindley on Part. 180–192.

The following opinion was filed January 10, 1888:

LYON, J. Most, if not all, of the material facts stated in the findings and opinion of the county judge are well sustained by the testimony, and will not be disturbed. The learned judge found that the wheat deal of 1882 and the lard deal of 1883 were illegal transactions, and held that no recovery can be had in this action, because the claim of the plaintiff grows out of such illegal transaction. Upon that theory, the findings of fact seem to be sufficiently full and comprehensive.   Much testimony, however, was given on the trial, directed to questions of fact upon which the findings are silent.   During the term at which the decision was rendered and the findings filed, counsel for *Mr. Wells*, the plaintiff, asked the court to make additional findings upon a large number of questions thus omitted therefrom.   "Whereupon [as stated in the bill of exceptions] the court ruled that the request should have been made before the findings had been made and filed by the court; and the court refused to pass upon the questions, and dismissed the application, and refused to look into or examine the requests submitted."

The ground upon which such refusal is rested is untenable. A party to an action in which it is the duty of the court to file findings of fact cannot know in advance of such filing what they will be.   He may rely upon the presumption that the court will discharge its duty by finding upon all disputed questions of fact involved in the case, and he cannot be put in default because he has failed to indicate to the court in advance the specific facts upon which he desires findings.   It is sufficient to secure a review by this court on appeal, if due exception be taken that the findings fail to cover and include certain specified material questions of fact litigated on the trial.

In the view we have taken of this case (which is hereinafter expressed), some of the omitted propositions of fact are material to a correct determination thereof.   At the risk of some repetition of what appears in the decision and findings of the county court, a statement of the case, including such omitted facts as the same appear in the pleadings, findings, and evidence, will now be made, after which the law of the case will be considered.

I.   From January 1, 1881, to June 16, 1883, the defendant, *Peter McGeoch,* was engaged in the city of Milwaukee in the business of a broker and commission merchant, dealing

in grain and other produce, under the name and style of
P. McGeoch & Co. During the same time, he was a partner in the firm of McGeoch, Everingham & Co., which was
engaged in a like business in Chicago, operating on the
board of trade in that city. There were four partners in
the firm, but *McGeoch* owned a one-half interest in its business and profits, and was the leading partner therein.

During the whole time aforesaid, the parties — *Wells* and
McGeoch — were jointly interested as partners in very extensive transactions in grain, lard, pork, and other commodities. These transactions were mostly in futures, that
is, purchases and sales for future delivery, and were conducted by *McGeoch* alone, through his said firm in Chicago
and his Milwaukee house. There were many hundreds of
such transactions, and they amounted in the aggregate to
many millions of dollars.

In February, 1882, the parties settled and adjusted their
previous dealings on joint account, and the profits of each
were found to be over $300,000. This sum includes the
profits of each, amounting to over $278,000, in an extensive
deal in pork and ribs. The parties then engaged in a wheat
deal in Chicago in connection with others. This speculation is known as the "April (1882) corner in wheat." It was
prosecuted with energy, sagacity, and courage, and resulted
in a successful corner of the market, and in a net profit to
Wells and *McGeoch* of $278,705.57, or $139,352.78 each.
The final result of this deal was reported by McGeoch, Everingham & Co., at Chicago, to the house of P. McGeoch &
Co., at Milwaukee, and the aggregate profit of the two parties was credited in the books of the latter house to XX account. It was not entered up to the credit of the respective
parties, because a suit was then pending which might result (but never did) in changing the figures somewhat.
The fact that the amount so entered had not been divided
between the parties on the books of P. McGeoch & Co.

seems to have been overlooked or forgotten, and so it remained therein as originally entered. *Wells'* share of the profit on the wheat deal of 1882 was left in the hands of *McGeoch* for future operations, and the credit of $278,705.57 to XX account was transferred to the credit of *McGeoch* alone on the books of the Chicago house.

The joint adventures of the parties, under the direction and management of *McGeoch*, were continued until the failure of the Chicago house, June 16, 1883. There was a large number of transactions during that time,—some of which resulted in profits to the parties; others, in loss. These were reported to the Milwaukee house, and *Wells'* share of such profits and loss were entered in the books of that house to his account, but stood to the credit of *McGeoch* on the books of McGeoch, Everingham & Co. On June 16, 1883, the aggregate of profits over losses in those transactions belonging to *Wells* (excluding the lard deal hereafter mentioned) amounted to $100,455.39.

Early in 1883 the parties inaugurated in Chicago what is called a "lard deal;" or perhaps, rather, *McGeoch* inaugurated it, and *Wells* soon thereafter took a joint interest therein with him. This was a deal in April, May, June, and July lard. Through the Chicago house they purchased cash lard and lard for future delivery in enormous quantities. Their transactions amounted to over $12,000,000. Of course, vast sums of money were required to carry on the deal. *Wells* authorized *McGeoch* to use in the deal all his funds in the hands of *McGeoch*, and the same were so used. They raised on their individual notes, from various banks, $950,000, and, by hypothecation of cash lard which they held, they raised nearly $4,000,000 more. To the above sums should be added any sums which *McGeoch* furnished and put into the deal. All these contracts for lard were made by the firm of McGeoch, Everingham & Co. as principal. No account with *Wells* was kept on the books of that firm, but the lard-deal account therein was designated as "41." Transactions relating to that deal were frequently, perhaps daily, transmitted to P. McGeoch & Co., at Milwaukee.

To carry the deal to a successful termination, *Wells* and *McGeoch* were forced to buy all the lard in the market. The quantity thrown upon the market was unexpectedly large, and additional large sums of money were required for such purchases, as well as for margins on purchases for future delivery. The financial ability of the operators was not equal to the emergency. The crisis came June 16, 1883. The parties were unable to furnish any more money to their brokers, and the latter could not put up certain large margins regularly required of them under the rules of the board of trade, to which they were subject; so the firm of McGeoch, Everingham & Co. failed and the lard deal collapsed, entailing an enormous loss upon its operators.

Many actions were at once brought against the parties, and against McGeoch, Everingham & Co., by the creditors of that firm, both in Illinois and Wisconsin. Both parties resided in Milwaukee. In one of the suits against the firm of McGeoch, Everingham & Co., a receiver, a Mr. Bensley, was appointed. The appointment was a most fortunate one for the parties interested. The receiver at once qualified and entered upon the duties of his office. He gathered in the scattered assets of the firm, and set himself to ascertain the extent of the disaster and the means of repairing it as far as possible. Before the end of June, he informed the parties that the debts of the firm, estimated at about $1,300,000 (over $1,000,000 of which was on account of the lard deal), could, in his opinion, be compromised at fifty cents on the dollar, if the money could be furnished soon; and that with $450,000 in cash, and the assets of the firm in his hands, estimated at something over $200,000, he could pay all the liabilities, and thus relieve not only the firm, but *Wells* and *McGeoch,* from the enormous indebtedness resulting from the failure of the lard deal. Thereupon negotiations were had between the parties, resulting in the contract of July 17, 1883, which is set out in full in the foregoing statement of facts. Each party paid to the receiver $225,000, as therein agreed; and with that money, and the proceeds of the assets of the firm which came to his hands (such proceeds amounting to nearly $340,000), the receiver procured the discharge of all the indebtedness of the firm, paid all costs in pending suits, and all expenses of his receivership, and paid a surplus of nearly $28,000 to the partners in that firm, other than *McGeoch*.

Thus far the transactions between the parties are narrated in the findings of the county court substantially as here stated, and perhaps more fully. We now proceed to state certain facts proved on the trial to which little or no reference is made in the findings.

Each party had invested a large sum of money in the lard deal, which was irretrievably lost. They jointly owed other large sums, for the payment of which both were legally liable. Utter financial ruin of both was imminent, and, naturally, both were anxious to avert it if possible. The receiver was pressing a compromise upon the creditors of McGeoch, Everingham & Co., and had expressed the opinion to the parties that with the assets in his hands, and $450,000 in cash additional, he could pay off the liabilities of the firm; most of which were incurred on account of the parties in the lard deal. Under these circumstances, the parties, aided by legal advisers, met, negotiated, and entered into the contract of July 17, 1883. Pending such negotiations, and as part thereof, *McGeoch* represented to *Wells* that the latter had a credit with him of a little over $100,000, being his share of the profits of their joint operations, and that he had invested it in the lard deal, pursuant to the authority which *Wells* gave him to do so. He also stated to *Wells* that he (*McGeoch*) had

invested $700,000 in the deal, including a note to a bank
of $250,000. The parties then owed to banks, on their
individual notes, $950,000, including the $250,000 just
mentioned. Each was a party to all these notes, either as
maker or indorser. *McGeoch* thereupon proposed to *Wells*
that he (*Wells*) should assume payment of the remaining
$700,000; *McGeoch* assuming payment of the $250,000 note.
As *McGeoch* represented the matter, this would make *Wells'*
payment on account of the deal, in round numbers, $800,000,
and *McGeoch's*, $700,000. To equalize these payments, it
was agreed, after some negotiation, that *McGeoch* should
pay $25,000 on one of the bank notes assumed by *Wells*,
and should give the indemnity contained in the contract of
July 17, 1883.

It may be observed here that on the above basis, to have
made the payments of these parties equal in amount,
McGeoch should have paid $50,000 to *Wells* or on his
account, whereas he paid $25,000. Thus, *Wells* allowed
McGeoch $25,000 for the indemnity just mentioned. It is
perfectly obvious that the result of this agreement was that
Wells assumed to pay $25,000 more, and *McGeoch* the same
sum less, than one half the losses of the deal. The sums
theretofore put in the deal by each party and the sums assumed by each on account of existing indebtedness to banks
having thus been adjusted and equalized on the basis of
McGeoch's representations, each party agreed to raise, and
did raise and pay to the receiver, his agreed proportion of
the amount estimated to be necessary to discharge the liabilities above mentioned. Such negotiations were had, and
the contract of July 17, 1883, was entered into, with the
express understanding between the parties that the money
of *Wells* in the hands of *McGeoch*, the $675,000 of bank in-
debtedness assumed by *Wells*, and the $225,000 paid by him
to the receiver, equaled one half the losses by the lard deal,
plus $25,000, including costs and expenses of closing out

the deal; and that the $275,000 assumed by *McGeoch*, the $225,000 paid by him to the receiver, and the sums put into the deal by him before the failure, would equal one half of such net loss, minus $25,000.

The evidence leaves no room for doubt that *McGeoch* represented to *Wells* that he had put into the lard deal $700,000, including the bank debt of $250,000 assumed by him, or $450,000 without it; and that the balance in his hands to the credit of *Wells* was but $100,455.59. His attorneys, to his knowledge, were notified in writing by the attorneys of *Wells*, before the contract of July 17th was executed, that *Wells* would execute it on the faith of these representations; and neither *McGeoch*, nor his attorneys for him, denied that he made such representations. Further, one of *McGeoch's* attorneys drew and delivered to the attorneys of *Wells* a memorandum in which, after referring to certain indebtedness, it is said that the same " is exclusive of $1,500,000 which the two parties, *Wells* and *McGeoch*, severally owe at the banks, or have raised," etc. The amount owing at the banks was $950,000; leaving $550,000 as the sum raised and put in the deal by both parties. Of this last sum it was stated by *McGeoch* that *Wells* had put in only a little over $100,000; thus leaving his *(McGeoch's)* investment in the deal nearly $450,000, exclusive of the $250,000 raised by him at the bank. This memorandum was so delivered before the contract was signed, and *McGeoch* saw it and made no objection to it. It has the force of a direct statement to *Wells* that he *(McGeoch)* had thus actually invested in the deal $700,000, including the bank debt of $250,000. Besides, the oral testimony alone, on the same subject, is quite sufficient to prove that such representations were repeatedly made by *McGeoch* to *Wells* during the negotiations.

II. The conclusions we have reached as to the law of this case render it necessary to determine the following questions: *First.* Were such representations true or false? If false, *second,* were they fraudulently made by *McGeoch?* And, *third,* did *Wells* rely upon them, and make and perform the contract of July 17, 1883, on the faith of them, believing them true?

1. Were the above representations true or false? It is admitted by all the counsel that *McGeoch* retained in his hands the share of *Wells* in the profits of the wheat deal of 1882, being $139,352.78, and that he invested the same by authority of *Wells* in the lard deal. Hence the representation by *McGeoch* that the amount of the money of *Wells* in his hands which he so invested was but $100,455.59, was not true; the actual amount was $239,808.17.

As to the representation by *McGeoch* that he had put into the lard deal $700,000, his counsel claim that it was substantially true. A large amount of testimony is directed to this point; and much argument has been employed, and many ingenious theories advanced, by both sides, to demonstrate the truth or falsity of this representation. To one not an expert accountant, the combination of figures and accounts involved in these theories, and pressed upon us in the argument, are quite bewildering, and it must be added that none of them are satisfactory. Fortunately, the record furnishes us the means of solving the question.

It is an admitted fact in the case that the losses in the lard deal amounted to $2,352,036.52. The proofs are very satisfactory that, by the compromise with the creditors of McGeoch, Everingham & Co., there was released on account of the indebtedness incurred in the lard deal $513,537.76. This appears in the testimony of Stoltz, the book-keeper of that firm, and by an account furnished by him, showing the entries made in the books of that firm, after its debts and the expenses of the receiver had been paid, to balance and close the accounts of the firm. It is undisputed. Moreover, it is just about the sum we should expect to find; for such indebtedness amounted to something over $1,000,000, and the amount released by the compromise was fifty per cent. thereof.   Deducting the amount released by the compromise from the total loss, we have $1,838,498.76, which is the amount paid by both parties on account of losses, including the costs and expenses above mentioned.   Of this last sum it is conceded that *Wells* paid $1,139,808.17.   As a matter of course, the difference between the two sums last mentioned, which is $698,690.59, is the total sum paid by *McGeoch*.   Deduct therefrom the sum afterwards paid by him to the receiver, and we have $473,690.59; which is the amount he had put into the lard deal when he represented to *Wells* that he had thus put in $700,000.   He therefore overstated his investment $226,309.41, in addition to the understatement of *Wells'* investment above mentioned. The following table will show the above computation in a more condensed form:

Total loss		$2,852,036 52
Released by the compromise		518,537 76
Paid by both parties		$1,838,498 76
Wells paid —		
To banks	$675,000 00	
In *McGeoch's* hands, admitted by him	100,455 39	
One half profit of wheat deal of 1882, in *McGeoch's* hands, not accounted for by him	139,352 78	
Paid to receiver	225,000 00	
		1,139,808 17
McGeoch invested in lard deal		$698,690 59
Deduct his payment to receiver		225,000 00
Paid by *McGeoch* before July 17, 1883		$473,690 59
McGeoch represented his investment to be		700,000 00
He actually had invested only		473,690 59
McGeoch overstated his payments		$226,309 41
He understated the amount of *Wells'* money in his hands		139,352 78
Total		$365,662 19

This method of ascertaining the amount paid into the lard deal by *McGeoch* renders it quite unnecessary to ascertain the sources from whence the money came. The amount may, probably does, include the capital of *McGeoch* invested in the firm of McGeoch, Everingham & Co., and his share of the commissions theretofore earned by that firm. It is maintained by counsel for *Wells* that, by the terms of the settlement between the parties, these items were not to be allowed to *McGeoch*. We do not so understand the proofs. The testimony on that subject was given by Mr. Winfield Smith, one of *Wells'* attorneys, who took a leading part for *Wells* in the negotiations which resulted in the contract of July 17, 1883. He testified that, during the negotiations (probably near the close thereof), he had a conversation with *McGeoch* and Mr. Finch (one of his counsel), in which *McGeoch* assented to the proposition that the capital stock of the firm " was not to be considered one of the debts due from the firm which *McGeoch* and *Wells* would have to assume or endeavor to pay, in whole or in part." This proposition seems to have been carried out. The representations made by *McGeoch* as to the amount he had invested in the lard deal were made before the above conversation took place; and, in order to determine whether such representations were fraudulent or not, *all* the money he so invested, no matter from what source derived, should be allowed him. Moreover, aside from the question of fraud, in an accounting between the parties of their investments in the lard deal, we do not think the above understanding or agreement as to capital is sufficiently broad to exclude the allowance to *McGeoch* of the proceeds of his share of capital and commissions which he had theretofore drawn out and invested in such deal. The allowance of these items to him does not seem to conflict with the agreement that the capital stock of the firm was not to be considered a debt of the firm which the parties were to assume or endeavor to pay. The agreement was satisfied when, by the failure of the firm, the partners therein, other than *McGeoch*, lost a large portion of the capital they had invested in the business. *McGeoch's* capital and his share of the commissions had already been drawn out and invested in the deal, and the amount thereof thereby ceased to be a liability of the firm. The agreement affects only such capital as remained a liability of the firm.

2. Having determined that *McGeoch*, in his own interest, overstated to *Wells* his investment in the lard deal, and understated the amount of *Wells'* money in his hands which he (*McGeoch*) invested in the same deal, and having determined, also, the aggregate amount thus overstated and understated, we will now proceed to consider whether such misrepresentations were fraudulently made by *McGeoch*.

This question requires but little discussion. If *McGeoch* knew that he was overstating his own investment or understating the amount of *Wells'* money in his hands which he invested in the lard deal, his representations were fraudulent. If such representations were made in ignorance of the real facts, they were equally fraudulent; the fraud in the latter case consisting in his assuming to know facts adverse to the interests of *Wells*, which he knew nothing about and which had no existence. *Miner v. Medbury*, 6 Wis. 295.

It would be unreasonable to hold *McGeoch* to the duty of exact knowledge of the amount of his investments, but it is not unreasonable to hold him to the duty of knowing approximately such amounts. The books of his two houses, at Chicago and Milwaukee, would have shown those facts with reasonable accuracy, had he consulted them; and it would not have been a difficult matter for him to obtain the information at very short notice. The county court found that he was no book-keeper, but this finding must be taken with some qualification; it probably means that he was not an expert book-keeper. It certainly cannot be truthfully said of a man who had capacity to conduct, and did conduct, commercial transactions amounting to millions of dollars in each year, usually with great success, and who can claim rank with the ablest business men in the country, that he has no knowledge of book-keeping. But, if he was unable to ascertain the amount of his investments by a personal examination of his own books, he had in his employment capable, expert book-keepers, who kept such books and knew all about their contents, who, if desired, would readily have given him the required information. In the circumstances of this case, there is no admissible theory upon which it can be truly said that such misrepresentations are consistent with honesty of purpose. He either knew that the representations were grossly false, or he made them recklessly, without stopping to inquire whether they were true or false. In either case, as before observed, the misrepresentations were fraudulent.

3. We are now to inquire whether *Wells* relied upon such false and fraudulent misrepresentations made by *McGeoch*, and made and performed the contract of July 17, 1883, on the faith of them, believing them to be true. The proofs tend to show that accounts of the transactions in Chicago in the lard deal were frequently transmitted to P. McGeoch & Co., at Milwaukee, and that *Wells* had free access to them. From this it is argued that he might have known, had he taken the trouble to investigate, the true condition of the deal at any given time, and that his failure to do so was negligence which is fatal to his right to recover in this action. It may be true that *Wells* had access to the means of thus ascertaining the condition of the deal and the amount invested therein by *McGeoch;* but it is certain that he did not do so. When we consider the extent and magnitude of the transactions of the deal, the length of time which they cover, and that none of them occurred

under the personal supervision of *Wells;* and the further facts, which clearly appear in the evidence, that *Wells* had most unbounded confidence in the ability and integrity of *McGeoch,* and in none of their numerous transactions had he given any personal attention thereto, but trusted entirely to *McGeoch,*— we cannot say that he was guilty of negligence in failing to keep himself personally advised of the condition of the deal. In other words, we think he had a right to rely upon the representations of *McGeoch* in respect to the amount of money invested by him in the deal, both of his own money and that of *Wells.*

As to the $139,000 of *Wells'* money in his hands, being the profit of the wheat deal of 1882, it is sufficient to say that *Wells* had not forgotten that he had that sum in the hands of *McGeoch,* but he supposed the dealings on their joint account, after the wheat deal, had reduced that amount to a little over $100,000. The representation of *McGeoch* in that behalf was, in effect (though not in words), that it had been so reduced. *Wells* had kept no account of those dealings; trusting, as he had a right to do, to the integrity of *McGeoch* to properly account for all sums in his hands. He was justifiably ignorant of the fact that their joint dealings, after the wheat deal, had resulted in a profit to him of over $100,000, which *McGeoch* had in his hands, leaving the $139,000 intact. *McGeoch* cannot now be heard to say, after *Wells* had trusted him so implicitly, that, although he grossly and fraudulently misrepresented the amount of their respective investments, still *Wells* had no right to believe his statements. We do not care to discuss this question further. The testimony convinces us that *Wells* had the right to rely upon the statement of *McGeoch* in the premises, that he did rely upon them implicitly, and that on the faith of them, and believing them to be true, he paid a very large sum of money to discharge their joint liabilities over and above what he ought to have paid on the basis upon which the transactions were settled, and what he would have paid had *McGeoch* truly stated his investments.

III. We are now to consider the law of the case applicable to the foregoing facts. The judgment of the county court is rested upon the propositions that the wheat deal of 1882 and the lard deal of 1883 contravened a statute of Illinois, and were illegal transactions; that *Wells* was obliged to trace his alleged right to recover in this action through such illegal transactions; and hence that he cannot recover therein.

In addition to pleading the illegality of those deals as defenses to the action, *McGeoch*, through his counsel, has expressed to us, in strong and earnest language, the wrong and injustice and the enormity of the evils which necessarily result from such illegal transactions, and has also denounced them as crimes against the public. Also, counsel cited several cases in which, in most impressive language, the immorality and illegality of such transactions are asserted. We cordially indorse all that was said to us on that subject in the arguments, as well as the language of the courts to which our attention has been called. When we said in *Melchoir v. McCarty*, 31 Wis. 252, that " all contracts which are repugnant to justice, or founded upon an immoral consideration, or which are against the general policy of the common law, or contrary to the provisions of any statute, are void; and that if a party claiming a right to recover a debt is obliged to trace his title or right to the debt through any such illegal contract, he cannot recover, because he cannot be allowed to prove the illegal contract as the foundation for his right of recovery," — we stated the rule as strongly as any court has stated it. To that rule this court has rigorously adhered. The rule is elementary, and we are not aware of any adjudication which has denied or shaken it. Numerous cases sustaining it will be found in the brief of the learned counsel for *McGeoch*. It is unnecessary to cite them here, but reference to them will be made in the report of the case. Thus far, we are in entire accord with *McGeoch*, his counsel, and the learned county judge.

We have no doubt the county court ruled correctly that the wheat deal of 1882 and the lard deal of 1883 were illegal transactions, under the statutes of the state of Illinois. They were also illegal at the common law, as against public policy. However, the nature of the wheat deal of 1882 seems to be of little importance in the case. *Wells'* share in the profits of that deal was left in the hands of *McGeoch*, and by him invested in the lard deal by consent and direction of *Wells*. Had *McGeoch* paid the $139,000 to *Wells*, and had *Wells* subsequently returned it, or a like amount, to *McGeoch*, to be invested in the lard deal, it would not be claimed, we think, by any one, that the illegality of the wheat deal would alone protect *McGeoch* from accounting to *Wells* for the money. We think the transaction which actually took place is, in legal effect, the exact equivalent of the one supposed.

2. If it be true, as the county court held, that, in order to establish his demand against *McGeoch*, *Wells* was obliged to trace his claim through such illegal transactions, the county court was right in dismissing the complaint. We are clearly of the opinion, however, that the ruling of the county court in this behalf is erroneous. The *gravamen* of this action is the fraud of *McGeoch* in misrepresenting to *Wells* the amount of their respective investments in the lard deal. Although, in form, the demand of the complaint is that the account of the transactions in that deal should be surcharged and corrected, yet, in substance and effect, the action is to recover damages suffered by *Wells* by reason of the fraud of *McGeoch*. The lard transaction is only involved incidentally in the case. It is resorted to only for

the purpose of ascertaining whether the representations made by *McGeoch* were true or false. There is no rule of law which prohibits a resort to an illegal contract for a purpose so purely incidental. The case is within the principle laid down in *Kiewert v. Rindskopf*, 46 Wis. 481. In the opinion by Mr. Justice Oᴙᴛᴏɴ, it is there said: " The *gravamen* of this action is the fraud practiced by the defendant in obtaining the two thousand dollars from the plaintiff by falsely representing that this sum was within and a part of the contract with Wight, and that the sum agreed to be paid to Wight was *three* thousand dollars, when in fact it was only *one* thousand dollars. Where money is so charged to have been obtained by fraudulent representations, the only material questions to be considered are: *First.* Were such representations intentional, material, and false? *Second.* Did they produce a false impression on the mind? *Third.* Were they the inducement of the payment? *Fourth.* Were they relied upon as being true? If these elements are present, they constitute a positive fraud without exception; and the matters to which such fraudulent representations relate, whether legal or illegal, will not lessen the fraud, or affect the liability of the guilty party. Kerr, Fraud & M. 73; *Smith v. Mariner*, 5 Wis. 551; *Kelley v. Sheldon*, 8 Wis. 258; *Reynell v. Sprye*, 21 Law J. Ch. 633."

There is no serious conflict of authority on this subject. Nearly all the cases involving the question are in harmony with *Kiewert v. Rindskopf*. Many of these cases are cited in the brief of counsel for *Wells*, and will be preserved in the statement of their argument in the report of the case.

All the conditions of a recovery required in *Kiewert v. Rindskopf* are established in this action; hence *Wells* is entitled to recover.

3. It is scarcely necessary to add that the full release of *McGeoch* by *Wells* from all claims and demands on

account of the lard deal, contained in the contract of July 17, 1883, is no obstacle to a recovery in this action; the contract having been obtained by the fraud of *McGeoch*. Such release may have excluded *Wells* from any share of the money remaining in the receiver's hands after his trust was executed, but it is not perceived how it can conclude *Wells* in this action, which is founded upon the fraud of *McGeoch*.

IV. The only remaining question is that of damages. The *gravamen* of the action being the fraud alleged, it is plain that *Wells* should recover all that he paid, by reason of such fraud, in excess of what he would have been required to pay on the agreed basis had *McGeoch* represented the investments truthfully. That is to say he may recover what he lost by reason of the fraud. But he cannot recover a sum which will reduce his payments on account of the lard deal below what he would have been required to pay on an accounting between the parties, for it cannot be correctly said that he has lost anything beyond that limit. The amount of such loss is easily ascertained. It is measured by the extent of the misrepresentations by *McGeoch* in his own favor, subject to the limitation just mentioned. We have already seen that these amount to $365,662.19 against *Wells*. Hence, in order to indemnify *Wells* for the consequences of *McGeoch's* fraud, the latter should pay *Wells* one half the amount last above stated, to wit, $182,831.10, less any sum necessary to be deducted in order to make *Wells'* payments equal the amount he ought to pay, as that amount would be ascertained were an account of the lard deal stated between the parties. This will place *Wells* in the same position that he would have been in had *McGeoch* represented their respective investments truly, and had the amount that each, upon the agreed basis, ought to have paid, been adjusted accordingly.

In order to find whether one half the aggregate of *McGeoch's* misrepresentations of the investments made by him in the lard deal for himself and for *Wells* exceeds the sum which *Wells* ought to recover, we will see how an account stated would stand:

Both parties paid..........	$1,838,498 76
One half is.........	$919,249 88
Wells agreed to pay, in addition........................	25,000 00
Wells ought to pay.................................	$944,249 38
He paid...	1,139,808 17
Wells overpaid..	$195,558 79
McGeoch ought to pay................................	$894,249 38
He paid only	698,690 59
McGeoch's deficiency..........................	$195,558 79

But there remained in the hands of the receiver after the business was closed and all demands paid, the sum of $27,836.32. In the absence of a special agreement to the contrary, this money belonged to the parties in equal shares. Hence, in the accounting, $13,918.16 should be deducted from *Wells'* overpayment, as above stated, to find the maximum limit of his recovery. Had there been no surplus, *Wells* would recover $182,831.10, and would be compelled to lose the difference between that sum and the amount he overpaid ($195,558.79), because of the illegality of the lard deal, which bars a recovery on an account stated. But, inasmuch as there was a surplus, we state the account in the interest of *McGeoch*, and find that the recovery should be reduced to $195,558.79 — $13,918.16= $181,640.63.

By the Court.— The judgment of the county court is reversed, and the cause will be remanded with directions to its successor, the superior court, to render judgment for the plaintiff for $181,640.63, and interest thereon at seven per cent. per annum from July 17, 1883, to the date of the judgment.

A motion by the respondent for a rehearing was denied March 27, 1888.

BROWN, Respondent, vs. PHILLIPS and others, Appellants.

January 13 — January 31, 1888.

(1–3) Constitutional law: Woman suffrage: Elections pertaining to school matters. (4) Pleading: Conclusions of law: Demurrer.

1. Under sec. 1, art. III, Const., the legislature may, by law approved by the people as therein prescribed, extend the right of suffrage to women.

2. An "election pertaining to school matters," within the meaning of ch. 211, Laws of 1885 (which gives to women the right to vote at such elections), is an election for the choosing of school officers or school employees. The mere fact that a city, county, or state officer, as incident to his office, is required to do some act which may affect schools (as where a mayor appoints school commissioners), does not make the election of such officer one pertaining to school matters.

3. *It would seem* that where school officers and other officers are required to be voted for upon the same ballot, the inspectors of election are not authorized to receive the votes of women even for such school officers.

4. In an action against inspectors of election for refusing to receive the vote of a woman, allegations of the complaint that the plaintiff "was a legally qualified elector . . . and was entitled to vote at such election," are held to be mere conclusions of law and not to be admitted by a demurrer.

APPEAL from the Circuit Court for *Racine* County.

The substance of the complaint is thus stated by Mr. Justice CASSODAY:

The complaint in this action alleges, in effect, that the plaintiff, a woman of lawful age and a citizen of the United States and of Wisconsin, was April 5, 1887, a resident of the Second ward of the city of Racine, and had so resided continuously for the nine years immediately prior thereto; that on said day the annual municipal election in and for said city was held in the several wards therein, for the election of mayor, city clerk and comptroller, justice of the peace, assessor, city marshal, an alderman for each ward, and a supervisor; that said election was one "pertaining to school matters;" that the defendants were the qualified and acting inspectors of election in and for said ward, constituting one of the election districts in said city, at said municipal election held on that day at the usual polling place in and for said ward; that the plaintiff was on said day a legally qualified elector at said election, and entitled to vote in said ward, and possessed none of the disabilities enumerated or referred to in ch. 211, Laws of 1885; that within the prescribed hours for voting, at said voting place in and for said ward, she did offer publicly to said inspectors, then present, a ballot with the names of candidates thereon for the respective offices of mayor, clerk and comptroller, alderman, and supervisor, and with the names of candidates stricken out thereon for the respective offices of justice of the peace, assessor, and city marshal; that said inspectors, acting as such, did then and there refuse to receive and rejected said ballot, and did then and there neglect and refuse to administer to the plaintiff the oaths and each of them prescribed by secs. 36, 38, R. S.; that she at the same time delivered to said inspectors her affidavit, together with the affidavits of two freeholders of the ward, proving her said residence and excusing her want of registration, and read the same to said inspectors, after which they did still refuse to receive said ballot from the plaintiff or permit her to vote at said election, to her damage $5,000, for which amount she demands judgment.

The defendants appealed from an order overruling a general demurrer to the complaint.

D. H. Flett, attorney, and *T. W. Spence*, of counsel, for the appellants, contended: (1) Ch. 211, Laws of 1885, does not confer the right of suffrage upon women except in elections pertaining directly and exclusively to school matters. (2) The legislature has no power under the constitution to confer the right of suffrage upon women. When the constitution prescribes the functions of departments of the government, or of its officers, or territorial limits for governmental subdivisions, or qualifications for the exercise of political rights, there is thereby secured to the public, protection from legislative change, enlargement, or circumscription of such departments, functions, or rights. See *Gough v. Dorsey*, 27 Wis. 131; *Van Slyke v. Trempealeau Co. F. M. F. Ins. Co.* 39 id. 390; *Chandler v. Nash*, 5 Mich. 409; *State ex rel. Crawford v. Hastings*, 10 Wis. 525; *McCabe v. Mazzuchelli*, 13 id. 534; *State ex rel. Kennedy v. Brunst*, 26 id. 412; *State ex rel. Wood v. Goldstucker*, 40 id. 124; *Att'y Gen. v. McDonald*, 3 id. 805; *People ex rel. Bolton v. Albertson*, 55 N. Y. 50; *Page v. Allen*, 58 Pa. St. 338; *Dells v. Kennedy*, 49 Wis. 556; *Minor v. Happersett*, 21 Wall. 163, 170, 172; Cooley on Const. Law, 251; *People v. Draper*, 15 N. Y. 543; Cooley's Const. Lim. (4th ed.), 104. The proviso in subd. 4, sec. 1, art. III, Const., under which the law in question was passed, provides that the legislature may extend, by law, the right of suffrage to persons not therein *enumerated*. The word *enumerate* is defined by Webster as " to number, to tell off, or count by numbers;" and it must refer to the four classes of persons distinctively numbered or told off in subd. 1–4 of the section. The legislature might, in the manner indicated, add to or enlarge those classes, but could not change the indispensable qualifications of sex, age, and residence in the state. This construction of the constitution has just been recognized by the legislature and the people by passing a constitutional amendment by which an express power has been vested,

within certain limits, to fix the necessary time of residence
of any voter in his election district. And the history of
the proviso and of the whole of art. III, in the constitutional
convention, shows that it was intended to limit the power
of the legislature within the provisions of the first paragraph of sec. 1.   (3) An inspector of election is not liable
to an action for damages to a person claiming to be an
elector, for refusing to receive his vote in a new and doubtful
case, in the absence of proof of malice. *Jenkins v. Waldron,*
11 Johns. 114; *Weckerly v. Geyer,* 11 Serg. & R. 35; *Caul-
field v. Bullock,* 18 B. Mon. 495; *Morgan v. Dudley,* id. 693;
Carter v. Harrison, 5 Blackf. 138; *Gordon v. Farrar,* 2
Doug. 411; *Peavey v. Robbins,* 3 Jones, Law, 339; *Rail v.
Potts,* 8 Humph. 225; *Fausler v. Parsons,* 6 W. Va. 486;
State v. M'Donald, 4 Harr. (Del.), 555; *Dwight v. Rice,* 5
La. Ann. 580; *Bevard v. Hoffman,* 18 Md. 479; *Zeiler v.
Chapman,* 54 Mo. 502; *U. S. v. Gillis,* 2 Cranch C. C. 44.
The sole reasoning upon which the decision of this question
in *Gillespie v. Palmer,* 20 Wis. 557-8, is founded, is inappli-
cable to the case at bar; and the opinion in that case has
been subjected to the animadversion of this court more than
once. See *Sawyer v. Dodge Co. Mut. Ins. Co.* 37 Wis. 524;
Bound v. Wis. Cent. R. Co. 45 id. 579.

For the respondent there was a brief by *Rowlands &
Rowland,* and oral argument by *W. W. Rowlands* and *I. C.
Sloan.* They contended, *inter alia,* that ch. 211, Laws of
1885, is a valid act.   A state constitution is not a grant but
a restriction upon the powers of the legislature; and the national and state constitutions impose the only limitations
upon the legislative power.   To warrant a court in declaring
an act of the legislature void and of no effect, there must be
a conflict between said act and these fundamental instruments, and such conflict must be clear and free from reasonable doubt. Sec. 1, art. III, Const. of Wis., therefore
confers upon all the persons mentioned therein the right of

suffrage, and this right the legislature cannot take away, abridge, or impair, except for crime. The proviso contained in subd. 4 of sec. 1, does not *confer* upon the legislature power to extend suffrage. That power already exists, and the object of the proviso is merely to *abridge* that power by declaring that no such law shall be in force until the same shall have been submitted to the people, etc.

Inspectors of election are ministerial officers, and malice in the rejecting of ballots by them need not be alleged or proved. *Gillespie v. Palmer*, 20 Wis. 544; *Lombard v. Olliver*, 8 Allen, 1; *Gates v. Neal*, 23 Pick. 308; *Capen v. Foster*, 12 id. 485; *Bacon v. Benchley*, 2 Cush. 100; *Goetcheus v. Matthewson*, 61 N. Y. 420.

The municipal election held in the city of Racine on April 5, 1887, was an election pertaining to school matters, such as was contemplated by ch. 211, Laws of 1885. The commissioners who constitute the board of education in Racine are appointed by the *mayor* and confirmed by the *common council.* All contracts entered into by the board, except the employment of teachers, are required to be countersigned by the *city comptroller.* The legislative functions of the county are exercised by the board of *supervisors*, in which the city is represented. For these officers the plaintiff attempted to vote; and it is manifest that an election at which they are chosen necessarily pertains to school matters. If women cannot vote at the municipal election, they can have no voice in the control or management of the schools of Racine; and the act of 1885 will be inoperative in that city and, indeed, in most if not all of the cities of the state. The only elections pertaining *exclusively* to school matters are to be found in school-district meetings. If the legislature had intended a limitation to school districts of this right of suffrage, they certainly would have used terms to designate such intent. The clear intention of the act is, in recognition of the vast importance to the state of school matters, and assigning that as a reason, to extend to women full and complete suffrage at all elections affecting in any manner the schools of the state.

The following opinion was filed January 31, 1888:

CASSODAY, J.   The plaintiff, a woman of lawful age and a citizen of this state and the United States, and long a resident of the Second ward of the city of Racine, claimed the right to vote under and by virtue of ch. 211, Laws of 1885; and accordingly offered to vote in that ward at the last annual municipal election in that city, for candidates for the respective offices of mayor, city clerk and comptroller, alderman, and supervisor.   The defendants, as inspectors of such election for that ward, refused to receive her vote or allow her to swear it in.   This action is to recover damages sustained by reason of such refusal.

1. It is contended on the part of the defendants that the chapter under which such right is claimed is wholly inoperative, because it was never adopted as required for an amendment to the constitution by art. XII, Const. of Wis. That article requires that any such amendment "shall be agreed to by a majority of the members elected to each of the two houses," in two successive legislatures, and then approved and ratified by the people, before it becomes binding.   The act in question was only so agreed to by one legislature, and then approved and ratified by the people at the general election in the following year.   There is no claim that such adoption was in compliance with that article of the constitution.   On the contrary, it is contended on the part of the plaintiff that under another article of the constitution it was competent to "extend, by law, the right of suffrage" to women, if "submitted to a vote of the people at a general election, and approved by a majority of all the votes cast at such election."   Subd. 4, sec. 1, art. III, Const. of Wis.   Such was manifestly the opinion of

the members of the legislature enacting it. It is conceded that the chapter in question was so agreed to, and then so submitted and so approved. The contention is, however, that women do not belong to the class of "persons" to whom "the right of suffrage" may thus be extended "by law." The argument is that such "right of suffrage" could only be so extended "by law" to such "persons" as were not "enumerated" in "classes" in that article, but otherwise having the qualifications therein required. That is to say, according to the argument, such right could only be so extended to such "male" persons, "of the age of twenty-one years or upwards," as had "resided in the state for one year next preceding any election," and did not belong "to either of the . . . classes" therein "enumerated." Sec. 1, art. III, Const. of Wis., amended by ch. 272, Laws of 1882. Omitting the clauses not bearing upon the question here being considered, and the section reads: "Every *male* person of the age of *twenty-one years* or upwards, *belonging to either of the following classes,* who shall have *resided* in the state for *one year* next preceding any election, shall be deemed a *qualified elector* at such election: (1) Citizens of the United States; (2) persons of foreign birth, who shall have declared their intention to become citizens; . . . (3) persons of Indian blood, who have . . . ; (4) civilized persons of Indian descent, not members of any tribe: *provided,* that the legislature may at any time *extend, by law,* the right of suffrage *to persons not herein enumerated,"* etc.

It will be observed that the section only declares such persons to be qualified electors as belong to one of the four enumerated classes, each of which must be composed of males of the requisite age, having the requisite duration of residence. Thus, it is said to have been within the power of the legislature to so extend the right of suffrage to "every male colored inhabitant," of the requisite age and duration of residence, by ch. 137, Laws of 1849, as was held, if not conceded, in *Gillespie v. Palmer*, 20 Wis. 544. This removed one of the conditions which formerly attached to the first class, which then read, "(1) *White* citizens of the United States."

The argument that the right of suffrage could only be extended in this way to other *classes* of persons not therein enumerated, but having the general qualifications mentioned, is certainly very plausible. But the language is not "that the legislature may at any time extend, by law, the right of suffrage to" such other "male" persons or classes having the general qualifications mentioned, but "to *persons* not *herein* enumerated." In neither of the four classes do we find the word "male," and yet it is only male persons of the classes described, and having the other qualifications mentioned, that are therein declared to be qualified electors. But the enumeration therein mentioned is not confined to such male persons thus classified, but extends to any persons therein "[*herein*] enumerated;" and may refer to any persons mentioned anywhere in the section. If this is so, then suffrage may be so extended to any persons not mentioned in the section. Certainly women were not therein enumerated when this chapter was enacted. "Every male person," however, was mentioned therein, and then by subsequent language his qualification as an "elector" was made to depend upon age, residence, and other conditions named.

It is true, as claimed, that this section of the constitution must be regarded as an implied limitation upon the legislative power of the state. Otherwise there would have been no object in making it a part of the constitution. But it contains a proviso which, to a certain extent, prevents such limitation from becoming operative. This is done by affirmatively declaring "that the legislature may at any time *extend, by law*, the right of suffrage to *persons not herein* enumerated." The power to thus extend the right of suffrage is certainly not in terms confined to males. Had it been so intended it could have been very easily so expressed. Such confinement can only rest on mere inference, if at all; and such inference must arise from the circumstance that only certain classes of male persons are therein made qualified electors, leaving other classes still disqualified. But the extension of such right was expressly authorized "to persons not" therein "enumerated," generally, without any mention of sex. This preservation of power to so extend the right of suffrage was manifestly intended to relieve the legislature to that extent from the limitations which otherwise would have fastened upon it. To that extent, then, the power of the legislature, when so approved, was left unlimited. The exercise of such power is not restricted to males, nor prohibited from being exercised as to females, unless by implication of a remote and argumentative character.

The question is not whether the constitution conferred the power to so extend the right of suffrage to women, but whether it anywhere expressly or by *necessary* implication prohibited the exercise of such power. It is not contended that there is any prohibition upon the exercise of such power in the constitution of the United States. There was a time when it was strenuously urged that the fourteenth amendment of that instrument, giving to all the right of citizenship, and prohibiting any state from abridging " the privileges or immunities of citizens of the United States," also conferred the right of suffrage upon women, but the supreme court of the United States held otherwise. *Minor v. Happersett*, 21 Wall. 162. According to their construction of the recent amendments, the matter of suffrage was left with the several states, subject to certain conditions. *Ibid.; U. S. v. Reese*, 92 U. S. 214; *U. S. v. Cruikshank*, 92 U. S. 542. The limitation upon the power to so extend the right of suffrage to women must, therefore, be found in the constitution and laws of this state, or it does not exist at all. It is certainly not to be found there in express terms. Nor do any of us think it can be found there by *necessary* implication. Mere inferences and doubts as to the true construction of the language employed will not justify the abrogation of a legislative enactment. To authorize the court to declare the act void, it should clearly appear to be in violation of the organic law. This is the established rule. We must hold the act in question to be a valid law.

2. Did ch. 211, Laws of 1885, confer upon the plaintiff the right to vote at the election mentioned for the officers named? The act is entitled: "An act relating to the exercise of the right of suffrage by women *upon school matters.*" The first section declares, in effect, that "every woman who is a citizen of this state, of the age of twenty-one years or upwards, . . . who has resided within the state one year, and in the *election district* where she offers to vote ten days next preceding *any election pertaining to school matters*, shall have a right to vote *at such* election." The second section provided for the submission of the act for the approval or disapproval of the electors of the state at the general election in November, 1886. The third section provided for taking the vote thereon "by separate ballot," and the form of such ballot in these words: "For woman suffrage *in school matters*," or "Against woman suffrage *in school matters.*" On the part of the defendants, it is claimed that such right only extends to the voting directly for school officers. Upon the part of the plaintiff, it is contended that such right extends to the voting for any officer having any duties pertaining to school matters however remotely.

In the city of Racine, unlike some cities in the state, the charter provides that "the public schools in said city shall be under the supervision and management of the board of education, consisting of one school commissioner from each ward. Such commissioners shall be appointed by the mayor.

subject to confirmation by the common council." Title XV, Charter. [See tit. XV, ch. 313, Laws of 1876, as amended by sec. 10, ch. 59, Laws of 1879, sec. 13, ch. 133, Laws of 1882, and sec. 15, ch. 122, Laws of 1887.] All contracts entered into by such board, except with teachers, are to be countersigned by the city comptroller, who is to keep an account of the liabilities incurred by the board for each current year, and report the same to the council. The board of supervisors, in which cities are represented, exercises all the legislative functions of the county as a body corporate. Secs. 662, 669, 670, R. S. For these reasons, it is claimed that the election of each of the four officers named — mayor, clerk and comptroller, alderman, and supervisor — was "an election pertaining to school matters," within the meaning of the act. It is moreover claimed that the words employed in the act were aptly chosen, and clearly express such right to vote at such municipal election for such officers. But when asked whether such right also extended to the election of governor and other state officers, the able counsel, notwithstanding his special study of the subject, frankly admitted that he was not yet prepared to answer the question. If the plaintiff had the right to cast the vote offered, then it would be very difficult, if not impossible, to give any substantial reason for rejecting her vote for most, if not all, state officers,— for they certainly perform duties no more remotely "pertaining to school matters" than such municipal officers, and some of them far more directly. The same is true as to the several county officers, members of the legislature, judges of the courts, and perhaps members of Congress. In fact, an appeal was made for such extended construction, based upon the supposed social, ethical, and political right to such suffrage. Had such appeal been addressed to the legislature, having power to act in the premises, it might have had the effect of securing the extended rights now contended for, and in such clear and unmistakable language that no one could fail to comprehend them. But, as conceded by counsel, courts have no power to grant suffrage to any one, but are confined to the exercise of judicial powers. To attempt, under the guise of a liberal construction, to extend the act to objects beyond its purpose, would be nothing less than the usurpation of powers not only belonging to the legislature but to the qualified electors of the state. The same would be true of any attempt, under the guise of a narrow construction, to withdraw the act from any of the objects within its legitimate scope. The plain duty of the court is, under the well-established rules of law, to declare the intention of the legislature as expressed in the act,— nothing adding, nothing subtracting. When the language of an act is clear and explicit, then construction is not permissible; or, rather, the act construes itself. But when the language is ambiguous, we may resort to the history of the bill in the legislature, as well as to the established rules of construction.

On March 10, 1885, "the special joint committee on woman suffrage," in the legislature, reported three several senate bills, numbered respectively 164, 208, 277, and one memorial to Congress, numbered 2, senate, with recommendations for and against. Senate Jour. 325. Bill No. 164 S. was "A bill to extend the right of suffrage to women," and was indefinitely postponed by the senate, March 11, 1885. Senate Jour. 347. The memorial to Congress, No. 2 S., was "for a sixteenth amendment to the constitution of the United States, granting the right of suffrage to women;" "was refused engrossment and third reading" by the senate, March 13, 1885, and thus defeated. Senate Jour. 366. Bill No. 277 S. was "A bill to grant municipal suffrage to women;" and "was indefinitely postponed," March 17, 1885. Senate Jour. 383. Bill No. 208 S. was "A bill relating to the exercise of the right of suffrage by women upon school matters;" and passed the senate, March 13, 1885. Senate Jour. 367. That bill subsequently passed the assembly with amendments, which were concurred in by the senate, and the same is the law in question.

Thus it appears that within a few days of the time when the bill incorporated into this law passed the senate, that body effectually defeated "a bill to extend the right of suffrage to women," a memorial to Congress for an " amendment to the constitution of the United States granting the right of suffrage to women," and " a bill to grant municipal suffrage to women." In view of these facts, can any impartial mind deliberately conclude that, notwithstanding the nature of the bills and memorial thus defeated, and some of them after a contest at a special hour previously fixed, the same body could for a moment suppose that by this enactment they were securing to women the same rights of suffrage thus proposed to be secured by the several bills and memorial thus defeated, or any of them? An affirmative answer to this question cannot be secured on the theory of the survival of the fittest. It can only be obtained by convicting an honorable body of intelligent men of the folly of defeating what they wanted to secure, or adopting what they wanted to defeat. Still, if such is the manifest purpose of the act as expressed in the language employed, then the courts are bound to so declare, any inferences arising from the history of the bill to the contrary notwithstanding.

Turning to the act itself, we are necessarily forced to the conviction that it was never intended thereby to extend an unlimited right of suffrage to women. If it had, the words, "upon school matters," never would have been embraced in the title; and the words, "pertaining to school matters," ever would have been left in the first section; and the form of the ballot in submitting the vote would not have contained the words, "in school matters." These several ex-

pressions are necessarily limitations upon the word "suffrage" and the word "election." While the words "suffrage" and "election" are each general in themselves, yet,
as here used, they must each, upon well-established rules of
construction, "be restrained unto the fitness of the matter,"— that is "school matters." *Gillespie v. Palmer*, 20
Wis. 559; *Webster v. Morris*, 66 Wis. 366. It was only
the right to vote at "any *election* pertaining to school matters" that was thereby attempted to be conferred. This is
in accordance with the action of the senate in defeating the
bill and the memorial, in each of which it was proposed to
give women the unlimited right of suffrage.

The bill, as it originally passed the senate, contained, in
place of the words, "and in the election district where she
offers to vote," now found in the act, the words, "and within
the city or town in which she claims a right to vote." The
striking out of these last words, and inserting the former,
was made by way of amendment in the assembly, March 26,
1885 (Assem. Jour. 814), and was concurred in the next day
by the senate (Senate Jour. 484). One of the apparent objects in making such change would seem to have been to
dispel any inference which might otherwise have arisen
favorable to the right of women to vote at town meetings
or municipal elections, the latter of which had been defeated
some ten days before. The change seemed to contemplate
that the voting would only be in "election districts," in con-
tradistinction to the election of officers generally in towns
and cities. School officers are mostly elected in districts.
Secs. 424–432, 703, R. S. Of course, a town, village, ward,
or city, or some subdivision thereof, may constitute an election district; and one object of making the change may
have been in view of the right of women to vote for all
school officers.

Much was said, upon the argument, as to the meaning of
the word "pertaining." It was claimed to be of ancient

origin. It is said to be a sacred word. That may depend upon its use, and the subject to which it is applied. Here it is applied to schools, than which few things are more sacred, and in which none are more interested than women. We apprehend, however, that the meaning of the word is well understood. Manifestly, such right to vote is only given at an "*election* pertaining" or relating "to school matters." It is only "at *such* election"— that is to say, at such qualified election — that such right of suffrage can be exercised. And what are we to understand by the word "election" as thus qualified? When standing alone it is defined as "(1) the act of choosing; choice; the act of selecting one or more from others. Hence, appropriately, (2) the act of choosing a person to fill an office or employment, by any manifestation of preference, as by vote, uplifted hands, or *viva voce.*" Imperial Dict. Webster gives substantially the same definition, but uses the word "ballot" instead of vote. Such qualified election, therefore, must mean "the act of choosing a person to fill an office or employment" in "school matters;" otherwise "*such* election" would not pertain or relate to school matters. An election for the choosing of any school officers or school employees would be an "election pertaining to school matters;" and after very careful consideration we are convinced that the choosing or selecting of any other officers is not an "election pertaining to school matters," within the meaning of the act.

It is the character of the *election itself* which determines the right of women to participate in it. The mere fact that a city, county, or state officer may, as incident to his office, be required to do some act which may more or less remotely affect schools, does not make the election of such officer one pertaining to school matters. The act of the person so choosing or selecting by vote or ballot, must itself relate to school matters. Under the charter of Racine the mayor was required to nominate, and

with the approval of the common council appoint, school
commissioners, whose duties pertained to school matters, but
the act of electing or choosing a mayor was in no sense the
act of electing or choosing such school commissioners.
Much less was it so with the other officers proposed to be
voted for on the ballot offered. In some cities such commissioners are elected by the people. Where the statutes
require such commissioners, or other school officers, to be
voted for upon the same "ballot or piece of paper," upon
which are the names of other "persons voted for by such
elector," it would seem that the inspectors of election are
not authorized to receive the votes of women, even for
such school officers, since to do so would open the door for
illegal votes to be cast for such other persons without any
possibility of prevention or detection. The obvious reason
for this is that such inspectors are expressly forbidden to
open any ballot, or to permit it to be opened or examined,
but are required to deposit the same in the box. Sec. 32,
R. S. After such deposit, it would, of course, become impossible to tell which ballots had been cast by electors
qualified to vote for all officers to be chosen at such election, and those which were cast by persons only qualified
to vote for such school officers. The oath of inspectors requires them to perform their duties as such, "according to
law." Sec. 28, R. S. Any departure might subject them
to severe punishment. It may, therefore, require further
legislation to secure the full benefits of the rights sought
to be conferred by ch. 211, Laws of 1885. In this respect,
it may be like many provisions of our state and national
constitution, which do not execute themselves, but require
legislation in order to become effective.

3. The complaint alleges that the plaintiff "was a legally
qualified elector at such municipal election, . . . and
was entitled to vote . . . at said election." These allegations must be regarded as mere conclusions of law from

JANUARY TERM, 1888.   255

Schilling, Adm'x, etc. vs. The Chicago, Milwaukee & St. Paul R. Co.

the facts therein stated. The demurrer was an admission of such facts, but not of such mere conclusions. *Pratt v· Lincoln Co.* 61 Wis. 62; *Williams v. Williams,* 63 Wis. 72.

By the Court.— The order of the circuit court is reversed, and the cause is remanded for further proceedings according to law.

A motion for a rehearing was denied March 27, 1888.

———

Schilling, Administratrix, etc., Appellant, vs. The Chicago, Milwaukee & St. Paul Railway Company, Respondent.

February 28 — March 27, 1888.

· *Railroads: Negligence: Injury to persons on track: Unlawful speed of train: Contributory negligence: Nonsuit.*

Plaintiff's intestate was killed upon the track of the defendant's railroad by a freight train approaching from behind him, but which he knew to be due about that time, and which could have been seen for a distance of nearly half a mile. When the train was about forty rods behind him he was walking along a pathway beside the track, and when it was within about forty feet of him he attempted to cross the track without having looked back or listened for the train. *Held,* that although there was evidence tending to show that the train was running at an unlawful rate of speed and that signals were not given by bell or whistle, a nonsuit was properly granted on the ground of the contributory negligence of the deceased. Taylor, J., dissents.

APPEAL from the Circuit Court for *Dodge* County.

Action to recover damages for the death of the plaintiff's husband alleged to have been caused by the negligence of the defendant. The facts are sufficiently stated in the opinion.

Harlow Pease, for the appellant, contended, *inter alia,*

that it cannot be presumed that the deceased did not look or listen. His negligence in that regard must be *proved*. *Hoye v. C. & N. W. R. Co.* 67 Wis. 1, 15; *Hoyt v. Hudson*, 41 id. 111; *Massoth v. D. & H. Canal Co.* 64 N. Y. 524–529; *Guggenheim v. L. S. & M. S. R. Co.* 9 Western Rep. 903, 33 N. W. Rep. 161. The fact that the train was run at an unlawful rate of speed is competent evidence of the *plaintiff's care.* He had a right to assume that the defendant would obey the law and not bring injury upon him by its violation. *Nutter v. B. & M. R. Co.* 60 N. H. 483-5; *State v. B. & M. R. Co.* 58 id. 408–410; *Clark v. B. & M. R. Co.* 10 Atl. Rep. (N. H.), 676; *Klanowski v. G. T. R. Co.* 57 Mich. 525; Whittaker's Smith on Neg. 419; *Haas v. C. & N. W. R. Co.* 41 Wis. 44–50; *Newson v. N. Y. C. R. Co.* 29 N. Y. 383. The evidence shows that when the deceased first came upon the track from the highway there was no train on the track which could have been seen by him, and that if the train had run at the lawful rate of speed he would not have been overtaken by it, but would have crossed the track in safety and would have left the track to go upon his own premises when the train was still sixty rods away. The unlawful speed of the train was therefore the direct, immediate cause of the injury, and the fact that the deceased walked on the track did not in any way contribute thereto.

Upon another principle the nonsuit was error. " Where a person walking on a railroad track is run over and killed by an engine belonging to the railroad company, the company is responsible in damages for such killing, though the deceased was guilty of a want of ordinary care and prudence in so walking on the track, *provided* it appear that the accident would not have occurred if the agents of the railroad company had used ordinary prudence and care (in running the engine which caused the killing) in giving reasonable and usual signals of its approach and in *keeping a reasonable lookout.*" *Baltimore & O. R. Co. v. State*, 36

Md. 366; *Brown v. H. & St. J. R. Co.* 50 Mo. 461; *Dunk-man v. W., St. L. & P. R. Co.* 10 West. Rep. (Mo.), 396–400.

For the respondent there was a brief by *John- W. Cary*, attorney, and *Burton Hanson*, of counsel, and oral argument by *Mr. Hanson*. To the point that the deceased was negligent in failing to look and listen before he went upon the track, they cited, besides cases cited in the opinion: *Railroad Co. v. Houston*, 95 U. S. 697; *Grethen v. C., M. & St. P. R. Co.* 22 Fed. Rep. 609; *Holland v. C., M. & St. P. R. Co.* 18 id. 247; *O'Donnell v. M. P. R. Co.* 7 Mo. App. 190; *Mulherrin v. D., L. & W. R. Co.* 81 Pa. St. 366; *Terre Haute & I. R. Co. v. Graham*, 12 Am. & Eng. R. Cas. 80; *Carlin v. C., R. I. & P. R. Co.* 37 Iowa, 316–323; *Murphy v. C., R. I. & P. R. Co.* 45 id. 661; *Chicago, B. & Q. R. Co. v. Olson*, 12 Bradw. 245; *Bresnahan v. M. C. R. Co.* 49 Mich. 410; *Lake Shore & M. S. R. Co. v. Hart*, 87 Ill. 534; *Frazer v. S. & N. A. R. Co.* 81 Ala. 185; *Mobile & O. R. Co. v. Stroud*, 64 Miss. 784.

ORTON, J. The undisputed facts of this case seem to be as follows: A very long and heavily loaded freight train of the company, being hauled by a very large and heavy engine, was going from the junction at Watertown north-westerly, a short time before 1 o'clock in the afternoon, somewhat behind the time of half-past 12 o'clock, the regular time of its passing at that place, and where and when it had passed, about on time, for about eleven years before. The wind was blowing strongly from the northwest,—the direction in which the train was moving. From the place where the accident occurred, and southeastwardly towards the junction, the track was open and straight for nearly half a mile, and the train could have been easily seen that distance by any one at the place of the accident, and any one on or near the track at such place could have been easily seen by the engineer on the train for that distance. When the train was about forty rods behind him, the deceased was walking on a pathway about three feet on the south side of the railroad track, and towards the northwest, and was so seen by the engineer. When the train came within about forty feet of him, the deceased attempted to cross over the track, apparently for the purpose of going towards his house, about 200 feet north or northwest of the track at that point, and where he had lived for a great many years. The attention of the engineer had been diverted by some duty to be performed in a place on the engine from which he could not look ahead on the track, until the train had come within said forty feet of the deceased, just as he attempted to so cross the track in front of the engine. Whether at that time signals were given by whistle or bell or both, is a question in dispute, as also whether the usual signals had been given in crossing the streets of Watertown in the vicinity and before arriving at that point. An attempt was made to stop the train before it reached the deceased, but it was too near him to be successful, and the train was stopped only after the locomotive had passed over and beyond him about eighty feet. The rate of speed the train was going at the time was also a question in dispute. The circuit court, on these facts, granted a nonsuit in the case.

The negligence of the company, if any, consisted in either the signals not having been given or the train having been run with greater speed than six miles an hour; and both of these questions, depending upon a conflict of evidence, were proper to be determined by the jury and not by the court. We presume, therefore, that the only ground upon which the nonsuit was granted was the contributory negligence of the deceased. The deceased knew that this freight train was due at that place about that time, and therefore had reason to expect and look out for it. It is quite evident that he did not look to see whether this train was coming towards him, in all that distance of at least forty rods, or he would have kept it within observation up to the time of his attempt to cross over the track; and that he did not look towards the train within' that last forty feet, or he would have stopped, or jumped from the track instantly to save his life. The conclusion is inevitable, therefore, that the deceased did not look, and did not listen. He used neither his eyes nor his ears in this place of great danger. The train made a great noise, and, as the engineer testified, as much as the whistle or bell could make. The strong head-wind may have prevented the sound of either coming to the deceased. But he was aware of this disadvantage, as well as of the fact that the train was due and might be expected at any moment. Was he guilty of a want of ordinary care and prudence in thus attempting to cross over the track without hesitating to listen, or look in the direction from which he had reason to expect the approaching train? Can we say that an ordinarily prudent man, with the same knowledge of the time when the train was due, and having lived so near the railroad at that place so long a time, would not have looked or listened before crossing the track? He took no precaution, and used no means whatever, to avoid the danger. He used no care and exercised no prudence whatever. He might as well have been blind and deaf. Did not his own want of common care and ordinary prudence contribute to the injury that resulted in his death? It seems to us that this is one of the clearest cases for the application of the rule that it was his duty to have looked or listened before he attempted to cross over the track,— a place of so much risk and danger. If he had looked back at any time within the distance of that forty rods, and especially before he turned to cross over the track, he would have saved himself from death.

Schilling, Adm'x, etc. vs. The Chicago, Milwaukee & St. Paul R. Co.

The cases in this court touching this question are sufficiently numerous and to the point, without at this time concerning ourselves about cases elsewhere. The last case in which this duty to "look or listen" has been considered, and which is cited by the learned counsel of the appellant with the positive assurance that it is authority in point against this nonsuit, is that of *Hoye v. C. & N. W. R. Co.* 67 Wis. 1. In that case the circumstances are very peculiar, and quite different from those of this case in most all respects. It is sufficient to cite the language of Mr. Justice CASSODAY, in the opinion in that case, to show its entire inapplicability to this. He said: "Undoubtedly she was bound *to use her eyes in looking and her ears in hearing,* and to act prudently upon the knowledge thus acquired." "This being the fixed rule of law, it cannot be conclusively presumed that Mrs. Hoye *did not, at the time and place in question, look and listen,* and prudently act upon the knowledge thus acquired." In this case, it *can* be conclusively presumed that the deceased did not look or listen, for, if he had done so, he would most certainly have avoided the danger. There can be no other possible conclusion. It will be noticed that in that case the rule is restated and reaffirmed that a person placed in such circumstances must use his eyes to look and see, or his ears to listen and hear, the approaching train, or be guilty of such a want of care and prudence, and of such contributory negligence, as to preclude a recovery. *Delaney v. M. & St. P. R. Co.* 33 Wis. 70; *Kearney v. C., M. & St. P. R. Co.* 47 Wis. 144; and *Williams v. C., M. & St. P. R. Co.* 64 Wis. 1,— are closely in point. In this last case, the counsel of the respondent has collated numerous decisions in this and other states affirming this rule. See, also, *Rothe v. M. & St. P. R. Co.* 21 Wis. 256; *Langhoff v. M. & P. du C. R. Co.* 23 Wis. 43; *Haas v. C. & N. W. R. Co.* 41 Wis. 44. If we should hold that the deceased was not guilty of contributory negligence in this case, it would vir-

tually overrule all of the above cases. We think that the
circuit court did not err in granting a nonsuit in the case.

TAYLOR, J. This action was brought to recover damages
for killing the husband of the appellant while walking upon
the track of the respondent's railroad within the limits of
the city of Watertown. The accident happened shortly
after noon on the 27th day of October, 1885. The following are the material circumstances shown on the trial:
The track of the road as it leaves the junction with the
Chicago & Northwestern Railway Company's track at
Watertown runs in nearly a westerly direction for about
100 rods and then turns to a northwesterly course. The
place where the accident happened is 153 rods from the
point where the track takes a straight line on its northwesterly course. This 153 rods is an up-grade, going to
the northwest, and the track is on an embankment three or
four feet above the surrounding surface of the land. When
the train came around the curve and started on the straight
course up the grade, the deceased was on the track or along
side of it on the westerly side, traveling to the northwest,
his back towards the train, about 120 rods ahead of the engine, and there is no evidence showing that he looked behind him from the time the train came around the curve
until he was struck and killed by it. There was a strong
wind blowing from the northwest in the face of the deceased and in the face of the engine. After the deceased
was discovered on the track by the engineer just as he
came to the straight track, until immediately before he was
struck, no notice was taken of his movements by any one
on the train or engine until the engine was within forty
feet of the deceased, when the engineer claims it was too
late to stop the train. No attempt seems to have been
made by the deceased to get off the track before he was
struck. The evidence on the part of the plaintiff tends

strongly to show that no whistle was sounded or bell rung on the engine before striking the deceased. The engineer testifies that the whistle was sounded and the bell rung when he discovered that he was within forty feet of deceased, and that efforts were then made to stop the train. The evidence is not very clear as to how far the train ran after the engineer says he saw the deceased on the track forty feet ahead of the train. He thinks the train was stopped eighty or ninety feet beyond the place where the deceased was struck, or from 120 to 130 feet from the place where he saw him within forty feet of the engine. There was other evidence tending to show that the train ran considerably farther before it was stopped. This fact was material only as tending to show the speed with which the train was running at the time, the plaintiff's evidence tending to show that it was running at the rate of from twelve to fifteen miles an hour, and the engineer claiming that it was running at the rate of about six miles an hour. The train was composed of thirty-two cars and a caboose, drawn by a ten-wheel engine, nineteen to twenty-six inches stroke, called by railroad men a " Mogul."

The evidence tended to show, and it was not controverted by the railroad company, that the track of their road, from what is called the plank-road crossing to the northwest as far at least as the house of the deceased, had been used for many years by the citizens of that part of the city lying northwesterly of the plank-road crossing as a foot way, to the knowledge of, and without objection by, the railroad company. Deceased was about sixty-two years old, a mechanic of ordinary intelligence, and had lived in the vicinity of the railroad track for many years. It was claimed by the plaintiff that the deceased was coming from his work in the city to his dinner, and that he came along the plank-road and then took the railroad track at the plank-road crossing to go to his home. If he came upon the track at that point, then he was between ninety and one hundred rods northwesterly of the curve on the track towards the junction, and could not see a train approaching from the junction unless it had passed the curve going on its way to the northwest. If he came on the track at that point, then it is evident that he could not have seen the train when he started to go on the track to his home, because the engineer testifies that when the engine came upon the straight track the deceased was thirty rods northwesterly of the plank-road crossing and within thirty rods of the place where the engine struck him.

If we take the evidence of the engineer as to where the deceased was when the engine came on the straight track, then the train must have run 150 rods while the deceased traveled thirty rods, and as the same evidence shows that the deceased had traveled along the track thirty rods northwesterly of the plank-road crossing when first seen by the engineer, and supposing the comparative speed of the train and deceased was the same, it would show that the train had not left the junction when the deceased first started to walk along the railroad track. The evidence shows that the whole distance from the place where the accident happened to the junction of the C. & N. W. Railway, was 268 rods. We think it may be fairly claimed, that the evidence shows that when the deceased started up the railroad track from the plank-road crossing the train was at the junction and about ready to start. The distance from the junction to the place where the engineer says the train was when he first saw the deceased alongside of the track, is not to exceed 120 rods. The point at which it is claimed the deceased first went upon the track was at least 200 rods northwesterly from the junction. The distance from the same point to the curve in the track beyond which the deceased, standing on the plank-road crossing, could not see

the train, is, according to the evidence, about twice the distance from the plank-road crossing to the point where the
deceased was intending to leave the track.

Now, if we suppose the deceased looked up the track
when he first started on it, as we are bound to presume
that he did until the contrary is shown by the evidence, and
saw no train in sight, and he believed, as the evidence
shows he had the right to believe, that the train had not
yet left the junction, can we say as a matter of law he was
negligent in walking along the track or even on the track
without looking again while he traveled about fifty-five
rods along the same? But it is a legitimate presumption,
in the absence of evidence to the contrary, that the deceased looked behind him after he had traveled on or along
the track twenty-five rods, and if he did, then, according
to the evidence, he could not have seen any train approaching from behind with a straight clear track for 120 rods in
full view. The deceased knowing that there was nothing
but a freight train coming from that direction,—admitting
that he was aware of that fact,—which, according to the
laws of the state regulating the rate of speed of trains, was
required not to travel to exceed six miles per hour, can we
say as a matter of law that he was guilty of negligence
because he walked on or along the track thirty rods farther
without looking behind again? I think not. And I think
that the weight of authority is that, under such or similar
circumstances, whether he was guilty of contributory negligence or want of ordinary care in not again looking behind him is a question of fact for the jury and not of law
for the court. The evidence of the engineer shows that if
the deceased had looked behind him at any time before he
got thirty rods northwesterly from the plank-road crossing
the train would not have been in sight; and whether it
would have been in hearing, no one speaks on that subject,

and with a very strong wind blowing away from the deceased and in the direction of the train, we certainly cannot say as a question of law that he would have heard it.

Viewing the evidence in the most favorable light for the plaintiff, and drawing all reasonable inferences in his favor in determining whether a nonsuit ought to have been granted,—a rule which it is unnecessary to cite authority to sustain—we have this case: The deceased traveling alongside of or upon a railroad track in a city in a place where people have been accustomed to travel for years, looking behind him over a clear track for at least 120 rods, sees no train in sight, turns around and walks on for a distance of thirty rods and is run down by a train approaching from behind without giving any warning, and killed. Can we say as a question of law that his negligence contributed to his death? If the man reasoned about the probabilities of a train overtaking him and running him down, the weight of the argument would be against the probabilities, and unless he was bound to take into consideration the fact that the train would be run twelve or fifteen miles an hour instead of the lawful rate of six miles, it could not possibly run over him while he was walking that distance. Why then, should he be continually looking for that which, in the orderly course of things, ought not to endanger his safety?

But it may be said he must have heard the approach of the train. Whether he heard it or not, under the circumstances, is a question of fact and not of law. Certainly all the presumptions are that he did not hear it. If he had heard it, the natural instinct of self-preservation would have induced him to have at least attempted to avoid it. But with a strong northwest wind blowing towards the approaching train and carrying all sounds with it away from the deceased, and with his back to the approaching train, there is no such certainty that he heard the train, or would have heard it if he had listened, as to justify a court, as a legal proposition, in holding either that he did hear it, or, if he did not, that he ought to have heard it or would have heard it had he listened.

The fact that the engineer testified that the deceased was walking alongside of the track when he first saw him, and that he stepped between the rails just before he was struck, ought not to change the situation. There is nothing which shows that the deceased was not in as dangerous a position walking alongside of the track as on the track. The only other witness who saw the deceased, says he was walking between the rails all the time she saw him, and her evidence tends strongly to show that she saw him before the engineer claims that he stepped on the track. The evidence also shows that the general custom was to walk on the railroad track and not beside it. Whether he was walking on the track or on the side of the track is clearly, under the evidence, a question of fact. It is also quite clear from the way in which the presiding judge granted the nonsuit that it was because there was no contradiction as to the fact that the deceased was walking on the track when he was killed, and not because the engineer testified that he had been walking beside the track until just before he was killed. The presiding judge having granted the nonsuit on the motion made at the close of the plaintiff's evidence, without any new motion made by the defendant, and without any announcement on the part of the defendant or of the plaintiff that no more evidence would be offered in the case, it should be held, I think, that the nonsuit, if to be sustained at all, should be sustained upon the plaintiff's evidence alone. The plaintiff was not permitted to disprove or rebut the evidence offered by the defendant, and it would be unjust to the plaintiff that the defendant's evidence should be considered on the motion for the nonsuit.

It is admitted that there was sufficient evidence in the

case to charge the railroad company with negligence, and
the only question is whether, upon the evidence, it is conclusively shown that the plaintiff's contributory negligence
concurred in producing the accident. In my view of the
case, the question was for the jury and not for the court.
In addition to the numerous cases cited by the learned counsel for the appellant in this and other courts upon the question that the contributory negligence of the plaintiff was,
under the evidence in this case, a question of fact for the
jury and not of law for the court, see *Weiss v. P. R. Co.* 79
Pa. St. 387; *Penn. R. Co. v. Weiss*, 87 Pa. St. 447; *Schum
v. P. R. Co.* 107 Pa. St. 8; *Penn. R. Co. v. Webber*, 76 Pa.
St. 157; *Scoville v. H. & St. J. R. Co.* 81 Mo. 434, 439; *Nor-
ton v. Ittner*, 56 Mo. 351; *Smith v. U. R. Co.* 61 Mo. 588;
Hill v. Fond du Lac, 56 Wis. 242, 246; *Townley v. C., M. &
St. P. R. Co.* 53 Wis. 632; *Loyd v. H. & St. J. R. Co.* 53
Mo. 509; *Thompson v. N. M. R. Co.* 51 Mo. 190; *Petty v.
H. & St. J. R. Co.* 28 Am. & Eng. R. Cas. 618, 625, 626;
Henze v. St. L., K. C. & N. R. Co. 71 Mo. 636.

This court has adopted the rule of Pennsylvania and
many other states that the defense of contributory negligence is a defense to be established by proofs and is not to
be presumed from the mere fact that the plaintiff does not
show affirmatively that he was in the exercise of ordinary
care at the time the accident occurred. It is defensive matter to be alleged and proved by the defendant (*McNamara
v. Clintonville*, 62 Wis. 209); and the plaintiff can only be
nonsuited on his evidence when such evidence clearly shows
that his negligence contributed to the accident.

That the deceased did not look behind him while traveling on or beside the track for thirty or thirty-five rods before he was struck by the train, may be fairly held to have
been proved by the evidence in the case, and this fact
should go to the jury on the question of his contributory
negligence, but it, as said above, is not conclusive. That

he did not listen for the train is not expressly shown by the evidence, and the circumstances are not such as to be conclusive that he would have heard the train if he had listened. His back was towards the train, and a very strong wind blowing from him and in the direction of the approaching train. The evidence is almost conclusive that he did not hear it. Had he heard the train every natural instinct would have prompted him to get out of its way. It seems to me that to sustain a nonsuit in this case upon the evidence, establishes the rule that in every case where a person walks on the track of a railroad or alongside of it in a position where a passing train would strike him, neither he nor his representative can recover. The fact that he is on the road or so near it as to be in danger from a passing train, and his failure to get out of the way, is conclusive evidence of his contributory negligence. This rule has certainly not been adopted by some of the most respectable courts of this country.

In the case of *Balt. & O. R. Co. v. State, use of Trainor*, 33 Md. 542, 554, the court say: "It is argued that if the deceased walked on the track, and his walking on the track was want of ordinary care, and the accident would not have happened if he had not walked on the track, then such walking was the proximate cause of the accident and the plaintiff cannot recover. This argument does not justly apply the rule in 29 Md. 421. By proximate cause is intended an act which directly produced or concurred directly in producing the injury. By remote cause is intended that which may have happened and yet no injury have occurred, notwithstanding that no injury could have occurred if it had not happened. No man would ever have been killed on a railway if he had never gone on or near the track. But if a man does imprudently and incautiously go on a railroad track, and is killed or injured by a train of cars, the company is responsible, unless it has used reasonable care and caution to avert it, and provided that, being on the track, he did nothing positive or negative to contribute to the immediate injury." In this case an employee of the railroad company was killed while walking on the track of the road in open daylight by a passenger train approaching him from behind, the same as in the case at bar. The only difference between the case at bar and that case consists in the fact that in the Maryland case the train was an extra and not a regular as in the case at bar, and that the deceased in the case cited was traveling along the railroad track where persons were not accustomed to walk, and where the deceased had neither an express or implied license from the company to walk. The plaintiff recovered on the trial and the judgment was affirmed by the supreme court. In this case as in the case at bar there was sufficient evidence to carry the case to the jury on the question of the negligence of the railroad company, and the only question was whether, under the admitted facts, the court should say as a matter of law the deceased was guilty of contributory negligence in not discovering the approach of the train and getting out of its way.

Frazer v. S. & N. A. R. Co. 81 Ala. 185, was also a case where a person was killed while walking upon the track of the railroad without any license express or implied from the company, and where the evidence apparently made a clearer case of negligence on the part of the deceased than in the case at bar, and the court held that notwithstanding such negligence the plaintiff might recover. The court makes the following statements: "Though it will be regarded as contributory negligence if a person goes on the track of a railroad or puts himself in a place so near in point of time to a collision with a passing train that preventive effort cannot avoid it, his so doing when danger is not immediate does not by itself constitute contributory negligence. It is a condition which remotely contributes to the subsequent injury, but is not in the legal sense the proximate cause. Such negligence will not disentitle him to recover, unless he could by ordinary care have avoided the consequences of the defendant's negligence."

But, admitting that the deceased was negligent and that his negligence contributed to the accident that caused his death, still, under the evidence in the case, I am constrained to think the court should have submitted the case to the jury upon the ground that the facts as proved tended to show that those in charge of the train were guilty of such gross carelessness as would justify a recovery notwithstanding the negligence of the deceased.

Taking the testimony of the engineer as true as to when he first saw the deceased and how the train was handled from that time until he ran over and killed the deceased, and another fact, which upon the evidence the jury would have been justified in finding, viz., that the train was running at least at the rate of twelve miles an hour, and we have this case: The engineer in charge of the train sees the deceased traveling on or so near the track as to be in a dangerous position, nearly or quite 120 rods ahead of him, with his back towards the train, and a high wind blowing directly from him towards the train, and without taking any measures to watch the man on the track, without giving any signals to warn him of his danger, without lessening his speed or taking any measures to control the speed of the train, and without looking for the man again until he is so near him that it is impossible to avoid running over him, runs over and kills him. Can this be said to be anything but gross negligence? Is human life of so little consequence as compared with the rights and privileges of railroad trains, even though rightfully running upon their own tracks, as to justify the railroad company in running down and killing the man on the track without making the least effort to avoid such a result? It does not help the engineer in this case to say that he tried to prevent the accident when it was too late to do so. The facts in this case show just as much neglect on the part of the engineer as if he had never seen the deceased after seeing him 120 rods ahead of him on the track until he had run over and killed him. That he saw him again when it was too late to avoid the accident, and then made efforts, if he did make any, to avoid the disaster, goes for nothing. The carelessness was in not watching the man and getting his train under control, and when he came within such distance of him as showed him that the deceased was, for some reason, in danger of being run over, warning him of his danger and, if necessary, stopping his train. I am not prepared to say that a railroad company may with impunity run down and kill any man who may be found walking along or on its tracks, no matter how careless or negligent such person may be. Having discovered the man on the track in time to prevent running over him, some kind of care on the part of those in control of the train must be shown to avoid the taking of human life. Certainly none was taken by those in charge of the train in this case, so far as disclosed by the evidence.

It cannot be said that this man walking on the track or alongside of it is in the same situation with regard to the care that those in charge of the train are bound to exercise as a man who is seen by those in charge of the train approaching a road crossing. In such case it may be said that those in charge of the train are not bound to slacken their speed or have the train in control so as to be able to stop the same suddenly, and may rest upon the presumption that the person approaching the track will stop before crossing it if the train is in sight and so near as to endanger him while crossing. In support of this proposition I am content to cite a brief abstract from the opinion in *Frazer v. S. & N. A. R. Co.* 81 Ala. 185, and the citation of the cases below. In the case of *Frazer v. S. & N. A. R. Co.*, the court say: "In order not to be misunderstood it may be observed that where the persons in charge of the train discover the peril, or are in a position where they ought to have discovered it, a position in which the circumstances, movements or condition of the person injured would manifest to a vigilant observer *that such person is unaware of his peril,* or if aware of it unable to extricate himself, a culpable omission to use the means in hand to prevent an accident, when a prompt resort thereto might have prevented it without endangering the freight or passengers being transported on the train, will be regarded as reckless or intentional negligence." The rule above stated is fully sustained by the following cases: *Balt. C. P. R. Co. v. McDonnell,* 43 Md. 534; *Northern C. R. Co. v. Price,* 29 Md. 420, 425; *St. Louis, A. & T. H. R. Co. v. Manly,* 58 Ill. 300; *Lake Shore & M. S. R. Co. v. Miller,* 25 Mich. 277; *Isabel v. H. & St. J. R. Co.* 60 Mo. 475; *Harlan v. St. L., K. C. & N. R. Co.* 65 Mo. 26; *Zimmerman v. H. & St. J. R. Co.* 71 Mo. 484; *Frick v. St. L., K. C. & N. R. Co.* 75 Mo. 542; *Kelley v. H. & St. J. R. Co.* 75 Mo. 140; *Werner v. C. R. Co.* 81 Mo. 368; *Welsh v. J. C. H. R. Co.* 81 Mo. 466; *Scoville v. H. & St. J. R. Co.* 81 Mo. 434; *Baumeister v. G. R. & I. R. Co.* 28 Am. & Eng. R. Cas. 476; *State v. M. & L. R. Co.* 52 N. H. 528, 557; *Isbell v. N. Y. & N. H. R. Co.* 27 Conn. 393.

I think the case should have been submitted to the jury both upon the question of the contributory negligence of the deceased and upon the question of the gross negligence of those in charge of the train.

By the Court.— The judgment of the circuit court is affirmed.

See note to this case in 37 N. W. Rep. 416.— REP.

BOSTWICK, Appellant, vs. ESTATE OF BOSTWICK, Respondent.

February 28 — March 27, 1888.

Parent and child: Evidence of contract to pay for services rendered by father to son.

Where aged parents have been living with a son as members of his family, having all their wants supplied by him, an agreement to pay for services rendered by the father during that time should be clearly shown in order to charge the estate of the son with a claim for such services.

APPEAL from the Circuit Court for *Monroe* County.

The following statement of the case was prepared by Mr. Justice TAYLOR as a part of the opinion:

This is an appeal from the judgment of the circuit court of Monroe county. The appellant presented two claims against the estate of. Edwin L. Bostwick, deceased, to the county court of Monroe county,— one for $555, for money alleged to have been loaned the deceased; and one for $1,360, for the services of the appellant at the rate of $25 per month, performed between the years of 1880, or 1881, to the death of the deceased in 1885. The county judge of Monroe county being an attorney for the plaintiff, the hearing of the case was transferred to the circuit court of said county for trial. In the circuit court the case was tried by the court without a jury, and the circuit judge found against both of the claims; and from the judgment rendered by the circuit court, disallowing said claims, the claimant appeals to this court.

The circuit judge made the following findings of fact and conclusions of law: "That *John Bostwick* [the claimant] was father of E. L. Bostwick, deceased; that for many years said *John Bostwick* lived in the family of said E. L. Bostwick as a member thereof, superintending the operation of his son's farm in his son's absence, selling the produce of said farm, receiving the avails thereof, and discharging the debts and liabilities growing out of the management of the farm; that during his son's absence said *John Bostwick* deposited in his own name, in the Bank of Tomah, various sums received by him from the sale of produce of said farm, the property of his said son; that on the 18th day of December, 1882, said *John Bostwick* turned over to his said son, E. L. Bostwick, the amount then remaining unexpended of said sums so deposited, which balance so turned over was not a loan, but was so turned over as the property of said E. L. Bostwick, which transaction constituted the alleged loan from said *John Bostwick* to said E. L. Bostwick; that no agreement was ever made for the repayment of said sum to *John Bostwick;* that all the services rendered by said *John Bostwick* in and about the superintending said farm were rendered by him as a member of the family of said E. L. Bostwick, and without express or other agreement for compensation; that just and equitable provision was made by the will of said E. L. Bostwick, deceased, for the support and maintenance of said *John Bostwick;* that said claimant has failed to prove any of the material allegations of his two several complaints." As conclusions of law the court finds "that said claims, and each of them, should be and are hereby disallowed."

For the appellant there was a brief by *Dickinson & Graham*, and oral argument by *Mr. S. N. Dickinson.*

George Graham, for the respondent.

TAYLOR, J.   The only question for the determination of this court is whether the findings of fact are supported by the evidence.   After reading the evidence in the case we have no hesitation in saying that the findings are not only supported by the evidence, but that every reasonable presumption arising upon the evidence sustains them.

As to the $555 claimed to have been loaned by the appellant to his son, by a transfer of that amount, standing to the credit of the appellant in the Bank of Tomah, to the credit of his deceased son, the evidence very clearly shows that the whole sum so standing to the credit of the appellant in said bank, and which was transferred as above stated, was, in fact, the money of the deceased which had been theretofore received by the appellant upon sales made by him of property of the deceased, as his agent, and deposited in said bank to his personal credit; and that the transfer was made to the credit of the deceased because the money belonged to him, and not as a loan to him.

The claim for services has no substantial support by the evidence in the case. The claimant is the father of the deceased. On January 1, 1881, the time he claims his services for which he has not been paid commenced, he was about seventy-seven years old, and was living in his son's family with his aged wife, eating at the same table, supplied with money to pay for his clothing, medical attendance, and other necessaries, by his son, no account being kept, either by the father or son, for services rendered or for money supplied to the father and mother for clothes, medical attendance, or other necessaries provided by the son, and no satisfactory evidence that there ever was any agreement on the part of the son to pay any wages for such services as the aged father was able to and did perform for him. It seems to us that a father and mother living in the family of a son, having all the necessary wants supplied by the son as members of his family, the father being of the age of seventy-seven years when he commenced so living, and living with him until he was about eighty-two years old, ought to make out a pretty clear case of an agreement on the part of the son to pay him wages for his services, when he seeks to charge the estate of such son with a claim for such services after his death. There certainly is no such clear evidence of a contract in this case as should take the case out of the general rule as laid down by this as well as all other courts in cases of this kind. *McGarvey v. Roods* (Iowa), 35 N. W. Rep. 488; *Byrnes v. Clark*, 57 Wis. 13, 21; *Tyler v. Burrington*, 39 Wis. 376; *Wells v. Perkins*, 43 Wis. 160; *Manseau v. Mueller*, 45 Wis. 430; *Pellage v. Pellage*, 32 Wis. 136; *Mountain v. Fisher*, 22 Wis. 93; *Leary v. Leary*, 68 Wis. 662, 671; *Geary v. Geary*, 67 Wis. 248. Most of the cases cited are cases where the son or daughter claims for services rendered for the father, but the same rule applies where the father claims for services rendered for the son under similar circumstances. See *Leary v. Leary, supra*, and *Harris v. Currier*, 44 Vt. 468; Schouler, Dom. Rel. (3d ed.), sec. 270, p. 379.

All the evidence in the case shows that the deceased son was disposed to and did deal with his aged father and mother in a dutiful and kindly way, during his life-time; and at his death he made, considering his ability, at least, no niggardly provision for the support of his father during the remnant of his days.

We find nothing in the record to impeach the justice of the findings and judgment of the circuit court.

By the Court.— The judgment of the circuit court is affirmed.

See note to this case in 37 N. W. Rep. 405.— REP.

Boyington, Respondent, vs. Squires, Appellant.

February 28 — March 27, 1888.

Watercourses: Mill-dams: Flowage of land: Injury to possession: Proof of title: Instructions to jury.

1. Proof of the plaintiff's actual possession and occupancy of land is sufficient *prima facie* proof of title and ownership to enable him to maintain an action to recover damages for negligence in the use of a mill-dam and water-power whereby such land was flowed and

injured and the growing crops thereon destroyed — such injury being merely to the possession. *Winchester v. Stevens Point,* 58 Wis. 350, distinguished.

2. In such an action it is not error for the court to instruct the jury that the right of the plaintiff to the use and enjoyment of his land is equal to the right of the defendant to the use and enjoyment of his dam and water-power; and that the defendant may pass the whole volume of water running in the stream at any time through his dam, but he may not so increase that volume from his mill-pond as to injure the lands of other owners below, which otherwise would not have been injured.

APPEAL from the Circuit Court for *Monroe* County.

Action to recover damages for the alleged negligence of the defendant in the use of a certain mill-dam and water-power on Mill creek, in Monroe county, by retaining the water of the stream in the pond created by the dam, and discharging the same therefrom, by means whereof the plaintiff's land below on the same stream was flowed and injured, and his crops growing thereon destroyed, etc., etc. The complaint charges that a portion of such damages was caused in June, 1883, and a portion in July, 1884, by the means aforesaid.

The answer denies the negligence charged, and that any damage was caused by the discharge of water through the dam; and alleges that from October 1, 1883, to October 1, 1885, the dam, water-power, and mill were in the possession of a tenant, and that such mill and water-power had been used and operated in the same manner for more than twenty years next preceding the commencement of this action.

A trial of the cause resulted in a verdict for the plaintiff for $50. The rulings and testimony on the trial are sufficiently stated in the opinion. A motion for a new trial was denied, and judgment rendered for the plaintiff pursuant to the verdict. The defendant appeals from the judgment.

For the appellant there was a brief by *G. C. Prentiss* and *Dickinson & Graham*, and oral argument by *Mr. Prentiss.*

For the respondent there was a brief by *George Graham* and *J. M. Morrow*, and oral argument by *Mr. Graham.*

LYON, J. 1. It is alleged in the complaint that the plaintiff is the owner in fee-simple, and in possession, of the land therein described and charged to have been injured, being sixty acres of land. The answer admits his ownership of forty acres thereof under a conveyance to him executed by the defendant, and denies his title to the remaining twenty acres. Probably the plaintiff did not prove a good record title to the twenty acres by competent evidence, but he did prove himself in the actual possession and occupancy of the whole sixty acres when the land was flowed and the injury . complained of inflicted. This is sufficient *prima facie* proof of title and ownership to enable the plaintiff to maintain this action, which is merely for injury to the possession, and not, as in *Winchester v. Stevens Point*, 58 Wis. 350, for a permanent and continuing injury to the freehold. See, also, *Reed v. C., M. & St. P. R. Co., post*, p. 399. It must be held that the plaintiff sufficiently established his title to the land injured to maintain this action.

2. The defense of a right by prescription to hold and discharge water by and through defendant's dam in the manner in which it was discharged when the injuries complained of were inflicted, and that the lessee of the mill is alone liable for the damages suffered in July, 1884, seem to have dropped out of the case. No instruction on these subjects was asked or given, and no point thereon was seriously urged in the argument in this court. It may be observed, however, that the testimony does not tend to prove any prescriptive right, if a prescriptive right could exist in such a case, and it was proved that defendant was in the actual

use of the mill property at or about the time the injury of July, 1884, was inflicted.

3. There was abundant testimany given on the trial tending to show that the defendant controlled the water in his mill-pond negligently, and discharged it in unreasonable quantities upon the plaintiff's land at the times alleged, and that the plaintiff was injured thereby to the amount of his recovery and more. The testimony is quite voluminous, and we cannot undertake to state it in detail. A statement of our conclusion of its character and effects, after a careful persual of it, must suffice.

4. The only exceptions to the charge of the judge to the jury are to passages therein to the effect that the right of the plaintiff to the use and enjoyment of his land was equal to the right of the defendant to the use and enjoyment of his dam and water-power; and that the defendant may pass the whole volume of water running in the stream at any time through his dam, but he may not so increase that volume from his mill-pond as to injure the lands of other owners below, which otherwise would not have been injured. This is nothing more than an application of the maxim *sic utere tuo ut alienum non lædas*. We think the maxim applicable to this case, and hence find no error in the charge.

By the Court.— The judgment of the circuit court is affirmed.

SPIESS, Appellant, vs. NEUBERG and wife, Respondents.

February 29 — March 27, 1888.

Public lands: Homestead entry: Mortgages: Pre-emption: Subsequently acquired title: Equity.

1. One C., having made a homestead entry of land, assigned the same and conveyed the land by warranty deed to the defendant, who mortgaged the land to one S., and afterwards gave second and

third mortgages to the plaintiff. The mortgage to S. was foreclosed, and the plaintiff, to save her own mortgages, purchased at
the foreclosure sale, received the sheriff's deed, and thereafter paid
taxes on the land. Subsequently the defendant took the land
from the plaintiff to work on shares, and, while so in possession
under the plaintiff, made a new homestead entry of the land, commuted the same by payment of the government price, and obtained
title from the United States, under sec. 2301, R. S. of U. S. *Held*,
that the mortgages given by the defendant were valid, and the
title subsequently acquired by him inured to the benefit of the
plaintiff.

2. Some of the facts which make such title inure to the benefit of the
plaintiff not being of record, she may maintain an equitable action to establish her right.

APPEAL from the Circuit Court for *La Crosse* County.
The following statement of the case was prepared by
Mr. Justice CASSODAY:

At some time prior to May 14, 1877, Hans C. Colstad had
taken and made a homestead entry of the E. ½ of N. E. ¼
of section 33, township 15 N., of range 5 W., the same
then being the property of the United States, and May 14,
1877, caused a receipt for the payment of the requisite
amount therefor to be recorded in the office of register of
deeds. On the same day Colstad sold and assigned to the
said defendant *John Peter Neuberg* his right or claim in and
to said homestead entry, and executed to him a warranty
deed of the land, which was recorded. February 28, 1879,
said *Neuberg* borrowed $1,200 of one Stephenson, to secure
which, with interest, the said *Neuberg* and wife executed
and delivered to said Stephenson their mortgage on 273
acres of land, including said eighty. June 27, 1879, the said
Neuberg borrowed of the plaintiff $125, to secure which,
with interest, the said *Neuberg* and wife executed and delivered to the plaintiff their mortgage on the 273 acres.
January 17, 1880, the said *Neuberg* borrowed of the plaintiff $100, to secure which, with interest, *Neuberg* and wife

executed and delivered to the plaintiff their mortgage on said 273 acres. *Neuberg* being in default, the Stephenson mortgage was foreclosed, and judgment of foreclosure and sale entered thereon, June 3, 1881, upon which judgment there was due for principal, interest, and costs, July 24, 1882, $1,812.58, for the payment of which the whole 273 acres was on said last-mentioned day sold, and bid in by the plaintiff, who paid the amount thereof, being compelled to do so to save her said two mortgages, upon which nothing had been paid. The plaintiff thereupon received a duly executed sheriff's deed on said foreclosure sale, and recorded the same, but failed thereby to get the legal title to said eighty acres, for the reason that the title was in the United States. The balance of the land was worth much less than the amount then due on the Stephenson mortgage. Since said sheriff's deed, the said *Neuberg* took said lands to work on shares from the plaintiff. The plaintiff had paid during that time $145.36 taxes on said lands. January 28, 1886, the said *Neuberg* made a United States homestead entry of said described eighty acres, and December 15, 1886, commuted the same, proved his occupation thereof, and paid the United States government price of $100, and received the title thereof from the United States, subject to the revision of his proof by the land department.

December 22, 1886, the plaintiff commenced this action to enjoin the defendants from disposing of or incumbering the eighty acres, and to have the title thereof so acquired by *Neuberg* adjudged to inure to the benefit of the plaintiff. The defendants answered, admitting most of the facts stated, but claiming the title free from said mortgages or any claim of the plaintiff. Upon the trial the court found, in effect, as conclusions of law upon the facts stated, that as to the eighty acres, said several mortgages were void, being in contravention of the provisions and policy of the United States homestead law; that the title subsequently acquired by *Neuberg* under said law did not inure to the benefit of the plaintiff; that the plaintiff had failed to establish a right to equitable relief, and therefore the action be dismissed. From the judgment entered thereon accordingly the plaintiff appeals.

John J. Cole, for the appellant, to the point that in cases both of homesteads and pre-emptions the courts have upheld the rights and equities of assignees and mortgagees, cited, besides cases cited in the opinion: *Whitney v. Buckman,* 13 Cal. 536; *Christy v. Dana,* 34 id. 548; *S. C.* 42 id. 174; *Douglas v. Gould,* 52 id. 656; *Camp v. Grider,* 62 id. 20; *Pierson v. David,* 1 Iowa, 23.

For the respondents there was a brief by *Prentiss & Miller,* and oral argument by *Mr. G. C. Prentiss.* They contended, *inter alia,* that land entered under the homestead law cannot become subject to a mortgage lien or be alienated prior to the issuing of a patent therefor. Secs. 2296, 2290, 2291, R. S. of U. S. The facts of this case cannot be construed as a contract to convey this land when entered. The courts have uniformly held that contracts violating a similar provision in the pre-emption laws are void. *Warren v. Van Brunt,* 19 Wall. 654; *Webster v. Bowman,* 25 Fed. Rep. 889; *Gile v. Hallock,* 33 Wis. 523; Jones on Mortg. secs. 177, 178. See, also, *Weber v. Zeimet,* 30 Wis. 283; *Paige v. Peters,* 70 id. 178. The plaintiff's title cannot be aided by the judgment of a court of equity. If the law has not given him the title, the court cannot. Having the legal title, and the defendant being in the adverse possession of the land, the plaintiff's remedy is by action of ejectment. He cannot maintain an action in a court of equity. *Lee v. Simpson,* 29 Wis. 333; *Gray v. Tyler,* 40 id. 579; *Remington v. Foster,* 42 id. 608; *Pennoyer v. Allen,* 51 id. 360.

CASSODAY, J.   Upon the facts stated the inferences are irresistible that *Neuberg* has been in the possession of the eighty ever since he bought out Colstad and received the warranty deed of the same, May 14, 1877; that he claimed the same by virtue of such purchase and deed and the prior homestead entry of Colstad until he lost the same by the sheriff's sale and deed.   There can be no question but what the several mortgages were given to create a lien upon whatever right, title, and interest *Neuberg* had in the eighty as well as the other lands, and that the respective mortgagees advanced their moneys thereon in good faith and with the expectation of thereby acquiring adequate security for the same.   With the same good faith and expectation, and to save her own mortgages, the plaintiff manifestly advanced the requisite amount of money on her purchase at sheriff's sale, and subsequently in paying taxes on the land.   Prior to 1886, there seems to have been no pretense but what the plaintiff had acquired whatever equitable right, title, and interest in the eighty *Neuberg* had previously possessed.   During that period of three and a half years, *Neuberg* had remained in possession under and in subordination to such equitable right, title, and interest of the plaintiff.   There can be no question but what *Neuberg* made the entry of January 28, 1886, and the commutation of the same, December 15, 1886, for the purpose of cutting off such equities of the plaintiff and converting the possession which he thus held under her into an adverse possession and hostile title.   This was held to be legitimate by the trial court, on the theory that the mortgages were given in contravention of the provisions and policy of the United States homestead law.

1. While the title remains in the United States, it is undoubtedly true that "no lands acquired under the provisions of" that law can "in any event become *liable* to the satisfaction of any debt contracted prior to the issuing of

the patent therefor." Such is the statute. Sec. 2296, R. S. of U. S. This court has held that prior to such issuance of a patent such lands were not liable to attachment, execution, or mechanic's lien. *Gile v. Hallock*, 33 Wis. 523; *Paige v. Peters*, 70 Wis. 178. In the case last cited it is said in the opinion, in effect, that the right of the occupant of such lands to mortgage his interest in the same does "not come within the prohibition of the federal statutes cited." That assertion is not only sustained by the authorities there cited, but others. *Nycum v. McAllister*, 33 Iowa, 374; *Fuller v. Hunt*, 48 Iowa, 163; *Kirkaldie v. Larrabee*, 31 Cal. 456; *Orr v. Stewart*, 67 Cal. 275; *Cheney v. White*, 5 Neb. 261; *Jones v. Yoakam*, 5 Neb. 265. We are not aware of any adverse decision in the supreme court of the United States.

2. But the same chapter of the Revised Statutes of the United States in effect provides that nothing therein "shall be so construed as to prevent any" homesteader "from paying the minimum price for the quantity of land so entered, at any time before the expiration of the five years, and obtaining a patent therefor from the government, *as in other cases directed by law*, on making proof of settlement and cultivation as provided by law, granting preemption rights." Sec. 2301, R. S. of U. S. Having commuted under that section, it is claimed that *Neuberg* is entitled to all the benefits and was subjected to all the restraints and prohibitions of chapter four of those statutes, entitled "Pre-emptions." Assuming for the present that when *Neuberg* made the several mortgages he was under the same disabilities that he would have been had he previously pre-empted the eighty, the question recurs whether such disabilities were such as to avoid the mortgages. That chapter provides, in effect, that "any grant or conveyance which" such pre-emptor "may have made, except in the hands of *bona fide* purchasers for a valuable consideration,

Spiess vs. Neuberg and wife.

shall be null and void," with an exception not material
here. Sec. 2262, R. S. of U. S. But that provision did not
operate as a disability, since the several mortgagees advanced their money in good faith, and the plaintiff bid in
the property on the foreclosure sale and paid thereon the
amount of money stated in good faith. The same section required such pre-emptor, before being allowed to enter the lands, to take the requisite oath, among other things,
to the effect that he had "not directly or indirectly made
any agreement or contract, in any way or manner, with
any person whatsoever, by which the title which he might
acquire from the government of the United States should
inure in whole or in part to the benefit of any person except himself." *Ibid.* And that chapter further provides
that "all assignments and transfers of the right hereby
secured, prior to the issuing of the patent, shall be null
and void." Sec. 2263, R. S. of U. S. According to the
supreme court of the United States, these provisions were
enacted to prevent such pre-emption rights from being acquired by land speculators. *Myers v. Croft*, 13 Wall. 291.
In that case Mr. Justice DAVIS, speaking for the court, said:
"In view of these facts, we cannot suppose, in the absence
of an express declaration to that effect, that Congress intended to tie up these lands in the hands of the original
owners until the government should choose to issue the
patent. If it had been the purpose of Congress to attain
the object contended for, it would have declared the lands
themselves unalienable until the patent was granted. Instead of this, the legislation was directed against the assignment or transfer of the right secured by the act, which was
*the right of pre-emption, leaving the pre-emptor free to sell
his land after the entry*, if at that time he was in good faith
the owner of the land and had done nothing inconsistent
with the provisions of the law on the subject." To the
same effect, *Lessee of French v. Spencer*, 21 How. 228;

Thredgill v. Pintard, 12 How. 24; *Landes v. Brant,* 10 How. 348. These views are in harmony with the adjudications of this court, wherein it has been held that such pre-emptor, having made the entry, paid his money, taken his receipt or certificate, and recorded the same (as Colstad did), has the entire equitable title and interest, which he may assign, transfer, and convey at pleasure; and that the legal title will vest in his grantee upon the issuing of the patent. *Dillingham v. Fisher,* 5 Wis. 475; *Stephenson v. Wilson,* 37 Wis. 489. In *Lamb v. Davenport,* 18 Wall. 307, it was held that, "unless forbidden by some positive law, contracts made by actual settlers on the public lands concerning their possessory rights, and concerning the title to be acquired in future from the United States, are valid as between the parties to the contract, though there be at the time no act of Congress by which the title may be acquired, and though the government is under no obligation to either of the parties in regard to the title." It follows from these several adjudications that Colstad was under no disability which prevented him from conveying his equitable title and interest in the land to *Neuberg,* and that the latter was under no disability which prevented him from creating valid liens thereon by way of mortgages, as he did. These things being so, there can be no question but what such equitable right, title, and interest passed to the plaintiff by such foreclosure sale and sheriff's deed.

3. The plaintiff having thus acquired such equitable right, title, and interest in and to the eighty, was she divested of the same by the subsequent entry and commutation by *Neuberg* while in possession as her tenant? To hold that she was, would be the consummation of a gross fraud under the guise of a legal right. This being so, it should not be sanctioned by the courts, unless forced to do so by positive law or binding authority. Here it has neither. The law on the subject seems to be pretty well settled to

the effect that where the owner of such equitable right, title, and interest transfers the same by way of mortgage or otherwise to a *bona fide* purchaser for a valuable consideration fully paid, and afterwards acquires the legal title by patent from the United States, such legal title at once inures to the benefit of such *bona fide* purchaser, and estops such patentee from claiming title as against such purchaser. This is sustained by the authorities already cited. This rule is well illustrated and strongly supported by *Thredgill v. Pintard, supra,* in which it was held that "where a settler upon the public lands had a pre-emption right to them, and sold them to a person who again sold them to a third party, the original vendor has a lien upon the land for the balance of the purchase money still due, and can enforce it by a bill in chancery, *notwithstanding the vendee has taken out a patent in his own name under a subsequent pre-emption law.*" So, in *Lessee of French v. Spencer, supra,* it was held that "a patent to the original beneficiary, who had previously sold his right, inured to the benefit of the purchaser, and related back to the date of the entry; and the heir of the grantor in such a deed is estopped from setting up a legal title under the patent." See, also, *Hughes v. U. S.,* 4 Wall. 232. In *Orr v. Stewart, supra,* the homesteader, after having mortgaged his right, title, and interest, and the mortgage foreclosed and bid in by the mortgagee, who obtained thereon a sheriff's deed, commuted his homestead entry into a cash entry, as here, and paid in full the price, and received a duplicate receipt and certificate of purchase therefor; but it was held that such after-acquired title by the mortgagor fed the mortgage, and inured to the benefit of the mortgagee and purchaser at such foreclosure sale.

4. Upon the principles stated it may seem that the plaintiff had an adequate remedy at law, and hence that there was no necessity to bring this action. But the patent

gave to *Neuberg* the apparent legal title of record; and some of the facts which make that title inure to the benefit of the plaintiff are not of record, and hence there is a necessity of establishing the plaintiff's right to the land by an adjudication.

By the Court.— The judgment of the circuit court is reversed, and the cause is remanded with directions to enter judgment in accordance with the prayer of the complaint.

REID and others, Appellants, vs. SOUTHWORTH, Respondent.

February 29 — March 27, 1888.

(1, 2) Judgment by confession for debt not due: Power construed.
(3) Setting aside unauthorized judgment.

1. Authority to confess judgment upon a debt not due must be given in clear and precise language.
2. A warrant of attorney to confess judgment upon a note "for such amount as may appear to be *unpaid* thereon," authorizes judgment to be confessed only for the amount actually *due.*
3. An unauthorized judgment will be presumed to affect substantial rights, and should be set aside.

APPEAL from the Circuit Court for *La Crosse* County. The case is stated in the opinion.

For the appellants there was a brief by *Prentiss & Miller*, and oral argument by *J. J. Cole* and *G. C. Prentiss*. To the point that the party moving to set aside a judgment entered upon warrant of attorney must show that he has been subjected to some injustice before the court will interfere, they cited *Van Steenwyck v. Sackett*, 17 Wis. 645, 657; *McIndoe v. Hazelton*, 19 id. 567; *Herfurth v. Biederstaedt*, 43 id. 633; *Pirie v. Hughes*, id. 531; *Rollins v. Kahn*, 66 id. 658.

For the respondent there was a brief by *Fruit & Brindley*, and oral argument by *Mr. J. J. Fruit*.

Reid and others vs. Southworth.

Cole, C. J.   This is an appeal from an order setting aside judgments between these parties. It is stipulated that the appeals from the order in each case be consolidated, and that they be treated as one appeal.   The judgments were entered upon warrants of attorney included in the same instruments with the promissory notes given by the defendant.   These notes were dated February 3, 1887, and became due, one in four months and the other in six months from date.   Judgments were entered on the warrants of attorney on each note, February 11th, eight days after the notes were given, and before anything was due upon them.   It is now claimed on behalf of the defendant that the warrants of attorney did not authorize the entry of judgment when nothing was due upon the notes.   This contention we think is sound, and must prevail.

The warrants of attorney, in effect, " authorize any attorney of any court of record to appear for the defendant in term time or vacation at any time [thereafter], and confess judgment without process in favor of the holder of the note, for such amount as may appear to be unpaid thereon, hereby expressly waiving all exemption under the laws of Illinois, and also waiving all errors in the proceedings." Now the obvious meaning of this language restricts the authority to confess judgment to the amount actually due upon the notes.   It is said on the part of the plaintiffs that it authorizes a confession of judgment, not only for the amount due, but for the amount to become due, at any time after the warrant of attorney was executed.   But this is not a fair construction of the instrument.   The language, "for such amount as may appear to be unpaid thereon," clearly refers to the amount which is actually due and payable.   It is doubtless true that the word "*unpaid*" sometimes means a debt or obligation not discharged, without regard to the time it matures.   But that is not the sense in which the word is used in the warrant of attorney.   It ap-

pears from the affidavits used on the part of the plaint
in resisting the motion to vacate the judgment that th
notes were given as extensions of other notes, and to exte
the time of payment of the debt. It may be possible tl
the defendant would have been willing and consented
have judgment entered immediately for the amount
cured by the notes, yet such a supposition is very unreas
able and highly improbable.

The remarks of Mr. Justice ORTON, in *Sloane v. Anders*
57 Wis. 123, are so pertinent to the point we are consid
ing that we cannot do better than quote them, as they fo
settle the construction which should be given to the w
rant of attorney. The warrant of attorney in that c
contained the precise language which is used in the one
fore us. Mr. Justice ORTON says: "The power of attorr
does not authorize the confession of judgment before
note is due, or for more than is due upon it. The langus
'for such amount as may appear to be *unpaid* thereon' d
not give such authority by the necessary meaning of
word 'unpaid,' or by any meaning that can be forced
its context." A power to confess judgment for a debt i
due should be "clearly granted and expressed, and not I
to mere inference or implication. The word 'unpaid
more commonly and properly applied to a debt *due* than
a debt *undue*, and may at least as well mean a debt due
undue; therefore no power to confess a judgment foi
debt undue is even implied by it. In *Dilley v. Van Wie*
Wis. 209, the warrant of attorney authorized the confessi
of judgment for the amount *appearing* to be due, and
attorney was held to the authority only to confess jut
ment for the amount *actually* due. See, also, *McCabe*
Sumner, 40 Wis. 386."

The law is well settled that, in entering up judgment
a warrant of attorney, the authority given by it must
strictly pursued. 1 Tidd, Pr. (9th ed.), 552. It seems to

it is impossible to say that authority was given in the warrant of attorney in this case to enter up judgment upon the
notes whether they were due or not.   As was said in the
Sloane Case, such authority should be given in clear and
precise language, and should not rest in inference or doubtful implication.   It is claimed by the learned counsel for
the plaintiffs that the authority given was to confess judgment at any time after the date of the warrant of attorney, without reference to the maturity of the debt, as was
done in *Sherman v. Baddely*, 11 Ill. 622; *Adam v. Arnold*,
86 Ill. 185; and *Thomas v. Mueller*, 106 Ill. 36.   In these
cases it was held that the warrant of attorney authorized
a confession of judgment at any time after the date of the
note, and that a judgment confessed before the maturity
of the note was valid.   It is obvious that these decisions
have no application to this case, in view of the construction
which we feel compelled to place upon the warrant of attorney. Authority is not here given to confess judgment at any
time after the date of the note, in express terms, or by any
unequivocal language; but it is to confess judgment in favor
of the holder of the note for such amount as may appear to
be unpaid thereon, which implies, as we have said, for the
amount which is actually due.   We are satisfied that this is
the proper construction of the warrant of attorney, but
will discuss the point no further.   It may well be, as counsel
contends, that courts have sustained confessions of judgments upon debts not due.   We do not deny but authority
may be given to confess judgment upon a debt not due, but
what we do hold is that such authority must be given in
clear and precise language.   It is certainly not so given in
this case.   And it would be contrary to all the facts and
probabilities of the case to suppose a merchant seeking an
extension would give his creditor authority to have judgment entered at once on his extended paper, without regard
to the time of its maturity, and thus effectually destroy

his credit in the commercial world. That would not be consistent with human conduct and experience, and we are quite confident it was not the intention of the defendant when he executed the warrant of attorney.

In this case, one of the notes was not due when the order vacating the judgment upon it was made. It is said the defendant should show that he is subjected to some injustice, before the court should interfere and set the judgment aside. We think he does show that when it appears that a judgment has been entered against him without any authority in law. It is fair to presume that substantial rights have been affected by the entry of judgment in that manner. This does not present a case of mere technical error or irregularity, but a judgment unauthorized, which would seriously affect the credit of the defendant.

By the Court.— The order of the circuit court is affirmed.

HAND and another, Respondents, vs. CONGER, Appellant.

February 29 — March 27, 1888.

Agency: Sale of land: Commissions.

Defendant employed H. to sell certain land. H. employed M. to find a purchaser, and M. employed plaintiffs, agreeing to divide commissions with them if they found a purchaser at a certain price. Plaintiffs found D., who agreed to take the land at the price named on certain terms, and paid $500 towards the purchase to M., who gave a receipt therefor stating the agreed terms of sale. M. paid the $500 to H., who gave him a receipt therefor for D., stating therein the terms of sale as reported by M. to H. At a meeting to consummate the sale H. and D. differed as to the terms. Defendant was willing to execute the contract as stated by H., but not as stated by D. The sale failed, and the $500 was repaid to D. There was no evidence that defendant ever employed plaintiffs, or authorized H. or M. to employ them, or ever ratified their acts in that behalf. *Held*, that defendant is not liable to plaintiffs for any commissions.

APPEAL from the Circuit Court for *Price* County.

This action is to recover commissions on a sale of pine lands in Price county belonging to the defendant *Conger*, alleged to have been earned by the plaintiffs as brokers. The action was originally brought against the defendant *Conger* and one McDonald, but was discontinued as to McDonald during the trial. Motions for a nonsuit, and that the court direct a verdict for the defendant, were denied. The case was submitted to the jury without instructions, by consent of parties. The jury found for the plaintiffs, and assessed their damages at the sum claimed. A motion for a new trial was denied, and judgment for plaintiffs entered pursuant to the verdict. A sufficient statement of the testimony will be found in the opinion. The defendant appeals from the judgment.

For the appellant there was a brief by *A. Haight*, attorney, and *George Gary*, of counsel, and oral argument by *Mr. Haight*.

For the respondents the cause was submitted on the brief of *Willis Hand*.

LYON, J. The only question presented for determination by this appeal is, Does the testimony tend to prove the defendant *Conger* liable for the commissions claimed.

Although the testimony is quite voluminous, the material facts which it tends to prove may be stated somewhat briefly as follows: The plaintiffs are real-estate brokers at Phillips, in Price county. In 1885 defendant *Conger* owned a tract of land in that county. He resides at Elkhorn, in Walworth county. During that year he employed Mr. Haight, residing in Oshkosh, to sell or aid in the sale of such land. Such employment was by parol. It does not appear that Haight had any authority to settle and fix the terms of sale, although *Conger* expressed his willingness to approve of what he might do in the matter. In September, 1885,

Haight employed McDonald (formerly a defendant her
to find a purchaser for the land, and told him he mi
have all he got for it over $12,000 as his compensat
therefor. It does not appear that any terms of sale of
than the price were stated by Haight to McDonald. '
latter thereupon agreed with the plaintiffs that if t
would find a purchaser of the land for $13,000, they she
have a commission of $500 out of the purchase mor
The plaintiffs soon found a person, one Davis, who wa
purchase the land and pay that price therefor on cert
terms and conditions. Davis paid McDonald $500 towa
the purchase, and McDonald, in his own name, gave hit
receipt therefor. The agreed terms of sale were writtet
the receipt. McDonald paid the $500 to Haight, who g
a receipt therefor to McDonald for Davis, stating thet
the terms of the sale as reported by McDonald to Haig
Thereafter McDonald, Davis, and one of the plaintiffs i
at Oshkosh to close the sale. Haight and Davis differed
to the terms. Haight refused to take the responsibility
accepting the terms insisted upon by Davis, and Davis-
fused to accept the terms insisted upon by Haight. Th(
upon the four went to Elkhorn and met *Conger*. The lat
was willing to execute the contract proposed by Haig
but Davis would not accept it. *Conger* refused to sign
contract proposed by Davis, and so the sale failed, and (
yer repaid Davis the $500. ·

There is no evidence that *Conger* ever employed
plaintiffs to sell his land or find him a purchaser theret
or that he ever authorized either McDonald or Haight ta
employ them. Neither is there any proof that *Conger* e
ratified the acts of McDonald or Haight in the matter.
may have learned during the interview at Elkhorn (but t
before) that if the sale was consummated at $13,000,
plaintiffs expected to receive and would claim a commiss
of $500 out of the purchase money, and probably he wa

have acceded to such claim. But it does not appear that he promised to do so, or ever authorized any one else to make such promise for him. There being no evidence to go to the jury on the question of *Conger's* liability for the commissions claimed, the motion for a nonsuit should have been granted, or a verdict for the defendant directed. Failing these, the motion for a new trial should have been granted.

By the Court.— The judgment of the circuit court is reversed, and the cause will be remanded for a new trial.

DAWSON, Respondent, vs. MEAD and others, Appellants.

February 29 — March 27, 1888.

Foreclosure of mortgage: Filing notice of lis pendens.

The filing of the notice of the pendency of an action to foreclose a mortgage is inoperative until the complaint is filed; and judgment cannot be rendered, therefore, until twenty days after the filing of the complaint. R. S. sec. 3187.

APPEAL from the Circuit Court for *Waupaca* County. The facts are sufficiently stated in the opinion.

For the appellants the cause was submitted on the brief of *F. C. Weed.*

[No appearance for the respondent.]

BY THE COURT. This is an action to foreclose a mortgage on real estate. It was commenced by the service of a summons June 23, 1885. Notice of the pendency of the action was filed in the proper office July 15, 1885. The complaint was filed with the clerk of the court in which the action was brought, October 14, 1885, and upon the same day judgment of foreclosure and for the sale of the

ortgaged premises was entered.   The defendants *Mead*
d *Butler* appeal from the judgment.

The judgment is premature.   Sec. 3187, R. S., provides
at such notice must be filed twenty days before judgment.
though this notice was in fact filed more than twenty
ys before the rendition of the judgment, yet, under the
me statute, the filing was inoperative until the complaint
is filed.   It was so ruled in *Flood v. Isaac*, 34 Wis. 423,
d again in *Olson v. Paul*, 56 Wis. 30.

Judgment reversed, and cause remanded for further pro-
edings according to law.

PORTER, Respondent, vs. DAY and others, Appellants.

February 29 — March 27, 1888.

*ming contracts: Horse racing: Premiums: Exclusion of horse from
race: Discretion: Fraud.*

The mere racing of horses is not illegal or against public policy ; and
where a premium or reward is offered by a third party, in good
faith and not as a cover for betting, to the winner in such a race,
the latter may recover the premium even though he paid an entrance fee which went to make up in part such premium.

Where the judges of a horse race had discretionary power to exclude
a horse violating a certain rule from further participation in the
race, their decision allowing the horse to proceed after a violation
should not be set aside except upon clear proof of fraud affecting
such decision.

APPEAL from the Circuit Court for *Eau Claire* County.
The following statement of the case was prepared by Mr.
istice TAYLOR as a part of the opinion:

This action was brought to recover a purse offered by the
fendants, as the president, secretary, treasurer, and man-
er of the Eau Claire Driving Park Association, an unin-

corporated society. The material allegations of the complaint are the following:

"That the said defendants, on or about the 22d day of September, 1885, promised the said plaintiff to pay the said plaintiff on the 24th day of September, 1885, the sum of $150, in consideration that and upon condition that the said plaintiff would pay the said defendants, or the said defendant *Putnam*, the sum of $30, called an 'entrance fee,' and would on the day last named, at an hour to be appointed by defendants, drive or cause to be driven over the race-track under the control of the said defendants, for the entertainment of the persons admitted thereto by the defendants upon payment to the said defendants of the admission price above mentioned, and of such other persons as the said defendants should choose to admit, the said plaintiff's horse, known as Sorrel George, in such manner and at such speed as to outstrip certain other horses driven in competition with the plaintiff's said horse over the said race-track at the same time, and to win, according to the decision of the three arbitrators or judges, so called, designated by the said defendants, a race described as a race of the 2:40 class. That thereupon the plaintiff paid the said defendant *Putnam*, as secretary of said Eau Claire Driving Park Association, the sum of $30, called an 'entrance fee,' and on the 24th day of September, 1885, at an hour appointed by defendants, caused to be driven over the race-track under the control of the defendants, for the entertainment of the persons admitted thereto by the said defendants, the said plaintiff's horse known as Sorrel George, in such manner and at such speed as to outstrip all other horses driven in competition with the plaintiff's said horse over the said race-track at the same time, and to win, according to the decision of the three arbitrators or judges, so-called, designated by the said defendants, a race described as a race of the 2:40 class, and duly performed all the conditions on his

part, whereby the said defendants became indebted to tl
plaintiff in the sum of $150. That the said defendants ha'
not, nor has any of them, paid the said plaintiff the sa
sum of $150, or any part of it." The complaint deman
judgment for the sum of $150, with interest and costs.

The answer, among other things, admits "that the Ei
Claire Driving Park Association offered to pay the own
of the horse who should win the 2:40 class race at the Se
tember meeting, when trotted under the rules of the Nation
Association, the sum of $150, if such rules were in all r
spects complied with, and towards which sum the own
should contribute the sum of $30," and "that the plaint
entered his said horse to compete in said race and for sa
stake and wager, and paid the said association the sum
$30 towards said stake." The answer then alleges that tl
plaintiff did not comply with the rules and regulatio
governing said race; "that his horse paced instead
trotted;" and that he "could not have won such race he
he trotted instead of paced." And further alleges that tl
plaintiff obtained the decision of the judges of the race
his favor by fraudulently representing to them that h
horse trotted when he well knew that he paced.

On the trial it was admitted that the plaintiff's hor
won the race, and the only question on that part of tl
case was whether he won it fairly. At the close of tl
evidence the learned circuit judge directed a verdict f
the plaintiff, and the defendants duly excepted. From tl
judgment entered in favor of the plaintiff, the defendan
appeal to this court.

W. F. Bailey, for the appellants, contended, *inter ali*
that the contract was void as against public policy. Mo
of the states, including Michigan and New York, ha'
specific statutes in regard to horse racing. Our statute (se
4538, R. S.) is general, but comprehensive enough to inclu
what is prohibited by the statutes of the other states. S

Bronson A. & B. Ass'n v. Ramsdell, 24 Mich. 441; *Hall v. Bergen,* 19 Barb. 122. The exception of contracts of insurance from the provisions of the section shows that the legislature considered contracts of this nature unlawful upon principle. If racing for premiums and purses was lawful, sec. 1779, R. S., authorizing certain corporations to offer such premiums, was wholly unnecessary. Purses made up in this way are in violation of the law and of the policy of the law relating to lotteries.

V. W. James, for the respondent.

TAYLOR, J. There were but two questions discussed by the learned counsel on the hearing of this appeal, viz.: (1) Was the contract set out in the complaint an illegal contract and void either at common law or under the statutes of this state? (2) Was there sufficient evidence of fraud on the part of the plaintiff to avoid the decision of the judges in his favor at the time the race was completed?

That the mere trotting or racing of horses, when done in a proper manner and not in the public streets or highways, is not an illegal act at common law, is well settled by the authorities, and it is equally well settled that betting on the result of a horse-race was not illegal at common law. See the following authorities: *Da Costa v. Jones,* Cowp. 729; *Good v. Elliott,* 3 Term, 693; *M'Allester v. Haden,* 2 Camp. 438; *Blaxton v. Pye,* 2 Wils. 309; *Gibbons v. Gouverneur,* 1 Denio, 170; *Van Valkenburgh v. Torrey,* 7 Cow. 252; *Bunn v. Riker,* 4 Johns. 426; *Campbell v. Richardson,* 10 Johns. 406. By the statutes of this state, trotting or racing horses is not declared illegal. It is only "betting and wagering upon a horse or other race" which is declared to be illegal. See secs. 4532, 4536, 4538, R. S. 1878. The only question on the first point made is whether competing for a reward, purse, or stake offered by a third party to one whose horse shall win in a running or trotting race, is illegal. It seems to us

this question must be answered in the negative. As state
above, the mere racing or trotting of horses, when conducte
in a proper place and in a proper manner, is not an illegal act
Offering a reward or premium to the successful competito
in such a race or trot is therefore just as lawful as the offei
ing a reward for competing in any other lawful business. I
the mere offering a premium or reward to the competitoi
in a lawful transaction is a violation of the laws agains
gaming and betting, then all the premiums offered by ou
state and county agricultural societies would be a violatio
of that law.

The fact that the parties competing for the reward o
premium offered are required to pay something in the wa!
of an entrance fee before they are allowed to compete doe
not make the transaction a betting or gaming transaction
All competitors for premiums in these societies are require
to pay an entrance fee, and these entrance fees go to mak
up in part the premiums offered to the competitors. It i
only when it is shown that the offering a reward or premiun
to the competitors is a mere subterfuge for betting an
gaming on a horse-race or any uncertain event, that i
comes under the law prohibiting betting and gaming. I
two or more men owning trotting horses should contribut
equally or otherwise a sum of money, and put it into th
hands of some other person for the purpose of offering it a
a premium or reward to them only, and to the owner of th
horse who should win the race, such a transaction woul
undoubtedly come within the rule which prohibits bettinf
on a horse or other race; and it was so held in the case o
Gibbons v. Gouverneur, supra. Where there is no claim
that the competitors are the sole contributors to the pre
mium or purse which is offered to them as competitors, we
are unable to find any decided case which holds that the
competing for such purse or premium is illegal or prohibited
unless the same be expressly prohibited by the laws of the

state in which such rewards are offered. On the other hand, in those states where the legality of offering rewards or premiums has been considered, and where they are not expressly prohibited by law, the courts have uniformly held the transaction a lawful one, and that it is not within the prohibition against betting and gaming. *Harris v. White*, 81 N. Y. 532; *Misner v. Knapp*, 13 Oreg. 135; *Delier v. Plymouth Co. Agr. Soc.* 57 Iowa, 481; *Alvord v. Smith*, 63 Ind. 58.

In *Harris v. White, supra,* the court state the difference between betting and gaming, and offering purses or premiums, as follows: " A bet or wager is ordinarily an agreement between two or more that a sum of money or some valuable thing, in contributing which all agreeing take part, shall become the property of one or some of them on the happening in the future of an event at the present uncertain, and the stake is the money or thing thus put upon the chance. There is in them this element that does not enter into a modern purse or premium, viz., that each party to the former gets a chance of gain from others, and takes a risk of his own to them. . . . A purse or premium is ordinarily some valuable thing, offered by a person for the doing of something by others, into the strife for which he does not enter. He has not a chance of gaining the thing offered; and if he abide by his offer, that he must lose it and give it over to some of those contending for it is reasonably certain." This is perhaps as good a statement of the difference between a bet and a premium or prize as can be given. And when a purse or prize is offered in good faith to the winner in a competitive contest, which contest is not unlawful in itself, the transaction is a lawful one, and the person offering the prize or premium will be held liable in the law to make good his offer to the winner. This appears to be the rule in all states where the statutes do not forbid the offering of such rewards or premiums. In the state of Michigan the law prohibits the offering of such rewards or

premiums in certain cases, and it is therefore held that
person competing for and winning such reward in a cas
prohibited by law cannot recover the same in an action a
law. See *Bronson A. & B. Ass'n v. Ramsdell*, 24 Mich
441–443.

That the speeding of horses is not illegal or against pub
lic policy in this state is evident from the fact that th
legislature expressly authorizes it to be done by certain cor
porate bodies. Sec. 1779, R. S. It is not to be presume
that the legislature would authorize corporate bodies to d
that which was against the public policy of the state. W
must hold therefore that the mere racing of horses is no
illegal or against public policy, and the offering of a pre
mium or reward to those competing in such races, whe
such rewards or premiums are not a mere cover or disguis
for betting on such races, is not illegal.

Upon the other point, we think with the learned circui
judge that the evidence entirely fails to make a case for set
ting aside the decision of the judges made at the time in
favor of the plaintiff. The evidence discloses the fact tha
the plaintiff's horse fairly won three of the five heats, and
the only doubt raised as to the right of the plaintiff to th
money is that in the third heat, when the plaintiff's hors
did not win, the horse was so managed by his driver tha
he violated the rules governing the race and should hav
been excluded from further competition for the reward
There is nothing in the evidence, taken most strongl
against the plaintiff, which, by the rules governing th
race, made it the imperative duty of the judges to exclud
the plaintiff's horse from further competition; and thei
decision made at the time, permitting him to continue in
the race, cannot now be overruled in order to give the re
ward to some other competitor, except by showing a clea
case of fraud on his part.

It is very clearly shown that in the third heat the plaint

iff's horse paced most of the way, but that fact being admitted, it was still in the discretion of the judges to permit him to go again in the race. The rule relied upon by the defendants for excluding the plaintiff's horse after the third heat provides that when a horse breaks from his gait in trotting or pacing the rider shall at once pull him to the gait in which he is to go in the race, and, the rider failing to do that, the horse shall lose the heat though he comes out ahead, and if he does not come out ahead all the other horses shall be placed ahead of him in that heat; "and the judges shall have discretionary power to distance the offending horse " and to fine the driver, etc. Now, it is evident that this discretionary power to exclude the offending horse from further participation in the race must be exercised by the judges before the next heat is run, and having exercised that power and permitted the horse to go again and win the race, nothing but the clearest evidence of fraud on the part of the owner of the horse should be allowed to set aside such decision of the judges.

The only claim that any fraud was practiced in the case by the plaintiff is the statement of one of the judges, that the driver made a false statement to them before they decided to let the horse go again, as to the extent of his pacing on the third heat. This is denied by the driver, and not positively testified to by either of the judges. We have great doubt whether the plaintiff is to be held liable for the statements made by his driver not in his presence or by his direction. But if he did make a misstatement as to the extent of the pacing done by his horse in the third heat, there is no clear proof that he would have been excluded had the driver made a more truthful statement. The witness *Day*, one of the judges of the race, testified: "If the truth was that the horse paced, he would have been distanced. That would not have been the result regardless of the fact whether he gained by it or not. The question would be whether he gained by it." The person who drove the horse testified that the horse could not pace as fast as he could trot, and that he lost ground by pacing. Against this evidence there was only the evidence of the witness Howard, who testified generally that the horse's fastest gait was pacing. He never drove the horse or saw the horse in a race before the race in question.

There is nothing in the evidence that shows satisfactorily that the horse would have been distanced and excluded from further contesting for the race had the exact truth been known to the judges when they permitted him to remain in the race. Their decision to permit him to remain in the race must therefore stand.

By the Court.— The judgment of the circuit court is affirmed.

Orton, J., dissents.

Valley Lumber Company, Respondent, vs. Smith and another, Appellants.

March 1 — March 27, 1888.

Contracts: Evidence: Purchase price: Value: Objections to account rendered: Instructions to jury.

1. Where there is a direct conflict of testimony as to the price orally agreed to be paid for property, evidence of its real value at the time of the contract is admissible.
2. There being a direct conflict in the evidence as to whether the defendants objected to a bill or account presented by the plaintiff, it was error for the court to ignore or suppress the evidence on the part of the defendants and to charge the jury that where no objections are made to a bill presented it is *prima facie* evidence of the correctness thereof.
3. One of the defendants testified that at the time of making a contract he made a memorandum of its terms in a book kept for such

Valley Lumber Co. vs. Smith and another.

purposes. The memorandum was introduced in evidence, and there was no evidence tending to impeach the credibility of the witness in respect thereto. *Held*, that it was error for the court, in charging the jury, to cast suspicion and doubt upon the defendant's testimony and to call special attention to the criticisms of plaintiff's counsel upon the memorandum.

APPEAL from the Circuit Court for *Eau Claire* County. The case is stated in the opinion.

For the appellants there was a brief by *J. H. Opdale* and *James Wickham*, and oral argument by *Mr. Wickham.*

W. F. Bailey, for the respondent.

ORTON, J. This action is brought to recover a certain sum for goods, wares, and merchandise, and $200 for the use or lease of certain logging camps during the winter of 1883 and 1884, situated on a certain forty acres of land belonging to the plaintiff, which had been denuded of its timber or stumpage. The only matter controverted on the trial was the claim for $200 for the use of said logging camps. This the defendants denied in their answer. The only witness for the plaintiff on that question was one Carson, the president of the plaintiff company, who testified that the contract for the use of the logging camps was *made* by him when he and *Smith*, one of the defendants, *were* alone, and that such was the contract. The defendant *Smith* testified with great positiveness that the defendants never made any such contract, but that the contract was that the defendants should pay the plaintiff $200 for a good title of the said forty acres of land, with the old camps thereon, which were dilapidated and of scarcely any value whatever. Another witness, who claimed to have been present when the contract was made, testified that the said Carson, the president of the company, said, "I will do better by you than by the other man. I will give you the logging camps and the forty acres of land the camps stand on for $200, and give you title." Another witness testified that he heard the said Carson substantially admit that he had sold the defendants the camps and the forty acres. The testimony tended to show that the defendants, the winter before, had been troubled by some one shutting up their roads across the said forty-acre lot, which they used in their logging business on other lands in the vicinity, and that they wished therefore to own and have full control of that lot, so as to prevent such annoyance. The said Carson on cross-examination testified that " *Smith's* object was to purchase those camps, and get the forty acres of land on which they stood, so that he might control the roads on account of this trouble;" and he further testified, "I would give him title to the forty acres of land if I had known he wanted it. It would not have been any detriment to have deeded it to him. I would not give him the title now if he paid the money. I never agreed to."

This is a sufficient statement of the case to show the pertinency of the exceptions. The jury rendered a verdict for the plaintiff of $238.62, presumably for the $200 for the use of the logging camps, and interest. To reverse the judgment rendered on this verdict, the appellants allege the following errors:

First. The appellants offered and asked questions tending to show the real value of the logging camps at the time, and that they were useless to 'the plaintiff, as the timber had all been cut off the forty acres, and that they were not in a condition to use until repaired, and that they were of no value whatever, for the purpose of corroborating the testimony of the defendant *Smith* and of the other witnesses as to what the contract was. The court sustained the objection of the plaintiff to such offer and questions. This was clearly erroneous. This was a very strong case for the application of the rule that such corroboration is proper when there is a direct conflict of the evidence as to the contract price to be paid for the property in question. If the logging camps were of the value of $200 or more, then the plaintiff's version of the contract would be quite probable as against the testimony for the defendants that such consideration was to include the title of the forty acres also. On the other hand, if the camps were of little or no real value to any one, then the testimony of the defendants would be quite probable as against the testimony for the plaintiff that the defendants agreed to pay $200 rent for the use of such camps for one winter. This is agreeable to common reason, and logical, and such evidence is approved by the authorities. The evidence disapproved in *Kvammen v. Meridean Mill Co.* 58 Wis. 399, was as "to the *usual* price for sawing laths the season before." It did not relate to the price or value of the thing itself which was the subject of the controversy and of the contract. In that case Mr. Justice CASSODAY said in the opinion: "It may be, as intimated by Mr. Justice COOLEY in *Campau v. Moran*, 31 Mich. 280, that where the evidence adduced upon both sides is in direct conflict, and pretty evenly balanced, as to the *contract price*, evidence that the cost of performance was greatly in excess or greatly below such price might afford some reasonable ground for believing that the contract was for the price nearest the cost." This is a clear exposition of the rule. Mr. Abbott, in his work on Trial Evidence, states the rule as follows: "Where the testimony is conflicting as to what was the price agreed upon in an oral sale, or as to whether there was any agreement as to price, it is competent to show the value of the property at the time of the sale as tending to show what the real contract was." Page 305. The following cases are cited by the appellants' counsel as supporting this rule: *Richardson v. McGoldrick*, 43 Mich. 476; *Misner v. Darling*, 44 Mich. 488; *Rauch v. Scholl*, 68 Pa. St. 234; *Allison v. Horning*,

22 Ohio St. 138; *Swain v. Cheney*, 41 N. H. 232; *Moore v. Davis*, 49 N. H. 45; *Kidder v. Smith*, 34 Vt. 294; *Johnson v. Harder*, 45 Iowa, 677; *Bradbury v. Dwight*, 3 Met. 31.

Second. The court, in charging the jury, after reciting the testimony of Carson, the president of the company, that he had presented to the defendants a bill or account containing this charge of $200 for the use of the camps, and that the defendants made no objections to it, but kept the bill, said to the jury: "Where a statement of account is rendered, and nothing is said about it, and no objections made, of course that is *prima facie* evidence of the correctness of the bill. . . . It is a sort of admission on his part of the correctness of the bill." Aside from the fact that this claim is not a matter of book-account, or of an account rendered or bill presented, but the subject of a special contract, and such a principle of law has no application to it, it was unfair for the court to ignore or suppress the testimony of the defendant *Smith*, that he did at the time object and insist that he had never hired or rented the camps, but that he had bought the forty acres, with the camps upon it. The jury might forget that evidence, and from this charge of the court take it for granted that the defendants had assented to the claim by not objecting to it, and might have been, and probably were, thereby misled as to the evidence.

Third. The defendant *Smith* testified that he made a memorandum of the contract of the purchase of the forty acres and the camps on it at the time in a memorandum book which he kept for such matters of business, and said memorandum was introduced in evidence. The court, in commenting upon this evidence to the jury, and after saying "that it tended to show that he *(Smith)* was not mistaken as to what the contract was," said, "Of course, *if he really made* that memorandum," etc. "You have heard the criticisms of counsel upon that memorandum. It is your duty to consider whether that was really a memorandum made *at that time.*" This was very unfair, as well as a very serious error. There was no evidence tending to impeach the credibility of the defendant *Smith* in respect to his having made at the time this memorandum, or tending to cast any suspicion upon his evidence in that respect. The court cast suspicion and doubt upon this evidence, without any other grounds than the unrestrained and groundless *criticisms* of the opposing counsel in his argument. The attention of the jury is not called to the testimony on this point, except with an unauthorized proviso, " if he really made the memorandum," and " whether it was really made at that time." But the special attention of the jury is called to " the criticisms of counsel upon that memorandum."

There are other errors assigned, but they may not occur upon another trial, and are not very material. We are inclined to think that if the above errors had not been committed, the verdict would have been in favor of the defendants.

By the Court.— The judgment of the circuit court is reversed, and the cause remanded for a new trial.

MANUFACTURERS' NATIONAL BANK OF RACINE, Appellant, vs. NEWELL and another, Respondents.

March 1 — March 27, 1888.

Negotiable instruments: Note discounted by bank: Bona fide *purchaser: Constructive notice of infirmity.*

1. A bank discounted a note for a company and credited it with the amount, the credit subsequently increasing, so that, at the time of suit on the note, the bank had parted with nothing of value for it. *Held,* that the bank was not a *bona fide* purchaser for value.

2. Where a note is given to a company, constructive notice of infirmity therein to the officers of the company does not in itself import

notice to a bank discounting the note, of which, also, they are directors and officers.

8. The mere fact that the officers of the bank knew, in a general way, that the company was in the habit of selling machinery and taking notes therefor, and then discounting the same at the bank, was not equivalent to actual notice of the infirmity attaching to this particular note.

APPEAL from the Circuit Court for *St. Croix* County.

The following statement of the case was prepared by Mr. Justice CASSODAY:

August 25, 1884, the J. I. Case Threshing-Machine Company, a corporation doing business at Racine, by its agent, sold to the defendant *P. F. Newell*, at Hammond, St. Croix county, a separator and steam-engine for threshing grain. At the same time, and in part consideration therefor, a note bearing that date, purporting to be executed by the said *P. F. Newell* and his brother, *M. J. Newell*, was made, wherein they promised to pay on or before November 15, 1885, to J. I. Case Threshing-Machine Company *or bearer* $800 at the bank of New Richmond, with interest at seven per cent. per annum from that date until paid. This action was commenced December 12, 1885, to recover the amount of the note, which the complaint alleged to have been duly sold, assigned, and transferred to the plaintiff, a banking corporation at Racine, by said company for a valuable consideration, before the same became due. The defendant *M. J. Newell* separately answered, and denied that he ever signed, executed, or delivered the note. The defendant *Peter F. Newell* separately answered, and admitted that he executed, signed and delivered the note. He also alleged, in effect, that he purchased the separator and steam-engine at the agreed price of $1,400, upon a warranty, upon which he relied, as to its good quality and efficiency; and that the machine was worthless, and that he had in consequence suffered loss greater in amount than such price of the machine; and that the plaintiff took and received the note with fair notice and knowledge of such breach and all the facts therein stated. After the close of the testimony, the court directed a verdict in favor of the defendants, which was returned accordingly. From the judgment entered thereon the plaintiff appeals.

For the appellant there was a brief by *H. C. Baker* and *J. B. Smith*, and oral argument by *Mr. Baker*. They contended, *inter alia*, that the burden was not upon the plaintiff of showing that it purchased the note for value before due. 1 Dan. on Neg. Inst. 596; 47 Wis. 433. Mere suspicion of defect of title, or of the existence of circumstances which would put a prudent man on inquiry, will not avail in defense. *Kelley v. Whitney*, 45 Wis. 110; *Brown v. Spofford*, 95 U. S. 474; *Goodman v. Simonds*, 20 How. 343; *Mitchell v. Catchings*, 23 Fed. Rep. 710; *Murray v. Lardner*, 2 Wall. 110; *Farrell v. Lovett*, 68 Me. 326. Notice to an officer of a bank, derived by him while not engaged officially in the business of the bank, cannot operate to the prejudice of the bank. *Nat. Bank v. Norton*, 1 Hill, 572; *Bank of U. S. v. Davis*, 2 id. 463; 87 N. Y. 291–307; 37 id. 320; *Mann v. Second Nat. Bank*, 34 Kan. 746. The placing of the amount for which the note was discounted to the credit of the Machine Company, and placing the note with the assets of the bank as a note discounted, made the bank a purchaser for value.

For the respondents there was a brief by *R. H. Start* and *L. P. Wetherby*, and oral argument by *Mr. Start*. To the point that the bank was not a *bona fide* purchaser for value, they cited Edwards on Bills & N. (1st ed.), 373; *Central Nat. Bank v. Valentine*, 18 Hun, 417; *Fulton Bank v. Phœnix Bank*, 1 Hall, 562; *Mann v. Second Nat. Bank*, 30 Kan. 412; *Platt v. Chapin*, 49 How. Pr. 318; *Dresser v. M. & I. R. C. Co.* 93 U. S. 92; *McBride v. Farmers' Bank*, 26 N. Y. 454; *Am. Exch. Bank v. Corliss*, 46 Barb. 19; *Clark v. Ely,* 2 Sandf. Ch. 166; *West v. Am. Exchange Bank,* 44 Barb. 175; *Garland v. Salem Bank,* 9 Mass. 408; *Holcomb v. Wyckoff,* 35 N. J. Law, 36; *Todd v. Shelbourne,* 8 Hun, 510; *Clarke Nat. Bank v. Bank of Albion,* 52 Barb. 592; *Parish v. Stone,* 14 Pick. 208; *Jordan v. Nat. S. & L. Bank,* 74 N. Y. 473; *Williams v. Smith,* 2 Hill, 301; *Hubbard v. Chapin,* 2 Allen, 328.

CASSODAY, J.   The name of *M. J. Newell* was signed to the note in question by his brother *Peter F.,* in the presence of the agent of the threshing-machine company, but apparently without any authority, express or implied.   The most that is claimed is that when *Peter F.,* some months afterwards, told him he had so signed his name, he made no response.   There is no claim that *M. J. Newell* was in business with his brother, nor that he had any interest in the purchase, nor that such agent was induced to believe or had any expectation of holding him liable in any other capacity than as mere surety, solely by virtue of his name being signed as stated.   Upon these admitted facts, it is evident that if the defense made by *Peter F. Newell,* as principal defendant, is available to him, then it is equally available to *M. J. Newell,* and the direction of the verdict was justifiable.   For the purposes of this case, it must be assumed that had the action been brought by the company, instead of the bank, the defense to the note made by *Peter F. Newell,* under the breach of the warranty on the purchase of the machines, would have been a complete and perfect bar to any recovery.   The only question for consideration, therefore, is whether it appears conclusively, from the undisputed evidence, that the plaintiff was not a *bona fide* purchaser of the note in suit for value before maturity.   If it was not such *bona fide* purchaser, then the court was justified in directing a verdict in favor of both defendants; otherwise, the judgment must be reversed.

The testimony on this point is undisputed. It consists of the depositions of B. B. Northrup and J. I. Case, taken on the part of the plaintiff, and offered and read in evidence by the defendants. These depositions, so far as material here, are to the effect that during the times in question Northrup was cashier, and Case president, of the plaintiff bank; that during the same times Case was director and president, and Northrup a director, of the company; that during the same times M. B. Erskine was a stockholder and director in the company, and also in the bank; that during the same times the Baker estate was a stockholder in the company, and also in the bank, and was represented by Northrup, as trustee thereof; that during the same times Charles E. Erskine was a stockholder, director, and treasurer of the company, and also a stockholder in the bank; that during the same times the bank had a capital stock of $250,000, of which $79,000 were owned by stockholders of the company, and of that amount Case owned $33,000; that during the same times the company did its banking business at the bank, and the bank was in the habit of collecting and also discounting notes taken by the company for machinery manufactured and sold by it; that October 8, 1885, Charles E. Erskine, as such treasurer of the company, took said note to the bank to be discounted, and for that purpose left the same with Northrup, as such cashier, who received the same, and stamped it as "Bills Discounted," and credited the amount thereof, including the interest thereon to that date, in the then current account of the company with the bank; that on that day there stood to the credit of the company on the books of the bank in that account a balance of $42,095.55; that October 9, 1885, there stood to the credit of the company on the books of the bank in that account a balance of $52,614.47; that December 9, 1885, there stood to the credit of the company on the books of the bank in that account a balance of $147,911.86;

that December 12, 1885, there stood to the credit of the
company on the books of the bank in that account a balance of $141,676.65; that Case had no personal knowledge
of the note in suit, nor of any of the circumstances under
which it was given, nor of either of the defendants, until
long after the commencement of this action; that Northrup
had no personal knowledge nor information concerning the
sale and purchase of said machinery, nor said warranty,
nor any of the circumstances under which said note was
given, nor the consideration thereof, until after the note
was so credited to the company on the books of the bank.

Upon these facts, can we hold that the plaintiff became a
bona fide purchaser of the note for value, before maturity,
by virtue of the amount thereof being credited to the company on the books of the bank, under the principles of the
law-merchant, or must we hold the reverse? The acts of
the agent in selling the machine and taking the note were,
in legal effect, the acts of the company. This being so, the
company must be presumed to have had constructive notice
of the infirmity of the note in question. But it does not
appear that, prior to its receipt of the note, any of the directors or officers of the bank had any actual knowledge or
information respecting such infirmity. The mere fact that
some of the directors and officers of the bank were also directors and officers of the company did not import to the
bank the same constructive notice as was chargeable against
the company. *Westfield Bank v. Cornen*, 37 N. Y. 320;
Atlantic State Bank v. Savery, 82 N. Y. 291; *Mann v. Second
Nat. Bank*, 34 Kan. 746. That fact of itself, therefore, was
not such, in law, as to preclude the bank from becoming a
bona fide purchaser of the note at the time of giving the
credit, had it then actually paid the amount of the note.
The mere fact that the officers of the bank knew, in a general way, that the company was in the habit of selling machinery, and taking notes therefor, and then discounting the

same at the bank, was not equivalent to actual notice of the infirmity attaching to this particular note. The ruling in *Gill v. Cubitt*, 3 Barn. & C. 466, to the effect that a mere suspicious circumstance would prevent a party from becoming a *bona fide* purchaser for value, seems to have been disapproved by later authorities, not only in this country but England. *Goodman v. Harvey*, 4 Adol. & E. 870; *Goodman v. Simonds*, 20 How. 367–369; *Murray v. Lardner*, 2 Wall. 110; *Brown v. Spofford*, 95 U. S. 478; *Farrell v. Lovett*, 68 Me. 326, 28 Am. Rep. 59; *Phelan v. Moss*, 67 Pa. St. 59; *Comstock v. Hannah*, 76 Ill. 530; *Fox v. Bank of Kansas City*, 30 Kan. 441. This is in harmony with the rulings of this court. *Kelley v. Whitney*, 45 Wis. 110; *Patterson v. Wright*, 64 Wis. 289. But here it conclusively appears that the bank did not pay the company the amount of the note at the time of giving the credit to the latter on its books, nor any part thereof; on the contrary, it was then owing the company over $40,000 on its bank-account. The taking of the note and giving the credit simply increased the amount of that indebtedness. The relation of the bank to the company continued to be that of debtor and creditor, as well after the receipt of the note as before. *Bank of the Republic v. Millard*, 10 Wall. 155; *Foley v. Hill*, 2 H. L. Cas. 28. Of course, there was an implied obligation on the part of the bank to honor the checks and drafts of the company to the extent of such indebtedness. *Ibid*. But there is not a particle of evidence that any such check or draft was ever given. On the contrary, we have the evidence of the officers of the bank to the effect that on the next day after the credit was given the indebtedness of the bank to the company had increased $10,000; and that on the day this suit was commenced such indebtedness was nearly $100,000 greater than when the note was received and the credit given. Whether the company checked the money out of the bank during the sixty intervening days between the dates given, does not appear. If it did, the fact could easily have been stated by the officers of the bank in giving their depositions in the case. Not having been thus stated, and it appearing affirmatively that the plaintiff received the note on a mere credit, which continued to increase, we must assume that the credit given to the company on account of the note was not paid by the bank when this action was commenced. At the time of the commencement of the action the note was several weeks past due. Up to that time the bank had parted with nothing of value for it. The defense interposed was substantial, and went to the merits. It was sufficient to bar any recovery, unless the bank is to be regarded as a *bona fide* purchaser for value of the note, by reason of the mere discount and credit. Such being the facts, we are constrained to hold that the plaintiff's remedy was to tender the note back to the company, and cancel the credit. The right to do so is certainly sanctioned by courts of high authority. *Lancaster Co. Nat. Bank v. Huver*, 114 Pa. St. 216; *Dougherty v. Cent. Nat. Bank*, 93 Pa. St. 227; *Dresser v. M. & I. R. Co.* 93 U. S. 92; *Scott v. Ocean Bank*, 23 N. Y. 289; *Cent. Nat. Bank v. Valentine*, 18 Hun, 417; *Clarke Nat. Bank v. Bank of Albion*, 52 Barb. 592; *Platt v. Chapin*, 49 How. Pr. 318; *Payne v. Cutler*, 13 Wend. 605; *Fulton Bank v. Phœnix Bank*, 1 Hall, 562; *Mann v. Second Nat. Bank*, 30 Kan. 412; *Balbach v. Frelinghuysen*, 15 Fed. Rep. 675. These adjudications are to the effect that such mere discount and credit does not constitute a *bona fide* purchaser for value. To be such, the holder of the note must actually part with something of value for it. If, after such discount and credit, such holder receives notice of the infirmity of the note, he is thereby incapacitated from becoming such *bona fide* purchaser by any subsequent payment. We have not overlooked the remark of the late learned master of the rolls, cited by counsel, in *Ex parte Richdale*, L. R. 19 Ch. Div.

417. But that was under a bankrupt act, and the rights of third parties were involved. We must hold that the bank was not a *bona fide* purchaser for value so as to be protected against the infirmity of the note.

By the Court.— The judgment of the circuit court is affirmed.

WEBSTER GLOVER LUMBER & MANUFACTURING COMPANY, Respondent, vs. ST. CROIX COUNTY and another, Appellants.

March 1 — March 27, 1888.

Appeal: Waiver: Accepting benefits of judgment.

In an action against a county to set aside certain taxes and restrain collection thereof, a part of the taxes were held valid, and it was ordered that the plaintiff pay such part into court, and that upon so doing it should have judgment enjoining the collection of the remainder. The plaintiff paid into court the required sum, and judgment was thereupon entered, adjudging the sum so paid to be in full payment, satisfaction, and discharge of all the taxes in question, and enjoining the collection of any further sum. The county procured an order that the money be paid to its treasurer, and it was so paid. *Held,* that by accepting the money the county waved its right to appeal from the judgment.

APPEAL from the Circuit Court for *St. Croix* County.

Action to set aside and have declared void all the state, county, town, school-district, and highway taxes levied upon the plaintiff's land in the town of Emerald, St. Croix county, for the year 1883. The cause was before this court on a former appeal. See 63 Wis. 647.

Upon the second trial the court found that the taxes in question amounted in the aggregate to $2,140.69, and that all of said taxes were valid, except the sum of $314.25 of school and road district taxes, which the court held invalid because the plaintiff's lands upon which the same were assessed were not legally embraced in said school and road districts.   An order was thereupon entered requiring the plaintiff to pay into court for the use of the defendants the sum of $1,826.44, with interest thereon at twelve per cent. from January 1, 1884, and that upon so doing the plaintiff take judgment perpetually enjoining the collection of said sum of $314.25, school and road district taxes.   The plaintiff having paid the required sum into court, judgment was entered, in pursuance of the order, adjudging the sum so paid to be in full payment, satisfaction, and discharge of all the taxes levied upon the plaintiff's lands for the year 1883, and enjoining the defendants from collecting the delinquent school-district and highway taxes assessed on said lands in that year, amounting to $314.25.

The defendant county procured an order that the amount paid into court by the plaintiff be paid over to the county treasurer, and it was so paid, the said treasurer giving his receipt therefor.

The defendants appeal from the order first above mentioned and from the judgment.

For the appellants there were briefs by *R. H. Start* and *L. P. Wetherby*, and oral argument by *Mr. Start*.

For the respondent there was a brief by *H. C. Baker* and *J. B. Smith*, and oral argument by *Mr. Baker*.

Cole, C. J.   From the view which we have taken of this case it is unnecessary to inquire whether the court below was right in holding the school and road district taxes in dispute invalid.   The judgment required the plaintiff to pay into court the sum of $1,826.44, and interest thereon at twelve per cent. from January 1, 1884, and that upon compliance with that condition it should take judgment perpetually enjoining the collection of the district school and road taxes, amounting to $314.25.   The court adjudged that the payment by the plaintiff of the sum specified should be

in full payment, satisfaction, and discharge of all the taxes
levied upon its lands for the year 1883. The record shows
that the plaintiff complied with this conditional judgment
by paying the money into court according to its terms.
The record further shows that subsequently, on the application of the defendants, this money was ordered to be paid
over to the treasurer of the county, who gave a receipt for
the same, which is likewise among the papers in the cause.
Now, the question is, Can the defendants, after having applied for and received the money which it was adjudged the
plaintiff should pay, appeal from the judgment and have it
reviewed?

The appeal is "from the whole and every part of the
judgment." The counsel for the plaintiff insists that the
defendants, by accepting the money, waived their right to
appeal from the judgment. We think this position is correct, and that the appeal must be dismissed. The case
comes fully within the principles decided in *Cogswell v.
Colley*, 22 Wis. 399; *Flanders v. Merrimac*, 44 Wis. 621;
Bennett v. Van Syckel, 18 N. Y. 481; *Murphy v. Spaulding*,
46 N. Y. 556; *Carll v. Oakley*, 97 N. Y. 633. These decisions go upon the ground that a party cannot proceed to
enforce and have the benefit of such portions of a judgment
as are in his favor, and appeal from those against him. In
other words, that the right to proceed on a judgment and
enjoy its fruits, and the right to appeal therefrom, are
totally inconsistent positions. The election to pursue one
course must be deemed an abandonment of the other. Here
the plaintiff paid all the taxes which it was adjudged it
should pay as a condition to enjoining those which the
court held illegal. The defendants have seen fit to apply
for and accept the money thus paid. By complying with
the provisions of the judgment, the plaintiff is forever
estopped from questioning the legality, either in law or in
equity, of the taxes paid. The defendant's contention is

that all the taxes levied upon the plaintiff's lands in 1883 should be held valid in equity. If they desired to appeal from the judgment which held illegal a portion of those taxes, they should not have accepted the money paid into court which was adjudged to be in full satisfaction of all the taxes in controversy. The defendants seek to receive and retain those taxes which the court held valid and just, and to enforce the collection of the taxes which the court held illegal. The provisions of the judgment are connected and dependent. As the defendants have accepted all that is of benefit to them, they should not at the same time ask to have the whole judgment reversed. Such a course is not open to them. The correctness of this view is fully demonstrated by the reasoning in the cases above cited, and we are relieved from any further discussion of the question.

The learned counsel for the defendants says the taxes were ordered to be paid into court for the use of the defendants; that they belonged to the county which was justly entitled to them; and that no condition was annexed to the acceptance of the money by the defendants. It is true the judgment does not provide that if the defendants apply for and accept the money paid into court this shall be a waiver of the right to appeal from the judgment. But the authorities above cited show that the law attaches that consequence to the acts of the defendants; that it will not allow them to enforce a right conferred by the judgment and at the same time prosecute an appeal from it. The acceptance of the money, under the circumstances, must be referred to the defendants' right to it under the judgment, and cannot be considered as a voluntary payment by the plaintiff, but as a payment in pursuance of the judgment. The defendants were not obliged to accept the money. They might have let it remain in court until the litigation was terminated, but they chose to apply for and receive it,

thus indicating, in a most positive manner, a purpose to
assert and claim all the benefit the judgment gave them.
To sustain the appeal, under the circumstances, would "be
contrary to that just principle which forbids one from
claiming under, and at the same time repudiating, any instrument." Mr. Justice PAINE, in *Cogswell v. Colley, supra.*
By the Court.— The appeal is dismissed.

THE STATE EX REL. THE TOWN OF SPRING LAKE, Respondent,
   vs. THE BOARD OF SUPERVISORS OF PIERCE COUNTY,
   Appellant.

March 1 — March 27, 1888.

Bridges: Towns: Counties: Mandamus: *Pleading: Place of trial:
   Judgment: Mandate of writ, when satisfied.*

1. The petition on behalf of a town for a writ of *mandamus* to compel
   a county to aid in building a bridge did not show that the officer
   applying for the writ was directed so to do by the electors of the
   town, or that a stream of water flowed through the ravine over
   which the bridge was to be built, but such facts were proved on
   the trial without objection. *Held,* that the petition might be
   amended at any time to correspond with the proofs, or that the
   variance might be disregarded.

2. Ch. 187, Laws of 1885, does not limit the bridges which the county
   may be required to assist in building, to such as cross streams of
   water.

3. When the return to an alternative writ of *mandamus* consists of
   denials of the material allegations in the relation, no answer to
   the return is required to raise the issues.

4. Under sec. 3452, R. S., and ch. 292, Laws of 1881, issues of fact in
   an action of *mandamus* in the Eighth judicial circuit may be tried
   at a special term of the court issuing the writ, held in another
   county.

5. In an action to compel a county to aid in building a bridge, the
   judgment directed the issuance of a writ of *mandamus* commanding the county board to meet and to levy the required tax

VOL. 71 — 21

upon the taxable property of the county, without appointing any
time for such meeting, and without excepting from liability to such
taxation certain cities which were not liable under the law. *Held.*
that the mandate of the writ would be satisfied if the county board
should perform the duty required of them at their first meeting after
service of the writ, and should levy the tax upon the taxable
property of the county subject thereto.

APPEAL from the Circuit Court for *Pierce* County.

This proceeding was commenced by petition by the town
of *Spring Lake,* praying that a *mandamus* issue to the *Board
of Supervisors of Pierce County* to compel them to levy a
tax on the taxable property of the county to aid said town
in the building of certain bridges therein. The proceeding
was instituted under ch. 187, Laws of 1885. Due petition
had theretofore been presented on behalf of the town to the
county board, containing a sufficient statement of the facts,
praying the board to make such appropriation and tax levy.
An alternative writ of *mandamus* was allowed and issued
upon such relation, and duly served. The county board
appeared, and moved to quash the writ for certain alleged
defects therein. The motion was denied, and thereupon
the board made return to the writ, denying many of the
material allegations of fact contained therein. The cause
was thereupon noticed for trial on behalf of the town, at a
general term of the circuit court for St. Croix county. A
motion was made to that court to strike the cause from the
calendar, for the reasons (1) that St. Croix was not the
proper county for the trial of the cause, but Pierce county,
in which the action was commenced; and (2) because no
issue was made by the pleadings. The motion was overruled. The cause was afterwards tried in St. Croix county,
the defendant county not appearing at the trial. Such trial
resulted in a judgment that a peremptory writ of *mandamus* issue to the *Board of Supervisors of Pierce County,*
commanding them to meet and appropriate one half of the

cost of the bridges in question (being $400), to cause the same to be levied upon the taxable property of the county, and to designate two of its members to act as its commissioners as required by sec. 1, ch. 187, Laws of 1885. Costs were also awarded against the defendant. The county board appeals from the judgment. The case is further stated in the opinion.

For the appellant there was a brief signed by *J. S. & F. M. White*, and oral argument by *Mr. J. S. White.* They contended, among many other things, that the board was entitled to judgment on the pleadings. There being no reply the affirmative allegations of the return stood admitted. 5 Wait's Pr. 589; *People ex rel. Bently v. Comm'rs,* 7 Wend. 475; *State ex rel. Cothren v. Lean,* 9 Wis. 290; *State ex rel. Christopher v. Portage,* 14 id. 550; *State ex rel. Taylor v. Delafield,* 64 id. 220.

R. H. Start, for the respondent.

LYON, J. 1. It was stated in the argument, and not controverted, that the ground upon which the *Board of Supervisors of Pierce County* refused to make the appropriation demanded was that the board were of the opinion the act of 1885 is unconstitutional and void. But for this opinion we suppose this appeal would not have been taken, although many other objections to the validity of the judgment were made and argued by counsel. Since this appeal was taken this court has decided that the statute in question is a valid law. *State ex rel. Baraboo v. Sauk Co.* 70 Wis. 485; *State ex rel. Woodland v. Sauk Co.* 70 Wis. 491; *State ex rel. Rochester v. Racine Co.* 70 Wis. 543. These decisions put at rest the question of the validity of this law.

2. The relation or petition for a *mandamus* states sufficient facts to entitle the town to the relief demanded, with perhaps two exceptions. One of these is, it is not alleged therein that the officer applying for the writ was directed

by the electors of the town to make such application. In the two cases against Sauk county, above cited, this was held a fatal defect unless supplied by amendment. The other exception is, the petition states that one of the bridges which the town proposed to build was across a ravine, without stating that it also crossed a stream of water. The act of 1885 does not limit the bridges which the county may be required to assist in building, to such as cross streams of water. A bridge may be as necessary across a dry ravine as it would be did a river flow through the ravine, and no good reason is perceived why any distinction should be made in the two cases.

Both of these alleged defects in the petition are cured by the subsequent proceedings in the case. The town proved on the trial (of course without objection, for the county was not present to object) that the electors of the town, at a town meeting therein, gave direction to its supervisors to institute this proceeding; and also proved that a stream of water flowed through the ravine in question most of the time. The rule in this state is that in such a case the defective pleading may be amended at any time to correspond with the proofs, or the variance or omission may be disregarded without actual amendment. This is so well settled that it would be an affectation to cite authorities to support the rule. Hence we must regard the petition as containing all the necessary allegations (if the same are true) to entitle the town to the relief demanded.

3. A very ingenious argument was submitted by counsel for the county board to show that in case the recitals of fact in the writ are defective, no resort can be had to the relation to supply such defects. Under several cases in this court this is probably an untenable proposition. The question is of no importance in this case, however, for the reason that the material allegations in the relation are sufficiently recited in the alternative writ.

4. No answer to the return was interposed. Because of this it is contended, on behalf of the county board, that there was no issue to be tried. The contention is that in the absence of such answer denying the allegations of the return such allegations must be taken as admitted.

It is probably the correct practice, where independent averments of fact are stated in the return, for the relator to answer and deny them if he wishes to make an issue thereon. But where, as in this case, the return consists of denials of material allegations in the relation, no such practice is required. In such a case an answer would be nothing more than a reiteration of the averments in the relation, which, of course, is unnecessary and absurd. So we conclude that the return raises issues upon all propositions of fact affirmed in the relation and denied in the return. This disposes of one of the objections made to the trial of the cause in St. Croix county.

5. Were the issues properly tried in the circuit court of St. Croix county? We think the question must be answered in the affirmative. It was tried at a general term of the circuit court of that county, and such term is a special term for the circuit court of Pierce county, both counties being in the Eighth judicial circuit. Laws of 1881, ch. 292. It is provided by statute (R. S. sec. 3452) that when a writ of *mandamus* shall be issued by any circuit court, any issue of fact therein may be tried at a special or general term thereof, and the court may summon a jury for the trial thereof. This cause, as we have seen, was tried at a special term of the circuit court of Pierce county, that being the county in which it was commenced. Ch. 292, Laws of 1881, is to the same effect. When read in connection with sec. 3452, the reasonable construction of it is that issues of fact arising in actions of *quo warranto* and *mandamus* may be tried at special terms.

6. It is objected that the judgment is not in proper form

in that it requires the board of supervisors of Pierce county to meet, and also to levy the required tax upon the taxable property of the county, without appointing any time for such meeting, and without excepting from liability to such taxation the two cities of Prescott and River Falls within that county, which, it is alleged, are not liable to such tax under the law of 1885. Under a fair construction of this judgment the mandate of the writ awarded by it will be satisfied if such board of supervisors perform the duty required of them by the peremptory writ, at their first meeting after the same shall be served upon them, and if they levy the necessary tax upon the taxable property of their county subject thereto. Probably the court has no power to order a special meeting of the board, and has not done so in this judgment.

7. Several other alleged errors were argued by counsel. Some of these have been overruled by former decisions of this court; others are predicated upon erroneous propositions of fact, and still others are purely technical and quite immaterial in the consideration of the case upon the merits. It is unnecessary to discuss or even to state the errors thus alleged.

Upon the whole case, we are satisfied that no material errors prejudicial to the county have been committed in the progress of the cause.

By the Court.—Judgment affirmed.

THE STATE EX REL. THE TOWN OF EL PASO, Respondent, vs. THE BOARD OF SUPERVISORS OF PIERCE COUNTY, Appellant.

March 2 — March 27, 1888.

Towns: Bridges: County aid: What valuation governs: Mandamus: *Pleading: Objection to evidence.*

1. Under ch. 187, Laws of 1885, providing for county aid to towns in building bridges whose cost exceeds one fourth of one per cent. of all the taxable property in the town "according to the last equalized valuation," the valuation of 1885 governs as to bridges authorized at the annual town meeting in April, 1886, although the county board was not called upon to act in the premises until after the assessment roll of 1886 had been made.

2. The petition on behalf of a town for a writ of *mandamus* failed to show that the proceeding had been authorized by the electors. On the trial, when the town records were offered in evidence to show that fact, the whole record was objected to as incompetent, irrelevant, and immaterial. *Held*, that the objection was too broad and general.

APPEAL from the Circuit Court for *Pierce* County.

This was a proceeding by *mandamus* to compel the *Board of Supervisors of Pierce County* to appropriate one half of the cost of the construction and repair of certain bridges in the town of *El Paso* in said county, and to cause the same to be levied upon the taxable property in said county subject thereto. The facts so far as they differ from those in the case of *State ex rel. Spring Lake v. Pierce Co., ante,* p. 321, are sufficiently stated in the opinion. The board appeals from a judgment in favor of the relator.

For the appellant there was a brief signed by *J. S. & F. M. White,* of counsel, and oral argument by *Mr. J. S. White.*

R. H. Start, for the respondent.

LYON, J. This case involves substantially the same questions determined in the case of *State ex rel. Spring Lake v.*

Pierce, Co., ante, p. 321, and, notwithstanding certain differences between the cases, which will presently be stated, is ruled by it.

The construction and repair of the bridges here in question were authorized by the town of *El Paso,* the relator, at its annual town meeting, in April, 1886. It is not denied that the estimated cost of such bridges and repairs exceeded one fourth of one per cent. of all the taxable property in said town according to the equalized valuation thereof in 1885. It is claimed, however, that because the county board of supervisors was not called upon to act in the premises until after the assessment roll of 1886 had been made, that roll governs, and it is alleged that the cost of such bridges and repairs does not exceed one fourth of one per cent. of the assessed valuation of the town in that year. We think the term employed in the act of 1885, "the last equalized valuation," relates to the last valuation before the annual town meeting in April, 1886, and hence that it refers to the valuation of 1885.

The only remaining difference in the two cases which it is deemed necessary to notice is that while no objection was made to the introduction of testimony showing that the electors of the town directed the case of the town of Spring Lake to be brought, in this case when the plaintiff offered the town records, which showed, among other things, the same direction, the whole record was objected to on behalf of the county board as incompetent, irrelevant, and immaterial. We think the objection too broad and general to be available to the county board. Had the objection to this particular portion of the town records been made on the ground that there is no averment in the relation that any such direction had been given, the objection should have been sustained, but with leave to the relator to amend the relation by inserting such an allegation. It would be unjust to allow the objection to prevail and thus defeat the

action, when the action could have been saved by amendment had the objection been made specifically.

We conclude that the differences between the two cases
do not take this case out of the rule of the *Spring Lake
Case.*

By the Court.— The judgment of the circuit court is affirmed.

DREVIS, Respondent, vs. WOODS and another, Appellants.

March 2 — March 27, 1888.

Court and jury: Contributory negligence.

1. In this action to recover the value of grain alleged to have been
   burned through defendants' negligence while they were threshing
   for the plaintiff with a steam-thresher, it is *held* that the evidence
   does not clearly show that the plaintiff was guilty of contributory
   negligence in permitting the defendants to continue threshing
   under the circumstances, and that the question was therefore properly submitted to the jury.
2. Where a statement made by one of the defendants to the plaintiff
   was of importance in determining the question of contributory
   negligence, and the language used, as testified to by the plaintiff,
   might have more than one meaning, it was error for the court, in
   charging the jury, to say what he supposed the defendant meant.

APPEAL from the Circuit Court for *St. Croix* County.
The following statement of the case was prepared by Mr.
Justice TAYLOR as a part of the opinion:

Action to recover the value of some barley which was
burned by sparks escaping from an engine used by the defendants. The evidence shows that at and before the time
the fire occurred the defendants were threshing grain with
a steam-threshing machine on the premises of the plaintiff,
and for him; that when the fire caught, and for some time
previous, the wind blew briskly from the direction of the

engine towards a stack or stacks of unthreshed barley, standing about seventy-five feet from the engine; that a fire was kindled in said barley from the sparks emitted from the smoke-stack of said engine, and the barley was destroyed. About these facts there is no dispute. About other matters the evidence is conflicting. On the part of the plaintiff it is claimed that he was entirely ignorant as to the dangers likely to result from the use of the steam-engine in the vicinity of the stacked grain, and he claims that he was informed by one of the defendants, before the threshing commenced, that the threshing could be done in the barn without setting it on fire. This is denied by the defendants. The defendants claim that, shortly before the fire occurred, they warned the plaintiff that it was danger-ous to continue threshing with the wind blowing towards the stacks, and that the plaintiff was anxious they should continue the work and finish up the job as soon as possible. This the plaintiff denies, and claims that nothing was said to him by the defendants or any other person as to the danger of continuing the work. There is also a conflict of evidence as to the quality of the wood provided by the plaintiff; the defendants claiming that he was to provide good, sound wood, and that the wood he in fact provided was unsound and rotten, and caused more sparks and fire to be emitted from the smoke-stack, and so increased the danger. On the part of the plaintiff it is claimed that the wood furnished was good, sound wood. Evidence was also given on the part of the plaintiff tending to show that there was a sprinkler attached to the engine, which, when kept in use, had the effect of greatly lessening the quantity of sparks emitted from the smoke-stack, and so lessening the danger therefrom; that this sprinkler was not used at and before the time the fire was kindled in the barley stacks, and that the reason given by the defendants for not using it was be-cause it took a large quantity of water to run it. On the

part of the defendants it was claimed that the reason it was
not used was because the quality of the wood furnished was
such that they could not get up sufficient steam to run the
machine and keep the sprinkler in use at the same time.
There was also some evidence in the case tending to show
that the defendants, after the fire, promised to pay the
damage done, by threshing in the future for the plaintiff,
and which they afterwards refused to do.

The case was submitted to the jury, who, under the direction of the court, found a special verdict, by which they
found, among other things, "that the plaintiff did not know
that it was dangerous to thresh on that day;" "that the
defendants, prior to the fire, did not notify the plaintiff
that it was dangerous to thresh on that afternoon;" "that
neither the plaintiff nor any of his workmen objected to
threshing on that day;" "that the wood furnished by the
plaintiff was a good, fair quality;" "that the plaintiff was
not guilty of any want of ordinary care in any way which
contributed to the accident;" and "that the defendants
were guilty of want of ordinary care in threshing, on the
occasion of the accident, and that such want of ordinary
care caused the fire." Upon the special verdict, judgment
was rendered in favor of the plaintiff for the value of the
barley burned.

The defendants appeal from such judgment, and allege
as errors (1) "that the court should have nonsuited the
plaintiff, as requested by them at the close of the evidence;
(2) that the court erred in refusing to direct a verdict for
the defendants upon the whole evidence, as requested by
them; (3) that the court erred in submitting the question
of the plaintiff's negligence or want of ordinary care to the
jury; (4, 5) that the court erred in his charge to the jury,
and in refusing to charge the jury as requested by the defendants; (6, 7) that the verdict is contrary to the law and
the evidence.

J. B. Smith, for the appellants.

For the respondent there was a brief by *Smith & Vannatta*, and oral argument by *Mr. C. Smith*.

TAYLOR, J. The questions whether the plaintiff should have been nonsuited at the close of his evidence, or whether a verdict should have been directed for the defendants at the close of the evidence, depend wholly upon the question whether the evidence, as a matter of law, showed that the plaintiff was guilty of negligence in permitting the defendants to continue threshing, under the circumstances detailed in the evidence. That there was sufficient evidence to justify a jury in finding the defendants guilty of negligence in continuing the threshing, under the circumstances, is not denied by the counsel for the appellants, and no exception is taken to the court's submitting that question. The evidence of the appellants themselves shows their negligence, and the only way they pretend to justify themselves in continuing the work as they did is by alleging that the respondent directed them to do so after they had informed him of the danger. This was denied by the respondent, and the jury found that they did not so inform him. · After a careful consideration of all the evidence in the case, we think it does not clearly show that the respondent was guilty of a want of ordinary care on his part which contributed to the accident; and that question was therefore properly submitted to the jury. To justify a court in directing a verdict for the defendants on the ground that the plaintiff is shown to have been guilty of negligence which contributed to the accident, it must appear that the evidence, giving it the most favorable construction for the plaintiff, still shows such want of ordinary care on his part. We do not think the evidence in this case, so construed, necessarily establishes the fact of the plaintiff's negligence.

This question of the contributory negligence of the plaintiff being the most important question in the case, and the one involving the most doubt upon the evidence, it was highly important that upon that question the learned circuit judge should have avoided, in his instructions to the jury, any statement, not clearly warranted by the evidence, which might influence them in determining that question. One of the questions submitted to the jury bearing directly upon the plaintiff's negligence was as follows: "Did the plaintiff know it was dangerous to thresh on that day?" It would seem, as a matter of course, if he knew it was dangerous and still permitted the threshing to continue without objection, and without being misled by any assurance to the contrary coming from the defendants, he would be held to have assumed the risks of such danger, and so have been held to a want of ordinary care on his part. In submitting this question to the jury, the learned circuit judge said: "That question I leave for you to answer yes or no; and that involves, perhaps, a consideration of some other circum·stances, and I may as well call attention to that now. (He claims here that he was informed by the defendants, some one, two, or three days before, that they could thresh in the barn without setting it on fire; by which, I suppose, he meant to be understood there was no danger of setting fire from the engine.) (Now, that is a circumstance, if the plaintiff here, ignorant of the peculiar qualities of this machine, and not an expert, perhaps,— not shown to be in the threshing business,— might perhaps very properly have relied on that statement.) That is one fact and circumstance, if you find that it is so, to be taken into consideration in passing on that question. Now, I think, had he known about that machine,— known that sparks would fly out of it,— and could see for himself that the wind was blowing from the engine down onto the stacks, and unless he had the information that these defendants must have had as owners of that machine, I think that he should have known that it was dangerous to thresh on that day. (I will leave this question to you, in view of the fact that there are some circumstances claimed here to show that the plaintiff was misled, perhaps, by the remarks of the defendants and his own ignorance of the qualities of that particular engine, and not being an expert in threshing.) It is question of fact for you to determine whether the plaintiff knew it was dangerous to thresh on that day." Those parts of these instructions inclosed in the parentheses were excepted to by the defendants. The first paragraph refers to some evidence given by the plaintiff himself on the trial, and, after stating the substance of that evidence, the court adds: "By which, I suppose, he meant to be understood there was no danger of setting fire from the engine." In the last clause of the paragraph, the learned judge assumes to give the jury the meaning of the evidence given by the witness We think this was error. It seems to us it was for the jury to say, and not the court, what the meaning of the language used by the defendant, as testified to by the plaintiff, was. The plaintiff was the only witness who testified as to what one of the defendants said as to threshing in or near the barn. On his direct examination he states it as follows: "While we were threshing near the barn I had a conversation with *Mr. Woods.* I asked him if there was any danger near the barn. He told me, ' Don't be afraid.' He said he would thresh right in the barn, and not be afraid of fire." On cross-examination he testified: " *Mr. Woods* told me before, when threshing by the barn, there was no danger; he threshed right in the barn." Again he said: "Up at the barn, I asked *Mr. Woods* if there was any danger on account of — you know we had threshed near the barn — about fire. He said, ' Oh, don't be afraid. I would thresh right in the barn, and would not be afraid it would catch fire.'" We do not think this statement of the defendant *Woods,* as detailed by the plaintiff, is susceptible of but one meaning, viz., that there was no danger of setting fire from the engine. It was for the jury, therefore, and not for the court, to say what the meaning of the language used was.

It cannot be said that the explanation given to the jury by the court of the words alleged to have been used by the defendant *Woods* was of little importance in the case. The learned judge was clearly of the opinion that they were of the highest importance in coming to a correct answer to the question above stated; and he strongly intimates, in the other part of his instructions upon this question, that they should find that the plaintiff did know it was dangerous to thresh under the circumstances, had it not been for the fact that the defendant *Woods* had made the statement in regard to the safety of using the machine which the plaintiff insisted he had made. Again, in instructing the jury upon the eighteenth question submitted to them, viz., " Was the plaintiff guilty of any want of ordinary care, in any way, which contributed to the accident?" the learned judge again calls the attention of the jury to this alleged statement of the defendant *Woods* to the plaintiff, as having a direct bearing upon the question of the plaintiff's negligence. In these instructions the learned judge says: " Of course you will take into consideration what had been said to him there by the defendants as to what they could do, if they find anything was said as to the condition of the engine and what they were to do without danger." This last instruction is not cited for the purpose of showing that there was any error in giving it in the form last above stated, but for the purpose of showing the prominence which was given to the fact that such a statement was made by the defendant to the plaintiff, as bearing upon the determination of those questions. Any improper instruction, therefore, by the learned circuit judge as to the meaning which the jury ought to give the language alleged to have been used by the defendant, must be held a prejudicial error and cause a reversal of the judgment.

By the Court.— The judgment of the circuit court is reversed, and the cause is remanded for a new trial.

See note to this case in 37 N. W. Rep. 256.— REP.

HUDDLESTON, Respondent, vs. JOHNSON, Appellant.

March 2 — March 27, 1888.

(1) Justice's court: Jurisdiction: Title to land. (2, 3) Land contract: Waste: Conversion: Evidence.

1. In an action in justice's court for the conversion of timber the complaint alleged that the title to the land from which the timber was cut was in the plaintiff's brother, who gave him license to cut the same. The answer denied the allegations of the complaint and alleged title to the land in the defendant. *Held,* that the title to land came in question, and the cause was properly removed to the circuit court, under sec. 3619, R. S.

2. The vendee in a land contract expressly stipulated that "he would not commit, or suffer any other person to commit, waste or damage to or upon said premises." He permitted his brother to cut in different places on the land several valuable trees for stave timber. Afterwards, having paid nothing on the contract, he assigned it back to the vendor to be canceled. The vendor took possession of the timber so cut. *Held,* that he was not liable in an action by the vendee's brother for a conversion of such timber.

3. In such a case the fact that the land was purchased for a farm, or that it would be worth more when cleared of trees, could not justify the promiscuous cutting of trees to make staves to be carried away and sold.

APPEAL from the Circuit Court for *Pierce* County.

The case is stated in the opinion. The defendant appeals from a judgment in favor of the plaintiff.

J. S. White, for the appellant.

For the respondent there was a brief by *Smith & Van-natta*, and oral argument by *Mr. C. Smith*.

ORTON. J.   This action was brought before a justice for the conversion of a lot of stave timber of the value of $25. The plaintiff alleges title to the land on which the stave timber was cut in his brother, Samuel Huddleston, who sold the timber to the plaintiff or gave him license to cut the same. The defendant denied the allegations of the complaint, and alleged title to the land in himself. The justice thereupon certified the case to the circuit court on the ground that the title was put in issue by the pleadings. The appellant claims that there was no ground for such removal of the case, and that the circuit court acquired no jurisdiction to try the same. It seems that the title was properly, if not necessarily, put in issue by the pleadings, and that it properly came in question on the trial. The title of the land was the foundation of the right of either party to the timber. Sec. 3619, R. S. The case was properly removed.

The facts in evidence were substantially as follows: On the 4th day of June, 1886, the defendant and the said Samuel Huddleston entered into an agreement under seal in respect to the land in question, as follows: the defendant, who was the owner of the land, stipulated that in consideration of $1 paid, and the payment of the further sum of $400 (with ten per cent. interest, payable annually) on the 4th day of June, 1890, according to a note then given by the said Samuel Huddleston to the defendant, he would convey said land to said Huddleston. The said Huddleston agreed to pay said note and interest promptly, and pay the taxes on said land, and that " *he would not commit, or suffer any other person to commit, waste or damage to or upon said premises.*" Time of payment is made the essence of the

contract, and default of ninety days was to cause a forfeiture of all the rights of Huddleston under the contract. It
is stipulated further that the right of possession should
remain in the defendant until the fulfilment of the contract, and that Huddleston should in the mean time be the
tenant of the defendant. The said Huddleston, soon after
said contract was entered into, cleared off about two acres,
in one corner of said land, of timber and underbrush. He
did nothing more with the land, and paid nothing on the
contract; and on the 23d day of September, 1886, he assigned back said contract to the defendant to be canceled.
In July of that year the said Samuel Huddleston gave the
plaintiff permission to go upon the land and cut stave timber; and, accordingly, the plaintiff did go on the land and
cut in different places several valuable trees suitable for
stave timber, or, as he testified on the trial, "The trees I
cut were scattered *promiscuously* all over the forty." Again
he testified. " I was chopping them for the purpose of getting staves, and for no other purpose." The cutting down
of these trees had nothing to do with the clearing of the
land. The timber, when so prepared, was piled up on the
premises and left there; and when the defendant received
back the contract to be canceled, in September, or soon
after, he removed said timber to another place near by, and
piled it up, and this was its condition when the suit was
brought. The plaintiff testified further that when he did
the cutting he knew that his brother held this land only by
this contract and had not paid for it.

The errors assigned are: (1) The plaintiff was allowed,
against objection, to testify in answer to the question, "For
what purpose did he [your brother] purchase it?" that " He
purchased it to make a farm of it." Can any one conceive how this evidence could affect the rights of the
parties under this contract under seal? If such evidence
could be allowed to change the terms of a written contract

in respect to the land,— which of course is preposterous,— how could it justify the cutting off the choice and selected trees, promiscuously, all over the tract, to make staves of to be carried away and used or sold? This is not the way to make a farm of the land, or to clear it off for a farm. The plaintiff had already testified that he cut the trees in this way " for the purpose of getting staves, *and for no other purpose.*" (2) The plaintiff was allowed, against objection, to answer the question, " Would this forty of land be worth more cleared, or with the trees standing on it?" that "It would be worth more cleared." Such evidence is never allowed as a justification for *waste.* Abb. Tr. Ev. 534; *McGregor v. Brown*, 10 N. Y. 114. An agreement to sell the land does not imply a license to cut down trees. *Mooers v. Wait*, 3 Wend. 106. It was for the defendant to say whether he wanted the timber cut off the land. On this evidence, the court directed the jury to render a verdict of $23.49 for the plaintiff. The defendant moved for a new trial, and the motion was denied.

The plaintiff showed no right whatever to the timber cut or uncut, but did show that, by permission of his brother, he committed *waste* upon the land of the defendant without the semblance of justification or excuse. The written contract fixed the rights of the parties, and that contains a stipulation against waste. Samuel Huddleston never obtained any rights in the land, legal or equitable, outside of the contract, and such rights as he had, or could have, he voluntarily surrendered. He certainly never had any title to the land beyond the mere right to purchase it. If the citation of any authorities is needed in such a very plain case in reason and common sense, reference may be had to *Heath v. Van Cott*, 9 Wis. 522; *Hoile v. Bailey*, 58 Wis. 455; *Rector v. Higgins*, 48 N. Y. 538. The circuit court, if a verdict in this case ought to have been directed either way, should have directed the jury to find for the defendant, rather than for the plaintiff.

By the Court.— The judgment of the circuit court is reversed, and the cause remanded for a new trial.

Coon and another, Respondents, vs. SEYMOUR and others, Appellants.

March 2 — March 27, 1888.

Vacating judgment: Jurisdiction of one court over judgments of another: Equity: Laches: Limitation of actions.

1. A circuit court in which a transcript of a judgment rendered by the municipal court of the city and town of Ripon has been filed and docketed, has no jurisdiction of an action to open and set aside such judgment, the said municipal court being a court of record, capable of granting the necessary relief.

2. Where a bill in equity discloses gross laches the court will, on its own motion, refuse relief even without such laches having been pleaded.

3. *It would seem* that a delay of fifteen years after knowledge of the entry of a judgment, before the commencement of an action to set it aside, would be such gross laches as to preclude equitable interference.

4. An action upon a judgment which may be brought within twenty years after the cause of action accrued, under sec. 4220, R. S., is an action to confirm and enforce the judgment, not an action to set aside and avoid it.

APPEAL from the Circuit Court for *Eau Claire* County. The following statement of the case was prepared by Mr. Justice CASSODAY:

It appears that July 1, 1864, the plaintiffs herein, *A. L. & S. E. Coon*, made and delivered to S. L. Sheldon & Bro., the payees therein, two promissory notes, one for $100, due

February 1, 1865, and one for $60, due January 1, 1866, each with interest at seven per cent., and accompanied by a warrant of attorney to confess judgment; that July 7, 1868, the said notes having been assigned and transferred to the firm of *Seymour, Morgan & Allen*, the defendants herein, the said *Seymour, Morgan & Allen* took and entered up judgment in their favor and against the said *Coons*, under and by virtue of such warrants of attorney, in the municipal court of the city and town of Ripon, the same being at the time a court of record in this state, for $235.54 damages and costs; that July 20, 1868, a transcript of said judgment was duly filed and docketed in the office of the clerk of the circuit court for Eau Claire county; that November 24, 1883, execution was issued thereon, with leave of the court, to the sheriff of Eau Claire county, who returned the same unsatisfied; that thereupon *Seymour, Morgan & Allen*, with the purpose of collecting the whole of said judgment, commenced supplementary proceedings against said *S. E. Coon* before a court commissioner at Eau Claire, in which he was required to appear, and did appear, before the commissioner, May 31, 1884, and answered, and an issue was made thereon, and that the same was still pending and undetermined when this action was commenced, about July 9, 1884, to set aside and vacate said judgment and to enjoin the collection thereof, and to enjoin said supplementary proceedings.

The allegations of the complaint are to the effect that the said *Coons* had sustained damage to the amount of $275 and the interest thereon, by reason of the breach of warranty on the machinery for which the notes were given, July 1, 1864; that February 1, 1865, the *Coons* paid on one of said notes $60, which was not deducted therefrom when the judgment was entered; that in 1869 the said *Coons* paid to the sheriff, upon an execution issued thereon, $50 in compromise and satisfaction of the judgment. The said *Seymour*,

Morgan & Allen answered, admitting the notes, warrants of attorney, judgment entered thereon, execution, and supplementary proceedings, but in effect denied each of such alleged payments; also denied the alleged compromise, or the authority of the sheriff or any one to make such compromise; also denied the making of any such warranty, or any consideration therefor.

Issues were submitted to the jury, which found, in effect, that said machinery was warranted, and that said *Coons* sustained damages by reason of the breach thereof in the sum of $190; that $60 was paid on the note February 1, 1865; that $50 was paid to the sheriff upon an execution in his hands, in December, 1869, for which the sheriff gave a receipt in full. The court confirmed such findings, and made others of fact above mentioned and admitted; and as conclusions of law the court found, in effect, that the said *Coons* were entitled to judgment canceling each of said notes and releasing them from all liability thereon; and that said *Seymour, Morgan & Allen*, and each of them, their agents and assigns, be perpetually enjoined from collecting, or attempting to collect, said judgment or any part thereof, and from prosecuting such supplementary proceedings; and that the docketing of the judgment in Eau Claire county be canceled and vacated, and for costs. And judgment was ordered thereon accordingly, which was entered, and from which the said *Seymour, Morgan & Allen* appeal.

T. F. Frawley, for the appellants, argued, among other things: (1) A judgment of confession has all the qualities, incidents, and attributes of other judgments, and is in legal contemplation and effect a judicial and final determination of a court in the exercise of its jurisdiction. Freeman on Judg. sec. 547; *Hoffman v. Coster*, 2 Whart. 453; *Braddee v. Brownfield*, 4 Watts, 474; *Hageman v. Salisberry*, 74 Pa. St. 286; *Farrington v. Freeman*, 2 Edw. Ch. 572; *Lanning v. Carpenter*, 23 Barb. 402; *Gifford v. Thorn*, 9 N. J. Eq.

702, note; *Iylehart v. Morris*, 34 Ill. 501; *Rising v. Brainard*, 36 id. 79; *Osgood v. Blackmore*, 59 id. 261; *Bush v. Hanson*, 70 id. 480; *Blaikie v. Griswold*, 10 Wis. 294; *Wells v. Morton*, id. 468; *Egan v. Sengpiel*, 46 id. 710. (2) Supplementary proceedings are equitable proceedings in the action,— a sort of additional equitable execution, penetrating farther than ordinary executions, and under the control of the court whose judgment is sought thereby to be enforced. *Ross v. Clussman*, 3 Sandf. 676; *Bank of Genesee v. Spencer*, 15 How. Pr. 412; *Gould v. Torrance*, 19 id. 560; *Wegman v. Childs*, 41 N. Y. 159; *Mann v. Blount*, 65 N. C. 99; *Barker v. Dayton*, 28 Wis. 367. (3) An action will not lie in one court to enjoin the collection of a judgment recovered in another court of concurrent jurisdiction. Freeman on Judg. sec. 95; High on Injunctions, sec. 265; *Ludington v. Peck*, 2 Conn. 700; *Amory v. Amory*, 3 Biss. 266; *Anthony v. Dunlap*, 8 Cal. 27; *Rickett v. Johnson*, id. 35; *Chipman v. Hibbard*, id. 268; *Gorham v. Toomey*, 9 id. 77; *Uhlfelder v. Levy*, id. 607; *Flaherty v. Kelly*, 51 id. 145; *Crowley v. Davis*, 37 id. 268; *Judson v. Porter*, 51 id. 562; *Poultney v. Treasurer*, 25 Vt. 168; *Johnson v. Harvey*, 4 Mass. 485; *Stearns v. Stearns*, 16 id. 171; *Brackett v. Winslow*, 17 id. 153; *Baker v. Judges*, 4 Johns. 191; *Grant v. Quick*, 5 Sandf. 612; *Wardell v. Eden*, 2 Johns. Cas. 258; *Simpson v. Hart*, 1 Johns. Ch. 91; *Smock v. Dade*, 5 Rand. 639; *Maclean v. Speed*, 52 Mich. 257; *Merril v. Lake*, 16 Ohio, 373; *La Crosse & Minn. P. Co. v. Reynolds*, 12 Minn. 213; *Johnston v. Paul*, 23 id. 46; *Lacock v. White*, 19 Pa. St. 497; *Boyd v. Miller*, 52 id. 431; *Newhart v. Wolfe*, 102 id. 566; *Ex parte Baldwin*, 69 Iowa, 502; *State v. Pauley*, 12 Wis. 538; *Parish v. Marvin*, 15 id. 247; *McDonald v. Falvey*, 18 id. 571; *Johnson v. Coleman*, 23 id. 452; *Platto v. Deuster*, 22 id. 482; *Endter v. Lennon*, 46 id. 300; *Fenske v. Kluender*, 61 id. 602. (4) Supplementary proceedings are in their nature equitable proceedings in the action, and cannot be enjoined by another equitable action commenced in a court other than the one whose judgment is sought to be enforced. *Gould v. Torrance*, 19 How. Pr. 560, and cases above cited. (5) Relief against fraudulent and unconscionable judgments is granted by the courts in the exercise of their equitable powers, and must be done in the nature of a bill of review, which must be brought in the court where the record remains. Story's Eq. Pl. sec. 426; *Arnold v. Styles*, 2 Blackf. 391; *Parish v. Marvin*, 15 Wis. 247; *Johnson v. Coleman*, 23 id. 452; *Fenske v. Kluender*, 61 id. 602.

Alexander Meggett, for the respondents, contended, *inter alia*, that to prevent the collection of a judgment at law by confession, not for irregularity but for merits *dehors* the record, *action* and not *motion* is the proper remedy and better practice. *McIndoe v. Hazleton*, 19 Wis. 567, 573; *Brown v. Parker*, 28 id. 21, 28. The circuit court had jurisdiction of the subject matter of the action, it being for the purpose of exercising a supervisory control over a judgment obtained by confession in a court of this state. *Blaikie v. Griswold*, 10 Wis. 293, 302; *Brown v. Parker*, 28 id. 21, 25; *Scheer v. Keown*, 34 id. 349, 363; *McCabe v. Sumner*, 40 id. 386, 389. The municipal court is not a court of concurrent and coordinate jurisdiction. Its power to act is confined to certain territorial limits, and is limited as to the amount involved; and its process must be served within its territorial jurisdiction. *Atkins v. Fraker*, 32 Wis. 514–517; *Zitske v. Goldberg*, 38 id. 217, 234. Under secs. 2900, 2942, R. S., the appellants, by docketing the judgment in the circuit court for Eau Claire county, voluntarily gave that court full control and jurisdiction over it as one of its own judgments. Otherwise, the appellants could not have invoked the aid of the court commissioner of the court below in supplementary proceedings to enforce collection of that judgment. Had this action been commenced in the municipal court, what power had it, as an inferior court of limited jurisdiction, to restrain or control proceedings supplementary in a court of superior and general jurisdiction, and especially to act beyond the jurisdictional limits of the former? The circuit court had, at least, injunctional jurisdiction over its own commissioner to prevent the enforcement of the judgment within its own immediate jurisdiction; and if it had jurisdiction for that purpose it had it for every other necessary to determine all the equities of the parties to the original judgment. *Sexton v. Mann*, 15 Wis. 162; *Lee v. Peckham*, 17 id. 383, 391; *Hamilton v. Fond du Lac*, 25 id. 490, 495.

CASSODAY, J. This is a bill in equity brought in the circuit court for the county of Eau Claire. Its purpose is to cancel notes given, with warrants of attorney to confess judgment, more than twenty years prior to the commencement of this action, and to perpetually enjoin the collection of the judgment entered thereon. One of its objects is to make available as a defense to such judgment damages sustained by reason of an alleged warranty on the sale of the machinery for which the notes were given. Another object is to make available two alleged payments,— one before judgment and nearly twenty years before the commencement of this action, and the other after judgment and more than fourteen years before the commencement of this action. Since the notes were necessarily merged in the judgment, the purpose of the action is essentially to set aside and nullify the judgment. It is admitted in the complaint that the plaintiffs knew of the entry of the judgment against them about fifteen years before the commencement of this action. These gross laches, appearing upon the face of the complaint, would seem to be sufficient of themselves to preclude equitable interference. *Sable v. Maloney*, 48 Wis. 331; *Hiles v. Mosher*, 44 Wis. 601; *Coddington v. Railroad Co.* 103 U. S. 409; *Graham v. B., H. & E. R. Co.* 118 U. S. 161. We do not understand this to be an action upon a judgment which may be brought within twenty years after the cause of action accrued, within the meaning of sec. 4220, R. S. Such an action is to confirm and enforce a judgment. This, on the contrary, is an action to avoid and set aside a judgment for alleged causes existing outside of the record. True, the defendants herein failed to plead the six years statute of limitation (subd. 7, sec. 4222, R. S.), or the ten years statute of limitation (subd. 4, sec. 4221, R. S.). But it has often been held that where a bill in equity discloses gross laches the court will, on its own motion, refuse relief even without such laches having been pleaded. *Sullivan v. P. & K. R. Co.* 94 U. S. 811; *Board of Comm'rs v. C., R. I. & P. R. Co.* 18 Fed. Rep. 209; *Frame v. Kenny's Heirs*, 2 A. K. Marsh. 145, 12 Am. Dec. 367, and notes; *Smith v. Thompson*, 7 Grat. 112, 54 Am. Dec. 126; *Skinner v. Deming*, 2 Ind. 558, 54 Am. Dec. 463, and notes.

But here the plaintiffs had a perfect remedy for their alleged grievances, by motion in the municipal court for the city of Ripon, which was a court of record. Jurisdiction therein could readily have been obtained by service upon the attorney of record in entering the judgment. This of itself was sufficient to require the refusal of equitable interference by any other court. *Graham v. B., H. & E. R. Co., supra; Henderson v. Mitchell*, 1 Bailey, Eq. 113, 21 Am. Dec. 526. As observed, the subject matter of this action is to open and set aside the judgment of the municipal court. The circuit court of Eau Claire county had no jurisdiction over such subject matter. This has, in effect, been recently decided by this court. *Orient Ins. Co. v. Sloan*, 70 Wis. 611. In that case Mr. Justice Lyon has so fully discussed the question presented in this case as to require nothing additional here.

By the Court.— The judgment of the circuit court is reversed, and the cause is remanded with directions to dismiss the complaint.

BOND, Respondent, vs. CARROLL, Sheriff, etc., and another, Appellants.

March 3 — March 27, 1888.

(1) Estoppel: Title of common grantor. (2, 3) Mortgages: Foreclosure by advertisement: Evidence.

1. Where both parties derive title from the same source the defendant is estopped to deny that the common grantor had title.

2. The printer's affidavit of the publication of the notice of sale on foreclosure of a mortgage by advertisement, with the notice attached, was in evidence, as was also the affidavit of the deputy sheriff who acted as auctioneer, stating the time and place of the sale, the sum bid, and the name of the purchaser. These affidavits were made and recorded pursuant to secs. 3586, 3587, R. S. The notice of sale stated that it was given by virtue and in pursuance of a power of sale contained in the mortgage. The sheriff's deed was also in evidence, which recited, among other things, that the mortgage contained a power of sale, and that the sale was made pursuant to such power. *Held*, sufficient, in the absence of evidence to the contrary, to prove that the mortgage contained a power of sale and that the proceedings to foreclose it were regular.

[3. Whether sec. 4154, R. S., applies to a sheriff's deed given upon the foreclosure of a mortgage by advertisement, not determined.]

APPEAL from the Circuit Court for *St. Croix* County. The facts will sufficiently appear from the opinion. The defendants appeal from a judgment in favor of the plaintiff.

Armstrong Taylor, for the appellants.

F. J. McLean, for the respondent.

COLE, C. J. This is an action to restrain the sale of real estate to satisfy a mechanic's lien in favor of the defendant *Clapp*. The plaintiff claims title to the land under a sheriff's deed given on the foreclosure of a mortgage. The mortgage foreclosure was by advertisement, and the sale was prior to the mechanic's lien. It is objected that the evidence does not show that the party giving the mortgage had title to the land and the right to mortgage it. This objection is not well taken, for this reason,— if no other existed,— that both parties derive title from the same source. Lawson H. Rice executed the mortgage in question in March, 1882, to one Jensen, and he afterwards conveyed an undivided half of the premises to Sweet, against whom the defendant *Clapp* claims a lien for lumber and materials furnished for the erection of a house on the premises, in the summer of 1883. Besides, the court below found that Rice was the owner of the premises when he executed the mortgage, and there is evidence to sustain this finding.

Now, if we comprehend the other objections taken to the judgment they all resolve themselves into the contention that the plaintiff failed to prove that the mortgage contained a power of sale and that the proceedings to foreclose it were regular. The bill of exceptions states that certain exhibits, attached thereto and marked, were put in evidence; also that certain abstracts of title were put in evidence without objection. Among the exhibits is an affidavit of the publication of a notice of sale, made by the printer of the newspaper in which the same was inserted, with the notice of sale attached thereto; and an affidavit of the deputy sheriff who acted as auctioneer at the sale, stating the time and place at which the same took place, the sum bid, and the name of the purchaser. These affidavits were made and recorded, so as to perpetuate the proof of the sale, pursuant to sec. 3536, R. S., and were made by statute presumptive evidence of the facts therein contained. Sec. 3537. The notice of sale states that it was given by virtue and in pursuance of a power of sale contained in the mortgage. The sheriff's deed was likewise put in evidence, which, among other things, recites that the mortgage contained a power of sale, and that the sale was made pursuant to such power. It seems to us that the evidence given was amply sufficient to establish a *prima facie* case that there had been a legal foreclosure of the mortgage. Certainly, in the absence of all evidence to the contrary, the presumption must be that the mortgage contained a power of sale and that the proceedings to foreclose the same were regular. The certificate of sale and the sheriff's deed were given in evidence, and the statute makes the former evidence of the facts therein contained. Sec. 3532. The sheriff's deed is very full in its recitals, stating that default was made in the payment of the sum secured by the mortgage; that notice of the sale was given and the sale made to the mortgagee, he being the highest and best bidder. The learned counsel for the plaintiff insists that sec. 4154 applies to the case, and declares what effect the sheriff's deed shall have as evidence. That section, in effect, provides that every conveyance of land which has been duly executed by any sheriff or other person by virtue of or in pursuance of any judgment, order, or license, shall be received, without any other proof of the previous proceedings, as presumptive evidence of the facts therein stated. We have great doubt whether this section applies to the deed in question; but, without deciding the point, upon the whole case we fully agree with the court below in the view that the testimony shows that the foreclosure and sale were made in substantial compliance with the statute.

As intimated, the proof shows that the mortgagee, Jensen, bid in the property at the foreclosure sale. It appears that he afterwards assigned the certificate of sale to the plaintiff, who received the sheriff's deed when due. An unsuccessful effort was made to show that the mortgage debt was paid to Jensen for the purpose of extinguishing the lien, but the court found against that view, and that the certificate was duly assigned to the plaintiff, who paid the amount due upon it. The evidence is most clear and satisfactory that the plaintiff bought the certificate, and intended, when he did so, to take the sheriff's deed upon it. He supposed that he had a subsequent mortgage on the same property which he wished to protect. It is evident he had no purpose of extinguishing the lien when he purchased the certificate, but intended to keep it alive. He has become the owner of the property under a prior and paramount lien, and is clearly entitled to the relief granted him by the court below.

The judgment of the circuit court must therefore be affirmed.

By the Court.— Judgment affirmed.

McClure, Assignee, etc., Appellant, vs. Campbell, Sheriff, etc., Respondent.

March 3 — March 27, 1888.

Voluntary assignment: Bankrupt act: Extra-territorial effect: Construction of laws of another state by its courts, when binding.

1. An assignment of property, made pursuant to a bankrupt act, the assignee being in effect an officer of the court, and the assigned property being *in custodia legis* and administered by or under the direction of the court, can have no legal operation out of the state in which such proceedings were had.

2. The decisions of the supreme court of Minnesota that ch. 148, Gen. Laws Minn. 1881, is a bankrupt act and that the assignee is in effect an officer of the court and the assigned property *in custodia legis*, are *held* binding upon this court.

[3. Whether a voluntary assignment for the benefit of creditors, executed in Minnesota by a resident of that state pursuant to ch. 41, Gen. Stats. of Minn., would pass to the assignee title to personal property named in such assignment having a *situs* in this state, not determined.]

APPEAL from the Circuit Court for *St. Croix* County.

This action is to recover $1,195, being the proceeds of a quantity of personal property seized in St. Croix county in this state, by the defendant, *Campbell*, as sheriff of said county, under and by virtue of a writ of attachment sued out by one Johnson against the property of Gillespie & Harper, a copartnership firm theretofore doing business in Minnesota and this state.   By an arrangement between the parties, the sheriff sold the property and retains the proceeds subject to the determination of this action.   Johnson obtained a judgment in his action against Gillespie & Harper, and issued execution thereon, which the sheriff levied upon such proceeds.   Johnson was named herein as a defendant, but the summons was not served upon him, and he has made no appearance.

The plaintiff, *McClure*, claims the proceeds of the property under an assignment executed to him by Gillespie & Harper in the state of Minnesota, pursuant to chapter 148 of the General Laws of that state for 1881.   The trusts specified in the assignment are that the assignee shall distribute the proceeds of the assigned property to those creditors of the assignors who shall file releases of their demands, and, if a surplus remains after paying such debts, he shall pay the same to the assignors.   The plaintiff, *McClure*, Johnson, and the members of the firm of Gillespie & Harper are residents of the state of Minnesota, and were such residents when the assignment was executed.   Gillespie & Harper had real and personal property both in Minnesota and this state.   The property thus seized and sold was, when seized, in use in and about a saw-mill in St. Croix county, owned and operated by Gillespie & Harper before such assignment, but was then in possession of the assignee.   No question is made on the pleadings, and there is no dispute as to the facts.

The circuit court held that the plaintiff took no title to the property in this state thus seized and sold, and hence was not entitled to the proceeds thereof, and gave judgment for the defendant accordingly.   The plaintiff appeals from the judgment.

For the. appellant there were briefs by *Fayette Marsh* and *Ray S. Reed*, and oral argument by *Mr. Marsh.* They contended, *inter alia*, that the assignment being valid in Minnesota, and all the parties in interest in this action being citizens and residents of Minnesota, the courts of Wisconsin, as an act of comity, should recognize the assignment as valid in this state as to any personal property here situate and in the actual possession of the assignee. *Smith v. C. & N. W. R. Co.* 23. Wis. 269; *In re Paige & Sexsmith Lumber Co.* 31 Minn. 136; *Bentley v. Whittemore*, 19 N. J. Eq. 469; *Moore v. Bonnell*, 31 N. J. Law, 90; *Einer v. Beste*, 32 Mo. 249–251; *Thurston v. Rosenfield*, 42 id. 474; *May v. Wannemacker*, 111 Mass. 208; *Dehon v. Foster*, 4 Allen, 545; *S. C.* 7 id. 57; *Train v. Kendall*, 137 Mass. 366; *Butler v. Wendell*, 57 Mich. 62; *Green v. Gross*, 12 Neb. 117; *Chafee v. Bank*, 71 Me. 514, 36 Am. Rep. 345; *Fuller v. Steiglitz*, 27 Ohio St. 355; *Natchez v. Minor*, 48 Am. Dec. 727; *Richardson v. Leavitt*, 45 id. 90; *Sanderson v. Bradford*, 10 N. H. 260. The supreme court of Minnesota and the U. S. circuit court for the district of Minnesota have disagreed as to whether an assignment made under the statute in question places the property *in custodia legis*, the latter holding that it does not and that the assignment is nothing more than a common-law assignment regulated by statute. *Lapp v. Van Norman*, 19 Fed. Rep. 406. But they agree that the assignment is a voluntary one and should have all the force and effect of a voluntary assignment. See *May v. Walker*, 35 Minn. 194, where the supreme court speaks of the assignment as a voluntary assignment under the insolvent law. Where courts seize upon the property of a debtor and convey it to an assignee without any voluntary act of the debtor, the law under which the property is seized having no extra-territorial force, the act of the court cannot operate to convey any property except such as is within its jurisdiction. But where the conveyance is voluntary, whether under an insolvent law or otherwise, it is operative to the same extent as an assignment at common law for the benefit of creditors. . Burrill on Assignm. sec. 304; *Shelby v. Bacon*, 10 How. 56; *Lapp v. Van Norman*, 19 Fed. Rep. 406; *Adler v. Ecker*, 2 id. 126; *Griswold v. Cent. Vt. R. Co.* 9 id. 797; *Lehman v. Rosengarten*, 23 id. 642. And it has often been determined by the courts that where a receiver has actually reduced the property placed in his hands by the order of the court to actual possession, the courts of a sister state will not interfere with the possession of the receiver, except to protect the rights of a citizen of that state, creditor of the person or corporation for whom the receiver is appointed. High on Receivers, secs. 47, 48.

H. L. Humphrey, for the respondent, argued, among other things, that an assignment may be questioned in any court of competent jurisdiction, state or federal. *Kohn v. Ryan*, 31 Fed. Rep. 636. The assignment here in question is an assignment of the copartners only, and is void under the laws of Minnesota. *May v. Walker*, 35 Minn. 194; *Citizens' Ins. Co. v. Wallis*, 23 Md. 182; Burrill on Assignm. (3d ed.), secs. 88, 111; *Merrill v. Wilson*, 29 Me. 58; *Fellows v. Greenleaf*, 43 N. H. 421; *Tiemann v. Molliter*, 71 Mo. 512. It is not good as a common-law assignment because it compels creditors to release their whole debts in order to share in the assets. *May v. Walker*, 35 Minn. 194; *Nat. Bank v. Lanahan*, 60 Md. 477. It is void under the laws of Wisconsin as to the property situate in this state because it does not conform to the laws of this state in respect to the transfer of property by voluntary assignment. See secs. 1694–96, R. S.; *Auley v. Osterman*, 65 Wis. 118; *King v. Glass*, 34 N. W. Rep. (Iowa), 820; *Richmondville Mfg. Co. v. Prall*, 9 Conn. 487. Title acquired under a foreign attachment cannot prevail against the rights of an attaching creditor under the laws of the state where the property is actually situated; and the fact that the creditor is a citizen of the state where the assignment was made,

can make no difference. *Hibernia Nat. Bank v. Lacombe,*
84 N. Y. 367; *Jenks v. Ludden,* 34 Minn. 482; *Warner v.
Jaffray,* 96 N. Y. 248; *In re Walker,* 33 N. W. Rep. (Minn.),
852; *Holmes v. Remson,* 20 Johns. 254; *Kelly v. Crapo,* 45
N. Y. 86; *S. C.* 16 Wall. 610; *Green v. Van Buskirk,*
5 id. 314; *S. C.* 7 id. 139; *Hervey v. R. I. L. Works,* 93 U. S.
664; *Paine v. Lester,* 44 Conn. 196; *Upton v. Hubbard,* 28
id. 275; *Osborn v. Adams,* 18 Pick. 245; *Milne v. Moreton,*
6 Bin. 361, 365; *Ingraham v. Geyer,* 13 Mass. 146; *Zipcey
v. Thompson,* 1 Gray, 243; *Moore v. Church,* 70 Iowa, 208,
59 Am. Rep. 439. Under the statute of Minnesota the assignee is under the control of the courts of that state and
must administer the trust under' their direction and in accordance with the laws of that state. He is therefore virtually a receiver, and the assignment does not vest in him
title to property situated outside of that state. See *Smith
v. C. & N. W. R. Co.* 23 Wis. 270. 271; *Booth v. Clark,*
17 How. 322.

LYON, J. Ch. 148, of the General Laws of Minnesota for
1881, under which the assignment in question was made, is
éntitled " An act to prevent debtors from giving preference
to creditors, and to secure the equal distribution of the property of debtors among their creditors, and for the release of
debts against debtors." The act provides that whenever
the property of any debtor shall be attached or levied upon
by any writ or process from a court of record of that state
in favor of any creditor, or garnishment made against any
debtor, such debtor may, within ten days after such levy or
garnishment, " make an assignment of all his property and
estate, not exempt by law, for the equal benefit of all his
creditors, in proportion to their respective valid claims, who
shall file releases of their debts and claims against such
debtors as hereinafter provided." The act then provides
that, upon such assignment being made, the attachments,

levy, or garnishments shall be dissolved, and the officer shall deliver the property to the assignee, unless the latter elect to retain the process for the benefit of all such creditors. Sec. 1. It is further provided in sec. 10 that "no creditor of any insolvent debtor shall receive any benefit under the provisions of this act, or any payment of any share of the proceeds of the debtor's estate, unless he shall first have filed with the clerk of the district court, in consideration of the benefits of the provisions of this act, a release to the debtor of all claims other than such as may be paid under the provisions of this act for the benefit of such debtor; and thereupon the court or judge may direct that judgment be entered discharging such debtor from all claims or debts held by creditors who shall have filed such releases."

Within ten days before the assignment to the plaintiff was executed, the property of Gillespie & Harper in Minnesota was seized by virtue of a writ of attachment issued out of a court of record of that state.

Another statute of Minnesota (ch. 41, Gen. Stats.) gives the procedure for making general assignments for the benefit of creditors. Its provisions are not unlike ch. 80 of our Revised Statutes, entitled "Of voluntary assignments."

The contention on behalf of the plaintiff is that the instrument under which the plaintiff claims to recover the proceeds of the property in question is essentially a voluntary assignment by Gillespie & Harper for the benefit of their creditors; and that it is a valid conveyance to the assignee of all the personal property of the assignors, wherever the same may be situated. In other words, their position is that, in respect to personal property, the *lex loci contractus* governs, and an assignment valid under the laws of the state in which it was executed is valid everywhere.

The contention on behalf of the defendant (who represents the creditor Johnson) is that the instrument is not a voluntary assignment for the benefit of creditors, within

the meaning of that term as used in the common law, or in
ch. 41 of the Minnesota statute, or ch. 80 of our Revised
Statutes, but is part of a statutory proceeding in insolvency,
looking to a full discharge of the debts of the insolvent
without full payment thereof,— a result which cannot follow
a voluntary assignment for the benefit of creditors; and,
further, such being the nature of the proceeding, the assignment has no effect beyond the territorial limits of the state
in which it is made and in which the assignor resides. It
is also denied that it has any such extra-territorial effect,
even though it be a voluntary assignment for the benefit of
creditors.

The question as to the character of the instrument under
which the plaintiff claims has been determined by the supreme court of Minnesota in *Jenks v. Ludden*, 34 Minn. 482,
and other cases therein cited. In *Jenks v. Ludden* the court
says: " Our act of 1881 is, as we have repeatedly held, a
bankrupt act; the assignee being, in effect, an officer of the
court, and the assigned property being *in custodia legis* and
administered by the court or under its direction. *Wendell
v. Lebon*, 30 Minn. 234; *In re Mann*, 32 Minn. 60; *Lord v.
Meachem*, 32 Minn. 66; *Bennett v. Denny*, 33 Minn. 530;
Simon v. Mann, 33 Minn. 412." Thus it will be seen that
although an assignment under ch. 148 of the Statutes of
Minnesota for 1881, in a certain sense is voluntary, in that
the debtor is not compelled to make it,— a feature common
to many, perhaps most, insolvent laws, including those of
this state (R. S. ch. 179),— still that court holds it to be, in
substance and legal effect, an assignment by operation of
the statute thus held to be a bankrupt law, executed as a
part of the procedure in the administration of that law.
We regard the above adjudications of the supreme court of
Minnesota, giving construction to their act of 1881, as binding upon this court, and hence shall not examine or discuss
the argument of counsel for the plaintiff against the accu-

racy of such construction. We will only say that our consideration of the subject has inclined us to think that the court construed the act correctly.

Our conclusion as to the character of the instrument in question renders it quite unnecessary to determine whether a voluntary assignment for the benefit of creditors executed in Minnesota by a resident of that state, pursuant to ch. 41, passes to the assignee title to personal property named in such assignment having a *situs* in this state. This question was very fully argued by the respective counsel, and their citations of authorities (to which we add *Mowry v. Crocker*, 6 Wis. 326) will be preserved in the official report of the case.

The only remaining question (and it is the controlling question in the case) is, Has an assignment of property, made pursuant to a bankrupt act, the assignee being in effect an officer of the court, and the assigned property being *in custodia legis* and administered by or under the direction of the court, any extra-territorial effect? That is to say, should the courts of this state recognize such an assignment as a valid transfer to the assignee of personal property in this state, and thus defeat an attachment levied upon it pursuant to the laws of this state by a creditor of the assignor? We think the question is not affected by the fact that the property, when seized, was in the possession of the assignee, or that the attaching creditor is a resident of the state in which the insolvency or bankruptcy proceedings were had.

The cases on this subject are very numerous. No review of them will here be attempted. While some of them may, under special circumstances, extend the rule of comity to such a case, and thus give an extra-territorial effect to somewhat similar assignments, we are satisfied that the great weight of authority is the other way. The rule in this country is, we think, that assignments by operation of law in bankruptcy or insolvency proceedings, under which debts may be compulsorily discharged without full payment thereof, can have no legal operation out of the state in which such proceedings were had. This rule is laid down in Burrill, Assignm. (5th ed.) p. 458, sec. 303, and numerous cases are cited in the note to that section in support of it.

An application of the above rule to this case negatives the plaintiff's right to recover in the action.

By the Court.— The judgment of the circuit court is affirmed.

See note to this case in 37 N. W. Rep. 343.— REP.

Geisinger, Appellant, vs. Beyl, Respondent.

March 3 — March 27, 1888.

Ejectment: Defect in defendant's tax deed: Payment of taxes, when a condition precedent to judgment: Presumption in support of judgment.

Under ch. 270, Laws of 1874, in an action of ejectment a finding by the court or jury that the plaintiff is entitled to recover by reason of a defect or insufficiency of a tax deed under which the defendant claims title, is essential in order to make payment by the plaintiff of the taxes therein mentioned a condition precedent to judgment in his favor. And an appellate court cannot assume the existence of that fact, in order to support a judgment for the defendant, where it was never put in issue, tried, or determined.

APPEAL from the Circuit Court for *Polk* County.

The following statement of the case was prepared by Mr. Justice Cassoday:

This action of ejectment for a quarter section of land described, in Polk county, Wis., was commenced February 12, 1876. The complaint is in the statutory form. The only answer is a general denial. On the trial of that issue before BARRON, J., and on September 28, 1876, the jury returned this verdict, and nothing more: "We, the jury empaneled to try the above-entitled action, find for the plaintiff that he is entitled to the possession of said premises, and that he is the owner thereof in fee-simple absolute."

October 26, 1876, the trial court made an order therein to the effect that the plaintiff have judgment to which he had shown himself entitled, upon the payment to the defendant, within ninety days, of the amount for which the premises had been sold, with penalty and interest, as provided by ch. 22, Laws of 1859, and also all taxes paid by the defendant subsequent to such sale, with interest; and that, if the plaintiff failed to pay said amounts within the time named, his action be dismissed with costs and any further action for the same cause be thereby barred. That order recited the verdict, and that the plaintiff had not made it to appear affirmatively that the premises were not liable to taxation for the tax for which they were sold, nor that the premises were redeemed from such sale, nor that such taxes had been paid.

February 9, 1877, and on motion of counsel for the plaintiff, a judgment was entered therein with the clerk upon said verdict, to the effect that the plaintiff recover possession of said premises, in accordance with said verdict, together with $34.67, the costs and disbursements of the action, and that execution issue therefor.

March 12, 1877, upon affidavits and the records, the plaintiff was ordered to show cause, at a time and place named, why said judgment should not be vacated, annulled, and set aside, and the action dismissed with costs, on the grounds that the plaintiff had failed to comply with said order of October 26, 1876, and that, even if he had complied with it, he could only have judgment upon application to the court. Upon the hearing of that motion the same was denied September 12, 1877. From that last order the defendant appealed to this court October 27, 1877; and June 28, 1878, the same was reversed (44 Wis. 258) on the ground that the order of October 26, 1876, though irregular, could not be treated as a nullity, and hence that such judgment was irregular and should have been set aside; and the *remittitur* therein was filed in the trial court December 20, 1878.

June 23, 1879, the trial court, BARRON, J., presiding, made an order setting aside said judgment, also denying a motion to set aside the order of October 26, 1876, and to grant leave to the plaintiff to enter judgment upon the verdict, with costs; and also that the motion of the defendant to dismiss the action with costs be denied without prejudice.

October 13, 1887, upon notice served, the trial court, CLOUGH, J., presiding, ordered, in effect, that the defendant have judgment therein dismissing the action with costs to be taxed. That order recited, in effect, the verdict, the order of October 26, 1876, and the failure of the plaintiff to comply with that order. October 17, 1887, on motion of the defendant's attorneys, judgment was entered therein dismissing the action, and that the defendant recover of the plaintiff $31.20, costs and disbursements as taxed; which judgment, in effect, recited the trial of the action, the rendition of said verdict, the making and the substance of said order of October 26, 1876, the plaintiff's failure to comply therewith, the order of October 13, 1887, and this further recital, and nothing more, to wit: " And it having appeared, upon the trial, that the defendant claimed title to the said premises by virtue of certain tax deeds issued by the county clerk of said Polk county." From this last judgment, so entered October 17, 1887, the plaintiff appeals.

Chas. C. Willson, for the appellant.

For the respondent there was a brief by *Pinney & Sanborn,* and oral argument by *Mr. A. L. Sanborn.*

CASSODAY, J.   This is an action of ejectment tried by a jury over eleven years ago.   The verdict was to the effect that the plaintiff was the owner in fee and entitled to the possession.   That verdict has never been set aside.   Notwithstanding these facts, the judgment appealed from was entered last October, and is in favor of the defendant, and dismissed the action with costs.   This is said to have been done by reason of the failure of the plaintiff to pay taxes as required by the order of October 26, 1876.   That order is said to have been made in pursuance of ch. 270, Laws of 1874, which, in effect, "*provided* that in all actions of ejectment now pending, or hereafter brought, when the *court or jury find* that the plaintiff is entitled to recover the lands claimed, . . . *by reason of a defect or insufficiency* of any tax deed *under which the defendant* claims title to such lands, . . . it shall be the duty of the court in which such action is tried, unless it shall be made to appear affirmatively by the plaintiff that such lands were not liable to taxation for the tax for which they were sold, or that such lands were redeemed from such sale, or that the taxes for which such lands were sold had been paid, to cause an order to be entered that the plaintiff have judgment to which he has shown himself entitled, upon the payment to the defendant, within ninety days, of the amount " of such taxes, interest, and penalty as therein prescribed, and that, if the plaintiff fail to so pay, then that his action be dismissed with costs, and any further action for the same cause be thereby barred.

The questions to be considered are — *First*, whether there is anything in the record to bring the case within the operation of this act, and, *secondly*, if not, whether the judgment is to be sustained upon mere presumption.   There is no bill of exceptions.   The appeal, therefore, only brings up for review the pleadings, verdict, judgment, and orders upon which it was based.   *Kelley v. C., M. & St. P. R. Co.*

53 Wis. 76; *Edleman v. Kidd*, 65 Wis. 21. Of course such orders are reviewable on appeal from the judgment. The charge of the court is printed. If we were at liberty to consider that as a part of the record, we might be forced to the conclusion that the jury must have found that the tax deed mentioned was acquired by the defendant while acting as the agent of the plaintiff to pay the taxes on this same land. If that were so, then such acquisition of the deed would have been, in legal effect, a payment of such taxes and an extinguishment of such tax deed. In that view of the case the act quoted would have no application here. But the charge of the court is no part of the record, and we are not at liberty to consider it. *Kirch v. Davies*, 55 Wis. 299. The pleadings are, of course, a part of the record. The complaint is simply in the statutory form, and makes no reference to such tax deed, nor any tax deed. The answer contains nothing but a general denial. The verdict is a part of the record, but that determines nothing but the simple issue of title and right to possession, made by the complaint and answer. There are no findings or finding by the court, except in so far as the recitals in the judgment and the orders upon which it is based are to be regarded as findings. The judgment recites all that is contained in such orders respectively, and more, as appears from the above statement of facts. It is sufficient to say that, assuming all such recitals to be findings by the court, still there is no finding by the court or jury that the plaintiff was entitled to recover " by reason of *a defect or insufficiency* of any tax deed." Under the act such finding was absolutely essential, even where it appeared from the pleadings that the defendant claimed title under a tax deed, in order to make such payment of taxes by the plaintiff a condition precedent to judgment in his favor. But, as observed, no such claim was put in issue or referred to by the pleadings, and such recitals are outside of the

issues and the verdict. While presumptions are frequently entertained in support of judgments, yet they are not to be indulged to the extravagant extent of assuming the existence of facts never put in issue, nor tried, nor determined. *Blossom v. Ferguson*, 13 Wis. 75; *Farrell v. Drees*, 41 Wis. 186; *Hogan v. C., M. & St. P. R. Co.* 59 Wis. 148. This court must deal with the issues actually tried, submitted, and determined, and not such as might have been but were not. *Murphy v. Martin*, 58 Wis. 280.

By the Court.— The judgment of the circuit court is reversed, and the cause is remanded with directions to enter judgment upon the verdict in favor of the plaintiff and against the defendant.

BRIDGE, Respondent, vs. THE CITY OF OSHKOSH, Appellant.

March 5 — March 27, 1888.

(1) Evidence: Personal injuries: Complaints. (2) Changes in physical or mental condition: Expert testimony. (3) Excessive damages: Former verdict for less amount.

1. Where personal injuries are the subject of inquiry and the basis for awarding damages, evidence of complaints made by the injured person either to his attending physicians or others is admissible.

2. In such case a witness who is not an expert, but who is acquainted with the injured person and has seen him frequently before and after the injury, may testify as to any changes either in his physical or mental condition.

3. Where on the first trial of an action to recover damages for personal injuries the plaintiff was prevented by the rulings of the court from fully presenting his case on the question of damages, and on the second trial, had nearly two years later, it was proved that he had not fully recovered from his injuries, a verdict on the first trial for $217 should have little weight in determining whether a verdict on the second trial for $1,800 is excessive. *Baker v. Madison*, 62 Wis. 137, distinguished.

APPEAL from the Circuit Court for *Marquette* County. The case is stated in the opinion.

Wm. H. Casey, for the appellant, contended, *inter alia*, that the evidence of the witnesses Anderson, R. W. Bridge, and Mrs. Bridge as to pain suffered by the plaintiff since the injury, and plaintiff's nervous condition, memory, etc., was wholly incompetent. *Insurance Co. v. Mosley*, 8 Wall. 397; *People v. Davis*, 56 N. Y. 95; *Ashland v. Marlborough*, 99 Mass. 48; Wharton on Evi. secs. 261–268; 1 Greenl. on Evi. sec. 110. Declarations made after convalescence, or when there has been an opportunity to think over the matter in reference to projected litigation, are inadmissible. *Kennard v. Burton*, 25 Me. 39; *Bacon v. Charlton*, 7 Cush. 581; *Chapin v. Marlborough*, 9 Gray, 244.

For the respondent there was a brief by *Weisbrod, Harshaw & Nevitt*, and oral argument by *Mr. A. W. Weisbrod.*

TAYLOR, J. The respondent brought this action against the city of *Oshkosh*, to recover damages for a personal injury sustained by falling upon one of the sidewalks of said city. The case has been twice tried. The first trial was in the Winnebago county circuit court, and resulted in a verdict in favor of the plaintiff for the sum of $217 damages. This verdict was set aside on motion of the plaintiff, and a new trial granted. An appeal was taken by the city from the order granting such new trial, and the order was affirmed by this court. See case reported in 67 Wis. 195. On the return of the record the place of trial was changed to Marquette county, where a second trial was had, and the jury returned a verdict in favor of the plaintiff for the sum of $1,800 damages. The defendant moved to set aside the verdict, and for a new trial, upon two grounds: *First*, that the court erred in admitting certain evidence offered by the plaintiff and objected to by the defendant; and, *second*, because the damages were excessive. The motion was overruled, exception duly taken by the defendant, and, after the judgment rendered upon the verdict, the city again appeals to this court.

The only errors alleged upon this appeal are the two stated above. That the street was out of repair, and had been for a long time previous to the accident, and that the accident was caused by the want of repair of the street, is admitted. The evidence which was objected to, and the admission of which is alleged to be error, is as follows:

The witness R. W. Bridge, a son of the plaintiff and a witness on his behalf, was asked the following question: "What was your father's general condition after the happening of the injury, so far as you can give it from what you have seen and observed? *Answer.* At times it has been impossible for him to do business, and at other times he can do a little something. He has been subject to more or less pain." The counsel for the defendant objects to that part of the answer which states, "He has been subject to more or less pain." To this objection the court remarked: "He complains of pain." "*Question.* What have you noticed in respect to his memory since the injury? *Answer.* I have noticed that since the injury his memory has at times been very bad." This the defendant moved to strike out, and the motion was denied.

The following questions and answers were allowed, by the witness Mrs. Bridge, wife of the plaintiff's son and intimately acquainted with the plaintiff: *Question.* "Have you observed any change in his condition since the happening of the injury?" Objected to because it is not shown that the witness is an expert, and the question calls for an opinion. The objection overruled, and the witness answered: "Yes, sir; very much in his nervous constitution, and in his health and mind." The witness also answered, under objection, that she had observed a difference in his memory. "His memory has not been so good as it was before." "I have noticed a peculiarity about his walk. He has been lame, or that is what I should call it. He calls it a kind of numbness, I believe. He does not walk the same as before." The court remarked upon the objections of the defendant: " It is difficult to distinguish on these answers. She can tell what she observes,— his physical condition in regard to walking, or sight, or memory, anything of that kind,— if she noticed anything. Her opinion, of course, is not of any value."

The witness Anderson, after testifying as to his relations to the plaintiff and how far he was acquainted with him, was asked: " What, if any, change in the physical condition of *Mr. Bridge* did you notice after the injury?" — and the question and answer were objected to by the defendant. The witness answered: " He seemed to be quite nervous. He didn't seem to have any memory; didn't seem to remember things. He seems to be very shaky,— nervous. His hands were shaking. He was trembling and nervous. If you would ask him a question, probably he would think a moment before answering." " Did you notice any change in his eyes?" This was also objected to. *Answer.* "I think I did, by his asking me at different times to read postal cards and letters." "How often a month did you observe that he had spells of nervousness?" Objected to. *Answer.* "I could not say how many times; of course, many times I heard him complain."

The foregoing is substantially all the evidence which was objected to by the appellant. The appellant also makes a general objection to the evidence of complaints made by the plaintiff to his physicians and others, as to his symptoms, pains, and ailments. There was some evidence given in the case, both by the physicians in attendance upon him and by others who were intimately acquainted with him, that the plaintiff had complained to them of pains in his head and back and a numbness of his limbs, and of other ailments.

Under well-established rules of law applicable to cases of this kind, where personal injuries to the plaintiff are the subject of inquiry and the basis for awarding damages, evidence of the kind admitted by the court in this case is clearly admissible. The admissibility of complaints made by the injured person, either to his attending physicians or others, is clearly sustained by the following authorities: *Insurance Co. v. Mosley*, 8 Wall. 397, 405–407; *Bridge v. Oshkosh*, 67 Wis. 195; *Quaife v. C. & N. W. R. Co.* 48 Wis. 513; *Bacon v. Charlton*, 7 Cush. 586; *Barber v. Merriam*, 11 Allen, 322–324; *Hatch v. Fuller*, 131 Mass. 574; 1 Greenl. Ev. (14th ed.), sec. 102, and cases cited in note *b*. The propriety of permitting a witness who is not an expert, but who is acquainted with the injured person and has seen him frequently before and after the injury, to testify as to any changes either in his physical or mental condition, is established by the following authorities: *Baker v. Madison*, 62 Wis. 137; *Wright v. Fort Howard*, 60 Wis. 119–123; *Sydleman v. Beckwith*, 43 Conn. 9; *Parker v. B. & H. Steamboat Co.* 109 Mass. 449; *Comm. v. Sturtivant*, 117 Mass. 122; *Thompson v. Stevens*, 71 Pa. St. 161; *Elliott v. Van Buren*, 33 Mich. 49; *Wilkinson v. Moseley*, 30 Ala. 562; *Smalley v. Appleton*, 70 Wis. 340. The evidence received over the objections of the appellant was properly received, and no error was committed by the court in that respect.

It is urged that the damages are excessive. If we take into consideration simply the evidence received on the second trial, as we certainly must, we cannot say the damages are excessive. On the contrary, they appear rather moderate, considering the fact that the plaintiff proved on the trial that he had expended something like $300 in paying medical attendants.

But the counsel urge that because upon the first trial a presumably fair jury awarded him only $217, it is evidence of prejudice on the part of the second jury to award him

$1,800 for the same injury.   Under the evidence in this case the first verdict should have very little effect in determining whether the verdict on the second trial was excessive.   On the first trial the plaintiff was prevented by the rulings of the trial court from fully presenting his case on the question of damages, and, in addition to that, the second trial was not had until nearly two years after the first, and it was then proven that the plaintiff had not fully recovered from the injuries he had sustained,— a fact which could not have been established with any certainty on the first trial.   Under this state of facts, what was said by this court in *Baker v. Madison*, 62 Wis. 137, 149, as to the weight the previous verdicts of juries in the same case should have in determining the question as to the excessiveness of the verdict on the final trial of the action, can have no application.   The case appears to have been fairly tried, and there is nothing in the amount of the verdict which would justify this court in setting it aside for any cause.

By the Court.— The judgment of the circuit court is affirmed.

See notes to this case in 37 N. W. Rep. 409.— REP.

Parker, Appellant, vs. Hull, Respondent.

March 5 — March 27, 1888.

Mistake: Degree of proof necessary: Instructions to jury.

The trial court, in charging the jury as to the proof of mistake necessary to change the amount of a promissory note, first instructed them that "in order to establish a mistake the proof thereof must be clear, satisfactory, and convincing," but subsequently said that the *burden of proof* was upon the party alleging it to establish the mistake, and by "burden of proof" was simply meant that he must establish the fact "*by a preponderance of the evidence,*" that is, his evidence "must be *more weighty, convincing, and satisfactory* than the proof adduced by the other party." *Held*, that the charge was erroneous, the correct rule first stated being afterwards overruled and changed.

APPEAL from the Circuit Court for *Sauk* County.

Action to recover the balance due upon a promissory note. The facts will sufficiently appear from the opinion. The plaintiff appeals from a judgment in favor of the defendant.

For the appellant the cause was submitted on the brief of *John Barker*.

G. Stevens, for the respondent, to the point that the whole charge should be considered together, cited *Sterling v. Ripley*, 3 Pin. 155; *Kenworthy v. Ironton*, 41 Wis. 647; *Hinton v. Wells*, 45 id. 268; *Woodruff v. King*, 47 id. 265; *State v. McCahill*, 72 Iowa, 111.

ORTON, J. This action is brought to recover the sum of $283, the balance due upon a certain $800 note given by the respondent to the appellant in part for the purchase of one third interest in a grist or roller mill in the city of Baraboo. The defendant claims that there was a mistake made at the time, in calculating the amount that should be put into said note, by not deducting from said amount of $800 the sum of $283 for certain profits that the mill had made, which at that time were not estimated or ascertained but were contemplated by the agreement of the parties. The jury found that such mistake was made, and therefore found for the defendant.

1. The appellant claims that the verdict is against the law and the evidence. We think that the evidence tended to prove that there was a mutual mistake of fact in determining the amount that should be put into the note as claimed by the respondent, and that there was sufficient

evidence to preclude our interference with the verdict on that ground.

2. The contention of the learned counsel of the appellant is that the learned judge before whom this cause was tried erroneously instructed the jury as to the degree or quantum of evidence necessary to establish the alleged mistake. At the request of the appellant's counsel the jury were first instructed that, "in order to establish a mistake, the proof thereof must be clear, satisfactory, and convincing." This was strictly correct. But this brief statement of an abstract legal principle, disconnected from any other part of the instructions, and made before the main and general instructions were in form addressed to the jury, would not be likely to make a very strong or lasting impression upon their minds. The following instruction was the last one given, and upon the declared subject of the "burden of proof," and would be likely to be intently listened to and well remembered, as the correct rule by which the testimony on behalf of the defendant should be measured. This, as the true rule, is stated deliberately, impressively, and at considerable length, and made specially applicable to the facts of the case, and it was illustrated and explained so that the jury must have clearly understood it. The instruction was as follows: "The *burden of proof* is upon the defendant to establish the fact that such a mistake as he claims was in fact made, and that this note was given for $283 more than it should have been by virtue of the terms of the contract between the plaintiff and the defendant. By *burden of proof* is simply meant this: When a party avers a thing which is denied by his opponent, we say the party who avers the fact to exist must take upon himself the trouble or burden of proving it; and when the burden of proof is upon a party he is bound to establish the fact which he alleges and the other party denies *by a preponderance of the evidence;* and by a preponderance of

the evidence is simply meant that the evidence which the party produces in favor of the fact which he affirmatively avers, and which is denied by his opponent, *must be more weighty, convincing,* and *satisfactory* than the proof adduced by the other party by way of answer or by way of overcoming such affirmative proof." The jury then retired with this rule fresh in memory.

It was incumbent upon the defendant to correct and surcharge an account, to reform a written instrument, or to establish a mistake. The rule recognized by all courts in such cases is that the party alleging the mistake must prove it clearly and satisfactorily, and, some courts hold, beyond a reasonable doubt. A mere *preponderance* of evidence is not sufficient. To be *more* weighty, convincing, or satisfactory than the evidence of the other party is not the rule; for that would be simply the rule of preponderance. Abb. Tr. Ev. 463; *Towsley v. Denison,* 45 Barb. 490; *Klauber v. Wright,* 52 Wis. 303; *Wells v. Ogden,* 30 Wis. 637; *Stockbridge Iron Co. v. Hudson Iron Co.* 102 Mass. 45; *Ely v. Early,* 94 N. C. 1, 25 Am. Law Reg. 342. In *Bond v. Dorsey,* 65 Md. 310, the language is that the evidence must be "clear and overwhelming;" citing *Groff v. Rohrer,* 35 Md. 327; *Mendenhall v. Steckel,* 47 Md. 454; *Beard v. Hubble,* 9 Gill, 430. The learned counsel of the respondent virtually admits in his brief that such is the rule, but contends that such rule was given in the first place, and the whole charge must be taken together. The trouble is that the correct rule, so briefly stated in the beginning, was afterwards overruled and changed, and the incorrect rule, of a mere preponderance of the evidence, substituted and impressed upon the jury, and they were quite probably influenced by it. Which rule should they regard,— the first or the last? To say the least of it, the evidence to establish the mistake was not of the clearest or most convincing character or beyond a reasonable doubt. On account of this error in the charge, the judgment will have to be reversed.

By the Court.— The judgment of the circuit court is reversed, and the cause remanded for a new trial.

AYRES and another, Respondents, vs. THE CHICAGO & NORTHWESTERN RAILWAY COMPANY, Appellant.

March 5 — March 27, 1888.

Railroads: Common carriers: Live-stock: Duty to furnish cars when able: Burden of showing inability: Notice to shipper of inability: Damages.

1. A railroad company engaged in the business of transporting live-stock and accustomed to furnish suitable cars therefor upon reasonable notice whenever it can do so, and which holds itself out to the public as such carrier for hire upon the terms and conditions prescribed in a special written contract with shippers, is a common carrier of live-stock with such restrictions and limitations of its common-law duties and liabilities as arise from the instincts, habits, propensities, wants, necessities, vices, or locomotion of such animals, under the contracts of carriage.

2. As such common carrier the company is bound to furnish suitable cars for live-stock upon reasonable notice whenever it can do so with reasonable diligence without jeopardizing its other business.

3. The burden of showing that it could not, in a particular instance, with such diligence and without jeopardizing its other business, have furnished cars at the time ordered and upon the notice given, is upon the railroad company.

4. Where a shipper makes application to a railroad company, as such common carrier of live-stock, for cars to be furnished at a time and station named, it is the duty of the company to inform him within a reasonable time if it is unable to furnish such cars; and if it fails to give such notice and induces the shipper to believe that the cars will be in readiness, and, relying upon such conduct of the carrier, the shipper is present with his live-stock at the time and place named, and no cars are there, the company is liable for damages.

5. In an action against a carrier for damages arising from delay in transporting live-stock to market, it appeared that the stock arrived on Friday evening in time for the market on Saturday. *Held*, that there could be no recovery for expense of keeping, shrinkage, or depreciation in value after Saturday.

APPEAL from the Circuit Court for *Sauk* County.

The following statement of the case was prepared by Mr. Justice CASSODAY:

This case was here on a question of pleading upon ·a former appeal. 58 Wis. 537. The amended complaint is to the effect that the defendant, being a common carrier engaged in the transportation of live-stock, and accustomed to furnish cars for all live-stock offered, was notified by the plaintiffs, on or about October 13, 1882, to have four such cars for the transportation of cattle, hogs, and sheep at its station La Valle, and three at its station Reedsburg, ready for loading on Tuesday morning, October 17, 1882, for transportation to Chicago; that the defendant neglected and refused to provide such cars at either of said stations for four days, notwithstanding it was able and might reasonably have done so; and also neglected and refused to carry said stock to Chicago with reasonable diligence, so that they arrived there four days later than they otherwise would have done; whereby the plaintiffs suffered loss and damage, by decrease in price and otherwise, $1,700.

The answer, in effect, admitted the defendant's incorporation with the privileges alleged; "that it was at times engaged in the transportation over its roads of live-stock when and if it was able to do so, and was accustomed to furnish suitable cars therefor upon reasonable notice when within its power to do so; and to receive, transport, and deliver such live-stock with reasonable dispatch, but only upon special contracts at the time entered into between the shipper and this defendant, and upon such terms and conditions as should be agreed upon in writing; that one of the lines of this defendant's railway is located as in said amended complaint stated." The answer also, in effect, alleged that "within a reasonable time, and as soon as it reasonably could, and as soon as it was within its power to do so," after the application of the plaintiffs for such cars, the defendant "forwarded four suitable and empty cars to La Valle," and "three suitable and empty cars to Reedsburg," which cars were severally forwarded with reasonable dispatch, and arrived in due course and as soon as they could with reasonable dispatch be forwarded over its line; that at the times of such respective shipments the plaintiffs entered into an agreement in writing with the defendant for the transportation of said stock at special rates, and in consideration thereof it was agreed that the defendant should not be liable for loss from the delay of trains not caused by the defendant's negligence.

At the close of the trial the jury returned a special verdict to the effect (1) that at the times named the plaintiffs were copartners at Reedsburg, engaged in buying and shipping live-stock to the Chicago market for sale; (2) that at the times stated the defendant was a common carrier, and as such engaged in the transportation of live-stock, and accustomed to furnish cars for and transport all live-stock offered for that purpose; (3) that one of its lines ran from La Valle and Reedsburg to Chicago; (4) that October 13, 1882, the plaintiffs, being fully apprised of the state of the Chicago market for live-stock and prices, proceeded to buy therefor seven car-loads of cattle, hogs, and sheep, four to be loaded at La Valle and three at Reedsburg; (5, 6, 7, 8, 9, 10, 14) that the plaintiffs notified the defendant's agents at the respective stations, October 13, 1882, to have such cars in readiness at said stations respectively, October 17, 1882, and that such notices were reasonable, and such agents promised to order the cars and have them in readiness at the time; (11) that two cars were furnished at Reedsburg,

October 17, 1882, and one October 19, 1882; (12) that the four were furnished at La Valle, October 19, 1882; (13) that the defendant furnished two as soon as it reasonably could, but five it did not; (15) that the plaintiffs received no notice before October 17, 1882, that the cars would not be furnished as ordered; (16, 17, 18) that prior to that time, and with the expectation that the cars would be on hand as ordered, the plaintiffs had bought sufficient stock to load said several cars, and had the same at said respective stations on the morning of October 17, 1882; (19) that the defendant, being able to furnish such cars, disregarded its duty as a common carrier of live-stock in not having the same on hand when ordered; (20) that had the cars been so furnished, they would have arrived at Chicago on the morning of October 18, 1882; (21) as it was two arrived there on Thursday, October 19, 1882, A. M., and five on Friday, October 20, 1882, at 5:45 P. M.; (22, 23, 24) that the market value of hogs in Chicago, on Friday, October 20, was $7.36 per hundred, on Saturday, October 21, was $7.11, and on Monday, October 23, $6.81; (25, 26, 27) that the loss on the hogs, by reason of depreciation of the market, was $140.08; that the total damages of the plaintiffs on all the stock were $825.97, made up of the following items, to wit: Taking care of and feeding stock, $50; shrinkage on hogs, cattle, and sheep, $408.35; depreciation in value on hogs and sheep, $172.58; and interest on the above sums until the rendition of the verdict, $195.04.

The defendant thereupon moved for judgment in its favor upon the verdict and record, which was denied. Thereupon the defendant moved to set aside the verdict, and for a new trial, upon the grounds that the verdict is against the weight of the evidence, and for errors of the court in its charge to the jury and in its rulings on the trial, and because the damages were excessive and contrary to the proofs, which motion was denied. Thereupon, and upon the motion of the plaintiffs, judgment was ordered in their favor on the special verdict for $825.97 damages and costs. From the judgment entered thereon accordingly the defendant appeals.

For the appellant there was a brief by *Jenkins, Winkler & Smith*, and oral argument by *Mr. J. G. Jenkins*. They contended, *inter alia*, that the fact that the railroad company had carried and still offered to carry live-stock for hire for all who desired, on terms as to duties, liabilities, and relations not recognized by the law of common carriers but in some respects variant and in others repugnant thereto, did not make it a common carrier of live-stock. *Cleveland & T. R. Co. v. Perkins*, 17 Mich. 296. Railroad companies become common carriers as to any particular kind of property only so far as they hold themselves out as such. *Oxlade v. N. E. R. Co.* 15 C. B. (N. S.), 68; *Johnson v. Midland R. Co.* 4 Exch. 367; *Bank v. Champlain Transp. Co.* 23 Vt. 186, 206. Railroad companies not being common carriers as to live-stock, and the common-law liability being thus changed, the burden of proof as to where the fault lies rests upon the plaintiff. Rorer on Railroads, 1247, 1248, and note 1; Id. 1261, and note 3; Id. 1399, 1400, and note 1; *Lamb v. C. & A. R. Co.* 46 N. Y. 271; *Perry v. D. S. W. R. Co.* 36 Iowa, 102; *Knight v. N. O., O. & G. W. R. Co.* 15 La. Ann. 105. Statutes like sec. 1798, R. S., do not apply to live-stock. Rorer on Railroads, 1300; *Mich. S. & N. I. R. Co. v. McDonough*, 21 Mich. 165. The company is not liable for shrinkage of the cattle. *Ohio & M. R. Co. v. Dunbar*, 20 Ill. 624, 628.

G. Stevens, for the respondents, argued, among other things, that as all the proof on the subject of the defendant's ability to furnish cars was within its own control the burden of proof was on it upon that question. To hold otherwise would be to place all shippers at the mercy of the railroad company, and would be a practical repeal of sec. 1798, R. S., so far as it relates to this subject. *Great Western R. Co. v. Bacon,* 30 Ill. 347; *Wheat v. State,* 6 Mo. 455; *Lovell v. Payne,* 30 La. Ann. 511; *Geuing v. State,* 1 McCord, 573; *Haskill v. Comm.* 3 B. Mon. 342.

CASSODAY, J. There is no finding of any agreement on the part of the defendant to have the cars in readiness at the stations on Tuesday morning, October 17, 1882. There is no testimony to support such a finding. One of the plaintiffs testified, in effect, that he told the agent that he would want the cars on the morning of the day named; that the agent took down the order, put it on his book, and said, "All right," he would try and get them, but that they were short because they were then using more cars for other purposes; that nothing more was said. It appears in the case that the cars were in fact furnished. It also appears that, as the shipments were made, special written contracts therefor were entered into between the parties, whereby it was, in effect, agreed and understood that the plaintiffs should load, feed, water, and take care of such stock at their own expense and risk, and that they would assume all risk of injury or damage that the animals might do to themselves or each other, or which might arise by delay of trains; that the defendants should not be liable for loss by jumping from the cars or delay of trains not caused by the defendant's negligence. The court, in effect, charged the jury that there was no evidence of any negligence on the part of the defendant causing delay in any train after shipment, and hence that the delay of the two cars admitted to have been furnished in time was not before them for consideration. This relieves the case from all liability on contract. It also narrows the case to the defendant's liability for the delay of two days in furnishing the five cars at the stations named, as ordered by the plaintiffs, and in the absence of any contract to do so.

In *Richardson v. C. & N. W. R. Co.* 61 Wis. 601, 18 Am. & Eng. R. Cas. 530, it was, in effect, held competent for a railroad company engaged in the business of transporting live stock to exempt itself by express contract "from damage caused wholly or perhaps in part by the instincts, habits, propensities, wants, necessities, vices, or locomotion of such animals." And it was then said: "Since the action is not based upon contract, the plaintiff must recover, if at all, by reason of the defendant's liability as a common carrier upon mere notice to furnish cars and a readiness to ship at the time notified. Did such notice and readiness to ship create such liability? We have seen that a carrier of live-stock may, to at least a certain extent, limit its liability. Whether the defendant was accustomed to so limit its liability, or to carry all live-stock tendered upon notice, without restriction, does not appear from the record. If it was accustomed to so limit, and the limitation was legal, it should at least have been so alleged, together with an offer to comply with the customary restriction. If it was accustomed to carry all live-stock offered upon notice and tender, and without restriction, then it would be difficult to see upon what ground it could discriminate against the plaintiff by refusing to do for him what it was constantly in the habit of doing for others."

In that case there was a failure to allege any such custom or holding out on the part of the defendant, or that reasonable notice had been given to the defendant to furnish suitable cars to the person applying therefor, or that the same was within its power to do so; and hence the demurrer was sustained. The allegations thus wanting in that case are present in this complaint. It is, moreover, in effect admitted that the defendant was at times, when able to do so, engaged in the transportation of live-stock over its roads, one line of which runs through the stations in question; that it was accustomed to furnish suitable cars therefor, upon reasonable notice, when within its power to do so; and to receive, transport, and deliver such live-stock with reasonable dispatch, but only upon special contracts at the time entered into between the shipper and the defendant, and upon such terms and conditions as should be agreed upon in writing. It is, moreover, manifest that the defendant actually undertook to furnish the cars at the time designated by the plaintiffs; that it succeeded in furnishing two of them on time; that there was a delay of two days in furnishing the other five; and that the plaintiffs were willing to, and did, submit to the terms and conditions of carriage imposed by the defendant by signing the special written contracts mentioned. It must be assumed, also, that such special written contracts were substantially the same as all contracts made by the defendant at that season of the year for the shipment of similar live-stock under similar circumstances. Otherwise the defendant would be justly chargeable with unlawful discrimination; the right to do which the learned counsel for the defendant frankly disclaimed upon the argument.

We are therefore forced to the conclusion that at the time the plaintiffs applied for the cars the defendant was engaged in the business of transporting live-stock over its roads, including the line in question, and that it was accustomed to furnish suitable cars therefor, upon reasonable notice, whenever it was within its power to do so; and that it held itself out to the public generally as such carrier for hire upon such terms and conditions as were prescribed in the written contracts mentioned. These things, in our judgment, made the defendant a common carrier of live-stock, with such restrictions and limitations of its common-law duties and liabilities as arose from the instincts, habits, propensities, wants, necessities, vices, or locomotion of such animals, under the contracts of carriage. This proposition is fairly deducible from what was said in *Richardson v. C. & N. W.*

R. Co., supra, and is supported by the logic of numerous cases. *North Penn. R. Co. v. Commercial Bank,* 123 U. S. 727; *Moulton v. St. P., M. & M. R. Co.* 31 Minn. 85, 12 Am. & Eng. R. Cas. 13; *Lindsley v. C., M. & St. P. R. Co.* 36 Minn. 539; *Evans v. F. R. Co.* 111 Mass. 142; *Kimball v. R. & B. R. Co.* 26 Vt. 247, 62 Am. Dec. 567; *Rixford v. Smith,* 52 N. H. 355; *Clarke v. R. & S. R. Co.* 14 N. Y. 570, 67 Am. Dec. 205; *South & N. A. R. Co. v. Henlein,* 52 Ala. 606; *Baker v. L. & N. R. Co.* 10 Lea, 304, 16 Am. & Eng. R. Cas. 149; *Philadelphia, W. & B. R. Co. v. Lehman,* 56 Md. 209; *McFadden v. M. P. R. Co.* 92 Mo. 343; 3 Am. & Eng. Cyclop. Law, pp. 1–10, and cases there cited. This is in harmony with the statement of PARKE, B., in the case cited by counsel for the defendant, that " at common law a carrier is not bound to carry for every person tendering goods of *any* description, *but his obligation is to carry according to his public profession.*" *Johnson v. Midland R. Co.* 4 Exch. 372. Being a common carrier of live-stock for hire, with the restrictions and limitations named, and holding itself out to the public as such, the defendant is bound to furnish suitable cars for such stock, upon reasonable notice, whenever it can do so with reasonable diligence without jeopardizing its other business as such common carrier. *Texas & P. R. Co. v. Nicholson,* 61 Tex. 491; *Chicago & A. R. Co. v. Erickson,* 91 Ill. 613; *Ballentine v. N. M. R. Co.* 40 Mo. 491; *Guinn v. W., St. L. & P. R. Co.* 20 Mo. App. 453.

Whether the defendant could with such diligence so furnish upon the notice given, was necessarily a question of fact to be determined. The plaintiffs, as such shippers, had the right to command the defendant to furnish such cars. But they had no right to insist upon or expect compliance, except upon giving reasonable notice of the time when they would be required. To be reasonable, such notice must have been sufficient to enable the defendant, with reasonable diligence under the circumstances then existing, to furnish the cars without interfering with previous orders from other shippers at the same station, or jeopardizing its business on other portions of its road. It must be remembered that the defendant has many lines of railroad scattered through several different states. Along each and all of these different lines it has stations of more or less importance. The company owes the same duty to shippers at any one station as it does to the shippers at any other station of the same business importance. The rights of all shippers applying for such cars under the same circumstances are necessarily equal. No one station, much less any one shipper, has the right to command the entire resources of the company to the exclusion or prejudice of other stations and other shippers. Most of such suitable cars must necessarily be scattered along and upon such different lines of railroad, loaded or unloaded. Many will necessarily be at the larger centers of trade. The conditions of the market are not always the same, but are liable to fluctuations, and may be such as to create a great demand for such cars upon one or more of such lines, and very little upon others. Such cars should be distributed along the different lines of road, and the several stations on each, as near as may be in proportion to the ordinary business requirements at the time, in order that shipments may be made with reasonable celerity. The requirement of such fair and general distribution and uniform vigilance is not only mutually beneficial to producers, shippers, carriers, and purchasers, but of business and trade generally. It is the extent of such business ordinarily done on a particular line, or at a particular station, which properly measures the carrier's obligation to furnish such transportation. But it is not the duty of such carrier to discriminate in favor of the business of one station to the prejudice and injury of the business of another station of the same importance.

These views are in harmony with the adjudications last cited.

The important question is whether the burden was upon the plaintiffs to prove that the defendant might, with such reasonable diligence and without thus jeopardizing its other business, have furnished such cars at the time ordered and upon the notice given; or whether such burden was upon the defendant to prove its inability to do so. We find no direct adjudication upon the question. Ordinarily, a plaintiff alleging a fact has the burden of proving it. This rule has been applied by this court, even where the complaint alleges a negative, if it is susceptible of proof by the plaintiff. *Hepler v. State*, 58 Wis. 46. But it has been held otherwise where the only proof is peculiarly within the control of the defendant. *Mecklem v. Blake*, 16 Wis. 102; *Beckmann v. Henn*, 17 Wis. 412; *Noonan v. Ilsley*, 21 Wis. 144; *Great Western R. Co. v. Bacon*, 30 Ill. 352; *Brown v. Brown*, 30 La. Ann. 511. Here it may have been possible for the plaintiffs to have proved that there were at the times and stations named, or in the vicinity, empty cars, or cars which had reached their destination and might have been emptied with reasonable diligence, but they could not know or prove, except by agents of the defendant, that any of such cars were not subject to prior orders or superior obligations. The ability of the defendant to so furnish with ordinary diligence upon the notice given, upon the principles stated was, as we think, peculiarly within the knowledge of the defendant and its agents, and hence the burden was upon it to prove its inability to do so. Where a shipper applies to the proper agency of a railroad company engaged in the business of such common carrier of live-stock for such cars to be furnished at a time and station named, it becomes the duty of the company to inform the shipper within a reasonable time, if practicable, whether it is unable to so furnish, and if it fails to give such notice, and has induced the shipper to believe that the cars will be in readiness at the time and place named, and the shipper, relying upon such conduct of the carrier, is present with his livestock at the time and place named, and finds no cars, there would seem to be no good reason why the company should not respond in damages. Of course, these observations do not involve the question whether a railroad company may not refrain from engaging in such business as a common carrier; nor whether, having so engaged, it may not discontinue the same.

The court very properly charged the jury, in effect, that if all the cars had been furnished on time, as the two were, it was reasonable to presume, in the absence of any proof of actionab e negligence on the part of the defendant, that they would have reached Chicago at the same time the two did — to wit, Thursday, October 19, 1882, A. M., whereas they did not arrive until Friday evening. This was in time, however, for the market in Chicago on Saturday, October 21, 1882. This necessarily limited the recovery to the expense of keeping, the shrinkage, and depreciation in value from Thursday until Saturday. *Chicago & A. R. Co. v. Erickson*, 91 Ill. 613. The trial court, however, refused to so limit the recovery, but left the jury at liberty to include such damages down to Monday, October 23, 1882. For this manifest error, and because there seems to have been a mistrial in some other respects, the judgment of the circuit court is reversed, and the cause is remanded for a new trial.

By the Court.— Ordered accordingly.

See note to this case in 87 N. W. Rep. 432.— REP.

THE STATE, Respondent, vs. HOGUE, Appellant.

March 5 — March 27, 1888.

CONSTITUTIONAL LAW: HIGHWAYS. *(1) Notice of meeting to locate state road under special act: When general law applies. (2) Oath of commissioners. (3) Bridges. (4) Width of highway. (5) Compensation for property taken.*

1. The fact that a special act for the laying out of a state road makes no provision for giving notice to resident owners of the time and place of meeting of the commissioners to locate the road, does not invalidate the act, as in such case the provisions of the Revised Statutes apply and regulate the manner of giving notice.

2. Nor is such an act invalidated by the failure to provide therein that the commissioners shall take an oath before entering upon the discharge of their duties, the legislature having power to exempt "inferior officers" from taking an oath.

3. A special act for the laying out of a state road which will cross a navigable river need not make any provision for building a bridge.

4. The report of commissioners appointed to lay out a highway failed to state the width of the highway, but the survey showed the centre line thereof. *Held*, that this was sufficiently definite under sec. 1264, R. S., which provides that all public highways shall be not less than four rods wide.

5. Sec. 1315, R. S., provides that all damages occasioned by laying out a state road shall be paid by the several counties in which it may be located, and that every person claiming such damages shall present his claim to the county board, and in case it is disallowed may appeal to the circuit court. Ch. 223, Laws of 1882, gave to the commissioners appointed therein the same power as to awarding damages as is conferred by law upon the county board. *Held*, that this was a sufficient provision for compensation for the property taken.

APPEAL from the Circuit Court for *Pepin* County.

Action to recover the statutory penalty for obstruction of a highway. Under the pleadings the issue was as to the existence of a highway at the point of obstruction, and this involved the validity of ch. 223, Laws of 1882, and the legality of the proceedings taken by the commissioners under that act. Said ch. 223 is entitled "An act to provide for laying out a state road from the village of Misha Mokwa in the county of Buffalo, to the village of Pepin in the county of Pepin." Its provisions will sufficiently appear from the opinion.

The court directed a verdict for the plaintiff, and from the judgment entered thereon the defendant appeals.

For the appellant there was a brief by *W. F. Bailey* and *C. M. Hilliard*, and oral argument by *Mr. Bailey.* They contended that ch. 223, Laws of 1882, is unconstitutional for the following reasons, among others: (1) It does not provide for giving notice. It should specify a personal notice to known resident owners, of the time and place of meeting to locate the road. *State ex rel. Flint v. Fond du Lac,* 42 Wis. 298; *Siefert v. Brooks,* 34 Wis. 443. It should provide for notice to the owners of the time and place of meeting for the assessment of damages. *Siefert v. Brooks,* 34 Wis. 443; *Powers v. Bears,* 12 id. 223; *Burns v. M. R. Co.* 15 Fed. Rep. 177; *In re Middletown,* 82 N. Y. 201; *Stuart v. Palmer,* 74 id. 183; *Beckwith v. Beckwith,* 22 Ohio St. 188. (2) It does not provide for compensation. It does not provide for ascertaining the damages before appropriation. *Bohlman v. G. B. & L. P. R. Co.* 30 Wis. 105; *Norton v. Peck,* 3 id. 714; *Powers v. Bears,* 12 id. 214; *Brock v. Hislen,* 40 id. 681. There is no provision for review of or appeal from the award of the commissioners, being a denial of the right to have the damages assessed by a jury. *Charles River Bridge v. Warren Bridge,* 11 Pet. 571. The award is not binding on the county. The right to sue is not compensation. Mills on Em. Dom. sec. 132; *Shepardson v. M. & B. R. Co.* 6 Wis. 614; *Norton v. Peck,* 3 id. 714. There is no provision for payment of the award, or fund provided in the hands of the commissioners to pay it from. An act almost similar in its provisions was held unconstitutional in *Langford v. Ramsey Co.* 16 Minn. 375.

The provisions of the act of 1882 are so dissimilar in all respects to the provisions of the Revised Statutes upon the subject that it was clearly the intent of the legislature that the authority of the commissioners was embraced in the act, and that it was complete and exclusive — independent of the general law. *Pettibone v. La C. & M. R. Co.* 14 Wis. 443; 2 Dillon on Mun. Corp. 613, 615, note 4.

. For the respondent there was a brief by *John Fraser* and *W. P. Bartlett,* and oral argument by *Mr. Bartlett.*

COLE, C. J.   It is evident this judgment must be affirmed if ch. 223, Laws of 1882, is a valid enactment.   So, the principal question to be considered is the constitutionality of that law.   The act appoints a board of commissioners to lay out and establish a state road from the village of Misha Mokwa in the county of Buffalo, on the most feasible route to the village of Pepin in the county of Pepin.   It gives the commissioners the same powers as are conferred by the general statute on county boards of supervisors, to award damages and settle with any parties who may feel aggrieved or sustain damages by the laying out and establishing the road; and it makes it the duty of the commissioners, within thirty days after they have laid out the road or such part thereof as in their opinion the public good requires,— but the same, in any event, must extend into both counties,— to cause to be filed in the office of the town and county clerks of the counties through or into which the road extends, a correct copy of the field-notes and plat of the survey thereof; and the act declares that on and after the filing of the said copy of the field-notes and plat of survey by the commissioners the road shall be a public highway and be deemed to be opened and established as a public highway.   The other section of the act relates to the compensation of the commissioners, but has no bearing upon the question as to the validity of the law.

Before proceeding to notice the objections taken to the act, it may be well to call attention to a remark made by Mr. Justice TAYLOR, in *Jensen v. Polk Co.* 47 Wis. 298, as to the power of the legislature to enact laws of this character. He says: "That the legislature has the power to appoint commissioners to lay out and establish state roads can only be questioned on the ground that it is prohibited from so doing by some positive provision of the constitution. Unless the power is taken away, it is clearly a legislative power, and can be exercised by the legislature. The power has been exercised by the territorial legislature during the existence of the territory, and by almost every legislature since the formation of the state. By the amendment of the constitution made in 1871, the power of the legislature is clearly recognized by limiting its exercise to certain specified cases. The language of the amendment, so far as it relates to this question, is as follows: 'The legislature is prohibited from enacting any special or private law . . . for laying out, opening, or altering highways, except in cases of state roads extending into more than one county.' This amendment of the constitution is a clear declaration that the power to pass acts for laying out, establishing, and opening state roads is a legislative power; and that part of the amendment was adopted for the express purpose of restraining and limiting the power previously exercised by the legislature."

There are a number of objections taken to the constitutionality of ch. 223, by the learned counsel for the defendant. He says truly that the law makes no provision for giving notice to the resident owners of the time and place of the meeting of the commissioners to locate the road. This he insists is a fatal defect, which invalidates the act. To this objection it is answered that as the special law is silent as to the giving of notice, the provisions of the general statute apply and regulate the manner of giving notice. It seems to us that this is a sufficient answer to the objection. Resort is often. had to a general provision as a guide and aid in the exercise of a special authority or jurisdiction over a particular subject, and we think such reference must be had here. Illustrations of the justness of this view will occur to any one on a moment's reflection. The Revised Statutes of 1878 contain provisions for laying out state roads where it is not otherwise specially provided by law. Sec. 1312 et seq. Provision is made for posting copies of the special law under which the commissioners act, and for giving notice of the time and place when they will meet to locate the road. The general statute is full and explicit on this point, and makes ample provision for giving notice to all affected by· the proposed highway. In this case the commissioners complied with sec. 1313, and gave the notice therein prescribed. That must be held sufficient as to notice.

But, again, it is objected that the law fails to provide that the commissioners should take an oath before entering upon the discharge of their duties. As a matter of fact it appears that the commissioners did take the oath prescribed by sec. 28, art. IV, of the constitution, to be taken by members of the legislature and other officers. But the general law makes no provision for the commissioners taking an oath, and the legislature doubtless had power to exempt them from the necessity of taking an oath in laying out a state road. The section of the constitution just referred to gives the legislature power to exempt " inferior officers " from taking an oath. The case of *Lumsden v. Milwaukee*, 8 Wis. 485, and *Bohlman v. G. B. & M. R. Co.* 40 Wis. 158, upon which counsel relies, have no application to this case. In the former case, where the constitution had provided that no municipal corporation shall take private property for public use against the consent of the owner without the necessity thereof being first established by a jury, it was held that the jury must first be sworn before determining such necessity. In the *Bohlman Case*, the general law required the commissioners to take the constitutional oath, and it was held that this was imperative, and that the commissioners had no right to act without taking it. The distinction between those cases and the one before us, where the legislature has seen fit to exempt the commissioners from taking an oath, is too obvious to need comment.

The road crosses a navigable river, and it is objected that the law makes no provision for building a bridge over the stream, so as to render the highway continuous. The special law certainly makes no provision for constructing or working the highway so as to render it fit for public travel, but the expense of opening it, of erecting bridges where necessary, would fall upon the towns, and in some cases partly upon the counties, in which it is located. The general law fully regulates these matters.

Further, it is said the return of the commissioners fails to state the width of the highway laid out. The survey shows the center of the highway as laid, and the general statute applies which prescribes that all public highways shall be not less than four rods wide. Sec. 1264, R. S. This is sufficiently definite as to the width of the highway.

The last objection is that the law fails to provide compensation for the property taken for the highway. The commissioners had the same power as to awarding damages for land taken as is conferred by law upon the county board of supervisors. When the county board lays out a highway and is unable to agree with the owner as to the damages, it assesses such damages for every parcel taken, which are to be paid by the town in which the highway is situated, or by such town and any other town or towns, in such proportion as the county board shall direct at the time of making the order laying out the highway, when the county board deem such other towns benefited thereby. Sec. 1303, R. S.

In respect to state roads, the general statute provides that all damages occasioned by laying them out and opening them shall be paid by the several counties in which the same may be located; and every person claiming any such damages shall present his claim therefor to the county board of the county in which his lands are situated; and such board is required to act upon such claims and allow the same or such part thereof as they shall deem just; and any person whose claim is disallowed in whole or in part may appeal to the circuit court as in other cases. Sec. 1315. So it will be seen that as to the amount of compensation the owner is not bound by the award of the commissioners, but may appeal to the circuit court when the county board fails to allow him what he deems just and equitable for his property taken. In the circuit court, of course, he has a judicial determination of the question as to compensation by a jury trial, which assesses his damages. But it is said that this is not making compensation to the owner for his land appropriated for public use, but is giving him a lawsuit to determine the compensation. In this state the law is firmly established that "where the property is taken for public use by a town or municipal corporation which is made liable to the owner for any damage sustained by reason thereof, the taxable property of such town or municipality constitutes a pledge or fund to which the owner may resort for payment in the manner prescribed with absolute certainty and safety, and that the providing of such a method of enforcing payment out of such a pledge or fund is the making of just compensation for the property taken, within the meaning of the constitution." *Smeaton v. Martin*, 57 Wis. 364. In the case of the taking of private property for public use by a private corporation, a distinction is made and a different rule obtains. But where the land is taken by a town or municipality for public use, the fact that the entire taxable property of the town or municipality is liable for its payment, and to which the owner may resort to enforce such payment, relieves the town or municipality from the necessity of making actual prepayment before appropriating the land to the use of the public. The highway law, and perhaps other laws found in the Revision or Session Laws, go upon that theory as to compensation, and they have been deemed valid in that regard since the early decision of *Norton v. Peck* (in 1854), 3 Wis. 714.

This disposes of all the material objections to ch. 223, Laws of 1882.

By the Court.— The judgment of the circuit court is affirmed.

Lusted, Respondent, vs. The Chicago & Northwestern Railway Company, Appellant.

March 6 — March 27, 1888.

Equity: Mistake: Release under seal: Failure to read: Negligence.

While plaintiff was suffering from injuries received in a collision on the railroad of the defendant, the agent of the latter procured him to execute, in consideration of $50, a release under seal of all claims against the defendant by reason of his property being destroyed at the time of the collision and also for personal injuries received at that time. The jury found that the subject of a release for the injuries was not talked about during the negotiations, and that neither the plaintiff nor the agent understood that the release covered the claim for such injuries. The value of the property destroyed exceeded $50. The release was not read to the plaintiff who was sick in bed, and when handed to him he tried to read it but could not by reason of dizziness caused by the injuries to his face and head. *Held*, that the release as to the personal injuries was not binding, and plaintiff's ignorance of its contents was not, under the circumstances, the result of such negligence as would preclude him from avoiding the release.

APPEAL from the Circuit Court for *Dane* County.

Action to recover damages for personal injuries received by the plaintiff in a collision on the defendant's railroad, alleged to have been caused by the negligence of the defendant's servants. The answer among other things alleges that after the collision and injury the plaintiff, in consideration of a sum of money paid to him, by an instrument under seal, released and discharged the defendant from all claims and demands by reason of the claim set up in the complaint.

There was a special verdict relating to the execution of the release, the substance of which is stated in the opinion. There was also a general verdict in favor of the plaintiff, assessing his damages at $3,500. A motion for a new trial was denied; and from the judgment entered on the verdict the defendant appealed.

For the appellant there was a brief by *Jenkins, Winkler & Smith*, and oral argument by *Mr. J. G. Jenkins*. They contended, *inter alia*, that the release, being under seal and absolute, can only be avoided for fraud. *Ellis v. Esson*, 50 Wis. 138, 146; *Randall v. Reynolds*, 52 N. Y. Super. Ct. 145; *Brown v. Cambridge*, 3 Allen, 474; *Hanley v. Noyes*, 35 Minn. 174. The failure of the plaintiff to read the release or have it read to him was such negligence that he cannot now ask for relief in equity. *Greenfield's Estate*, 2 Harr. 496; *Fuller v. Madison M. Ins. Co.* 36 Wis. 603–4; *Sanger v. Dun*, 47 id. 615, 620; *Gulliher v. C., R. I. & P. R. Co.* 59 Iowa, 422–3; *Wallace v. C., St. P., M. & O. R. Co.* 67 id. 547; *Pennsylvania R. Co. v. Shea*, 82 Pa. St. 198, 202. The plaintiff, having acted upon the agreement as executed by him, having received and spent the money, and having never tendered a return until after this action was commenced, cannot now be heard to dispute the settlement or be permitted to recover. *Gould v. Bank*, 86 N. Y. 75; *Ludington v. Miller*, 38 N. Y. Super. Ct. 478; *Kellogg v.*

Richards, 14 Wend. 118, 119. See, also, *Stapleton v. King*, 33 Iowa, 31–35; *State v. Gott*, 44 Md. 341–349; *Coon v. Knap*, 8 N. Y. 402; *Eggleston v. Knickerbacker*, 6 Barb. 458; *Hinkle v. M. & St. L. R. Co.* 31 Minn. 434; *Stockton v. Frey*, 4 Gill (Md.), 406, 424; *Kansas City & O. R. Co. v. Hicks*, 30 Kan. 288.

For the respondent there was a brief by *Rogers & Hall*, and *Geo. W. Bird*, and oral argument by *Mr. Bird* and *Mr. W. H. Rogers*. To the point that the release does not prevent a recovery for the personal injuries in this action, they cited *Woodman v. Clapp*, 21 Wis. 350; *Butler v. Regents*, 32 id. 124; *Smith v. Schulenberg*, 34 id. 41; *Schultz v. C. & N. W. R. Co.* 44 id. 645; *Bussian v. M., L. S. & W. R. Co.* 56 id. 325; *Catlin v. Wheeler*, 49 id. 507; *O'Neil v. L. S. I. Co.* 30 N. W. Rep. (Mich.), 688; *C., R. I. & P. R. Co. v. Lewis*, 13 Ill. App. 166, 109 Ill. 120; *Eagle Packet Co. v. Defries*, 94 Ill. 598; *Codding v. Wood*, 112 Pa. St. 371.

COLE, C. J. Unless the plaintiff is barred from a recovery in this action by the release given in evidence, the judgment appealed from must be affirmed. The plaintiff was a mail-agent, and was injured while traveling on the defendant's road, by a collision which occurred solely through the negligence of an engineer in charge of and running an engine on its road. It is not claimed that the plaintiff was at fault, or contributed in any way through want of care to produce the injuries he sustained. When injured he was in the discharge of his duties as mail-route agent, and doubtless held the relation of a passenger to the company at the time of the collision. Besides personal injuries, the plaintiff lost some money and property in consequence of the car taking fire on which he was riding. The accident happened in the forenoon on the 26th of October, 1886, soon after the regular passenger train going east had left Pine Bluff station.   The' plaintiff rode on the train to Madison, and was first taken to the Sisters' Hospital, where his wounds were dressed by Drs. Fox and Boyd.   He had a scalp wound, or cut on the head, but there was no apparent injury to the skull, and his face, neck, and hands were burned or scalded to some extent.   Soon after his wounds were dressed, he was taken in a carriage to the residence of Mr. Rogers, in this city, a brother-in-law.   There he remained, from Tuesday of the week he was hurt, until the following Friday afternoon, when he returned to his home in Lancaster.   On Thursday, the 28th of October, Mr. Richards, the claim-agent of the defendant, in company with Dr. Boyd, visited the plaintiff at the house of Mr. Rogers, and, after some negotiations, the plaintiff signed an instrument under seal, which was in substance as follows: "In consideration of the sum of fifty dollars, to me in hand paid by the *Chicago & Northwestern Railway Company*, the receipt whereof is hereby confessed, I hereby release and forever discharge said railway company from all claims and demands which I now have or may have against it by reason of property belonging to me which was burned in a wreck near Pine Bluff, October 26, 1886, and for injuries received by me at the same time; said wreck caused by an engine colliding with the train upon which I was riding."   The instrument was dated and signed.

The testimony is conflicting as to what conversation was had between the plaintiff and Mr. Richards, the claim-agent, prior to the signing of this release, and as to the circumstances attending its execution.   The jury found, in answer to questions submitted, that the money was not paid upon the understanding, by the claim-agent, that it was in full of all claims growing out of the accident; that the plaintiff signed the release without knowing it contained a clause releasing claims for personal injury, and that he would not have signed it had he known it contained such a clause; and that the subject of a release for personal injuries was not talked about during the negotiations; that the plaintiff at the time of the negotiations was conscious and rational, and had an opportunity to read and understand the contents of the release; that he used the money received, and never tendered it back to the defendant until after the commencement of this action.

The learned circuit judge declined to submit a question whether the defendant's agent made any false representations to the plaintiff as to the contents of the release when it was signed, because he thought there was no evidence that any false statements or representations in express terms were made. It is true that there is no evidence that any actual fraud was practiced by the agent to procure the plaintiff's signature to the paper; still it is difficult to conceive how the clause releasing all claims for personal injuries was inserted therein without the knowledge of the agent, who himself drew up the instrument, as we understand the testimony. But, in view of the finding of the jury, we must assume that the agent inserted that clause by mistake; for it is found that neither the plaintiff nor the agent understood or knew that the instrument contained a clause releasing the claim for personal injuries. The conclusion is inevitable that the clause releasing the claim for personal injuries was inserted in the release either through pure mistake, or by error on the part of the agent of the defendant in reducing it to writing, who did not intend any actual wrong or bad faith. Upon either hypothesis, the question is, Does the release bind the plaintiff, or may he show that he did not understand it and would not have signed it had he known that it contained that clause?

The learned counsel for the defendant insists that the release is binding unless it appears that it was procured by fraud; consequently that the evidence admitted against objection, that the plaintiff did not read or understand the release when he executed it, was incompetent, and should have been excluded. We suppose the doctrine is well settled that courts relieve against mistakes, as well as frauds, in written instruments. A mistake is a ground for setting aside settlements; or where there is a material mistake in a written instrument, either through the error of the draughtsman in reducing the agreement to writing or by the omission or insertion of a stipulation contrary to the intention of the parties, courts relieve against and correct the mistake. A strong illustration of this is afforded by the case of *Green Bay & M. Canal Co. v. Hewitt*, 62 Wis. 316, where a deed was corrected and reformed so as to accord with the intention of the parties. Indeed, the cases are numerous of the correction of a mistake made in reducing an agreement to writing, as well as of avoiding the effect of an instrument entered into through mistake or ignorance of its real character, where such ignorance is not attributable to the negligence of the ignorant party. It certainly cannot be necessary to cite authorities in support of these familiar propositions. We are confident the learned counsel for the defendant would not controvert them.

As to the case before us, the decided weight of testimony supports the conclusion that the matter of personal injuries was not talked about or considered when the release was executed. The explanation may be (probably is) that such injuries were not deemed serious. The agent himself says, in substance, that in their negotiations the plaintiff seemed to place the most stress upon his property lost and the expense of his sickness, and did not dwell upon his personal injuries. If his real pecuniary loss was made good, and his doctors' bills paid, he seemed satisfied, "and would call it even." Dr. Boyd did not remember that anything was said in the conversation about personal injuries. The plaintiff remarked that $50 was paying for the personal property, and that the government would allow him for his time lost,

Lusted vs. The Chicago & Northwestern R. Co.

and that would compensate him, it being understood that the defendant would pay the doctors' bills. The jury was fully warranted in finding that the subject of a release for personal injuries was not talked about during the negotiations; also, that the plaintiff did not know that the instrument contained the clause releasing all claim for personal damages when he signed it. It is perfectly clear that the $50 paid only made good in part the loss of personal property. It certainly was not intended to apply on any claim of damages for personal injury. The loss in property considerably exceeded, according to the plaintiff's testimony, $50.

The further question then arises, Was the ignorance of the plaintiff of the clause contained in the instrument releasing all claim of personal injury, the result of such negligence on his part as precludes him from avoiding it? As to that point we are constrained to say, without imputing to the agent who obtained the release any conscious bad faith in the transaction, that he obtained it at such a time and under such circumstances as show that he acquired an undue advantage, akin in law to a species of fraud. Therefore we are satisfied from all the evidence that it would be against good conscience to allow the defendant to have the benefit of the release thus acquired and hold the plaintiff to its terms. The parties were not standing upon an equal footing in the negotiation. The plaintiff was sick in bed; suffering from an injury to his face and head, which proved to be serious. True, he was conscious and rational, and his recollection of events was clear, but the interview was quite brief, and it is a fair inference that the plaintiff was in no condition to read and fully comprehend the release. He says, in regard to his condition, that the release was not read to him, but handed to him to read; that he tried to read it and could not. He adds: " I had tried three times to get up that morning. Each time I raised up I was seized with dizziness and could not see anything, and would lie down each time. The time the paper was handed me the same dizziness came upon me as it had before, and I could not see anything; everything was a blur before my eyes. For that reason I did not read the paper." It is quite probable he might have been less on his guard in signing the paper because so little (if anything) had been said about his personal injuries. He supposed he was being paid merely for his property lost. Under these circumstances, we think the ignorance of the plaintiff of the contents of the release cannot be said to be the result of such want of diligence on his part as to preclude him from the right to avoid it. The case, in all of its features, comes strictly within the decision of *Schultz v. C. & N. W. R. Co.* 44 Wis. 638, and *Bussian v. M., L. S. & W. R. Co.* 56 Wis. 326. In those cases there was a release and discharge of all claim for personal injuries, under seal; yet it was held that the plaintiff was not bound by it. We think the cases were rightly decided, and are not disposed to overrule them, notwithstanding criticisms made upon them. In the cases of *Fuller v. Madison Mut. Ins. Co.* 36 Wis. 599, and *Sanger v. Dun*, 47 Wis. 615, the parties were not relieved from the agreements in consequence of being ignorant of their contents, because such ignorance was justly attributable to gross negligence on their part. The cases are clearly distinguishable, in fact and principle, from those in 44 and 56 Wis.

The trial court in effect held that the burden of impeaching the release was upon the plaintiff, who must show with reasonable certainty that it was not intended to include the claim for personal injury; and the jury were told that if the plaintiff signed it after the subject of his injuries was talked over, understanding that it was a release of that claim, whether he then knew the extent of his injuries or not,— if he executed the instrument understandingly,— he was bound by it. Under the charge, the jury found the verdict which we have referred to. There is no ground for charging the plaintiff with culpable neglect in failing to read and know the contents of the release. Ignorance of its contents, under the circumstances, is not prejudicial to his rights. It would be against good conscience and all rules of fair dealing to allow the defendant to have the advantage of the release obtained in the manner it was. The agent seemed to be conscious that he made a sharp bargain in the transaction. He says: "I paid him $50. I did think I got out of it pretty cheap." It would be most inequitable and unjust to hold the release conclusive in view of all the facts disclosed in the record. This disposes of the material question in the case.

By the Court.— The judgment of the circuit court is affirmed.

Reed, Respondent, vs. The Chicago, Milwaukee & St. Paul Railway Company, Appellant.

March 6 — March 27, 1888.

(1, 2) Negligence: Injury to land by fire: Proof of title. (3) Evidence: Certificate of clerk of commissioners of public lands. (4, 5) New trial: Mistake of law: Discretion: Review on appeal.

1. In an action to recover damages for negligence in setting a fire which burned over vacant and uncultivated land (and especially where continuing damage by reason of reduced productiveness is claimed), it is incumbent upon the plaintiff to prove his title.

2. In such an action a quitclaim deed to the plaintiff, together with oral testimony (admitted without objection) that he owned the land, and evidence that through an agent he gathered the crop of cranberries therefrom, is *held* to prove, *prima facie*, his title, and to cast upon the defendant the burden of proving that the plaintiff was not the owner.

3. A certificate signed by the chief clerk of the commissioners of the public lands, and having the seal of such commissioners affixed, to

the effect that at a certain time a person named purchased certain lands from the state, and that patents therefor were duly issued to him, is not admissible in evidence.

4. If a new trial be granted solely by reason of a misapprehension of the law, the order granting the same will be reversed on appeal. But it must clearly appear that such was the sole ground of the order.

5. In this case the plaintiff introduced considerable testimony for the purpose of proving the alleged negligence of the defendant, and which had a bearing on that question; and it is probably true that there is some doubt as to what inferences may properly be deduced from such testimony. The circuit court having held, on a motion for a new trial, contrary to its ruling on the trial, that the testimony was sufficient to send the question to the jury, this court affirms the order granting a new trial, without reviewing such conflicting rulings of the court below.

APPEAL from the Circuit Court for *Juneau* County.

The complaint alleges, in substance, that the plaintiff is the owner in fee of a tract of land consisting of seven forty-acre lots, described in the complaint, through which tract the railway of the defendant company is constructed and operated; that through the negligence of the railway company, its servants and employees, fire was communicated from its locomotives, at three several times, to dry grass and other combustible materials which the company had negligently suffered to accumulate and remain on its right of way, from whence the fires spread and burned over portions of the plaintiff's land, destroying large quantities of cranberry vines, shoots, and berries growing thereon, of great value, and greatly injuring and decreasing the productiveness of such land. The damage occasioned by each fire is stated as a separate cause of action. These are alleged to have occurred in August, 1883, July 6, 1886, and July 24, 1886, respectively. The damages claimed for the first fire are $5,000; for the second, $11,500; and for the third, $1,918.

The answer denies the plaintiff's title to the land described in the complaint, and the negligence charged therein; also that the plaintiff was damaged by the fires.

At the close of the trial the court held that there was no testimony tending to prove the negligence of the defendant company in respect to the two fires of July, 1886, and submitted to the jury only the question of the liability of the company for the damages caused by the fire of 1883. The jury returned a verdict for the plaintiff, assessing his damages at six cents. Thereupon the plaintiff moved the court to set aside the verdict and for a new trial. The motion was granted. The order granting the same was as follows: "After a careful examination of a portion of the testimony written out by the reporter, and authorities to which I have been referred since the motion of the plaintiff's counsel to set aside the nonsuits and the verdict and for a new trial, I have come to the conclusion that in the present state of the testimony the nonsuits, and especially that on the second count in the complaint, ought not to have been granted; that the question whether or not there was negligence on the part of the defendant company in consequence of the condition of its right of way at the time of the fire in July, ought to have been submitted to the jury. For this reason the entire motion is granted, and a new trial granted on the entire complaint." The defendant appeals from such order.

For the appellant there was a brief by *John W. Cary*, attorney, and *Burton Hanson* and *John T. Fish*, of counsel, and oral argument by *Mr. Fish*.

For the respondent there was a brief by *Carter & Carter*, and oral argument by *Mr. C. S. Carter*.

LYON, J. I. The title to the lands alleged to have been injured by the negligence of the defendant company is put in issue by the pleadings. Such lands were vacant and uncultivated. On the authority of several cases heretofore adjudicated by this court, it was incumbent upon the plaintiff to prove his title. *McNarra v. C. & N. W. R. Co.* 41 Wis. 69; *Hungerford v. Redford,* 29 Wis. 345. Moreover, the plaintiff claims for continuing damage by reason of the reduced productiveness of his land. Probably, on the authority of *Winchester v. Stevens Point.* 58 Wis. 350, it was incumbent upon him to prove his title, even though he was in actual possession of the land at the time of the alleged injury.

It is maintained on behalf of the defendant that the plaintiff made no proof of any title to the lands in question, and that a motion for a nonsuit, made during the progress of the trial, although based only upon the alleged want of proof of defendant's negligence or of damage to the plaintiff, should have been granted for such want of proof of the plaintiff's title. Counsel for the defendant invoke the rule laid down in *Maxwell v. Hartmann,* 50 Wis. 660, and since followed in many cases, that the respondent's exceptions are available to sustain a judgment in his favor.

To prove his title, plaintiff offered in evidence a certificate signed by the chief clerk of the state commissioners of public lands, to which was affixed the seal of such commissioners, to the effect that in October, 1873, one Thomas Miller purchased the lands described in the complaint from the state, and that patents were duly issued to him therefor. This certificate was received in evidence against the objection and exception of the defendant. It is very clear that the admission of this document was error. We are aware of no law giving the force of evidence to such a certificate.

The plaintiff also read in evidence a quitclaim deed of the same land, duly executed by Miller to him June 22, 1881, and testified, without objection (as did several other witnesses), that he owned such land. It also appeared that he had an agent in the vicinity to look after the land, and that he contracted with such agent to gather the berries therefrom in 1885 and 1886. The crop was gathered by the agent in 1885, and the plaintiff received a share thereof pursuant to such contract. The crop of 1886 was destroyed by the fires.

We think the above testimony, excluding such certificate, proved, *prima facie*, the title of the plaintiff, and cast the burden of proof upon the defendant to show, if it could, that some other person was the owner of the land. To hold otherwise, especially when there was no suggestion of an adverse title, would be altogether too strict and technical an application of the rules of evidence on the subject of proof of title in actions for injuries to real property.

II. It is well settled that if a new trial be granted solely by reason of a misapprehension of the law, the order granting the same will be reversed on appeal. *Bushnell v. Scott*, 21 Wis. 451; *Jones v. Evans*, 28 Wis. 168; *Duffy v. C. & N. W. R. Co.* 34 Wis. 188; *Walter A. Wood R. & M. M. Co. v. Stenel, ante*, p. 71. But the above cases, or at least some of them, hold that it must clearly appear that such was the sole ground of the order. Failing in this, the hypothesis that the discretionary power of the court was also exerted is not excluded. It is elementary that the exercise of discretion by the court in a proper case will not be disturbed unless it clearly appears that the court has exercised its discretion improperly. We are of the opinion that this rule is unaffected by the circumstance that the order granting a new trial is based in part upon an erroneous proposition, either of law or of fact.

True, the order appealed from in the present case recites, in substance, that the judge was of the opinion that there was sufficient testimony tending to prove the negligence of the defendant, as charged in the second and third causes of action in the complaint, to send that question to the jury; but it does not state, and there is nothing in the record to warrant the inference, that this was the sole ground upon which the new trial was granted.

Without going into an extended discussion, it may justly be said there is sufficient in the case to preclude a ruling that the granting of a new trial was an abuse of discretion; but, without determining the question whether the testimony does or does not tend to show that the fires were negligently set, we are constrained to sustain the order as a proper exercise of the discretion of the court. Considerable testimony was introduced on the trial by the plaintiff for the purpose of proving the alleged negligence of the defendant as charged, and which had a bearing upon that question. It is probably true that there is some doubt as to what inferences may properly be deduced from such testimony. In such a case, if the circuit court holds, on a motion for a new trial, contrary to his ruling on the trial, that the testimony was sufficient to send the question to the jury, we are inclined to think, and for the purposes of this case we hold, that the appellate court should not review such conflicting rulings on an appeal from an order granting a new trial, but should permit the case to go to another jury unembarrassed by any intimation of an opinion upon the weight and effect of the testimony given on the former trial.   ·   •

For these reasons we must sustain the order granting a new trial, without determining the question of negligence.

By the Court.— Order affirmed.

See note to this case in 87 N. W. Rep. 225.— REP.

McMILLEN, Administrator, etc., Appellant, vs. MASON and others, imp., Respondents.

March 7 — March 27, 1888.

Equity: Cancellation of mortgage: Adequate remedy at law.

1. In an action to cancel a mortgage which had been assigned to the defendants and which was a lien superior to any claim of the plaintiff, a complaint showing that the mortgage was valid when given, and not showing that it had been paid or anything which should preclude the defendants from purchasing it, is *held* not to state a cause of action.

2. Equity will not interfere where there is a complete and adequate remedy at law.

APPEAL from the Circuit Court for *Marquette* County.

The following statement of the case was prepared by Mr. Justice TAYLOR as a part of the opinion:

This is an appeal from a judgment entered upon an order sustaining a demurrer to the amended complaint. The following are the facts alleged in the complaint: (1) That the plaintiff is the administrator of the estate of Robert McMillen, deceased, who died January, 1885. (2) That in September, 1865, Owen White died possessed of 160 acres of land (describing it); that he left a widow and two children (daughters); that he died testate, leaving a will by which he devised to his daughter Margaret Boyle one half of said land, the other half to his widow, Bridget White, during her life-time, with remainder in fee to his said daughter Margaret Boyle. (3) That afterwards, and on the 31st of December, 1874, Margaret Boyle and her husband, Daniel Boyle, and Bridget White, conveyed all the 160 acres of land, by warranty deed, to one R. C. Rockwood, and received back from said Rockwood a bond for a deed, conditioned to convey said land to Bridget White and Margaret Boyle on the payment of $400 and interest thereon according to the terms of said bond, and the said Bridget White and Margaret Boyle agreed to pay said sum of $400 and the interest. (4) In August, 1879, Rockwood conveyed said land to one Cornelius O'Keefe, subject to said bond. (5) That after the conveyance to O'Keefe, and probably before the 21st of October, 1879 (the exact time is not stated in the complaint), in order to prevent the forfeiture of said bond, and at the request of Daniel Boyle and Margaret Boyle, his wife, Robert McMillen procured the money to pay the sum due on said bond, as follows: $300 from one Robert Mitchell, $150 from one Ernest Bothin, and $55 he furnished of his own money. This $505 was due on said bond, and was all paid to said O'Keefe, and thereupon said O'Keefe conveyed said land to Daniel Boyle and Margaret Boyle, his wife. That, to secure the payment of the $300 furnished by the said Robert Mitchell, a mortgage was given upon said lands by Daniel Boyle and Margaret Boyle. To secure the payment of the $150 furnished by Ernest Bothin, Robert McMillen and Daniel Boyle gave their joint promissory note. For the money furnished by Robert McMillen, viz., $55, no security was given. (6) October 21, 1879, Daniel Boyle conveyed all his interest in the land to his wife, Margaret Boyle, and it is charged in the complaint that this conveyance was without consideration and was intended as a fraud upon the creditors of Daniel Boyle. (7) Afterwards, but at what particular time is not stated, Margaret Boyle died intestate, leaving her husband, Daniel Boyle, surviving her, and seven minor children as her heirs at law, and that Daniel Boyle was appointed her administrator.

Thus far the complaint shows this state of facts: The title to the whole 160 acres of land in Margaret Boyle at the time of her decease, subject to the mortgage of $300 given to Robert Mitchell, and her estate subject to the payment of the $55 advanced by Robert McMillen, at her request, to pay off the old claim against the lands, and also subject to the payment of the $150 advanced by Bothin, and for which her husband and Robert McMillen had given their joint note.

The complaint further shows that for the $55 advanced by McMillen he presented a claim against the estate of Margaret Boyle, deceased, which was finally allowed against said estate. After the death of Margaret Boyle, Robert McMillen was compelled to pay the $150 to Bothin, and after paying it he commenced an action against Daniel Boyle and the heirs of Margaret Boyle, deceased, to recover the amount of said $150, and the interest thereon. After the commencement of this last action, Robert McMillen died, and the plaintiff in this action, as administrator of said Robert McMillen, was substituted as plaintiff in said action against Daniel Boyle and the heirs of said Margaret Boyle, and it is alleged in the complaint that in such action this plaintiff recovered a judgment against Daniel Boyle and the heirs of the said Margaret Boyle for the sum of $329 damages and costs, and that by the same judgment the court set aside the deed from the defendant Daniel Boyle to his wife, Margaret Boyle.

The complaint then goes on to allege, in a general way, that *Patrick Mason* and *Mary Mason*, his wife (who was the other daughter of Owen White), intending to cheat and defraud Robert McMillen out of the money advanced by him to pay said bond and prevent its forfeiture, and to defraud Daniel Boyle and the heirs of said Margaret Boyle, deceased, out of their interest in said real estate, procured the removal of Daniel Boyle, as the administrator of the estate of Margaret Boyle, and procured the proper court to appoint *Morgan Riley* in his place. It then charges that said *Masons* and *Morgan Riley*, combining to defraud said McMillen out of his just claims against said estate, fraudulently procured the allowance of certain pretended claims against said estate, especially one for the sum of $25, and then made applications to the court to direct a sale of the estate of said Margaret Boyle to pay such illegal and unjust claims; alleges that the said *Masons* and *Riley* wrongfully procured from the county court an order to sell said real estate, and that *Morgan Riley*, pretending to act under said order, pretended to sell an undivided half of said real estate to the defendants *Patrick* and *Mary Mason* for the sum of $500, and executed a deed to them therefor; that such deed has never been recorded, and that the defendants the *Masons* have paid no consideration therefor.

The complaint then alleges that *Patrick* and *Mary Mason* have wrongfully procured Robert Mitchell to assign said $300 mortgage to them, and that afterwards they procured Bridget White, the widow of said Owen White, to make a deed of an undivided half of said lands to the said *Mary Mason*, and that said *Mary Mason* and *Patrick Mason* are now in possession of said lands belonging to the estate of Margaret Boyle, and have been in such possession thereof for more than two years last past, claiming to own the same in fee; and further alleges that by reason of the wrongful conduct of said *Masons* and *Morgan Riley*, the plaintiff is unable to collect his debts against the estate of Margaret Boyle and said heirs, and prays judgment — *First*, that the pretended administrator's sale and the deed made by *Riley* be declared null and void; *second*, that the court construe the will of said Owen White and the acts of said parties hereto in relation to the other undivided half of said lands, and determine therefrom what, if any, interest the said defendants *Patrick* and *Mary Mason* acquired in said lands by virtue of the deed from Bridget White to the said *Mary Mason; third*, that the court order the $300 mortgage given by Mitchell, and by him assigned to *Mary Mason*, to be delivered up and canceled of record, and determine what, if any, interest the defendants *Patrick* and *Mary Mason* have in the purchase money for said mortgage as against the said plaintiff; *fourth*, and that the undivided half of said premises be sold under the order of this court, and out of the proceeds thereof the costs of this action and sale be first paid, and the judgment of this plaintiff, and the residue, if any, be distributed as the equities of the defendants may appear.

To this complaint the defendants demurred, upon the following grounds: (1) that the court had no jurisdiction of the subject of the action; (2) that there was a defect of parties defendant; (3) that there was another action pending; (4) that several causes of action were improperly joined; (5) that the complaint did not state facts sufficient to constitute a cause of action. The court sustained the demurrer to the amended complaint, and ordered judgment in favor of the defendants, dismissing the complaint with costs. The plaintiff appeals.

H. W. Lee, for the appellant.

For the respondents *Mary Mason* and *Patrick Mason* there was a brief by *G. J. Cox;* for the respondent *Riley*, a brief by *John Brickwell;* and the cause was argued orally by *Mr. Cox.*

TAYLOR, J. Upon a careful reading of the complaint, it is difficult to find any sufficient allegations in the complaint which would entitle the plaintiff to any relief from a court of equity. There is certainly nothing in the case made by the complaint which would justify the court in granting the relief prayed for as to the $300 mortgage. There are no allegations which tend to show that it ever has been paid, and nothing stated which could hinder the defendants the *Masons* from purchasing it. It was a lien on the premises to which all other claims against the estate of Daniel Boyle and Margaret Boyle are subject, and superior to any claim of the plaintiff against said estate. Admitting that the $300 and the $150 and $55 were all advanced to redeem the land from the claim of O'Keefe, there can be no priority of the claim over the mortgage, especially in the absence of any allegation that there was an agreement made between the parties that all the money so advanced should be equally a lien upon the lands redeemed. The complaint is entirely silent as to any such agreement, and simply alleges that after the money was furnished a mortgage was given to secure the payment of the $300. There is not enough in the complaint to show that the plaintiff was entitled to a lien on the land for either the $150 advanced by Bothin or for the $55 advanced by himself. There is certainly nothing stated in the complaint showing any necessity for the construction of the will of White, and if there was anything stated which would make a construction of the will a proper relief it would seem that the widow White should have been made a party defendant.

Taking all the allegations together, they do not call for the interference of a court of equity.

The plaintiff shows that his claim for the $55 and interest has been allowed against the estate of Margaret Boyle, and that the estate is ample to pay the claim. His remedy is clear in the county court. He can compel the administrator to pay the debt out of the estate which has come to his hands, if there was sufficient personal estate for that purpose, or from the proceeds of the sale of the real estate, if the same has in fact been lawfully sold, and if it has not he could procure an order from the county court for the sale of the real estate to pay the debt, unless he has lost that right by delay.

As to the claim for the $150 and interest, if his complaint be true, he has a judgment which not only subjects to sale thereon all the interest Daniel Boyle has in the 160 acres of land, but also all the interest the heirs of said Margaret Boyle have in said lands; and, so far as the sufficiency of the complaint is concerned, we must judge of it by what is alleged therein. We remark that as to the nature of the judgment obtained for the $150 there is not enough stated in the complaint to show very clearly what it is, nor upon what grounds he was able to and did sustain his action against Daniel Boyle and the heirs at law of Margaret Boyle, deceased, and we only decide in this case that if the general allegations of the complaint are true in regard to this judgment, then plaintiff does not need the aid of a court of equity to enforce it. We think the demurrer was properly sustained.

By the Court.— The judgment of the circuit court is affirmed.

THE STATE, Respondent, vs. THE CITIZENS' INSURANCE COMPANY OF MOBILE, ALABAMA, Appellant.

March 7 — March 27, 1888.

Insurance corporations: Penalty for failure to file annual statement: Pleading: Unlicensed company.

In an action to recover the penalty prescribed by sec. 1920, R. S., for failure by a foreign fire insurance corporation to file the annual statement therein mentioned, if the complaint undertakes to state the particular facts constituting the cause of action it must state all the material facts necessary to constitute such cause of action, including the fact that the defendant company was licensed to do business in this state. So *held* on appeal from a judgment rendered on default.

APPEAL from the Circuit Court for *Dane* County.
The case is sufficiently stated in the opinion.
For the appellant there were briefs by *Cotzhausen, Sylvester & Scheiber*, and oral argument by *Mr. F. Scheiber*.
H. W. Chynoweth, for the respondent.

ORTON, J.   This action is brought to recover the penalty provided for in sec. 1920, R. S., of $500, on account of the failure of the defendant company and its officers to prepare and deposit in the office of the commissioner of insurance a statement of the business of said corporation, etc., during the year, etc., required by said section, in the month of January, 1884, and of an additional $500 for every month thereafter. There was no appearance of the defendant company, and judgment was rendered, on default and proofs, for $16,500 and costs.   From that judgment this appeal is taken.

The only error assigned is that the complaint failed to state a cause of action against said company for the penalty provided for in the above section.   There can be no question but that the decision in the recent case in this court, of *State v. U. S. Mut. Accident Ass'n*, 69 Wis. 76, rules this case.   The two cases are substantially alike, *mutatis mutandis*, and the provisions of the statute relating respectively to these two kinds of insurance companies are *in pari materia*.   The learned counsel of the respondent concedes that sec. 1920, relating to foreign fire insurance companies, and sec. 1954, R. S., relating to foreign life or accident insurance companies, are substantially alike.   The other sections referred to in the opinion in that case to sustain the construction given to sec. 1954, that it related only to foreign companies that had been licensed to do business in this state, are substantially the same as other sections respecting the latter companies.   In both cases the same foreign insurance companies that are required to file such statement and are liable to the penalty for failure to do so, are made liable to have their *licenses* or *certificates authorizing them to transact business in this state revoked* by the commissioner.

But it is contended that said case, aside from the above substantial similitude to the present case, does not rule this case, in consequence of certain legal principles applicable to the form and manner in which the same defect of the complaint is sought to be taken advantage of in this case. That case was decided on demurrer to the complaint for not stating a cause of action. Here it is sought to reverse the judgment on the same ground. And it is contended: (1) That it was an admitted fact in the other case that the insurance company had never procured a license. Such an admission may have been made by the learned counsel himself, but it is very certain that this court did not decide the question raised by the demurrer in view of any such admission. The chief justice opens the opinion in that case by saying: "The main question in this case is, Does the complaint state a cause of action?" That was the only question decided, and it was not and could not have been decided upon any such admission of fact. The learned counsel properly says that there is no such admission in this case. If there was any such admission on the argument of this appeal, it certainly would not and could not be considered, for it is foreign to the only question here, which is precisely the same as it was in the other case,— Does the complaint state a cause of action? In K—— $v.$ H——, 20 Wis. 239, the judgment was reversed because the complaint did not state a cause of action, although the material facts omitted from the complaint were proved upon the trial without objection. The complaint must state all the material facts necessary to entitle the plaintiff to recover, or the judgment for that reason will be reversed, whether it was rendered on default or on trial. The complaint must support the judgment, or it has no foundation whatever, and should be reversed. This has been so many times decided in this state as to have become elementary. *Larkin v. Tibbitts,* 1 Wis. 500; *Goodrich v. Compound School Dist.* 2 Wis. 102; *Johnson v. Johnson,* 4 Wis. 135; *Harris v. Harris,* 10 Wis. 467; *Thurber v. Jones,* 14 Wis. 16; *Hays v. Lewis,* 17 Wis. 210; *Brookins v. Shumway,* 18 Wis. 98; *Smith v. Whitney,* 22 Wis. 438; *Fifield v. Marinette Co.* 62 Wis. 532.

(2) It is contended that the complaint is sufficient because, according to sec. 3295, R. S., it need state only "that the defendant is indebted to the plaintiff in the amount of the forfeiture claimed, according to the provisions of the statute which imposes it, specifying the section and chapter containing such statute," and the complaint does so state. After a particular statement of all the facts deemed sufficient to constitute a cause of action, the complaint closes as follows: "*Thereby* the defendant has become, and still is, indebted to the plaintiff in the sum of $16,500, according to the provisions of sec. 1920, ch. 89, R. S. 1878." This is a mere conclusion from the facts before stated. "*Thereby*," that is, by or from the previous statement of facts, "the defendant has become, and still is, indebted," etc. When the complaint undertakes to state the particular facts constituting the plaintiff's cause of action, it must state every material fact necessary to constitute a cause of action. *Teetshorn v. Hull*, 30 Wis. 162. In *State v. Egerer*, 55 Wis. 529, the pleading is very similar, and the conclusion only refers to the statute as in this case. After a particular statement of the facts to show that the defendant had become liable to the forfeiture or penalty, it closes as follows: "That the defendant *thereupon* became indebted to the plaintiff in the sum of fifty cents a day from and after and since the 5th day of November, 1881, according to the provisions of secs. 1330, 1331, R. S." The cases are alike in this respect. Mr. Justice LYON says, in the opinion: "The complaint assumes to state the specific grounds of the action. . . . If, therefore, those facts do not constitute a cause of action, the demurrer was properly sustained." This precise question having been so recently decided by this court, we need not look elsewhere for authority. But I understand this to be the rule of all the courts. This form of pleading was the same in *State v. U. S. Mut. Accident Ass'n, supra*. After stating the facts specifically, it

closes by a similar conclusion: "*Whereby* it has become liable or indebted, etc., according to the provisions of sec. 1954," etc. And yet the complaint was held not to state a cause of action.

The third and fourth positions assumed by the learned counsel may be considered together: (3) That the defendant insurance company was not licensed implies a negative that the plaintiff need not aver, but which must be proved by the defendant; and (4) that the complaint should receive a liberal construction, and that the averment of "doing business in this state" implies lawful authority. This last suggestion was made and disposed of in the other case. There is no such rule as allows a complaint upon an appeal from the judgment to be more liberally construed as to material averments than upon a demurrer. This is an action for a penalty, and every fact necessary to show that the defendant has incurred the penalty must be stated. Such material facts cannot rest in presumption or mere inference, or appear by implication. There is no rule of liberal construction that will dispense with the statement of every fact that creates the liability. In this case the complaint should have stated all such facts as are necessary to show that the defendant company or its officers were required to make such annual statement, the failure to make which would make the company and its officers liable to the penalty. The company was not required to make such statement unless licensed to do business in this state. Therefore such material and essential fact must be stated. It is not a negative, but a positive, averment. In the case of *State v. Egerer*, 55 Wis. 529, the fact necessary to be stated to make the defendant liable to the penalty was that he had been notified in a certain way to remove the encroachment. Mr. Justice LYON says: "The question is, therefore, whether the facts stated *specifically* in the complaint show a cause of action against the defendant for the penalty claimed. A person is liable to the penalty of the statute only when he fails to remove the encroachment within thirty days after the supervisors' order to do so is served upon him." This allegation was absent from the complaint, and it was therefore held insufficient. So here, the company was required to make such statement, and became liable to the penalty for not making it, only after being *licensed* to do business in this state, and therefore such fact must be stated. The cases are alike in principle. In *Jensen v. State*, 60 Wis. 577, the complaint was held not good against the defendant for the penalty, because it did not state that he was engaged in the business of selling or retailing intoxicating liquors. His *status* in this respect, that brought him within the statute, was not stated. So here, the *status* of the company as a *licensed* company is not stated. "The plaintiff must show facts bringing the case *clearly* within the terms of the statute fairly and reasonably construed." *Allen v. Stevens*, 29 N. J. Law, 509; *Verona C. C. Co. v. Murtaugh*, 50 N. Y. 314. "The conditions upon which the penalty attaches must be affirmatively shown to have existed." *Comm'rs of Pilots v. Vanderbilt*, 31 N. Y. 265. "If the penalty is imposed for conduct or neglect in a particular *capacity*, it must be stated that the defendant was acting in that capacity." *Trowbridge v. Baker*, 1 Cow. 251; Abb. Tr. Ev. 771.

This is sufficient to dispose of the positions assumed by the learned counsel of the respondent in his brief and urged by his able and plausible argument to show that this case is not ruled by the previous decision. The complaint is fatally defective for not having shown that the defendant company was authorized by license to do business in this state, and therefore required to make the statement provided for in sec. 1920, R. S., and liable for the penalty fixed in said section for the failure to do so.

By the Court.— The judgment of the circuit court is reversed, and the cause remanded for further proceedings according to law.

BAYLEY, Respondent, vs. ANDERSON and another, imp., Appellants.

March 7 — March 27, 1888.

Contracts: Sale of chattels: When title passes.

Plaintiff agreed to furnish to T., a contractor, the iron work for certain buildings, according to the plans and specifications of the architect. The specifications were a part of the contract for the construction of the buildings, and provided that all materials used should be subject to the approval of the architect and superintendent. The contract provided that T. should be paid for his work as it progressed, at a certain rate, upon estimates made by the superintendent, but that no material should be estimated or paid for until used in the permanent construction of the buildings. After the buildings were partly constructed, the contract was declared forfeited for nonperformance, and the defendants entered into a contract to complete the buildings. Certain iron beams which had theretofore been furnished by plaintiff to T., but which had not been accepted or approved by the superintendent, were used by the defendants in completing the buildings, and were then accepted, and the defendants were paid therefor. *Held*, that the specifications of the original building contract became a part of the agreement between the plaintiff and T.; that the title to the iron work remained in the plaintiff until the same was used in the building and accepted; and that the defendants are therefore liable to the plaintiff for the beams used by them.

APPEAL from the Circuit Court for *Dane* County.

Action to recover the value of twenty-nine iron beams alleged to have been sold and delivered by the plaintiff to the defendants and to have been used by them in and about the construction of a chemical laboratory building for the University of Wisconsin. The defendant Trumbull had, in June, 1885, taken the contract to erect such laboratory and other buildings for the university; and the plaintiff had made to him the following proposition, which he had accepted: "June 25, 1885. We will furnish the iron work for the boiler-house, laboratory, and machine-shop, according to the plans and specifications by H. C. Koch & Co., for the sum of $2,850. Yours respectfully, WILLIAM BAYLEY & Co." The provisions of the contract between Trumbull and the regents of the university are sufficiently stated in the opinion. In January, 1886, the regents declared that contract forfeited by reason of Trumbull's failure to perform. The buildings were then partially constructed. The defendants *Anderson* and *Littlejohn*, who had been the sureties on Trumbull's contract, on January 29, 1886, jointly with said Trumbull, entered into a new contract with the regents, by the terms of which they were to complete the buildings according to the original contract with Trumbull, with certain exceptions as to time, etc., not important here.

The twenty-nine iron beams mentioned in the complaint had been delivered by the plaintiff to Trumbull in the fall of 1885,-but it appeared that only ten of them had actually been wrought into the building prior to January 29, 1886. The remaining nineteen were used by the defendants in completing the laboratory after that date.

The cause was tried by the court without a jury. The court found as facts that the allegations of the complaint were true except as to ten of the iron beams mentioned therein, and as a conclusion of law, in effect, that the defendants were indebted to the plaintiff for the nineteen beams used by them in completing the building. From the judgment entered accordingly the defendants *Anderson* and *Littlejohn* appealed.

For the appellants there was a brief by *Pinney & Sanborn*, and oral argument by *Mr. A. L. Sanborn.* They contended that the title to the beams passed to Trumbull when they were delivered to him by the plaintiff. Benj. on Sales, secs. 315 *et seq.*, 360; *Goddard v. Binney*, 115 Mass. 450; *Merchants' Nat. Bank v. Bangs*, 102 id. 291; *Hayden v. Demets*, 53 N. Y. 426; *Hunter v. Wetsell*, 84 id. 549; Blackburn on Sales, 128; *Wigton v. Bowley*, 130 Mass. 254; *Pratt v. Peck*, 70 Wis. 620; *Dunning v. Gordon*, 4 U. C. Q. B. 399. The fact that the contract for the beams was "according to the plans and specifications" can have no effect upon the passing of the title. It is merely a warranty on the part of the plaintiff that the iron shall answer the specifications, for the breach of which Trumbull might have either claimed damages or rescinded the contract and returned the beams. *Woodle v. Whitney*, 23 Wis. 55; *Fisk v. Tank*, 12 id. 303; *Boothby v. Scales*, 27 id. 637, and cases cited; *Gammon v. Abrams*, 53 id. 323; *Bryant v. Isburgh*, 13 Gray, 607; *Fairfield v. Madison Mfg. Co.* 38 Wis. 346; *Hunt v. Wyman*, 100 Mass. 198; *Wilkinson v. Hoffman*, 61 Wis. 637.

H. W. Chynoweth, for the respondent, argued that the original contract between Trumbull and the regents became a part of the plaintiff's contract. *Price v. Garland*, 6 Pac. Rep. (New Mex.), 474; *Dawes v. Powers*, 5 Mont. 59; *Denver & N. O. Const. Co. v. Stout*, 8 Colo. 61. The contract of the defendants was a continuation of that of Trumbull; an assumption by them of all the obligations imposed upon Trumbull and all of the conditions. The sale of the iron under the contracts in question was a sale subject to approval, and the title was not to pass or the plaintiff to be paid until the iron was actually wrought into the building and accepted.

COLE, C. J. In the proposal of the plaintiff made to Trumbull, he agreed to furnish the iron-work for the buildings named, according to the "plans and specifications" of the architect. The specifications referred to were a part of the original contract between Trumbull and the regents of the university, and required that all the materials used in the construction of the building should be of the best quality of their respective kinds, subject to the approval of the architect and superintendent. The contractor was to be paid for his work as it progressed, at a specified rate, upon estimates made by the superintendent, but the contract provided that no material was to be estimated or be paid for until used in the permanent construction of the building. It was one of the duties of the superintendent to decide upon the fitness of all materials used; and the work done was to be to his entire satisfaction, without reference to any other person. We think these plans and specifications of the original contract became a part of the contract between the plaintiff and Trumbull, and that the parties contracted with reference to them. These facts are material as bearing upon the question discussed as to when the title passed of the iron beams in controversy. The learned counsel for the defendants claims that the title to them passed as soon as they were delivered on the university grounds and Trumbull had an opportunity to inspect them; consequently, that they were Trumbull's property when the supplemental contract for completing the building was entered into by the defendants. On the other hand, it is insisted that the sale of the beams, under the contract, was subject to the approval of the superintendent, and they did not become the contractor's property until such approval was had; that, in fact, the beams were not actually wrought into the building and accepted by the superintendent, either expressly or impliedly, before the defendants entered into the contract of January 29, 1886. Therefore, it is said, the beams were not the property of Trumbull, and he could not have transferred them to the defendants even if he had attempted to do so. We are inclined to adopt this view of the transaction.

There can be no doubt but parties may make a valid sale of an article dependent upon the approval of another person; in such case there is no absolute sale until the approval is given. This is familiar law. Here the contracts clearly provide that the iron beams furnished by the plaintiff were to be subject to the approval of the superintendent, and the evidence shows that the superintendent did not accept or approve of them until they were wrought into the building. The superintendent did not even examine them while they were lying on the ground, and did nothing, in fact, in respect to them, which could be deemed an approval. The sale was a conditional one in the strict sense of the term; the vendee was not bound to pay for the beams unless the superintendent was satisfied with them. See *Exhaust Ventilator Co. v. C., M. & St. Paul R. Co.* 66 Wis. 218. The superintendent had the right to reject the beams even after they were placed in the building, if they did not answer the contract. But when the beams were permanently wrought into the building, and the superintendent made estimates for them, this should be deemed an acceptance and approval. Until that was done, the property was in the plaintiff and at his risk. The defendants entered into a contract to complete the building after the regents declared the Trumbull contract forfeited by reason of his failure to perform. The nineteen beams, for the value of which a recovery was had, were then upon the ground. They were used in the building by the defendants, were accepted by the superintendent, and the defendants were paid for them. They seek to avoid liability to the plaintiff on the ground that by the sale the property passed to Trumbull, and that he alone is responsible for it. The court below, in effect, decided that, as these beams were used by the defendants in and about the construction and completion of the building, they were liable to the plaintiff for their value. We think that view is correct, and the judgment is therefore affirmed.

By the Court.— Judgment affirmed.

PRICHARD and others, Supervisors, etc., Appellants, vs. BIXBY and others, Respondents.

March 7 — March 27, 1888.

(1–3) Drains: Appeal: Commissioners must all act: Jurisdiction: Liability on bond to pay costs: Witness fees. (4) Towns: Supervisors: Form of judgment.

1. If one of the commissioners selected under sec. 1362, R. S., upon an appeal from the decision of town supervisors in relation to a drain, fails to appear and qualify, the remaining commissioners have no jurisdiction of the subject matter of the appeal.

2. If, by reason of their want of jurisdiction of the subject matter, the decision of the commissioners on such appeal is a mere nullity, *quære* whether the appellant is liable upon his bond conditioned to pay all costs arising from such appeal in case the determination of the supervisors shall not be reversed. If so liable, he is not liable, in such a case, for the expenses incurred by the supervisors in procuring the attendance of witnesses.

3. *Quære*, whether the expenses of procuring witnesses are in any case covered by the bond of the appellant given under sec. 1362, R. S.

4. An action upon a demand alleged to be due a town was brought by, and judgment for costs therein was rendered against, "G. W. P., F. R. U., and H. H., supervisors of the" said town. *Held*, that the judgment was not a personal judgment against the persons named, but was against the town and could be enforced only in the manner prescribed by sec. 781, R. S.

APPEAL from the Circuit Court for *Dane* County.

This action was brought to recover certain witness fees, the claim for which arose out of the following facts: In September, 1886, the defendant *Bixby* and other citizens of the town of Rutland, having the qualifications prescribed by statute, made application in writing to the supervisors of that town pursuant to sec. 1359, R. S., to lay out therein a certain ditch or drain described in the application. Proceedings were thereupon had pursuant to the statute, which resulted in the making and filing by such supervisors of an order denying the application. The defendant *Bixby* thereupon took an appeal from the decision of the supervisors pursuant to sec. 1362; and commissioners were duly selected and summoned to meet at a time and place specified in the summons to hear and determine the matter embraced in such appeal. He also filed the bond required by the statute, in which the other defendants, *Soule* and *Nye*, were the sureties.

Four of the commissioners met at the appointed time (the remaining commissioner not appearing), and, by consent of parties, after being duly sworn, proceeded to determine such appeal. They took the testimony of witnesses produced before them, heard arguments, and made and signed their decision in writing, affirming the order of the supervisors. Such decision was duly filed in the office of the town clerk, as required by the statute.

The defendant *Bixby* thereupon paid the fees of the commissioners and justice, and of the constable who served the summons, but refused to pay the fees of certain witnesses produced on the hearing by the supervisors. This action is upon the appeal bond to recover the costs and expenses of procuring the attendance of such witnesses on the hearing of the appeal. The amount claimed is $38.53.

The action was brought before a justice of the peace, and resulted in a judgment for the plaintiffs for $30.14 and costs. The defendants thereupon appealed to the circuit court, where the cause was tried without a jury. The foregoing facts were stipulated, and upon them the court found that the plaintiffs were not entitled to recover. Judgment for costs and disbursements was accordingly rendered for the defendants. The plaintiffs appeal from the judgment.

For the appellants there was a brief by *Lamb & Jones*, and oral argument by *Mr. F. J. Lamb*. They contended, *inter alia*, that the judgment is against *Prichard, Usher*, and *Hanson, de bonis propriis*, and is erroneous for that reason. *Ladd v. Anderson,* 58 Wis. 591; *Hei v. Heller,* 53 id. 415. Judgment in favor of the plaintiffs for the costs would not be in any sense affirming the decision of the four commissioners. This suit is a distinct and collateral proceeding, and ought to be sustained on each of three grounds: (1) The parties agreed to proceed with four commissioners, without the fifth, and in fact did so. (2) The statute required the bond to provide, and the bond does accordingly provide, that the appellant would pay the town all costs arising on said drain appeal in case the determination of the supervisors *shall not be reversed* (R. S. sec. 1362), and there is no pretense that it was reversed. (3) The decision of the commissioners is involved only collaterally, and until reversed by direct proceedings stands as the decision on the drain appeal.

For the respondents there was a brief by *Luse & Wait,* attorneys, and *C. E. Estabrook,* of counsel, and the cause was argued orally by *Mr. L. K, Luse.*

Lyon, J. On the authority of *State ex rel. Luderman, v. Findley,* 67 Wis. 86, it must be held that the decision and order of the four commissioners, in the absence of the fifth who did not appear, is void. It is quite immaterial that the supervisors and the defendant *Bixby* consented that the four might thus act. In the absence of the fifth commissioner there was no jurisdiction of the subject matter, and consent could not confer jurisdiction. This is elementary. Hence the case stands as though the commissioners had made no order, and the decision of the supervisors has been neither affirmed nor reversed. The condition of the bond is that the principal therein, the defendant *Bixby,* shall pay all costs arising from such appeal in case the determination of the supervisors shall not be reversed. But the statute is that "if the determination or judgment of the supervisors shall be affirmed by the decision of the commissioners, the party appealing from such determination or judgment shall pay all costs and expenses of the proceedings had in the matter." Sec. 1362, R. S. It will thus be seen that while the bond, in form, renders the obligors therein liable for such costs and expenses unless the determination of the supervisors is reversed, the statute seems to make such liability dependent upon an affirmance of such determination. There are very plausible, perhaps good, reasons for holding that, notwithstanding the form of the bond, the statute relieves the obligors from liability unless there is an actual affirmance. We do not find it necessary, however, to determine the question here suggested, but, for the purposes of this case, we choose rather to assume that the failure to obtain a valid determination by the commissioners renders the obligors liable upon their bond according to its terms. This brings us to the question, Does the bond cover and include the expenses of the town in procuring witnesses to testify on the hearing before the commissioners?

The statute (sec. 1363) requires the commissioners to view and examine the lands described in the notice of appeal, and to hear any reasons which may be offered for and against the determination of the supervisors. It also authorizes, but does not require, them to "examine witnesses upon any point relating to the subject matter submitted to them." The commissioners may examine witnesses, or not, in their discretion. Probably in most cases the view of the land and the arguments in behalf of the town and interested parties would give them all the information necessary to an intelligent determination of the appeal, without resorting to the testimony of witnesses. Hence it could not be known in the present case whether the attendance of witnesses would be required until the commissioners had met and indicated their views upon that subject. The attendance of the witnesses in question on behalf of the town was procured on the day appointed in the summons for the commissioners to meet, and, as a matter of course, before the supervisors could know that their testimony would be called for or received. We think, therefore, that the expenses incurred by the town in that behalf were prematurely incurred. The supervisors should have waited until they ascertained whether the persons named as commissioners would all appear and qualify as such, and whether, after being duly qualified, they would examine any witnesses. By producing their witnesses when they did, they took the risk that the hearing of the appeal might fail for any cause, or that no witnesses would be examined. Hence, if we assume that the bond in suit covers the expenses of witnesses necessarily obtained by the town, it must still be held, for the reasons above suggested, that it does not cover the expenses therefor incurred in the present case.

In view of the fact that the statute provides expressly for the fees of the commissioners, justice, and constable, and is silent in regard to the expenses of procuring witnesses, the argument is quite persuasive that such expenses were not intended to be covered by the bond. But we do not determine the point.

It is claimed on behalf of the plaintiffs that the judgment herein is a personal judgment against the three supervisors named as plaintiffs, upon which the defendants are entitled to an execution *de bonis propriis*, and hence that the judgment is irregular. We do not so understand this judgment. We are of the opinion that the action is substantially by the town of Rutland, or, what is the same thing, by the supervisors of that town in their official capacity, upon a demand alleged to be due the town, and that the action has no feature of a personal action by the supervisors in their individual capacities. The insertion of their personal names as plaintiffs may be rejected as surplusage. The irregularity is harmless. Had other persons become supervisors of that town pending the action, the suit would not have abated. The judgment is, in form, "against *George W. Prichard, F. R. Usher*, and *Hans Hanson*, supervisors of the town of Rutland, Dane Co., Wisconsin." But the names of the supervisors inserted in the judgment is equally surplusage, and does not render the judgment a personal one against them. It merely follows the summons and complaint, and has no more effect in one than in the other. The foregoing views are sustained by the case of *Cairns v. O'Bleness*, 40 Wis. 469, and cases there cited.

It may be an irregularity that the action was brought in the name of the supervisors, instead of the town of Rutland (see sec. 773, R. S.); but, if so, it was committed by the plaintiffs, and they cannot be heard to complain of it. We are of the opinion that the judgment, although in form against the supervisors, is substantially against the town, and that it can be enforced only in the manner prescribed by sec. 781, R. S.

Our conclusion is that the case was correctly decided by the circuit court, and hence that the judgment should not be disturbed.

By the Court.— Judgment affirmed.

ELLSWORTH, Respondent, vs. HAYES, Appellant.

March 7 — March 27, 1888.

Slander: Miscount of votes by election inspector: Intention in making charge: Privilege: Instructions to jury.

1. In an action for slander the complaint alleged that the defendant falsely and maliciously spoke of the plaintiff, an election inspector, the following words: "He counted four votes which were cast for E., for B., for sheriff. . . . It is true; there is no doubt about it. There was a man standing looking right over [plaintiff's]

shoulder, and saw him do it. It is a swindle;" and that the defendant thereby falsely and maliciously charged the plaintiff with having knowingly violated the provisions of the law governing the duties of inspectors of election. *Held*, that the language used might fairly be construed as charging a wilful and fraudulent miscount, not a mere mistake, and that the complaint therefore stated a cause of action.

2. In such a case, there being no evidence which would justify the jury in finding that the defendant honestly and in good faith made such statements for the purpose of having a recount of the votes under the provisions of ch. 464, Laws of 1885, instructions to the effect that if they were made for such purpose, without malice, the plaintiff cannot recover, were properly refused.

APPEAL from the Circuit Court for *Dane* County.

The following statement of the case was prepared by Mr. Justice TAYLOR as a part of the opinion:

This action was brought to recover damages for slanderous words alleged to have been uttered and published by the defendant. Upon the trial of the action in the circuit court, the plaintiff had a verdict in his favor for $100 damages, upon which verdict judgment was entered in his favor, with costs of the action. From this judgment the defendant appealed to this court.

The plaintiff alleges in his complaint that he was one of the supervisors of the town of Oregon, in Dane county, in the the years 1885 and 1886, and that as such supervisor, at the general election held in said town on the 2d of November, 1886, he acted as chairman of the board of inspectors of such election, and was duly qualified as such inspector. It then alleges that, at such election, one John M. Estes was a candidate on the Republican ticket for the office of sheriff of Dane county, and that Phillip Barry was the candidate for such office on the Democratic ticket; that the plaintiff was a member of the Democratic party, and took an active interest in that election; that the defendant was a member of the Republican party, and that he was active in behalf of John M. Estes, the republican candidate for sheriff of said county. The complaint then alleges that the defendant, *Hayes*, wickedly contriving, etc., to injure the plaintiff, etc., and cause it to be suspected and believed by his neighbors and others that plaintiff was guilty of the offenses and misconduct hereinafter mentioned and charged, in a certain conversation, etc., held in said town on the second day of November, 1886, concerning the number of votes which had been counted for the said John M. Estes, as sheriff, and the said Phillip Barry in said town, "falsely and maliciously spoke of and concerning this plaintiff, these false, malicious, and defamatory words, that is to say: 'He [meaning the plaintiff] counted four of the votes which were cast for Estes [meaning John M. Estes, the candidate for sheriff on the Republican ticket] for Barry for sheriff [meaning the said Phillip Barry, who was the candidate for sheriff on the Democratic ticket].'" The complaint then alleges that several persons hearing the statement remarked that they did not believe that *Ellsworth* was that kind of a man, and thereupon the defendant further stated to the persons then present: "It is true; there is no doubt about it. There was a man standing looking right over *Mr. Ellsworth's* shoulder, and saw him do it. It is a swindle." The complaint then alleges that the defendant thereby falsely and maliciously charged the plaintiff with having knowingly violated the provisions of the law governing the duties of the inspectors of election, etc.

The second cause of action stated in the complaint was for the following statement, made by the defendant on the 6th day of November, 1886, in the village of Oregon, in the presence of divers persons, concerning said election and counting the ballots by the said *Ellsworth:* "I have been informed by a man who stood right by and watched *Ellsworth* count the votes, and he counted four of Estes' votes for Barry for sheriff." The complaint also charges a repetition of these conversations at other times and places before the commencement of the action.

The defendant answered, admitting the fact that plaintiff was one of the inspectors of the election on November 2, 1886, and that he assisted in counting the votes at such election; the candidacy of Estes and Barry for sheriff,— Estes as the Republican, and Barry as the Democratic, candidate. He also admits that the plaintiff was acting with the Democratic party, and he with the Republican party. The answer then makes the following allegations:

"Defendant, further answering said complaint, alleges that immediately after the fall election of 1886, in the said village of Oregon, one of the voting precincts at which the said Estes and the said Barry were voted for as candidates for sheriff of Dane county, it was freely, openly, and publicly suggested and charged, by divers and sundry of said electors and tax-payers of said voting precinct, that the said plaintiff had made a mistake in counting the votes cast at the said voting precinct for the office of sheriff; that it was freely and openly considered and discussed by said electors, in good faith, the question whether a recount should not be made of said votes, and that the defendant, as one of the electors and tax-payers at said voting precinct, in good faith and with malice towards none, at said time and place, in Monk's hotel, in answer to a question propounded by one Mr. Patchin, also an elector and tax-payer of said precinct, namely, '*Hayes*, what is there about that vote business?' said: 'All I know about it is what I have heard, and that is this: There was a man who said in my presence, in the post-office, that he saw four votes that had Barry's name scratched off, and Estes' name written on them, and they were counted for Barry; and that he stood right behind *Ellsworth* when the vote was counted, and he said he noticed that one of the tickets was torn;' that said Patchin replied that he did not believe *Ellsworth* would do that; that this defendant replied: 'I don't believe that he did it either; I don't believe that anybody believes that he did it;' that this defendant uttered these words, answering said interrogatory of said Patchin in good faith, and in the exercise of his rights as an elector of said precinct to see that the votes cast at said precinct should be counted as cast.

"Defendant, answering said second alleged cause of action, admits that he joined in a conversation in the presence of one Peter Peterson, respecting a canvass of the votes cast at said precinct of Oregon, the 2d day of November, 1886, for the said John Estes and the said Philip Barry, as candidates for the office of sheriff; that the said Peter Peterson and the others present were electors and tax-payers of said precinct of the village of Oregon, and with him (the defendant) interested in a fair count of the votes cast at said precinct; that the defendant at the said time and place, in answer to the question addressed to him by one of the electors of said precinct, said: 'It is intimated that *Ellsworth* made a mistake of four votes; that a man claimed to have stood right behind *Ellsworth* while the votes were being counted, and saw the ballots with Barry's name scratched off and Estes' name written on counted for Barry;' that defendant further stated that, 'I did not think *Ellsworth* would do that, and in justice to him the votes ought to be recounted; and if I see him I will tell him.' That defendant used no other or different language, at the said time and place, than above set forth, respecting the matters and things alleged in the said complaint; that said statements were made calmly and dispassionately, with no ill motive towards the plaintiff, but wholly in good faith, and solely in the exercise of the defendant's right, as an elector and tax-payer of said voting precinct of said village of Oregon, to discuss the question of alleged mistake by the board of inspectors in canvassing the votes cast at said precinct, and for the purpose of promoting the public welfare by insisting that the ballot shall always be counted as cast."

The answer denies everything else stated in the complaint.

On the trial in the circuit court the defendant objected

to the admission of any evidence under the complaint, on the ground that it did not state facts sufficient to constitute a cause of action. This objection was overruled, and exception taken. At the close of the plaintiff's evidence the defendant moved for a nonsuit, which was denied, and exception taken. These rulings of the court are alleged as error by the appellant upon the hearing of this appeal.

For the appellant there was a brief by *Rogers, Luse & Hall*, and oral argument by *W. H. Rogers* and *F. W. Hall*. They contended, *inter alia*, that there is nothing slanderous *per se* in the words charged in either count. Words are only actionable when in their most obvious and natural sense they impute a crime. *Montgomery v. Deeley*, 3 Wis. 709; *Geary v. Bennett*, 53 id. 444. The words used were conditionally privileged, that is, though they may be false they do not on that account imply malice. See *Van Wyck v. Aspinwall*, 17 N. Y. 193; *Larkin v. Noonan*, 19 Wis. 83; *Lewis v. Chapman*, 16 N. Y. 369; *State ex rel. Lanning v. Lonsdale*, 48 Wis. 348; *White v. Nichols*, 3 How. 236; Townshend on Slander, 350–357; *Bradley v. Heath*, 12 Pick. 163; *Bays v. Hunt*, 60 Iowa, 251; *Marks v. Baker*, 28 Minn. 162; *Bronson v. Bruce*, 59 Mich. 467, 26 N. W. Rep. 675, note; *Noonan v. Orton*, 32 Wis. 106; *Servatius v. Pichel*, 34 id. 292.

For the respondent there was a brief by *John M. Olin* and *J. L. O'Connor*, and oral argument by *Mr. Olin*. They argued, among other things, that if the language used was capable of a slanderous meaning, or might become so when explained by surrounding circumstances and the collateral acts and declarations of the defendant and those to whom the language was addressed, the ruling of the court admitting evidence under the complaint was correct. *Weil v. Schmidt*, 28 Wis. 137; *Cottrill v. Cramer*, 43 id. 242; *Campbell v. Campbell*, 54 id. 90; *Lathrop v. Hyde*, 25 Wend. 448; *Rowand v. De Camp*, 96 Pa. St. 493; 8 Atl. Rep. 230.

Language which imputes crime or corruption to a person in official capacity is not privileged unless it appears that it was directed exclusively to the authority which has the power of removing such officer or of taking other definite legal action upon the communication, and for the purpose of inducing *such authority to such action.* *Thorn v. Blanchard,* 5 Johns. 508; *Sewall v. Catlin,* 3 Wend. 292; *Vanderzee v. M'Gregor,* 12 id. 545; *Fawcett v. Charles,* 13 id. 473; *Howard v. Thompson,* 21 id. 319; *O'Donaghue v. M'Govern,* 23 id. 26; *Larkin v. Noonan,* 19 Wis. 82; *Gray v. Pentland,* 2 Serg. & R. 23; *Rowand v. De Camp,* 96 Pa. St. 493; *Foster v. Scripps,* 39 Mich. 376; *Bodwell v. Osgood,* 3 Pick. 379; *Smith v. Higgins,* 16 Gray, 251; *State v. Burnham,* 9 N. H. 34; *Wilson v. Collins,* 5 C. & P. 373; *Parsons v. Surgey,* 4 F. & F. 247. In such cases the courts have held that the petition containing the libelous charges is in the nature of a judicial or a *quasi*-judicial proceeding, and consequently privileged. *Larkin v. Noonan,* 19 Wis. 82. One may criticise the public acts and conduct of an officer more freely than the acts and conduct of a private person, but any imputation of unjust or corrupt motives is equally slanderous in either case. *Spiering v. Andræ,* 45 Wis. 330; *Dodds v. Henry,* 9 Mass. 262; *Comm. v. Clap,* 4 id. 163; *Hamilton v. Eno,* 81 N. Y. 116; *Seely v. Blair,* Wright (Ohio), 358; *McDonald v. Woodruff,* 2 Dill. 244; 6 M. & W. 105; *Rearick v. Wilcox,* 81 Ill. 77; *Palmer v. Concord,* 48 N. H. 211; *Bronson v. Bruce,* 59 Mich. 467; *White v. Nichols,* 3 How. 266; *Crane v. Waters,* 10 Fed. Rep. 619; *Barr v. Moore,* 87 Pa. St. 385; *Neeb v. Hope,* 111 Pa. St. 145; *Comm. v. Wardwell,* 136 Mass. 164.

TAYLOR, J. It is argued that the language used by the defendant, as stated in the complaint, does not charge any unlawful or wilful miscounting of the votes cast at the election by the plaintiff, but simply that he made a mistake in

counting the votes cast thereat. The language set up in
the complaint is not so clearly a simple allegation of mistake as to justify the court in saying that it did not have a
different meaning, and that the persons to whom it was
addressed did not understand it as charging the plaintiff
with a false and fraudulent count, as stated in the innuendo.
If the words are fairly susceptible of the meaning which it
is claimed by the plaintiff was intended by the defendant
in uttering them, then it is clear that they sufficiently charge
the plaintiff with a crime under the statute, which declares
what shall constitute an offense by an inspector of elections
(see secs. 4544, 4545, R. S.), and are actionable *per se* when
spoken of his acts as an inspector of elections, and the court
properly refused to exclude the plaintiff's evidence. The
same is true of the refusal of the motion for a nonsuit. The
evidence made a clearer case of an intention on the part of
the defendant to charge the plaintiff with a wilful miscounting of the votes cast at said election than is made by the
statements set out in the complaint. The court would not
have been justified in granting a nonsuit. The following
cases sustain the rulings of the circuit court to which the
exceptions were taken: *Geary v. Bennett,* 53 Wis. 444, 447;
Weil v. Schmidt, 28 Wis. 137; *Campbell v. Campbell,* 54
Wis. 90; *Rowand v. De Camp,* 96 Pa. St. 493, 501; *Singer
v. Bender,* 64 Wis. 169.

In the instructions of the learned circuit judge to the
jury, he expressly told them that the plaintiff could not recover in the action if they found that the defendant simply
charged the plaintiff with ar unintentional miscount of the
votes; "that it was not slander for the defendant to say
that the plaintiff counted votes for one candidate that were
cast for another, unless the words were stated under such
circumstances as that a fair and ordinary interpretation of
the words spoken, by the persons hearing them, would be
that the plaintiff knowingly or wilfully so miscounted the

ballots; and, if you find that the words used by the defendant did not so charge, your verdict should be for the defendant." This submitted the questions raised by the motions to exclude the evidence of the plaintiff and for a nonsuit fairly to the jury; and upon the reading of the evidence there can be no question but that there was enough in the case to require the trial judge to submit the question as to what the defendant meant by the words uttered by him.

The learned counsel also alleged for error the refusal of the court to instruct the jury that, under the evidence, they might find the statements made by the defendant conditionally privileged. There is no contention that the second and fourth instructions asked by the defendant were improperly refused by the court, as both instructions ask the court to say, as a matter of law, that the words uttered by the defendant were privileged. It cannot be contended that the evidence is so clear as to the intent with which the defendant uttered the words as would justify the court in stating, as a matter of law, that they were privileged or conditionally privileged. The third and fifth instructions asked would have been proper instructions to the jury, had there been any evidence to sustain the claim made by the defendant.[1] After a careful examination of the evidence,

---

[1] The third and fifth instructions asked by the defendant were as follows:

"3. The law permits all persons who are interested as electors or taxpayers to comment upon the official acts of their public officers so long as they do so *bona fide* and not for the purpose of injuring the person spoken of; hence, if the defendant was induced from any cause to believe that the plaintiff did what the defendant is alleged to have said he did, and mentioned it to others with a view of correcting the evil, and without malice toward the plaintiff, his acts would be justifiable, and the plaintiff cannot recover.

"5. Every qualified voter of Dane county was interested in the subject of a fair and correct count of the ballots cast for the respective candidates for the office of sheriff of Dane county, at the village of Oregon,

Ellsworth vs. Hayes.

we do not find anything in it which would have justified the
jury in finding that the defendant honestly and in good
faith made the statements he is shown to have made, for
the purpose of having a recount of the votes .cast at such
election, under the provisions of ch. 464, Laws of 1885. He
does not show that he made the statements with the purpose of procuring a recount of the vote; nor did he ever
take any legitimate steps towards obtaining such recount;
nor is it shown that any other elector or electors in said
town were at the time taking, or about to take, any measures to have the vote recounted; nor does he show, as
alleged in his answer, that it was openly and publicly suggested and charged immediately after such election, by
divers and sundry of the electors of said voting precinct,
that the plaintiff had made a mistake in counting the votes
cast at such election. The evidence does not disclose that
any one made the charge except himself and one other man,
nor that any one except himself suggested that a recount
ought to be made. There was not enough in the evidence
to justify the court in submitting the proposition embraced
in the instructions asked to the consideration of the jury.
We think the case was fairly submitted to the jury, and
there is no reason, upon the whole evidence, for disturbing
their verdict.

By the Court.—The judgment of the circuit court is
affirmed.

at the November election of 1886, and if you find from the evidence that
the defendant, *Hayes*, in good faith, without malice toward the plaintiff, *Ellsworth*, expressed himself on the subject in question in the manner set forth in the complaint to persons having a like interest in the
communication, namely, electors of said county, no presumption of
malice arises from the speaking of the words, and, therefore, this action
cannot be maintained without you further find that the defendant was
actuated by express malice toward the plaintiff at the time the said
words were spoken."— REP.

JANUARY TERM, 1888. 437

Littlejohn vs. The Regents of The University of Wisconsin.

LITTLEJOHN, Appellant, vs. THE REGENTS OF THE UNIVER-
SITY OF WISCONSIN, Respondent.

March 8 — March 27, 1888.

*Reference: Action, tort or contract? Fraud: Long account: Discre-
tion.*

**An action to recover a balance claimed to be due upon a building
contract and for extra work and materials, but which, it is alleged,
has been fraudulently disallowed by the superintendent — who,
by the terms of the contract, was constituted sole arbitrator to determine conclusively all matters pertaining to the contract, including the amount to be allowed for extra work and materials,— is an
action *ex contractu,* and if it involves the examination of a long
account all the issues therein, including that of fraud, may be referred in the discretion of the trial court.**

APPEAL from the Circuit Court for *Dane* County.
The facts will sufficiently appear from the opinion.
For the appellant there were briefs by *Pinney & San-
born,* attorneys, and *J. V. Quarles,* of counsel, and oral argument by *Mr. A. L. Sanborn.* They contended, *inter alia,*
that the action is one of tort. *Ross v. Mather,* 51 N. Y.
113; *Matthews v. Cady,* 61 id. 651; *People v. Dennison,* 19
Hun, 137; *People v. Peck,* 57 How. Pr. 315; *Berrian v.
Mayor,* 15 Abb. Pr. (N. S.), 208; *Peck v. Root,* 5 Hun, 547.
An action of tort cannot be referred without consent. ·
Clark v. Candee, 29 Hun, 139; *Welsh v. Darragh,* 52 N. Y.
590; *Verplanck v. Kendall,* 45 N. Y. Super. Ct. 525; *Wood
v. Hope,* 2 Abb. N. C. 186; *Townsend v. Hendricks,* 40
How. Pr. 143; *Silmser v. Redfield,* 19 Wend. 20; *Dede-
rick's Adm'rs v. Richley,* id. 110; *Godfrey v. W. C. F. Ins.
Co.* 12 Abb. Pr. (N. S.), 250; *Freeman v. A. M. Ins. Co.* 13
Abb. Pr. 124; *Dewey v. Field,* 13 How. Pr. 437; *Cameron
v. Freeman,* 10 Abb. Pr. 333; *Ross v. Mayor,* 32 How. Pr.
164; *Messenger v. Broom,* 1 Pin. 630. Whether the action
is in tort or on contract, it should not be referred, because

the substantial and preliminary issue to be determined before any account is necessary, is a question of fraud or mistake. *Read v. Lozin*, 31 Hun, 286; *S. C.* 96 N. Y. 647; *Morrison v. Horrocks*, 40 Hun, 428;. *Morrison v. Van Benthuysen*, 103 N. Y. 675; *Claflin v. Drake*, 38 Hun, 144; *Camp v. Ingersoll*, 86 N. Y. 433; *Evans v. Kalbfleisch*, 36 N. Y. Super. Ct. 457. The action involves difficult and important questions of law, on which the parties are entitled to the experience and judgment of the court. *Druse v. Horter*, 57 Wis. 644; *Magown v. Sinclair*, 5 Daly, 70. In any event, the whole action should not be referred, but only the question of accounting and value of work and material.

For the respondent there were briefs by *Lamb & Jones*, attorneys, and *Geo. W. Bird*, of counsel, and oral argument by *Mr. F. J. Lamb* and *Mr. Bird*. They argued, among other things, that the allegations of fraud or mistake in the complaint do not constitute the cause of action, but are necessary to make out the cause of action on the contract. The decisions of the superintendent adverse to the plaintiff and his claims are a bar to the action, unless impeached for fraud or mistake. *Bausen v. Baehr*, 7 Wis. 520; *Hasbrouck v. Milwaukee*, 17 id. 266; *Hudson v. McCartney*, 33 id. 331; *Tetz v. Butterfield*, 54 id. 242. But if the fraud or mistake were proved the plaintiff cannot recover anything *therefor.* He could only recover *on the contract.* *Cairns v. O' Bleness*, 40 Wis. 469; *Norton v. Rooker*, 1 Pin. 195; *Fifield v. Sweeney*, 62 Wis. 204; *Western Ass. Co. v. Towle*, 65 id. 247; *Littlejohn v. Jacobs*, 66 id. 600; *Austin v. Rawdon*, 44 N. Y. 63, 68; *Welsh v. Darragh*, 52 id. 590; *Conaughty v. Nichols*, 42 id. 83'; *Byxbie v. Wood*, 24 id. 607, 610, 611; *Vilmar v. Schall*, 61 id. 564. Although the issue of fraud is raised in the manner indicated, still the cause should be referred. *Devlin v. Mayor*, 54 How. Pr. 50; *People v. Peck*, 57 id. 315; *S. C.* 77 N. Y. 630; *Bensel v. Galt*, 5 N. Y. Sup. Ct. 186; *S. C.* 2 Hun, 678; *Sheldon v. Wood*, 3 Sandf. 739; *Kingsley v.*

Brooklyn, 1 Abb. N. C. 108; *Maryott v. Thayer,* 39 N. Y. Super. Ct. 417; *Whitaker v. Desfosse,* 7 Bosw. 676; *Mills v. Thursby,* 11 How. Pr. 113; *Atocha v. Garcia,* 15 Abb. Pr. 303; Hoffman on Referees, 11, 12; *Austin v. Rawdon,* 44 N. Y. 63; *Vilmar v. Schall,* 61 id. 564. The issue of fraud cannot be separated from the other issues and tried by jury. The fraud itself involves the examination of the accounts, and can be established only by showing that the superintendent did not allow plaintiff enough. And the courts have decided the issues inseparable. *Devlin v. Mayor,* 54 How. Pr. 50; *Dane Co. v. Dunning,* 20 Wis. 210; *Carpenter v. Shepardson,* 43 id. 406. Whether all the issues or only part of them should be referred, is left wholly to the discretion of the court below. Sec. 2864, R. S. The ruling on that question will not be interfered with unless there has been a gross and manifest abuse of such discretion. *U. S. Rolling Stock Co. v. Johnston,* 67 Wis. 182; *Wheeler & W. Mfg. Co. v. Monahan,* 63 id. 194; *Jefferson Co. Bank v. Robbins,* 67 id. 68.

ORTON, J. As near as I can apprehend the object of this action from the statements, allegations, and prayer of the complaint, it is to recover the balance due upon the performance of a written contract between the plaintiff and John Trumbull and Gilbert Anderson of the one part, and the defendants of the other part, for constructing certain buildings for the university, of the contract price, and for extra work and materials, now owned by the plaintiff alone. In order to remove all obstruction to such recovery, it is alleged that the superintendent of said work,— appointed by the defendants according to said contract, and who was constituted thereby sole arbitrator to adjudge, adjust, and determine *conclusively* all matters pertaining to said contract, including what should be allowed for extra work and materials and what should be deducted from the contract price for any deficiency of said work, and all matters of difference between the parties in relation thereto,— by reason of bias, mistake, or fraud, refused to make and did not make just and proper allowance to the plaintiff of what was honestly and fairly due on said contract and for such extra work and materials, and deducted therefrom certain items of unjust charges against the plaintiff; and that there is due to the plaintiff for such balance so corruptly deducted or disallowed, the sum of $18,291.11, for which judgment is demanded. The answer denies the fraud, and other material averments of the complaint, and alleges that the plaintiff submitted all such matters to said superintendent, and that he adjusted and determined the same, and what was so found due to the plaintiff was duly paid and satisfied, and that such determination of the superintendent is *conclusive* upon the parties.

There are long bills of particulars of the numerous items of account involved on both sides appended to the pleadings. Upon affidavit, showing that the trial of said issue or issues will require the examination of a long account, according to subd. 1, sec. 2864, R. S., and upon rule to show cause obtained by the defendants, the circuit court made an order that the action be, and the same hereby is, referred to Robert G. Siebecker, Esq., to hear, try, and determine; and that the said Robert G. Siebecker, Esq., is hereby appointed referee herein, and directed to hear and decide the whole issue and all the issues, both of law and fact, in this action. • The plaintiff appealed to this court from said order. Against said order, the contention of the learned counsel of the appellant is —

First. That this is an action in tort, and therefore not referable. The statement of what we understand to be the object of this action has already indicated our view upon this question. The written contract between the parties, the balance due thereon, and the extra work and materials

JANUARY TERM, 1888.   441

Littlejohn vs. The Regents of The University of Wisconsin.

contemplated thereby, and the value thereof, constitute the main grounds of the action, and what is justly due thereon and therefor is what is sought to be recovered. The fraud alleged is an incidental or collateral issue, and must be proved to entitle the plaintiff to recover, not as damages arising from the fraud, but as money due upon the contract and for extra work and materials. To illustrate this issue: If the plaintiff had alleged what was due on the contract and for extras, and demanded judgment therefor, and the defendant had set up the fact that by the contract the determination of the matter by the superintendent was *conclusive* and a bar to any recovery, and the plaintiff had replied that such determination was corrupt and made by bias, mistake, and fraud, could there be any doubt that the action was *ex contractu*, and not *ex delicto?* And yet the same issue is here presented, only the plaintiff has seen fit to anticipate and answer the defense by his complaint. The general issue would be *non assumpsit;* and the determination and the fraud of the arbitrator the subject of a special plea and replication in the same action. But the classification of such an action as one of contract, by this court, in similar cases, is sufficient authority. *Fifield v. Sweeney,* 62 Wis. 204; *Western Assurance Co. v. Towle,* 65 Wis. 247; *Littlejohn v. Jacobs,* 66 Wis. 600, and many other cases cited in the brief of respondent's counsel. We do not decide whether an action *ex delicto* may be the subject of a compulsory reference under our statute, for it is not in the case.

Second. That the special issues other than the long account and what is due thereon, ought not to have been referred. We do not understand that the learned counsel contends that such issues, and all of them, cannot be referred with the accounting, but that such important and complicated questions ought to be reserved, and tried in court before a jury. It does not seem possible that there could be any doubt but that the court could, together with the accounting, refer any or all the issues in such a case.

" *All or any* of the issues in the action, whether of fact or law, or both, may be referred," etc., is the language of the statute.   As a matter of course such issues as are not referred are reserved to be tried by the court or jury.   This language imports the fullest discretion as to what issues may be referred or what reserved.   There may well be issues in an action, the trial of some of which would require the examination of a long account and for that reason is referred, that ought not to be submitted to a referee.   Such are questions of *constitutional law*, or, as in *Ives v. Vandewater*, 1 How. Pr. 168, of the *validity* of certain "articles of association of forwarders on the Erie canal," which the court refused to refer; or, as in *Shaw v. Ayrs*, 4 Cow. 52, of the *construction* of a certain agreement.   It is certain that the court has a wide discretion in the matter as to what other issues should be referred, and it would seem that "important issues requiring the discretion, experience, learning, and judgment of the court" ought not to be referred, as held in *Druse v. Horter*, 57 Wis. 644; and we do not wish to reconsider what is said upon that subject in that case, although it might not have been necessary to its decision.   It would seem that such a discretion ought to be exercised in actions at law as well as in equity cases, as to what other issues in the case ought to be referred.   The question then recurs, Was it an abuse of such a discretion for the court to refer the question or issue of fraud or other issues in this case, together with the matter of the long account?   We think that it was not.   Those questions are not difficult or complicated, and may be readily decided on the evidence; and besides, it is important that such issues be kept together with the main issues in the case, if they can be as well; and we see no good reason for separating them in this case, any more than there was in *Dane Co. v. Dunning*, 20 Wis. 210, or in *U. S. R. Stock Co. v. Johnston*, 67 Wis. 182, and in other cases cited in the brief of the respondent's counsel. It is not only in the discretion of the court as to what other issues should be referred, but it is clearly in the discretion of the court as to whether the case should be referred, even if it is referable. There is no reason of construction that should make the word " may," in the last clause of sec. 2864, R. S., mean *shall*, or imperative, more than the same word in the first clause. We do not think a full reference of this case was an abuse of such discretion. It is not a matter of transcending importance, anyway, whether a case be referred or not; for the circuit court may review the report and, on motion, render judgment thereon, or set aside, alter, or modify it, or require the referee to amend it. The learned counsel of the appellant does not question the right or propriety of referring the matter of account in this case. What is due the plaintiff on the contract and for extra work and materials is involved in such accounting, and that is the main issue in the case. That being referred, there is no good reason why the subordinate, incidental, or collateral issues of the case should not also be referred, so that the report of the referee may dispose of the whole case.

By the Court.— The order of the circuit court is affirmed, and the cause remanded for further proceedings according to law.

Biemel vs. The State.

Biemel, Plaintiff in error, vs. The State, Defendant in error.

March 8 — March 27, 1888.

Criminal Law and Practice. *(1) Murder: Justifiable homicide: Setting aside verdict. (2, 3) Counsel to assist district attorney: Employment by private persons: Milwaukee municipal court.*

1. In a prosecution for murder, where the accused admits the killing and the only defense is that it was justifiable homicide, the evidence must be very clearly in favor of the accused to justify this court in setting aside a verdict against him which has been sustained by the trial court.

2. An attorney employed by and expecting compensation from private persons should not be permitted, even at the request of the district attorney, to appear and aid in the prosecution of a person charged with a crime punishable by imprisonment in the state prison.

3. Ch. 354, Laws of 1887, providing for the appointment of counsel to assist the district attorney, is applicable to the municipal court of Milwaukee county and the judge thereof.

ERROR to the Municipal Court of *Milwaukee* County. The case is stated in the opinion.

For the plaintiff in error there were briefs by *Markham, Williams & Bright,* attorneys, and *Edward S. Bragg,* of counsel, and oral argument by *Mr. A. H. Bright.* To the point that counsel receiving pay from private parties should not have been permitted to assist in the prosecution, they cited, besides cases cited in the opinion, *Comm. v. Wilson,* 2 Cush. 590; *Comm. v. Tuck,* 20 Pick. 364; *People v. Hendryx,* 58 Mich. 319.

For the defendant in error there was a brief by the *Attorney General* and *L. K. Luse,* Assistant Attorney General, and oral argument by the *Attorney General.* To the point that it was not error to permit private counsel to assist the district attorney in prosecuting the case, they cited *Rounds v. State,* 57 Wis. 45; *Lawrence v. State,* 50 id. 507; *State v. Bartlett,* 55 Me. 200; *State v. Wilson,* 24 Kan. 189; *Griffin v. State,* 15 Ga. 476; *Jarnagin v. State,* 10 Yerg. 529; *Martin v. State,* 16 Ohio, 364; *Burkhard v. State,* 18 Tex. App. 599; *Wood v. State,* 92 Ind. 269; *People v. Blackwell,* 27 Cal. 65; *U. S. v. Hanway,* 2 Wall. Jr. 139; *Edwards v. State,* 47 Miss. 581; 1 Bish. Crim. Proc. sec. 281; Whart. Crim. P. & P. sec. 555.

TAYLOR, J.　The plaintiff in error was tried upon an information for the murder of one Pagel, in the municipal court of Milwaukee county.　On the trial, the plaintiff in error was convicted of manslaughter in the third degree. The plaintiff in error, upon the return of the verdict, moved the court to set aside the verdict, and grant a new trial, upon the minutes of the court, for the following reasons: (1) That the court erred in refusing to permit the defendant to show the employment of Mr. R. N. Austin, the attorney who appeared for the state, and his payment by private parties; and that the court erred in holding that counsel for the state receiving pay from private parties should be permitted to take part in the trial on behalf of the state. (2, 3) That the verdict is contrary to the evidence and to the charge given by the court.　(4) That the verdict is perverse and contrary to the law and facts.　(5) That justice has not been done the defendant.　The motion was overruled, and the defendant excepted; and after judgment was pronounced upon the verdict he settled a bill of exceptions in the case and brings the judgment and proceedings on the trial to this court upon a writ of error for review.

As we have concluded that the learned judge of the municipal court erred in refusing to permit the defendant to show that Mr. Austin, who appeared and assisted the district attorney in prosecuting on behalf of the state, was employed and paid by private parties to aid in such prosecution, we shall not pass upon the other causes of error assigned by the learned counsel for the plaintiff in error, further than to say that when the accused admits the killing, and the only defense is justifiable homicide, the evidence would have to be very clearly in favor of the accused upon the question involved in order to justify this court in setting aside the verdict against the decision of the trial judge refusing a new trial upon that ground.

The question involved in the first assignment of error has not heretofore been presented to this court in the form presented in this case, and we are now called upon for the first time to determine whether, upon the trial of a person accused of a high crime involving his imprisonment in the state prison for life or for a term of years, private persons may employ counsel, whether from good or bad motives, and send them into our courts to prosecute persons accused of such crimes, and whether the courts may allow such paid attorneys to prosecute the accused against his consent. We think public policy, and the fair, just, and impartial administration of the criminal law of the state, make it the duty of the courts to exclude the paid attorneys of private persons from appearing as prosecutors. That public policy is against permitting them to prosecute, is, we think, clearly indicated by the several provisions of our laws upon the subject of criminal prosecutions.

The statutes provide for the election in each county of a prosecuting attorney, and they make it his duty to appear and prosecute all persons informed against or indicted for crimes in the courts of his county, and when for any reason there is no public prosecutor in the county, the court in which the prosecution is pending shall appoint some one to prosecute the accused. Sec. 752, R. S., says it shall be the duty of the district attorney to prosecute all criminal actions in the circuit courts of his county, etc., and all criminal actions, except for common assault and battery and actions for breaches of the peace by the use of abusive or threatening words, before any magistrate, when requested by the magistrate before whom the action is pending, and upon like request to attend all criminal examinations before any magistrate; and at the request of a grand jury to appear before them and examine witnesses, to give advice, to draw all bills of indictment and informations, and issue subpœnas and other processes for the attendance of witnesses. Sec. 754 reads as follows: "No district attorney shall receive any fee or reward from or on behalf of any prosecutor or *other individual,* for services in any prosecution or business to which it shall be his official duty to attend; nor be concerned as attorney or counsel for either party, other than for the state or county, in any civil action depending upon the same state of facts upon which any criminal prosecution commenced but undetermined shall depend; nor shall any district attorney while in office be eligible to or hold any judicial office whatever." Sec. 750 provides for the appointment of a person in the place of the district attorney when the office is vacant, or when the district attorney is absent from the court unable to attend to his duties, or when he shall have acted as attorney for or be near of kin to the accused, and when the person shall be so appointed by the court he shall for the time being perform all the duties and have all the powers of the district attorney. Sec. 4649 directs that all informations for crimes shall be signed by the district attorney and filed by him.

In addition to these provisions, the legislature, recognizing the propriety of giving the district attorney the aid of other counsel in the prosecution of important or intricate cases, by ch. 354, Laws of 1887, has provided "that the circuit judges, within their respective circuits, are authorized in their discretion to appoint counsel to assist the district attorney in the prosecution of persons charged with crime in all cases when the crime charged is punishable by imprisonment in the state prison. Such additional counsel shall be paid in the same manner as now provided by law for the payment of counsel for indigent criminals." This last act was undoubtedly passed, recognizing the fact that in some criminal cases there was great propriety if not a necessity for furnishing the district attorney aid in their prosecution. The propriety of such aid had been recognized by this court in the cases cited below; and it may be reasonably inferred that this act was passed to sanction the custom of the courts which had grown up in the state of allowing the district attorneys the aid of assistant counsel in difficult cases, and at the same time to regulate and limit it to the appointment of counsel who are not paid by private parties but from the public funds, thereby placing the assistant attorney in the same impartial and unprejudiced position as the prosecuting attorney.

It cannot be claimed that either before or since the passage of the act of 1887 private parties could thrust their hired attorneys into the courts to take charge of or assist the district attorney in the prosecution of any criminal case, without the consent of the court and the district attorney. Whenever attorneys other than the district attorney have been heretofore permitted to appear in a criminal case, they have come in by the consent of both the court and the district attorney, and not upon any claim of right to be there by the employment of private individuals. Heretofore no case has come before this court where the trial judge has permitted any one to appear as the assistant of the district attorney when it was shown that he was employed by private parties and came into court at their request. In this case, defendant, by his counsel, offered to show on the trial of this case the *status* of Mr. Austin, who appeared in court to aid in the prosecution of the defendant.

Before entering upon the trial the counsel for the defendant stated to the court: "I desire, before counsel other than those employed by the state proceed to take part in the trial of this case by act or conduct, to raise the question

so that it shall appear upon the record that on behalf of
the defendant we enter our protest and objection against
the appearance on behalf of the state of any person employed for reward by any private association or private
person.   Such we charge to be the condition which the
counsel who has just risen for the state occupies, and we
offer — unless it be admitted — to prove that fact upon the
record, so that we may have the ruling of the court."   To
this proposition the learned judge of the municipal court replied: "This court has always refused to go into the investigation as to compensation of counsel."   The counsel for
the defendant answered: "We do not desire to prove the
amount of compensation the attorney is to receive, but offer
to show that he is employed by an organization known as
the 'Sailors' Union,' so that we stand in fact defending ourselves against the Union."   The court then remarked:
"What do the gentlemen say on the other side?"   The
district attorney replied: "The only thing I can say about
the matter is, Mr. Austin appears in this case to assist me
at my request."   In a further conversation between the
counsel for the defendant and the district attorney, it was
stated that Mr. Austin appeared at the preliminary examination of the accused, but not at the request of the district
attorney; that the district attorney did not request him to
go there, and did not know that he was employed by the
Sailors' Union.   The attorney for the defense then offered
to prove that Mr. Austin was employed by private parties.
The court refused to permit the proofs, and the counsel for
the defendant duly excepted.

The evidence in the case shows that the person alleged to
have been killed by the defendant was a member of the
Sailors' Union, and there was also evidence in the case tending to show that Pagel, the deceased, and another Union
sailor, came on the vessel where the defendant was and
where Pagel was shot, for the purpose of removing the de-

fendant off the vessel. For the purposes of this decision, we must treat the case as though the defendant had proved by competent evidence that Mr. Austin, who appeared and assisted in the prosecution by the permission of the court, was employed for that purpose by the Sailors' Union or by some other private parties, and that he was to receive a compensation for his services from such Union or other private parties, and from them only. The question for determination is whether it is in accord with the statutes and laws of the state and with public policy that the court should permit an attorney employed by and expecting compensation from private parties to appear and aid in the prosecution of a person charged with a crime punishable by imprisonment in the state prison.

We think it is quite clear from the reading of our statutes on the subject, as well as upon public policy, that an attorney employed and paid by private parties should not be permitted either by the courts or by the prosecuting attorney to assist in the trial of such criminal cases. The laws have clearly provided that the district attorney, who is the officer provided by the laws of the state to initiate and carry on such trials, shall be unprejudiced and unpaid except by the state, and that he shall have no private interest in such prosecution. He is an officer of the state, provided at the expense of the state for the purpose of seeing that the criminal laws of the state are honestly and impartially administered, unprejudiced by any motives of private gain, and holding a position analogous to that of the judge who presides at the trial. Such is the view taken of the office of the prosecuting attorney by the courts of this country as well as of England, and we think it is the true view of his position. *Hurd v. People*, 25 Mich. 416. In this case the court say: "The only legitimate object of the prosecution is to show the whole transaction as it was, whether its tendency be to establish guilt or innocence. The prosecuting officer represents the public interests, which can never be promoted by the conviction of the innocent. His object, like that of the court, should be simply justice; and he has no right to sacrifice this to the pride of professional success." *Maher v. People*, 10 Mich. 225, 226; *Regina v. Chapman*, 8 Car. & P. 559; *Regina v. Orchard*, 8 Car. & P. 565, note. These cases clearly indicate the duty of the prosecuting attorney to proceed with all fairness in presenting the cause of the state to the jury, and in prosecuting the whole case, even though parts of the case as presented should make in favor of the innocence of the accused. This method of presenting a case is not that favored or pursued in civil cases, where the paid attorneys of the respective parties conduct them. And criminal cases are not likely to be so presented if the prosecution is permitted to be conducted by the paid attorneys of parties who from passion, prejudice, or even an honest belief in the guilt of the accused, are desirous of procuring his conviction.

The statutes of this state having carefully provided that the prosecuting attorney shall, like the judge on the bench, be free from prejudice of private interest in conducting the trial of criminal cases, it would seem to be eminently proper that the courts, in permitting or selecting assistants to the public prosecutor under the authority of the new law upon the subject, viz., ch. 354, Laws of 1887, should permit or select only such assistants as are as unprejudiced and impartial as the prosecutor provided by law. This question has been fully considered by the courts of Michigan and Massachusetts,— states in which the laws prescribing the duties of public prosecutor are substantially like ours,— and the courts of these states have uniformly held that attorneys employed by private parties ought not to be permitted to aid the district attorneys in the conduct of criminal cases. *Meister v. People*, 31 Mich. 99; *Sneed v. People*, 38 Mich. 248; *People v. Hurst*, 41 Mich. 328; *Comm. v. Knapp*,

10 Pick. .477, 482; *Comm. v. Williams*, 2 Cush. 582, 584; *Comm. v. King*, 8 Gray, 501; *Comm. v. Gibbs*, 4 Gray, 146. In this last case the court holds that where an attorney is appointed to prosecute a case in the absence of the attorney general, the person so appointed ought to have the same general qualifications of the attorney general; and that the appointment of an attorney to prosecute a criminal case depending upon the same facts as a civil action in which such attorney had been previously employed, was a sufficient ground of error to reverse the judgment. In *People v. Hurst* it was held error to allow an attorney to assist in prosecuting a criminal action against whom the accused had testified in the matter out of which the prosecution grew. In *Sneed v. People* the court, speaking of the right of the prosecuting attorney to employ counsel to assist him in the prosecution of a criminal action, and stating that the service so rendered would be a proper charge against the county, and that the counsel so employed are acting for and on behalf of the public, as much so and with as much impartiality as the prosecuting attorney, then add: " It is quite different, however, where such counsel are employed by the complaining witness or the party injured or by private individuals. Counsel so employed can in no fair sense be said to be employed by or on behalf of the people, even though the prosecuting attorney may consent to or even request that counsel be so employed."

In the courts of Texas and Kansas counsel employed by private parties have been permitted to appear and assist in the prosecution of criminals. The Texas courts say it has been the practice to permit private counsel to appear in criminal cases from the earliest history of the state, and justify the continuance of the custom on the ground that the legislature, knowing of the custom, had not seen fit to prohibit it. *Burkhard v. State*, 18 Tex. App. 599, 618. In Kansas the practice seems to have been tolerated in the case of *State v. Wilson*, 24 Kan. 189, and in Maine the court, without expressly approving the practice, refused to reverse a judgment where an attorney was permitted to assist on the trial who had been spoken to by private persons to assist; but on the trial the counsel who had been so spoken to by the private parties declared that he had no agreement for compensation, and should leave the question of compensation to the will of those who had requested him to appear in the case. *State v. Bartlett*, 55 Me. 200, 203, 204.

Among the conflicting opinions of the courts upon the propriety or impropriety of permitting counsel employed by private persons to assist the district attorney in the trial of criminal actions where the punishment is imprisonment in the state prison, we are inclined to hold that under the laws of this state, since the legislature has given the trial judge the power of appointing assistant counsel where he thinks the public interest requires it, and providing that such assistant counsel shall be paid out of the public funds, counsel should not be permitted to appear in the case, even at the request of the district attorney, when it appears that such counsel has been employed to appear by private parties, at whose request such counsel appears in the case, and from whom he expects to receive compensation for his services. The cases in this court cited by the attorney general *(Lawrence v. State*, 50 Wis. 507, and *Rounds v. State*, 57 Wis. 45) are not in conflict with this ruling, and the cases both arose previous to the enactment of ch. 354, Laws of 1887.

It is said that ch. 354, Laws of 1887, is not applicable to the municipal court of Milwaukee or to the judge thereof. We think it does apply to that court and the judge thereof. It is a general law regulating the trial of criminal cases in circuit courts, and all such laws are made applicable to the municipal court of Milwaukee county. See sec. 2, ch. 256, Laws of 1879; *State v. Hirth*, 67 Wis. 368.

Had the learned judge of the municipal court, acting under the authority of ch. 354, Laws of 1887, appointed Mr. Austin as counsel to assist the district attorney in the prosecution, notwithstanding his previous employment by private parties, and Mr. Austin had accepted such appointment and acted under it, a different question would be presented. It might be urged that in such case the acceptance of the appointment by the counsel and acting under it would be a renunciation of his previous employment, and his services thereafter rendered would be solely for the state, and the only compensation he could legally demand would be that provided by the act of 1887. But the learned judge declined to act under the law, and permitted the counsel to appear on the mere statement of the district attorney that he appeared at his request, after the defendant had offered to prove that he was employed by private parties and with the expectation of receiving his sole compensation for his services from said private persons. In such case, we think he was not a proper attorney to prosecute the case on behalf of the state. For this error the judgment of the municipal court is reversed, and the cause is remanded for a new trial.

By the Court.— Ordered accordingly.

The Oshkosh Gas Light Company and another, Respondents, vs. The Germania Fire Insurance Company, Appellant.

March 27 — April 17, 1888.

(1) Insurance against fire: Several policies: Total loss: Measure of damages. (2) Forfeiture: Waiver. (3) Evidence: Immaterial error.

1. Where several concurrent policies of insurance upon real property have been written with the consent of the respective companies, and the property is wholly destroyed, the aggregate amount of

such insurance must, under sec. 1943, R. S., "be taken conclusively to be the true value of the property when insured, and the true amount of loss and measure of damages when destroyed."

2. Where the agent of an insurance company, with knowledge of a forfeiture of the policy, continues to recognize its validity, and enters into negotiations for a settlement of the loss, whereby the insured incurs expense or trouble, the forfeiture will be deemed waived.

8. The admission of incompetent evidence to prove a fact established by other evidence which was competent, is an immaterial error.

APPEAL from the County Court of *Winnebago* County. The following statement of the case was prepared by Mr. Justice CASSODAY:

February 8, 1885, the defendant issued to the plaintiffs its policy of insurance, whereby it insured the plaintiffs against loss by fire to the amount of $750 in several sums, upon six separate pieces of property, some of which were real estate, and some personal property, including "$180 on the frame store-house building and shed adjoining, including scales." By the terms of the policy, "$15,000 concurrent insurance" was "permitted," in the aggregate, on the whole property covered by the policy. "There was other insurance upon this property, amounting, in the aggregate, to $11,250." December 18, 1885, a fire occurred, as shown by the evidence and found by the jury, wholly destroying "the frame store-house building and shed adjoining, as well as the scales, and also damaged slightly some of the other property." The aggregate amount of insurance upon the property so destroyed at the time of the fire was $2,700, in seven different companies, including the defendant company, which carried one fifteenth of the risk thereon. The nature of the defense will appear from the opinion. On the trial, August 18, 1887, the jury returned a verdict of $220.63. From the judgment entered thereon the defendant appeals.

For the appellant there was a brief by *Jenkins, Winkler Fish & Smith,* and oral argument by *Mr. C. H. Van Alstine.* They contended, *inter alia,* that sec. 1943, R. S., does not declare that the *aggregate* insurance written in *several policies* shall be taken to be the true value, etc. So construed the statute would foster and encourage over-insurance, instead of preventing it as intended. The legislature had in mind the issuance of but one policy. There cannot consistently be more than one " true value " to one piece of property. And when several policies are issued in different amounts, and the several values are in excess of the actual true value of the property, a provision for scaling down those values to the actual true value does not conflict with the statute, but rather makes that certain which would otherwise be uncertain.

For the respondents there was a brief by *Finch & Barber,* and oral argument by *Mr. Charles Barber.* As to the construction of sec. 1943, R. S., they cited, besides cases cited in the opinion, *Thompson v. St. Louis Ins. Co.* 43 Wis. 459; *Harriman v. Queen Ins. Co.* 49 id. 71; *Oshkosh P. & P. Co. v. Mercantile Ins. Co.* 31 Fed. Rep. 200; *Queen's Ins. Co. v. Jefferson Ice Co.* 64 Tex. 578; Wood on Ins. sec. 41.

CASSODAY, J. 1. Upon the verdict of the jury it must be assumed that the building mentioned was wholly destroyed by the fire. At the time of such destruction it was insured in seven different companies, in the aggregate $2,700, one fifteenth of which was in the defendant company. The evidence tended to show that the value of the building at the time of the fire was about $1,200. The defendant concedes that, if it is liable at all, it should pay its proportionate share of the true value of the building, but insists that it is not bound to pay the amount specified in the policy. The contract of insurance was made under a statute which declared that " whenever any policy of insurance shall be written to insure any real property, and the property insured shall be wholly destroyed without criminal fault on the part of the insured or his assigns, the amount of the

insurance written in such policy shall be taken conclusively
to be the true value of the property when insured, and the
true amount of loss and measure of damages when destroyed." Sec. 1943, R. S.   Under this statute it is settled
by frequent adjudications that the actual value of such real
estate when insured or destroyed, and the consequent *actual
loss* to the insured, is wholly immaterial.   *Reilly v. Franklin Ins. Co.* 43 Wis. 449; *Thompson v. Citizens' Ins. Co.* 45
Wis. 388; *Cayon v. Dwelling House Ins. Co.* 68 Wis. 515,
516.   This is the necessary result of the language of the
statute making " the amount of the insurance written in such
policy " conclusive between the parties to the contract, not
only as to " the true value of the property *when* insured," but
also as to " the true amount of loss and measure of damages
when destroyed."

The statute must be regarded as a part of the contract of
insurance, and the amount written in the policy as liqui-
dated damages agreed upon by the parties conclusively in
such contract.   The several concurrent policies were each
written with the consent of the respective companies.   This
being so, the aggregate amount of such insurance written
in the several policies is the value of such property as stipulated in each contract, and hence, as between the parties,
must be regarded as conclusive, not only as to " the true
value of the property when insured," but also as to " the
true amount of loss and measure of damages when destroyed."   This must be so, or the statute would be wholly
ineffectual whenever there is more than one policy on the
same property.   And this is so notwithstanding other clauses
in the policies inconsistent therewith.[1]   The result is that the

---

[1] The policy in suit contained, among other clauses, the following:
"In case of any other insurance upon the property hereby insured,
whether made prior or subsequent to the date of this policy, the insured
shall be entitled to recover of this company no greater proportion of
the loss sustained than the sum hereby insured bears to the whole
amount insured thereon, whether by specific or floating policies."— REP.

exceptions to such portions of the charge as, in effect, directed the jury that in case they found the building to have been wholly destroyed, then the plaintiffs were entitled to recover the full amount written in the policy, must be overruled.

2. The policy contained a clause to the effect that any increase of hazard by reason of any change in the use or occupancy of the building, or by the erection of neighboring buildings, without being specifically agreed upon, should avoid the policy. It appears that after the contract of insurance and before the fire, the plaintiffs, without the consent of the defendant, erected another building within twenty feet of the one in question, and put a steam-boiler therein of about seventy horse power, and used the same for making steam and running an electric-light plant. There was evidence tending to show that, after the fire and proofs of loss had been furnished to the defendant, an adjuster, having knowledge of the erection of such other building and the putting in of such boiler and use of the same, and with authority from the defendant, negotiated with the agent of the plaintiffs respecting the adjustment and settlement of such loss under the policy, whereby the plaintiffs incurred expense and trouble. Under these circumstances we think there was no error in charging the jury, in effect, that if they found that such adjuster was the agent of the defendant, and, with knowledge of such forfeiture and without insisting upon the same, continued to recognize the validity of the policy, and entered into negotiations for, and efforts at, a settlement of such loss, whereby the plaintiffs incurred expense or trouble, then there was a waiver of such forfeiture. Such waivers have so frequently been sanctioned by this court as to require no discussion, much less a restatement of the law. *Webster v. Phœnix Ins. Co.* 36 Wis. 67; *Northwestern Mut. L. Ins. Co. v. Germania F. Ins. Co.* 40 Wis. 446; *Gans v. St. Paul F. & M. Ins. Co.* 43 Wis. 108;

Cannon v. Home Ins. Co. 53 Wis. 585; *Hollis v. State Ins. Co.* 65 Iowa, 454.

3. Assuming that the declarations of the adjuster were not admissible to prove his authority from the defendant, yet, as his testimony established such authority, their admission affected no substantial right of the defendant, and hence is not 'ground for reversal. Sec. 2829, R. S.

By the Court.— The judgment of the county court is affirmed.

SAXTON, Respondent, vs. McNAIR and another, Appellants.

March 27 — April 17, 1888.

Contracts: Consideration: Restoration of distrained cattle: Defective proceedings.

In order to obtain possession of cattle which had been distrained by the plaintiff while they were doing damage to his crops, the owner induced the defendants to execute an undertaking for the return of the cattle to the plaintiff or the payment of the damages, etc. *Held,* that although the proceedings upon the distress were technically defective and the owner might have maintained replevin, yet the restoration of the cattle to the owner was a sufficient consideration for the undertaking.

APPEAL from the Circuit Court for *Florence* County.

The facts will sufficiently appear from the opinion. The defendants appealed from a judgment in favor of the plaintiff.

For the appellants there was a brief by *Fairchild & Fairchild,* and oral argument by *Mr. H. O. Fairchild.*

For the respondent there was a brief by *Webster & Wheeler,* and oral argument by *Mr. W. H. Webster.*

COLE, C. J. From the view which we have taken of this case it will be unnecessary to consider the objections taken to the proceedings under the original distraint and appraisement. There was a demurrer *ore tenus* to the complaint, which was overruled. The complaint was founded upon the written undertaking set forth therein. The undisputed facts relating to the giving of this undertaking are these: Nine head of cattle belonging to one Thomas La Montagne were taken or distrained by the plaintiff, October 20, 1886, while doing damage to his crops on his farm in the town of Florence. The cattle were driven from the plaintiff's premises, and left with one Malloy, to be fed and taken care of. They remained in the charge of Malloy until after proceedings for the appraisement of the damage done by them were completed. On the evening of the 21st of October, one Cleary, who was employed in working and had charge of the farm of La Montagne, in Florence county, from which the cattle escaped, arranged with Malloy for the restoration of the cattle to his possession, and obtained them by agreeing to give the undertaking sued on. The next morning the defendants executed the undertaking, whereby they promised and agreed in consideration of the delivery of the cattle to Cleary, the agent of La Montagne, that the cattle should be returned to the possession of the plaintiff in case La Montagne refused or neglected to pay the amount of damages as appraised, together with costs and expenses, or that they would pay such damages, costs, and expenses. A breach of the undertaking is alleged.

Now, the learned counsel for the defendants insists that the complaint shows no consideration for the undertaking. Independent of the recitals in the instrument, he says, the complaint does not allege nor state the circumstances in regard to the plaintiff's possession of the cattle, nor does it set forth the facts which show that he had the right to the possession of them, so as to afford a sufficient consideration for the undertaking. This objection is not well founded. It appears with sufficient clearness and certainty that the

cattle were in the possession of the plaintiff under a distraint proceeding, and that the undertaking was given for
the sole purpose of obtaining a restoration of the cattle to
the possession of the agent of the owner. It seems to us
that the surrender of the possession of the cattle by the
plaintiff, under the circumstances, to the owner or his agent,
was a valid consideration for the agreement. It may be
conceded that the distraint proceeding was technically defective, and that the owner might have maintained trespass
on the refusal of the plaintiff to surrender them or might
have acquired possession of his cattle by an action of replevin, but this course he did not see fit to pursue. His
agent, in order to obtain the possession, induced the defendants to execute the undertaking, thereby waiving, for
the owner, all objection to the validity of the distraint proceeding; and the defendants obligated themselves to pay
the amount fixed in the event the owner of the cattle did
not pay it or refused to return the cattle. We can conceive of no valid objection to enforcing the obligation.
Upon the facts, we must assume that La Montagne ratified
the acts of his agent in procuring the undertaking to be
executed, and that he deemed it for his interest to obtain
his property by the arrangement made. Now suppose, as
suggested by the plaintiff's counsel, La Montagne, in order
to obtain the possession of his cattle, had seen fit to pay
the damages appraised, could he turn round and recover his
money back by showing that the distraint proceeding was
irregular or defective in some particular? It seems to us
he could not do this, for the plain reason that, knowing his
rights, he had chosen to settle the matter by causing the
undertaking to be executed and in that way secure a return
of his cattle. Again, suppose the plaintiff, after surrender-
ing the cattle and accepting the undertaking, had brought
an action for the damages done by the cattle, would he not
be held to have waived his right to such an action by ac-

cepting the obligation of the defendants to pay the amount fixed or restore the cattle?

These supposed cases furnish strong reasons for enforcing the obligation given by the defendants to secure a benefit for the owner of the cattle. The defendants assumed the responsibility voluntarily, and no reason is perceived why they should not abide by it. The arrangement made was in the nature of a settlement of a controversy, and it is not claimed that it was brought about by any artifice or fraud. This is not a case of giving an undertaking *in invitum*, as in *Shevlin v. Whelen*, 41 Wis. 88, but is more like the case of *Mason v. Nichols*, 22 Wis. 376. Bearing in mind the fact that at the time the undertaking was given, even if the cattle were held under a defective distraint proceeding, still the owner might have obtained the possession of them by an action of replevin, but that he did not choose to resort to that remedy, but rather to secure their possession, and settle for the trespass, induced the defendants to enter into this obligation, it seems now eminently just to hold that it is binding upon them. We think the facts show a sufficient consideration to support it. Where a bond is voluntarily given it is held binding upon the parties. *Lewis v. Stout*, 22 Wis. 234. See *Griswold v. Wright*, 61 Wis. 195.

It results from these views that the judgment of the circuit court must be affirmed.

By the Court.— Judgment affirmed.

CANTWELL, Respondent, vs. THE CITY OF APPLETON, Appellant.

March 27 — April 17, 1888.

MUNICIPAL CORPORATIONS: PLEADING: NEGLIGENCE. *(1) Claim for damages: Appeal: When formal pleadings necessary. (2) Defective sidewalk: Actual notice: Liability for injury: Charter construed. (3) Contributory negligence.*

1. The plaintiff, having been injured by reason of a defective sidewalk, filed with the city clerk a claim for damages containing all the essential elements of a good complaint. The claim not being allowed, she appealed to the circuit court. *Held*, that there was no error in refusing to require a formal complaint to be filed in said court.

2. The charter of a city provided that it should not be liable for any damages arising from accidents occasioned by reason of the sidewalks or streets being in a defective or dangerous condition, unless one of the officers of the city had actual knowledge of the defect for three days prior to the accident. *Held*, that where officers of the city had actual knowledge of a dangerous excavation in a sidewalk, and neglected to erect a barrier or warning to prevent people from falling therein, the city was liable for the consequences of such neglect, even though the defect had existed but a few hours.

3. The fact that the plaintiff in broad daylight walked into an excavation extending across a sidewalk on the principal thoroughfare of a city, there being no barriers and no dirt or other object upon the sidewalk to indicate the presence of the excavation, is *held* not to be conclusive proof of contributory negligence.

APPEAL from the Circuit Court for *Outagamie* County. During the forenoon of June 18, 1885, as the plaintiff was walking east on the north side of College avenue, which is one of the principal streets in the defendant city, she fell into an excavation extending across the sidewalk, and was injured. On the 20th of the same month she filed with the city clerk a notice of such injury, specifying the place where it occurred and the nature of the defect in the sidewalk which occasioned it. On July 22, 1885, she also filed in the office of such city clerk a claim for $2,000 damages for such injuries. This claim contained all the essential requisites of a complaint in an action to recover such damages. On the same day the common council referred such claim to a committee. After the expiration of sixty days from the presentation of such claim, the council having failed to take any further action thereon, the plaintiff duly appealed to the circuit court pursuant to the provisions of the city charter. Laws of 1876, ch. 47, subch. 5, secs. 25–27.

The cause being called for trial in the circuit court, a motion was made on behalf of the defendant that the plaintiff be ordered to file and serve a complaint in the action. This motion was denied, and the cause was tried without further pleadings.

It appeared on the trial that the excavation was made by the Appleton Water-Works Company, on the morning of the day on which the plaintiff was injured, for the purpose of making connections in a store abutting the sidewalk at the place of the injury. It was about two and one-half feet wide, and six feet deep, and extended across the walk, which was about twelve feet in width. The water-works company had authority, under an ordinance of the city, to make the excavation for that purpose. No barrier was placed on either side of the excavation to prevent persons passing along the walk from falling into it. An objection to the admission of any evidence under the complaint was overruled, and a motion for a nonsuit denied. No exceptions were taken to the instructions given by the court to the jury, and no instructions were proposed on behalf of the defendant. The jury found for the plaintiff, and assessed her damages at $600. A motion for a new trial was denied, and judgment entered pursuant to the verdict. The defendant city appeals from the judgment.

Samuel Boyd, for the appellant, contended, *inter alia:*

(1) The court should have required a formal complaint to be filed, so as to allow the defendant to answer, demur, or interpose any of the defenses allowed by statute, as in other cases. The writing treated as a complaint in this case is simply a bill or account in which the plaintiff is creditor and the defendant debtor. It does not give the title of the cause, specify the name of the court in which the action is brought, the name of the county in which it is to be tried, or the names of the parties — plaintiff and defendant — as required by sec. 2646, R. S. (2) A nonsuit should have been granted, there being no proof that any city official had knowledge of the defect, if any, for three days prior to the accident. *McFarlane v. Milwaukee*, 51 Wis. 691; *Raymond v. Sheboygan*, 70 id. 318, and cases cited. (3) If the persons making the excavation were guilty of negligence, the plaintiff was still bound to use ordinary care and prudence to avoid the injury. *Hassa v. Junger*, 15 Wis. 598; *Ward v. M. & St. P. R. Co.* 29 id. 144; *Montgomery v. Scott*, 34 id. 338; *Achtenhagen v. Watertown*, 18 id. 331. If she had made ordinary and proper use of her eyes she would have avoided the injury. See *Seefeld v. C., M. & St. P. R. Co.* 70 Wis. 216.

Leopold Hammel, for the respondent, argued, among other things, that the section of the city charter relied upon by the defendant is invalid as an attempt to relieve a particular corporation from its liability under the general law, and as repugnant to fundamental principles of justice. *Durkee v. Janesville*, 28 Wis. 464; *Whittaker v. Janesville*, 33 id. 90; *Hincks v. Milwaukee*, 46 id. 559; *State v. Bartlett*, 35 id. 287; *Johnson v. Waukesha Co.* 64 id. 281. It contravenes sec. 9, art. I, of the constitution. If the section is held valid it should be construed strictly against the city and in favor of the public, and should not be held to relieve the city from liability in this case where the city officials had actual notice of the danger and could easily have protected the plaintiff and other travelers. *Parish v. Eden*, 62 Wis. 272; *Bloor v. Delafield*, 69 id. 273; *Harper v. Milwaukee*, 30 id. 365; *Weisenberg v. Appleton*, 26 id. 56; *Bailey v. Spring Lake*, 61 id. 227; *Jaquish v. Ithaca*, 36 id. 108; *Winn v. Lowell*, 1 Allen, 177; *Harriman v. Boston*, 114 Mass. 241. The city is liable because of its omission of duty — because of the neglect of its officers, after actual knowledge, to protect the public from accident. See *Colby v. Beaver Dam*, 34 Wis. 285; 2 Dillon on Mun. Corp. secs. 730, 1024; *Boucher v. New Haven*, 40 Conn. 460; *Russell v. Canastota*, 98 N. Y. 496; *Requa v. Rochester*, 45 id. 129; *Klatt v. Milwaukee*, 53 Wis. 196; *Seward v. Milford*, 21 id. 485; *Alexander v. Oshkosh*, 33 id. 277; *Prideaux v. Mineral Point*, 43 id. 513; *Hubbell v. Viroqua*, 67 id. 343; Wood on Nuisances, sec. 783; *Chicago v. Robbins*, 2 Black, 422; *Rehberg v. New York*, 91 N. Y. 137.

Lyon, J. I. The refusal of the court to order the plaintiff to file a formal complaint is assigned for error. The court might have done so in its discretion; but we are aware of no rule of law which requires, in a case like this, that formal pleadings shall be interposed. The claim for damages filed with the city clerk contains all the essential elements of a good complaint. It alleges the corporate character of the defendant city, gives the location of the excavation and its dimensions, sufficiently describes the injuries the plaintiff received, charges the city with negligence in respect to the excavation, and alleges the giving of the notice of the injury required by law. Had a complaint been ordered to be filed, it would have been but a mere repetition of the contents of such claim for damages. Hence, further pleadings on behalf of the plaintiff were entirely unnecessary. The papers returned by the city clerk on the appeal to the circuit court gave the defendant all necessary information of the nature and amount of plaintiff's claim. We think the alleged error is not well assigned.

II. The motion for a nonsuit was based upon two general propositions. These are, *first*, that under a provision of the charter, which will presently be stated, there was no cause of action against the city; and *second*, that the plaintiff was guilty of contributory negligence.

1. The clause of the charter above referred to is as follows: "The city shall not be liable for any damages arising or resulting from accidents occurring by reason of the sidewalks, streets, drains, sewers, gutters, ditches, bridges, or public grounds in the city being out of repair or in a defective or dangerous condition, unless it be shown that, prior to the happening of such accident, one of the officers of the city had actual knowledge of the defect causing the accident for three days prior to such accident."

Of course no city official could have notice of such excavation three days before the accident, because it had existed but a few hours. It was proved, however, that two aldermen of the city met near the excavation, shortly before the plaintiff fell into it, and conversed concerning its dangerous character, and one of them called the attention of the person who superintended the work to the same. The city marshal also knew of the excavation. Notice thereof to the aldermen was notice to the city; hence the city had actual notice of the excavation. It is very clear that the above provision of the charter has no application to this case. Here was a dangerous obstruction to travel upon the sidewalk, which the jury might well find called for prompt and immediate action by the city authorities. If it be conceded that the charter gave the city the right to leave the excavation there three days without incurring any liability, it certainly did not relieve the city from the duty of immediately putting up some kind of a barrier or warning to prevent people falling into the pit, if the jury were of the opinion (as they doubtless were) that some barrier should have been erected. The two aldermen who met there could have erected the same in a few moments, as the materials therefor were at hand. The jury having found the barrier necessary to the safety of travelers there, it would be a vicious and most unreasonable construction of the charter provisions above quoted to relieve the city from liability for the consequences of the neglect of its officials to cause such barrier to be immediately erected. The case, in this particular, is like *Parish v. Eden*, 62 Wis. 272, and many other cases in this court.

2. Was it conclusively proved that the plaintiff was guilty of negligence which contributed directly to the injury of which she complains? Presumably the question of her negligence was submitted to the jury and by the jury determined in her favor. True, the plaintiff walked into the pit in broad daylight. It is not claimed that her eye-sight was defective. From these facts it was argued that she was negligent. Had the jury so found, their verdict could not be disturbed. But the proof tends to show that there was no dirt or other object upon the sidewalk to indicate the presence of the excavation. The plaintiff walked slowly, looking straight ahead, and did not see that the sidewalk had been disturbed. No one was working there at the time, and she did not know of the pit. A gentleman walking but a few feet behind her also failed to see the excavation until the plaintiff fell. Her attention might have been momentarily diverted at the time by any one of many causes, without raising a conclusive presumption of negligence against her. Moreover, she was passing along the principal thoroughfare of the city, and had no reasonable cause to fear or suspect that such an unguarded pitfall would be allowed in her path. Many facts were proved bearing upon the question of the alleged contributory negligence of the plaintiff, from which different inferences may reasonably be drawn. In such a case the authorities all agree that the question of negligence is for the jury.

We conclude, therefore, that the motion for a nonsuit was

properly overruled. This disposes of all the alleged errors adversely to the defendant.

By the Court.— The judgment of the circuit court is affirmed.

WEST, Appellant, vs. VANDEN BROOK, Respondent.

March 27 — April 17, 1888.

Appeal from J. P.: Reversal of judgment on question of fact: Facts taken for granted on trial before justice.

1. On appeal from a judgment rendered upon the verdict of a jury in justice's court, if a new trial upon the merits is waived and no error in the proceedings is shown, the judgment will not be reversed if there was evidence which, uncontradicted, would support it.

2. Where it was taken for granted on the trial in justice's court that the plaintiff's claim arose out of a certain leasing,— the defendant claiming that the action should abate because his co-lessee was not made a party, and the plaintiff relying upon the alleged fact that the defendant was a several and not a joint lessee,— a judgment that the action abate should not be reversed on appeal on the ground that there was no evidence to show that the plaintiff's claim arose out of such leasing.

APPEAL from the Circuit Court for *Outagamie* County. The following statement of the case was prepared by Mr. Justice TAYLOR as a part of the opinion:

The plaintiff commenced an action in a justice's court to recover the value of certain personal property, for the value of which the defendant was indebted to him; alleges the value of the property to be the sum of $81.12; and demands judgment for said sum, less $15.36, which is admitted to have been paid. A bill of particulars was filed by the plaintiff, showing that the demand was for farm products, labor, and team work. The defendant did not deny the claim; but answered that the supposed cause of action, if

any existed, all and singular arose out of transactions and
dealings had by the defendant and one Frank Fabrick
jointly as copartners, and that said Fabrick is still living in
the city of Appleton, Wisconsin, where this action is now
pending, and demands judgment that said action abate.

Upon these pleadings the parties proceeded to trial in the
justice's court, and a jury was summoned and impaneled to
try the issue in the case. After hearing the evidence, the
jury returned a verdict as follows: "We, the jury, find for
the defendant that the plea in abatement made by the defendant's answer is well taken, and the liability of the defendant, if any exists, is a joint and not a several liability."
Upon this verdict the justice rendered judgment that the
action abate, and that the defendant recover of the plaintiff
the costs of the action, which were taxed at $26.58.

From this judgment the plaintiff duly appealed to the
circuit court of said county, but did not file the necessary
affidavit under sec. 3768, R. S., to entitle him to a new trial
in said circuit court. The justice made his return, upon the
appeal, of all the proceedings in the case before him, and
of the testimony produced by the parties on the trial.
Afterwards the case was tried in the circuit court upon the
proceedings and evidence so returned by the justice upon
said appeal. Upon such last trial the circuit court affirmed
the judgment of the justice, and from the judgment of the
circuit court the plaintiff appealed to this court.

The cause was submitted for the appellant on briefs by
Henry D. Ryan and *John Goodland*, and for the respondent on the brief of *H. Pierce*.

TAYLOR, J. It is insisted by the learned counsel for the
appellant that there is no evidence to support the judgment
rendered in the justice's court, and that it was error for the
circuit court to affirm such judgment.

The plaintiff in the action having appealed from the

judgment of the justice, and having waived the right to a new trial upon the merits in the circuit court, and there being no error shown in the proceedings in the justice's court, the only question for the circuit court was to determine whether there was any evidence to support the verdict rendered by the jury on the trial in the justice's court. That there was evidence given on the part of the defendant tending strongly to show that all claims arising ·in favor of the plaintiff under the lease of the farm mentioned in the proceedings, was a joint claim against the defendant and Frank Fabrick, cannot well be controverted. It may be said that the preponderance of the evidence, as returned by the justice, appears to be against the claim of the defendant; but, there being evidence which, uncontradicted, supports the judgment, the question was one of fact for the jury and not of law for the court. The same rule must apply to a judgment in a justice's court when heard upon an appeal to the circuit court, and no new trial is had in that court, as is applied upon an appeal from a trial and judgment in the circuit court to this court; and when there is evidence which, uncontradicted, supports the judgment, all questions of credibility of witnesses and preponderance of proofs are for the jury, and not for the court. *Campbell v. Babbitts*, 53 Wis. 276, 279, 280; *Persons v. Burdick*, 6 Wis. 63; *Martin v. Beckwith*, 4 Wis. 219, 243; *Hassa v. Junger*, 15 Wis. 598, 600.

It is claimed, however, by the counsel for the appellants that, admitting that there was some evidence to support a finding that all matters in relation to the leasing of the farm were joint matters between the plaintiff on the one side, and the defendant and Fabrick jointly on the other side, still there is an entire absence of any evidence tending to show that the plaintiff's claim grew out of or has any connection with such leasing of the farm. From reading the evidence it appears to us that it was taken for granted on the trial in the justice's court that the plaintiff's claim grew out of such leasing. The plaintiff himself was on the stand as a witness, and made no claim to the contrary; but, on the other hand, relied upon the alleged fact, to defeat the answer of the defendant, that the leasing of the farm was a several and not a joint contract with the defendant and Fabrick; and he also introduced Fabrick as a witness to sustain his construction of the contract. Under this state of the evidence, it appears to us that it would be unjust to permit the plaintiff to reverse the judgment upon appeal upon a question not raised or controverted before the justice. If the plaintiff thought injustice had been done by the verdict of the jury upon the facts of the case, he should have made the proper affidavit and have taken a new trial in the circuit court.

By the Court.— The judgment of the circuit court is affirmed.

QUACKENBUSH, Administratrix, etc., Respondent, vs. WISCONSIN & MINNESOTA RAILROAD COMPANY, Appellant.

March 28 — April 17, 1888.

Railroads: Fences: Constitutional law.

Sec. 1810, R. S., as amended by ch. 193, Laws of 1881, makes a railroad company *absolutely* liable for all damages occasioned by the failure to erect fences along its road as therein required, and excludes the defense of contributory negligence; and such act is constitutional. *Quackenbush v. W. & M. R. Co.* 62 Wis. 411.

APPEAL from the Circuit Court for *Chippewa* County.

Action to recover damages for the death of the plaintiff's intestate, alleged to have been caused by the failure of the defendant to fence its railroad as required by law. An order overruling a general demurrer to the complaint was affirmed on a former appeal. See 62 Wis. 411. Upon the trial the jury returned a special verdict and also found generally in favor of the plaintiff, assessing her damages at $5,000. From the judgment entered on the verdict in favor of the plaintiff the defendant appeals. Other facts are stated in the opinion.

For the appellant there was a brief by *Edwin H. Abbot*, attorney, and *David S. Wegg* and *Howard Morris*, of counsel, and the cause was argued orally by *Mr. Morris* and *Mr. Wegg*.

H. H. Hayden, for the respondent.

ORTON, J. The facts of this case are substantially and briefly as follows: The plaintiff was the wife, and brings this suit as administratrix, of Edward C. Quackenbush, deceased. The deceased was the conductor on a train of flat cars engaged in ballasting the railroad of the defendant between the stations of Thorp and Cadott, east of Chippewa Falls, about the 8th day of July, 1881. That part of the road had been open for general business since November, 1880. The flat cars had been loaded with surfacing material at a pit lying westerly of Cadott, and was pulled by the engine to a point between the stations of Thorp and Stanley, and there unloaded, and was then being pushed by the engine back towards Stanley station. When about three miles west of said station, the train collided with a heifer upon the track, and was derailed, and the lifeless remains of the deceased were found among the wreck. At the moment of the collision the deceased was on the westerly portion of the train. It was claimed by the appellant that so pushing the train on that part of the track was a violation of the rules of the company, to the knowledge of the deceased.

At about 600 feet easterly from the place of the accident one MacDonough had established a place for the delivery of piles cut from adjoining land on the defendant's right of way for shipment on the road. MacDonough had cut roads into the country opposite, on which material to be there shipped was hauled, and these logging roads extended three-quarters of a mile on both sides of the railroad into the country. The nearest highway crossing was a mile and a half from the place of the accident, and the nearest farm crossing was from a half mile to three quarters of a mile east, or, some witnesses say, a mile and a half east, and the nearest cultivated farms were half a mile distant either way. The railroad of the defendant on both sides opposite the place where the animal was run over by the train, and as is claimed by the respondent where it got upon the track, had never been fenced, although such places were outside of depot grounds and not at farm or highway crossings, and there was no pond, water-course, ditch, embankment, or other sufficient protection rendering a fence unnecessary at such places to prevent cattle from straying upon the right of way of the defendant, and although the road had been built and operated more than three months, in violation of sec. 1810, R. S., as amended by ch. 193, Laws of 1881. The jury found that this was the condition of the road where the accident occurred and where the animal got upon the track. There was some argument by the learned counsel of the appellant that it was not shown that the place where the animal got upon the right of way was required to be fenced. But we think the evidence warranted the jury in so finding. The jury found also that the death of the deceased was occasioned by the negligence of the defendant in having failed to erect fences at the place where the animal got upon the right of way of said road.

The vital and important questions in the case are — *First.* Whether the statute makes the defendant *absolutely* liable for the damages caused by the failure to so fence its road; and, *second*, if the statute does make the company so absolutely liable, whether it is constitutional. It is true the jury found that there was no want of ordinary care and prudence on the part of the deceased that operated as a cause contributing to his death, and we are inclined to think that such finding was warranted by the evidence; but the main argument of the counsel on both sides was as to the construction and validity of the above statute, and but little was said as to contributory negligence. For that reason alone the case ought not to rest on that finding, but the above questions ought to be treated as *necessarily* in the case, and so decided. It is contended by the respondent's counsel that these questions are *res adjudicata* in this case on the former appeal from the order overruling the demurrer to the complaint. .But on the other hand it is contended by the learned counsel of the appellant that they are not *res adjudicata* on the former appeal, because not necessary to the decision of the demurrer, as the complaint alleged that the plaintiff was in the exercise of ordinary care when the train was thrown from the track, and this court intimated that these questions might not be strictly in the case. It might as well be said that these questions are not now in the case on account of the above finding that the plaintiff's intestate was not guilty of any contributory negligence. But on the other appeal it is very significant that the learned counsel of the appellant made their briefs and arguments on these questions almost alone, and asked for their decision; and so also they have done on this appeal. If that statute makes the company *absolutely* liable, then the question of contributory negligence is an immaterial issue in the case, and ought not to be regarded, and is not lawfully in the case. We must therefore hold that said questions were in the case on the former appeal, and are in the case on this appeal, and that they are *res adjudicata*, and may not again be raised on this appeal. This court fully considered those questions on the former appeal, and the opinion of the chief justice is full and com-

prehensive as to the construction and constitutionality of
the statute. It was held "that the statute imposes an *absolute* liability in such a case;" and "that it excludes the defense of contributory negligence when the corporation fails
to perform the duty which the statute prescribes in the first
instance;" and "that it is in the nature of a penalty," etc.;
and that such a law falls within the police power of the
legislature and is constitutional and valid.

We find no error in the record.

By the Court.— The judgment of the circuit court is affirmed.

SWIFT, Respondent, vs. THE STATE LUMBER COMPANY and
others, Appellants.

March 28 — April 17, 1888.

*Equity: Debtor and creditor: Deed absolute in form: Mortgage: Assign-
ment: Redemption: Accounting: Parties: Trusts and trustees.*

1. The legal title to plaintiff's undivided interest in certain lands was
held by one J., who had purchased jointly with him, as security
for moneys advanced for plaintiff on such purchase. J. conveyed
plaintiff's interest and a part of his own to B. and L., who loaned
to plaintiff the money wherewith to repay the advance made by J.,
and agreed to convey to the plaintiff the title to his interest in the
lands when they should receive from him, or from the sale of timber cut from the land, the amount of the loan, with interest,
expenses, etc. B. conveyed his interest to persons having full
knowledge of the equities, and afterwards, by conveyances from
J., L., and the grantees of B., the entire legal title became vested
in the defendant corporation, which, through its officers, had like
knowledge of the equities. In an action to have the deed from J.
to B. and L. declared a mortgage, for an accounting for timber cut
and sold, etc., and to compel a conveyance to plaintiff of his interest in the land, *held:*

   (1) The relation between the plaintiff and B. and L. was, in effect,
   that of mortgagor and mortgagees, and the subsequent conveyances must in equity be regarded as assignments of any balance

, remaining unpaid on the mortgage at the times they were respectively made.

(2) Grantees of B. through whom the title passed to the defendant company, and the personal representatives of B., are not necessary parties, and there was no error in refusing to require them to be brought in.

2. One who held the legal title to land merely as security for a debt due him, conveyed the same to his son by deed absolute in form. It was claimed that the conveyance was intended as a trust for the benefit of the grantee and his brothers. *Held*, that the grantee was at least a trustee of an express trust, within the meaning of sec. 2607, R. S., and his brothers need not be joined as defendants in an action by the debtor to redeem the land as from a mortgage.

APPEAL from the Circuit Court for *Chippewa* County. The following statement of the case was prepared by Mr. Justice CASSODAY:

This action was commenced against the *State Lumber Company, Edward Bradley* and *Allen P. Lovejoy*, about May 5, 1886. It appears from the complaint that prior to October 14, 1871, the plaintiff, *Swift*, and one Jenkins jointly purchased the 17,000 acres of land described; that, in doing so, Jenkins, at the request of *Swift*, advanced and paid thereon for him $10,000, upon the express agreement that the equal undivided three-fourths of said lands should belong to Jenkins and the other equal undivided one-fourth should belong to *Swift*, that Jenkins should take the legal title to the whole of said lands and hold three fourths thereof as his own and the other one-fourth thereof as security for the money so advanced and loaned by him to *Swift;* that on the day and year named he so held the legal title to the whole of said lands; that October 14, 1871, Jenkins, from his own share, bargained and sold to D. W. Bradley and *Lovejoy* the undivided one-half of all said lands, and conveyed the same by warranty deeds to them, together with the undivided one-fourth which in equity belonged to *Swift;* that by such deeds D. W. Bradley took the undivided twelve-twentieths of all said lands, and said *Lovejoy*

the undivided three-twentieths thereof; that this was done
in pursuance of an agreement between *Swift*, D. W. Bradley, and *Lovejoy*, whereby they were to and did advance to
Swift, as a loan, $10,000, with which he paid his indebted-
ness of that amount to Jenkins, and for the security of the
repayment of which, with interest, they were to hold the
title to *Swift's* said one-fourth; that upon such conveyance
D. W. Bradley and *Lovejoy* gave back an agreement, dated
October 14, 1871, reciting the facts stated, and wherein they
agreed, in effect, to reconvey to *Swift*, his heirs or assigns,
his one-fourth of the whole, whenever requested by him, his
heirs or assigns, at any time after they should receive from
Swift, or the sale of said lands, or from the proceeds of timber cut from the same, the said $10,000, with annual interest
thereon at ten per cent. from May 1, 1872, together with
one third part of all necessary expenses or expenditures they
might incur in managing and protecting the three-fourths
of the whole land to which they thus received title, provided
Swift or Jenkins should pay all taxes on said lands, including the taxes of 1871, and also all interest as it had or should
become due on three notes signed by Jenkins, and payable
to Palms, as per agreement made by Jenkins and *Swift;*
and *Swift* was annually to pay all taxes on his share of said
lands so conditionally conveyed, and in the event of his
failure in any year, and they paid the same, then *Swift* was
to refund to them such advances, with annual interest at ten
per cent., before they should be required to so reconvey; that
it was therein agreed, in effect, that D. W. Bradley and *Lovejoy* should have the right to sell, or permit to be cut and removed from said lands, at any and all times, timber, until
they were fully paid as aforesaid and saved harmless from
such taxes and interest, at such prices as they might deem
expedient and might obtain for their own interest in the
same timber; and the net proceeds of timber so received
should be applied as such payments, but they were not to

sell any of *Swift's* interest in said lands, without his written
consent, during the six years next after the date of said
agreement; that *Swift* was to look after the land and timber thereon, and, when requested by them, to sell, or permit on the same, or make contracts for, the cutting and
removing of the timber, etc., and supervising the same; that
July 13, 1872, D. W. Bradley sold and conveyed the undivided four-twentieths of said lands to A. P. & D. Kelley, of
Chicago, who took the same with actual knowledge of the
plaintiff's right, title, interest, and equities in the land; that
April 15, 1875, D. W. Bradley, without any consideration,
made a voluntary conveyance, by quitclaim deed, of his remaining eight-twentieths of the land to his son, *Edward
Bradley*, who took the same with notice of said agreements
and of the plaintiff's right, title, interest, and equities in the
lands; that in 1876 the said D. W. Bradley died intestate
at Muskegon, Mich., where he at the time resided, and that
no administrator of his estate has ever been appointed in
Wisconsin; that said company was incorporated and organized October 6, 1882; that in October and November, 1882,
the said Jenkins, *Edward Bradley*, *Lovejoy*, and the Kelleys conveyed, by quitclaim deeds, all of said lands (except
fourteen forties in Price county from which the timber had
been cut, and the lands abandoned) to the defendant the
State Lumber Company; that at the times of taking the
same, and prior thereto, the said lumber company and its
officers and stockholders had full knowledge and notice of
the said right, title, interest, and equities of the plaintiff in
said lands; that the plaintiff paid all said taxes and interest
up to and including 1877, and the highway taxes of 1878,
and that the defendants, or their predecessors in interest,
have paid them since; that said *Edward Bradley* has a full •
account of all matters mentioned, and of all taxes and interest paid, and of all moneys received for timber cut or removed from the lands and the expenses thereof, and of all

dealings with the lands; that the defendants have cut and removed from the lands large amounts of timber, and re. ceived large amounts of money on account thereof; that the net amount so received by the defendants was more than enough to pay off and extinguish said indebtedness from the plaintiff to D. W. Bradley and *Lovejoy,* and the interest thereon and taxes; that the plaintiff has frequently demanded of the defendants an accounting, but that they have and still do refuse to account. The complaint prayed judgment that the deeds from Jenkins be declared a mortgage as to the plaintiff's share, and the plaintiff the owner thereof subject to the mortgage; and for an accounting, paying over, and reconveyance.

The answer of the defendants admitted some things, restated others, and denied any knowledge or information sufficient to form a belief as to others, and then, in effect, denied the payment or satisfaction of the plaintiff's indebtedness, or his right to any accounting or proceeds of timber or reconveyance. The answer also alleged, in effect, that D. W. Bradley and *Lovejoy* took said one-fourth interest absolutely, and subject only to the plaintiff's right to repurchase the same upon terms stated, which had never been done; that the plaintiff had, from time to time, with consent of those holding the title, procured large portions of the timber to be cut from the lands, and had or received the benefit of his share of the proceeds thereof; that in 1877 the plaintiff had accountings with the Kelleys and also *Edward Bradley* and *Lovejoy;* that in 1880, and since, large amounts of timber had been cut and sold from the lands with the knowledge of the plaintiff, and the results and the distribution of the proceeds thereof, and that there was a large balance still due from the plaintiff.

October 26, 1887, the plaintiff was ordered to show cause why the defendants should not be allowed to amend their answer, and why said A. P. & David Kelley, William H.

Bradley, and James W. Bradley, named in such proposed amended answer and affidavits, should not be made parties defendant, and the summons and complaint be amended accordingly. The proposed amendment to the answer alleged, among other things, in effect, that, at the time of the conveyance to the Kelleys, D. W. Bradley made a contract with them whereby they took such lands subject to the contract with the plaintiff, and agreed to share the burdens as well as the benefits thereof; that the Kelleys still resided in Chicago, that they participated in cutting, removing, and selling the timber, and in the moneys received therefor, and were interested in the subject matter of the action; that said *Edward Bradley* took said deed from his father in trust for the equal benefit of himself and his two brothers,— the said William H. and James W., who reside in Milwaukee; that D. W. Bradley left a will which had been duly proved and admitted to probate in Michigan. The plaintiff responded to the order to show cause, by affidavit; and, upon hearing the motion, the same was overruled and denied,. and the order to show cause discharged, with costs against the defendants. From that order the defendants appeal.

For the appellants there were briefs by *Stark & Sutherland*, and oral argument by *Mr. Joshua Stark*. They contended, *inter alia*, that all who, as assignees of D. W. Bradley, or purchasers from him, were at any time in possession and in receipt of the rents and profits of the one-fourth interest in lands to which the plaintiff had an equitable claim, and participated in the sale of that interest and shared in the proceeds of the same, are interested in the accounting and should be made parties. *Armstrong v. Pratt*, 2 Wis. 306; Story's Eq. Pl. secs. 72, 76a, 138, 160,. 192; *Posten v. Miller*, 60 Wis. 494, 499; *Eldredge v. Putnam*, 46 id. 205; *Burhop v. Milwaukee*, 18 id. 431; *Burhop v. Roosevelt*, 20 id. 338.

For the respondent there was a brief by *Levi M. Vilas*,.

attorney, and *M. Griffin*, of counsel, and oral argument by
Mr. Vilas.

CASSODAY, J.   Upon the facts stated, and numerous deci-
ions of this court, we must hold that the plaintiff was, in legal
effect, the owner of the undivided one-fourth of all the lands
in question, October 14, 1871, subject to the payment of
the $10,000 mentioned; and that when D. W. Bradley and
Lovejoy advanced the amount of money named and received
the conveyances from Jenkins, they took and received the
title to such undivided one-fourth as security for the money
so advanced, and such interest, taxes, etc.; and hence, under
the agreement mentioned, the relation between the plaintiff
and them was, in legal effect, that of mortgagor and mortgagees. *Starks v. Redfield,* 52 Wis. 352, 353; *Hoile v.
Bailey,* 58 Wis. 448; *Schriber v. Le Clair,* 66 Wis. 579;
and cases cited in these references.   By such conveyances
D. W. Bradley got the legal title to twelve twentieths of
the lands, and *Lovejoy* three twentieths, while the other five
twentieths remained in Jenkins.   July 13, 1872, D. W.
Bradley sold and conveyed to the Kelleys four twentieths
of the lands, and September 15, 1875, he made a voluntary
conveyance of his other eight twentieths to his son *Edward.*
November 10, 1882, Jenkins, *Edward Bradley,* the Kelleys,
and *Lovejoy* conveyed the whole of the lands, except fourteen forties apparently worthless, to the defendant company.   These several conveyances must each in equity be
regarded as an assignment of a fractional part, or the whole,
of any balance that may have remained unpaid on the mortgage at the times they were respectively made.   Whether
or not there were any such unpaid balances can only be
determined by an accounting and trial upon the merits.
This action, therefore, is essentially a bill for an accounting
by these defendants, and for a redemption from the mortgage, and a reconveyance from the defendant company.

The principal contention is that there is a defect of parties defendant. It is claimed that, as a matter of fact, *Edward Bradley* took such title from his father in trust for himself and his two brothers, William H. Bradley and James W. Bradley, who should be made parties defendant. Since the deed to *Edward* was absolute in form, it would seem that, even upon the showing of the defendants, he was at least a trustee of an express trust, within the meaning of the statutes. Sec. 2607, R. S. *Winner v. Hoyt*, 66 Wis. 234, 235; *State v. Wettstein*, 64 Wis. 243; *Platteville v. Hooper*, 63 Wis. 383; *Poor v. Guilford*, 61 Am. Dec. 749; *Johnson v. Catlin*, 62 Am. Dec. 622. This being so, he could maintain an action in relation to the land without joining his brothers. *Ibid.* Having the right to thus sue alone, we perceive no reason why he may not with equal propriety defend the title thus acquired, without joining his brothers as defendants. Certainly, the conveyance to him carried with it all the title his father had in the lands at the time it was made, and that same title has since been conveyed to the lumber company. Since neither William H. nor James W. has any legal title or interest in the land, and no attempt is made to charge them personally, they cannot be regarded as necessary parties to this action.

The same is true respecting the personal representatives of the D. W. Bradley estate, and also both of the Kelleys. Certainly it is unnecessary for the assignor of the mortgage to be made a party in an action to redeem from the mortgage. That is practically what is sought to be required here. Neither the Kelleys, nor any of the other absent parties mentioned, have submitted themselves to the jurisdiction of the court and sought to be made parties. The burden is upon the plaintiff to show that the mortgage has been paid, and hence that he is entitled to a reconveyance. Such payment is claimed by reason of his share of the net proceeds of timber removed and sales of timber and land.

If the plaintiff's share of such net proceeds were at any time sufficient to pay off and satisfy such indebtedness, interest, taxes, etc., in accordance with the contract, then the mortgage thereby became extinguished, and the plaintiff thereby became entitled to a reconveyance of his share of the land; and if, thereafter, any timber was removed from the land, or any timber or land sold, then the plaintiff would be entitled to recover his share of such excess from the party removing or selling, or authorizing or causing such removal or sale.   But, even in that event, these defendants, in the absence of any liability created by contract, could only be chargeable with so much of such share of such excess as should arise from such removal or sales by themselves. While the plaintiff, therefore, may possibly be interested in holding some one liable for his share of such excess who is not a party to this action, yet it is not perceived that the defendants are interested in, or are prejudiced by, the absence of such party.   Even if the Kelleys or some other absent party is liable on contract to some of the defendants for timber removed or sold, yet it does not appear that the plaintiff has become bound by any such contract, and if not, he certainly cannot be coerced into making it available in this action.   The plaintiff is now only proceeding against these defendants, and for an accounting and reconveyance. The answer filed seems to be sufficient to protect the defendants and to raise all equities in which any of them are concerned.   If it should appear otherwise upon the hearing, the trial court would undoubtedly allow such amendments as might appear to be just.   We are unable to say that there was any abuse of discretion in disallowing the proposed amendment.

. *By the Court.*—The order of the circuit court is affirmed.

FARWELL and others, Appellants, vs. WEBSTER, Garnishee, etc., Respondent.

March 28 — April 17, 1888.

Voluntary assignment: Perfecting insufficient bond, etc.: Execution by one partner on Sunday. '

1. The sureties upon the bond of an assignee for the benefit of creditors failed to justify as the statute requires, and the court commissioner omitted to indorse upon the bond and copy of the assignment the proper certificates. The bond was not left with the court commissioner, but was filed with the clerk of the circuit court by some other person. Afterwards the bond was withdrawn and redelivered to the assignee, and was then perfected, and the perfected bond, with a copy of the assignment, with the proper indorsements, was again filed with the clerk, three days after the first filing, and before the rights of any creditors had intervened. *Held*, that the failure to comply with the statute in the first instance should not avoid the assignment, notwithstanding sec. 1695, R. S., requires that the bond shall, "*immediately* after its execution," be filed, etc.

2. A voluntary assignment duly executed and delivered by one of two partners on a secular day is not invalidated by the fact that the other partner signed it on Sunday.

APPEAL from the Circuit Court for *Barron* County.

Garnishment. The plaintiffs, who are judgment creditors of John Lindstrom and William Cholerton, appealed from a judgment in favor of the garnishee. The facts will sufficiently appear from the opinion.

For the appellants there was a brief by *C. D. Tillinghast*, and oral argument by *H. H. Hayden*.

[No appearance for the respondent.]

COLE, C. J. The garnishee claimed to hold the property of the principal debtors under a voluntary assignment made by them for the benefit of creditors. The assignors, Lindstrom and Cholerton, were doing a mercantile business

at Chetek, in Barron county.   We infer from the evidence
that Lindstrom had charge of the business and managed
it for the firm, and that his partner resided at Richland
Center, quite a distance from Chetek.   It appears that
Lindstrom executed the assignment at Chetek on Saturday,
the 24th of January, 1885, and Cholerton executed it on
Sunday, at Richland Center.   On Monday, the 26th, the
assignment was delivered to the garnishee, being the assignee, who attempted to qualify by giving the requisite
bond and taking possession of the assigned property.   But
the sureties of the bond failed to justify as the statute requires, and the court commissioner omitted to indorse upon
the bond and copy of the assignment the proper certificates.
Nor was the bond left with the court commissioner, as it
should have been, but was retained by the assignee, or by
some one for him, and was filed by some one with the clerk
of the circuit court on the 26th of January.   The assignee,
learning that the bond was defective, afterwards took it
from the files and redelivered it to Lindstrom, who delivered
it back to the assignee.   The sureties justified before the
commissioner, and the perfected bond, with a copy of the
assignment with the proper certificates or indorsements
thereon, was filed with the clerk on the 29th of January.
The assignee surrendered the possession of the property to
Lindstrom, and did not interfere with it until he had made
and filed the perfected bond.   The garnishee proceedings
in this case were not commenced until some fourteen days
after all this was done.

    Now, the question arising upon these facts is, Was the
garnishee liable to the plaintiffs, or had he the right to hold
and dispose of the assigned property under the assignment?
We concur with the court below in the opinion that he was
not liable as a garnishee, and that the assignment was good
to transfer the title to the property, notwithstanding the
defects in the execution of the assignment as originally

made; for while the statute provides that the bond "shall *immediately* after its execution, together with a full and true copy of the assignment," be filed by the officer taking the same in the office of the' clerk of the circuit court, yet this language must have a reasonable construction, and was not intended to prevent or preclude the assignee from perfecting his bond without unreasonable delay, when he had failed to comply with some requirement of the statute in the first instance. The bond as first executed was clearly insufficient for want of the justification of the sureties, and the assignee had no right to take possession of the assigned property under it; but still, without delay, an unobjectionable bond was executed and filed in the proper office, before the rights of any creditor had attached to the assigned property. We think the assignee substantially complied with the statute, and that the assignment should not be avoided by reason of his failure to comply with its requirements in the first instance. Had the rights of the plaintiffs intervened before a good bond was executed and filed, a different question as to the liability of the garnishee would be presented.

But there is a further objection taken to the assignment, which is that Cholerton executed it on Sunday. Does that fact render the assignment void? Lindstrom was the partner managing the business; Cholerton, the other partner, not being present. It may well be that Lindstrom, under the rule established in this state, would not have the power to execute the assignment without the consent of his partner. This certainly is so where the partner is present and can be consulted in the matter. *Brooks v. Sullivan*, 32 Wis. 444. But where one partner has absconded, or is absent so that he cannot be consulted, and the responsibility of the business is thrown entirely upon the remaining partners, a different rule prevails. Burrill, Assignm. (5th ed.), 107 *et seq.* And the law is well settled that a general as-

signment without preferences, made by one partner in the
name of the firm, by the authority or with the consent of
his copartners, will have the same effect as if made by all.
Ibid. This proposition is so clear as to require neither authority nor argument to support it. The act of the partner
making the assignment in such a case is, in legal contemplation, the act of all. In this case, of course, the assignment was made with the assent of both partners. The deed
of assignment was intrusted by Cholerton, after its execution, with his partner, with implied authority to deliver it
to the assignee; and it was so delivered and redelivered on
a secular day. Under the circumstances, though Cholerton
signed the instrument on Sunday, yet that fact should not
invalidate the assignment, when it is obvious he intended
to assent to the assignment, and impliedly gave authority
to Lindstrom to make a good delivery of it. Where the
non-assigning partner is not consulted, yet ratifies the act
of his partner in making the assignment, or the circumstances are such as to furnish reasonable grounds for infer-
ring that he intended to confer upon the assigning partner
authority to do the act for the firm, there the assignment,
if fairly made, will be held *prima facie* valid. In *Rumery
v. McCulloch*, 54 Wis. 565, there was an assignment, with
defective justification of the sureties, of partnership property, executed by both partners. One of the partners left
the state, and the other partner afterwards, without the
knowledge of the absent partner, executed in the firm name
a second assignment of the same property to the same assignee, to correct the defect in the first, and the assignment
was held valid for all purposes. Mr. Justice Orton, in his
opinion, says: "We may presume and infer from the execution of the first assignment by Parks [the absent partner]
his design and intention to make an effectual assignment,
and imply therefrom authority and consent that such assignment should be made by Bigler effectual for the pur-

poses expressed in it, and to correct the same, if necessary to that end, either by another assignment or in any other proper way; and we think it proper to hold in this case that such authority and consent are clearly implied, because Parks has never made any objection to either assignment, and no rights have intervened between the first and second assignments which would render the making of the second, for the purpose of correcting the first, wrong or improper." In *Coleman v. Darling*, 66 Wis. 155, an assignment was made by one partner without the knowledge of the other partners, who were present at their place of business and might have been consulted. The question in the case was whether the non-assigning partners afterwards assented to and ratified the assignment. The implication from the opinion is that such ratification might be made, but was not made in that case until after the rights of third parties had intervened. In the light of the authorities, we therefore conclude that, though Cholerton signed the assignment on Sunday, yet this fact alone did not invalidate it. The instrument would not take effect until delivered, and there was a good delivery upon a secular day by Lindstrom, who had undoubted authority to make such delivery and bind the firm.

We do not understand that any other objection is taken to the assignment; consequently we hold it sufficient to convey the property of the partnership to the assignee for the purposes specified in the instrument.

By the Court.—The judgment of the circuit court is affirmed.

TANNER, Respondent, vs. GREGORY and another, Appellants.

March 29 — April 17, 1888.

Equity: Delivery of stock certificates: Pleading: Appeal to S. C.

1. A judgment for equitable relief against one of two defendants, who, after his general demurrer was overruled, took no further steps in the action except to join in the appeal, must be affirmed if the complaint states a cause of action for equitable relief and the judgment can be sustained upon the facts stated.

2. A complaint which alleges that the plaintiff is the owner of certain shares of stock in the defendant corporation, and that the corporation has recognized him as such but refuses to deliver to him the certificates therefor, states an equitable cause of action.

3. An answer upon the merits is a waiver of the objection that the complaint does not state an equitable cause of action.

4. A defendant cannot complain because the plaintiff has taken judgment against him for less relief than he was entitled to.

APPEAL from the Circuit Court for *Ashland* County.

The following statement of the case was prepared by Mr. Justice TAYLOR as a part of the opinion:

The respondent commenced an action in the circuit court for Ashland county against the appellants, and filed and served the following complaint in such action:

" [Title of case.]

" The plaintiff respectfully alleges and shows to this court:

" 1. That the said defendant the *Caledonia Iron Mining Company* is a corporation duly organized by and pursuant to the laws of the state of Wisconsin.

" 2. That the said defendant *J. T. Gregory* and certain other persons, on or about October 1, 1885, entered into and formed a joint-stock company, known as the 'Section 6 Iron Mining Company,' for the purpose of prospecting for and mining iron ore, and to sell, ship, manufacture, deal in, and smelt the same, and to purchase, acquire, sell, lease, and rent options, mining leases, and mineral lands; that the capital stock of said company consisted of and was 20,000 shares, of the par value of $25 per share; that the said *J. T. Gregory* was the owner and holder of 2,500 shares of said stock.

" 3. That on November 11, 1885, the said *J. T. Gregory,* for a valuable consideration to him in hand paid by this plaintiff, sold and assigned to this plaintiff 150 shares of said stock, and in writing agreed to deliver to this plaintiff the certificates for said 150 shares of stock so soon as the· same should be issued; and this plaintiff was duly acknowledged the owner of said stock by said company and by said defendant corporation, and said transfer was so entered on the books of said company and corporation, and said plaintiff has paid all assessments made upon said stock since November 11, 1885, and the said company and corporation accepted the same.

" 4· That on or about December 9, 1885, the said company was duly reorganized as and became a corporation, being the above named defendant, pursuant to and by virtue of the laws of the state of Wisconsin, under the name of the *Caledonia Iron Mining Company,* with a capital stock of 40,000 shares, of the par value of $25 per share,— each of said stockholders in said Section 6 Iron Mining Company becoming the owner of and entitled to a *pro rata* share of the stock of said defendant corporation, according to the amount of stock held by him in said Section 6 Iron Mining Company; and this plaintiff thereupon became the owner of and entitled to 300 shares of the stock of said defendant corporation.

" 5· That this plaintiff has repeatedly demanded of said defendant corporation, and prior to the commencement of this action, his certificates for the said 300 shares of stock; but, although the said company has issued certificates of stock to all the other stockholders of said corporation, it has refused and neglected, and still does refuse and neglect, to issue the said certificates to this plaintiff, to his great and irreparable damage.

"6. That the said defendant *J. T. Gregory* falsely and fraudulently denies the right of this plaintiff to said certificates, and claims that this plaintiff is entitled to certificates for only 150 shares of said stock.

"Wherefore this plaintiff demands judgment against said defendants (1) that the plaintiff is the owner of and entitled to 300 shares of the said capital stock of said defendant company; (2) that the said defendant company issue and deliver to this plaintiff the said 300 shares of stock; (3) that the plaintiff may have such other and further relief as he may show himself entitled to, together with the costs of this action."

The defendant *Gregory* answered the complaint, denying its material allegations, and the *Caledonia Mining Company* demurred to the complaint for the reason that the complaint does not state facts sufficient to constitute a cause of action. The demurrer of the *Caledonia Company* was overruled, and the case was tried upon the issues made by the answer of the defendant *Gregory;* and, after hearing the evidence, the court found "(1) that the allegations of the complaint were true; (2) that the allegations of the answer are not true;" and, as conclusions of law, "(1) that the plaintiff is the owner of and entitled to 300 shares of the capital stock of said defendant corporation; (2) that the said company issue and deliver to the plaintiff the said 300 shares of stock; (3) that the plaintiff is entitled to judgment in accordance with the above findings, and for the costs of this action against the defendant *J. T. Gregory.*"

Upon the findings, judgment was entered as follows: "It is hereby adjudged (1) that the plaintiff is the owner of and entitled to 300 shares of the capital stock of said defendant corporation, the *Caledonia Iron Mining Company;* (2) that the said defendant the *Caledonia Iron Min-*

ing Company issue and deliver to the said plaintiff, *S. W. Tanner*, 300 shares of the capital stock of said defendant company; (3) that the plaintiff recover of the defendant *J. T. Gregory* forty and 45–100 dollars, costs of this action, and may have execution therefor." The defendants appealed from the judgment.

For the appellants there was a brief by *Miles & Shea*, and oral argument by *Mr. J. J. Miles*. They contended, *inter alia*, that the Section 6 Company was nothing more than a partnership in which *Gregory* held an eighth interest. *Durkee v. Stringham*, 8 Wis. 1; *Bergen v. Porpoise F. Co.* 13 Am. & Eng. Corp. Cas. 1. Even if it had been a corporation, and *Gregory* a stockholder, it would not be bound by his contract to deliver stock. *Joslin v. Stokes*, 5 Am. & Eng. Corp. Cas. 98, 38 N. J. Eq. 31. The officers of the defendant company, by assenting to plaintiff's claim, did not assume any liability for the company or bind it for the delivery of the stock. The consideration was paid to *Gregory*, and the company cannot be compelled to perform his agreement.

For the respondent there was a brief by *Tomkins & Merrill*, and oral argument by *Mr. W. M. Tomkins*.

TAYLOR, J. The mining company did not take any further steps in the case after the demurrer was overruled, except to appeal from the judgment. It took no exceptions to the evidence offered on the trial, nor did it except to the findings of fact or conclusions of law made by the court after hearing the evidence. If the complaint states an equitable cause of action against the company, then the judgment, as to the company, must be affirmed if the judgment can be sustained upon the facts stated in the complaint. All other exceptions to the proceedings in the case were waived by its failing to appear further in the case and take exceptions therein. See *State ex rel. Spring Lake v. Pierce*

Co., ante, p. 321. Although the allegations in the complaint 'are not very specific, yet, giving them a liberal construction, there appears to be enough alleged to show that the corporation, after its organization, recognized the plaintiff as the owner of the 300 shares of the capital stock of said corporation, as claimed by him. If he was such owner of the shares of stock, and recognized as such owner by the corporation, then the corporation held the shares of stock as trustee for the plaintiff, and a court of equity would enforce the delivery of the certificates of such stock. See *Dousman v. Wisconsin & L. S. M. & S. Co.* 40 Wis. 418, 420. So far as the claim against the corporation is concerned, the complaint shows a trust, and not a sale of the stock by the company to the plaintiff. The case, as between the plaintiff and the corporation, does not involve the question whether a court of equity will enforce a specific performance of a contract for the sale of shares of stock in a private corporation. See *Hill v. Rockingham Bank,* 44 N. H. 567; *Cowles v. Whitman,* 10 Conn. 121; *Pollock v. Nat. Bank,* 7 N. Y. 274.

The defendant *Gregory,* having answered the complaint, has waived the objection that the complaint does not state an equitable cause of action. *Peck v. School Dist.* 21 Wis. 516, 522–3; *Tenney v. State Bank,* 20 Wis. 152, 163. The court might have rendered judgment against him, upon the evidence in the case, for the value of the stock he had agreed to deliver to the plaintiff, had the plaintiff desired such judgment, with the costs of the action; and he has no ground of complaint that the plaintiff chose rather to take a judgment against the· company for the delivery of the stock than a money judgment against him for the value. Upon the evidence found in the record, it is sufficiently shown that, as between the plaintiff and *Gregory,* the plaintiff was entitled to the 300 shares of the mining company's stock, and *Gregory* cannot complain that the plaintiff *took* judgment against him for less relief than he was entitled to.

By the Court.— The judgment of the circuit court is affirmed.

LYON, J., took no part.

THE BERLIN MACHINE WORKS, Appellant, vs. PERRY, Respondent.

March 29 — April 17, 1888.

Contracts: Public policy: Sale of patents, etc.: Covenant in restraint of trade.

The defendant, a carpenter and joiner and inventor of sand-papering machines, sold his interest in certain patents upon such machines and in the business of a firm engaged in the manufacture and sale thereof. In the contract of sale he covenanted that he would not thereafter "manufacture, sell, or cause to be sold any sand-papering machines of any description," unless with the consent of the purchaser of said patents, etc. *Held:*

(1) The restriction upon the manufacture and sale of the machines cannot be held to be applicable only to this state.

(2) If the defendant should invent and patent a new sand-papering machine, not infringing on the patents sold, and should sell the patent therefor to one who should manufacture and sell machines under it, he would thereby *cause* the machines *to be sold,* within the meaning of the covenant.

(3) The restriction being greater than is reasonably necessary to protect the purchaser in the enjoyment of the patents and business purchased, and prohibiting the defendant from pursuing his trade or profession of inventing sand-papering machines, is void as against public policy, although it affects only a single class of machines.

APPEAL from the Circuit Court for *Jefferson* County. This appeal is by the plaintiff from an order sustaining a general demurrer to the complaint. The case stated in the complaint is substantially as follows:

In February, 1884, and previously, the defendant, *James*

L. Perry, and one Charles A. Mather were engaged, at Berlin, Wis., as partners, in the manufacture and sale of wood-polishing and sand-papering machines of which *Perry*, either solely or jointly with others, was the inventor, and upon which he then held and owned five letters patent issued to such inventors by the United States. These machines were bulky and expensive, a large capital was required to carry on the successful manufacture and sale of them, and they were only sold and used in large cities. It is not alleged that the business extends beyond the United States. In February, 1884, *Perry* sold his interest in such business, with the good-will thereof, also in all the property of the firm, in the letters patent before mentioned, and *in* an application for another patent then pending before the United States commissioner of patents, for the sum of $20,000. The contract of sale contained a stipulation by *Perry* to apply for letters patent on another invention of his, being "improvements in sand-paper machines and planer combined, for cleaning sashes, doors, and blinds," etc., and, when obtained, to assign such letters patent to Mather. This stipulation is of no importance on this appeal. The material stipulation in the contract of sale is to the effect that *Perry* "will not hereafter manufacture, sell, or cause to be sold any sand-papering machines of any description" unless with the consent of Mather. The plaintiff corporation has acquired, by mesne assignments and transfers, the whole interest in the business, including the interest thus sold by *Perry* to Mather, and the benefit of the stipulation last above mentioned, and is now carrying on the business under the same letters patent, at Berlin aforesaid. *Perry* is a carpenter and joiner by education and trade, and formerly carried on a certain business in that line. He is the inventor, solely in some cases, and jointly with another person in others, of the devices and machines covered by the letters patent above mentioned. He resides in Watertown, Wis., sixty miles distant from Berlin aforesaid.

The cause of action alleged in the complaint, and the prayer for relief, are that "Notwithstanding said promise and agreement on the part of the defendant as aforesaid, whereby, for the consideration aforesaid, he promised and agreed not to manufacture, or sell, or cause to be sold, any sand-papering machines of any description, without the written consent of said Mather, the defendant, without the consent in writing or otherwise of said Mather, his heirs, or representatives, or any of the assigns of said agreement (including this plaintiff), wrongfully and unjustly, and contrary to his said undertaking, promise, and agreement, and to the great past, present, and prospective injury and damage of this plaintiff, has since several weeks before the commencement of the suit been, now is, and threatens to continue to be, engaged, at Watertown aforesaid, in the manufacture and sale of sand-papering machines of the same general character and for the same purpose as the sand-papering machines now and heretofore manufactured by plaintiff under said patents in the carrying on of said business as aforesaid, but which machines so manufactured by defendant are constructed so slightly different from the devices described and claimed in said patents as to evade liability under the laws of the United States enacted to protect patentees, their heirs and assigns, from infringements of their patents; which machines so manufactured and being manufactured by defendant, defendant has been and is still wrongfully and unjustly offering for sale, and, as plaintiff is informed and believes, has at Watertown aforesaid, sold several of said machines, among others to Nonnast & Co., of Chicago, Ill., and to Meyers & Co., also of Chicago, Ill., and to other persons, residents in Wisconsin and elsewhere, whose names are unknown to the plaintiff; all of which has been and is of great pecuniary injury and damage to plaintiff, in the sum of several thousands of dollars; and the manufacture and sale of such machines by

The Berlin Machine Works vs. Perry.

defendant, if continued, will be of great and irreparable injury to the plaintiff, in and by taking away and depriving him of his trade, lessening his business, reducing his profits, increasing his expenses, and otherwise damaging his said business and interests. Wherefore plaintiff prays that defendant be enjoined from manufacturing, selling, or causing to be sold, by himself, his servants, or agents, any sand-papering machines of any description whatever, and the plaintiff have judgment for his damages, and costs and disbursements herein, and for such other relief as appears just and proper."

For the appellant there were briefs by *Erwin & Benedict*, attorneys, and *Joshua Stark*, of counsel, and oral argument by *Mr. C. T. Benedict*.

For the respondent there were briefs by *Hall & Skinner*, attorneys, and *Gregory, Bird & Gregory*, of counsel, and oral argument by *Daniel Hall* and *Geo. W. Bird*.

LYON, J.   The only object of this action is to obtain an injunction perpetually restraining *James L. Perry*, the defendant, "from manufacturing, selling, or causing to be sold sand-papering machines of any description," which he covenanted with Charles A. Mather not to do, but which he has done and threatens to continue to do, contrary to the terms of such covenant. Counsel for defendant maintain that the covenant is not assignable, and hence that no one but Mather can have an action for the breach of it. We do not determine the question, but assume, for the purposes of the case, that the plaintiff corporation may maintain an action for such breach, just as Mather could have done had he not assigned his interest in the covenant.

Thus assuming the assignability of the covenant, the only question to be determined is whether it is binding upon the defendant. That is to say, Is it a covenant which it was competent for the defendant to make? or is it invalid as against public policy? The covenant is general and unrestricted. It binds the defendant, unless Mather consent in writing that he may do so, not to "manufacture, sell, or cause to be sold, any sand-papering machines of any description." The prohibition is not qualified or limited by time, place, or circumstance. It is as general and comprehensive as can be expressed by language. It has no relation to the sale of a business secret, or any infringement of a trademark or patent.

The law undoubtedly is that the covenant under consideration, *prima facie* at least, is void, and will be so held on demurrer unless the party asserting its validity has averred facts in his complaint from which the court can say the restriction is not larger than is reasonably necessary for the protection of Mather in the enjoyment of the business and patents he purchased of the defendant. If it extends beyond that it is unreasonable and the covenant is void. In view of the averments of the complaint we think the restriction does extend far beyond that limit. It would be a breach of the covenant were the defendant to manufacture, sell, or cause to be sold any kind of sand-papering machines in Canada or Mexico, or at any point in the eastern hemisphere, although the complaint shows that the plaintiff's business, assigned to it by Mather, is confined to the United States. Again, should the plaintiff abandon its business, and should the manufacture and sale of machines under the patents thus sold by defendant to Mather cease entirely, it would still be a breach of the covenant were the defendant to manufacture and sell a sand-papering machine in any place, although it did not infringe any of such patents. Furthermore, the covenant does not limit the prohibition to such machines as would or might come in competition with Mather's business. The defendant might be able to invent a sand-papering machine applicable to uses to which those made by Mather and the plaintiff were not adapted. What reason can there be for restricting him from doing so, if he is not in competition with the business he sold to Mather? We perceive none.

But it is claimed that this case is not within the above rule for several reasons. These will now be considered.

1. An argument is predicated upon the averment in the complaint that the defendant is a carpenter and joiner and had formerly worked at that trade. It is claimed that no restraint he might impose upon himself in respect to any other business or employment could be unlawful. There is no such rule of law. Besides, the complaint shows that he is also an inventor of sand-papering machines. The law would protect him against illegal restrictions in respect to the latter business just as readily as it would against such restrictions affecting his business as a carpenter and joiner, and on the same principles. The point is scarcely worthy of notice.

2. It is also urged that there is nothing in the covenant in question which interferes with the right of the defendant to invent other sand-papering machines, not infringing the patents sold to Mather, and to sell the inventions. It is said that such purchaser might manufacture and sell the after-invented machines without working thereby a breach of the covenant. It seems to us that this would be a very dangerous concession for the plaintiff to make were the covenant valid. It points out an easy way to make the covenant worthless. But we think the concession improvidently made. We are quite clear that if the defendant invents a machine for which he obtains letters patent, and sells the patent to one who makes and sells machines under it, the defendant thereby causes the machine to be sold, within the meaning of his covenant with Mather.

3. Neither is the position tenable that the courts of this state will consider the restriction as applicable only to Wisconsin. Were the covenant valid, our courts would take

The Berlin Machine Works vs. Perry.

cognizance of a breach thereof committed in any other state or country the same as though committed in this state.

4. An alleged rule to the effect that restrictions of the character under consideration, if made as incidental to the sale of patents and a business thereunder, are valid, no matter how general and unlimited such restrictions may be, is invoked to uphold this covenant. But the cases cited to sustain such a rule do not sustain it as broadly as claimed. They hold that such restriction is valid only when, in the judgment of the. court, it is not unreasonable, due regard being had to the subject matter of the covenant. Tested by that rule we have seen that the restriction in this case is not a reasonable one, because not necessary to the protection of the covenantee. In other words, this restriction is not, in any correct sense of the term, incidental to the sale of patents and a business thereunder, but reaches far beyond the point of just and lawful protection to such business.

5. It is also urged that because the restriction affects only a single class of machines, and does not cover the trade of a machinist, it is not within the rule which vitiates contracts in restraint of trade. The position cannot be sustained. While the restriction relates only to sand-papering machines, the defendant is an inventor of such machines, and the covenant unreasonably and unnecessarily prohibits him from pursuing his trade or profession. It is, therefore, within the rule that such covenants are void.

We do not feel called upon to go into a discussion of the history of the law concerning contracts in restraint of trade, or the grounds upon which the rules above stated are founded. It would be an agreeable task to elaborate these subjects, did the exigencies of the case require it. This has been well done, however, in a late treatise of much merit. Greenhood on Public Policy, part XIV, ch. 6. The author has there cited and collated practically all the cases in England and this country on the subject of contracts in restraint of trade. These cases are very numerous. The most of the materials for the very elaborate and able briefs of the respective counsel seem to have been drawn from this treatise. We have deemed it unnecessary to cite cases to each rule laid down in this opinion, believing it sufficient to refer to Mr. Greenhood's work where the cases will be found intelligently classified and arranged under proper heads.

By the Court.— The order sustaining the demurrer to the complaint is affirmed.

THE STATE EX REL. VAUGHN, Respondent, vs. THE MAYOR AND COMMON COUNCIL OF THE CITY OF ASHLAND, Appellants.

March 29 — April 17, 1888.

Municipal corporations: Assessments for street improvements: Bridges: Certiorari: *Appeal from common council.*

1. Under a city charter making the " grading, graveling, paving, planking, or macadamizing " of any street chargeable to the lots abutting thereon, the expense of raising a street to the established grade by the construction of a pile bridge over a ravine is not so chargeable, especially where the charter further provides for paying the expense of building bridges by levying a special tax.
2. Where the board of public works and common council of a city have attempted, without authority of law, to charge upon private property the cost of building a bridge, their proceedings may be reviewed on *certiorari*, although the city charter has provided that an appeal shall be the only remedy of the owner for the redress of any grievance he may have by reason of the making of an improvement or of the amount of the cost thereof charged upon his land.

APPEAL from the Circuit Court for *Ashland* County. The following statement of the case was prepared by Mr. Justice CASSODAY:

April 30, 1887, the city surveyor estimated the cost of an entirely new pile bridge on Second street, between Lake street and Vaughn avenue, in Ashland, at $2,036. May 16, 1887, the board of public works in the city reported that they had viewed and considered the lots and lands abutting on Second street which they deemed would be benefited by placing Second street, between Lake street and Vaughn avenue, at the established grade, and that in their opinion the city at large should be charged with one third of the cost of such improvement on account of said street being crossed at that point by a ravine, and that the remaining two thirds of the cost should be charged to lots 1 to 12, inclusive, in block 73, and lots 12 to 24, inclusive, in block 113, all in Vaughn division, which in their opinion would be actually benefited by such improvement when completed as per the surveyor's estimate. May 17, 1887, the common council directed the board of public works to view said several lots and consider the amount to be made chargeable according to law against said lots for such improvement, and to give public notice of such assessment for review and correction, and to advertise for bids for doing such work. On the same day the said board thereupon assessed said several lots as directed, on the basis of the surveyor's estimated cost of $2,036, of which $678 was to be paid by the city, and $1,358 chargeable to said lots, with descriptions, etc., in detail. May 18, 1887, the board gave public notice of such assessment of benefits and damages for placing said portion of said Second street at the established grade, " by causing a new pile bridge to be built," and that such report would be open for review and correction at a place and times named, when all persons interested would be heard by said board. June 14, 1887, the common council, by resolution, confirmed the assessment of the board of public works made upon the lots abutting upon Second street, between Lake street and

Vaughn avenue; and on the same day the common council, by resolution, authorized the board to enter into a contract on behalf of the city " for the building of said bridge with the lowest responsible bidder; said contract to be signed by the mayor."

June 28, 1887, a writ of *certiorari*, issued by the circuit court to said mayor and common council upon the verified petition of said Emiline E. Vaughn, a resident and tax-payer of said city and the owner of a large number of said lots, was served on said mayor. July 12, 1887, the said board reported to the common council that they had examined and approved the said new pile bridge constructed under contract, and that the actual cost thereof exceeded said estimate by $36.41. July 18, 1887, the city authorities made return to the writ in substance as above stated. Upon the hearing of the matter, the court held, in effect, that, in so far as the proceedings attempted to charge the cost of such improvement against the lots fronting thereon, they could not be sustained, and accordingly that the assessments against said lots should be reversed. From the judgment entered thereon accordingly, the mayor and common council appeal.

For the appellants there was a brief by *Dockery & Kingston*, and oral argument by *Mr. E. J. Dockery*. They contended, *inter alia*, (1) that *certiorari* is not the proper remedy, and the relator should have resorted to an independent action; (2) that the improvement in question is not a bridge; and (3) that the city is not excluded by the charter from building bridges by assessments against abutting lot-owners. At least it may charge the benefits derived from such bridges to the property benefited. To the point that the ravine is not a watercourse and the city would have had a perfect right to have raised an embankment of sand, gravel, or any other proper material in grading said street to the proper level, and to have assessed the benefits to the abutting lots as here, they cited *Hoyt v. Hudson*, 27 Wis. 656, 660, *et seq.*; *Smith v. Milwaukee*, 18 id. 63, 67.

For the respondent there was a brief by *Miles & Shea*, and oral argument by *J. J. Miles* and *W. M. Tomkins*.

Cassoday, J. The improvement mentioned consisted almost wholly in building an entirely new pile bridge across the ravine mentioned. The only additional improvement suggested is a sidewalk on the north side of the street; but the cost of that is not given, and must have been comparatively small. The surveyor's estimate, which appears to have been acted upon throughout, gives the total cost at $2,036, of which 64,000 feet of board measure timber is given at $1,536, and $500 for piles as completed in the structure, including iron spikes and price of driving the piles. If the lots were not chargeable with the building of the bridge, then the whole assessment, made under the circumstances stated, was unauthorized. The rule is well settled that the corporate authorities of a city possess only such powers as are expressly granted by legislative enactment, and such others as are necessarily or fairly implied in or incident to the powers thus expressly granted, or essential to the declared objects and purposes of the corporation. *Bell v. Platteville, ante*, p. 139. By the charter, the common council were empowered "to order and contract for the making, grading, paving, and repairing and cleaning all streets and parts of streets, . . . and to provide for the construction of sidewalks, or the repair of the same, *in the manner" therein mentioned.* Sec. 2, subch. 11, ch. 127, Laws of 1887. "The grading, graveling, paving, planking, or macadamizing to the center of any street or alley, and the grading, graveling, and macadamizing, planking, or paving of any sidewalk, the paving of any gutter, and the construction of cross-walks, where there is no intersection of streets, shall be chargeable to and payable by the lots fronting or abutting upon such street, alley, sidewalk, or gutter, to the amount which such grading, graveling, macadamizing, planking, or paving shall be adjudged by said board to benefit such lots: provided, however, that, in case of paving a street, a portion of the cost, not exceeding, however, one third thereof, may be paid by the city at large if the common council so determine." Sec. 4, Id. Certainly, it cannot be seriously claimed that the building of a pile bridge of the character indicated comes within the description of "grading, graveling, paving, planking, or macadamizing," thus authorized to be charged to the several lots fronting thereon; and nothing else is so chargeable. It is argued with much force and ingenuity by the learned city attorney that the common council had a discretionary power in selecting the material with which to bring the street to grade through and over the ravine in question. Undoubtedly they have such discretion so long as they keep within the powers thus granted; but they have no authority whatever, much less such discretionary authority, outside of the powers so granted by the charter. Besides, the charter expressly provides for paying the expense of building bridges by levying a special tax. Sec. 3, subch. 8, Id. It is claimed that this only applies to bridges over some stream of water. But it does not say so, and we have recently held that bridges over ravines stand upon the same footing as bridges over streams. *State ex rel. Spring Lake v. Pierce Co.*, ante, p. 321. It follows that the special assessments against the lots in question, for paying a portion of the expenses of the bridge, were without authority of law, and therefore void.

2. But it is urged by the learned city attorney that a writ of *certiorari* will not lie where there is another adequate remedy, and that the charter gives a remedy by appeal, and makes it exclusive. Secs. 9, 10, subch. 11, ch. 127, Laws of 1887. But, as we understand, this remedy

by appeal is only given by the charter as to matters within the jurisdiction of the common council. Certainly it was not designed to take away the remedy given by writ of *certiorari*. The jurisdiction of the circuit court to issue such writ is secured by the constitution of the state, and of course cannot be taken away by legislative enactment. Sec. 8, art. VII.

By the Court.— The judgment of the circuit court is affirmed.

Tipping and others, Appellants, vs. Robbins, Respondent.

March 30 — April 17, 1888.

(1) Appeal: Remittitur: *New findings. (2, 3) Mines and mining: License by one tenant in common: Revocability.*

1. Where a judgment is reversed and the cause remanded, a new and additional finding of facts by the trial court, there being no further evidence given or trial had, is unauthorized.

2. A license to work a new and unopened mine, granted by one tenant in common, does not confer any right thus to mine without the concurrent license of the other tenants in common.

3. Sec. 1647, R. S., providing that no license to a miner shall be revocable after a valuable discovery or prospect has been struck, does not apply to a license granted by only one of several joint owners of the land.

APPEAL from the Circuit Court for *Green* County.

The cause was before this court on a former appeal, and is reported in 64 Wis. 546, where a sufficient statement of the facts will be found. This appeal is by the plaintiffs from the judgment entered in the court below after the filing of the *remittitur* from this court on the former appeal. The substance of that judgment is stated in the opinion.

For the appellants there was a brief by *Orton & Osborn,* and oral argument by *Mr. P. A. Orton.*

For the respondent there was a brief by *M. M. Cothren* and *P. B. & J. B. Simpson*, and oral argument by *Mr. Cothren*.

COLE, C. J. When this cause was here on a former appeal (64 Wis. 546) it was decided that the defendant acquired no right to mine on the plaintiffs' land by virtue of the Tipping lease mentioned in the case; that whatever right he had acquired rested upon the parol authority or license given him by the plaintiff *Fox* as to his interest. *Fox* was the owner, as tenant in common, of an undivided two-thirds of the tract in question. The other undivided one-third belonged to the infant plaintiffs, *Irene* and *William Tipping*, subject to the dower of their mother, Mary. As to this undivided one-third owned by the infants it was said there was no proof whatever that any license had been given which could affect their rights or bind them in any manner. The effect of the statute (sec. 1647, R. S.) upon a license granted by one tenant in common was not much discussed in the case, but there is a distinct intimation in the opinion that the parol license granted by *Fox* as to his two thirds was of no practical value unless a further license was obtained which should bind the infants. That question, however, was not definitely settled, but purposely left open for further consideration. The cause was remanded for further proceedings. On filing the *remittitur* from this court in the court below a motion was made by the plaintiffs for a judgment. The circuit court, without any further testimony having been given or any new trial had, made another finding of facts, which in the main affirmed the finding on the first trial. In the final judgment the court decided that the plaintiffs could not maintain this action against the defendant; dissolved the injunction which had been granted, and dismissed the action, saving to the infant plaintiffs and their mother their rights in the net proceeds arising from the sale of the one-third part of the lead ore taken from their ground by the defendant, after deducting the reasonable value of the labor expended in raising such ore, not including the expense of the level run by the defendant to reach their premises. The court further decided and decreed that the defendant had the legal right to work the mine on the plaintiffs' ground, and to receive the avails of two thirds of the mineral raised therefrom, subject to the duty of paying the one-eighth to the owner of the ground as rent from the time of the discovery of the range of mineral.

The learned counsel for the plaintiffs criticises the practice adopted by the circuit court in making a new and additional finding of facts. As there was no further evidence given or trial had, the necessity for such a finding is not obvious. As counsel suggests, it was perhaps harmless to reaffirm the former finding, but certainly there was no ground for incorporating in the new finding additional facts, and such practice we deem unauthorized.

The important question arising on this appeal is the one left undecided on the former appeal, which is, What effect must be given to a parol license granted by one tenant in common to a miner to open and work a new and unopened mine upon land which he owns in common with other tenants who refuse, or for any reason fail, to grant any such license? In other words, does the license of a co-tenant confer any right thus to mine without the concurrent license of the other co-tenants interested in the ground? The right of the defendant in this case is rested entirely upon the statute, which enacts in substance that no license or lease, verbal or written, made to a miner shall be revocable by the maker thereof after a valuable discovery or prospect has been struck, and the discovery of a crevice or range containing ores or minerals shall entitle the discoverer to the ores or minerals pertaining thereto, subject to the

rent due his landlord, before as well as after the minerals
are separated from the freehold. Sec. 1647, R. S. It seems
to us that the statute implies and means that the license
thus protected is granted by the owners of the land, who
own it and have the right to subject the property to the
use of mining. It was not intended to apply to a case
where only one of several joint owners of the land had
granted the license, and it would be unreasonable to give
the statute any such construction. Counsel agree in the
proposition that the right of a tenant in common extends
to the whole and every part of the estate; that he has the
right to the common possession and enjoyment thereof.
The right to work the mine is in its nature entire and indi-
visible and cannot well be enjoyed without exclusive possession. It would certainly be impossible to sever and
remove the interest of one tenant in common in the ores
and leave the interest of the other tenant undisturbed. Nor
could one tenant work the same crevice with the licensee
unless they did it jointly, though they might by arrangement work distinct parts of the crevice, and divide the minerals removed on some equitable basis. But it is entirely
settled as a principle of law that the conveyance of any
separate estate by a tenant in common by metes and
bounds is void as against his co-tenant. Authorities need
not be cited to so elementary a proposition. The license
granted by *Fox* to mine upon the common estate cannot
bind the infant plaintiffs, and the statute does not aid or
increase the efficacy of such license. The learned counsel
for the defendant says the statute is based on the idea of
giving to the discoverer of a mineral range the right to
work it and have the benefit of his discovery. So undoubtedly it is where the miner goes to work under a license
granted by the owners of the property and makes a valuable discovery. It is not in the power of the landlord to
deprive him of the benefit of that discovery while he pays

his rent and incurs no forfeiture by mining usages. But, as we have said, the statute assumes and implies that the license is granted by the owners of the ground, not by one of several co-tenants, each one of whom has the same right to the possession and enjoyment of the common property as his co-tenants.

It follows from these views that the license of *Fox* confers no right to work the mine without the concurrent license of the infant plaintiffs, lawfully obtained. We cannot doubt but this is the proper and only admissible construction of the statute. The counsel for the defendant suggests that it may be greatly for the interests of the infants to have this mine worked and the mineral removed; that instead of destroying the value of their property, the infants would be benefited by it. This view of the matter may be correct, but still their guardian, on their behalf, asks that the defendant be restrained from unlawfully mining upon the ground in which they are interested. It seems to us they are entitled to that relief under the circumstances. If this shall render the license which the defendant obtained from *Fox* of no value to him, the result is unavoidable. He should have seen to it that he had a valid license from all the owners of the land before he commenced to work upon it. For it is only such a license that comes within the purview and protection of the statute. *Fox* has united in this action, and has asked relief which the evidence shows he is not entitled to; but this does not prevent the court from granting the infant plaintiffs protection of their rights and such relief as may be consistent with equity and good conscience. An injunction seems to be the only adequate remedy to restrain the wrongful acts of the defendant and prevent him from digging and carrying away the mineral from the ground. It is evident that repeated actions of trespass for damages would be a very inadequate remedy.

We have not deemed it necessary to consider the question

whether it would be waste for one tenant in common to open and work a new mine on the common estate without the permission or assent of his co-tenant. The counsel for the plaintiffs insists that a co-tenant has not that right at common law, and he has referred to many authorities which sustain his position. One of his authorities states the law upon the subject in the following language: "Coparceners, joint tenants, and tenants in common, are also liable to each other for waste; and actions of account are maintainable for the receipt of more than the proper share of profits. All such owners may also be restrained by injunction from the wilful destruction of the common property. But they may all concur as among themselves in an act of waste. This concurrence must include all. In one case five of the owners had authorized the construction of a railroad on the land held in common, against the wishes of the remaining owner, who proceeded to remove the rails, and the court of chancery refused to restrain him." Bainb. Mines (4th ed.), 23. There are many authorities which state the law substantially the same way, some of which are cited in briefs of counsel, but we need not dwell upon them. The right of the defendant to mine is not rested upon any relation existing between tenants in common and the right which a lease or license given by one confers at common law, but it is based upon the provisions of the statute alone. It was insisted that under the statute the license of *Fox* gave the defendant the right to mine upon and remove the mineral which he had discovered, as against the infant plaintiffs, because the statute secured to him that right. But this we deem an erroneous view, which we cannot sanction. *Fox* conferred no right capable of a successful assertion against the other co-tenants.

In respect to the mineral which has been dug and removed by the defendant from the plaintiffs' premises, the rights of *Fox* have been already determined. He must take his rent in two thirds of such mineral. As to the infant plaintiffs, they are, entitled to one third of such mineral, less one third of the expense of digging it out and removing it from the mine. It is but equitable to charge them with their share of the expense, but they should not be charged with any expense of running the level to their ground. We see no reason for charging them with the costs of the litigation. They had to come into court to vindicate their rights in the property against the unlawful acts of the defendant. We have already said they were entitled to a perpetual injunction restraining the defendant from further working the mine or from removing mineral from their premises. There must be an account taken of the quantity and value of mineral taken from the plaintiffs' land and sold, and also of any unsold which may now be in the level and which came from their land, upon the basis stated in this opinion.

By the Court.— The judgment of the circuit court is reversed, and the cause is remanded with directions to enter a decree in conformity with this opinion.

♦

Jones, Appellant, vs. Jones, imp., etc., Respondent.

March·30 — April 17, 1888.

(1) Appeal to S. C.: Partial reversal: New judgment: Equity. (2) New findings by trial court after remittitur. (3) Lack of findings not ground for reversal. (4) Dower: Allowance of gross sum: Damages for withholding. (5) Costs: Discretion.

1. Where in an equitable action only a portion of the judgment was reversed, a new judgment entered by the trial court is not erroneous because it contains no order as to that part of the prior judgment which was undisturbed, where it is apparent from the record that the new judgment is in substance, though not in form, merely a modifying or additional one.

VOL. 71 — 33

2. It was held by the trial court and, on appeal, by this court that a widow was entitled to recover, as damages for the withholding of dower, one third of the rents and profits of certain land, deducting the amount paid for taxes, insurance, and repairs. The judgment of the trial court did not determine the amount so to be deducted. That judgment was reversed for errors in other particulars, and the cause was remanded with direction to render judgment in accordance with the opinion of this court. *Held*, that on filing the *remittitur* the trial court properly proceeded to take testimony and determine the amount to be so deducted for taxes, insurance, and repairs.

8. If, in an equity case, the judgment is supported by the evidence, the lack of or defects in the findings of fact will not work a reversal.

4. The grantee in a conveyance made by the defendant's husband, just prior to the marriage, in fraud of her dower rights, brought an action to quiet the title and bar the claim for dower. The defendant, by counterclaim, asked to have the conveyance set aside and to recover dower and damages for the withholding thereof. *Held*, that in such action the court might render a money judgment against the plaintiff for damages for the withholding of dower, and might also, with the defendant's consent, allow a gross sum of money in lieu of dower.

5. In equitable actions costs may be allowed or not to any party, in the discretion of the court.

APPEAL from the Circuit Court for *Jefferson* County. The following statement of the case was prepared by Mr. Justice CASSODAY:

May 14, 1874, the plaintiff, *Richard Jones*, became the owner of the undivided one-half of the premises described (except the east six inches), by deed from Peter Bertholf and wife to said *Richard Jones* and Thomas D. Evans, reciting a consideration of $3,800, and the same was recorded. May 14, 1874, *Richard Jones* and Thomas D. Evans gave back to Bertholf a mortgage on all of the premises conveyed by that deed, of $3,000, and the same was recorded. August 25, 1874, the Bank of Watertown conveyed to *Richard Jones* and Evans said six inches, and the same was recorded. July 3, 1875, *Richard Jones* and wife conveyed to Thomas

C. Jones the said undivided one-half of all. said premises
(except said six inches), in consideration of natural love and
affection and by way of advancement, subject to an unpaid
balance of said mortgage of $1,500, which, with the inter-
est thereon from May 14, 1875, the said Thomas C. Jones
thereby assumed and agreed to pay and satisfy, and subject
to all leases of the store and the rooms in the building
thereon already made; and the one-half of the rents reserved in said leases was thereby assigned to Thomas C.
Jones. Said deed was not delivered, but was retained by
said *Richard*, with the understanding that he should continue in possession notwithstanding such deed. November 13, 1877, the said Thomas C. Jones obtained the said
deed, and had the same recorded. November 19, 1877;
Richard Jones and wife deeded the six inches to Thomas C.
Jones, and the same was recorded December. 3, 1877. November 19, 1877, Thomas C. Jones (then unmarried), gave
to *Richard Jones* a mortgage back on all the premises so
conveyed to him, conditioned for the payment of $2,500
within ten years from date, with interest thereon annually
at eight per cent. according to a note described, with
the usual covenants to pay taxes, etc., which mortgage
was recorded December 3, 1877. January 24, 1880, the
Bertholf mortgage was satisfied of record. March 13, 1880,
in the forenoon, Thomas C. Jones (still unmarried), by
warranty deed conveyed all of said lands back to *Richard
Jones*, and delivered the same to him; but it was lost and
never recorded. March 13, 1880, in the evening, and after
the delivery of said last-named deed, Thomas C. Jones
was married to the defendant *Amanda L. Jones*. May 3,
1881, Thomas C. Jones died testate, leaving no children,
but leaving his said wife, *Amanda L. Jones*, him surviving. July 19, 1881, said will was admitted to probate and
Price Lewis was appointed executor thereof, and thereby
the said Thomas C. gave one third of all his property to

said *Amanda L.* in lieu of dower, and the other two thirds to his father, *Richard Jones.* April 20, 1882, the said *Amanda L. Jones* renounced the will, and elected to take under the statutes. Claims to the amount of $7,393.71 were allowed against the estate of Thomas C. Jones; and the allowance to the widow, and expenses incident to allowing said claims, were about $1,000. The estate, exclusive of exemptions and household furniture turned over to the widow, did not exceed in value $3,000. No part of the Bertholf mortgage was ever paid by Thomas C., but was wholly paid by *Richard Jones* before it was so satisfied. Thomas C. Jones never paid any of the principal or interest on the $2,500 mortgage. The value of the premises was $6,000, and the annual rental value $560, and the taxes, insurance, and repairs were paid by *Richard Jones* ever since July 3, 1875.

The facts above stated were, in effect, found before the first appeal. On the appeal from the original judgment, this court, among other things, in effect held that the deed from Thomas C. Jones to *Richard Jones* was made in fraud of the said *Amanda L. Jones'* right of dower in said premises, and that she was entitled to such dower therein notwithstanding said deed, subject only to said $2,500, but free and discharged of the Bertholf mortgage; that the said *Amanda L. Jones* was entitled to one third of the rents and profits of said premises, deducting taxes, insurance, and reasonable cost of necessary repairs, from the time of her answer in this case, August 18, 1882. 64 Wis. 311, 312. That judgment was reversed, and the cause was remanded with direction to render judgment in accordance with the opinion. Upon the *remittitur* being filed, both parties moved for judgment, and thereupon the trial court ordered proofs to be taken of the rents and profits, and of taxes, insurance, and reasonable cost of necessary repairs, and the same were taken accordingly. Thereupon, and on

March 29, 1887, and without any new findings of fact, the
court caused judgment to be entered as of September 21,
1886, to the effect that said lost deed of March 13, 1880,
from Thomas C. Jones to *Richard Jones* be, and the same
was thereby, established as a valid conveyance of the premises in fee-simple, subject, however, to the right of dower of
said *Amanda L. Jones;* that said *Amanda L.* was entitled
to one third of the rents and profits of said premises, after
deducting taxes, insurance, and repairs, from August 18,
1882, to the date of. such judgment; that the said *Amanda
L.* have and recover from the plaintiff $269.92 as and for
said one third of said rents and profits from August 18, 1882,
to September 21, 1886, the same being her damages for the
withholding of her said dower; that the said *Amanda L.*
was entitled to dower in said premises, subject only to the
payment of said $2,500 mortgage, and was entitled to have
the same admeasured and assigned to her in this action by
way of a money recovery; that said *Amanda L.* do have
and recover from the plaintiff the further sum of $828.85
as and for her said dower in said premises, which, together
with said $269.92, made the sum of $1,098.77 as her damages herein; that said *Amanda L.* also recover from the
plaintiff $258.53 for her costs in this action, making her
aggregate recovery $1,357.30; that the same be a lien upon
said premises until fully paid; that she have execution to
enforce the payment thereof; that upon such payment she
be forever barred of any and all right or interest in the said
premises and every part thereof; and that the executor of
the will of said Thomas C. Jones be forever barred of all
right and claim of whatever nature in or to the premises
and every part thereof. From that part of said judgment
favorable to the said *Amanda L. Jones*, and unfavorable to
the plaintiff, he appeals.

For the appellant there were briefs by *I. W. & G. W.
Bird* and *Gregory, Bird & Gregory*, and oral argument by

Mr. G. W. Bird. To the point that where either party objects a gross sum should not be allowed in lieu of dower, they cited *Herbert v. Wren*, 7 Cranch, 370; *Beavers v. Smith*, 11 Ala. 20; *Johnson v. Elliott*, 12 id. 112; *Francis v. Garrard*, 18 id. 794; *Lewis v. James*, 8 Humph. 537.

Harlow Pease, for the respondent, to the point that, with the consent of the widow, the court might properly give a gross sum in lieu of dower, cited 2 Scribner on Dower, ch. 24, pp. 653–697; *Kyle v. Kyle*, 67 N. Y. 400, 404; *Smith v. Jackson*, 2 Edw. Ch. 28, 35, 36; *Hawley v. Bradford*, 9 Paige, 200, 202; *Jennison v. Hapgood*, 10 Pick. 70; *Van Gelder v. Post*, 2 Edw. Ch. 577–9; *Hale v. James*, 6 Johns. Ch. 258; Willard's Eq. Jur. 699; *Campbell v. Erving*, 43 How. Pr. 258; *Mole v. Smith*, 1 Jac. & W. 665, 673; *Taylor v. Bentley*, 3 Redf. Surr. 34; *Hazen v. Thurber*, 4 Johns. Ch. 604–5; *Wood v. Keyes*, 6 Paige, 478; *Wright v. Young*, 6 Wis. 127, 133; *Maccubbin v. Cromwell*, 2 Har. & G. 443, 457; *Dorsey v. Smith*, 7 Har. & J. 345, 366–7; *Goodburn v. Stearns*, 1 Md. Ch. Dec. 420, 440, 441; *Lewis v. James*, 8 Humph. 537; *Bank v. Dunseth*, 10 Ohio, 18, 23; *Unger v. Leiter*, 32 Ohio St. 210, 214; *Matthews v. Duryee*, 45 Barb. 69; *Fulton v. Fulton*, 8 Abb. N. C. 210, 213.

CASSODAY, J.   The learned counsel for the plaintiff is undoubtedly correct in claiming that the judgment on the former appeal was reversed on the sole ground that the widow's dower had been adjudged subject to the $1,500 mortgage as well as the $2,500 mortgage, when it should only have been subject to the latter mortgage. That appeal was by the widow alone, and, although in form from the whole judgment, yet in substance only from that part of the judgment against her. Her counsel merely asked for a modification of the judgment. As indicated, the decision on that appeal only related to her rights under the statutes. Technically, the mandate of the court should in form have limited such reversal to such particular part of the judgment; but it is manifest from the opinion and the *status* of the record at the time that the decision of this court was necessarily confined to such particular part of the judgment. The result is that that part of the judgment adjudging costs to the plaintiff against the executor as such, and payable out of the estate, was not before us nor considered on that appeal, and hence remained as though no such appeal had been taken.

1. Error is now assigned because such costs are omitted from what is termed "an entirely new judgment," and which may fairly be regarded as such in form. But such new judgment recites the first trial, the making and filing of the findings of fact and conclusions of law, the judgment entered thereon, the appeal by the widow, the reversal, and the mandate thereon, and then orders and adjudges as indicated. This is a case in equity; and, in harmony with the old practice in such cases, it would have been competent to add to the original judgment or decree; and, as that part of the original judgment between the plaintiff and the estate remained unreversed, it would seem that nothing was left to the trial court but to modify the judgment as indicated. True, such new judgment does not in form purport to be such further or additional judgment, as it should have done, yet, in view of the *status* of the record, we think it must in substance be so regarded. Thus regarding it, the judgment of the plaintiff against the estate for costs remains as before.

2. Error is assigned because the court adjudged that the widow was entitled to recover, by reason of her dower, as damages for withholding her share of the rents and profits from August 18, 1882, to the entry of the final judgment, September 21, 1886, the sum of $269.92. On the trial it was found, and in the original judgment it was adjudged, that the annual rental value of the premises was $560, and

that the plaintiff had received the rents since July 3, 1875, and had always paid the taxes, insurance, and repairs. It was also found and adjudged in said original judgment, in effect, that in any accounting for rents received by the plaintiff after August 18, 1882, he was entitled to have deducted from the gross receipts of said rents all sums paid for taxes, insurance, and reasonable repairs; but there was no finding or determination as to the amount of such taxes, insurance, or repairs. Since there could be no final determination of the matters in controversy without first ascertaining the amount of such taxes, insurance, and repairs, it is manifest that the original judgment was not a final judgment. This being so, the determination of such amounts was necessarily open for the trial court upon the filing of the *remittitur* on the former appeal. Accordingly the court properly took testimony as to such amounts. True, the court made no findings thereon; but, if the judgment is supported by the evidence, such want of findings is no ground for reversal. *Wilkinson v. Wilkinson,* 59 Wis. 560; *White v. Magann,* 65 Wis. 86; *Pier v. Prouty,* 67 Wis. 223. In support of the contention that the amount so allowed was too large, it is claimed that the plaintiff was entitled to interest at eight per cent. on the $2,500 mortgage from November 19, 1877, to August 18, 1882, as well as since. But we do not think the plaintiff was entitled to such interest during the time he received such rents and profits without being held liable to account therefor,— especially as they were much more annually than such interest. With this view of the question suggested, and without going into details, we must hold that the evidence was sufficient to support the allowance to the widow of $269.92 as damages for withholding dower prior to the final judgment. That she was entitled to a money judgment for that amount there can be no question. The statutes expressly authorize such damages for such withholding. Secs. 2175, 2176, R. S.;

Munger v. Perkins, 62 Wis. 499. Such right to recover damages is not limited to cases in which the husband died seized of the lands, but extends to the alienee of the husband, or one who has become vested of his title by operation of law. *Ibid.* So the mere fact that the husband, prior to his marriage, conveyed to his father, in fraud of the dower rights of this widow, does not take the case out of the operation of the rule stated.

3. This brings us to the question whether it was error to adjudge the widow entitled to have her dower admeasured to her in this action by way of a money recovery, and to fix the amount thereof, in addition to the damages named, at $828.85. The amount cannot be claimed to be objectionable if there was any authority to so fix it. The subject of such authority has elicited much discussion and a contrariety of opinion in the past. We have no disposition to renew the old discussion. It is said by Mr. Story that, " as dower is a strictly legal right, it might seem at first view that the proper remedy belonged to courts of common law. . . . But the result of the various decisions upon this subject is that courts of equity will now entertain a general concurrent jurisdiction with courts of law in the assignment of dower in all cases." 1 Story's Eq. Jur. § 624; Pom. Eq. Jur. §§ 185, 1382. This is especially true where, as in this state, the two jurisdictions are combined in the same court, and the statutes expressly authorize a plaintiff to " unite in the same complaint several causes of action, whether they be such as were formerly denominated legal or equitable, or both " (sec. 2647, R. S.), and to counterclaim a similar cause of action (secs. 2655, 2656). This seems to be the view of courts in other states having similar statutes. *Van Name v. Van Name,* 23 How. Pr. 247; *Brown v. Brown,* 31 How. Pr. 481; *Townsend v. Townsend,* 2 Sandf. 711; *Starry v. Starry,* 21 Iowa, 254; *Thomas v. Thomas,* 35 N. W. Rep. (Iowa), 693. The extent of such jurisdiction, and

whether such right of the widow must be confined to a
third of the net annual use of the property, or, in case it is
converted into money, to such third of the annual income
therefrom, or a definite amount in gross, seems to depend
largely upon the policy of local statutes and the equitable
rights of parties in each particular case.   In this state there
seems to be no statutory impediment to allowing such
amount in gross in a proper case.   As already observed,
the statutes expressly authorize the recovery of a money
judgment for damages for withholding dower.   So, in case
of a forced sale of premises subject to dower in an action of
partition, such right and interest is barred in the premises
and transferred to the proceeds.   Secs. 3102, 3119–3121,
R. S.   The same is true respecting any surplus on foreclosure sale of land, where the widow would otherwise be en-
dowed.   Secs. 2164, 2165; *Hawley v. Bradford*, 9 Paige,
200; *Campbell v. Erving*, 43 How. Pr. 258.   So, where there
is a dower right in lands of infants which have been sold
by proceedings in court, the widow may have a gross sum
in lieu of such dower.   Sec. 3514, R. S.   The same is true
where lands subject to such dower right are sold for the
payment of debts.   Sec. 3885, R. S.

The facts in the record present a case peculiarly justify-
ing a broad exercise of equitable jurisdiction.   The premises consist of an undivided one-half of a building or block.
Manifestly, there can be no actual partition, or setting off
a portion of the premises for the use of the widow.   The
only way of making a partition, therefore, would be by a
forced sale of the premises and an equitable distribution of
the proceeds.   The husband did not die seized of the land.
Neither the mortgage nor the deed was given by him to
the plaintiff during coverture.   Both were made before
marriage.   The widow's right of dower was not a right
apparent at law upon the death of the husband.   It was
only established by an adjudication upon evidence *aliunde*

the deed, showing that it was made on the eve of marriage and as a fraud upon her rights as such proposed wife. Having been thus established in equity at the suit of such fraudulent grantee to extinguish her right as a cloud upon the title, it would seem peculiarly fitting that a complete determination of the rights of all the parties should be made in the same action, unless forbidden by some settled rule of law. As observed, there seems to be no statutory impediment. On the contrary, it seems to be the general policy of the statutes cited, not only to allow a money judgment by way of damages for withholding dower, but, on the distribution of estates subject to dower, to allow, with her consent, a gross sum in lieu of dower. The rules applicable to the trial court contemplate that whenever a party, as tenant in dower, is entitled to the interest or income of any sum, she may accept a gross sum in lieu of such annual interest or income for life, and that the same shall be estimated according to the then value of an annuity of six per cent., as shown by the annuity tables therein mentioned. Circuit Court Rule XXXII. That a widow entitled to dower may in equity have a gross sum in lieu of dower, where the property has been actually sold and converted into money, would seem to be elementary. 1 Washb. Real. Prop. marg. pp. 243–250, subd. 25–27; 3 Pom. Eq. Jur. §§ 1382, 1383; 2 Scrib. Dower, ch. 24, pp. 653–697, and cases there cited, as well as those in briefs of counsel. The same would seem to be true where the property is held in trust, and sold by the trustee, who bids in the property for his own benefit, and the widow acquiesces in such purchase. *Ibid.* It is said, in effect, in these authorities, that in certain cases a gross sum may be accepted and allowed as compensation in lieu of dower, without any sale being made. In the case at bar the plaintiff controverted the defendant's right of dower, and insisted that he had the absolute title to the premises by virtue of the deed given in fraud of her rights.   This being so, he certainly stands in no more favorable position in equity than he would in respect to the fund had the premises been actually sold and converted into money.   In other words, the plaintiff, having wrongfully withheld the widow's dower, under the peculiar circumstances stated, is, as a participant in such fraud, estopped from now disclaiming his acquisition of such absolute title, and responding in damages for the value of such dower in gross thus converted.

4. In equitable actions, costs may be allowed or not to any party, in the discretion of the court· and, when such discretion has not been abused by the trial court, its judgment as to costs will not be disturbed. *Portz v. Schantz,* 70 Wis. 497.   We cannot say there was any abuse in allowing costs to the widow.   On the contrary, we think it was eminently just.

By the Court.— The judgment of the circuit court is affirmed.

ROUNDY and others, Appellants vs. CONVERSE and another, Garnishee, etc., Respondents.

March 31 — April 17, 1888.

DEBTOR AND CREDITOR. *(1) Chattel mortgage: Sales by mortgagor: After-acquired property. (2) Exemptions: Proceeds of sale of stock in trade.*

1. The fact that a chattel mortgage authorizes the mortgagor to sell the goods and replace them with others to be paid for out of the proceeds of such sales, does not affect the validity of the security, there being no agreement or understanding that he may dispose of the proceeds of the sales for his own use and benefit. But the attempt to extend the security of the mortgage over the after-acquired goods is probably unavailing, except, perhaps, as a license to seize such goods.

2. The exemption of a debtor's stock in trade not exceeding $200 in value, under subd. 8, sec. 2982, R. S., does not extend to the proceeds of a sale thereof. Thus, a mortgagor who made no reservation of exemptions in a mortgage of his stock in trade, and claimed none when the property was sold under the mortgage, cannot claim any exemption in the balance of the proceeds of such sale remaining in the hands of the mortgagee after payment of the mortgage debt.

APPEAL from the Circuit Court for *Rock* County.

For some time previous to April, 1886, down to March, 1887, the defendant *C. N. Converse* was carrying on business as a merchant at Milton, in Rock county. Previous to the date first above mentioned, one James Pierce, who was the administrator of the estate of one G. W. Hamilton (the deceased son of the garnishee defendant, *Hannah B. Hamilton*), loaned to *Converse* $1,100 of the moneys of the estate of his intestate. *Mrs. Hamilton* was her deceased son's sole heir. *Converse* executed his note to Pierce for the loan, also a chattel mortgage, to secure it, on his stock of goods. The loan was made at the request of *Mrs. Hamilton*. The estate was duly settled in the county court about the middle of April, 1886, and the mortgage and note given for the loan were transferred to *Mrs. Hamilton*. A daughter of the latter, Mrs. Emma H. Cary, was the general agent of her mother, and had the whole charge and management of her business, *Mrs. Hamilton* being quite aged.

On December 23, 1886, *Converse* executed to *Mrs. Hamilton* a new note for the same loan, secured by a new mortgage of that date executed to her by him on his stock of goods, and thereupon she surrendered to him the original note and mortgage executed to Pierce. The mortgage last executed was duly filed in the proper clerk's office. The mortgaged property is described therein as follows: "All my stock of goods, including the entire stock of goods in the store kept by me in the Hamilton store in Milton, including fixtures in store, and goods in store now, and those purchased to replace any which may be sold out." The mortgage also contains the usual clause authorizing the mortgagee to take possession of the mortgaged property at any time she may deem herself insecure, and to sell the same.

On March 3, 1887, Mrs. Cary was informed that an attachment against *Converse* had been, or was about to be, levied upon his stock of goods, and she thereupon went to the store of *Converse*, and found there a deputy-sheriff with such writ of attachment, who was about to close the store. She asserted the right of *Mrs. Hamilton* to the goods by virtue of the mortgage, and the deputy-sheriff and *Converse* yielded to her the possession of the store and goods. Thereupon all further proceedings under the attachment ceased, and the writ was never returned. The plaintiffs (who were such attaching creditors) afterwards commenced this garnishee proceeding against *Mrs. Hamilton*.

After giving due notice, as required by the mortgage, Mrs. Cary, for and on behalf of her mother, sold the stock of goods for a little more than $1,600.

Before this action was commenced, garnishee process was served upon *Mrs. Hamilton* in an action brought by another creditor against *Converse*, in which action she was charged, as a garnishee, to the amount of $160.88 by the judgment of the court.

The plaintiffs having recovered judgment against *Converse*, the present action came on for trial July 1, 1887, and was then tried. At this time the defendant *Converse* first appeared, and obtained leave of the court to answer, claiming exemptions of $200 stock in trade, and $200 worth of provisions for his family for one year. The trial resulted in quite voluminous findings of fact, substantially in accordance with the facts above stated. The court allowed *Converse* $200 for his exemptions, and allowed *Mrs. Hamilton*

$1,150.32 on account of her unpaid demand against *Converse*, and the $160.88 with which she had been charged in the other garnishee suit. The mortgage was held to be a valid security. The balance of the proceeds of the sale, being $78.10, *Mrs. Hamilton* was adjudged to pay to the plaintiffs, together with $47.10, the costs and disbursements of the action,— amounting in all to $125.25. The plaintiffs appeal from the judgment.

For the appellants there was a brief by *Fethers, Jeffris & Smith,* and oral argument by *Mr. M. G. Jeffris.* To the point that the mortgage from *Converse* to *Mrs. Hamilton* was void as against the creditors of *Converse,* they cited *Anderson v. Patterson,* 64 Wis. 557; *Wilson v. Voight,* 13 Pac. Rep. (Col.), 726; *Chynoweth v. Tenney,* 10 Wis. 397; *Single v. Phelps,* 20 id. 398; *Case v. Fish,* 58 id. 56.

For the respondent *Hannah B. Hamilton* there was a brief by *Winans & Hyzer,* and oral argument by *Mr. E. M. Hyzer.*

LYON, J. Two questions were litigated on the trial. These are, (1) Is the mortgage of December 23, 1886, a valid security? and, if so, (2) Should *Converse* have been allowed any exemptions?

1. There is nothing upon the face of the mortgage in question to impeach its validity, although the fair inference from its terms is that the mortgagor was authorized to sell the goods and replace them with others to be paid for out of the proceeds of such sales. Probably the attempt to extend the security of the mortgage over after-acquired goods was unavailing, except, perhaps, as a license to seize such goods. This clause does not affect the validity of the security. Such is the purport and effect of the opinion by RYAN, C. J., in *Hunter v. Bosworth,* 43 Wis. 583, and of the cases there cited.

A persistent effort was made upon the trial to show that,

at the time of the execution of the mortgage, there was
some agreement or understanding between the parties
thereto that the mortgagor might dispose of the proceeds
of sales of the mortgaged property for his own use and
benefit, thus bringing the case within the rule of *Anderson
v. Patterson*, 64 Wis. 557. A careful examination of the
testimony satisfies us that the plaintiffs failed to establish
this proposition, and failed also, we think, to show that the
mortgage was tainted with fraud. The circuit court so
held, thus establishing the validity of the mortgage. The
ruling cannot be disturbed. We hold, therefore, that the
mortgage was a valid security.

2. The ruling of the circuit court allowing *Converse* $200
out of the proceeds of the sale of the mortgaged property,
as and for his exemptions, cannot be upheld. He made no
reservation of exemptions in his mortgage to *Mrs. Hamilton*, and claimed none when she sold the property. Conceding that he was entitled to exemptions had he claimed
the same while the property remained in the hands of
Mrs. Hamilton (which is, to say the least, quite doubtful),
he certainly lost all right thereto after the property was
sold, and the proceeds thereof in the hands of *Mrs. Hamilton* attached by the plaintiffs. The exemption is of the
specific property enumerated in the statute, that is to say,
of $200 worth of the goods constituting the stock in trade,
and does not extend to the proceeds thereof. R. S. sec. 2982,
subd. 8. In this respect the case is unlike one which involves the proceeds of money arising from insurance upon
exempt property destroyed by fire (subd. 17), or money
arising from the sale of a homestead (sec. 2983). Such
moneys are specially exempted by the statutes. We are
aware of no provision of law which extends the exemption
of stock in trade to the proceeds of such stock realized upon
a sale thereof. It was error, therefore, to allow any exemptions to *Converse* out of the moneys in the hands of

Mrs. Hamilton. The result is that the plaintiffs' judgment against the garnishee should be increased $200.

It appeared that *Mrs. Hamilton* took, under the mortgage, goods of the value of $133 not covered by it. The circumstance is immaterial, because the plaintiffs recover of *Mrs. Hamilton* more than the value of such goods.

By the Court.— The judgment is reversed, and the cause remanded with directions to the circuit court to render judgment for the plaintiffs in accordance with this opinion.

NORWEGIAN PLOW COMPANY, Respondent, vs. HANTHORN, Appellant.

March 31 — April 17, 1888.

SALE OF CHATTELS: STATUTE OF FRAUDS: EVIDENCE. *(1) Payment: Credit on debt. (2) Delivery: Receipt. (3) Cross-examination: Re-examination. (4-8) Debtor and creditor: Fraudulent conveyance: Evidence: Conversion by sheriff: Demand: Instructions to jury.*

1. Where goods are sold or transferred in part payment of a debt due from the vendor to the vendee, and the latter credits the value thereof upon the account, this is such a payment for the goods as will take the sale out of the statute of frauds (sec. 2308, R. S.).

2. *It would seem* that although goods sold are left in the possession of the vendor, if he gives a written receipt acknowledging that he holds them subject to the order of the vendee, this is a sufficient delivery and acceptance to take the sale out of the statute.

3. A witness for the plaintiff who has testified on cross-examination that he had seen a credit on the plaintiff's books, may be asked on re-examination what was the date of such credit.

4. The question being whether a transfer of goods from L. to the plaintiff was fraudulent as to other creditors of L., evidence of the consideration L. had paid to his former partner for the latter's interest in the goods is irrelevant, in the absence of evidence connecting the plaintiff with that transaction or showing his knowledge of its particulars.

5. In an action against a sheriff for the conversion of plaintiff's goods which had been seized and sold by defendant's deputy as the property of a third person in whose possession they were found, an instruction that if the officer levied upon and sold the property in good faith the plaintiff cannot recover unless, before the sale, he demanded the goods from the officer, is *held* to have been properly refused, the levying officer not being the defendant, upon whom a demand was made, and the evidence not showing that the goods in question were so mingled with those of said third person as not to be readily separated. *Smith v. Welch,* 10 Wis. 91, distinguished.

6. The court having, at the request of the defendant and again in the general charge, instructed the jury that if the sale in question was, with the knowledge of the vendee, made with intent to hinder or delay or defraud the creditors of the vendor it was void, the omission of the words "hinder or delay," in calling attention to it again, and the use of the expression "his creditors generally," without adding "or any of them," are *held* not to have been misleading.

[7. *Quære,* whether a creditor who in good faith takes the property of his debtor in payment or part payment of an honest debt can be held to have committed a fraud upon other creditors because he may know or believe that the debtor is paying his debt to avoid paying other creditors,— especially where the creditor only receives goods which he has sold the debtor, and the debt is the purchase price of such goods.]

8. The question being as to the validity of a sale of goods which were left in the possession of the vendor, the court called attention to the fact that they were so left, and, after reading sec. 2310, R. S., instructed the jury that under that section the presumption was that the sale was fraudulent, but that if the vendee paid full value for the goods that fact would rebut the presumption of fraud. *Held,* that when taken in connection with the other instructions given this instruction was not erroneous as giving the jury to understand that proof of a full consideration paid would conclusively rebut all the evidence of fraud in the case.

APPEAL from the Circuit Court for *Rock* County.

The case is sufficiently stated in the opinion.

For the appellant there was a brief by *Fethers, Jeffris & Smith,* and oral argument by *Mr. M. G. Jeffris.*

For the respondent there was a brief by *Dunwiddie & Goldin,* and oral argument by *Mr. B. F. Dunwiddie.*

TAYLOR, J.   The respondent commenced this action in the municipal court of Rock county to recover the value of certain agricultural implements alleged to belong to the respondent company, which had been taken and converted by the defendant.   The answer alleges that the defendant is the sheriff of Rock county, and that he took said property by virtue of an execution which, as such sheriff, he held against W. A. Lints and Byron Atwood; that the property was, at the, time of the taking of the same, the property of said Lints & Atwood, and if any transfer of said property had been made to the respondent by Lints & Atwood, or either of them, such transfer had been made with intent to hinder and delay the creditors of said Lints & Atwood, to the knowledge of said respondent, and that said company colluded with said Lints & Atwood in their fraud.   After a trial in the municipal court, the case was appealed to the circuit court of Rock county, where the case was again tried by the court and a jury, and a verdict rendered in favor of the plaintiff and respondent for the value of the property.   From the judgment entered on such verdict an appeal was taken to this court.

On the trial, at the close of the plaintiff's evidence, the defendant moved for a nonsuit, which was denied, and exceptions taken.   The ruling of the circuit judge on this motion is alleged as error.   It is also alleged that the court erred in the admission and rejection of evidence, and in the instructions given to the jury.   The material facts as shown on the trial were as follows:

The respondent company had sold the property in question to the firm of Lints & Atwood on credit.   Afterwards the firm of Lints & Atwood was dissolved, and the property of the firm was transferred to said Lints, he assuming the debts of the firm.   After the dissolution of the firm, and on the 17th day of August, 1886, the general agent of the respondent called upon Mr. Lints for payment or settle-

ment of his account with the company. The firm of
Lints & Atwood was then indebted to the respondent in
the sum of $445.85 for goods sold and delivered to them.
On said 17th day of August, Lints had on hand and unsold of said goods, purchased of the respondent, which
amounted in value, at the selling price to the firm, to the
sum of $225.56. Mr. Lints, being unable to pay the debt
due the company, proposed to the agent that he would return to the company their goods then on hand in part payment of the debt due the company. This offer was finally
agreed to by the agent of the company. The agent then
credited the amount on the account against Lints & Atwood
of the value of said goods, and immediately informed the
company of what he had done, and the company gave Lints
& Atwood the same credit on the books of the company,
and the agent at the same time delivered the account with
the credit given thereon to the said Lints. At the same
time Lints gave the company the following receipt for the
goods:

"Received of the *Norwegian Plow Company*, of Dubuque,
Iowa [here follows a particular description of the prop-
erty]; all having been manufactured by the said *Norwegian
Plow Company;* the aggregate net value of all said property being $202.56. Said property to be held by the said
W. A. Lints, free of storage costs, and subject always to the
order and complete control of said *Norwegian Plow Company.*   W. A. LINTS.
"*Dated at Edgerton, Wis. August 17, 1886.*"

The agent of the company explained on the stand, as a
witness, that the amount stated in the receipt was, by a
mistake in adding up the value of the different articles, less
by $23 and some cents than the real value, and that he at
once corrected the credit to Lints, and informed the company, which also corrected the credit on its books. The
sheriff seized the property on the execution against Lints &

Atwood, while the same was still in the warehouse of Lints, on the 20th day of August, 1886.

There was a claim made on the part of the appellant that this transaction between Lints and the agent of the company was not a *bona fide* transaction, but was made for the purpose of hindering, delaying, and defrauding the other creditors of said Lints & Atwood. The question of the *bona fides* of the transaction was submitted to the jury, and found in favor of the plaintiff.

Upon the argument in this court, the learned counsel for the appellant insist that the circuit court should have granted the nonsuit on their motion, because the evidence of the repurchase of the goods by the company from Lints did not show a valid purchase in the law; that there was no sufficient written memorandum of the sale, and no payment for the goods or delivery and acceptance of the same, sufficient to make a valid sale under sec. 2308, R. S. It seems to us very clear that there was sufficient evidence in the case to show that these goods were transferred by Lints to the plow company, and accepted by the company in part payment of its debt against Lints & Atwood. The general agent of the company testified that such was the fact; that he at once gave credit for the value of the goods on their account, and that the company gave credit on its books for the value of the goods on the 19th of August. Giving such credit, if made in good faith, is as much a payment for them as though the money had been paid over for them. *Gleason v. Day,* 9 Wis. 498; *Dow v. Worthen,* 37 Vt. 108, 113; *Walker v. Nussey,* 16 Mees. & W. 302; *Sharp v. Carroll,* 66 Wis. 62, 66; *Matthiessen v. McMahon's Adm'r,* 38 N. J. Law, 536; *Artcher v. Zeh,* 5 Hill, 200; *Ely v. Ormsby,* 12 Barb. 570; *Brabin v. Hyde,* 32 N. Y. 519; *Teed v. Teed,* 44 Barb. 96; *Mattice v. Allen,* 3 Keyes, 492; *Walrath v. Richie,* 5 Lans. 362; Benj. on Sales, §§ 192, 194. The general agent of the company testified that, at the time of the resale of the property to the company by Lints, he credited the amount upon the account of Lints & Atwood, and delivered to him the account with the credit in writing thereon. It is true, it is claimed by the defendant that this was not the fact; but that was a question of fact, and not of law. The fact that the company immediately gave credit to Lints & Atwood on its books shows sufficiently that the agent was authorized to give the credit as he testified he had. Under the authority of the cases cited, this credit was a payment of the purchase price within the meaning of the statute. It would seem that the giving of a written receipt for the goods by Lints, acknowledging that he held the goods subject to the order of the company, and the acceptance of such receipt by the company, was a sufficient delivery and acceptance of them by the company to take the case out of the statute. Benj. on Sales, § 182, and cases cited in the notes to said section; *Janvrin v. Maxwell*, 23 Wis. 51; *Smith v. Bouck*, 33 Wis. 33; *Marvin v. Wallace*, 37 Eng. L. & Eq. 6. The motion for a nonsuit was therefore properly denied.

It is alleged as error that the court permitted the agent of the company to testify that the credit for the goods was given on the plaintiff's books on the 19th of August. This evidence that a credit was given by the company on its books was drawn out on a re-examination of the witness, and after he had testified upon the cross-examination by the defendant that he had seen the credit on the plaintiff's books. The witness was asked by the plaintiff what was the date of the credit on said books. In this state of the case it was not error to permit the plaintiff to ask what was the date of the credit. As original evidence for the plaintiff it was probably inadmissible; but as a re-examination of the witness as to new matter drawn out on cross-examination it was not error to admit the answer.

The rejection of evidence as to the consideration that

Lints paid his partner when he bought him out was clearly proper, as the evidence offered had no tendency to show that the sale to the plaintiff company was fraudulent. There is no evidence that the plaintiff had any connection with that sale, or that it or its agent knew anything about the particulars of that sale, either at the time of the sale or afterwards.

It is alleged as error that the court refused to instruct the jury as follows: "If you believe, from the evidence in the case, that the officer levied on and sold the goods in question in good faith, he having found them in the possession of Lints and believing that they belonged to him, then you must also find that before the sale a demand for the goods was made upon him by a person representing the plaintiff, and that the officer knew that said person represented the' plaintiff, or was so informed by said person, or the plaintiff cannot recover." This instruction was properly rejected, for at least two good reasons: (1) The officer who levied on the goods in this case was not the defendant in this action, and the proof shows that a demand was made upon the defendant; (2) the evidence does not show that the plaintiff's goods were so mingled with the goods of the defendants in the execution under which the seizure was made that they could not be readily separated from the goods of such defendants. The evidence does not bring the case within the rule laid down by this court in *Smith v. Welch*, 10 Wis. 91.

The appellant insists that the court erred in instructing the jury as follows: "Did Lints by that transfer intend to defraud his creditors generally, and did Burdick, the plaintiff's agent, have knowledge of that intent? If he did, the plaintiff is not entitled to recover; so that is the real question for you to determine." It is urged that because the court did not insert in the charge the words, "or hinder or delay his creditors," and because it did not also state, "his creditors generally" "or any of them," it was erroneous. The court had already, at the request of the defendant, given such instruction, and had again repeated it in his general instructions, and in calling the attention of the jury to this part of the case a third time we do not think the jury could have been misled by what is claimed as an omission in the instruction. The instructions were fully as favorable to the defendant as was justifiable. It is quite doubtful whether a creditor who in good faith takes the property of his debtor in payment or in part payment of an honest debt can be held to have committed a fraud upon the other creditors, because he may know or believe that the debtor is paying his debt to avoid paying some other creditor or creditors, and more especially when the creditor receives only goods which he has sold the debtor, and his debt is the purchase price of such goods. A creditor in procuring pay from his insolvent or embarrassed debtor stands in a different relation to such debtor than a stranger who purchases the goods of such debtor knowing his embarrassment and his desire to avoid the payment of his creditors. See *Gage v. Chesebro*, 49 Wis. 486, 491.

The learned circuit judge made the following statement to the jury: "It is conceded that these goods were in the warehouse of Lints or under the control of Lints, and that they remained there after this sale where they had been before, and that calls in review this statute, which I will now read." The learned judge then read sec. 2310, R. S., and then continued: "These goods being left in the warehouse the same as they were before, under the control of Mr. Lints, the presumption, under this statute I have just read, is that the retransfer of those goods was fraudulent, and it was incumbent upon the plaintiff, therefore, to show that he took them in good faith. If you shall believe that he paid the full value for these goods, even although he left them there, that would rebut the presumption of fraud; so that if he had not paid the full value, but had agreed to, and there was some sufficient reason for his leaving them there, that would rebut the presumption of fraud." This the learned counsel for the appellant claims was an erroneous instruction as to the effect of the statute quoted upon the transaction. It is said that under this instruction the jury must have understood the court to mean that, if the plaintiff had given full value for the property in question, then all evidence of fraud in the case was conclusively rebutted and the plaintiff was entitled to recover. This instruction, taken in connection with the other instructions given by the court, could not have been so understood by the jury. The meaning of the instruction is simply that the legal presumption of fraud arising out of the mere fact that the property was left in the possession of the vendor is rebutted by proof of a full consideration paid for the same, and not that it rebutted all other evidence of fraud which may have been proven in the case. So understanding the instruction, it was not erroneous. See *Williams v. Porter*, 41 Wis. 422, 429; *Bullis v. Borden*, 21 Wis. 137; *Livingston v. Littell*, 15 Wis. 222; *Sargeant v. Solberg*, 22 Wis. 132; *James v. Van Duyn*, 45 Wis. 512, 518; *Semmens v. Walters*, 55 Wis. 675, 684; *Kalk v. Fielding*, 50 Wis. 339, 346, 347; Benj. on Sales, § 740, and notes. See especially the cases cited from Massachusetts: *Ingalls v. Herrick*, 108 Mass. 351; *Thorndike v. Bath*, 114 Mass. 116; *Hobbs v. Carr*, 127 Mass. 532; *Russell v. O'Brien*, 127 Mass. 349, and numerous other cases. In view of all the evidence in this case, we think there was no error in the instruction above quoted. The evidence as a whole would hardly justify a verdict different from the one rendered by the jury.

The case appears to have been fairly tried, and the evidence fully sustains the judgment.

By the Court.— The judgment of the circuit court is affirmed.

See note to this case in 37 N. W. Rep. 830.— REP.

SHEKEY, Appellant, vs. ELDREDGE and others, Respondents.

March 31 — April 17, 1888.

(1) Evidence: Number of witnesses. (2) Positive and negative testimony. (3) Appeal: Question of fact: Credibility of witnesses.

1. The rule that the majority of equally credible witnesses ought to prevail is not recognized in this state.
2. Where one witness testifies that a certain agreement was made and another testifies as positively, and with the same means of knowl-edge, that it was not made, the rule that positive testimony should prevail over that which is negative does not apply.
3. The question in this case, whether a certain agreement was or was not made, depending mainly upon the credibility of the witnesses, this court declines to disturb the finding of the trial court.

APPEAL from the Circuit Court for *Rock* County.

Action to restrain the collection of a judgment in favor of the defendants *Eldredge* and *Radcliffe*, against Margaret and Owen McDermott, claimed to be a lien upon the plaint-iff's homestead, and to have such judgment declared to be void and of no effect. The facts are stated in the opinion. The plaintiff appeals from a judgment in favor of the defendants.

For the appellant there was a brief signed by *Dunwiddie & Goldin*, and oral argument by *B. F. Dunwiddie* and *Geo. W. Bird.* To the point that the affirmative testimony of even one credible witness to a fact is entitled to more weight than that of several who testify negatively, they cited *Ralph v. C. & N. W. R. Co.* 32 Wis. 177; *Cook v. Racine*, 49 id. 243; *Pennoyer v. Allen*, 56 id. 502; *Kelley v. Schupp*, 60 id. 76; *Draper v. Baker*, 61 id. 450; *Bohan v. M., L. S. & W. R. Co.* id. 391; *Hinton v. Cream City R. Co.* 65 id. 323.

Joseph B. Doe, Jr., for the respondents.

ORTON, J. The history of this case appears to be this: The plaintiff purchased the premises at an administrator's sale as the property of the estate of Margaret McDermott, deceased, and has improved the same, and now occupies it as his homestead.   In the life-time of said Margaret McDermott, there had been a judgment rendered against her and her husband, Owen McDermott, before a justice of the peace, in favor of the defendants *D. H. Edredge* and *W. J. Radcliffe*, by default; and the defendants in said judgment had taken certain steps, by giving notice, filing the necessary affidavit, and paying the fees or costs, to appeal the case to the circuit court, but the case had not been transmitted to the circuit court, and it has so remained.   The plaintiffs in said judgment filed a transcript of the same, and docketed it in the circuit court, and issued an execution thereon, and the sheriff had levied the same upon said premises and threatened to sell the same.   The proceedings are sought to be enjoined, and said judgment declared void and of no effect, on the following grounds, as stated in the complaint: The attorney of the said plaintiffs in the action before the justice agreed with the attorney of said Margaret McDermott, who had taken such steps to take an appeal from said judgment, that if the said Margaret McDermott would discontinue the appeal so taken and not prosecute the same any further, he would pay the costs and fees so paid to the justice on taking said appeal, and would release the judgment against the said Margaret McDermott so filed and docketed in the circuit court, and he did so reimburse said costs.   The circuit court found that no such agreement of the counsel of the parties had ever been made, and dissolved the preliminary injunction, dismissed the complaint, and allowed the defendants to issue an *alias* execution on the judgment so docketed in the circuit court. The only evidence on the question whether such an agreement was made consisted of the testimony of the two attorneys who were alleged to have made it, and that of another attorney at law, together with some supposed cor-

roborating circumstances. Some exceptions were taken by
the plaintiff's counsel to the rejection of what was claimed
to be the evidence of other corroborating facts. But the
case was tried by the court without a jury, and such exceptions are of no avail. Such evidence, if admissible, will
be considered by this court the same as if allowed by the
court below in passing upon the question of fact.

The two attorneys who are alleged to have made such an
agreement testified directly in opposition to each other;
one asserting that such an agreement was made, and the
other asserting with equal positiveness that no such agreement was ever made and that the costs of the appeal had
never been reimbursed. The testimony of the other attorney at law was, substantially, that he had occasion to examine the title of said premises, and found this judgment
an incumbrance thereon, and that he called upon the attorney for the plaintiff in the said justice's suit, and upon the
justice; and, on inquiry of them, " he learned from both of
them that the suit had been discontinued and the judgment
discharged and would be canceled of record," and that he
so informed the plaintiff in this suit. This evidence is also
denied most positively by the attorney of the plaintiffs in
the case before the justice. The justice has no reliable
recollection of the appeal or of this interview with the
other attorney at law. This court is asked to reverse the
judgment mainly on the question of the credibility of these
witnesses. It is claimed by the appellant's counsel that
there are at least two witnesses against one as to the main
fact. This is not so. The fact testified to by the other attorney at law is an independent fact, not testified to by the
attorney of the defendant in the judgment. There are two
facts, one of which was the making of the agreement, and
the other was what the other attorney at law learned from
the attorney of the plaintiffs in the judgment. There is
only one witness against one as to each fact. But the rule

that the majority of equally credible witnesses ought to prevail is not recognized in this state. *Bierbach v. Goodyear Rubber Co.* 54 Wis. 208.

It is claimed, further, by the learned counsel, that the testimony of one of the said attorneys is *positive* or affirmative, and that of the other is *negative,* and that the positive or affirmative evidence ought to prevail. This is not so in the sense that is the reason of the rule. One witness testified that such an agreement was made, and the other testified as *positively,* and with the same means of knowledge, that such an agreement was not made. This kind of testimony is not within the rule invoked by the learned counsel. *Elkins v. Kenyon,* 34 Wis. 93; *Sobey v. Thomas,* 39 Wis. 317.

It is nearly a universal rule that this court will not reverse the finding of a court or verdict of a jury on the mere credibility of witnesses or conflict of evidence. The trial court is in much better situation to apply the usual tests of credibility. It sees the witnesses, hears them testify, and observes their manner of testifying and appearance on the witness stand, and in fact knows more of them every way. We do not think the corroborating evidence on either side, received or offered, throws much weight into the scales, or at least makes any difference in this case as to the application of the usual rule. The court below decided this question of credibility for reasons of its own. If this court should decide the question either way, it would be more or less arbitrary and without reasons. We shall decline to decide the question one way or the other, but leave it with the trial court, where it more properly belongs. All we can say is that there is no such clear preponderance of the evidence against the finding of the court as would justify our interference with it.

By the Court.— The judgment of the circuit court is affirmed.

PICKETT, Appellant, vs. NELSON, Respondent.

March 31 — April 17, 1888.

Boundaries: Agreement: Estoppel.

Where, a boundary line being in dispute or uncertain or unascertained, the adjoining owners locate a line with the obvious intention of making it the permanent line between them, and the same is acquiesced in for a long time and recognized by permanent improvements, such location of the line is binding upon the parties and those claiming under them, without any formal agreement.

APPEAL from the Circuit Court for *Green* County.

The following statement of the case was prepared by Mr. Justice CASSODAY:

This is an action for damages for breaking and entering the plaintiff's close, described as seventy-four acres, on or about May 1, 1885. The answer is a general denial. The court charged the jury, in effect, that the seventy-four acres described was off from the west side of fractional lots 1, 5, 6, and 8, in section 6 described, and all lying on the east side of the line running north and south through the center of the section; that both parties claimed title to the *locus in quo* under Hanson Irion; that it appeared from the undisputed evidence that Irion went into possession of those lots under a deed from Erastus Corning in November, 1863; that they contained 174.86 acres; that while Irion was in possession, and on November 29, 1867, he entered into a contract in writing with Wemple to sell him the same premises for $2,500; that Wemple went into possession under that contract, and remained in such possession until in 1869, when, under an agreement between him and Irion, he, by a deed of quitclaim, released all his right, title, and interest in the premises under such contract to Irion; that in the fall of 1868 the plaintiff, *Pickett,* went into possession of other fractional lots, 2, 3, 4, 9, and 11, in the same section, and all lying on the west side of the said north and south line running through the center of the section, under a contract of purchase, and remained in such possession since; that the evidence tended to show that the plaintiff had fulfilled such contract and become the absolute owner of said lots 2, 3, 4, 9, and 11 in 1872; that the undisputed evidence showed that November 8, 1875, Irion sold to Edward Whitehead the said 174.86 acres of land, and January 10, 1879, Edward Whitehead conveyed to Turner Whitehead the said seventy-four acres off the west side thereof; that November 23, 1881, Turner Whitehead conveyed the same seventy-four acres to the plaintiff; that August 6, 1885, Joseph W. Whitehead, who had then become the owner of all of said 174.86 acres except said seventy-four acres, conveyed the same to the defendant, *Nelson*, by deed, stating that the land therein conveyed contained 100 acres *more or less;* that the real contention between the parties was as to the location of the north and south section line; that the plaintiff claimed it to be seventeen rods further east than the defendant admitted it to be; that the plaintiff claimed that in 1868 he and Wemple and Irion made a parol agreement under which they had a survey made, and as a part of it the quarter section line was located, and that they made their fences on the line thus established, and that the plaintiff had maintained the same on his part until the defendant became such owner. From the judgment entered on the verdict in favor of the defendant, the plaintiff appeals.

For the appellant there was a brief by *B. Dunwiddie,* and oral argument by *B. F. Dunwiddie* and *B. Dunwiddie.* For the respondent there was a brief by *A. S. Douglas* and *Orton & Osborn,* and oral argument by *Mr. P. A. Orton.*

CASSODAY, J. The record is not certified to contain all the evidence. This being so, the facts stated above, and taken from the charge, must be treated as verities. At the time of the alleged trespass, the parties to this action were, respectively, the owners of adjoining farms. There was a dispute as to the north and south line between such farms. The plaintiff owned the farm on the west side of the line, and the defendant the farm on the east side of the line. The claims of the respective parties as to the location of such line at the north end differed some seventeen rods. The Wemple contract with Irion was made November 29, 1867, and called for 174 acres, more or less, and was all on the east side of the line running north and south through the center of the section. Wemple appears to have made some payment on that contract. That contract was surrendered by quitclaim deed from Wemple to Irion, August 9, 1869, in consideration of $200 paid by the latter. There was evidence tending to prove that, in the spring or summer of 1868, the parties all being ignorant as to the true location of the north and south line running through the center of the section, *Pickett* and Wemple, with the knowledge and consent of Irion, then owning the legal title subject to such contract, employed a surveyor by the name of West to establish such line for the purpose of building a partition fence thereon; that such surveyor did establish such line with the assistance of *Pickett*, Wemple, and Irion, the latter carrying the chain; that Wemple and *Pickett* thereupon respectively built portions of such partition fence upon the line so established; that upon the south half of such established line, and after Wemple had so surrendered, a public highway was laid out, and *Pickett* and Irion built road fences on their respective sides of such highway; that subsequently, and in the spring of 1871, Irion and *Pickett* built about ninety rods of such partition fence upon such established line north of such highway, each building one half, and which for several years they respectively maintained. November 23, 1881, the plaintiff obtained the title to the seventy-four acres off the west side of said fractional lots 1,

5, 6, and 8. The real controversy was whether the east line of the plaintiff's land prior to such purchase, or, which is the same thing, the west line of the seventy-four acres thus purchased, was the one so located by West, or a line some seventeen rods west of it at the north end, and coming much nearer to it at the south end, and which appears to have been run by Dodge and Stuntz. Of course, the finding of the one or the other to be the true line would make a corresponding difference in the location of the east line of the seventy-four acres so purchased, which is the partition line here in dispute.

These statements of fact are sufficient to appreciate the exceptions to certain instructions to the jury. At the request of the defendant, the jury were, in effect, told that if they were satisfied from the evidence that the survey made by Dodge and Stuntz correctly established the east line of the plaintiff's land according to the government survey, independent of all *agreements* between the parties, then their verdict must be for the defendant, unless they were further satisfied from the evidence that an *express agreement was entered* into between *Pickett* and Irion that they would be bound by the boundary line between the east and west half of section 6 as established by Mr. West; that the mere recognition of the line thus established by West, and the building of the partition fence and road fences as indicated, and the maintenance of the same by the plaintiff and Irion and his grantor until the plaintiff so purchased the seventy-four acres, was not such evidence of an express agreement between the parties as would justify them in finding that such contract was made. These instructions may well have led the jury to believe that the parties were not bound by the line located by West, unless it was found from the evidence that *Pickett* and Irion formally entered into an express contract to that effect. This we think was

misleading. Even an express contract may be inferred,
and hence proved by circumstances. *Geary v. Geary*, 67
Wis. 248. The mere acquiescence by adjoining owners,
through mutual ignorance and mistake, in a supposed divid-
ing line, and the building of a fence thereon, is not conclusive upon the parties. *Hass v. Plautz*, 56 Wis. 105;
Hacker v. Horlemus, 69 Wis. 280. But this does not prevent
such parties, when the location of the true line is in dispute
or uncertain or knowingly unascertained, from binding
themselves by mutual agreement, either alone or through
the agency of a surveyor, as to what should constitute the
true location of such line. *Vosburgh v. Teator*, 32 N. Y. 561;
Tobey v. Secor, 60 Wis. 310. We do not wish to be understood, however, as holding that parties can only bind themselves, in such cases of disputed, uncertain, or unascertained
location, by express contract. On the contrary, we think
that where such location is made by the parties concerned
with the obvious intention of making it the permanent line
between them, and the same is continued by long acquiescence and recognition in the making of permanent improvements, it will be binding upon such parties without any
formal agreement. *Jackson v. Van Corlaer*, 11 Johns. 123;
Brown v. Caldwell, 10 Serg. & R. 114, 13 Am. Dec. 662;
Beecher v. Parmele, 9 Vt. 352, 31 Am. Dec. 633; *George v.
Thomas*, 67 Am. Dec. 616; *Clark v. Tabor*, 28 Vt. 222;
Blair v. Smith, 16 Mo. 273; *Turner v. Baker*, 64 Mo. 218;
McArthur v. Henry, 35 Tex. 801. In other words, the conclusiveness of such location may, in certain cases, rest upon
the doctrine of estoppel *in pais*, rather than upon contract.
Ibid. The same is true respecting those claiming under
such parties. *Ibid.* This must be so, since the subsequent
conveyances to those claiming under Irion should be construed with reference to the actual rightful state of the
property at the time they were respectively executed.
Whitney v. Robinson, 53 Wis. 309; *McMillan v. Wehle*, 55

JANUARY TERM, 1888.   547

Given vs. The Wisconsin Odd Fellows' Mutual Life Ins. Co.

Wis. 695. That was ascertainable by extrinsic evidence in aid of such construction. *Ibid.*

By the Court.— The judgment of the circuit court is reversed, and the cause is remanded for a new trial.

GIVEN, Appellant, vs. THE WISCONSIN ODD FELLOWS' MUTUAL LIFE INSURANCE COMPANY, Respondent.

April 2 — April 17, 1888.

Life insurance: Appointment of beneficiary: Revocation by death: Married women: Mutual benefit society.

1. Unless a policy of life insurance points out to whom the insurance money shall be paid in case the beneficiary die before the assured, the appointment of the beneficiary is revoked by his death. This rule is not abrogated, where the beneficiary is the wife of the assured, by sec. 2347, R. S.

2. The by-laws of a mutual benefit company provided that on the death of a member "the person designated before death, or his widow, child, or children, mother, sister or sisters," etc., "as the case may be, *and in the order named,*" should receive the insurance. One G., a member, directed that his insurance be paid to S., his wife. S. died, and G. thereafter married the plaintiff, whom on his death he left surviving. *Held,* that the appointment of S. as beneficiary was revoked by her death, and the insurance was payable, under the by-laws, to the plaintiff.

3. It is not probable that sec. 2347, R. S., was intended to affect an insurance by a purely benevolent association upon the life of a member for the benefit of those dependent upon him.

APPEAL from the Circuit Court for *Jefferson* County.

The defendant is an incorporated company carrying on the business of life insurance on the mutual benefit plan, but confines its membership to members in good standing in the Independent Order of Odd Fellows in this state, and certain female relatives of Odd Fellows, and grants insurance for the benefit of the families of the insured.

The rules and by-laws of the company provide that any member thereof " may, at any time before his or her death, notify the secretary, in writing, to whom his or her insurance shall be paid after his or her death, which notice the secretary shall keep on file in his office, and in all such cases the said insurance shall be paid directly to the person designated in such notice." It is further provided therein that, on the death of the member, " the person designated before death, or his widow, child or children, mother, sister or sisters, father, brother or brothers, as the case may be, *and in the order named*, if not otherwise directed by the deceased previous to death, shall receive, out of the funds of the company, . . . the sum of $1,000, ninety days after due proof of death." And, further: " If the deceased member leaves no such relatives, nor any direction for the payment of the money, the company shall pay the expenses of his burial, if there be sufficient funds, and any surplus shall be paid to the lodge of which deceased was a member, to be placed in the widow and orphan's fund of such lodge."   · .   .

One Simeon S. Given was a member of such company, and, at the time of his death, held a valid certificate of such membership. When the certificate was issued to him, he directed, in due form, that the insurance be paid to " Sarah Given, my wife." He never changed or recalled such direction. He became a member of the company in 1881. His wife, Sarah Given, died in 1884. March 9, 1885, he married the plaintiff, *Lizzie Given*, and December 20, 1885, died, leaving surviving him his widow, the plaintiff, and two children by his wife Sarah. A child of the last marriage was born March 1, 1886, and is still living. The defendant refuses to pay the insurance money to the plaintiff, and she brings this suit to recover it.

The foregoing facts, and all the other facts essential to show the liability of the company for the insurance on the life of Simeon S. Given, are alleged in the complaint. The court sustained a general demurrer to the complaint, and from the order in that behalf the plaintiff appeals.

For the appellant there was a brief by *Whitman & Spencer* and *John Bottensek*, and oral argument by *Mr. Bottensek*. They contended, *inter alia*, that it is a well-established rule respecting beneficiaries of insurance in the mutual benefit, co-operative, or assessment insurance associations, that whenever the charter, by-laws, or certificate of membership authorizes the insured, without the knowl-edge or consent of the beneficiary already named, to change the beneficiary of such insurance, then such beneficiaries have no vested right, no property, but an expectancy only in such insurance, during the life-time of the insured, which expectancy ceases and becomes naught on the death of the beneficiary leaving the insured surviving, and the insured himself has no other right in that respect than that of a mere power of appointment of beneficiary. *Gentry v. S. L. K. of H.* 20 Cent. L. J. 393, and notes; *Richmond v. Johnson*, 28 Minn. 447; *Hellenberg v. Dist. No. 1, I. O. of B. B.* 94 N. Y. 580; *Arthur v. Odd Fellows' B. A.* 29 Ohio St. 557; *Masonic Mutual R. A. v. McAuley*, 10 Wash. L. R. 124, 2 Mackey, 70. When the charter of the company or the contract of insurance itself prescribes the persons or classes of persons who shall receive the insurance, and the order in which, in case of the death of some, the others shall take, then the contract controls, and the insurance must be paid to such beneficiaries only and in the precise order named. *Arthur v. Odd Fellows' B. A.* 29 Ohio St. 557; *Masonic Mutual R. A. v. McAuley*, 10 Wash. L. R. 124; 2 Mackey, 70; *Ballou v. Gile*, 50 Wis. 614; *Gentry v. S. L. K. of H.* 20 Cent. L. J. 393.

For the respondent there was a brief by *Gregory, Bird & Gregory*, and oral argument by *Mr. Geo. W. Bird.* To the point that the effecting of the insurance payable to Sarah

Given vested in her an actual subsisting interest therein, which, upon her death, unrevoked by the assured, passed to her two minor children and heirs at law, and the assured having died without having designated any other person as the beneficiary, the sum due was payable to said children, they cited, *Foster v. Gile,* 50 Wis. 603; *Continental L. Ins. Co. v. Webb,* 54 Ala. 688; *Drake v. Stone,* 58 id. 133; *Williams v. Williams,* 68 id. 405; *Waldrom v. Waldrom,* 76 id. 285; *Continental L. Ins. Co. v. Palmer,* 42 Conn. 60; *Phœnix Mut. L. Ins. Co. v. Dunham,* 46 id. 79; *Libby v. Libby,* 37 Me. 359; *Hutson v. Merrifield,* 51 Ind. 24; *Harley v. Heist,* 86 id. 196; *Lockwood v. Bishop,* 51 How. Pr. 221; *Hull v. Hull,* 62 id. 100; *Lee v. Page,* 8 Ky. Law Rep. 602; *Connecticut Mut. L. Ins. Co. v. Fish,* 59 N. H. 126; *Goodrich v. Treat,* 3 Colo. 408; *Myers v. Keystone M. L. Ins. Co.* 27 Pa. St. 268; *Anderson's Estate,* 85 id. 202; *Ricker v. Charter Oak L. Ins. Co.* 27 Minn. 193; *Fletcher v. Collier,* 61 Ga. 653; *Olmstead v. Masonic Mut. B. S.* 37 Kan. 93; *Day v. Case,* 43 Hun, 179.

LYON, J. The defendant company concedes its liability to pay the insurance on the life of Simeon S. Given, and that the complaint sufficiently shows such liability, but claims that the same is payable to the legal representative of the deceased Sarah Given, and not to the plaintiff. Whether it is so payable is the only question raised by the demurrer to the complaint. The question was very fully and ably argued by the respective counsel, and numerous authorities bearing upon it were cited and discussed by them. We find it unnecessary to consider these authorities at length, for the reason that the question has already been decided by this court in *Foster v. Gile,* 50 Wis. 603.

In that case a policy of insurance had been issued by the Penn Mutual Insurance Company of Pennsylvania on the life of one Walter H. Ballou, and by the terms of the policy the insurance money was payable to the two children of the insured, named therein, in equal shares, and to "their guardians, executors, administrators, or assigns." Both beneficiaries died before their father. Ballou died without making any change in the beneficiaries named in the policy. The contest was between the administrator of the insured and the administrator of the beneficiaries. It was held that the administrator of the beneficiaries was entitled to the insurance money, on the sole ground that the same was made payable, not only to them, but to "their guardians, executors, administrators, or assigns." The rule there laid down is that, unless the policy points out to whom the insurance money shall be paid in case the beneficiary die before the insured, the appointment of the beneficiary is revoked by his death. It was so held in analogy to the rules relating to lapsed legacies. Had the words "their guardians, executors, administrators, or assigns," or equivalent words, been omitted from the clause of the policy naming the beneficiaries, the judgment would have been that the administrator of the insured was entitled to the money. The question was very carefully and fully considered in that case; and although there was some difference of opinion between the members of the court, the judgment must be taken as a settlement of the question in this state until the rule is changed by competent authority.

In the case of *Ballou v. Gile*, 50 Wis. 614, there were no words of inheritance or transmission in the appointment of a beneficiary, and hence the case might as well have been decided upon the rule of *Foster v. Gile*. Probably it would have been but for the difference in the opinions of the justices in the latter case. *Ballou v. Gile* was a case of insurance in a benevolent company, under whose rules the money was payable only to those dependent upon the insured. If no such persons survived the insured, the insurance lapsed, and the liability of the company therefore ceased. So the judgment in that case went upon the restricted liability of the insurer, because we could all concur in placing it upon that ground.

Our attention was called by counsel to sec. 2347, R. S., as sustaining the contention of the company. It is not probable that the section was intended to affect an insurance by a purely benevolent association upon the life of a member for the benefit of those dependent upon him. In such case it would seem that the beneficiaries appointed by the charter or by-laws of the association would be entitled to the insurance money, even though the insured member may have attempted to appoint a different beneficiary. But, however this may be, we do not think the statute (were it here applicable) would take this case out of the rule of *Foster v. Gile*. Certainly it would not, unless it vested in the original beneficiary, Sarah Given, the absolute right to the insurance money as her separate property or estate. That a statute which, in principle, was like sec. 2347, did not work such a result, was held by this court in *Kerman v. Howard*, 23 Wis. 108.

Applying the rule of *Foster v. Gile* to the present case, the death of the wife, Sarah Given, during the life of the insured, abrogated the direction that the insurance money be paid to her, and left it to be paid to the person entitled thereto under the rules and by-laws of the company. That person is the widow of the insured, the plaintiff in this action. It follows that the complaint states a cause of action in her favor, and hence that the demurrer thereto should have been overruled.

By the Court.— The order sustaining the demurrer is reversed, and the cause will be remanded with directions to the circuit court to overrule the demurrer.

See note to this case by J. R. Berryman in 27 Am. Law Reg. 374, 377.— REP.

JOHNSON, Respondent, vs. THE ASHLAND WATER COMPANY, Appellant.

April 2 — April 17, 1888.

MASTER AND SERVANT. *(1) Temporary and gratuitous service. (2) Failure to employ sufficient number of men.*

1. One who at the request of the man in charge temporarily assists in defendant's work, not expecting any pay, is, for the time being, a servant of the defendant and entitled to the same protection as any other servant.

2. When the failure to employ a sufficient number of men to perform a particular work in a reasonably safe manner is the proximate cause of an injury to a servant engaged in such work, the master is liable unless the servant may fairly be said to have assumed the risk incident to carrying on the work with an insufficient number of men.

APPEAL from the Circuit Court for *Ashland* County. The following statement of the case was prepared by Mr. Justice TAYLOR as a part of the opinion:

Action to recover damages for personal injury sustained by the plaintiff while in the employ of the defendant. The defendant demurred to the complaint on the ground that it did not state facts sufficient to constitute a cause of action. The demurrer was overruled by the circuit court, and from the order overruling it defendant appeals to this court. The following is the substance of the complaint.

First. The complaint alleges that the defendant is a corporation, under the name stated in the title of the action.

Second. That John Johnson and G. W. Furville made an oral contract with the defendant to dig a ditch in Water street, in the town of Ashland, for a stipulated price per foot; that such ditch was a part of the work necessary for the construction of the water-works the defendant was constructing under its charter.

Third. That plaintiff was employed by said John Johnson and G. W. Furville, and engaged in digging said ditch, on the 14th day of October, 1885, and that at the same time the defendant was engaged in the work of calking and laying iron pipes in the ditch which plaintiff was engaged in digging; that one W. C. Pooley was the superintendent of said defendant, and as such superintendent had charge of the said work of calking and laying iron pipes, and employed men to do such work; that on said 14th day of October George Gandsey and several other men were engaged in calking and laying pipes, under the direction of said Pooley, superintendent, etc.; and that when said Pooley was not present personally directing and superintending said work the said George Gandsey was authorized by said Pooley to have control of the work and of the men who were assisting in said work.

Fourth. That while plaintiff was engaged in digging said ditch, and said Gandsey was, during the absence of said Pooley, engaged in calking said iron pipes, the said Gandsey called the plaintiff and directed him to raise one of the pipes upon which the said Gandsey was working; that the plaintiff responded to the request and instructions of said Gandsey, and raised one end of said pipe; and that while the plaintiff was so obeying the directions of said George Gandsey, without any fault or neglect on his part, the said iron pipe rolled from the blocks upon which it lay, and fell upon the plaintiff, breaking his leg and causing other severe injuries.

The remainder of the complaint is as follows: "That the tools, implements, and apparatus with which the defendant was doing said calking at that time and place were defective and unsafe, and said work was performed in an improper and unsafe manner, of all of which plaintiff had no knowledge. That in doing said calking at the time plaintiff was injured as aforesaid, the defendant and its servants carelessly and negligently laid the iron pipes upon shingle blocks; and when said pipes were so placed upon shingle blocks they were insecure and were liable to roll off at any time. That while the said pipes were so placed upon shingle blocks it was unsafe to work upon them or move them, and that two men could not properly and safely handle and work upon said pipes when the said pipes were placed as above mentioned, of all of which plaintiff had no knowledge. In doing said work of calking and laying iron pipes it was the defendant's duty to this plaintiff to use proper and safe tools, implements, and apparatus, and to employ a sufficient number of servants to do said work in a safe and proper manner, and to use due care in all respects in doing said work; but the defendant failed to perform its said duty in so much that it did not furnish and use proper and safe tools, implements, and apparatus, and that it did not keep and use a sufficient number of servants to do said work in a safe and proper manner, by reason whereof, and by reason of the negligence of defendant's said servant, George Gandsey, plaintiff was injured as aforesaid, to his damage $3,000."

For the appellant the cause was submitted on a brief by *Tomkins & Merrill*. They contended that the demurrer to the complaint should have been sustained because it appears by such complaint that the plaintiff was a mere volunteer, and the defendant owed no duty to him in the premises. The precise danger in the handling of the iron pipe in question was plain and apparent and must have been known to the plaintiff, and he must be held to have assumed such known risks. Such being the case, he cannot maintain an action against the defendant even if the relation of such master and servant were shown to exist between them. *Kelly v. C., M. & St. P. R. Co.* 53 Wis. 74; *Naylor v. C. & N. W. R. Co.* id. 661; *Behm v. Armour*, 58 id. 1. Moreover, if the relation of master and servant is held to exist, the injury was caused by the negligence of a fellow servant, and the master is not liable.

A. E. Dixon, for the respondent.

TAYLOR, J.   It is claimed by the learned counsel for the appellant that the complaint does not state a cause of action because it shows that the plaintiff was a mere volunteer in the work in which he was engaged 'at the time he received his injury.   Under the allegations of the complaint, the plaintiff was engaged in the defendant's work at the request of the man in charge of the work; and, although it may be said that his employment was for a mere temporary purpose, and that the plaintiff was not expecting any pay for the work done, and in that sense the employment was voluntary, still, being in the defendant's employment at the request of its servant or foreman, he was not a trespasser, and he was, for the time being, the servant of the defendant, and entitled to the same protection as any other servant of the defendant, and probably subject to the same risks of injury from the negligence of his fellow-servants. This seems to be the rule established by the authorities, and is supported by considerations of justice.   Elwell's Evans on Agency, 682; Wood on Mast. & Serv. 909, sec. 455; *Degg v. M. R. Co.* 1 Hurl. & N. 773; *Potter v. Faulkner,* 31 Law J. Q. B. 30; *Warburton v. G. W. R. Co.* L. R. 2 Exch. 30, 36 Law J. Exch. 9; *Wiggett v. Fox,* 11 Exch. 832; *Abraham v. Reynolds,* 6 Jur. (N. S.), 53; *Flower v. P. R. Co.* 69 Pa. St. 210; *New Orleans, J. & G. N. R. Co. v. Harrison,* 48 Miss. 112, 12 Am. Rep. 356; *Street R. Co. v. Bolton,* 43 Ohio St. 224, 226.

Conceding that the complaint shows that the plaintiff stood in the relation of a servant or employee of the defendant at the time the accident happened, does it state other facts which, if proved on the trial, would make the defendant responsible to him in damages for the injury received?   We think this question should be answered in the affirmative.   Laying out of view all other allegations in the complaint, the allegations contained in the last paragraph thereof are sufficient to make out his cause of action.   If he proves on the trial that his injury resulted from the defendant's failure to employ a sufficient number of men to do the work in a safe and proper manner, and by reason of such want of men he was injured, then he is *prima facie* entitled to recover.

The courts have uniformly held that it is a duty which the employer owes his servants, when set to do any particular work, that he shall provide a sufficient number of men to do the work in a reasonably safe manner.' This duty is placed on the same ground which requires the employer to furnish safe implements and appliances for doing the work and a reasonably safe place in which the work is to be done. Wood, in his work on Railway Law (Vol. 3, p. 1487, sec. 381), says: "The term 'appliances' of the business embraces not only machinery, premises, and all the implements of every kind used in and about the business, but also the persons employed to operate them; and the master must furnish a sufficient number of persons competent to perform the labor safely; and, when the failure to employ a sufficient number of hands to perform the particular service is the proximate cause of the injury, the master is liable unless the servant may fairly be said to have assumed the risk incident thereto."   This is a reasonable and just rule, and has been approved by all the courts in which the question has been raised, except in cases where the employee knew at the time that there was a want of sufficient help, and, notwithstanding such knowledge, entered into the employment. *Flike v. B. & A. R. Co.* 53 N. Y. 549, 554; *Hayes v. W. R. Corp.* 3 Cush. 270; *Mad R. & L. E. R. Co. v.*

Barber, 5 Ohio St. 541, 563; *Skipp v. E. C. R. Co.* 9 Exch. 223; *Booth v. B. & A. R. Co.* 73 N. Y. 39.

The facts stated in the complaint negative any presumption that the plaintiff was aware of the fact that there was a want of sufficient men to perform the work safely, which he was suddenly called upon to assist in doing. It cannot be said, therefore, from the facts stated in the complaint that the plaintiff assumed the dangers incident to carrying on the work with an insufficient number of men. We think the complaint states a good cause of action, and the demurrer to the same was properly overruled.

By the Court.— The order of the circuit court appealed from is affirmed, and the cause is remanded for further proceedings.

See note to this case in 87 N. W. Rep. 828.—REP.

OLSON, Respondent, vs. THE CITY OF CHIPPEWA FALLS, Appellant.

April 2 — April 17, 1888.

Municipal corporations: Defective street: Unguarded precipice: Unmanageable horses: Proximate cause of injury.

Horses ordinarily quiet and steady, attached to a wagon, were standing·in a public street, when they became suddenly frightened and unmanageable and backed the wagon over a steep embankment within the limits of the street, which had negligently been left unguarded by the city, and the plaintiff, who was in the wagon, was injured. *Held,* that in the absence of contributory negligence the city is liable for the injury. The frightened and unmanageable condition of the horses was not such an independent cause of the injury as to prevent a recovery.

APPEAL from the Circuit Court for *Chippewa* County.

Action to recover damages for personal injuries and the loss of personal property sustained by reason of the defective and unsafe condition of a highway in defendant city. The facts will sufficiently appear from the opinion.

At the close of the trial the jury returned a general verdict in favor of the plaintiff, assessing her damages at $650; also a special verdict as follows: (1) " *Question.* Was the highway at the place of the accident in a condition of insufficiency? *Answer.* Yes. (2) *Q.* Was Mr. Walker in the exercise of ordinary care in leaving the team in front of the mill, in charge of the plaintiff, in the manner and under the circumstances he did? *A.* Yes. (3) *Q.* Did the team, while in the plaintiff's charge, become unmanageable? *A.* Yes. (4) *Q.* If you answer 'yes' to the last above question, did the team become more than momentarily unmanageable? *A.* No. (5) *Q.* Did the plaintiff exercise ordinary care by making proper efforts to arrest the backing of the team? *A.* Yes."

From the judgment entered on the verdict, in favor of the plaintiff, the defendant appeals.

For the appellant there was a brief signed by *J. A. Anderson,* city attorney, and oral argument by *J. J. Jenkins.* They contended that the fright and unmanageable condition of the team constituted the primary cause of the accident, for which the city would be in nowise responsible. *Houfe v. Fulton,* 29 Wis. 296; *Kelley v. Fond du Lac,* 31 id. 179; *Moore v. Abbot,* 32 Me. 46; *Taylor v. Woburn,* 130 Mass. 499. It being established that the unmanageableness of the team was not in any manner chargeable to the defendant, there can be no recovery even though the driver was in no fault. *Marble v. Worcester,* 4 Gray, 401-2; *Murdock v. Warwick,* id. 180; *Rowell v. Lowell,* 7 id. 102; *Titus v. Northbridge,* 97 Mass. 264; *Houfe v. Fulton,* 29 Wis. 305-7; *Jackson v. Bellevieu,* 30 id. 258; *May v. Princeton,* 11 Met. 444; *Kelley v. Fond du Lac,* 31 Wis. 179. It is the duty of the traveler to remain in the traveled portion of the highway, and if he leaves the same and injury ensues he cannot recover. *Kelley v. Fond du Lac*, 21 Wis. 186–7; *Sykes v. Pawlet*, 43 Vt. 446. Where the plaintiff's unskilfulness or negligence primarily contributes to the injury, a recovery is barred. *May v. Princeton*, 11 Met. 442; *Delaney v. M. & St. P. R. Co.* 33 Wis. 75; *Davis v. Dudley*, 4 Allen, 560; *Otis v. Janesville*, 47 Wis. 423; *Cronin v. Delavan*, 50 id. 375; *Rowell v. Lowell*, 7 Gray, 100; *Stickney v. Salem*, 3 Allen, 374. And the question of want of care and unskilfulness is not one for the jury when it is plainly the cause of the accident. *Achtenhagen v. Watertown*, 18 Wis. 331; *Hill v. New Haven*, 37 Vt. 501; *Barber v. Essex*, 27 id. 62; *Teipel v. Hilsendegen*, 44 Mich. 461; *Pzolla v. M. C. R. Co.* 54 id. 273.

Arthur Gough, for the respondent, argued, among other things, that the highway was, as found by the jury, "in a condition of insufficiency." *Palmer v. Andover*, 2 Cush. 600; *Hayden v. Attleborough*, 7 Gray, 338; *Pittston v. Hart*, 89 Pa. St. 389; *Stevens v. Boxford*, 10 Allen, 25; *Chicago v. Gallagher*, 44 Ill. 295; *Wilson v. Atlanta*, 60 Ga. 473; *Alger v. Lowell*, 3 Allen, 402; *Adams v. Natick*, 13 id. 429; *Davis v. Hill*, 41 N. H. 329; *Prideaux v. Mineral Point*, 43 Wis. 514, 523; *Wheeler v. Westport*, 30 id. 392; *Hart v. Red Cedar*, 63 id. 634, 641. To the point that there was no negligence on the part of the plaintiff, and that the question of negligence was for the jury, he cited *Britton v. Cummington*, 107 Mass. 347; *Kenney v. Cohoes*, 100 N. Y. 623; *Black v. Brooklyn City R. Co.* 108 N. Y. 640; *Hull v. Kansas City*, 54 Mo. 598; *Cobb v. Standish*, 14 Me. 198; *Griggs v. Fleckenstein*, 14 Minn. 81; *Albert v. B. S. R. Co.* 2 Daly, 389; *Myers v. I. & St. L. R. Co.* 113 Ill. 386; *Pool v. C., M. & St. P. R. Co.* 56 Wis. 227; *Stilling v. Thorp*, 54 id. 528.

ORTON, J. The facts of this case appear to be substantially and briefly these: Prairie street of said city passes over a bridge that spans quite a large stream of water, called "Duncan Creek," in a northwesterly direction towards the country. About forty-five feet from the north end of the bridge is a large flouring-mill, called the "Star Mills;" and running from the corner of the bridge to the end of the mill in a somewhat circular form is the steep embankment of the creek, twenty feet above the water (which is about three feet deep), within the boundary of the street, and about twenty feet from its center. The surface of the street descends towards this embankment, and the embankment is entirely unguarded by fence, wall, or other barrier. The street passes on in front of the mill, the platform of which is within the street, and then passes on towards the country. A man by the name of Walker, who lives several miles in the country, and a farmer, had been to the city on business with a two-horse team and wagon. The plaintiff, who was a Norwegian girl about thirty years of age, and quite lately an emigrant from Norway, stout and healthy, was being carried by the said Walker to his home for the purpose of becoming his servant. She sat on the seat with him when they passed over said bridge and stopped in the street in front of the mill, where he got out to go into the mill on some business of his own, and left the plaintiff in the wagon holding the team, with the rear end of the wagon towards the embankment, when suddenly, without the least warning, the horses became frightened at something about the mill, perhaps a corn-sheller, which suddenly appeared to them with motion and noise, immediately in front, and as suddenly they backed the wagon over the embankment into the creek, by which the plaintiff was seriously injured, and came near losing her life. The team was an ordinarily quiet and steady team, and not unusually skittish or restless. The plaintiff did what she could in the sudden emergency to keep the team from backing, but failed. The street as it leaves the bridge and passes in front of the mill is considerably narrower than the other streets of the city, and less than four rods wide.

It is common observation that people having business at such a mill leave their teams standing in front of it, as Walker did, and that any team of horses, however steady and well broken, is liable to become frightened suddenly by some object in front, and begin to back away from the apparent danger; and that when any such team begins to back it is extremely difficult if not impossible to stop them within the distance of twenty feet, and even whipping may not do it. This was an extremely dangerous place in the street, and the negligence of the city authorities in not guarding such an embankment by some proper barrier is apparent. But the jury were allowed by the court to view this place and surroundings, and this court would be unable to revise their findings on the condition of the place. All the exceptions, except that to the admission of improper testimony, relate to the merits of the case, such as refusing a nonsuit, refusing to instruct the jury to find for the defendant, and to grant a new trial. The evidence admitted against objection related to the repair of the defect complained of, by placing a barrier at the precipice to keep teams from backing over since the accident, and *that* the jury must have seen on their view whether there had been testimony of it or not, and this could not be helped.

The main ground for a reversal of this judgment on the merits is that the frightened and unmanageable condition of the team as an independent cause of the injury in this case prevents a recovery, and the learned counsel cites a great many cases supporting this doctrine, as they understand it, and among them the case of *Houfe v. Fulton*, 29 Wis. 296. That case is almost exactly parallel to this, and that is the only authority that need be considered on that question. The driver and another man were riding in a cutter over a bad bridge without a barrier on one side at least. The horse became suddenly frightened, or excited, or shocked, and *started* and *shied* as suddenly; at something or for some cause, and went over the bridge sideways, and the plaintiff was injured. The horse was unusually safe and kind, and was being driven properly until it unexpectedly stopped and shied and ran off the bridge sideways, and the driver was unable to prevent it. In that case it was uncertain whether the horse was frightened or had a fit, and it would make no difference as to its being an independent cause of the accident. Chief Justice Dixon makes a thorough examination of the authorities upon this very question of horses becoming frightened and unmanageable while being driven on a highway that is defective, and points out clearly the exception to that rule and holds that the case he was considering was within the exception. He says: "But whatever the true ground of such decisions may be, or whether they are sound or not, it is unnecessary to inquire here, since a recognized exception to them is that a horse is not to be considered uncontrollable that merely *shies or starts or is momentarily not controlled by his driver.* Such was the fact in the present case." He then refers to the case of *Titus v. Northbridge*, 97 Mass. 264, as being like that case, and approves the opinion of the chief justice in that case. That case is still closer in point with the present case. The doctrine is in both cases, and in all cases, that where the horse (or horses) suddenly and merely shies, or starts, or backs, or goes sideways, and is momentarily not controlled or uncontrollable, and goes over a bridge or embankment negligently remaining without a reasonable guard or barrier, and the driver does his best to prevent it, and the horses are usually steady and kind and not more liable to sudden starts or fright than common horses, the driver, if injured by such defect, may recover. The case of *Houfe v. Fulton, supra,* was sustained on this ground, and that case rules this in every particular. The other authorities cited by the learned counsel of the appellant are not at all applicable to this case.   This accident happened in a most natural way in view of such a dangerous embankment open and unguarded.   The team was stopped before the mill in the usual manner, and left in the care of a competent person to hold them until the owner should transact his business in the mill and return.   The team instantly and suddenly became frightened by some suddenly appearing object, probably a corn-sheller near the mill, and as instantly and suddenly backs the wagon over the embankment, and the driver is utterly unable to stop them.   The plaintiff was wholly without fault, and if that embankment had been properly guarded no harm would have resulted from the backing of the team.   Such a movement of any team would not be at all uncommon under such circumstances, and so the city might have anticipated when it left the steep bank of the creek so unguarded in such a place. Any common team with any common driver would be likely to do as this team did.

The only other ground for a reversal of the judgment urged by the appellant's counsel is the contributory negligence of the plaintiff as the driver of the team.   The evidence seems to be very clear that she did all that any driver would have done under the circumstances.   Whipping horses within a few feet of a precipice of a river's bank twenty feet in perpendicular height would be extremely hazardous. They might start forwards or they might go backwards still faster.   It would be difficult to drive any team into the front face of an object by which they were so frightened as to suddenly go backwards to avoid it.   We think the case a very clear one on its merits, and that the verdict was warranted by the evidence.

.*By the Court.*— The judgment of the circuit court is affirmed.

See note to this case in 37 N. W. Rep. 575.— REP.

McHugh, Respondent, vs. Robinson, Appellant.

April 3 — April 17, 1888.

Replevin against officer: Possession.

Cattle in the possession of a constable under an attachment were replevied by the owner. After the constable had given an undertaking which entitled him to have the cattle returned to him, the
replevin suit was dismissed, but the cattle were never actually
returned to the possession of the constable, and he afterwards disclaimed such possession and refused to accept the delivery of the
cattle upon any condition. *Held,* that the owner could not maintain a second action of replevin against the constable.

APPEAL from the Circuit Court for *Marathon* County.
Replevin. The facts are sufficiently stated in the opinion. The defendant appeals from a judgment in favor of
the plaintiff.

For the appellant there was a brief by *Neal Brown* and
L. A. Pradt, and oral argument by *Mr. Brown.*

For the respondent the cause was submitted on the brief
C. F. Crosby and *R. B. Salter.*

Cole, C. J. This action was brought to recover the possession of a yoke of oxen. It appears that the oxen were
originally taken by the defendant, as constable, on a writ
of attachment against the plaintiff. The plaintiff then commenced an action of replevin against the defendant to recover the possession of the oxen, claiming that they were
exempt. On the 5th of February, 1886, the return day of
the writ of replevin, that action was dismissed by the justice for want of jurisdiction, and the property was ordered
to be returned to the defendant. The plaintiff then filed
an affidavit with the justice that he intended to appeal from
the judgment. On the 8th of February the defendant executed the requisite undertaking prescribed by sec. 3759,

R. S., and on the same day the justice entered an order in his docket directing the constable, Prossor, to return the oxen to the defendant. On the same day the plaintiff in that case and in this paid up the costs in justice's court, and that action was dismissed, and no further proceedings were taken therein. The constable, Prossor, made an effort to return the oxen to the possession of the defendant, and indorsed on the order of the justice that he delivered the oxen back to the defendant on February 9th, at Spencer, by placing them in the building from whence he took them, and leaving a written notice at the residence of the defendant of such delivery. It does not appear that there was any actual delivery of the oxen into the possession of the defendant, and we are satisfied from the evidence that there was not. Upon this point the defendant testified that he never took charge of them, that he never saw them, and that they never came into his possession after they were first taken from him. He also said that he saw the plaintiff, and had a talk with him, and told him "I had nothing to do with the cattle, and for him to go and get them, for I would not accept them." It does not clearly appear at what precise day this conversation between the parties occurred, but we infer that it was about the time the present action was commenced. At all events we are satisfied from the evidence that the defendant had not possession of the cattle, nor did he exercise any control over them whatever when this suit was commenced. For the plaintiff himself testified that he drove the cattle from Colby to Spencer, the same night the affidavit for the writ of replevin in this case was made. He says: "I took them as far as what they call 'Diamond Street.' I took them to Spencer. I waited until I got a wagon, and I was walking about four feet from the nigh ox. The cattle were walking with their heads tied together, and Mr. Prossor walked between us, and pulled out a paper from his pocket, and says,

'I hold these cattle in this litigation,' and he drove the cattle off. . . . I drove them out to my place,— out to Clark county. I started from Colby to my place, and from my place to Spencer. I drove them from my place to Spencer. Mr. Prossor did not go with me." There is some further testimony of statements made by the attorney of the defendant to the effect there would be no claim that the delivery by Prossor to the defendant was not good; but still we are satisfied that the defendant did not have any such possession or control of the oxen as will support this action against him. This action goes upon the ground that the property which is to be replevied has been taken and is detained by the defendant; that it is in the actual or constructive possession of the defendant or under his control. No such possession or control was shown to be in the defendant when the suit was commenced. On the contrary, it appears he disclaimed all such possession, and refused to accept the delivery of the cattle upon any condition. It is true, he had given an undertaking in the first replevin suit, which entitled him to have the cattle returned to him, but they never were in fact delivered. They seem rather to have remained in the legal custody and possession of Prossor, the constable, or in the possession of the plaintiff himself.

In *Johnson v. Garlick*, 25 Wis. 705, it is held that an action to recover the possession of personal property will not lie against one who was not in the actual possession and control of it, and who disclaimed title or right of possession upon demand made. To the same effect is *Libby v. Murray*, 51 Wis. 371. See, also, *Brockway v. Burnap*, 12 Barb. 347. If the plaintiff is to be believed, he was in the actual possession of the oxen when Prossor seized them on the writ in the present case. Thus the strange anomaly is presented of a party bringing a replevin for chattels in his actual possession and under his control. It is needless to say that such an action cannot be maintained. The provisions of the statute presuppose that the defendant in the action is in possession of the goods and unjustly detains them; and it would be contrary to all authority, reason, and common sense to suppose it was intended to give this remedy to one who already had possession of the property. We therefore think the court below erred in refusing to grant the defendant's motion for a nonsuit. The plaintiff had really proved himself out of court by his own testimony.

By the Court.— The judgment of the circuit court is re-reversed, and the cause is remanded for a new trial.

FARNHAM, Appellant, vs. SHERRY and another, Respondents.

April 3 — April 17, 1888.

(1) Taxation: Public lands: Unauthorized cancellation of land-warrant after location: Withholding patent. (2) Suspension of entry: Filing of certificate. (3) Ejectment: Judgment.

1. A military bounty land warrant was located on certain lands by one W. in 1857, and the usual certificate of such location was issued. In the same year the commissioner of pensions notified the commissioner of the general land office that said warrant and its assignment to W. were impeached as forgeries, and requested that the patent be withheld. The request was complied with, and no further action was taken until in June, 1863, when the commissioner of pensions assumed to cancel the warrant. The commissioner of the land office acquiesced in such cancellation, and withheld the patent until 1882, when, it having been decided by the secretary of the interior that the cancellation of the warrant was unauthorized, he caused the patent to be issued to W. The lands were sold in May, 1863, for nonpayment of the taxes assessed thereon in 1862. *Held,* that from the location of the warrant in 1857 until the tax sale in 1863 the entire equitable title to, and beneficial interest in, the land was in W., and hence that the land was taxable in 1862. *Calder v. Keegan,* 30 Wis. 127, distinguished.

2. Under ch. 105, Laws of 1861, providing that where entries of land had been suspended such lands should not be subject to taxation until such suspension was removed, the filing of a certificate of such suspension, as provided in sec. 8 of the act, was a condition precedent to the right of the owner to claim the benefit of the exemption.

3. A plaintiff in ejectment who established no title to the land cannot complain because the judgment awards to the defendants the possession of the whole of the land and not merely of that part to which they proved title.

APPEAL from the Circuit Court for *Wood* County.

Ejectment for 160 acres of land in Wood county. To establish her title to the land claimed the plaintiff put in evidence a patent therefor, dated December 20, 1882, issued by the United States to one Watkins, pursuant to a location thereon of a military bounty land warrant numbered 50,308; and also a quitclaim deed of the same land, dated December 24, 1883, executed by Watkins to her.

The defendants put in evidence two tax deeds of the land, executed in due form to one Samuel Hanson, and duly recorded,— one on the tax sale of 1863 for nonpayment of the taxes of 1862, executed and recorded in 1866; and the other on the tax sale of 1865 for nonpayment of the taxes of 1864, executed and recorded in 1869; and also mesne conveyances of the land, or some portion of it, from Hanson to defendants. The defendants further proved, on the trial, that on October 28, 1857, Watkins located the land warrant No. 50,308 on the land, and the local government land officers issued the usual certificate of such location, and transmitted the warrant to the land department at Washington.

November 21, 1857, the commissioner of pensions notified the commissioner of the general land office that such warrant, and the assignment thereof to Watkins, had been impeached as being forged documents, and requested the latter to withhold the patent thereon. June 15, 1863, the commissioner of pensions, by an indorsement on the warrant to that effect, assumed to cancel the land warrant on the ground that the same, together with the assignment thereof to Watkins, were forgeries, and he thereupon returned the warrant to the commissioner of the general land office, with notice of such cancellation.

No formal action was taken by the commissioner of the general land office in the matter, but it appears, by correspondence had in 1865 and 1868 between the commissioner and the agents of Watkins, that the former acquiesced in such cancellation, and withheld the patent. At the same time, however, he informed such agents that Watkins might locate another land warrant on the land, or enter the same for cash at the government price. Watkins did not avail himself of this privilege, and nothing further was done in the matter until December, 1882, when, under a decision of the secretary of the interior to the effect that the commissioner of pensions had no power to cancel the land warrant, the commissioner of the land office caused the patent to be issued to Watkins for the land. This is the patent introduced in evidence by the plaintiff, as above stated. A letter by the commissioner to Watkins, dated December 5, 1882, contains this passage: " This location was suspended from patent on account of objections presented by the commissioner of pensions against the issue of warrant and assignment thereof. Upon a present review of the case, and in accordance with the rulings of the honorable secretary of the interior, I find that no valid reason exists against the satisfaction of the case in question. I have therefore directed that as soon as practicable the said location, which is intact upon the plats of this office, should be passed for patent, and the same, when issued, will be transmitted for delivery to the register of the land office at Wausau, Wis., unless you previously file the duplicate certificate of location in this office; in which event the patent will be sent directly to your address."

Upon the above facts, the substance of which is stated in the findings of fact by the court (a jury having been waived), the court found, in effect, that Watkins was the owner of a taxable interest in the land in 1862, when it was essed and taxed, and in May, 1863, when it was sold for npayment of such taxes, and that the tax deed executed Hanson in 1866, on the certificates of the sale of 1863, ested in him a valid title to the land, available to the de- endants to defeat this action. No mention is made in the ndings of the tax deed of 1869. Judgment was thereupon rdered and entered for the defendants pursuant to such ndings. The plaintiff appeals from the judgment.

For the appellant there were briefs by *Neal Brown* and *A. Pradt*, attorneys, and *Silverthorn, Hurley, Ryan & A. Ges,* of counsel, and the cause was argued orally by *Mr. Geo. Hurley* and *Mr. Brown.*

atkins' right to a patent for all the lands in question be- ame complete in 1857, and hence the equitable title was hen fully vested in him so as to subject said lands to taxa- on in the following year, cited *Wis. Cent. R. Co. v. Price Co.* Wis. 588, 594; *Ross v. Outagamie Co.* 12 id. 26; *Cornelius Kessel,* 58 id. 237; *Tucker v. Ferguson,* 22 Wall. 527; *Wheeler v. Merriman,* 30 Minn. 379; *Whitney v. Gunderson,* Wis. 359; *Hall v. Dowling,* 18 Cal. 619; *People v. Shearer,* id. 645; *Witherspoon v. Duncan,* 4 Wall. 210.

L. *Williams,* for the respondents, to the point that

LYON, J. The learned counsel for the plaintiff with much ingenuity of argument maintain that the judgment of the circuit court herein is erroneous because (1) on general prin- ciples of law the absolute title of the land in controversy was in the United States in 1862, when the tax was levied thereon which is the basis of the tax deed of 1866, and hence the land was not then taxable; and (2) if plaintiff then owned an interest in the land otherwise taxable, the same was exempt from taxation by ch. 105, Laws of 1861. An additional objection to a full recovery by defendants is founded upon an alleged want of title in them of the whole 160 acres under mesne conveyances from Hanson. These propositions will be considered in their order.

I. Laying out of view for the present the effect of ch. 105, Laws of 1861, the first question to be determined is, Had Watkins a taxable interest in the land in 1862? In considering this question it must be borne in mind that Watkins, the plaintiff's grantor, made an effectual entry or location of the land in 1857, paid therefor, and received the usual certificates thereof from the proper local land officers of the government. That this vested in Watkins the entire equitable title to the land and beneficial interest therein, the United States holding only the naked legal title in trust for him, is settled in this state beyond controversy. Of course Watkins' interest was taxable.

What happened before 1862 that divested Watkins' title, and thus relieved the land from liability to taxation? Nothing whatever except that in 1857 the commissioner of pensions without authority notified the commissioner of the general land office that the validity of the land warrant No. 50,308, located on the land in controversy, was impeached, and requested the latter to withhold the patent therefor. The commissioner of the land office complied with such request, and no further action was taken in the matter until June 15, 1863. It requires no argument to show that these acts did not and could not affect the title of Watkins to the land. At most they merely delayed him in obtaining the legal title which the United States then held in trust for him, and which in its own good time it conveyed to him.

The case of *Wis. Cent. R. Co. v. Price Co.* 64 Wis. 579, in principle is identical with the present case. The railroad company was entitled to patents from the United States

for certain specific lands.   The government land officers refused to issue such patents, claiming that the railroad company was not entitled thereto, yet the equitable title was
held to be in the railroad company, and the lands were held
taxable although patents were refused.   See, also, the recent cases of *Wis. Cent. R. Co. v. Wis. River Land Co.*,
ante, p. 94; *Spiess v. Neuberg, ante*, p. 279.   The question
under consideration was fully discussed in those cases by
Mr. Justice CASSODAY, and numerous authorities cited bearing upon it.   The opinions and judgments therein are conclusive of the question, and relieve us from the necessity of
further discussion thereof.   It is only necessary to add a
few observations upon the case of *Calder v. Keegan*, 30 Wis.
127, upon which counsel for plaintiff seem to rely.   That
was a case of suspended entry under a spurious land warrant.
After the suspension, the person making the entry purchased
the land and paid for it in cash, as Watkins had the privilege of doing in the present case.   Such purchase was held
to be a new entry, the purchaser taking no title whatever
under the first entry because the warrant was spurious.   A
tax levied intermediate the two entries was held void.
Clearly the case is not in point here.

   We hold that, from the location of the land by Watkins
in 1857 down to the sale thereof in 1863 for nonpayment of
taxes, the entire equitable title to, and beneficial interest in,
the land in controversy was in Watkins, by virtue of his
entry, location, and purchase thereof, and hence that the
same was taxable in 1862 unless exempted from taxation by
the act of 1861.

   II. We are now to determine whether ch. 105, Laws of
1861, exempted the land from taxation in 1862.   It is provided in sec. 1 of the act that in all cases where entries of
land, made at any of the United States land offices within
this state, have been suspended by authority of the secretary of the interior, the commissioner of the general land

office, or the department of the interior, except in certain cases not material here, such land shall not be subject to taxation until such suspension is removed and the title confirmed to the original applicant. By the terms of the act such exemption is limited to two years from the date of the passage of the act, which was March 25, 1861. Sec. 2 provides that in all cases where lands situated as stated in sec. 1 have been sold for taxes while the entry thereof was suspended, all tax certificates of sale and tax deeds issued in pursuance of such sale for taxes are null and void. Sec. 3 is as follows: "All persons claiming relief under the provisions of this act, where the entries of land were suspended at the date of the passage hereof, shall, within one year from the passage of this act, cause to be filed in the office of the clerk of the board of supervisors of the county in which such suspended lands are located a certificate of such suspension from the general land office or from the local land office where such entries were attempted to be made; and all persons claiming such relief on account of the suspension of entries hereafter made shall file a like notice with the said clerk within one year from the time of such suspension."

It is very doubtful, to say the least, whether the entry or location of the land in controversy was ever suspended by any authority specified in sec. 1. But, assuming for the purposes of the case that such entry or location was so suspended, the suspension occurred November 21, 1857, when the commissioner of pensions requested the commissioner of the land office to withhold the patent, which request was complied with. This occurred before the passage of the act of 1861. Sec. 3 of the act required Watkins to file the certificate specified therein with the clerk of the board of supervisors within one year from the passage of the act, that is to say, by March 25, 1862. There is no proof in the case that this was done. We think the provisions of sec. 3

are mandatory, and that it was essential for Watkins to file such certificate within the prescribed time in order to avail himself of the provisions of secs. 1 and 2. Doubtless the legislature foresaw that, without some such provision as that contained in sec. 3, the taxing officers would or might be entirely in the dark as to what suspensions had been made, without adequate means of ascertaining the fact. The result would naturally be that lands exempt from taxation under the act would continue to be assessed and taxed and sold for nonpayment of taxes. Parties would invest their money on the faith of the validity of the taxes, perhaps make valuable improvements upon the land believing they had a good title thereto, when the original owner at his own convenience would bring forth from the archives of the land office at Washington evidence of a suspension of the entry, and thus defeat the title of the purchaser. In view of these and other considerations, it must be held that the filing of the certificate pursuant to sec. 3 is a condition precedent to the right of the original owner to claim the benefit of the exemption of sec. 1. Hence we conclude that the act of 1861 does not aid the claim of the plaintiff in this action.

III. It is claimed on behalf of the plaintiff that the defendants established on the trial a title under Hanson to but an undivided one-half of the land in controversy, and that it was error to give them judgment for the possession of the whole. It is elementary that the plaintiff in ejectment recovers (if at all) upon the strength of his own title, and not upon the weakness of that of his adversary. The plaintiff failed to establish any title to the land, and was necessarily defeated in the action no matter who was the owner. The land was entirely vacant and unimproved. Yet, although it was not in the actual possession of any one, the statute required the plaintiff to allege in her complaint that the defendants unlawfully withheld the possession thereof from her. R. S. sec. 3077. It is this constructive possession, and this only, that the judgment awards to the defendants. Whether the judgment in this respect is regular or irregular is quite immaterial, for it can result in no harm to the plaintiff.

Upon the whole case we conclude that the judgment of the circuit court is correct,and should be affirmed.

By the Court.— Judgment affirmed.

McCONKEY and others, Respondents, vs. McCRANEY, Appellant.

April 3 — April 17, 1888.

(1) Service of summons. (2) Judgment by default: Entry by clerk out of term.

1. Leaving a summons with defendant's foreman and informing him of the contents thereof, where such foreman is not a member of defendant's family nor at his usual place of abode, is not a valid service under subd. 4, sec. 2636, R. S.
2. The clerk has no power under sec. 2891, R. S., to enter judgment out of term when the process is not personally served on defendant.

APPEAL from the Circuit Court for *Marinette* County.

The following statement of the case was prepared by Mr. Justice TAYLOR:

The respondents commenced an action in the circuit court of Marinette county to recover upon contract. A summons was issued, and placed in the hands of the sheriff of said county, and he made the following return of service thereon:

"*State of Wisconsin, Marinette County:* I hereby certify that on the 25th day of October, 1887, at the town of Peshtigo, in said county, after diligent search and inquiry,

I have been unable to find the within-named defendant, *D. M. McCraney*, within my county, and thereupon I duly served the within summons and complaint by delivery to and leaving with Anthony Renner, personally, a true copy of summons and complaint thereof, who was then and there known to be the foreman of said defendant, he being a person of suitable age and discretion, to whom I explained the contents thereof.

"Services, $1,
"Copy (7 folios), $1.

———

"$2.   PATRICK CLIFFORD, Sheriff."

The defendant did not appear in the action, and on the 17th day of October, 1887, the plaintiff applied to the clerk of the circuit court for judgment, and took judgment by default against the defendant for the amount claimed in his complaint, and $166 costs. From this judgment the defendant appeals to this court, and alleges as error that it appears on the face of the record that the court did not have jurisdiction of the person of the defendant. The respondents have not submitted a brief upon this appeal.

For the appellant the cause was submitted on the brief of *B. F. Simpson* and *Eastman, Scudder & Mountain*.

[No appearance for the respondents.]

PER CURIAM. It is clear that the service of the summons and complaint, as shown by the record, was a void service. The sheriff failed entirely to serve the papers as required by subd. 4, sec. 2636, R. S., when the defendant cannot be found. It is equally clear that the clerk had no authority to enter judgment out of term, had the service been made as required by said section. See sec. 2891, R. S. That the service was void and gave the court no jurisdiction of the person of the defendant, see *Weis v. Schoerner*, 53 Wis. 72; *Hall v. Graham*, 49 Wis. 553; *Matteson v. Smith*, 37 Wis.

338; *Sayles v. Davis*, 20 Wis. 302; *Pollard v. Wegener*, 18 Wis. 569. That the clerk has no power to enter judgment out of term when the process is not personally served on the defendant, see *Northrup v. Shephard*, 26 Wis. 220; *Moyer v. Cook*, 12 Wis. 335; *Morrison v. Austin*, 14 Wis. 601; *Northrup v. Shephard*, 23 Wis. 513.

The judgment of the circuit court is reversed, and the cause is remanded.

Dodd, Appellant, vs. Dunne and another, Respondents.

April 4 — April 17, 1888.

Promissory note: Delivery: Negligence of maker.

Upon the evidence in this case — showing, among other things, that the defendants had signed in the evening a note which was to be delivered to a real-estate agent in payment of his commissions on a sale of the defendants' land which was expected to be consummated the next morning; that the payee, without the consent of the defendants, but without objection being made by them, took the note from their desk where it had been signed, saying "I will take charge of this," put the note in his pocket and went out; that on the next morning he sold the note to a *bona fide* purchaser; and that the contemplated sale of the land was never made — it is *held* that the jury were justified in finding that there had never been any delivery of the note, conditional or otherwise, so as to give it a legal existence, and that the defendants were not guilty of such negligence in permitting the payee to take the note as would render them liable thereon to an innocent holder.

APPEAL from the Circuit Court for *Rock* County.

Action upon a promissory note for $1,000, alleged to have been executed and delivered by the defendants to James H. Wheeler and F. L. Stevens, copartners, in their firm name of Wheeler & Stevens. The complaint alleges that the note was assigned by the payees to one S. A. Dean and by Dean to the plaintiff.

The answer denies that the defendants ever executed or delivered the note in suit, and, on information and belief, denies that it was ever assigned as stated. By way of counterclaim it alleges, among other things, the following facts:

The defendants had authorized Wheeler & Stevens to sell a farm owned by them. On or about the date of the note Stevens informed them that one Austin had proposed to purchase the farm for $26,000, of which $1,600 was to be paid in cash at the date of the sale, and that Austin had signed a written contract for the purchase on said terms. The defendants then informed Stevens that if Wheeler & Stevens would take the defendants' note for $1,000 in full payment for their services in effecting the sale, they (the defendants) would, on payment of said sum of $1,600 by Austin, accept the proposal of the latter and execute the contract for the sale. Afterwards, in the evening of the same day, Stevens came to the defendants and represented to them that Austin, who lived outside of the city, had then gone home but would be in the city early the following morning and pay the defendants the said sum of $1,600. Stevens urged the defendants to sign the contract then so that it might be ready for delivery when Austin should come in the morning and pay said $1,600, and the defendants thereupon signed such contract, upon the express understanding that it should not be delivered or take effect until said $1,600 was paid to them. At the same time, at the urgent request of Stevens and upon his assurance that Austin would complete the contract early the next morning, the defendants signed the note in suit at a desk in their store, but did not deliver it, nor did they intend to deliver it until said $1,600 was paid to them and the sale of the farm consummated. As soon as the defendants had signed said note, "Stevens wrongfully and fraudulently reached and took said note from said desk, saying, as he did so, ' I will take charge of that,' and immediately walked out of said store, taking said note with him, without the consent of the defendants or either of them, and against their will.".

The counterclaim further alleges that said Austin has refused to pay said sum of $1,600, or to recognize said contract as binding, claiming that he never agreed to the terms thereof or delivered the same; that on the day after the transactions above stated the defendants demanded said note from Stevens, but he refused to deliver the same to them, claiming to have sold it to Mr. B. F. Dunwiddie; and that, upon demand, Mr. Dunwiddie refused to deliver the note to them. Judgment is demanded on the counterclaim that the note be adjudged to be null and void and be delivered up to be canceled.

In reply to the counterclaim the plaintiff alleged that the note was executed and delivered by the defendants to Stevens after the contract for the sale of the land to Austin had been fully consummated and the commissions fully earned.

The jury found a special verdict to the effect that the note had never been delivered to, or intrusted to the keeping of, Stevens by the defendants or either of them or by their attorney or agent; that the signing of the note by the defendants was procured by the fraudulent acts or representations of Stevens, and that the note was wrongfully and fraudulently taken from their store by Stevens without their consent, either express or implied; that B. F. Dunwiddie purchased the note in good faith for S. A. Dean, with S. A. Dean's money, and that he had no knowledge that it was obtained from the defendants by fraud and no notice that the payees were not the rightful and lawful holders and owners of the same; that the defendants were not guilty of any negligence in not preventing Stevens from taking the note from their store; that B. F. Dunwiddie was not guilty of any negligence in purchasing the note from Wheeler & Stevens; that the note was transferred to the plaintiff before it fell due, but that she was not the lawful holder and owner of it at the time of the commencement of this action.

From the judgment entered on the verdict, in favor of the defendants, the plaintiff appeals.

William Smith, attorney, and *Edward M. Hyzer*, of counsel, for the appellant, argued that if there was no delivery of the note, or no intention to deliver it, then ,the defendants' negligence in permitting the payee to take the note from their store and in their presence without objection was sufficient to prevent them from defending against an innocent purchaser, and the court should have directed a verdict for the plaintiff. *Greenfield's Estate*, 14 Pa. St. 496; Daniels on Neg. Inst. sec. 850; *Kellogg v. Steiner*, 29 Wis. 626–631; *Nebeker v. Cutsinger*, 48 Ind. 436; *Kellogg v. Curtis*, 65 Me. 59; *Williams v. Stoll*, 79 Ind. 80. This question of negligence goes further than mere want of ordinary care; the defendants were bound to show affirmatively that they were guilty of no *laches or negligence*. *Chapman v. Rose*, 56 N. Y. 137; *Ross v. Doland*, 29 Ohio St. 473; *Mackey v. Peterson*, 29 Minn. 298; *Ort v. Fowler*, 31 Kan. 478; *Walker v. Ebert*, 29 Wis. 194. If there was a delivery upon condition, the condition was void as to the plaintiff; for the delivery of a negotiable promissory note to the payee, to take effect upon the happening of a future event, followed by transfer to an innocent purchaser for value before due, binds the maker of the note, although the transfer was fraudulent as between the original parties. Daniels on Neg. Inst. secs. 855, 856; *Massmann v. Holscher*, 49 Mo. 87; *Clark v. Thayer*, 105 Mass. 216; *Collins v. Gilbert*, 94 U. S. 753; *Stoddard v. Kimball*, 6 Cush. 469; 102 U. S. 442–444; *Davy v. Kelley*, 66 Wis. 452; *Platt v. Beebe*, 57 N. Y. 339; *Bank of N. Y. v. Vanderhorst*, 32 id. 553; *Stalker v. M'Donald*, 6 Hill, 93; *Coddington v. Bay*, 20 Johns. 637;

Park Bank v. Watson, 42 N. Y. 490; *First Nat. Bank v. Hall*, 44 id. 395; *Essex Co. Bank v. Russell*, 29 id. 673; *Merchants' Nat. Bank v. Comstock*, 55 id. 24; *Van Duzer v. Howe*, 21 id. 531; *Comstock v. Hier*, 73 id. 269; *Farmers' & C. N. Bank v. Noxon*, 45 id. 762; *Clarke v. Johnson*, 54 Ill. 296; Randolph, Comm. Paper, sec. 1888. It cannot be argued that this note was delivered in escrow, for a note cannot be delivered to the payee in escrow. Such delivery becomes absolute. *Steward v. Anderson*, 59 Ind. 385; *Johnson v. Branch*, 11 Humph. 521.

Wm. Ruger, for the respondents.

COLE, C. J.   If this were an action between the original parties to the note in suit, it is plain there could be no recovery, because it appears that the sale of the farm was not completed.   Austin refused to pay the $1,600, and the contract was abandoned, so that the commissions, which were the sole consideration of the note, were not in fact earned, which would be a perfect defense.   But it is claimed that the plaintiff is an innocent purchaser of the note for value, and is not affected by any equities which may exist between the original parties to the paper.   We assume, as a fact, that the plaintiff is such a holder, and the case will be considered in that light.   Very elaborate briefs have been filed, and numerous errors are assigned to the rulings of the trial court.   It would be burdensome to attempt to notice in detail these various assignments of error, and we do not deem it necessary that we should do so for a proper disposition of the case.   There are really but two questions to be considered: (1) Was there a delivery of the note, conditional or otherwise, so as to give it a legal existence?   (2) If not, were the defendants guilty of such negligence in suffering or in not preventing Stevens from taking and retaining the note as renders them liable for its payment in the hands of an innocent party?

Now, as to the delivery, the jury found, in answer to

questions submitted, that the defendants never made a delivery of the note; that they did not intrust it to the keeping of Stevens; that Stevens wrongfully and fraudulently took it from the store of the defendants, without their consent either express or implied. These findings are not only sustained by the testimony, but are in accord with the clear, distinct, and overwhelming weight of evidence relating to that question. We are fully satisfied with the verdict, and do not well see how any other result could have been reached. The learned circuit court gave a full charge bearing on the question of delivery, stating, as it appears to us, the law very fairly which was applicable to the facts disclosed on the trial. The court finally closed its charge on that point by instructing the jury that if they found from the evidence that the defendants, either in person or by their agent or attorney, in any manner delivered the note to Stevens as evidence of a subsisting debt, and that the plaintiff was a *bona fide* purchaser for value, before maturity, their verdict must be for the plaintiff.

The question as to the defendant's negligence was likewise submitted to the jury upon all the evidence. The jury found that the defendants were not guilty of any negligence in not preventing Stevens from taking the note from the store. It appears that the note was signed by the defendants at their store on the evening of its date, and it is conclusively shown that, while it lay on the desk where it had been signed, Stevens, of his own motion, without the consent, either express or implied, of the defendants, took the note from the desk, saying, as he did so, " I will take charge of this," put the note in his pocket, and went out of the store. The next morning he sold the note to Mr. Dunwiddie. Mr. Sale, who had drawn up the contract for the sale of the farm, and who had acted in the transaction, to some extent at least, as the attorney of the defendants, was in the store at the time Stevens took the note, as was Mr.

Galbraith, the husband of one of the makers. The note
had been signed that evening at the strong solicitation of
Stevens, with the expectation that the contract for the sale
of the farm to Mr. Austin would be completed and delivered the following day. The contract was intrusted to Mr.
Sale to keep until Mr. Austin came in and paid the $1,600
provided for in the contract, but the safe-keeping of the
note seems to have been strangely overlooked. This may
be accounted for by the fact that all parties expected that
the business would be consummated the next morning. No
objection or protest was made by the defendants, or their
attorney, Judge Sale, or by Mr. Galbraith, to Stevens' taking the note into his possession and carrying it away as he
did. They all say they did not think anything about it at
the time or were surprised at his conduct. Still, as Stevens
had acted as the agent of the defendants in making the
sale, it is not, perhaps, strange that they did not object to
his taking the charge of the note until morning. It is now
insisted by the counsel for the plaintiff that the court should
have held, as a matter of law, that the defendants were
guilty of gross negligence in permitting Stevens to take
and go away with the note. Upon all the facts, we think
it was clearly a question for the jury whether due prudence
and caution had been exercised as to the possession of the
note. We have just referred to the fact that Stevens was
acting as the agent of the defendants in making sale of the
farm, and there does not seem to have been anything in his
conduct in the matter which would excite suspicion or doubt
as to his integrity or trustworthiness. It would have been
quite natural, and according to the usual course of transacting such business, to have intrusted all the papers to him,
as a depositary, until the business was completed the next
morning. Indeed, we see little ground for imputing negligence to any one in permitting Stevens to take the note, in
view of the relation which he had occupied and still held

to the defendants. When it is seen how dishonorably he has acted, and how grossly he has betrayed the rights of his principals, it is easy to make the inference that no ordinarily prudent man would have intrusted him with the safe-keeping of the note. But our conclusion upon the whole case is that the question of negligence, as well as that of delivery, was fairly submitted upon the evidence, under proper instructions, and we see no reason for disturbing the verdict. The judgment of the circuit court must therefore be affirmed.

By the Court.— Judgment affirmed.

STANLEY, Appellant, vs. SULLIVAN, Respondent.

April 4 — April 17, 1888.

Execution: Writ of assistance: Homestead: Divorce: Lien of judgment.

1. A writ of assistance, under sec. 3025, R. S., to put the purchaser in possession of land sold on execution should not be issued where there is a *bona fide* contest as to his right to the possession of the land under such sale,— as where the defendant in good faith claims that the premises were his homestead and as such exempt from sale on execution.

2. A judgment in a divorce action that the plaintiff wife recover a certain sum of money,— it not being declared that the same is for alimony or in lieu of alimony, or that the judgment shall be a lien upon any of the defendant's real or personal estate,— is a mere money judgment, and execution thereon cannot be levied on the defendant's homestead.

APPEAL from the Circuit Court for *Chippewa* County. The appeal is from an order denying a writ of assistance. The facts are stated in the opinion.

John Randall, for the appellant.

For the respondent the cause was submitted on the brief of *Stafford & Connor*.

TAYLOR, J.   This was an application by the appellant for a writ of assistance to put the applicant into the possession of a parcel of real estate which he claims had been sold on an execution issued upon a judgment in an action for divorce brought by Mary J. Sullivan, as plaintiff, against her husband, *Daniel Sullivan*, the respondent in this appeal. Upon such execution sale a sheriff's deed had been issued to the applicant.   Possession of the premises had been demanded of the defendant, *Daniel Sullivan*, by the applicant, and he refused to surrender the possession to him. The respondent resisted the motion for the writ on the ground that the property sold on the execution was his homestead at the time the judgment was rendered and docketed, as well as at the time of the sale thereof upon said execution.   The circuit court refused to order the writ to issue, but without prejudice to the right of the applicant to bring an action of ejectment to recover said lands.

The application for the writ was made under the provisions of sec. 3025, R. S. 1878.   Previous to the enactment of said section in 1878, the courts had never had the right, or, if they had, had never exercised the right, to issue a writ of assistance to put a purchaser of real estate upon an ordinary execution sale into the possession of the real estate so purchased by him.   Previous to the passage of this law the purchaser's only remedy in this state was by action of ejectment against the party in possession, if he refused to surrender the possession.

Courts of equity have from the earliest times exercised the right to issue the writ of assistance in actions in equity brought for the purpose of determining the rights of the litigants to the title or possession of real estate, after judgment declaring such rights, as well as in cases for the foreclosure of or redemption of mortgages.   In such cases the courts of equity having jurisdiction of the persons and property in controversy have, after determining the rights of the parties litigant to the title or possession of real estate, rightfully assumed the power to enforce their judgments by the writ of assistance to transfer the possession, instead of turning the party over to a court of law to recover such possession. *Roberdeau v. Rous*, 1 Atk. 543; *Penn v. Lord Baltimore*, 1 Ves. Sr. 444; 2 Eden on Injunctions (Waterman's ed.), 425; *Stribley v. Hawkie*, 3 Atk. 275; *Huguenin v. Baseley*, 15 Ves. Jr. 180; *Garretson v. Cole*, 1 Har. & J. 387; *Buffum's Case*, 13 N. H. 14; *Devaucene v. Devaucene*, 1 Edw. Ch. 272; *McKomb v. Kankey*, 1 Bland, 363; *Kershaw v. Thompson*, 4 Johns. Ch. 610; *Valentine v. Teller*, 1 Hopk. Ch. 422; *Diggle v. Boulden*, 48 Wis. 477; *Schenck v. Conover*, 13 N. J. Eq. 220. In these cases the writs only issued when the rights of the respective parties to be affected by it had been fully determined by the judgment in the action. In the case of *Schenck v. Conover*, *supra*, it is said: "It is scarcely necessary to add that the exercise of the power rests in the sound discretion of the court. It will never be exercised in a case of doubt, nor under color of its exercise will a question of legal title be tried or decided." This limitation upon the exercise of the right to issue a writ of assistance is recognized by all the authorities. See *Langley v. Voll*, 54 Cal. 435; *San Jose v. Fulton*, 45 Cal. 316; *Henderson v. McTucker*, 45 Cal. 647; *Barton v. Beatty*, 28 N. J. Eq. 412; *Vanmeter v. Borden*, 25 N. J. Eq. 414; *Thomas v. De Baum*, 14 N. J. Eq. 41.

We think the rule under the statute is no broader than the rule at common law when applied to cases coming within the statute. The statute extends the power to issue the writ to cases not coming within the common-law rule, but it was clearly not intended that the power should be exercised in a case where there was a *bona fide* contest as to the right of the purchaser at the execution sale to the possession of the lands under such sale. The statute starts out by declaring that "whenever a *title* shall have been perfected in any person to any real estate sold by virtue of an execution, or to any part thereof or interest therein, and the person against whom such execution issued, or any other person claiming under him by title arising subsequently to the docketing of the judgment upon which it issued, shall be in possession of any such real estate, or part thereof, or interest therein," etc. We think it is evident that this section, read in connection with our law in regard to homestead exemptions, could not have been intended to compel the court to issue the writ of assistance in favor of the purchaser of such exempted homestead upon an execution issued against the owner of the homestead in possession thereof at the time of its issue and sale and at the time the writ was applied for. The letter of the statute might be said to apply to such a case, but it seems to us very clear that such is not the spirit or meaning of the act. In the case of the sale of the homestead there would, under the law exempting it, be a failure on the part of the purchaser at the execution sale *to acquire a title* thereto by virtue of such sale. If, on the application for the writ in such case, there be a *bona fide* contention on the part of the defendant for the homestead exemption, we think it is eminently proper that the court should refuse the writ, and leave the parties to settle the right in an action at law, where the merits of the claim of the defendant may be passed upon by a full trial before a court and jury.

In order to obtain the writ of assistance under the statute the applicant must show that at the time the judgment was docketed the defendant in such execution had an interest in the real estate upon which the judgment so docketed was a lien, and that such defendant, or some one claiming under him by title acquired subsequently to the docketing of such judgment, is in possession and refuses to surrender such possession to the purchaser. On the application for this writ the respondent meets the claim by alleging that the judgment and execution under which the applicant for the writ claims the land never was a lien thereon, and that the property never was subject to sale upon such execution. The claim made by the respondent is not so clearly unfounded as to justify the court in holding, upon this application, that it is not made in good faith, or that it is so frivolous, either in fact or in law, that it should be ignored and the writ issued.

The learned counsel for the appellant claims that the judgment rendered in the divorce case against the defendant in the execution, the respondent on this appeal, is a lien upon the homestead. That presents a question of law, and might perhaps be determined upon the application for a writ of assistance under the statute; and if it must be held as a question of law that it was a lien upon the homestead of the respondent, and that such homestead was subject to sale on such judgment, as any other real estate owned by him, there would then seem to be no good reason for turning the appellant over to his action of ejectment to recover the possession of said premises. The judgment in the divorce case under which the execution was issued and the sale made, after adjudging that the said Mary J. Sullivan be divorced from the said *Daniel Sullivan*, proceeds to adjudge as follows: "And it is hereby further ordered and adjudged that the plaintiff be allowed, and have, and recover of the said defendant, *Daniel Sullivan*, by a judgment of this court, the sum of eight hundred dollars, and fifty dollars as attorney's fees, and the costs of this action, taxed at sixty-two and 90-100 dollars, and that execution issue therefor."

It will be seen that this is a mere money judgment, upon which execution is directed as in ordinary money judgments. It is not even declared that the $800 is for alimony or in lieu of alimony, and it does not declare that the judgment shall be a lien upon any of the defendant's real or personal estate. If a lien upon his real estate at all, it became so by docketing it as a money judgment. An execution issued upon this judgment can have no other efficacy than an execution issued upon any other money judgment. A homestead of the defendant is exempt from sale upon any execution issued upon any judgment for the recovery of money. See sec. 2983, R. S. The judgment upon which the execution in this case issued did not declare on its face that it should be a lien upon the homestead of the defendant, as the court probably might have declared it to be, and, in the absence of any such declaration of the court, it must be treated as having the same force as an ordinary judgment. We do not hesitate to say that, upon the showing made by the record introduced on the hearing, the judgment was not a lien upon the homestead of the defendant, if he had one, and that the writ of assistance was properly refused on that ground. Whether, as a matter of fact, the premises in question were and are the homestead of the respondent *Sullivan* was not determined by the court on the application for the writ; and, because the fact whether it was or was not a homestead was a matter of uncertainty upon the proofs offered upon the hearing of the motion, the court was right in refusing the writ. See cases above cited.

It is said by the learned counsel for the appellant that the circuit court had adjudged, in a former proceeding in the divorce action, that the premises in question were not a homestead. After a careful reading of these proceedings it appears to us that the question of homestead was not in issue in said proceedings, and was not passed upon by the court. The proceedings referred to by the learned counsel were the proceedings upon a motion made by the defendant, *Daniel Sullivan*, in the divorce suit, after judgment, to set aside said judgment, or that part of it which adjudged that he should pay the plaintiff, Mary J. Sullivan, the sum of $800 and the costs of the action. The grounds of the motion were that the judgment was for too large an amount, considering his ability to pay, and on the further ground that there was an agreement before judgment was entered, between the attorneys of the parties, that no judgment for alimony or allowance for the plaintiff should be taken in the action. The question of the liability of the homestead to be sold for the payment of the judgment was not discussed or considered by the court, so far as we are able to discover from the proceedings.

By the Court.— The order of the circuit court is affirmed.

MENDELSON, Appellant, vs. PASCHEN, Respondent.

April 4 — April 17, 1888.

(1, 2) Execution: Levy subject to mortgage: Estoppel: Amendment of return. (3) Debtor and creditor: Fraudulent conveyance: Evidence: Perverse verdict.

1. A sheriff who has levied an execution subject to a certain mortgage, and has so stated in his return, is estopped to question the validity of the mortgage; and he has no right in such case to take the property from the possession of the mortgagee.

2. If the return of the sheriff in such case is amendable it can be amended only upon proof that it was made by mistake and that it is untrue, with due notice to the parties interested in it, and by the court in which it is a part of the record.

3. The verdict of the jury in this case that a chattel mortgage was not given in good faith to secure an actual indebtedness, but was given with intent to hinder, delay, and defraud creditors, is *held* to have been clearly unwarranted by the evidence.

APPEAL from the County Court of *Milwaukee* County. Action against a sheriff for the conversion of personal property. The facts are stated in the opinion. There was a verdict for the defendant; a motion for a new trial was denied; and from the judgment entered on the verdict the plaintiff appealed.

W. C. Williams, for the appellant.

For the respondent there was a brief by *Somers, Somers & Dorr* and *Burke & Meyers,* and oral argument by *T. F. Somers.* To the point that the sheriff should be permitted, before or after judgment, to amend his return to process, in accordance with the facts, they cited *In re Remington,* 7 Wis. 643; *Moyer v. Cook,* 12 id. 335; *Bacon v. Bassett,* 19 id. 45; *Northrup v. Shephard,* 23 id. 513; *Robertson v. Kinkhead,* 26 id. 560; *Wait v. Sherman,* 61 id. 119; *Decker v. Armstrong,* 87 Mo. 316.

ORTON, J. One Augusta Boaz was a merchant in millinery goods, and had a stock of the value of about $2,232. She was being pressed by some creditor, and asked the plaintiff for a loan of $830 to be secured by a mortgage on said stock. He gave her the money by giving his check to the attorney of such creditor, and said check for such amount was paid by the bank on which it was drawn, and the claim of such creditor was in this way paid and discharged. Augusta Boaz gave the plaintiff her judgment notes for such sum, and secured the same by a chattel mortgage on said stock of goods. The plaintiff, deeming himself insecure, took possession of said stock on the mortgage, and was selling the same at retail to obtain his money. This was the condition of things when the defendant as sheriff levied certain executions which he held, issued on judgments against said Augusta, upon said stock of goods, *subject* to the said mortgage of the plaintiff, and made his return on said executions accordingly, and took full possession of said stock upon such levy, and sold the whole, thereof to satisfy in part the said executions. The plaintiff thereupon brought this suit against said defendant for the conversion of said goods. The defendant alleges in defense that the plaintiff's said mortgage is void, as having been given with intent to hinder, delay, or defraud the creditors of said Augusta.

The executions and other records and the mortgage and notes were in evidence, and the testimony showed the above facts. The jury found specially, *first*, that said mortgage was not given in good faith to secure an actual indebtedness due from Mrs. Boaz to the plaintiff; *second*, that the plaintiff did not loan to her the sum of $830 at the date of said mortgage, to take up the claim against her, as alleged, and that said mortgage was given with intent to hinder, delay, or defraud the creditors of the mortgagor; and then found the value of the goods, and generally for the defendant. There are several exceptions to the charge of the court to the jury, and to its refusal to instruct the jury as requested, but they mainly relate to the legal effect of the evidence, and we may as well decide the case upon its merits on the overruling of the motion to direct a verdict for the plaintiff, to set aside the verdict, and to grant a new trial.

We cannot but think that the verdict in this case is perverse, arbitrary, and unwarranted by any evidence. We can scarcely find any evidence whatever of the plaintiff's intent to defraud the creditors of Augusta Boaz, and the fact of the *bona fide* and actual existence of the debt which the mortgage was given to secure was established by the most conclusive evidence. It requires clear and satisfactory evidence to establish fraud in such a case, and yet there was nothing above a bare and ungrounded suspicion of it in this case. The sheriff levied upon the stock of goods *subject* to this mortgage, and so made his return on the executions. In other words, he levied only upon the interest which the mortgagor, Augusta Boaz, had in the property after satisfying said mortgage, and so made his return. He is therefore estopped from questioning the mortgage. He has no interest in questioning it; for he only levied upon the interest of the mortgagor over and above the mortgage, and can claim no other or greater interest in it. He had no right, by his limited levy subject to the mortgage, to take possession of the property, and much less to take it from the possession of the plaintiff, the mortgagee. He could only sell the interest of the mortgagor in it over and above the mortgage claims upon it, or the overplus after the satisfaction of the mortgage. He is concluded by his return, and he is not permitted to question it. These principles have been so long recognized by the courts as to be elementary. *Cotton v. Marsh*, 3 Wis. 221; *Cotton v. Watkins*, 6 Wis. 629; *Eastman v. Bennett*, 6 Wis. 232; *Frisbee v. Langworthy*, 11 Wis. 375; *Saxton v. Williams*, 15 Wis. 292; Freem. Exec. § 363; Crock. Sher. § 45; Binm. Sher. § 280; Smith, Sher. 216, and notes of cases; *Ohlson v. Pierce*, 55 Wis. 205; *Irvin v. Smith*, 66 Wis. 113. It is very questionable whether such a return is amendable; but if so, it must be done upon proof that it was made by mistake and that it is untrue, with due notice to the parties interested in it, and by the court in which it is a part of the record. There was no proof of any proper amendment of the return indorsed on the exceptions, and it stands as a verity in the case. *Arnold v. Nye*, 23 Mich. 296; *Haynes v. Knowles*, 36 Mich. 409; *Townsend v. Olin*, 5 Wend. 207; *Browning v. Hanford*, 5 Denio, 586; *Langdon v. Summers' Adm'r*, 10 Ohio St. 77. The verdict was most clearly unsupported by the evidence.

By the Court.— The judgment is reversed, and the cause remanded to the superior court of Milwaukee county for a new trial.

THE STATE EX REL. TURNER VS. THE CIRCUIT COURT FOR
OZAUKEE COUNTY.

March 27 — May 12, 1888.

Jurisdiction: Criminal law: New trial after affirmance of judgment.

The circuit court has jurisdiction, under sec. 4719, R. S., to grant a
new trial in a criminal case within the time therein prescribed, although, after a previous motion for a new trial had been denied,
judgment was entered and such judgment has been affirmed by
the supreme court on writ of error. ORTON, J., dissents.

CERTIORARI to the Circuit Court for *Ozaukee* County.
The facts are stated in the opinion. The case of *Town
of Saukville v. The State* is reported in 69 Wis. 178.

For the relator there was a brief signed by *Eugene S.
Turner*, special district attorney, with *Geo. W. Foster* as
counsel, and the cause was argued orally by the *Attorney
General*.

For the defendant there was a brief by *Turner & Timlin*,
and oral argument by *Mr. W. H. Timlin*.

COLE, C. J. The town of Saukville was indicted for not
repairing a bridge, and was found guilty. A motion was
made to set aside the verdict and for a new trial, which
motion was denied, and the defendant town was sentenced
to pay a fine of $250. The cause was then brought to this
court on a writ of error, and the judgment of the circuit
court was affirmed. On the return of the record to the circuit court the defendant made a motion, founded upon a
petition and affidavits, for a new trial, which motion was
granted. A common-law writ of *certiorari* was then issued
from this court to review the order of the circuit court
granting a new trial. A motion is now made to quash the
writ because it was improvidently granted, and that motion
is the matter to be considered. The rule is well settled in
this court that the only question arising on the motion is

the question of jurisdiction. Where the writ issues to review the proceedings of a court, that is the only question which will be examined, though it is otherwise when it issues to review the proceedings of officers or bodies not proceeding according to the common law. It is not necessary to cite our decisions where these principles have been adjudicated and settled.

Had, then, the circuit court power or jurisdiction to grant a new trial in this cause? For the purposes of the case, jurisdiction may be defined to be the power to hear and determine the cause or controversy before the court, or the power to grant the motion for a new trial. See *Wanzer v. Howland*, 10 Wis. 16; *Pollard v. Wegener*, 13 Wis. 569; *Arnold v. Booth*, 14 Wis. 180; *Hauser v. State*, 33 Wis. 678. Sec. 4719, R. S., reads as follows: " The circuit court may, at the term in which the trial of any indictment or information shall be had, or within one year thereafter, and in either case before or after judgment, on the petition or motion in writing of the defendant, grant a new trial for any cause for which, by law, a new trial may be granted, or when it shall appear to the court that justice has not been done, and on such terms as the court may direct." It appears that a proper motion was made within one year from the judgment, upon the grounds addressed to the discretion of the circuit court, and a new trial was undoubtedly granted under the special authority conferred by the above statute; and the question now is, Had the court power to grant it? We can only consider the question of the power or jurisdiction of the court in the matter, not whether it exercised that power wisely or granted the motion on insufficient grounds, for the court may have erred, but error does not affect its jurisdiction.

This statute was probably borrowed from Massachusetts. See Pub. Stats. of Mass. 1882, ch. 114, sec. 128; *Comm. v. Peck*, 1 Met. 428; *Comm. v. McElhaney*, 111 Mass. 439;

Comm. v. Scott, 123 Mass. 418. Also Terr. Stats. of Wis. (1839), p. 377, sec. 6; R. S. 1849, ch. 149, sec. 6; R. S. 1858, ch. 180, sec. 6. We do not well see upon what grounds the power of the court to grant the new trial can be denied if the provision is valid. The fact that the judgment has been affirmed by this court furnishes no sufficient reason for denying that power. It is said by the affirmance of the judgment it became a finality, a final determination of the cause and sentence of the law. That view certainly would be correct had not the legislature conferred this special authority to grant a new trial upon a proper cause shown. On affirmance of a judgment in a civil case no new trial could be granted unless the statute authorized it. Only where the statute does authorize it can a new trial after affirmance be granted, either in a civil or criminal cause. In actions of ejectment the circuit court can grant a new trial even after affirmance by this court, and this by virtue of a statute upon the subject. *Haseltine v. Simpson*, 61 Wis. 427. Consequently we can perceive no sufficient grounds or reasons for denying the validity of the statute to grant a new trial after judgment has been affirmed in this court, any more in a criminal than in a civil cause. So under sec. 2832, R. S., a large discretionary power is vested in the court to relieve a party within a year from a judgment through mistake or excusable neglect. In the *McElhaney Case*, it was held that a new trial might be granted in a capital case after sentence of death passed and exceptions had been overruled by the supreme court, which was equivalent to an affirmance of the conviction. True, in that case a new trial was refused, but still the court distinctly affirm the point stated. It may be conceded that independently of the statute the court would have no power to grant a new trial after the affirmance of the judgment. But as the statute expressly authorizes it, the circuit court may, either before or after judgment, grant a new trial within a year.   This right the legislature has seen fit to extend to the convicted party, and we do not see that the provision is obnoxious to any consti-tutional objection.   The reason and policy of this statute are stated by Mr. Justice TAYLOR in *Ohms v. State*, 49 Wis. 421. Chief Justice SHAW, in *Comm. v. Peck*, 1 Met. 428, gives some reasons in vindication of the wisdom and necessity of the statute.   He says: "It may sometimes occur that from the discovery of new evidence it would be perfectly in the power of the defendant to establish his innocence by plenary evidence, if he could avail himself of an opportunity to bring it before a jury.   Between the trial and sentence it might be discovered that the conviction was the result of con-spiracy and perjury, which could be fully demonstrated on another trial."   It was doubtless some such considerations which induced the legislature to enact the provision, and effect should be given to it in a proper case.

Quite an elaborate argument is made on behalf of the relator to establish the position that the court ought not to have granted a new trial on the case presented.   It may be that the court erred in its decision, but for the reasons be-fore indicated we cannot consider that point.   On this writ we do not review the decision for error, but merely the question whether the court had jurisdiction to make it. Upon that point we confess we are entirely clear that the court, in granting a new trial, did not exceed its jurisdic-tion, even though it may have erred in granting the trial upon the case presented.   *Hauser v. State*, 33 Wis. 678; *In re Semlar*, 41 Wis. 517.   It seems hardly necessary to add that the power of the court is rested exclusively upon the au-thority conferred by the statute, and not upon its general jurisdiction.

It follows from these views that the motion to quash the writ must be sustained.

ORTON, J. The undersigned most respectfully hereby dissents from the decision of the motion in this case. The cause of *The State v. The Town of Saukville* had been tried before a jury on a plea of not guilty on its merits. The jury found the defendant guilty, and the court sentenced it to pay a fine of $250 and costs. In due time the defendant made a motion to set aside the verdict and to grant a new trial in the cause, which was overruled, and the defendant excepted. On writ of error to this court and bill of exceptions said judgment was affirmed, absolutely, and without any reservation. After the *remittitur*, the circuit court granted a new trial in the cause ostensibly on the ground that certain evidence which had been given and considered at the trial did not appear in the bill of exceptions in this court, and for other reasons. This was done, as claimed, by virtue of sec. 4719, R. S., which provides that the circuit court may, at the " term in which the trial of any indictment or information shall be had, or within one year thereafter, grant a new trial for any cause for which, by law, a new trial may be granted, *or when it shall appear to the court that justice has not been done.*" The new trial was evidently granted under the power given by this last clause of the section, for the cause stated was not sufficient as the ordinary ground of a new trial.

This proceeding was brought to this court by *certiorari*. The defendant moved in this court to quash the writ, on the ground that the circuit court had the power and jurisdiction under the above statute to grant such new trial. This court sustained the motion, holding that the circuit court had such power and jurisdiction under said statute, notwithstanding the affirmance of the judgment on the writ of error. The motion was submitted on the brief of the defendant's counsel, and on a brief of an attorney for the state, the attorney general for some reason omitting to file any brief or cite any authorities on behalf of the state.

In my opinion this motion involved, and the decision has disposed of, the most important question of jurisdiction ever presented to this court. The constitutional jurisdiction of this court not only embraces its power to hear and determine causes coming before it within its appellate jurisdiction and general control over inferior courts, but it embraces also the legal effect of its judgments as *res adjudicatæ*. The legislature, in carrying out the provision of the constitution conferring its jurisdiction, provided that it "may reverse, *affirm*, or modify the judgment, etc., and may, *if necessary or proper*, order a new trial," and "shall remit its judgment or decision to the court from which the appeal or writ of error was taken, *to be enforced accordingly*." Sec. 3071, R. S. This statute does not confer any jurisdiction upon the court, but it is an interpretation of the constitutional provision, and gives it practical effect. Its jurisdiction and judgments are therefore supreme, *dernier*, final, and conclusive, not only as to the subject matter and parties, but also as to all inferior courts in respect thereto. Any law which abridges, impairs, or limits this jurisdiction is void. For instance, if a law should provide for another court that should have a superior appellate jurisdiction and the power to hear and determine appeals and writs of error from this court, and to reverse, affirm, or modify its judgments, or to revise in any manner its proceedings, it would be void. So, also, any law which should give to the circuit court or any other inferior court the power to affect or impair the finality or conclusiveness of its judgments, either by review or by a new trial in the action, or directly or indirectly, would be equally void. The judgment of *affirmance* by this court makes the judgment of the court below its judgment, and such judgment is final and conclusive, and, when remitted to the court below, it is "to be enforced accordingly." This is the clear and unquestionable constitutional effect of a judgment of *affirmance*, or it has no effect whatever. A statute that should allow the court below to grant a new trial in the action after such judgment of affirmance, would utterly destroy its constitutional effect. If the new trial should result in the same judgment as on the first trial, on the second appeal to this court there might be another judgment of affirmance, but on new grounds, or a judgment of reversal and a new trial ordered. But even that second judgment of affirmance is not *final*, for under this statute the circuit court might grant another new trial, under that broad ground " that justice has not been done," and so on *forever*. · In case of an appeal from the judgment on the second trial, if it should be reversed by this court, then its final judgment of affirmance is effectually wiped out. This court on *reversal* may grant another new trial, or the circuit court may grant a new trial within one year from any subsequent judgment, and so on *ad infinitum*. Can there be any doubt that such a statute would be unconstitutional for having destroyed the effect of the final judgments of this *supreme* appellate court? To give the court below this unlimited control of judgments of affirmance by successive new trials, would practically make litigation in the same action interminable, when the constitution has provided a supreme tribunal in which it shall end forever. In criminal cases such retrials and delays after affirmance of the conviction by this court, would destroy the ultimate certainty of final conviction, and defeat the prompt execution of the criminal laws by the escape of prisoners, the death or removal of witnesses, the loss of testimony, and the increased chances of acquittal, that would justify the present extreme public opinion that criminals escape punishment through the delays and uncertainties of trial, through the meshes and endless circumlocutions of the law. But the *practical* effect of the violation of this principle of the absolute finality and conclusiveness of a judgment of affirmance upon appeal or writ of error from a final judgment of the court below by which the *whole case* is brought to this court, is not the question. The question is one of the *jurisdiction* of this court, as to the effect of its judgments, within the constitutional power to hear and *determine* cases vested in this court of *final* appeal and of *last* resort. It is the violation of this principle that will be followed by these practical and ruinous consequences, and which no doubt constituted the reason for its establishment, which is the only matter to be considered.

If the judgments and orders of the inferior court which are not final but only interlocutory, as intermediate steps in the proceedings, are brought to this court, then, of course, the judgment of affirmance by this court is limited to the precise matter appealed, and is final only as to that alone, while the main case remains all the time in the court below. It is only where the judgments appealed are final and fully dispose of the whole cause, as in this instance, that the affirmance thereof has the effect for which I contend. But as to such judgments the affirmance thereof must necessarily be *res adjudicata*, and final as to the whole case, both as to the law and facts.

So far I have contended that any mere law which should authorize the lower court to do anything which would destroy or impair the finality and conclusiveness of a judgment of affirmance in such cases, is void. But the statute referred to has no reference whatever to such cases. It refers to cases which have remained in the lower court, and over which it has full jurisdiction before any such final determination in this court. In criminal cases the statute provides two methods of bringing them to the attention of this court without a writ of error, which brings the whole record and the whole case to this court, and they are, *first*, by special exceptions; and, *second*, by special questions of law certified to this court. In the first case the exceptions are sustained or overruled, and in the second the questions or interrogatories of the court below are specifically answered. Secs. 4720, 4721, R. S. These proceedings are *special*, and the action of this court is confined strictly to them. Neither an appeal nor writ of error is taken from the judgment, and the main case remains in the court below, and there is no judgment of affirmance or reversal in this court. The special exceptions or questions are alone considered and disposed of. If there is a judgment in the court below, it is neither reversed nor affirmed by this court, but remains to be otherwise disposed of. To show the wide difference between such cases and those brought to this court by writ of error it is only necessary to notice the proviso of sec. 4723, which is as follows: "But the proceedings here prescribed shall not deprive any party of his *writ of error* for any error or defect appearing of *record*." I speak of the obvious differences between such cases and this case, in which the final judgment of conviction and sentence on a verdict of guilty was affirmed on a *writ of error* by this court, because the only authority which could be found in all the books claimed to have any such effect, and that is cited in the opinion to sustain this ruling, is the case of *Comm. v. McElhaney*, 111 Mass. 439. That case was disposed of by the supreme court of that state on just such *special exceptions* as we have mentioned, and not at all analogous even to an affirmance of the judgment on a writ of error. It is claimed that our statute (sec. 4719, R. S.) was borrowed from that of Massachusetts, and should have the same construction. Admitting that to be so, that case has no application to or is any authority in this case, for the above reasons. But our statute has one very significant clause that is not found in the Massachusetts statute, which limits our statute to exclude even the power in the circuit court to grant a new trial after such special exceptions are disposed of by this court, without the *mandate* of this court, and most clearly shows that the statute does not in its terms extend to cases in which the final judgment of the court below has been affirmed on writ of error. That clause is, " *before or after judgment.*" This language can mean nothing else than to refer to cases which are in the circuit court and remain there without the intervention of a writ of error or a judgment of affirmance or even of special exceptions.

We conclude, therefore, that the decision of this motion is absolutely without *authority* as well as in violation of reason and the constitution. This statute, in its general terms, is no broader in its application to criminal cases than the statutes which authorize the circuit court to grant new trials generally or in civil cases, or even as broad, by reason of the above clause, which clearly limits its operation to cases which have continued all the time in the circuit court, and within its full jurisdiction, " before or after judgment." In civil cases a new trial may be granted on the minutes of the court, or upon exceptions, for newly-discovered evidence, the verdict being contrary to the law or evidence, or for excessive damages, and other causes, with the only limitation that the " motion must be heard at a special or regular term." R. S. sec. 2878, *et seq.* The court or judge of the circuit court may relieve a party from a judgment " through mistake, inadvertence, surprise, or excusable neglect," with the only limitation of " one year after notice thereof." Sec. 2832, R. S. There is no exception made of any such cases as have been *affirmed* on appeal or writ of error by this court, whether civil or criminal. They all stand alike in this respect. It follows, therefore, that this decision is a *binding precedent* as to the power of the court below to grant new trials in *all* cases, after an absolute and unqualified *affirmance* of the final judgment by this court. The statutes and the reasons are the same in all possible cases, and the circuit courts and other courts of record may grant new trials *ad libitum* in all cases after an appeal from the final judgment of the whole case, and affirmance thereof by this court without qualification or mandate, for any of the causes named in the statute, within the time limited.

These consequences of the decision may not be ignored, even if they were overlooked, or however *insidious* the precedent, and they will be more serious and deplorable in criminal cases than in civil, because they affect the prompt and certain execution of the criminal law for the protection of the peace and good order of society, by opening the *vista* of an interminable series of trials after the affirmance of the final judgment of conviction by this court, by which the criminal may finally escape. But more important than even these practical consequences is the emasculation or destruction of the constitutional power and jurisdiction of this court, as the court of *last resort*, to render judgments of finality. Already this court has four times decided, in the strongest language possible, that its judgments of *affirmance* are final as to the subject matter appealed, and that the court below can take no step or do anything to impair or change it in the least particular. If the *whole* case be appealed, or is taken by writ of error from the final judgment, then the judgment of affirmance by this court is final and conclusive as to the *whole* case, and the court below, on *remittitur*, can do nothing in the case, or with it, except to execute this final judgment of this court. In *Smith v. Armstrong*, 25 Wis. 517, Mr. Justice PAINE says in the opinion: "This very judgment, having been rendered and *affirmed* on appeal to this court, has become *final* between the parties, and even though it were conceded that there *were errors* in it, they are no longer subject to correction in the circuit court under the *guise* of amendment." In *Stevens v. Clark Co.* 43 Wis. 36, Chief Justice RYAN said: "We know of no case in this court, or indeed elsewhere, in which a judgment of *affirmance* has directed a new trial. Indeed affirmance of a judgment, *ex vi termini*, seems to preclude a new trial. . . . There is neither statute to authorize, nor practice to sanction, a *discretion for a new trial, upon affirmance.* Such a discretion would convert *affirmance* into reversal." In *Wells v. Am. Exp. Co.* 55 Wis. 23, one of the parties sought to get rid of an order allowing the withdrawal of a stipulation which dispensed with the production of certain evidence which was then supposed to be easily obtainable, which had been affirmed by this court. It was afterwards found that said evidence was not obtainable, and that the order was so made under a mistake. It was held that the affirmance was *res adjudicata*, and there was no relief against it. In *Mowry v. First Nat. Bank*, 66 Wis. 539, it was held that after a judgment had been in part reversed and in part *affirmed* by this court, the part reversed was subject to further trial in the court below, but the part *affirmed* was *res adjudicata* and not subject to further litigation in the court below. In numerous cases in this court it has been held that all the judgments of this court, whether of reversal or affirmance, are final and conclusive except by the express mandate of this court which authorizes further action by the court below. *Luning v. State*, 2 Pin. 215; *Parker v. Pomeroy*, 2 Wis. 112; *Downer v. Cross*, 2 Wis. 371; *Cole v. Clarke*, 3 Wis. 323; *Ranney v. Higby*, 6 Wis. 28; *Miner v. Medbury*, 7 Wis. 100; *Hill v. Hoover*, 9 Wis. 15; *Eastman v. Harteau*, 12 Wis. 267; *Du Pont v. Davis*, 35 Wis. 631; *Hutchinson v. C. & N. W. R. Co.* 41 Wis. 541; *Mohr v. Tulip*, 44 Wis. 274; *Mills v. Evansville Seminary*, 52 Wis. 669, and many other cases.

In other states where the jurisdiction of the supreme court in respect to appeals and writs of error is the same as ours, it has been uniformly held that after a judgment of affirmance the court below can do nothing in the case except to execute such judgment, and no case can be found where it is held otherwise. All objections to the judgment not brought before the supreme court by writ of error and finally disposed of by judgment of *affirmance* are waived, and the judgment is final as to the whole case. *Rider v. Union India Rubber Co.* 4 Bosw. 169. A judgment of affirmance upon an equal division of the judges is equally final, and cannot be set aside by the court below. *Mason v. Jones*, 3 N. Y. 375. In *Lyon v. Merritt*, 6 Paige, 473, the defendant moved in the court of chancery to alter or modify its decree which had been affirmed on appeal by the court for the correction of errors, on affidavit of new facts and newly-discovered evidence. It was held that the chancellor had no such power, and that the judgment of *affirmance* was *res adjudicata* between the parties and as to the subject matter, and that unless the judgment of affirmance reserved such right it was gone forever. After the order of the chancellor has been affirmed on appeal, the chancellor has no power to correct even errors in calculation. *Utica Ins. Co. v. Lynch*, 2 Barb. Ch. 573. After judgment of affirmance, no other or different judgment can ever be entered in the case in any way or by any proceeding. It is *res adjudicata*. *De Agreda v. Mantel*, 1 Abb. Pr. 130. When a judgment is brought into the highest court of the state by appeal or writ of error, and affirmed therein, the final judgment is in the latter court, and the inferior court has nothing to do with it except to carry out and execute it, and can take no step in the case that might result in affecting it in any way. *Eno v. Crooke*, 6 How. Pr. 462. In this case it was held also that the court below could do nothing except to issue execution to enforce the judgment of affirmance. In New York this important principle is held so strictly that an *affirmance* of the judgment upon the dismissal of the appeal or writ of error, is equally a finality, and must be executed by the lower court. *Union India Rubber Co. v. Babcock*, 4 Duer, 620. When a judgment of the supreme court of New York is affirmed by the court of errors, such judgment of *affirmance* is *res adjudicata*, and conclusive as to every question it embraced and upon which, in a subsequent suit, the right of the plaintiff to recover, or the validity of the defense, is found to depend, *under any state of facts* or *under any evidence*. *Birckhead v. Brown*, 5 Sandf. 134. In this case the affirmance was upon an equal division of the judges, and the question was very fully considered as one of jurisdiction.

When a judgment or decree of a circuit court of the United States has been affirmed by the supreme court, even by a division of the judges, it is final and conclusive, and nothing remains for the lower court to do in the case except to execute it, and this is the doctrine of *affirmance* by the House of Lords on appeal in England. *Durant v. Essex Co.* 7 Wall. 107. A judgment is *affirmed* because it is correct in itself, and is therefore final and conclusive. *Whiting v. Root*, 52 Iowa, 292; *Jamison v. Perry*, 38 Iowa, 14. A judgment of *affirmance* will be conclusive upon all questions which might have been raised in the court below. If they are brought up by the appeal they are finally disposed of, and if not so brought up they will be treated as waived, and the affirmance must be final in all cases. *Grimes v. Hamilton Co.* 37 Iowa, 290. When the plaintiff failed to plead over or to prosecute his suit on overruling his demurrer to the answer, but appealed from the order overruling the demurrer, and the order is *affirmed*, the judgment of the supreme court is final beyond relief. *Dunlap v. Cody*, 31 Iowa, 260. When a judgment of the lower court has been affirmed by the supreme court, the judgment of affirmance is the final judgment, and not the judgment appealed from, and can only be set aside or modified by the supreme court, if at all. *Griffin v. Seymour*, 15 Iowa, 30. After an affirmance of a judgment on an appeal which brings up the whole case or on its merits, there can be no trial *de novo*. *Trescott v. Barnes*, 51 Iowa, 409. Where a judgment against several must be reversed as to some of the appellants, and ought to be affirmed as to others, the supreme court will *reverse* the whole judgment as to all, lest a judgment of affirmance as to some, by reason of its being *res adjudicata*, might have the effect to embarrass or hinder the new trial of the other appellants. *Gaar v. Millikan*, 68 Ind. 208. A complaint to *review* a judgment after affirmance must be on *new matter*, but not on *newly-discovered evidence*. The complaint must make a *new case*, and be filed within a certain time. *Hill v. Roach*, 72 Ind. 57. Newly-discovered evidence is not such new matter as to entitle a party to review a judgment. *Fleming v. Stout*, 19 Ind. 328; *Rousch v. Layton*, 51 Ind. 106; *Webster v. Maiden*, 41 Ind. 124. On a *remittitur* from the court of appeals of New York of a judgment of *affirmance*, not even a matter of costs can be corrected by the court below. The lower court can do nothing in the case except to execute the judgment of affirmance. *McGregor v. Buell*, 33 How. Pr. 450. On a judgment of reversal the court below cannot grant a new trial unless ordered by the supreme court, and on a judgment of affirmance no new trial can be had from the very nature of the judgment as a finality. *Davidson v. Dallas*, 15 Cal. 75. From the consequences of a judgment of affirmance as *res adjudicata* the parties cannot in any way be relieved by the lower court. *Phelan v. San Francisco*, 20 Cal. 45. After a judgment of affirmance by the supreme court of the United States the same case cannot be further litigated so as to ever come to the supreme court again by any proceeding. *Washington Bridge Co. v. Stewart*, 3 How. 413.

A judgment of the supreme court is a finality on every fact and question that came before it on the appeal, and it is the *facts*, and not the *evidence* of the facts, that enter into the *estoppel*. *Gill v. Morris*, 11 Heisk. 614. The decision of the supreme court is a finality, and the same case embraced in the appeal can never again come before the court by any proceeding in the court below. *Rector v.*

Danley, 14 Ark. 304.   On reversal of a decree by the supreme court the lower court can do nothing except to carry out the *mandate* of the court.   It has no further original jurisdiction in the case.   *Himely v. Rose*, 5 Cranch, 313. The supreme court having original jurisdiction of writs of error, there can be no action taken in the cause by the court below after judgment on the writ of affirmance or of reversal without mandate, even if the statute would seem to allow it.   *Enos v. Boardman*, 2 Tyler, 271.   After judgment in the supreme court there can be no rehearing after the term, because after the term it is *res adjudicata*, binding upon all courts.   *Overton v. Bigelow's Adm'r*, 10 Yerg. 48. The judgment of the supreme court is *res adjudicata* as to all matters which came before the court below, or might have come before that court in the case.   *The Santa Maria*, 10 Wheat. 431.   Judge STORY enforces this principle by allusion to the consequences of its violation, such as " grossest laches and delays, the keeping in question and doubt important property rights, the protraction of litigation indefinitely, endless appeals to the supreme court in the same case, and the infliction upon the innocent of all the evils of *protracted* and expensive litigation."   A judgment of a supreme court establishes an unalterable rule in the case, and an unalterable precedent for other cases, and by it the rights of persons and property are unalterably fixed. Wells. Res. Adj. ch. 42.

References like the above could be extended to a great length, for the principle established in these cases has been asserted by nearly all of the supreme courts of the states.   I desired to see whether there was any exception in the cases, and could find none.   This court, on the decision of this simple motion, has established the only exception that can be found to the effect that the circuit court or court below, after a judgment of affirmance by this court on a writ of error and bill of exceptions bringing before this court the whole case together with the order of the court below over-

.ruling a motion for a new trial on the merits as well as for errors, may grant a new trial. The case was not here on special exceptions or questions merely under the statute, while the main case remained in the court below, like that in Massachusetts, but was here on the *whole* *record* by a writ of error. If there can ever be in any case a judgment of affirmance that shall be *res adjudicata* and final, it was the judgment of affirmance in this case. It follows, therefore, that the decision takes away, destroys, and emasculates the constitutional jurisdiction of this court, as the *supreme* court, the court of *last* resort, and the *dernier* resort of litigation.

There is no force even in the argument of convenience that the defendant ought to have justice done him under this statute when newly-discovered evidence shows him not guilty. The limitation of one year after judgment may be as much a denial of justice. Every case must at some time be ended. Criminals may safely be left to the mercy of the executive for relief from punishment when their innocence can be made to appear by newly-discovered testimony after a final judgment by this court. As long as this decision stands, the appellant in every appeal, and the plaintiff in every writ of error, in any case, civil or criminal, may, after judgment of affirmance by this court, obtain from the court below a new trial for any of the causes named in the statute, within the time fixed by the statute after the rendition of the judgment in said court, without regard to the judgment of this court. This is the only reasonable and logical effect of the decision as a *precedent* to be followed in other cases. If the decision is sought to be limited to criminal cases, and by the most glaring inconsistency, its effect in destroying the finality of a judgment of affirmance by this court follows as a consequence, and its effect in making criminal trials endless, as well as most uncertain in result, will also follow as a consequence to be deplored.

The importance of this question of the constitutional jurisdiction of this court must be the apology for this long dissenting opinion.

By the Court.— The motion to quash the writ of *certiorari* is sustained.

GISKIE, Plaintiff in error, vs. THE STATE, Defendant in error.

April 4 — May 12, 1888.

Criminal law: Murder: Pleading: Conviction of lesser offense: Instructions to jury: Reading statutory definition.

1. An information for murder in the first degree will sustain a conviction of murder in the second degree.
2. It was not error for the court to state to the jury that it was conceded by the prosecution that there was doubt as to the sufficiency of the proof of deliberation and premeditation to sustain a verdict of murder in the first degree, and hence they did not ask such a verdict, but claimed and insisted that the evidence was sufficient to warrant a verdict of murder in the second degree; such charge being manifestly designed to prevent a verdict of murder in the first degree, not sustainable by the evidence.
3. It was not error for the court to read to the jury the statutory definition of murder in the second degree, and state that it was plain, simple, and easily intelligible, and as well understood by them as by any lawyer; that it was so plain as to need no construction; and that they were simply to determine whether or not the facts proved, if any, came within such definition.
4. A charge that if the jury did not think the evidence had established murder in the second degree, as defined by the statute, there was another section which would authorize them to find defendant guilty of manslaughter in the second degree, though, standing alone, it might seem to intimate that the evidence was such as to authorize such finding, is not misleading or erroneous if followed by explanations of what constitutes the lesser crime, and instructions to determine from all the evidence whether such crime was committed.

ERROR to the Circuit Court for *Green Lake* County.

The plaintiff in error was tried upon an information charging her with having, on January 2, 1886, wilfully, feloniously, and of her malice aforethought killed and murdered one Peter Armstrong. Upon such trial she was convicted of murder in the second degree; and thereupon she was sentenced to the state prison for the term of eighteen years. To review the judgment of conviction she has sued out this writ of error. The facts are sufficiently stated in the opinion.

William Kennedy, for the plaintiff in error.

For the defendant in error there was a brief by the *Attorney General* and *L. K. Luse*, Assistant Attorney General, and oral argument by the *Attorney General*.

CASSODAY, J. It is undisputed that the deceased was a boy of about fifteen years of age, and came to his death by a bullet fired from a revolver in the hands of the accused. The accused was at the time about twenty-eight years of age, had separated from her husband, and was in the employ of one Davis as housekeeper. She had a child about three years of age. The house where she lived was a two-story frame building. It was situated near the depot in Appleton, and came up to the sidewalk. The upper part of it was occupied by Davis. From the front door of the house a stairway led directly to the upper part of the house. About 7 o'clock in the evening the deceased, his elder brother, and a boy of Davis, about eight years of age, walked from the depot to the front door of the house near the foot of the stairway, when a conversation took place between one or more of them and some person upstairs in the house. Thereupon the accused fired the fatal shot from the head of the stairway, and killed the deceased. There was no light in the house at the time, and it was dark outside.

There can be no question but what the information for

murder was sufficient to sustain the conviction for murder
in the second degree. The rule is that where the offense
charged in form includes another of a lower grade, the information will sustain a conviction of such lesser offense.
" Thus," it is said, that "one indicted in the usual form for
murder may be convicted of manslaughter, because, if the
averment that the killing was with malice aforethought be
negatived or stricken from the indictment, there remains a
sufficient charge of manslaughter." *Kilkelly v. State*, 43
Wis. 608; *State v. Shear*, 51 Wis. 462; *State v. Burwell*, 34
Kan. 315; *State v. Yanta, post*, p. 669.

Here the exceptions are confined to the charge of the trial
court to the jury, It certainly was not error prejudicial to
the accused for the court to state to the jury, in effect, that
it was conceded by the prosecution that there was doubt as
to the sufficiency of the proof of deliberation and premeditation to sustain a verdict of murder in the first degree, and
hence they were not asking for such a verdict, but claimed
and insisted that the evidence was sufficient to warrant a
verdict of murder in the second degree. Such charge, manifestly, was designed to prevent a verdict for the higher offense not sustainable by the evidence.

Nor was there any error in reading sec. 4339, R. S., and
then stating, in effect, the statutory definition of murder in
the second degree as being plain, simple, and easily intelligible, and as well understood by them as any lawyer; that
it was so plain, simple, and concise as not to admit of construction; that it was simply a question for them to determine whether or not the facts proved, if any, came within
such definition.

The jury were, in effect, told that no premeditated
design or malice aforethought was necessary to constitute
murder in the second degree, but that if there was a killing, and it was perpetrated by an act imminently dangerous
to others, and evincing a depraved mind, regardless of

human life, then it came within such definition; that they
were to examine the facts bearing upon that question
whether it was such an act; that if they found all those
things to have occurred, then they might convict of murder
in the second degree. The court then said: "If in your
judgment, however, that is not the offense which the evidence has established, then there is another section which
you may consider, and that is one which would authorize
you to find the defendant guilty of manslaughter in the
second degree." This sentence, standing alone, might have
misled the jury into the belief that the court meant to be
understood as saying, in effect, that the evidence was such
as to authorize them in finding the accused guilty of manslaughter in the second degree. But immediately after the
court read the section (sec. 4351) and the charge then continued: "That section is also simple,— if a person kills
another while resisting an attempt by such other person to
commit a felony. In this case that is not claimed, that
this Armstrong boy was engaged in an attempt to commit
a felony, but it is claimed that he was engaged in an unlawful act; that he pushed in the door of this woman when
it was barred; that his act was unlawful. That is for you
to determine. Examine all the evidence bearing upon that
question, and if you should find that this first section which
I have read to you was not applicable to the case, but
should find that the proof here brings it within the last
section of the statute which I have read to you,— that this
boy was engaged in the commission of an unlawful act, and
was unnecessarily killed by this woman,— then you would
be justified in finding the defendant guilty of manslaughter
in the second degree. If you find her guilty of any offense
at all, you must find her guilty of one of these two offenses.
It is claimed on the part of the defense that this woman
was not guilty of any offense at all; that the killing, which
is conceded, was justifiable homicide." Then, after defin-

ing and explaining the law of justifiable homicide as applicable to the case in a way to elicit no exception, the question whether the evidence brought the case within it was fairly submitted to the jury for determination. *Loew v. State*, 60 Wis. 564. The killing was admitted, and it seems to us that the whole charge, when taken together, fairly submitted to the jury three questions — whether the accused was guilty of murder in the second degree as charged, or of manslaughter in the second degree, or whether the case was one of justifiable homicide. In fact such were the three forms of verdict submitted.

It appears from the record that the accused was ably defended by counsel in the trial court, and with commendable fidelity to his client the same counsel has sought to make every objection available in this court. But after a careful examination of the whole record we are forced to the conclusion, not only that the verdict is sustained by the evidence, but that there is no material error in the record.

By the Court.— The judgment of the circuit court is affirmed.

HENKER, Respondent, vs. THE CITY OF FOND DU LAC, Appellant.

April 17 — May 12, 1888.

Municipal corporations: Defective sidewalk: Primary liability of lot-owner: Constitutional law.

The charter of Fond du Lac (secs. 1–8, subch. 18, ch. 152, Laws of 1883) makes it the duty of the lot-owner to keep the sidewalk in front of his lot in a safe condition, and makes him liable for all injuries resulting to any person from his neglect to perform that duty. It also provides that the city shall not be liable for any such injury until after the injured party has exhausted his remedy against the lot-owner. *Held*, that these provisions of the charter are valid, and a person injured by the negligent omission of a lot-owner to keep a sidewalk in repair must first exhaust his remedy against such lot-owner before he can maintain an action against the city.

APPEAL from the Circuit Court for *Washington* County. The action was brought in the circuit court for Fond du Lac county to recover damages for personal injuries alleged to have been sustained by reason of a defective sidewalk in the defendant city. The answer set up two separate defenses. The substance of the first is stated in the opinion. The second consisted of a general, denial. A general demurrer to the first defense was sustained. Thereafter the venue was changed to Washington county, and a trial was there had upon the issue made by the general denial. An objection to the admission of any evidence under the complaint was overruled. The trial resulted in a verdict for the plaintiff; a motion for a new trial was denied; and the defendant appealed from the judgment entered on the verdict.

P. H. Martin, City Attorney, for the appellant.

For the respondent there were briefs by *Gerpheide & McKenna*, and oral argument by *Mr. H. J. Gerpheide*. To the point that the demurrer to the first defense was properly sustained, they quoted the opinion of the circuit judge,[1]

---

[1] The opinion of the judge of the circuit court for Fond du Lac county was as follows:

"From the lapse of time the sidewalk in question has been used by the public with the knowledge and acquiescence of the city the latter must be held to have adopted the same as one of its ways, and is in a proper case liable for damages happening by reason of a defect therein, to the same extent as if the city had originally directed the sidewalk to be built. It is very clear from the facts stated in the complaint that the alleged defective condition of the walk at the place where it is claimed the plaintiff was injured was caused by natural decay from the length of time the walk had been constructed. Certainly it was not caused by any direct act of negligence on the part of the adjacent land owner. Entertaining this view of the pleadings I think the demurrer

Henker vs. The City of Fond du Lac.

and argued that the facts of this case, as shown by such opinion, distinguish it from the case of *Hiner v. Fond du Lac, ante,* p. 74.

COLE, C. J. The plaintiff, in September, 1884, was injured through a defect in the sidewalk in the city of Fond du Lac. In the notice which he filed with the city clerk he stated that this injury was sustained by him on the west side of Lincoln street, from a defective sidewalk in front of property owned by Ernst Haentze, fully describing the property. In its answer the city set up as a defense and relied upon the provisions of its charter, which made it the duty of the lot-owner to keep the walk in front of his lot in a safe condition, and made such owner liable for all damages resulting to any person by reason of the owner's neglect to thus maintain the walk; and the charter also, in effect, provided that the city should not be liable for any such injury

---

to the first defense stated in the answer should be sustained upon the authority of *Papworth v. Milwaukee,* 64 Wis. 389, and the cases there cited.

" If the provisions of the charter relied on by counsel for the defendant made the owner of adjoining property primarily liable for mere negligent omission to repair (which it does not in my opinion), I should be inclined to hold the act void to that extent, on the very convincing reasoning of the supreme court of Minnesota in *Noonan v. Stillwater,* 33 Minn. 198, to the effect that the municipality cannot be permitted to shift its governmental duty and responsibility in respect to streets upon adjacent land owners, and make them liable in damages for injuries happening to travelers from defects not directly occasioned by the fault of such owners, not merely in amount equal to or less than the value of the land adjacent to the place of injury, but personally and, in some cases, far in excess of such value. However, with the limitation placed upon similar provisions in the charter of other cities, it is not necessary to hold the charter of Fond du Lac, on this subject, in violation of the constitution. Our court rightly held, I am convinced, that the statute was intended to cover cases like that of *Hundhausen v. Bond,* 36 Wis. 29, and with that construction the part of the answer demurred to states no defense to the plaintiff's cause of action." — REP.

until after the failure of the injured party to recover and collect his damages against the lot-owner. On the return of an execution, issued on a judgment against the lot-owner, unsatisfied, the injured party might, within six months, bring an action against the city to enforce its liability. See secs. 1–3, subch. 18, ch. 152, Laws of 1883, p. 435.

Now, the insuperable difficulty in the way of maintaining this action is that it does not appear that the plaintiff has exhausted his remedy against the lot-owner, who is made primarily liable by these charter provisions, before this action was brought, but the contrary fact is shown. We do not perceive how this objection or defense can be overcome or avoided. In the case of *Hiner v. Fond du Lac, ante,* p. 74, this point was presented, and it was clearly and distinctly decided that the city was not liable, under its charter, for an injury resulting from a defective sidewalk, until the person injured had exhausted his remedy against the lot-owner. It is true, that case arose under the charter of 1879 (ch. 240, Laws of 1879), but the charter of 1883 is quite as express and strong upon this subject as the charter of 1879. It seems unnecessary to discuss here the question as to the liability of the city, because the intent of the charter is perfectly manifest, and requires the injured party to exhaust his remedy "against the lot-owner as a condition precedent to the right to maintain the action" against the city.

An attempt was made to distinguish this from the *Hiner Case,* on the grounds that the provisions of the city charter of 1883 were different from that of the charter of 1879, and because the facts of the two cases were dissimilar. The provisions in the charter of 1883 go into more detail than the former charter, but they are as clear and precise as language can express that it is the duty of the lot-owner to keep the sidewalk in front of his lot in a safe condition, and make him liable for all damages of every nature resulting from a neglect to perform that duty, and require the in-

jured party to exhaust his remedy to recover and collect
his damages from the lot-owner before commencing an action to enforce the liability of the city. Nor do we see anything in the facts that can take this case out of the decision
in the *Hiner Case*, and this judgment cannot be affirmed
without overruling that decision.

We were referred on the argument to *Noonan v. Stillwater*, 33 Minn. 198, which holds that a charter that imposes
the duty on the lot-owner to construct and maintain in good
repair sidewalks in front of his lot, and makes such owner
liable for all damages resulting from his default or neglect
in not keeping such sidewalks in good repair, was, as to this
latter provision, which makes the owner liable to others
than the city, unconstitutional. We have great respect for
the decision of that court, but the doctrine of that case is
in direct conflict with the law as established in this state
in many cases. Assessments for local improvements have
been sustained here from an early day; and the liability of
the lot-owner for damages resulting from his failure to perform the statutory duty of keeping the sidewalk in front
of his lot in repair is in the nature of a penalty to enforce
such duty, and is incident to the burden imposed by the
local assessment. We have no doubt of the power of the
legislature to impose the liability upon the lot-owner, and
to relieve the city from such liability until the injured party
exhausts his remedy against the lot-owner. The validity of
such a provision in city charters has been affirmed in many
cases, and must be deemed a settled question in this state.
See cases referred to in *Raymond v. Shebnygan*, 70 Wis. 318.

In this case the city not only relied upon the defense in
its answer, but offered to show on the trial that no judgment against the lot-owner had been obtained, when this
fact was admitted on the part of the plaintiff, that no judgment had been obtained against Mr. Haentze for damages.
The circuit court sustained a demurrer to the first defense

set up in the answer, which was contrary to the views we have expressed. For this error, and for the refusal of the court to set aside the verdict and grant a new trial, the judgment is reversed, and the cause is remanded for further proceedings according to law.

By the Court.— Ordered accordingly.

O'NEILL and others, Appellants, vs. THE PLEASANT PRAIRIE MUTUAL FIRE INSURANCE COMPANY, Respondent.

April 17 — May 12, 1888.

Town insurance companies: Insurable property: "Farm building."

An incubator building, erected on an acre of ground leased for that purpose, and used in carrying on the business of hatching chickens by artificial means and rearing them for the market, is not a "farm building" within the meaning of sec. 2, ch. 421, Laws of 1885, and is not insurable by a town insurance company.

APPEAL from the Circuit Court for *Kenosha* County.

Action upon a policy of insurance. The defendant insurance company is a corporation duly organized under the provisions of R. S., ch. 89, secs. 1927–1941, and the several acts amendatory thereof. In November, 1885, it issued its policy of insurance to the plaintiffs, in and by which it insured them for the term of five years against loss or damage by fire to the amount of $2,000, as follows: "$800 on incubator building; $800 on fixtures in above building; $400 on fowls and chickens in above-mentioned building,— all situated in the town of Pleasant Prairie, county of Kenosha, and state of Wisconsin, on section 2, town 1, range 22 east." In April, 1887, the insured property was destroyed by fire. The value of the property so destroyed probably exceeded the insurance thereon.

It appeared on the trial that the building was erected by the plaintiffs on one acre of land leased by them for that purpose. They carried on in the building the business of hatching chickens by artificial means and rearing them for the market. There was considerable testimony given on the trial tending to show that after the policy was issued additional fixtures were placed in the building without the consent of the company, which materially increased the risk of loss by fire.

The circuit court held that the statute conferred no authority upon the defendant company to insure the incubator building and its contents; also that the undisputed evidence proved that the plaintiffs had materially increased the risk after the issuing of the policy, without the consent of the insurance company. Thereupon the court nonsuited the plaintiffs, and rendered judgment against them, dismissing the action, with costs. The plaintiffs appeal from the judgment.

T. L. Cleary, for the appellants.

For the respondent there was a brief by *Cavanagh & Quarles*, and oral argument by *Mr. Charles Quarles*.

LYON, J. The first question presented by this appeal is, Was the town insurance company, the defendant, authorized by the statute to insure the building in question and the property therein?

The limitations upon the power of the defendant company to insure property against loss or damage by fire, at the time the policy in suit was issued, may be found in sec. 2, ch. 421, Laws of 1885, and are as follows: "No such corporation shall insure any property out of the town or towns in which said corporation is located: provided, that any such corporation, at its annual meeting, may, by a majority vote of the members present, authorize its directors to insure any farm property, or detached dwelling-house and contents, in any adjoining town or towns, or in any incorporated city or village which is located in any adjoining towns in which such town insurance corporation is located: provided, such farm property or dwelling or contents shall be detached at least one hundred feet from exposure. No such corporation shall insure any property other than detached dwellings and their contents, farm buildings and their contents, live-stock in possession or running at large, farm products on premises, and farming implements: provided, that no loss of any live-stock insured by such corporation shall be recoverable if occurring while such stock was kept or confined in any building which such corporation could not insure under this section. But such corporation, at its annual meeting, may, by a majority of all the votes cast by its members present, authorize its directors to insure country stores and their contents, school-houses, churches, town and society halls, country hotels, and water-mills; but such risks shall not exceed twenty-five hundred dollars in any one case."

It is certain that the company had no power to effect this insurance, under the above statute, unless the insured building is a "farm building" within the meaning of the statute; for it is not claimed that the corporation ever specially authorized its directors to insure buildings of this class.

We are of the opinion that the learned circuit judge construed the law correctly when he held that the incubator building was not a farm building within the meaning of the statute. We think the reasons given by him for such conclusion are sound, and we cannot do better than to reproduce them here as a satisfactory expression of our own views upon the question. The judge said: "As to the construction of the words 'farm buildings,' I am of the opinion that this point is also well taken. Words must be construed to mean in their ordinary, usual, common acceptation. When words are used which are ordinarily and commonly in use among the people, when they are used in the statute, unless some different construction is applied by the statute, we must construe them as they ordinarily are used. Now, these companies, it appears, all through the state, are organized for the purpose of allowing farmers to insure themselves. They are farm insurance companies. This is practically what they are, and the word 'farm' appears frequently; the word 'farmer' and 'farms' and 'farm.' Now, those words seem to me, in this state, to have a well-recognized and definite meaning; that is, a man who cultivates a considerable tract of land. Whether it is necessary that he should till practically I am not quite certain; but at least a man is not called a 'farmer,' and his place is not called a 'farm,' unless he has some considerable tract of land, and cultivates it, or uses it in some one of the usually recognized ways of farming. Were these men farmers? Was this place a farm? I do not think that, in the ordinary, common acceptation of that term, it can possibly be said that they were farmers, or that it was a farm, or that this building was a farm building. It seems to me that the suggestion with regard to growing seed is extremely applicable. Most farmers, I suppose, grow some seed,— seeds of vegetables to raise from,— and collect them in the fall, sometimes. Most farmers keep some hens and get some eggs. But if a man leased an acre of ground, whether it was on a farm, or whether it was not on a farm, and went to raising seed as a business in hot-houses, he could not be called a 'farmer,' and his place could not be called a 'farm,' nor his buildings be called 'farm buildings.' Construing that in what seems to me its natural, usual, and ordinary meaning, and what the statute seems to suggest as its meaning, that can hardly be called a 'farm building.' Now, it is of some significance that the legislature have deemed it necessary to put into their excepting clause here the words 'cheese factory.' If an incubator, a building like this, is a farm building, a cheese factory must be a farm building. I do not see any distinction — any rational ground — between the two; but the legislature have construed it, evidently, not to be a farm building." The statute above referred to, concerning cheese factories, is ch. 217, Laws of 1887.

We conclude, therefore, that the nonsuit was properly granted for the reason that the contract of insurance was prohibited by the statute. Having reached this conclusion, it is unnecessary to consider whether the court ruled correctly in respect to the increase of the risk after the policy was issued.

By the Court.— The judgment of the circuit court is affirmed.

WOODARD, Appellant, vs. WEST SIDE STREET RAILWAY COMPANY, Respondent.

April 17 — May 12, 1888.

Street railways: Injury to passenger: Failure to stop: Slippery track: Instructions to jury: Contributory negligence: Proximate and remote cause.

1. Plaintiff, in attempting to get on a moving street-car, fell, and was dragged by the car some distance before the car stopped. It was in the winter, snowing, and the car was on a down grade. The testimony of the driver that he set the brakes and held the horses back as soon as he heard the signal to stop, and that the car slid on the track, was contradicted by several witnesses. There was evidence that in winter, when the track was slippery, the cars would slide on the track at that place with the brakes set. *Held*, that a charge that it must be taken as established in the case that cars would, in the winter, on the down grade, slide on the track with the brakes set, and be beyond the control of the driver, was misleading as making no qualification as to the state of the track, and conveying the idea that the fact was established that the cars did slide on the occasion in question.

VOL. 71 — 40

2. Where plaintiff, in attempting to get on a moving street-car, fell, and was dragged some 160 feet before the car stopped, he would be entitled to recover, even though guilty of negligence in attempting to get on a moving car, if the driver could have avoided the injury by the exercise of reasonable care in stopping the car after he was notified that plaintiff had fallen and was being dragged by the car.

APPEAL from the Circuit Court for *Milwaukee* County. Action to recover damages for personal injuries alleged to have been sustained by reason of the negligence of the driver of a car upon the street railway operated by the defendant, and by reason of the defective and insufficient construction of the platform and handle upon said car, and the failure of the defendant to employ a conductor on such car. The evidence given on the trial and the instructions to the jury are sufficiently stated in the opinion.

The jury returned a special verdict as follows: (1) Did the plaintiff at the time and place in question signal the driver of the defendant's car to stop? Yes. (2) Did the plaintiff take hold of the handle of the car for the purpose of entering it as a passenger? Yes. (3) Was the platform at the entrance of the car insufficient and unsafe for passengers? No. (4) Was the handle of the car, in which the plaintiff's hand was caught, insufficient and unsafe for persons to use in getting onto said car? No. (5) When the plaintiff fell down was the driver immediately notified to stop the car? Yes. (6) Was the driver guilty of negligence in not stopping the car when he was notified that the plaintiff had fallen? No. (6½) Did the driver of the car wilfully or maliciously refuse to stop the car, and cause the plaintiff to be dragged? No. (7) Was the plaintiff in the exercise of ordinary care at the time he was injured? No. (8) Is the plaintiff's injury permanent? No. (8½) Do you find for plaintiff or defendant? Defendant.

From the judgment entered on the verdict, in favor of the defendant, the plaintiff appeals.

Harlow Pease, for the appellant.

For the respondent there was a brief by *Jenkins, Winkler & Smith*, and oral argument by *Mr. F. C. Winkler*.

TAYLOR, J. The appellant brought this action against the respondent to recover damages for an injury received by him under the following circumstances: On the 9th of February, 1885, the appellant was at the office of E. D. Holton, at No. 613 Grand avenue, in the city of Milwaukee. At about 10:30 A. M. on that day he left the said office, which is on the south side of said avenue, and about the middle of the block between Seventh and Sixth streets, which cross said avenue, running north and south, for the purpose of taking the street car going east on the avenue. Mr. James Holton accompanied the appellant from the office to see him off. The appellant and Mr. Holton both testify that they hailed or signaled the driver to stop and permit the appellant to get on the car; that the driver paid no attention to their signals, although he appeared to be looking towards them; and that he did not stop the car. The appellant went towards the car, and took hold of the handle at the side of the car, by the platform, and attempted to get on the car, but by some means his foot slipped from the step, and he fell at the side of the car, and his third finger, on which he had a heavy ring, caught in the handle in such manner that he could not get his hand loose from the handle of the car, and he was drawn along by the side of *it*, hanging by his finger, for about 160 feet, to the middle of Sixth street, where the car was stopped and he was released. His finger was injured so that it is permanently flexed inward.

The evidence on the part of the plaintiff shows that as soon as he fell, he called out to stop the car; that those in the car called to stop the car, and rang the car-bell violently; that other persons on the walk called to the driver to stop the car; and that finally two persons ran in front of the horses, about the middle of Sixth street, and threw up their hands to stop the horses, and that the horses and car then stopped. Several witnesses testified that they were on the sidewalk within thirty feet of the car, and that the driver made no effort to stop the car or horses; that the horses were pulling the car, and the wheels of the car were turning; that the car was not sliding; that it was snowing; that there was a high wind from the east, the direction in which the car was going; and that there was considerable snow on the track at the time. These witnesses also testified that the driver seemed to pay no attention to anything which was going on about him, but looked straight before him, apparently without making any attempt to stop the horses or the car. These statements of the plaintiff's witnesses as to the apparent inattention of the driver as to what was going on about him, are to some extent corroborated by the evidence of the driver himself. He testifies that he did not see either Holton or the appellant signal to him to stop the car; that he did not know that any one got on the car, or attempted to get on it, between Seventh and Sixth streets; that he heard no one call him to stop the car, and saw no one in the street in front of the horses when they stopped on Sixth street; that after the horses were stopped, he did not see the appellant, or know that he was injured, or how he was injured; but he does testify that when he was about 120 feet from where the horses stopped he heard the bells ring violently as though something was the matter, and he immediately set the brakes so as to stop the wheels of the car from turning, and held up his horses, but that the car slid, and he could not stop it until it stopped in the middle of Sixth street.

The main contention of the plaintiff on the trial was that the driver was negligent in not stopping the car immediately after the plaintiff slipped and fell, and that he wrongfully and negligently dragged him, while hanging by the finger to the car, for a long distance, by reason of which he was greatly injured. It was also claimed by the appellant that the car handle was not constructed in a proper manner, and that it was negligence on the part of the defendant that no conductor was on the car. On the trial, however, these charges of negligence were not claimed by the plaintiff to have been established by the evidence, and his counsel relied mainly upon the negligence of the driver as a ground upon which to base a recovery. The charge of negligence of the driver was the main question in the case, and was met by the company with the claim that on account of the condition of the track and the descent in the grade at the place, the driver could not stop the car by the use of all reasonable means and appliances sooner than it was stopped; that the plaintiff was dragged as he was, and the distance he was, because it was impossible for the driver to stop the car, and not because the driver neglected the use of any proper means for stopping the same. Against the testimony of several apparently credible witnesses, who had ample opportunity of seeing what was done, and who testified that the horses were not held up, but were drawing the car until stopped by the men in front of them in the middle of Sixth street, and that the car did not slide, but the wheels were turning,—the driver alone had testified that he set the brakes so as to stop the wheels, that the car slid, and the horses were held back by him. In this state of the evidence the court allowed the respondent to introduce witnesses showing the descending grade of the track between Seventh and Sixth streets, and also showing that at times in the winter season, when the track was slippery, the cars would slide down that grade, notwithstanding the brakes were set and the horses held up. Admitting that this evidence was competent as tending to confirm the testimony of the driver that the car slid down the grade at the time the accident happened, it was certainly far from being conclusive upon the question whether it did in fact slide at the time in question. Whether it would slide at the time in question depended upon the condition of the track at the time. If, as claimed by the appellant, there was considerable snow on the track at the time, with the wind blowing at the rate of thirty miles or more directly in the face of the car, there was no evidence given on the part of the defendant except the evidence of the driver, that it did slide although the brakes were properly set and the horses held back. In this state of the evidence the learned circuit judge instructed the jury as follows:

"The jury are instructed that if they find from the evidence that the plaintiff attempted to board the car without the knowledge of the driver, the car being reasonably safe for the use of this road, and in so doing slipped before he got upon the car, and the finger with the ring upon it caught and became fastened in the handle, thereby causing him to be dragged; if the car was upon the down grade upon Grand avenue; if the driver, so soon as he was notified by the bell or noise that something was the matter, set the brakes as tightly as he could, and made all reasonable and proper efforts to stop the car, but that on account of the weather and the slippery condition of the track the car continued to descend the hill, dragging the plaintiff until it was stopped at Sixth street,— then, and in such case, the plaintiff cannot recover in this action, and your verdict must be for the defendant.

"With respect to the question whether the cars would slide when upon the down grade of Grand avenue when the brake is firmly set, and the car be for a time beyond the control of the driver, the jury are instructed that the defendant has presented the testimony of some six witnesses who testified to a practical knowledge, acquaintance, and experience with the subject, and have testified positively that such is the fact.

"The testimony of the plaintiff on that subject is simply to the fact two or three witnesses have testified that they never have noticed cars so slide. The testimony of the defendant's witnesses on that subject is positive. The testimony on the part of the plaintiff in that regard is simply negative testimony, and amounts to but little more than, so to speak, a mere *scintilla* of evidence, and does not justify the jury in disregarding the positive and otherwise unimpeached testimony that such sliding does occur.

"The evidence in this case, therefore, justifies the court in instructing you that it is established by the evidence in the cause that, in the winter season, cars coming upon the down grade of Grand avenue will slide even when the brake is completely set, and the car for a time, until its momentum is overcome by the resistance of the brake, passes beyond the control of the driver to stop it. The jury must take that as an established fact in this case, and determine the questions submitted to it in the light of such established fact."

We think this charge was misleading. The question for the jury in the case was not whether, under certain conditions, a car would slide upon the tracks with the brakes set and the horses held back, but whether it did slide with the brakes set and the horses held back at the time in question and under the conditions shown by the evidence. In the second and third paragraphs excepted to the learned judge instructs the jury that it is conclusively established "that cars would slide when on the down grade of Grand avenue when the brake is firmly set, and the car be for the time beyond the control of the driver." The learned judge does not state what the condition of the track must be when the cars on that grade would be beyond the control of the driver, but declares generally that it is conclusively established "that the cars would slide when on the down grade," without regard to the condition of the track or the weather. In the last paragraph of the instructions excepted to the learned judge qualifies his statement by saying that it is conclusively established that the cars will slide in the winter season with the brakes firmly set, without any other qualification as to the condition of the track or state of the weather, and then concludes the instruction by saying that "the jury must take that as an established fact in this case, and determine the questions submitted to it in the light of such established fact."

It seems to us that when the court instructed the jury that they must take it as an established fact in the case they were considering, that, in the winter season, cars coming down the grade of Grand avenue would slide, though the brakes were set firmly, and for a time be beyond the control of the driver, the jury might well understand the instructions to mean that, in the case they were trying, it was established that the car did slide as testified to by the driver. The car was conclusively shown to be coming down the grade of Grand avenue, and it was in the winter season that the accident happened. We are very clear that, under the evidence in this case, it was error for the court to instruct the jury that the car was beyond the control of the driver at the time the accident happened, and that, under the instructions given, the jury would be very likely to understand that the court so intended to instruct them.

It is said by the counsel for the respondent that if the instructions above quoted were not strictly correct under the evidence, yet, as there was a special verdict and the jury have found that the plaintiff was not in the exercise of ordinary care when he was injured, no harm was done, as the plaintiff, under the finding, cannot recover in any event. It is evident that this finding, if it can be supported by the evidence, must relate to the want of care on the part of the plaintiff at the time he attempted to board the car, and could not relate to any want of ordinary care on his part after he fell and was dragged by the car. The learned judge properly instructed the jury on that subject as follows: "But it is contended, as you will observe, in this case that the injury may have been occasioned, not by the fall, but by the dragging of the plaintiff. That circumstance enables me to give you this instruction: Even if the plaintiff was guilty of negligence in attempting to get on the car while it was in motion, yet if the jury find from the evidence in the case that the driver was notified that the plaintiff had fallen and was being dragged at the tail of the car, and the jury also find that the driver could have avoided the injury by the exercise of reasonable care, then the defendant is liable." It is upon the theory set forth in this instruction that the plaintiff sought a verdict in this case, and it is very clear that there is no evidence even tending to show that the plaintiff was not in the exercise of such care as it was possible for him to exercise after he fell and was caught by his finger. The material question in the special verdict was the sixth question, viz.: "Was the driver of the car guilty of negligence in not stopping the car when he was notified that the plaintiff had fallen?" The instructions above quoted, and to which exceptions were taken, have peculiar reference to this question, and, as we think, must have been understood by the jury as tantamount to a direction to find that the driver was not guilty of negligence in not stopping the car, because the evidence was conclusive that he could not control it at the place where the accident happened.

By the Court. — The judgment of the circuit court is reversed, and the cause is remanded for a new trial.

See note to this case in 38 N. W. Rep. 847. — REP.

RUEGE and another, Respondents, vs. GATES, Appellant.

April 18 — May 1₤, 1888.

(1, ₤) Practice: Pleading: Opening case to jury: Amendment of plead-ing: Waiver. (3) Instructions to jury. (4) Evidence: Court and jury. (6) Contracts: Modification: Consideration.

1. Plaintiff's counsel in opening the case to the jury made some re-marks to which defendant objected. The court reserved its ruling until the evidence was offered, and defendant excepted. Evi-dence to substantiate the remarks was then introduced without objection, but plaintiff's request for leave to amend the complaint to correspond with such evidence was, on objection by defendant, refused by the court. *Held,* that the error, if any, of not declar-ing the remarks of plaintiff's counsel improper, was cured by the refusal of leave to amend the complaint, even if there was not a waiver of the exception by not objecting to the testimony of the same effect.,

2. An exception to the allowance of an amendment to a complaint is waived by asking a continuance as the terms thereof.

8. Where the jury has just been told that they must determine what is the truth between the parties "from all the testimony," a charge that they may decide a question as they think "truth and justice between the parties require," is not erroneous as instructing them to determine what is *just* rather than what is according to the contract and the evidence.

4. Plaintiffs' counsel stated on the trial that the price they were to pay for certain feed was as defendant claimed, and such statement was assented to by one of the plaintiffs on the witness stand, but it did not clearly appear that the statement and assent were intended to be conclusive, and both parties afterwards introduced evidence to show what the feed was worth. *Held,* that it was not error to submit the question as to the value or price of the feed to the jury, who might consider the admission, if any, with the other testi-mony.

5. Parties can agree to change or modify their contracts without any new consideration.

APPEAL from the Circuit Court for *Clark* County.

Action to recover the sum of $110.52, being the balance alleged to be due to the plaintiffs on a contract for cutting, hauling, and banking pine logs. The facts are sufficiently stated in the opinion. There was a verdict for the plaintiffs for $106.66, and from the judgment entered thereon the defendant appeals.

I. W. Mason, for the appellant.

James O'Neill, for the respondents.

ORTON, J. This action is brought to recover the contract price for cutting, hauling, and banking 838,390 feet of pine logs, at $2 per thousand. In the written contract there is a clause requiring the plaintiffs "to break the rollways in the spring." The plaintiffs gave the defendant credit in their complaint for payments on the contract of $1,566.26. The defendant answered that the plaintiffs cut, hauled, and banked only 797,000 feet of logs, and that they had been paid therefor the sum of $1,686.66, and that they had failed to break the rollways in the spring as required by said contract, to the damage of the defendant of $50. At the trial the plaintiffs' counsel, in opening their case to the jury, before any evidence was given, stated substantially that the plaintiffs signed the contract without knowing that said clause requiring them to break the rollways in the spring was in it, and that the defendant read the contract to them, omitting said clause. This was objected to by the defendant's counsel, and the court reserved its ruling on the subject until the evidence was offered, and this was excepted to. The plaintiff *Ruege*, as a witness, testified without objection as follows: "He [*Gates*] made a contract, and I could not read it at all. He was reading it to us, and when he read it he jumped that line about breaking the rollways in the spring; he did not read that to me." The plaintiffs' counsel thereupon asked leave to amend the complaint by inserting an allegation that said clause was not read or understood by the plaintiffs at the time, and that it was in the contract by mistake or fraud.

This was objected to by the defendant's counsel, and leave to so amend was refused by the court. The only exception taken and the only error assigned in respect to the above was that the court did not declare the above remarks of the plaintiffs' counsel to the jury improper. This error, if any, was cured by the refusal of leave to so amend the complaint, by which the whole matter was excluded from the jury, if there was not a waiver of the exception by not objecting to the testimony of the same effect.

2. The plaintiffs were allowed to amend the complaint by alleging that the defendant waived the performance of the stipulation contained in said clause, and this was excepted to by the defendant's counsel who at the same time asked for a continuance to procure witnesses to meet this new issue. The court took a recess, that the defendant's counsel might prepare the necessary affidavit for such continuance. After recess the defendant's counsel stated to the court that he had concluded not to present any affidavit for continuance, and thereupon the trial proceeded. The exception to the allowance of the amendment was waived by asking a continuance as the terms thereof, and the amendment itself was properly allowed according to sec. 2830, R. S. And yet the learned counsel for the appellant insists in his brief that allowing the amendment without terms was error, when he refused to make an affidavit of surprise, or that he was misled by the amendment, or that he desired or needed a continuance.

3. Exception is taken to the following part of the instructions to the jury: "You have heard the testimony of Mr. Currier as to the character of his scale of the logs, and of the manner in which the lumber inspector diminished the amount which he ascertained." It is complained that there was no evidence as to the *manner* in which the lumber inspector, Mr. Young, diminished the amount Mr. Currier had ascertained it to be. The learned counsel must have failed to notice the testimony of Mr. Currier as to the *manner* in

which Mr. Young diminished his scale of the logs.   He testified that Young came there only once, and about the time he was through with the scaling, and examined only a part of the logs, and made an arbitrary deduction of his scaling of from eight to ten per cent.

4. The instruction that the jury might determine the question as to whether the plaintiffs ought to have broken the rollways, and the cost of doing so, as they might think "truth and justice between the parties require," is complained of as erroneous, because they were instructed to decide what was *just* rather than what was according to the contract or the evidence.   The jury could not have so understood, for they had just been told that they must determine what was the truth between the parties, "from all the testimony."

5. It is complained that the court left the question to the jury as to what was the intention and understanding of the parties as to the price the plaintiffs should pay for certain feed which they obtained of Coburn & Co. on the order of the defendant to apply on the contract, after the plaintiffs' counsel had stated on the trial that it was $20 per ton and that was assented to by one of the plaintiffs as a witness on the stand.   Whether such statement and assent were meant to be a determination of that matter it is difficult to say from the form and manner in which they were made. It seems that the parties did not think it conclusive, for they both introduced evidence afterwards to show what the feed was worth per ton, and it was in evidence that Coburn & Co. charged the defendant for the same only $18 per ton.   Under such circumstances it does not seem to have been improper for the court to leave the whole question of its value or price to the jury.   That was certainly fair and just, and the jury could take into consideration the admission, if any, with the other testimony, to determine what the plaintiffs ought to pay for the feed.

6. There was a colloquy between the defendant's counsel and the court as to what the testimony was concerning the waiver of the clause requiring the plaintiffs to break the rollways. The counsel insisted that the testimony was that the defendant waived it only in consideration that it should be a final settlement of all matters between the parties, and the court asserted that such was not the testimony. The court was clearly right about it. The defendant did not testify that there was any understanding or agreement between the parties that such waiver was to be a final settlement or in consideration of it. His testimony was only as to what *he* thought or intended, and was not that any such thing was said or talked about when he told the plaintiffs that they need not break the rollways. In connection with this exception to the charge or statement of the court the learned counsel of the appellant rather inconsistently argues in his brief that the waiver of the performance of that clause in the contract was without *any* consideration and void. Parties can agree to change or modify their agreements without any new consideration. *Brown v. Everhard,* 52 Wis. 205.

There were numerous other exceptions taken to the charge of the court, but they are not insisted upon in appellant's brief. The instructions appear to have been very full and fair, and the evidence was of such a character that we think the jury were warranted in finding as they did in favor of the plaintiffs. The testimony on behalf of the plaintiffs was sufficient to entitle them to the verdict which the jury found in their favor, and that affords a sufficient reason for this court not to disturb it.

By the Court.— The judgment of the circuit court is affirmed.

RINDSKOPF, Appellant, vs. MYERS and another, Respondents.

April 19 — May 12, 1888.

Debtor and creditor: Fraudulent conveyance: Evidence.

1. The issue being whether the sales of certain goods to the plaintiff and to his vendor, N., were fraudulent as to the creditors of N. and his vendor, it was error to admit evidence of representations made by an agent of N.'s vendor to one of the defendants from whom he borrowed money in the name of such vendor, regarding the financial condition of his principal.

2. The plaintiff testified that he borrowed $2,000 from his brother L. to pay for the goods which the defendants claimed were transferred to him in fraud of creditors, and a deposition of L. to the same effect was read. The judgment rolls in certain actions against L. were then introduced by the defendants to show that L. was insolvent at the time of the alleged loan. L. was not asked whether these judgments had been paid or satisfied or to make any explanation in regard to them. *Held,* that it was error to admit such judgment rolls in evidence.

APPEAL from the Circuit Court for *Eau Claire* County. The action was brought by *Elias Rindskopf* against *Henry Myers*, the sheriff of Clark county, and *Richard Dewhurst*, for trespass in taking and carrying away a quantity of clothing of the value of $1,200, on the 2d of August, 1884. The facts will sufficiently appear from the opinion. The trial resulted in a verdict and judgment for the defendants. The plaintiff appealed.

R. J. MacBride, for the appellant.

James O'Neill, for the respondents.

COLE, C. J. We think there must be a new trial in this case because of the admission of incompetent testimony. A number of exceptions were taken to the rulings of the trial court in admitting or excluding testimony. We shall not notice all of these exceptions, but confine our attention to those taken to the admission of the statements or representations made by the witness Stumes to *Dewhurst* as to the financial condition of his father-in-law, E. M. Nathan, and the admission of the judgment rolls against Louis Rindskopf in favor of different parties.

The main issue in the case was as to the validity of the sale made by Hyman Nathan to the plaintiff. The sheriff, representing the creditors of Hyman Nathan and E. M. Nathan, claimed that this transfer was fraudulent and void. The sheriff justified seizing the goods in controversy (1) under an attachment in favor of *Dewhurst* against E. M. Nathan; (2) under an attachment in favor of the Neillsville Bank against Hyman Nathan; and (3) by virtue of an execution on a judgment against Hyman Nathan, which judgment was rendered more than twenty days after the taking of the goods, and some time after this action was commenced. There was evidence which tended to prove that E. M. Nathan, who originally owned the goods, or in whose name the business was transacted, had sold them to the vendor of the plaintiff in June, 1883, and that Hyman sold them to the plaintiff on the 1st of August, 1884. An effort was made to impeach the *bona fides* of these transfers.

It appears that E. M. Nathan resided in Milwaukee, and the business at Neillsville was under the management of one Stumes, as his agent or in some other capacity. Some time in May or June, 1883, Stumes applied to *Dewhurst* for a loan of $300. The loan was effected in the name of E. M. Nathan; and *Dewhurst* was permitted to testify, against the plaintiff's objection, that, at the time, Stumes represented his father-in-law, E. M. Nathan, was worth from $12,000 to $20,000, and gave as a reason for wanting the $300 that there were some store debts for merchandise coming due, and that he did not then wish to call upon his father-in-law for money, for reasons which he gave. It seems to us too plain for argument that this evidence as to the representations of Stumes had nothing to do with the case on trial, and should have been excluded. It was calculated to mislead the jury from the real issue. That issue was, as we have said, whether the sale to the plaintiff was fraudulent as to the creditors of Hyman Nathan. The facts about the loan, or the financial condition of E. M. Nathan, had no bearing whatever on that issue. It is attempted to justify the admission of this evidence on the ground that there was a scheme or conspiracy on the part of Stumes, E. M. and Hyman Nathan, the plaintiff, and his brother Louis Rindskopf, to defraud creditors; but the evidence entirely fails to sustain any such theory. There is really no evidence which tends to show that the plaintiff had anything to do with Stumes when he purchased, or that he then knew that E. M. Nathan ever owned the goods. The sale was made to the plaintiff by Hyman Nathan, who was in possession of the goods, claiming to own them, and who received the purchase price. The evidence is quite clear and satisfactory establishing these facts. If it conclusively appeared that Stumes was acting as the agent of E. M. Nathan in the management of the business in May or June, 1883, how could his representations as to the financial condition of his principal be pertinent evidence in this case? We confess we are unable to understand upon what rule they were admissible. It seems to us they were clearly incompetent, and should have been excluded. It is true, the defendants attacked the validity of the sale from E. M. Nathan to his son Hyman, as well as that from the latter to the plaintiff. But, still, we think the statements of Stumes were inadmissible for any purpose in the case.

Again, the plaintiff offered evidence tending to prove the consideration he paid for the goods. He was examined at considerable length on that point, and testified that he paid $2,500 in cash, and gave his note for $1,500. He was asked where and how he obtained the money to make the cash payment, and he said he borrowed $2,000 of his brother

Louis. The deposition of Louis was read, on the part of the plaintiff, to prove that he let the plaintiff have the $2,000, as had been testified to by the latter. On the part of the defendant, certain judgment rolls in causes against Louis Rindskopf were offered in evidence, under objection. The manifest object of this testimony was to disprove the fact that the plaintiff obtained the $2,000 from his brother, by showing that Louis was insolvent at the time. No question was asked the witness Louis whether these judgments had been paid or satisfied in any way, or to make any explanation in regard to them. Under the circumstances, it is obvious that the evidence was prejudicial to the plaintiff's case, and should not have been received.

The learned counsel for the defendants insists that all the facts and circumstances attending the transaction so clearly proved fraud in the transfer that the judgment should be affirmed upon the record, without regard to any technical errors which may have intervened on the trial. We do not feel justified in adopting that view. True, there are some suspicious or unusual circumstances attending the sale made to the plaintiff; but whether they are sufficient to show that the transfer was fraudulent was a question for the jury upon the evidence. The plaintiff was entitled to a fair trial of the question as to the validity of the sale, without any improper testimony being admitted to influence the minds of the jury against his claim. We think he has not had such a trial because of the errors in the proceedings which we have noticed; and therefore, without passing upon the other questions involved, we reverse the judgment and send the cause back for a new trial.

By the Court.— Ordered accordingly.

THE TOWN OF WILLIAMSTOWN, Respondent, vs. DARGE, imp., Appellant.

April 20 — May 12, 1888.

Appealable order: Criminal contempt.

An order adjudging a defendant in criminal contempt for the violation of an injunction is not appealable. *In re Murphey*, 39 Wis. 286, followed.

APPEAL from the Circuit Court for *Dodge* County.

The appellant was adjudged to be guilty of contempt in violating an injunctional order restraining him and others from further building a bridge across Rock river, and was ordered to pay a fine and the costs of the contempt proceedings, and to be imprisoned in the county jail until such fine and costs were paid, the term of such imprisonment not to exceed thirty days.

For the appellant there was a brief by *Eli & C. E. Hooker* and *James E. Malone*, and oral argument by *Mr. Malone*.

For the respondent there was a brief by *F. M. Lawrence* and *James J. Dick*, and oral argument by *Mr. Dick*.

PER CURIAM. This is an appeal from an order adjudging the appellant in contempt for the violation of an injunction. It is for misconduct and a wilful disregard of the order of the court, and is consequently a criminal contempt. It was held in *In re Murphey*, 39 Wis. 286, that such an order was not appealable. It is said in that case that this question of practice must be deemed settled. The appeal must therefore be dismissed.

RIEDEBURG and another, Respondents, vs. SCHMITT, imp., Appellant.

April 20 — May 12, 1888.

PARTNERSHIP: *Who are partners: Property chargeable with losses.*

S. and M. owned jointly a distillery. Without the knowledge of S., M. entered into partnership with the plaintiffs and furnished as his capital in the firm the said distillery for the use of the firm, and the agreed value thereof was entered as his capital on the partnership books. Afterwards S. assented to the agreement so made by M., and also gave his consent to the United States authorities that the property should be used by the firm for the purposes of a distillery, and subjected it to all claims of the government which might grow out of such use. The firm thereafter paid the taxes and insurance upon the property. S. was refused admittance to the firm, but M. agreed to divide with him his share of the profits of the partnership business. The business of the firm was unprofitable and was closed up. *Held:*

(1) S. was not a partner in the firm so as to render him personally liable to the members thereof for any part of the losses.

(2) As against S. the entire beneficial ownership of the distillery property must be deemed to have been in M. when he contributed it for the use of the firm and as his capital therein, and it was therefore firm property and is subject to the payment of the share of the losses chargeable to M.

APPEAL from the Circuit Court for *Milwaukee* County. The following statement of the case was prepared by Mr. Justice TAYLOR as a part of the opinion:

This action was brought by the respondents in the circuit court of Milwaukee county against the appellant and one William T. Marshall, for an accounting in respect to the partnership business of the late firm of H. Riedeburg & Co. The business of the said firm was operating a distillery in Milwaukee, known as the "White Malt Distillery." The plaintiffs charge in the complaint that the appellant was a member of the firm in fact, although his name did not appear in the articles of agreement signed at the time when the partnership was created. They seek to charge him, as such partner, personally for one third of the losses of the firm, and they also seek to charge the distillery fixtures, and the lands upon which the same is situated, with one third of the losses of the firm.

The important facts in the case are: (1) That previous to the 31st day of January, 1882, the said *Schmitt* and Marshall had purchased property in the city of Milwaukee, and constructed a distillery thereon, but as yet had not entered upon the business of distilling. That the agreement between *Schmitt* and Marshall was that they should be equally interested in the business. When they were about ready to start the business of distilling, Marshall, who was in Milwaukee and in charge of the affairs of *Schmitt* and Marshall there, ascertained that they could not prudently enter upon the business contemplated, by reason of some arrangements which had been made by *Riedeburg* and *Bodden* with the brewers in said city from whom the said *Schmitt* and Marshall expected to receive their supplies for the distillery; and in consequence of such interference on the part of *Riedeburg* and *Bodden*, and for the purpose of starting the works constructed by *Schmitt* and Marshall, Marshall, without the knowledge of said *Schmitt*, on the 31st day of January, 1882, entered into the following written contract with the said *Riedeburg* and *Bodden*, viz.:

"This agreement, made and entered into the 31st day of January, 1882, by and between William T. Marshall, *Henry Riedeburg*, and *A. G. Bodden*, witnesseth, that said parties have agreed to form, and do hereby enter into and form, a copartnership to operate a distillery, to be known as the 'White Malt Distillery,' in the city of Milwaukee, under the firm name of H. Riedeburg & Co., upon the following terms and conditions: Said William T. Marshall furnishes and contributed for the use of copartnership his real estate, consisting of lots two (2) and three (3), in block F, and the land in rear thereof running back to the Milwaukee river, in the First ward of the city of Milwaukee, and all buildings, improvements, machinery, fixtures, and apparatus thereon and used in connection with the same, including also the buildings Nos. 929 and 931 on North Water street in said city. Said property so furnished by said Marshall is valued at the sum of eleven thousand five hundred and fifty dollars, which is considered the capital of said Marshall in the firm. Said *Henry Riedeburg* and *A. G. Bodden* agree to furnish the necessary capital to carry on the business and operate the distillery. Each partner is to be allowed annually interest at the rate of seven per cent. per annum on the amount of capital by him invested in the copartnership. Said *Henry Riedeburg* and *A. G. Bodden* are to have the management of the business at the city of Milwaukee. All profits and losses of the business are to be shared by and between the said three partners equally. The term of the copartnership shall be three years from the 1st day of February, 1882. Said William T. Marshall also agrees at any time within said three years, upon the request of said *Henry Riedeburg* and *A. G. Bodden*, to sell and convey an undivided two-thirds of all the property, real and personal, by him furnished to the firm as aforesaid, for two thirds of the sum first herein mentioned.

"In witness whereof the parties hereto have hereto set their hands and seals this 31st day of January, 1882.

"WILLIAM T. MARSHALL.   [Seal.]

"HENRY RIEDEBURG.   [Seal.]

"A. G. BODDEN.   [Seal.]

"I, *Emil Schmitt*, of Cincinnati, Ohio, having an interest in the property mentioned in the foregoing agreement with said William T. Marshall, hereby give my consent to said agreement, and I agree to join with said Marshall in conveying such property in accordance with said agreement, upon the request of the other parties thereto as therein stated.

"*Dated February 14, 1882.*   EMIL SCHMITT."

It will be seen that, after the partnership was formed between *Riedeburg, Bodden,* and Marshall, and on the 14th of February, 1882, *Schmitt* assented to the contract made by Marshall, so far as he had undertaken to deal with the distillery and fixtures which at the time belonged to *Schmitt* and Marshall as joint owners. The firm of Riedeburg & Co. was reported to the United States authorities as composed of *Riedeburg, Bodden,* and Marshall, as required by sec. 2259, R. S. of U. S. *Schmitt* afterwards gave his written consent to the United States authorities that the property should be used by said firm for the purposes of a distillery, and subjected said real estate to all claims of the United States which might grow out of the use of said property as a distillery by said firm, as required by sec. 3262, R. S. of U. S. The firm of H. Riedeburg & Co. entered upon the business of distilling spirits under the above-named agreement, and continued it for about one year, when it was discovered that it was not profitable, the business of distilling stopped, and the business was finally closed up. The plaintiffs sold and disposed of the products of the business, and paid up all the liabilities of the firm, showing a loss of about $18,000, including interest on the plaintiffs' advances. By this action they seek to charge *Schmitt* personally with one third of said losses, and also to subject the distillery, and the lands on which it is situated, to the payment of the said one-third of the losses. The learned circuit judge, after hearing the evidence in the case, rendered a judgment in favor of the plaintiffs for the one-third of said losses, against the said *Schmitt* and Marshall, and appointed a receiver of the property, with directions to sell the same and apply the proceeds of the sale to the payment of the one-third of said losses; and, in case the proceeds of such sale should be insufficient to pay the amount found due the plaintiffs,

that an execution should issue against the property of said
Schmitt and Marshall, or either of them, for the unpaid
balance.   From this judgment the defendant *Schmitt* appeals to this court.   Marshall did not answer in the case,
and judgment was taken against him by default.   The evidence shows that he is pecuniarily irresponsible.

For the appellant there was a brief by *Dey & Friend*, and
oral argument by *Mr. C. C. Dey.*   To the point that *Schmitt*
was not a partner in the firm they cited, besides cases referred to in the opinion, *Frost v. Moulton*, 21 Beav. 596;
Bray v. Fromont, 6 Madd. 5; *Fitch v. Harrington*, 13 Gray,
468; *Murray v. Bogert*, 14 Johns. 318–322; *Setzer v. Beale*,
19 W. Va. 274; 1 Bates on Partn. secs. 159, 164, and cases
cited; 1 Lindley on Partn. (4th ed.), ch. 1, sec. 3, p. 55.   The
law is well settled that an agreement to use real estate for
partnership purposes or *as partnership property* is not sufficient to convert it into partnership stock, in the absence of
evidence of such intention.   *Alexander v. Kimbro*, 49 Miss.
529; *Ware v. Owens*, 42 Ala. 212; *Frink v. Branch*, 16
Conn. 261; *Theriot v. Michel*, 28 La. Ann. 107; 2 Lindley on
Partn. (4th ed.), 652 *et seq.*, and cases cited in notes.   And it
is also well settled that it does not follow that real estate
used for partnership purposes is partnership property.   A
contrary presumption prevails when the title is not in the
firm, and to rebut that presumption it must appear either (1)
that the property was paid for with firm money and used for
partnership purposes, or (2) that it was by proper agreement
actually brought into the firm; and (3) the latter must be
determined by the intention, derived from the agreement
and the acts and conduct of the partners.   *Shafer's Appeal*,
106 Pa. St. 49; *Hogle v. Lowe*, 12 Nev. 286; 1 Bates on
Partn. sec. 280.   The facts in this case clearly show that
the property should not be subject to the losses of the firm.
Gordon v. Gordon, 49 Mich. 501; *Adams v. Bradley*, 12 id.
346; *Robertson v. Corsett*, 39 id. 777.

For the respondents there was a brief by *Jenkins, Winkler*

& Smith, and oral argument by *Mr. F. C. Winkler.* To the point that under the facts in this case *Schmitt* was a partner in the firm, they cited *Meaher v. Cox*, 37 Ala. 201; *Upham v. Hewitt*, 42 Wis. 85; *Fordyce v. Shriver*, 115 Ill. 530; *Ault v. Goodrich*, 4 Russ. 430; *Stowell v. Eldred*, 39 Wis. 614; *Goddard v. Hodges*, 1 Crompt. & M. 33; Collyer on Partn. sec. 194, and note.

TAYLOR, J. The learned counsel for the appellant insists that the circuit court erred in finding that the appellant, *Schmitt*, was a partner in the firm of H. Riedeburg & Co., and that it was error to charge him personally with any part of the losses of said firm; and he also insists that the court erred in holding that the distillery property should be charged with the payment of any part of the debts of said firm. Upon the question as to the personal liability of *Schmitt* as a partner in the firm of H. Riedeburg & Co., . we think that, upon the evidence in the case, the court erred in holding *Schmitt* a partner. In the first place, the written articles of agreement exclude him from the partnership; and, again, within three months after the partnership articles had been signed and the business commenced, *Schmitt* applied to be admitted as a partner in the business, and his application was rejected by *Riedeburg* and *Bodden*, except upon a condition which he refused to comply with. It is urged by the learned counsel for the respondents that, notwithstanding these plain and admitted facts, he must be held as a partner, because he recognized the right of Marshall to put his property into the firm business, and that Marshall for that privilege agreed with *Schmitt* that he should have one half of his third of the profits of the business of the firm. It does not appear very clearly that this arrangement between *Schmitt* and Marshall was known to *Riedeburg* and *Bodden;* but, if it was known to them, it would not make him their partner. His arrangement with

Marshall did not give him any right to interfere with the business of the partnership, or impose any duty on the other partners to see that the half of the one-third of the profits which belonged to Marshall were paid over to *Schmitt*. If A. loans B. $5,000 with the understanding that B. shall invest it in forming a partnership with C., and, instead of charging B. with interest on the money loaned, he agrees to receive of B. one half of the profits he shall realize from the partnership business, it seems to us very clear that A. does not become a partner with B. and C. The evidence does not in this case show any arrangement between *Schmitt* and Marshall materially different from the one above stated. As between *Schmitt* and Marshall, there was no agreement that *Schmitt* should pay any part of the losses which might fall upon Marshall by reason of the partnership business, but simply that, if any profits accrued to Marshall from the business of the firm, he should have one half of them as compensation for the privilege of putting his property in the firm business during the three years it was to exist.

The true rule, in cases of this kind, is concisely stated by the court of appeals in New York, in *Burnett v. Snyder*, 81 N. Y. 555. Speaking of a contract made by a third person, not a member of the firm, with one of the members of the firm, to share in the profits derived by such member from the firm, and of the liability of such third person, even to the creditors of the firm, the court say: " But the participation in the profits of a trade which makes a person a partner as to third persons is a participation in the profits as such, under circumstances which give him a proprietary interest in the profits, before division, as principal trader, . . . and a right to an account as partner, and a lien on the partnership assets in preference to the individual creditors of the partner." The facts of that case were much stronger in favor of holding the third party as a partner than in the case at bar; yet the court held he was not a partner, even as to creditors of the firm, much less as between himself and the members of the firm. The general and universal rule is that, as between the parties comprising a partnership, no act of one partner, or any number of the partners less than the whole, can bring a new partner into the firm. In the case at bar a partnership was formed by a written agreement, by which only three were to compose the firm, and all profits of the firm were to be divided equally between the three. Now, it is clear that a fourth man cannot be brought into the firm as a member without the consent of all; and there is an entire absence of any evidence in the case showing that *Schmitt* was ever admitted to the firm as a member thereof with the assent of all parties. The evidence would appear to negative the idea that he was ever so admitted. The following, among many other authorities, sustain the contention that the evidence in this case does not make *Schmitt* a partner in the firm of H. Riedeburg & Co.: *Burnett v. Snyder*, 76 N. Y. 344; *S. C.* 81 N. Y. 550, 555; *Reynolds v. Hicks*, 19 Ind. 113; *Freeman v. Bloomfield*, 43 Mo. 392; *Rockafellow v. Miller*, 107 N. Y. 507; *Bybee v. Hawkett*, 12 Fed. Rep. 649; *Ex parte Hamper*, 17 Ves. 404; *Champion v. Bostwick*, 18 Wend. 184; *Richardson v. Hughitt*, 76 N. Y. 55; 1 Bates on Partn. § 164; 1 Lindley on Partn. (4th ed.), 55.

We are of the opinion that the circuit court erred in holding the appellant, *Schmitt*, personally liable to account to the plaintiffs for the one-third of the losses of the firm, or for any part of such losses, and that the part of the judgment holding him so liable must be reversed.

The only other question in the case is whether the real estate, viz., the distillery, the lands on which it is situated, and the personal property and fixtures therein, were a part of the firm property, so that in equity they must be held chargeable with a share of the losses of the firm in a final accounting between the members of the firm. Although

the title to this property was not in Marshall, who undertook to bring it to the firm at the time the partnership was
organized, we are of the opinion that under the evidence it
must, as against the appellant, *Schmitt,* be treated as though
the entire beneficial ownership had been in Marshall at the
time he undertook to give the partnership control of it.
We come to this conclusion from the fact that, after Marshall made the partnership agreement in writing by which
he, in explicit terms, furnishes and contributes for the use
of the copartnership his " real estate, consisting," etc., and
declaring that the property so furnished is of the value of
$11,550, "which is considered the capital of said Marshall
in the firm," the appellant, *Schmitt,* in writing, consented to
the contract made by said Marshall, and afterwards, in further execution of said contract, *Schmitt* conveyed or released
to the United States all his interest in said real estate, distillery, and fixtures, so far at least as to give the United States
a preference as to all claims the United States might thereafter have against the firm of H. Riedeburg & Co. If,
treating the distillery and fixtures as the property of Marshall at the time the partnership was formed, it became a
part of the property belonging to the firm as between Marshall and the other members thereof, and became liable to
contribute to the payment of the losses of the firm in a final
accounting between the partners, then it must be held liable
to contribute as against the appellant, *Schmitt.* This distillery must be treated as essentially real estate, and the question is whether, notwithstanding its character as real estate,
and notwithstanding that the title was not conveyed to the
firm by any of the usual forms of conveyance, it may still
be treated in equity as a part of the partnership assets, and
so liable to contribute as such to the payment of the losses
of the firm. The rule is universal that real estate purchased
with partnership funds for partnership purposes and used
for such purposes, although the title be taken in the name

of one of the partners, will be treated in equity as partnership assets, and be held for the benefit of the creditors of the partnership instead of the creditors of the individual partner in whose name the title appears; and so, in winding up the business of the firm, it must be used in payment of losses instead of going to the creditors of the individual. 1 Bates on Partn. §§ 280, 281, and cases cited. In cases of this character the authorities are very much in accord; but the rule is not so well settled as to the rights of parties to real estate which is brought into the firm business at the time of its organization, and used in the business of the firm thereafter. Whether real estate owned by one or more members of a firm at the time of the organization of the firm, and which is to be used by the firm thereafter, becomes firm property for all purposes, depends mainly upon the question whether the person bringing the property into the firm contributes it to the firm as his part of the joint stock, and has credit with the firm for the value thereof as the whole or a part of his contribution to such joint stock. This is the rule as stated by Bates, in his work on Partnership, §§ 280, 281. Mr. Bates also says, in section 280: "Whether real estate is partnership or individual property is purely a question of the intention of the partner, and, as this is rarely expressed in the deed, is a matter of inference and evidence."

Is there sufficient evidence in this case to show that the distillery and fixtures were contributed by Marshall, as his part of the joint stock, to be used by and for the use of the firm? After a careful consideration of the evidence, we think the finding of the court on that question is sustained by the evidence. We have, first, the articles of copartnership, by which Marshall put in the distillery and fixtures as his contribution to the joint stock of the partnership at a fixed valuation. He is to be paid interest on its value, as a part of the capital stock invested in the business, before

any profits are to be divided; the other partners to be paid
the same rate of interest on the capital furnished by them.
Afterwards, *Schmitt* and Marshall secure the lien of the
United States upon this property as the property of the distilling firm. The firm pay the taxes and the insurance on
the property as the property of the firm, although nothing is said in the partnership articles upon that subject.
Although *Schmitt* in his testimony denies generally that
the distillery was put in as firm property, and insists, as
Marshall does, that nothing but its use was transferred
to the company, still he says: "I was simply to allow them
to use the property for distilling purposes. Marshall was
allowed to put it in as working capital in the distillery."
It is very likely that *Mr. Schmitt* did not understand the
contract made by Marshall as conveying to the company
the distillery as the part of the joint capital which Marshall
was to contribute and did contribute for the use of the
firm. Still, his misunderstanding of the legal effect of the
contract cannot relieve him from its operation. There was
another piece of evidence in the case which is almost conclusive of the intent of the parties to make the distillery the
property of the firm; and that is the fact that it was entered on the books of the firm to the credit of Marshall as
his capital invested in the business. This court held, in the
case of *Bergeron v. Richardott*, 55 Wis. 129, that such an
entry upon the books of the firm, with the knowledge and
assent of the separate owner of a store building in which
the business of the firm was carried on, was almost conclusive evidence that the property was firm property, though
the title was never conveyed to the firm. We think, upon
the whole evidence, the circuit court rightly found that the
distillery was in equity firm property, so far as to subject it
to the payment of the share of the losses chargeable to
Marshall. The judgment, in that respect, must be affirmed.
The following cases sustain the judgment in that respect:

Wiegand v. Copeland, 14 Fed. Rep. 118; *Arnold v. Wainwright,* 6 Minn. 358; *Bergeron v. Richardott, supra; Sigourney v. Munn,* 7 Conn. 11; *Way v. Stebbins,* 47 Mich. 296; 1 Bates on Partn. §§ 280, 281; *Shafer's Appeal,* 106 Pa. St. 49; *Black's Appeal,* 89 Pa. St. 201; *Marsh v. Davis,* 33 Kan. 326; *M'Dermot v. Laurence,* 7 Serg. & R. 443; *Ludlow v. Cooper,* 4 Ohio St. 1, 8; *Duryea v. Burt,* 28 Cal. 569, 580; *Hogle v. Lowe,* 12 Nev. 286.

By the Court.— That part of the judgment of the circuit court which adjudges the appellant personally liable for the one-third of the losses of the firm is reversed, and the remainder of said judgment is affirmed; the appellant to recover the costs of this appeal. ·

See note to this case in 38 N. W. Rep. 836.— REP.

MCMILLAN, Respondent, vs. PAGE, Appellant.

April 20 — May 12, 1888.

Master and servant: Compensation: Implied contract.

The plaintiff, when a young girl, entered the home of defendant, a stranger to her, as a hired servant for a fixed period. For years after the expiration of that period she continued to work for him without receiving other compensation than a home, board, and clothing. *Held,* that in the absence of any express agreement to the contrary, the law would imply a promise on the part of the defendant to pay her for such services what they were reasonably worth.

APPEAL from the Circuit Court for *Columbia* County. The case is stated in the opinion. The defendant appeals from a judgment in favor of the plaintiff.

For the appellant there was a brief by *Rogers & Hall* and *Geo. W. Bird,* and oral argument by *Mr. W. H. Rog-*

ers and *Mr. Bird.* They contended, *inter alia*, that the court erred in relieving plaintiff of the burden of proving an express agreement that she was to receive something in addition to board, clothing, etc., and in casting upon the defendant the burden of proving an express agreement that she was to receive nothing in addition to board, clothing, etc. A person making another's house his home as a member of the latter's family, can recover for services only upon proving an express contract to that effect by positive and direct evidence. And the burden is upon the party claiming the compensation to prove the contract by *such* evidence. Clear and satisfactory evidence may be neither. *Fisher v. Fisher,* 5 Wis. 472; *Mountain v. Fisher,* 22 id. 93; *Kaye v. Crawford,* id. 320; *Hall v. Finch,* 29 id. 278; *Pellage v. Pellage,* 32 id. 136; *Wells v. Perkins,* 43 id. 160; *Geary v. Geary,* 67 id. 248; *Cowan v. Musgrave,* 35 N. W. Rep. (Iowa), 496; *McGarvey v. Roods,* id. 488; *Smith v. Myers,* 19 Mo. 433; *Maltby v. Harwood,* 12 Barb. 473; *Andrus v. Foster,* 17 Vt. 556; *Wilhelm v. Hardman,* 13 Md. 140; *Stone v. Dennison,* 13 Pick. 1; *Hays v. McConnell,* 42 Ind. 285.

For the respondent the cause was submitted on a brief by *John S. Maxwell.*

ORTON, J. The plaintiff's claim is for work and labor from October 1, 1879, to December 1, 1885, for $100 for the first year, and $200 for the subsequent years. The plaintiff, at the commencement of such work and labor for the defendant, was only sixteen years of age. Her mother had died, and her father had neglected to support or care for her, and she was dependent upon her own labor for support, when she commenced to work out in the city of Chicago at her own instance and without interference of her father; and she so worked about four years, when she came to her uncle's at Fall River in this state, where she had a home, in the spring of 1879, and where and when the defendant came and employed her to work for him for the ensuing summer. For such service the defendant paid her at the rate of ten shillings per week. He then employed her, as she alleges, to continue to work for him for an indefinite time, and agreed to pay her well when she got through, and she continued in his service until late in the fall of 1885. The defendant in his answer alleges, in effect, that the agreement was that the plaintiff should have a home with him, and that he should board, clothe, and care for her in sickness, and pay her doctor bills, as long as she saw fit to live with him, and that she should work for him according to her ability as the full and entire consideration of and complete compensation for such home, board, clothing, and care in sickness, and that beyond that he should pay her nothing for her labor.

The defendant was a single man, about fifty years of age, and owned and conducted a farm of 260 acres, and kept house thereon with a housekeeper. The plaintiff testified, substantially, that during the first summer she worked part of the time on the farm, and part of the time in the house; and that after she and the defendant settled and she received her ten shillings per week, the defendant said to her that he would like to have her stay with him right along, and that he would pay her well when she got through, and that she stayed and worked under that contract six years. The first winter she worked in the house most of the time. In the spring she plowed and dragged until the crops were in, and then she worked in the corn until harvest, and then worked in harvest on the harvester, and then did fall plowing and husked corn. In 1883, she plowed about 100 acres, and in 1884 about 120 acres, and in 1885 about 100 acres. She worked three horses all the time. She generally got to her work, in the spring, summer, and fall, at 4 o'clock in the morning, and her breakfast was sent to her in the field.

McMillan vs. Page.

She sometimes plowed until 10 o'clock at night, and sometimes all night by changing teams, and worked all the next
day, late in the fall. She had good and suitable clothing
when she commenced to work for the defendant, and when
they were worn out she was clothed with coarse, stout
cloth, called "demings," the same as men's overalls. She
was strong and healthy, and never needed a doctor. In
this way she continued until December 1, 1885, and then
quit work and asked the defendant to pay her for her labor,
and he refused to pay her anything except to offer her an
acre of beans. She thinks she received, during her term of
service, in all, about $15. She sometimes asked for a few
dollars, and was refused. One of the defendant's neighbors,
whose land adjoined his own, testified that the plaintiff
worked for the defendant about six or seven years, doing
all kinds of farm work, such as plowing, dragging, working
in harvest, binding, pitching bundles, etc.; that he employed
hired men on his farm; and that she did as much as a man,
and her services were worth $200 per year; and that the
defendant said that his women could do as much work as
his men, and that he would rather hire them because he
could get them cheaper. Another adjoining neighbor testified that she did as much work as a man in all kinds of
farm work, and that the defendant told him that he could
not afford to hire men, and that he could get women
cheaper, and get more out of them; and she worked for defendant over six years, and her services were worth $200
per year. Another adjoining neighbor testified the same as
to her labor and the time she worked for the defendant,
and that the defendant said to him that his girl could do
more work than his man, and asked how much he paid, and
then said that he, the witness, paid too much, and that he
could hire women cheaper, and that he should pay the
plaintiff all he possibly could.
    In view of the hard, rough, and constant work out of

doors, exacted of this poor young girl, under the guise
and pretext of giving her a home and boarding and clothing her suitable to her sex and condition, the conclusion is
almost irresistible that the defendant violated, in both letter and spirit, the very agreement that he alleges in his
answer, and upon which he relies in defense of her action.
Is that the kind of a *home* he agreed to give her? Is that
boarding and clothing her suitable to her age and sex?
Were such the female services she was to render as the consideration for such advantages, or for such "privileges of a
home," as they are called in the defendant's answer? Most
emphatically not. Although this view of the case is not
urged by the learned counsel of the respondent, yet it
stands out in such bold relief, and is so apparently conclusive against the defense set up in the defendant's answer,
that I could not help noticing it as preliminary to the consideration of the contract which the plaintiff alleged as the
foundation of her action. If this view of the case had been
taken by the court and the jury, it might have appeared
as a sufficient reason for the verdict. Such unusual, unnatural, and most unsuitable work and labor that she did for
the defendant were clearly not within the reasonable intent
and meaning of the contract which the defendant alleges
in his defense to her action. They rest, therefore, upon a
quantum meruit, if the plaintiff has not established any
other agreement than that alleged by the defendant.

But the contract, as stated by the plaintiff, was sufficiently proved by her own testimony, so corroborated by the
testimony of her witnesses. The defendant testified that
the only contract made was the one set up in his answer,
and there was some evidence that the plaintiff had made
statements to the same effect. The jury had the right to
believe the plaintiff. The father of the plaintiff left her
to hire herself out, receive her own wages, and generally to
take care of herself, at a very feeble age and when she was

a mere child, and deserted and abandoned her. He had given her her own time as if she were of age, and had to all intents and purposes emancipated her, as the jury found. But, after the plaintiff had so hired herself out, as she testified, this unnatural father appeared upon the scene. He visited her in the field where she was at work. He had an interview with the defendant at his house. An agreement in writing is made between them, to the effect that the father leaves the plaintiff, as his "daughter *Anna*," with the defendant for one year, with the privilege of his keeping her five years if he chooses, and to let her work for her board and clothes as long as she remains in his employ, and in case she goes away he gives the defendant power to take her and bring her back if she could be found. But that is not all. The defendant about the same time prepared a written proposition and signed it, to the effect that he would give the plaintiff a home, and board, clothe, and pay her doctor bills as long as she remains *in his home* peaceably, and when she leaves she can take only what belongs to her, and that he will not look after her any further, or pay any bills, etc. This written proposition appears in evidence, with the plaintiff's written acceptance and consent appended thereto; and the defendant testified that she signed it, and his testimony is corroborated by that of his housekeeper, one Mrs. Lord. But the plaintiff most positively testified that she never signed it, and that she never consented that her father should "bind her out," or contract with the defendant for her services. The jury found that she did not sign it, and they had the right to believe her if they chose to do so. The jury found, further, that the plaintiff made no such agreement as the defendant had alleged in his answer, and that no part of her services were rendered under any such understanding; and they assessed the plaintiff's damages at $800. The court rendered judgment upon this special verdict for the plaintiff.

This is really all there is of this case. There are no exceptions to the admission of evidence, and the only exceptions are to the instructions of the court to the jury, in effect as follows: (1) That this is not a case where a party claiming the compensation has the burden of proving an express agreement for compensation, in addition to home, board, clothing, etc.; (2) that the burden was upon the defendant to prove an express agreement that the plaintiff was to receive only a home, board, clothing, etc.; (3) that the jury might assess damages for the whole time from October, 1879, to December, 1885, if they found that she was entitled to recover for the whole amount of that time.

The first two exceptions embrace really but one legal proposition, and that is whether the relations between the parties were such that the plaintiff must prove an express contract to recover for her services. If the principle can ever be extended to embrace strangers, or those not of kindred relationship, as members of the same family, which may be doubtful, most certainly there should be such circumstances of family relationship as would imply that the plaintiff's services should be gratuitous. But in this case the plaintiff was an entire stranger to the defendant, and was not a member of his family until she was employed by him to work for a compensation; and when that time of employment was at an end she continued to work for him in the same general way but more laboriously. And if she did so without any express agreement, the law would imply from their former relations a promise on his part to pay her therefor what her services were reasonably worth. In other words, she was not a member of his family except as a hireling; and if she continued in his family the law would imply that she was still a hireling. There was nothing to create any other relation between them except that of employer and employee. Her being a minor cuts no figure in the case; for the defendant employed her first as if she had been of age and of full self-control, capable of contracting and being contracted with.   Indeed, minority has nothing to do with the question as to whether kindred of the same family can recover compensation of each other for personal services.   The same obligation to render to each other gratuitous service continues beyond minority.   The authorities cited by the learned counsel of the appellant are inapplicable to the case.   There is absolutely nothing in this case that should take it out of the general rule of one person doing work and labor for another to be compensated by the rule of *quantum meruit.*

It follows, therefore, that if the defendant wishes to take this case out of the general rule he must prove an express agreement to that effect, or that the plaintiff should receive only, as compensation, her board, clothing, and medical care, according to his answer.   But, again, there is no such question in this case.   The pleadings must determine the attitude of the parties to each other.   The plaintiff seeks to recover by proof of an express contract of employment, and the defendant seeks to defeat her action by proof of an express contract, not that he did not hire or employ her to work for him, but to work for him for the compensation only of a home and of board, clothing, and care in sickness. The jury found the contract as alleged by the plaintiff, and that no such contract as alleged by the defendant was ever made; and that was the real issue between the parties.   The question of gratuitous service in consequence of family relationship is not in the case.

The third exception, as stated in the brief of the defendant's counsel, is modified by the full instructions of the court as to the time for which the plaintiff might recover. It is guarded by all proper conditions, so that the jury could find for the whole time' or any part of it, and make proper deductions.   We cannot see any objection to that part of the charge, or, indeed, to any part of it.   The whole case was submitted to the jury very fully and impartially, and we think correctly. If there was any seeming error in the proceedings it was quite immaterial, and may well be disregarded as not affecting the substantial rights of the appellant. Sec. 2829, R. S. The case made for the plaintiff on the evidence has great merit, and the defense was rather technical than substantial, if not unconscionable. We have stated the facts more fully, that the merits of the case may be apparent, and to show the real bearing of the exceptions, as the point is made that the verdict is not supported by the evidence, with a view of obtaining a new trial.

By the Court.— The judgment of the circuit court is affirmed.

OLSON, Respondent, vs. SOLVESON, Appellant.

April 21 — May 12, 1888.

(1) Practice: Jurors: Full panel: Peremptory challenges. (5, 6) Statements by counsel and by presiding judge during trial: Reversal of judgment. (2) Breach of promise to marry: Evidence: Immaterial error. (3) Mutuality of contract: Court and jury. (4) When formal demand unnecessary. (7) Evidence of defendant's pecuniary circumstances. (8) Damages: Instructions to jury. (9) Excessive damages: Appeal.

1. An objection to proceeding with a trial on the ground that, two juries being out and one juryman excused, only eleven jurors of the regular panel are left, cannot be sustained. The lack of jurors may be supplied as provided in sec. 2538, R. S.; and the peremptory challenges given by sec. 2851 apply to a full panel of jurors thus called, as well as to the regular panel.

2. In an action for the breach of a promise of marriage, where the defendant concedes the promise and the refusal to marry, an error in admitting improper evidence to prove such promise, even if not cured by striking out such evidence, will not work a reversal.

3. Where the contract to marry is conceded, the question of its mutuality need not be submitted to the jury.

4. An absolute refusal to marry the plaintiff obviates the necessity of a formal demand.
5. The mere fact that the plaintiff's counsel, in opening the case to the jury, stated that judgment had been taken in the action by default at a former term, defendant's counsel having just before stated the same fact, is not ground for reversal.
6. It was not error for the court to announce that it could not wait until a certain jury came in before proceeding with the trial; nor to inquire the object of a certain line of cross-examination, and to state wherein it was immaterial, and to restrict the same; nor to state that it appeared in evidence that defendant was not a poor man, where such was the undisputed fact, and defendant had testified, in his own behalf, that he was probably worth between five and six thousand dollars.
7. In an action for the breach of a promise of marriage, evidence of the defendant's pecuniary circumstances is competent as affecting the question of damages.
8. In an action for the breach of a promise of marriage, the court refused an instruction that, under the complaint, the plaintiff was simply entitled to compensatory damages; but it submitted to the jury the question as to what sum should be given to the plaintiff *by way of compensation* for the injury sustained by the breach of the contract, charging them that they were to get at the damages from the evidence, the situation of the parties, what occurred between them, their condition and surroundings, and then give such sum as in their judgment the evidence would warrant — not an unreasonable or exorbitant sum, but a just, reasonable, and fair sum. *Held*, that the question of damages was fully and fairly presented to the jury.
9. In such a case this court will not interfere on the ground that the damages are excessive, unless it is made apparent that the jury were actuated by undue motives.

APPEAL from the Circuit Court for *Waukesha* County. The following statement of the case was prepared by Mr. Justice CASSODAY:

This is an action for damages for an alleged breach of a promise made October 26, 1885, whereby the defendant agreed to marry the plaintiff, and then refused. The answer was a general denial. Upon the trial the jury returned a verdict in favor of the plaintiff, and assessed her damages at $1,500. From the judgment entered upon such verdict the defendant appeals.

For the appellant there was a brief by *Morris Wittig*, attorney, and *David W. Small*, of counsel, and oral argument by *Mr. Small*.

Oscar F. Jones, for the respondent.

CASSODAY, J. The verdict is abundantly sustained by the evidence. In fact, the promise and refusal are both conceded. The several errors assigned will be considered.

1. Two juries were out, and one juryman had been excused at the time the cause was called for trial. This left but eleven names in the box, and the defendant objected to proceeding with the trial for that reason. It was never intended that the business of the court should be suspended merely because the regular panel of jurors should be thus exhausted. On the contrary, the statutes expressly provide that " when, by reason of challenge or otherwise, a sufficient number of jurors, duly drawn and summoned, cannot be obtained for the trial of any cause, civil or criminal, the court shall cause jurors, duly qualified, to be returned from the by-standers, or from the county at large, to complete the panel for such trial, and the court may, in its discretion, order a special *venire* to issue for that purpose, or such jurors may be returned by the sheriff . . . without writ." Sec. 2538, R. S. The lack of jurors was supplied as thus prescribed. The three peremptory challenges to which each party is entitled apply to a full panel of jurors thus called, as well as to the regular panel. Sec. 2851, R. S.; *Gilchrist v. Brande*, 58 Wis. 184. The exceptions thereto must be overruled.

2. The plaintiff testified, in effect, that she was at Mrs. Rockwell's, October 26, 1885; that her sister then lived there; that the defendant was there on that day, and agreed to marry her. She was then cross-examined by the defend-

ant's counsel, and, after being told to get down to the agree
ment made with the defendant, she was asked: "Who was
there besides you and *Martin? Answer*. No one." Thereupon the sister testified to the effect that the plaintiff and defendant were both there, and then, in answer to the question whether there was anything unusual in the appearance
of either, which was objected to, she stated what was said
between her and the plaintiff, but the same was immediately stricken out by the court. Assuming that the admission of such conversation was error, not cured by striking
out the testimony, which it would be difficult to maintain,
yet, as the defendant conceded the engagement and his refusal to marry, it affected no substantial right of the defendant, and hence is no ground for reversal. Sec. 2829,
R. S.

3. The mere fact that the plaintiff's counsel, in opening
the case to the jury, stated, in effect, that judgment had
been taken in the action by default at a former term, when
the defendant's counsel had just before stated the same fact,
is not ground for reversal. Nor do we find anything in the
remarks of counsel characterizing the evidence which should
work a reversal.

4. Numerous exceptions are taken to the remarks of the
learned judge who presided at the trial. But the right to
preside at all necessarily includes, within certain limits, a
discretionary right to direct the proceedings. He must
necessarily rule upon questions presented; the admission or
rejection of testimony; indicate the line of examination or
cross-examination to be pursued; and to limit or restrict the
same when unnecessarily extended, or when there is any
departure. It is impossible to perform such duties without
oral communications which may at times characterize the
question or testimony, or some part of it. It was certainly
not error for the court, in effect, to announce that it could
not wait until a certain jury should come in before proceed-

ing with the trial; nor to inquire the object of a certain line of cross-examination, and to state wherein it was immaterial, and to restrict the same; nor in stating that it appeared in evidence that the defendant was not a poor man, since such was the undisputed fact, as appeared from the defendant's letters in evidence. Besides, in the same connection, the defendant was recalled in his own behalf, and testified, in effect, that he had taken an inventory a year prior to the previous January, and that upon that basis he would then be worth between five and six thousand dollars. This estimate was really higher than the evidence would otherwise have authorized. That it was competent, upon the subject of damages, to prove the defendant's pecuniary circumstances, there would seem to be no doubt. *Bennett v. Beam*, 42 Mich. 346, 36 Am. Rep. 442; *Hunter v. Hatfield*, 68 Ind. 416; *Lawrence v. Cooke*, 56 Me. 187; *Reed v. Clark*, 47 Cal. 194; *James v. Biddington*, 6 Car. & P. 589.

5. The defendant having absolutely refused to marry the plaintiff, obviated the necessity of any formal demand.

6. The court was requested to give a certain instruction to the jury to the effect that, under the complaint, the plaintiff was simply entitled to compensatory damages. The court failed to give such instruction in form, or to hear an authority read which is said to be in support of it. But the court did fairly submit to the jury the question as to what sum, from all the evidence, ought to be given to the " plaintiff *by way of compensation* for the injury sustained by the breach of this contract." They were, moreover, told, in effect, that the only essential question for them to determine was the amount of damages they should award to the plaintiff for the breach of the contract; that this question of damages, generally, in actions of this kind, was a difficult and delicate one, upon which the law had failed to furnish any rule by which they could measure the same by dollars and cents, but that they were to get at the damages

from the evidence, the situation of the parties, what occurred between them, their condition and surroundings, and
all about it, and then give such sum by way of damages as
in their judgment the evidence would warrant; that they
were not to give an unreasonable or exorbitant sum, but a
just, reasonable, and fair sum,— such as they thought, from
a fair consideration of all the evidence and all the surroundings, the plaintiff should have and the defendant ought to
pay. Such is the substance of the portions of the charge
to which exceptions were taken. The charge nowhere authorized punitive damages. On the contrary, it only authorized compensatory damages. It fully and fairly presented
the question of damages, which was really the only question in the case.

7. It is claimed that the damages are excessive. But this
court will not interfere in such a case upon that ground
merely, unless it is made apparent that the jury have been
actuated by undue motives. *Smith v. Woodfine*, 87 Eng. C.
L. 660; *Richmond v. Roberts*, 98 Ill. 480; *Royal v. Smith*,
40 Iowa, 615; *Waters v. Bristol*, 26 Conn. 398.

8. The contract of marriage being in effect conceded,
there was no error in refusing to submit to the jury the
question of its mutuality.

Upon a careful examination of the whole record we find
no material error.

By the Court.— The judgment of the circuit court is
affirmed.

THE STATE vs. YANTA and others.

April 23 — May 12, 1888.

Criminal law: Pleading: Assault with intent to kill: Conviction of lesser offense.

An information charging that defendants "did then and there wilfully, maliciously, and feloniously assault, cut, stab, and wound one W., with intent wilfully, maliciously, and feloniously, and with malice aforethought, him, the said W., to kill and murder," will not sustain a conviction of an assault with intent to do great bodily harm, because the averments do not in form include the lesser offense.

REPORTED from the Circuit Court for *Portage* County. This case comes here on the certificate of the judge of the Seventh judicial circuit submitting to this court for determination certain questions of law pursuant to sec. 4721, R. S. The information charges that one John Pulchinski, at a time and place therein named, being armed with a dangerous weapon, to wit, a jack-knife, "did then and there, wilfully, maliciously, and feloniously assault, cut, stab, and wound one Mike Walski, with intent wilfully, maliciously, and feloniously, and with malice aforethought, him, the said Mike Walski, to kill and murder." The information then attempts to charge the defendants *Nick* and *Charles Yanta* and *John Schulist* with being then and there present, and feloniously aiding, abetting, counseling, procuring, and commanding the said Pulchinski to so kill and murder the said Walski.

The jury found the three defendants *Nick* and *Charles Yanta* and *John Schulist* guilty, as principals in the first degree, of an assault upon the said Walski with intent to do him great bodily harm. A motion in arrest of judgment was interposed, whereupon the court certified the case for answers to the following questions: "*First.* Does the information herein charge the defendants *John Schulist,*

Charles Yanta, and *Nick Yanta* with any criminal offense? *Second.* If it does, can the defendants, under the information herein, be convicted as principals in the first degree? *Third.* Under the information herein could the defendants lawfully be convicted of an assault with intent to do great bodily harm?"

The cause was submitted for the plaintiff on the brief of the *Attorney General* and *L. K. Luse,* Assistant Attorney General, and for the defendants on the brief of *Raymond & Haseltine.*

For the plaintiff it was contended, *inter alia,* that the rule is well settled in this state that one may be convicted of a lesser offense when charged with a greater, provided the greater offense includes all of the elements of the lesser, so that an information properly charging the greater offense would necessarily include the allegations sufficient to charge the lesser crime. *State v. Erickson,* 45 Wis. 86; *State v. Shear,* 51 id. 460; *State v. Hooks,* 69 id. 182; Whart. Crim. Pl. & Pr. sec. 246. In *Kilkelly v. State,* 43 Wis. 604, it was decided that one charged with intent to murder could not be convicted of an assault to maim, for the reason that the intent was of an entirely different character. But a reference to secs. 4372, 4373, R. S. (the sections there construed) will show that the offender must necessarily be charged with the intention to do one or more specific injuries therein prohibited. The doing of some physical injury would not constitute an offense under those sections, even if it might be a great bodily injury, for the reason that the injury might not be to any of the members of his person described in the sections prohibiting maiming. On the other hand, it would be impossible to murder a person without committing great bodily harm or great bodily injury upon him, and the ruling that the intent to do great bodily harm is necessarily included in the intent to murder is wholly consistent. *Beckwith v. People,* 26 Ill. 500; *Peo-*

ple v. Congleton, 44 Cal. 92. It has frequently been held that an assault to commit manslaughter in hot blood is included in an assault to commit murder. *State v. White*, 45 Iowa, 325; *State v. Reed*, 40 Vt. 603; *Keefe v. People*, 40 N. Y. 348; 1 Whart. Crim. Law, sec. 641.

LYON, J. The third question propounded to us, to wit, "Under the information herein could the defendants lawfully be convicted of an assault with intent to do great bodily harm?" was answered in the negative by this court in the case of *Kilkelly v. State*, 43 Wis. 604. The rule was there stated to be that where offenses are included one within another, a person indicted for a higher one may be convicted for one below, *provided the averment in the indictment, in form, charges the lesser offense as well*, and not otherwise. So it was there held that a charge of an assault with intent to murder will not warrant a conviction of an assault with intent to maim or disfigure,— the latter intent not being included in the former. 1 Bish. Crim. Law, § 794.

Kilkelly v. State was followed, and the same rule applied, in *State v. Shear*, 51 Wis. 460. Mr. Justice ORTON there says: "The lesser offense must be included in the greater *by necessary words of description*, so that, if the words defining the greater offense are stricken out of the information, there would remain a sufficient description of the lesser offense."

The third question, being thus answered in the negative, is decisive of the case, and it is unnecessary to answer the other two questions, which relate to the sufficiency of the information. The cause will be certified back to the circuit court, and that court advised to grant the motion in arrest of judgment.

By the Court.— Ordered accordingly.

TAYLOR, J., dissents.

THE STATE VS. WACKER.

April 23 — May 12, 1888.

Excise laws: Sales of liquor on Sunday: Nuisance.

A sale of intoxicating liquor "in violation of law," within the meaning of sec. 1563, R. S., is a sale prohibited by the *excise law;* and
sales made on Sunday by a licensed saloon-keeper, not being prohibited by that law, do not render the place in which they are made
a public nuisance, which, upon the conviction of the keeper thereof,
may be shut up and abated.

REPORTED from the Circuit Court for *La Crosse*
County.

The case is stated in the opinion.

For the plaintiff there was a brief by the *Attorney General* and *L. K. Luse,* Assistant Attorney General, and oral
argument by the *Attorney General.* They contended, *inter
alia,* that a sale of liquors on Sunday is illegal and prohibited by sec. 1564, R. S. This court has already given
its sanction to similar provisions of the law, and held that
the offense was distinct and separate from the sale of liquors
without license, and has directed judgment to be entered
abating the nuisance. *State v. Gumber,* 37 Wis. 298; *Faust
v. State,* 45 id. 273. A license to do business does not permit the person licensed to do that business in an improper
manner, or shield him from the consequences of conducting
such business in a manner to disturb the neighborhood, and
if he does so conduct his business, he is indictable for maintaining it as a nuisance, the same as though it were not
licensed. *State v. Buckley,* 5 Harr. 508; *State v. Mullikin,*
8 Blackf. 260; *U. S. v. Elder,* 4 Cranch, C. C. 507; *Wood
on Nuis.* sec. 38; 2 Whart. Cr. Law, sec. 1449, note 4. Regardless of the provisions of sec. 1563, it has frequently
been held that keeping a place of business where intoxicating liquors are habitually sold in violation of law will con-

stitute the place a public nuisance, and that the keeper may
be indicted and the place abated. 1 Bish. Cr. Law, sec. 1113
et seq; 2 id. sec. 967; *Stats v. Williams,* 30 N. J. Law, 102;
Comm. v. Shea, 14 Gray, 386; *Kroer v. People,* 78 Ill. 294;
State v. Waynick, 45 Iowa, 516; *Smith v. Comm.* 6 B. Mon.
21; *Wilson v. Comm.* 12 id. 2; *Comm. v. Cogan,* 107 Mass.
212; *Comm. v. Mitchell,* 115 id. 141; *Comm. v. Kerrissey,*
141 id. 110.

For the defendant there was a brief by *J. W. Losey* and
C. L. Hood, attorneys, and *G. M. Woodward,* of counsel,
and oral argument by *Mr. Losey.*

COLE, C. J.   The defendant was a keeper of a saloon at
the city of La Crosse, and engaged in the business of selling
intoxicating liquors at such saloon, having a license therefor.   He was charged in an information, and was found
guilty by a jury, of selling, at his saloon, intoxicating liquors on the several Sundays named, and also of usually
keeping open his saloon on Sunday.   The circuit court has
reported the case, under the statute, for the decision of this
court upon this question: "Does the selling of intoxicating
liquor on Sunday at a licensed saloon by the keeper of it,
make a saloon building a public nuisance within the meaning of section 1563 of the Revised Statutes or at common
law, and authorize a judgment, on conviction of the keeper,
directing the nuisance to be abated and the building closed?"

I am in some doubt as to what answer should be given
the question, but my brethren are of the opinion that it
should receive a negative answer, and I defer to their views.
It is not seriously claimed on the part of the state that an
information would now lie at common law for the sales of
liquor on Sunday; for, as suggested by the defendant's counsel, the legislature has enacted laws on the subject of excise,
prescribing penalties for all violations of the same, and this
legislation supersedes the common law on the subject.   Be-

sides the statute expressly declares that all punishments prescribed by the common law for any offense specified in the statutes of this state and the punishment whereof is prescribed therein, are prohibited. Sec. 4634, R. S. We have, then, but to consider the provisions of ch. 66, R. S., and the amendments thereto, so far as they have a bearing upon the question reported.

Sec. 1563 enacts that all places, of whatever description, in which intoxicating liquors are sold in violation of law, shall be held and are declared public nuisances, and shall, upon the conviction of the keeper thereof, be shut up and abated. Now, what is the meaning of this provision? It is said on the part of the state that the language is free from ambiguity; and, if we are governed in its construction by the ordinary meaning of the words used, we can arrive at no other conclusion than that it covers the case at bar and authorizes the trial court to direct that the saloon building be shut up and abated. But it is not always safe to follow the strict literal reading of a statute, because cases often arise which, though within the letter, are not within the intent and spirit, of the law. We are to carry out the intention of the legislature in enacting this provision. In *State v. Gumber*, 37 Wis. 298 (decided in 1875), it was held that the keeper of a saloon or place of public resort where intoxicating liquors were sold without first having a license therefor, came within this provision, which at the time was sec. 19, ch. 179, Laws of 1874. That decision was followed in *Faust v. State*, 45 Wis. 274. We have no doubt whatever that a person keeping a saloon or place of any other description where intoxicating liquors are sold without a license makes such saloon or building a public nuisance. That is undoubtedly a sale *in violation of law*, which it was one object — perhaps the main object — of the statute to prohibit and prevent. But, in the case before us, the defendant was a holder of a license. He had the right to sell intoxicating liquors at his saloon six days in the week to proper parties. Was a sale, then, made by him on Sunday, such a violation of law as the legislature had in mind; being an act which would not only forfeit his license but render his place of business liable to be abated as a public nuisance? That is the precise question we have to solve.

A person obtaining a license has to give a bond, conditioned that he will, during the continuance of such license, keep and maintain an orderly and well-regulated house; will permit no gambling with cards, dice, or any device or implement for that purpose within his premises or any outhouse appertaining thereto; that he will not sell or give away any intoxicating liquor to any minor, having good reason to believe him to be such, unless upon the written order of the parent or guardian of such minor; will not sell to persons intoxicated or bordering upon intoxication, or to habitual drunkards; and will pay all damages, etc. Sec. 1549. A breach of the bond in any of the specified conditions, or a failure to observe and obey any order made pursuant to law by the supervisors, trustees, or aldermen of the town, village, or city, is made a ground for revoking the license, on notice to the holder thereof. Sec. 1558; *Common Council v. State ex rel. Perkins*, 59 Wis. 425. Now, it is a significant fact that a sale on Sunday is not a breach of the bond, nor is it made a ground for revoking the license. That is to say, the statute does not, in express language, make a sale of liquor on Sunday a cause for revoking the license. We are inclined to hold that sec. 1563 has an effect co-extensive with sec. 1558, and that an act which would be a breach of the bond, or would be a cause for revoking the license under the latter section, would be a violation of law within the meaning of the former section. So, if the licensee keeps a disorderly house, or permits gambling on his premises, or sells intoxicating liquor to a minor, having good reason to believe him to be such, or sells to a person intoxicated, or to an habitual drunkard, that then his house or place of business becomes a public nuisance liable to be abated on the conviction of the owner of the offense under this provision. But the defendant is not charged with having violated the law in any of these particulars. True, there is a further clause in the bond by which the licensee binds himself to observe and obey the lawful orders of the supervisors or aldermen of the town or city granting the license; and a refusal to obey such order is made a ground for revoking the license. Now, whether the common council of the city of La Crosse adopted an ordinance prohibiting the sales of intoxicating liquors within the city limits on Sunday, does not appear, and we cannot presume such was the fact, in the absence of proof. The statute is penal in its character, and we would not be justified in presuming that a person has incurred its penalties without some evidence of the fact. This provision, making all places where unlawful sales of liquor are made a public nuisance, was first enacted, we believe, in 1872 (sec. 3, ch. 127, Laws of 1872), and has ever since constituted a part of the excise law. We have no doubt of the power of the legislature to enact such a provision, and subject persons and property to its penalties or forfeitures in a proper case. But the essential thing or fact to be shown under the law is that a sale of intoxicating liquors has been made in violation of law within the meaning of the section.

But sec. 1564 is relied on as showing that the sale in question, made by the defendant on Sunday, was in violation of law. The answer to this argument is, that in *Jensen v. State*, 60 Wis. 578, that section was construed as applying only to " tavern keepers " and persons of a similar class. The complaint in that case charged the defendant with selling intoxicating liquors on Sunday, and it was held that the complaint set forth no offense, because the section did not include all persons, but only a particular class. Mr.

Justice Taylor, in the opinion, traces the origin and history of this provision. He shows that it was enacted in 1859, and that the evil to be suppressed or at least mitigated by the law was to prevent the drunkenness and disorder which generally resulted from the unrestricted sale of intoxicating liquors on election days and town-meeting days, and to secure peace, quiet, and good order on Sunday. It was an independent provision relating to these matters, and was not incorporated in the excise law until the Revision of 1878. It does not appear whether the defendant in that case had a license to sell liquors on a secular day or not, and that fact renders the decision of more decisive weight here. But there is a general statute which prohibits any person from keeping open his shop or from doing any kind of business on Sunday, except works of necessity or charity. Sec. 4595. My doubt in this case grows out of the existence of that statute. I have had difficulty in reaching the conclusion that it did not apply to the case and make any sale of intoxicating liquors on Sunday a violation of law. But it is suggested that this general statute, which has been in force since the state was organized, and which is intended to apply generally to all citizens of the state and all business transactions, was not in the mind of the legislature when it enacted the excise law, or, rather, that the legislature had no reference to it. It is a forced construction to hold that the sale of intoxicating liquors on Sunday is in violation of law, within the intent of the special provision upon the subject, because it is prohibited in this general manner. There is much force in the view that the safe construction of sec. 1563 is to hold that it relates solely, and was intended only to apply, to a violation of the excise law itself, which was the subject matter before the legislature and about which it was making regulations and prescribing penalties. By this construction a sale in violation of law must be understood to mean a sale prohibited by the provisions of the excise law itself, either expressly or by implication; and, as we have said, as that law does not expressly prohibit a sale on Sunday, the saloon building of the defendant is not a public nuisance within the meaning of sec. 1563.

The question reported by the circuit judge must therefore be answered in the negative, and the cause remanded to the circuit court with a certified copy of this opinion for its action.

By the Court.— Ordered accordingly.

THE STATE VS. DEAN.

April 23 — May 12, 1888.

CRIMINAL LAW. *(1) Pleading: Unlawful assembly: Riot. (2) Positive and negative testimony: Court and jury: Instructions.*

1. An information stating that at a certain time and place the defendants, to the number of three and more, "then and there being together, did then and there, in a violent, unlawful, and tumultuous manner, to the disturbance of the peace and to the terror and disturbance of others then and there present, assault," etc., is held to charge an offense under sec. 4511, R. S.
2. The evidence being conflicting as to whether a defendant charged with riot did or did not kick a certain drum, it was error for the court to charge the jury, in effect, that where two persons are at the same place, and one swears that a particular fact happened, and the other that it did not, the affirmative witness must be believed.

EXCEPTIONS from the Circuit Court for *Rock* County.

The defendant *Dean* was found guilty under an information charging that on May 28, 1886, at the city of Beloit, he and other persons named to the number of three and more, "then and there being together, did then and there in a violent, unlawful, and tumultuous manner, to the disturbance of the peace and to the terror and disturbance of others then and there present, assault, strike, wound and beat [persons named], and did then and there, in a violent, unlawful, and tumultuous manner, break, injure, and destroy a bass drum and a violin and bow then and there in the possession of said [persons named], and did also in like manner then and there injure and tear the clothing of said [persons named], and other wrongs to the said [persons named] and others then and there present, then and there, violently, unlawfully, and tumultuously did, to the great damage of the said [persons named] and others then and there present, and against the peace and dignity of the state of Wisconsin."

The persons assaulted and whose property was destroyed were members of the so-called "Salvation Army." Other facts are stated in the opinion.

For the plaintiff there was a brief by the *Attorney General*, and *L. K. Luse*, Assistant Attorney General, and oral argument by *Mr. Luse*. They contended, *inter alia*, that an innocent and lawful assembly may become unlawful upon attempting to do or in doing an unlawful act in the manner prohibited in sec. 4511, R. S., and such is the rule at common law. *Bonneville v. State*, 53 Wis. 684; 2 Whart. Cr. Law, secs. 1535, 1540; *State v. Snow*, 18 Me. 346; Whart. Cr. P. & P. sec. 2220. It is the settled rule of evidence that a witness who swears positively to some circumstance which occurred and was directly observed by him, is entitled to more weight than one who testifies negatively that he did not observe the occurrence testified to by the affirmative witness. *Pennoyer v. Allen*, 56 Wis. 513; *Ralph v. C. & N. W. R. Co.* 32 id. 177; *Draper v. Baker*, 61 id. 450; *Bohan v. M., L. S. & W. R. Co.* id. 391; *Hinton v. C. C. R. Co.* 65 id. 337; *Stitt v. Huidekopers*, 17 Wall. 384; *Johnson v. Scribner*, 6 Conn. 185; 1 Phil. Ev. 598; 1 Starkie, Ev. 867.

For the defendant there was a brief by *J. G. Wickham* and *Joseph B. Doe, Jr.*, and oral argument by *Mr. Doe*. They argued, *inter alia*, that the information should have been quashed because it does not. charge riot as defined by the statute. There can be no riot unless there is first an unlawful assembly, and there can be no unlawful assembly without a common design. The information in this case charges neither the one nor the other; it does not charge that the defendant, with others, was engaged in any unlawful assembly, nor does it charge a common design. The unlawful assembly may have existed but a moment, but it must exist before there can be a riot. Again, if three or more persons, " being together," do acts of violence without any common design, it is not riot; and allegations of each and all of the necessary ingredients of the crime should be contained in the information. Sec. 4511, R. S.

Taylor, J. The defendant *Dean* was informed against for being engaged in a riot or riotous assembly in the city of Beloit. Upon such information he was tried in the circuit court of Rock county with others. After hearing the evidence and the instructions of the court, the jury found him guilty as charged in the information. During the progress of the trial the defendant took exceptions to·the ruling of the court upon a motion to quash the information for insufficiency.

The learned circuit judge instructed the jury as follows upon the question of positive and negative testimony: "Where there is an apparent inconsistency or contradiction in the testimony of witnesses, it is a general rule that such construction or interpretation shall be put upon it as to make it agree if possible, for the law will presume that everybody swears to the truth and no man will be guilty of perjury. If such construction can be given as will reconcile their testimonies, it shall be preferred to a construction that will make them disagree; but if the testimony cannot be reconciled, as where one testifies in the affirmative, as that he saw a person kick a drum, and the other testifies negatively that he did not see him kick the drum, the affirmative witness is to be believed. For it is a general principle or rule of evidence that one witness thus testifying affirmatively outweighs several who thus give negative testimony. The negative witness only swears that he did not see the fact. Therefore, the fact which the affirmative swears to be true may be so, while the other did not see it and knows nothing of it. When two persons are at the same place, and one swears that a particular fact happened, and the other that it did not, this makes the contradiction to be more express than if he said that he did not see it, for it is possible that the situation may be such that a witness may know with as much certainty that a fact did not happen as it could be known that it did. But even in such cases the affirmative witness is to be believed, for the fact may have happened and the negative witness did not see it, or may have forgotten it, but the affirmative witness could not see and remember a fact that did not happen. He must therefore be believed or be supposed to be guilty of perjury, while it is unnecessary to entertain any such suspicion of the other." This instruction was duly excepted to by the defendant.

There was a motion for a new trial for the alleged errors in the refusal to quash the information, and the error in giving the above instructions, and that the verdict was against the evidence, which was overruled and exceptions taken. There was also a motion for a new trial on the minutes and upon affidavits showing newly-discovered evidence. This motion was also overruled, and exceptions taken. The case was certified to this court by the learned circuit court upon the exceptions above taken as provided in sec. 4720, R. S.

The exception taken to the motion to quash the information, we think, was properly overruled by the learned circuit judge. The information clearly charges an offense under sec. 4511, R. S.[1]

After carefully reading the evidence in this case connecting the defendant *Dean* with the riotous proceedings in the streets of Beloit upon which the information was based, we think the learned circuit judge erred in the instructions excepted to, and undue weight was given by the learned judge to the rules of law applicable to affirmative and negative evidence. The evidence to which the instructions related was evidence tending to show that the defendant *Dean* had during the riotous proceedings in a violent manner kicked and crushed a certain drum. This fact, if established, was the main fact which connected the defendant in any manner with the riot. The evidence clearly established the fact that the drum had been kicked about the street in a violent manner, and was reduced to a complete wreck. The evidence also tended to show, and it did show, that several persons other than the defendant had struck and kicked the drum, and the attempt on the part of the state was to show that the defendant *Dean* was one of the persons engaged in kicking and destroying the drum. To our minds the question was one involving the question of the identity of the person who in fact did the kicking more than anything else. There was evidently a great crowd and considerable excitement, to say the least, and it would be very easy for an honest witness to have been mistaken as to

---

[1] Sec. 4511, R. S , is as follows: " Any three or more persons, who shall assemble in a violent or tumultuous manner to do an unlawful act, or, being together, shall make any attempt or motion towards doing a lawful or unlawful act, in a violent, unlawful, or tumultuous manner, to the terror or disturbance of others, shall be deemed an unlawful assembly ; and if they commit such acts in the manner and with the effect aforesaid, they shall be deemed guilty of a riot, and shall be punished in either case by imprisonment in the county jail not more than one year; or by fine not exceeding five hundred dollars."— REP.

the identity of the person committing the violent acts under the circumstances. If the evidence had established the fact that the drum had been kicked but once, and some of the witnesses had testified that *Dean* kicked it, and some that another person did the kicking, the question of affirmative and negative evidence would not have been in the case at all; it would have been a question of identity.

But admitting that the case presents the question of affirmative and negative testimony, and that the question whether the defendant *Dean* at a certain time and place kicked the drum was not in any way mixed up with the identity of the person or persons doing the injury, we are still very clearly of the opinion that the instructions given are erroneous. The learned judge did not instruct the jury simply that the testimony of the affirmative witnesses was entitled to greater weight in determining the fact than the testimony of the witnesses giving the negative testimony, but he substantially instructed the jury that the testimony of the affirmative witnesses must be believed. In this the learned judge very clearly invaded the province of the jury. It is for the jury and not the court to say what witnesses or testimony is to be believed, especially in a criminal action. Had there been no evidence for the defendant on the trial except his own testimony, it would have been error to instruct the jury that they must believe the evidence of the witnesses for the state on the ground that their evidence was affirmative and the testimony of the defendant negative. It is not probable that the learned circuit judge really intended to assume any such position in his instructions in the case at bar, but we think the instructions as given might be so understood by the jury, and the defendant may therefore have been greatly prejudiced thereby.

If, however, we should construe the instructions as simply meaning that the affirmative evidence should have greater weight with the jury in determining the question at issue than the negative, we are still of the opinion that the instructions as given were misleading. The instructions, as given, lay down an arbitrary rule without regard to the character of the affirmative and negative testimony, and not qualified by the circumstances surrounding the witnesses or their opportunities for seeing and knowing what did and what did not take place at the given time and place. The limitations and qualifications to the general rule on the subject of affirmative and negative testimony have been stated by this court in *Urbanek v. C., M. & St. P. R. Co.* 47 Wis. 59, and *Eilert v. G. B. & M. R. Co.* 48 Wis. 606. The qualifications of the rule as stated in these cases seem to have been ignored by the learned circuit judge in the instructions given in this case. The exceptions of the defendant to the instructions should have been sustained, and it was error to overrule them.

By the Court.— The case is remanded to the circuit court with instructions to grant the defendant a new trial.

INDEX.

For injuries to person from failure to restore street, 41.
For injuries to person through negligence, 64, 114, 391, 553, 625.
For death of person caused by negligence, 255.
For death of person caused by failure to fence railroad track, 472.
For slander, 427.
Ejectment, 88, 94, 358, 568.
To recover dower, 513.
Replevin, 565.
Garnishment, 485, 524.
For penalty for obstructing highway, 384.
For penalty for failure by foreign insurance company to file statement, etc., 411.
Certiorari to review action of common council in charging cost of improvements to abutting lots, 502.
Certiorari to review order granting new trial, 595.
Mandamus to compel county to aid in building bridge, 321, 327.
Contempt proceeding, for violation of injunction, 64³.
Probate of will, 83.
Application for writ of assistance, 585.
For an accounting, etc., as to partnership business, 644.
To compel issuance and delivery of corporate stock, 490.
To·bar dower right, 513.
To enforce lien for labor and materials, 11.
To foreclose mortgage, 181, 295.
To cancel or reform release of mortgage, 191.
To have deed declared a mortgage, for an accounting, etc., 476.
To establish title to land and restrain alienation, 279.
To restrain collection of tax, have town bonds declared void, and restrain disposal thereof, 59.
To restrain city from letting public hall, 139, 155.
To restrain vacating and closing up of street, 173.
To restrain sale of land to satisfy lien, 347.
To restrain manufacture and sale of machines, 495.
To restrain digging and removal of lead ore, 507.
To restrain building of bridge, etc., 643.
To set aside judgment and restrain its collection, 340, 588.
To set aside fraudulent conveyances of land, 148.
To set aside taxes, 317.
To set aside administrator's sale and deed, construe will, and cancel mortgage, 405.
Information for murder, 444, 612.
Information for assault with intent to kill, 669.
Information for selling liquor on Sunday, 672.
Information for riot and unlawful assembly, 678.

ADMINISTRATORS AND EXECUTORS. See ESTATES OF DECEDENTS.

ADMISSIONS. See EVIDENCE, 15.

AFFIDAVIT.
Of prejudice of judge. See CHANGE OF VENUE.
Of posting notice of tax sale. See TAX TITLES.

AGENCY.

See VENDOR, ETC. OF LAND, 2.

1. Parol agency to charge a principal's realty ought to be express and clearly established. *Engfer v. Roemer,* . 11

APPEAL.

and it was so paid. *Held*, that by accepting the money the county waived its right to appeal from the judgment. *Webster-Glover L. & M. Co. v. St. Croix Co.*   317

5. If a new trial be granted solely by reason of a misapprehension of the law, the order granting the same will be reversed on appeal. But it must clearly appear that such was the sole ground of the order. *Reed v. C., M. & St. P. R. Co.*   399

6. In this case the plaintiff introduced considerable testimony for the purpose of proving the alleged negligence of the defendant, and which had a bearing on that question; and it is probably true that there is some doubt as to what inferences may properly be deduced from such testimony. The circuit court having held, on a motion for a new trial, contrary to its ruling on the trial, that the testimony was sufficient to send the question to the jury, this court affirms the order granting a new trial, without reviewing such conflicting rulings of the court below.   *Ibid.*

7. A judgment for equitable relief against one of two defendants, who, after his general demurrer was overruled, took no further steps in the action except to join in the appeal, must be affirmed if the complaint states a cause of action for equitable relief and the judgment can be sustained upon the facts stated. *Tanner v. Gregory.*
                                                                      490

8. A defendant cannot complain because the plaintiff has taken judgment against him for less relief than he was entitled to.   *Ibid.*

9. Where a judgment is reversed and the cause remanded, a new and additional finding of facts by the trial court, there being no further evidence given or trial had, is unauthorized. *Tipping v. Robbins,*
                                                                      507

10. Where in an equitable action only a portion of the judgment was reversed, a new judgment entered by the trial court is not erroneous because it contains no order as to that part of the prior judgment which was undisturbed, where it is apparent from the record that the new judgment is in substance, though not in form, merely a modifying or additional one. *Jones v. Jones,*   513

11. It was held by the trial court and, on appeal, by this court that a widow was entitled to recover, as damages for the withholding of dower, one third of the rents and profits of certain land, deducting the amount paid for taxes, insurance, and repairs. The judgment of the trial court did not determine the amount so to be deducted. That judgment was reversed for errors in other particulars, and the cause was remanded with direction to render judgment in accordance with the opinion of this court. *Held*, that on filing the *remittitur* the trial court properly proceeded to take testimony and determine the amount to be so deducted for taxes, insurance, and repairs.   *Ibid.*

12. If, in an equity case, the judgment is supported by the evidence, the lack of or defects in the findings of fact will not work a reversal.   *Ibid.*

13. The question in this case, whether a certain agreement was or was not made, depending mainly upon the credibility of the witnesses, this court declines to disturb the finding of the trial court. *Shekey v. Eldredge,*   538

From Justices' Courts.

14. On appeal from a judgment rendered upon the verdict of a jury in justice's court, if a new trial upon the merits is waived and no

error in the proceedings is shown, the judgment will not be reversed if there was evidence which, uncontradicted, would support it. *West v. Vanden Brook*, 469

15. Where it was taken for granted on the trial in justice's court that the plaintiff's claim arose out of a certain leasing,—the defendant claiming that the action should abate because his co-lessee was not made a party, and the plaintiff relying upon the alleged fact that the defendant was a several and not a joint lessee,—a judgment that the action abate should not be reversed on appeal on the ground that there was no evidence to show that the plaintiff's claim arose out of such leasing. *Ibid.*

From Common Council.
See MUNICIPAL CORPORATIONS, 14. PLEADING, 4.

From Town Supervisors.
See DRAINS.

APPEALABLE ORDER.

An order adjudging a defendant in criminal contempt for the violation of an injunction is not appealable. *In re Murphey*, 89 Wis. 286, followed. *Town of Williamstown v. Darge*, 648

APPLETON CITY CHARTER. See MUNICIPAL CORPORATIONS, 11.

ASHLAND CITY CHARTER. See MUNICIPAL CORPORATIONS, 13, 14.

ASSAULT. See CRIMINAL LAW, 9, 10.

ASSESSMENTS. See MUNICIPAL CORPORATIONS, 13, 14.

ASSIGNMENT.
Of mortgage. See EQUITY, 6.
· For benefit of creditors. See VOLUNTARY ASSIGNMENT.

ASSISTANCE, WRIT OF. See EXECUTION, 2.

ATTORNEY AT LAW. See CRIMINAL LAW, 2, 3. NEW TRIAL, 1. PRACTICE, 1, 4.

BANKRUPT ACT. See VOLUNTARY ASSIGNMENT, 1, 2.

BANKS AND BANKING. See BILLS AND NOTES, 2–4. EQUITY, 1.

BILLS AND NOTES.

See JUDGMENT, 1, 2. VENDOR, ETC. OF LAND, 1.

1. Where a promissory note made by the plaintiff is set up as a counterclaim, interest thereon should be allowed by the referee to the date of his report at the rate specified in the note. *Thorn v. Smith*, 18

2. A bank discounted a note for a company and credited it with the amount, the credit subsequently increasing, so that, at the time of suit on the note, the bank had parted with nothing of value for it. *Held*, that the bank was not a *bona fide* purchaser for value. *Manufacturers' Nat. Bank v. Newell*, 309

3. Where a note is given to a company, constructive notice of infirmity therein to the officers of the company does not in itself import notice to a bank discounting the note, of which, also, they are directors and officers. *Ibid.*

4. The mere fact that the officers of the bank knew, in a general way, that the company was in the habit of selling machinery and taking

notes therefor, and then discounting the same at the bank, was not equivalent to actual notice of the infirmity attaching to this particular note.   *Ibid.*

5. Upon the evidence in this case — showing, among other things, that the defendants had signed in the evening a note which was to be delivered to a real-estate agent in payment of his commissions on a sale of the defendants' land which was expected to be consummated the next morning; that the payee, without the consent of the defendants, but without objection being made by them, took the note from their desk where it had been signed, saying "I will take charge of this," put the note in his pocket and went out; that on the next morning he sold the note to a *bona fide* purchaser; and that the contemplated sale of the land was never made — it is *held* that the jury were justified in finding that there had never been any delivery of the note, conditional or otherwise, so as to give it a legal existence, and that the defendants were not guilty of such negligence in permitting the payee to take the note as would render them liable thereon to an innocent holder. *Dodd v. Dunne,* 578

BONA FIDE PURCHASER. See BILLS AND NOTES, 2–5. FRAUDULENT CONVEYANCES. MUNICIPAL BONDS, 2.

BONDS. See DRAINS, 2, 8. MUNICIPAL BONDS. VOLUNTARY ASSIGNMENT, 4

BOUNDARIES

Where, a boundary line being in dispute or uncertain or unascertained, the adjoining owners locate a line with the obvious intention of making it the permanent line between them, and the same is acquiesced in for a long time and recognized by permanent improvements, such location of the line is binding upon the parties and those claiming under them, without any formal agreement. *Pickett v. Nelson,*   543

BREACH OF PROMISE of marriage. See CONTRACTS, 9, 10. DAMAGES, 4–6. EVIDENCE, 16.

BRIDGES.

See HIGHWAYS, 3.

1. Ch. 187, Laws of 1885, does not limit the bridges which the county may be required to assist in building, to such as cross streams of water. *State ex rel. Spring Lake v. Pierce Co.*   321

2. In an action to compel a county to aid in building a bridge, the judgment directed the issuance of a writ of *mandamus* commanding the county board to meet and to levy the required tax upon the taxable property of the county, without appointing any time for such meeting, and without excepting from liability to such taxation certain cities which were not liable under the law. *Held,* that the mandate of the writ would be satisfied if the county board should perform the duty required of them at their first meeting after service of the writ, and should levy the tax upon the taxable property of the county subject thereto.   *Ibid.*

3. Under ch. 187, Laws of 1885, providing for county aid to towns in building bridges whose cost exceeds one fourth of one per cent. of all the taxable property in the town "according to the last equalized valuation," the valuation of 1885 governs as to bridges authorized

at the annual town meeting in April, 1886, although the county
board was not called upon to act in the premises until after the
assessment roll of 1886 had been made. *State ex rel. El Paso v.
Pierce Co.* 827

BURDEN OF PROOF. See EVIDENCE, 8. INSTRUCTIONS TO JURY, 7.
    MUNICIPAL CORPORATIONS, 8. RAILROADS, 8.

CARRIERS. See RAILROADS, 1-5.

CASES DISTINGUISHED, ETC.

1. *Amos v. Fond du Lac,* 46 Wis. 695 (as to failure to exhaust remedy
against lot-owner for injury by defective sidewalk), distinguished.
Hiner v. Fond du Lac, · 74, 79, 80

2. *Anderson v. Patterson.* 64 Wis. 557 (as to fraudulent conveyance),
distinguished. *Roundy v. Converse,* 528

3. *Baker v. Madison,* 62 Wis. 137 (as to when previous verdict shows
damages to be excessive), distinguished. *Bridge v. Oshkosh,* 363,
368

4. *Bell v. Platteville,* 71 Wis. 139 (as to authority of city to let public
hall), followed. *Stone v. Oconomowoc.* 155, 159

5. *Bohlman v. G. B. & M. R. Co.* 40 Wis 157. See No. 14.

6. *Bussian v. M., L. S. & W. R. Co.* 56 Wis. 325. See No. 9.

7. *Calder v. Keegan,* 30 Wis. 126 (as to when land becomes taxable),
distinguished. *Farnham v. Sherry,* 568, 573

8. *Francis v. Evans,* 69 Wis. 115. See No. 15.

9. *Fuller v. M. M. Ins. Co.* 36 Wis. 599; *Sanger v. Dun,* 47 id. 615 (as
to relief from instruments executed in ignorance of their contents),
distinguished; *Schultz v. C. & N. W. R. Co.* 44 id. 638, and *Bussian v. M., L. S. & W. R. Co.* 56 id. 325, reaffirmed. *Lusted v. C. &
N. W. R. Co.* 398

10. *German Bank v. Leyser,* 50 Wis. 258 (as to action to set aside fraudulent conveyance by decedent), distinguished. *Andrew v. Hinderman,* 151

11. *Hoye v. C. & N. W. R. Co.* 67 Wis. 1 (as to negligence of person
crossing railroad track), distinguished. *Schilling v. C., M. & St. P.
R. Co.* 260

12. *Kvammen v. Meridean Mill Co.* 58 Wis. 899 (as to evidence), distinguished. *Valley Lumber Co. v. Smith,* 307

13. *Lawrence v. State,* 50 Wis. 507; *Rounds v. State,* 57 id. 45 (as to
counsel assisting district attorney), distinguished. *Biemel v. State,*
453

14. *Lumsden v. Milwaukee,* 8 Wis. 485; *Bohlman v. G. B. & M. R. Co.*
40 id. 157 (as to taking of oath by commissioners, etc.), distinguished. *State v. Hogue,* 388

15. *McLeod v. Evans,* 66 Wis. 401, and *Francis v. Evans,* 69 id. 115 (as
to priority of payment from debtor's assets), followed. *Bowers v.
Evans,* 133, 135

16. *N. W. Iron Co. v. Crane,* 66 Wis. 567 (as to change of venue), distinguished. *Will of McCrory,* 83, 87

17. *Plum v. Fond du Lac,* 51 Wis. 393 (as to notice of injury from defective street, etc.), distinguished. *Hiner v. Fond du Lac,* 74, 79

18. *Rounds v. State,* 57 Wis. 45. See No. 13.

19. *Sanger v. Dun,* 47 Wis. 615. See No. 9.

20. *Schultz v. C. & N. W. R. Co.* 44 Wis. 638. See No. 9.

21. *Smith v. Welch,* 10 Wis. 91 (as to demand before action against officer for conversion), distinguished. *Norwegian Plow Co. v. Hawthorn,* 530, 535

22. *Winchester v. Stevens Point,* 58 Wis. 350 (as to proof of title in action for injury to land), distinguished. *Boyington v. Squires,* 277, 278

CAUSE OF ACTION. See ACTION.

CERTAINTY.
In judgment. See REPLEVIN, 2.
In pleading. See PLEADING, 1.

CERTIORARI. See MUNICIPAL CORPORATIONS, 14.

CHALLENGES of jurors. See PRACTICE, 2.

CHANGE OF VENUE.

Though the party applying for a change of venue under sec. 2625, R. S., on the ground of the prejudice of the judge, states in his affidavit that the judges of certain other judicial circuits are also prejudiced, this is not conclusive of that fact, and the place of trial may nevertheless be changed to one of such circuits. *N. W. Iron Co. v. Crane,* 66 Wis. 567, distinguished. *Will of McCrory,* 83

CHARGING THE JURY. See INSTRUCTIONS TO JURY.

CHATTEL MORTGAGES.

See EXECUTION, 1, 4, 5.

The fact that a chattel mortgage authorizes the mortgagor to sell the goods and replace them with others to be paid for out of the proceeds of such sales, does not affect the validity of the security, there being no agreement or understanding that he may dispose of the proceeds of the sales for his own use and benefit. But the attempt to extend the security of the mortgage over the after-acquired goods is probably unavailing, except, perhaps, as a license to seize such goods. *Roundy v. Converse,* 524

CIRCUIT COURTS. See CRIMINAL LAW, 4. JURISDICTION. MANDAMUS, 8.

CITIES. See MUNICIPAL CORPORATIONS.

COGNOVIT. See JUDGMENT, 1, 2.

COMITY. See VOLUNTARY ASSIGNMENT, 1–3.

COMMON CARRIERS. See RAILROADS, 1–5.

COMPENSATION for land taken. See HIGHWAYS, 5.

COMPLAINT. See APPEAL, 7. EQUITY, 2, 8. INSURANCE, 1. MORTGAGES, 5, 8. MUNICIPAL CORPORATIONS, 8, 9. PLEADING, 3–6. PRACTICE, 1. NEGLIGENCE. REFERENCE, 8. SLANDER, 1. SUFFRAGE, 4.

CONDITION PRECEDENT.
To maintenance of action. See CONTRACTS, 10. ESTATES OF DECEDENTS. MUNICIPAL CORPORATIONS, 8, 16.
To judgment. See EJECTMENT, 1, 6, 7.
To claim of exemption. See TAXATION, 4.

CONFLICT OF LAWS. See VOLUNTARY ASSIGNMENT, 1–3.

CONTRACTS.

4. The first paragraph of a written contract stated that in consideration of $13,000 the plaintiff had sold a steamboat and certain real estate to the defendants, the deeds thereof being executed on the same day as the contract. The second paragraph stated that the plaintiff had further agreed to sell and convey certain other land for $2,000, to be paid when a deed of said land could be procured under a proper order of court for the sale of the same; that the plaintiff would use due diligence in procuring the guardian of the minor owner to make application for an order for such sale; and that in the event that such land, at its offer at public sale under such order, should not bring over $2,000, the same should be sold to the defendants for that sum; but in case the plaintiff should fail to make such title good to the defendants he should suffer no other forfeiture than in the contract mentioned. The third paragraph provided for the payment of $12,000, and that the defendants should retain $1,000 until the plaintiff should cause to be executed and delivered to them a conveyance of the land mentioned in the second paragraph, founded upon a proper order of court; and upon delivery of such conveyance the defendants should pay to the plaintiff said $1,000 as well as the $2,000 purchase money of said land; and if the plaintiff should entirely fail to cause said land to be conveyed to the defendants, the said $1,000, part of the $13,000 first aforesaid, should be forfeited to the defendants as liquidated damages for such breach. The land mentioned in the second para-

graph sold at the public sale for more than $2,000, and the plaintiff was unable to purchase it for that sum. Nearly twenty years later he brought this action to recover the $1,000 retained by the defendants. *Held*, on demurrer:

(1) The contracts in the first and second paragraphs were separate and distinct contracts, for separate and distinct considerations; and the $1,000 was retained not as a part of the consideration for the land mentioned in the second paragraph, but merely as security for the performance of the contract as to such land.

(2) The contract for the conveyance of the land mentioned in the second paragraph was upon the condition that such land could be purchased for $2,000 at the public sale.

(8) Upon the demurrer the delay in bringing the action should not be considered as showing the construction which the parties themselves put upon the contract. *Ibid.*

5. The parties had made large profits out of a successful corner of the wheat market, and the plaintiff's share was left with the defendant and afterwards invested by him in a lard deal by direction of the plaintiff. *Held*, that the illegality of the wheat deal would not protect the defendant from accounting for the money. *Wells v. McGeoch,*   196

6. In order to obtain possession of cattle which had been distrained by the plaintiff while they were doing damage to his crops. the owner induced the defendants to execute an undertaking for the return of the cattle to the plaintiff or the payment of the damages, etc. *Held*, that although the proceedings upon the distress were technically defective and the owner might have maintained replevin, yet the restoration of the cattle to the owner was a sufficient consideration for the undertaking. *Saxton v. McNair,*   459

7. The defendant, a carpenter and joiner and inventor of sand-papering machines, sold his interest in certain patents upon such machines and in the business of a firm engaged in the manufacture and sale thereof. In the contract of sale he covenanted that he would not thereafter " manufacture, sell, or cause to be sold any sand-papering machines of any description," unless with the consent of the purchaser of said patents, etc. *Held:*

(1) The restriction upon the manufacture and sale of the machines cannot be held to be applicable only to this state.

(2) If the defendant should invent and patent a new sand-papering machine, not infringing on the patents sold, and should sell the patent therefor to one who should manufacture and sell machines under it, he would thereby *cause* the machines *to be sold*, within the meaning of the covenant.

(8) The restriction being greater than is reasonably necessary to protect the purchaser in the enjoyment of the patents and business purchased, and prohibiting the defendant from pursuing his trade or profession of inventing sand-papering machines, is void as against public policy, although it affects only a single class of machines. *Berlin Machine Works v. Perry,*   495

8. Parties can agree to change or modify their contracts without any new consideration. *Ruege v. Gates,*   684

9. Where the contract to marry is conceded, the question of its mutuality need not be submitted to the jury. *Olson v. Solveson,*   663

10. An absolute refusal to marry the plaintiff obviates the necessity of a formal demand. *Ibid.*

COSTS.

CRIMINAL LAW AND PRACTICE.

to warrant a verdict of murder in the second degree; such charge being manifestly designed to prevent a verdict of murder in the first degree, not sustainable by the evidence. *Ibid.*

7. It was not error for the court to read to the jury the statutory definition of murder in the second degree, and state that it was plain, simple, and easily intelligible, and as well understood by them as by any lawyer; that it was so plain as to need no construction; and that they were simply to determine whether or not the facts proved, if any, came within such definition. *Ibid.*

8. A charge that if the jury did not think the evidence had established murder in the second degree, as defined by the statute, there was another section which would authorize them to find defendant guilty of manslaughter in the second degree, though, standing alone, it might seem to intimate that the evidence was such as to authorize such finding, is not misleading or erroneous if followed by explanations of what constitutes the lesser crime, and instructions to determine from all the evidence whether such crime was committed. • *Ibid.*

9. An information charging that defendants "did then and there wilfully. maliciously, and feloniously assault, cut. stab, and wound one W., with intent wilfully, maliciously, and feloniously, and with malice aforethought, him, the said W., to kill and murder," will not sustain a conviction of an assault with intent to do great bodily harm, because the averments do not in form include the lesser offense. *State v. Yanta,* 669

10. An information stating that at a certain time and place the defendants, to the number of three and more, "then and there being together, did then and there, in a violent, unlawful, and tumultuous manner, to the disturbance of the peace and to the terror and disturbance of others then and there present, assault," etc., is held to charge an offense under sec. 4511, R. S. *State v. Dean,* 678

11. The evidence being conflicting as to whether a defendant charged with riot did or did not kick a certain drum, it was error for the court to charge the jury, in effect, that where two persons are at the same place, and one swears that a particular fact happened, and the other that it did not, the affirmative witness must be believed. *Ibid.*

CROSS-EXAMINATION. See EVIDENCE, 11. PRACTICE, 8.

DAMAGES.

See DOWER. HIGHWAYS, 5. INSURANCE, 4. PLEADING, 1. RAIL-ROADS, 5. TELEGRAPH COMPANIES, 2.

1. The railroad car in which the plaintiff was riding was derailed, and she was thrown upon the floor and, while attempting to rise, was again thrown backwards in a sitting position. She was a large woman, weighing about 200 pounds. The evidence tended to show that she was rendered unconscious for a long time; that for several months she was quite helpless, could not be moved without making her scream, and had frequent fainting spells; that she suffered from pain in her spine and womb, and at times from pain and numbness in her left arm and limb; and that up to the time of the trial, about thirteen months after the accident, she had been confined to her bed most of the time. The physicians who examined her found a displacement and laceration of the womb, but agreed

that these were not caused by the shock or fall in the car. It did not satisfactorily appear that there was any permanent injury to the spine. There was evidence that the plaintiff was of unchaste character. *Held*, that a verdict awarding $7,000 should have been set aside on the ground that the damages were excessive. *Abbot v. Tolliver,* 64

2. The fact that the plaintiff is of unchaste character may be considered by the jury in assessing compensatory damages for personal injuries caused by negligence. *Ibid.*

3. Where on the first trial of an action to recover damages for personal injuries the plaintiff was prevented by the rulings of the court from fully presenting his case on the question of damages, and on the second trial, had nearly two years later, it was proved that he had not fully recovered from his injuries, a verdict on the first trial for $217 should have little weight in determining whether a verdict on the second trial for $1,800 is excessive. *Baker v. Madison,* 62 Wis. 137, distinguished. *Bridge v. Oshkosh,* 363

4. In an action for the breach of a promise of marriage, evidence of the defendant's pecuniary circumstances is competent as affecting the question of damages. *Olson v. Solveson,* 663

5. In an action for the breach of a promise of marriage, the court refused an instruction that, under the complaint, the plaintiff was simply entitled to compensatory damages; but it submitted to the jury the question as to what sum should be given to the plaintiff *by way of compensation* for the injury sustained by the breach of the contract, charging them that they were to get at the damages from the evidence, the situation of the parties, what occurred between them, their condition and surroundings, and then give such sum as in their judgment the evidence would warrant — not an unreasonable or exorbitant sum, but a just, reasonable, and fair sum. *Held*, that the question of damages was fully and fairly presented to the jury. *Ibid.*

6. In such a case this court will not interfere on the ground that the damages are excessive, unless it is made apparent that the jury were actuated by undue motives. *Ibid.*

DARLINGTON CITY CHARTER. See MUNICIPAL CORPORATIONS, 10.

DEBTOR AND CREDITOR. See AGENCY. APPEAL, 1. BILLS AND NOTES. CHATTEL MORTGAGES. CONTRACTS, 5. EQUITY, 1, 6, 7. ESTATES OF DECEDENTS. EVIDENCE, 1, 12. EXECUTION. FRAUDULENT CONVEYANCES. FRAUDULENT REPRESENTATIONS. INSTRUCTIONS TO JURY, 1, 5–7. JUDGMENT, 1–3. LIENS. LIMITATION OF ACTIONS. MORTGAGES. MUNICIPAL BONDS. PARTNERSHIP. PAYMENT. REFERENCE, 2, 8. SURETYSHIP. VOLUNTARY ASSIGNMENT.

DECEIT. See FRAUDULENT REPRESENTATIONS.

DEED.

See EQUITY, 6. EVIDENCE, 8. MORTGAGES, 1, 3, 6, 7. VENDOR, ETC. OF LAND, 1.

1. On the day of the date of a deed the grantor and grantee named therein, and the defendant and one W. were together in the office of W. W. drew the deed and also two mortgages, one on other lands, to secure the purchase money. The instruments were signed and acknowledged in the presence of W., and then laid by

him on a show-case in his office. A discussion arose as to the description and title of the land covered by one of the mortgages, and as to how some one in possession of the land deeded might be removed. Finally the defendant took the papers from the show-case, without authority or objection from either of the parties thereto, and said that he would examine the title and ascertain whether everything was all right. Afterwards, when the grantee demanded the deed, the defendant refused to give it to him, but offered to give him back the mortgages. *Held,* that there had been no delivery of the deed sufficient to pass the title, and that the grantee could not maintain replevin therefor. *Flannigan v. Goggins,* 28

2. *It seems* that if replevin will lie in any case for a deed in possession of a stranger, there should be no question as to whether the deed had been so delivered as to be a valid conveyance. That question should only be tried in an action to which the grantor is a party, and, since it involves the title to land, cannot be tried in replevin. *Ibid.*

8. In replevin to recover a deed its value must be proved. *Ibid.*

DEFAULT. See JUDGMENT, 3. SERVICE OF SUMMONS, 1.

DEFINITIONS. See WORDS AND PHRASES.

DELAY. See CONTRACTS, 4 (3). EQUITY, 2, 3. RAILROADS, 5. SALE OF CHATTELS, 1. TELEGRAPH COMPANIES.

DELIVERY. See BILLS AND NOTES, 5. DEED, 1, 2. EJECTMENT, 8. FRAUDULENT CONVEYANCES, 2.

DEMAND. See CONTRACTS, 10. INSTRUCTIONS TO JURY, 5.

DEMURRER. See CONTRACTS, 4 (3). MUNICIPAL CORPORATIONS, 9. PLEADING, 1. SUFFRAGE, 4.

DESCRIPTION. See REPLEVIN, 2.

DISCRETION. See COSTS. HORSE RACING, 2. MUNICIPAL BONDS, 1. NEW TRIAL, 1. REFERENCE, 8.

DISTRESS. See CONTRACTS, 6.

DISTRICT ATTORNEY. See CRIMINAL LAW, 2, 8.

DITCHES. See DRAINS.

DIVORCE. See EXECUTION, 8.

DOWER.

See APPEAL, 11.

The grantee in a conveyance made by the defendant's husband, just prior to the marriage, in fraud of her dower rights, brought an action to quiet the title and bar the claim for dower. The defendant, by counterclaim, asked to have the conveyance set aside and to recover dower and damages for the withholding thereof. *Held,* that in such action the court might render a money judgment against the plaintiff for damages for the withholding of dower, and might also, with the defendant's consent, allow a gross sum of money in lieu of dower. *Jones v. Jones,* 518

DRAINS.

1. If one of the commissioners selected under sec. 1862, R. S., upon an appeal from the decision of town supervisors in relation to a drain,

EQUITY.

ESTOPPEL.

See BOUNDARIES. EVIDENCE, 1. EXECUTION, 4. MORTGAGES, 2.

1. In ejectment for lands which were taxed as the property of the plaintiff company and sold for nonpayment of the taxes, the defendants who claim title under such tax sale are estopped from claiming that the plaintiff cannot recover because the patent from the United States has not yet been issued to it. *Wis. Cent. R. Co. v. Wis. R. Land Co.* 94

2. Where both parties derive title from the same source the defendant is estopped to deny that the common grantor had title. *Bond v. Carroll,* 347

EVIDENCE.

See AGENCY, 1. APPEAL, 1, 13–15. CHANGE OF VENUE. CRIMINAL LAW, 11. DAMAGES, 2, 4. FRAUDULENT CONVEYANCES, 5, 6. INSTRUCTIONS TO JURY, 1, 4, 7. MANDAMUS, 1. MILLS AND MILL DAMS, 1, MORTGAGES, 6, 7. NEGLIGENCE. PAYMENT. PRACTICE, 1, 8. RAILROADS, 3. STREET RAILWAYS, 1. VENDOR, ETC. OF LAND.

1. In an action to enforce a mechanic's lien for repairing a house and building a barn, the defendant admitted that she had authorized the repairs, but claimed that the barn was built without her knowledge or consent, and there was no direct proof that she had authorized it to be built. A bill for the whole work had been presented to her, and there was evidence that she then told the plaintiff that he must look to the tenant for his pay for the barn, because she had not authorized it to be built and did not want it. *Held,* that the mere fact that she received the bill and retained it for a long time would not warrant the inference that she assented to it or acknowledged her liability to pay for the barn. *Engfer v. Roemer,* 11

2. Where the court had erroneously sustained objections to a large number of questions asked for the purpose of proving a certain fact, the subsequent withdrawal of a similar question which was not objected to does not cure the error. *Conover v. Manke,* 106

3. Where there is a direct conflict of testimony as to the price orally agreed to be paid for property, evidence of its real value at the time of the contract is admissible. *Valley Lumber Co. v. Smith,* 304

4. The petition on behalf of a town for a writ of *mandamus* failed to show that the proceeding had been authorized by the electors. On the trial, when the town records were offered in evidence to show that fact, the whole record was objected to as incompetent, irrelevant, and immaterial. *Held,* that the objection was too broad and general. *State ex rel. El Paso v. Pierce Co.* 327

5. Where personal injuries are the subject of inquiry and the basis for awarding damages, evidence of complaints made by the injured person either to his attending physicians or others is admissible. *Bridge v. Oshkosh,* 363

6. In such case a witness who is not an expert, but who is acquainted with the injured person and has seen him frequently before and after the injury, may testify as to any changes either in his physical or mental condition. *Ibid.*

7. In an action to recover damages for negligence in setting a fire which burned over vacant and uncultivated land (and especially where

EXCISE LAWS.

A sale of intoxicating liquor "in violation of law," within the meaning of sec. 1563, R. S., is a sale prohibited by the *excise law;* and sales made on Sunday by a licensed saloon-keeper, not being prohibited by that law, do not render the place in which they are made a public nuisance, which, upon the conviction of the keeper thereof, may be shut up and abated. *State v. Wacker,* 673

EXECUTION.

1. The exemption of a debtor's stock in trade not exceeding $200 in value, under subd. 8, sec. 2982, R. S., does not extend to the proceeds of a sale thereof. Thus, a mortgagor who made no reservation of exemptions in a mortgage of his stock in trade, and claimed none when the property was sold under the mortgage, cannot claim any exemption in the balance of the proceeds of such sale remaining in the hands of the mortgagee after payment of the mortgage debt. *Roundy v. Converse,* 534

2. A writ of assistance, under sec. 3025, R. S., to put the purchaser in possession of land sold on execution should not be issued where there is a *bona fide* contest as to his right to the possession of the land under such sale,— as where the defendant in good faith claims that the premises were his homestead and as such exempt from sale on execution. *Stanley v. Sullivan,* 585

3. A judgment in a divorce action that the plaintiff wife recover a certain sum of money,— it not being declared that the same is for alimony or in lieu of alimony, or that the judgment shall be a lien upon any of the defendant's real or personal estate,— is a mere money judgment, and execution thereon cannot be levied on the defendant's homestead. *Ibid.*

4. A sheriff who has levied an execution subject to a certain mortgage, and has so stated in his return, is estopped to question the validity of the mortgage; and he has no right in such case to take the property from the possession of the mortgagee. *Mendelson v. Paschen,* 591

5. If the return of the sheriff in such case is amendable it can be amended only upon proof that it was made by mistake and that it is untrue, with due notice to the parties interested in it, and by the court in which it is a part of the record. *Ibid.*

FRAUDULENT CONVEYANCES.

See CHATTEL MORTGAGES. ESTATES OF DECEDENTS. EVIDENCE, 12. INSTRUCTIONS TO JURY, 5–7.

1. Where goods are sold or transferred in part payment of a debt due from the vendor to the vendee, and the latter credits the value thereof upon the account, this is such a payment for the goods as will take the sale out of the statute of frauds (sec. 2308, R. S.). *Norwegian Plow Co. v. Hanthorn,*   529

2. *It would seem* that although goods sold are left in the possession of the vendor, if he gives a written receipt acknowledging that he holds them subject to the order of the vendee, this is a sufficient delivery and acceptance to take the sale out of the statute.   *Ibid.*

[3. *Quære*, whether a creditor who in good faith takes the property of his debtor in payment or part payment of an honest debt can be held to have committed a fraud upon other creditors because he may know or believe that the debtor is paying his debt to avoid paying other creditors,—especially where the creditor only receives goods which he has sold the debtor, and the debt is the purchase price of such goods.]   *Ibid.*

4. The verdict of the jury in this case that a chattel mortgage was not given in good faith to secure an actual indebtedness, but was given with intent to hinder, delay, and defraud creditors, is *held* to have been clearly unwarranted by the evidence. *Mendelson v. Paschen,*   591

5. The issue being whether the sales of certain goods to the plaintiff and to his vendor, N., were fraudulent as to the creditors of N. and his vendor, it was error to admit evidence of representations made by an agent of N.'s vendor to one of the defendants from whom he borrowed money in the name of such vendor, regarding the financial condition of his principal. *Rindskopf v. Myers,*   639

6. The plaintiff testified that he borrowed $2,000 from his brother L. to pay for the goods which the defendants claimed were transferred to him in fraud of creditors, and a deposition of L. to the same effect was read. The judgment rolls in certain actions against L. were then introduced by the defendants to show that L. was insolvent at the time of the alleged loan. L. was not asked whether these judgments had been paid or satisfied or to make any explanation in regard to them. *Held*, that it was error to admit such judgment rolls in evidence.   *Ibid.*

FRAUDULENT REPRESENTATIONS.

1. The parties were jointly interested in an unsuccessful attempt to corner the market for lard. In arranging between themselves for a settlement of their losses, the defendant overstated the amount invested by himself in the deal, and understated the amount invested by him for the plaintiff. Relying upon such statements the plaintiff paid more than his share in the settlement of the losses, and also gave the defendant a full release from all claims and demands on account of the deal. *Held:*

(1) The statements by the defendant were fraudulent, whether he knew them to be untrue or made them in ignorance of the real facts.

(2) Notwithstanding the illegality of the attempt to corner the

market, the plaintiff may recover from the defendant such a sum
as will reduce his payment to the amount he would have been required to pay on an accounting between the parties.

(3) The release, fraudulently obtained, is no obstacle to such
recovery. *Wells v. McGeoch,*   196

2. The plaintiff had for a long time had joint transactions of great magnitude with the defendant, in whom he had unbounded confidence and to whom he had trusted their entire management. The
business was done by defendant's firm in Chicago, but the accounts
were sent to his Milwaukee house, and the plaintiff had free access
to them. The plaintiff's share of the profits had been left with the
defendant, and were afterwards invested by him in a lard deal by
direction of the plaintiff. *Held*, that in arranging for a settlement
of the losses by such deal the plaintiff had a right to rely upon the
defendant's statement of the amounts invested therein by himself
and for the plaintiff.   *Ibid.*

8. As a result of the unsuccessful deal in lard a firm in which the defendant was a partner failed. It was agreed between the parties
that the capital stock of such firm was not to be considered a debt
of the firm which the parties were to assume or endeavor to pay.
Held, that such agreement affected only such capital as remained
a liability of the firm, and in an accounting between the parties of
their respective investments in the deal the defendant was entitled
to be allowed his capital which he had drawn out of the firm and
invested in the deal.   *Ibid.*

GAMING CONTRACTS. See CONTRACTS, 5. FRAUDULENT REPRESENTA-
TIONS. HORSE RACING, 1.

HIGHWAYS.

See MUNICIPAL CORPORATIONS, 1, 3, 4, 10-13, 15, 16.

1. The fact that a special act for the laying out of a state road makes
no provision for giving notice to resident owners of the time and
place of meeting of the commissioners to locate the road, does not
invalidate the act, as in such case the provisions of the Revised
Statutes apply and regulate the manner of giving notice. *State v.
Hogue,*   384

2. Nor is such an act invalidated by the failure to provide therein that
the commissioners shall take an oath before entering upon the discharge of their duties, the legislature having power to exempt
"interior officers" from taking an oath.   *Ibid.*

8. A special act for the laying out of a state road which will cross a
navigable river need not make any provision for building a bridge.
                                                                 Ibid.

4. The report of commissioners appointed to lay out a highway failed
to state the width of the highway, but the survey showed the centre line thereof. *Held*, that this was sufficiently definite under
sec. 1264, R. S., which provides that all public highways shall be
not less than four rods wide.   *Ibid.*

5. Sec. 1315, R. S., provides that all damages occasioned by laying
out a state road shall be paid by the several counties in which it
may be located, and that every person claiming such damages
shall present his claim to the county board, and in case it is disallowed may appeal to the circuit court. Ch. 223, Laws of 1882,

gave to the commissioners appointed therein the same power as to awarding damages as is conferred by law upon the county board. *Held*, that this was a sufficient provision for compensation for the property taken. *Ibid.*

HOMESTEADS. See EXECUTION, 2, 3. MORTGAGES, 8.

HORSE RACING.

1. The mere racing of horses is not illegal or against public policy; and where a premium or reward is offered by a third party, in good faith and not as a cover for betting, to the winner in such a race, the latter may recover the premium even though he paid an entrance fee which went to make up in part such premium. *Porter v. Day,* 296

2. Where the judges of a horse race had discretionary power to exclude a horse violating a certain rule from further participation in the race, their decision allowing the horse to proceed after a violation should not be set aside except upon clear proof of fraud affecting such decision. *Ibid.*

HUSBAND AND WIFE. See INSURANCE, 6, 7. VENDOR, ETC. OF LAND, 2.

ILLEGAL CONTRACTS. See CONTRACTS, 5. FRAUDULENT REPRESENTATIONS.

INDEFINITENESS.
In pleading. See PLEADING, 1.
In judgment. See REPLEVIN, 2.

INFORMATION. See CRIMINAL LAW, 5, 9, 10.

INJUNCTION. See APPEALABLE ORDER. MUNICIPAL BONDS, 1. MUNICIPAL CORPORATIONS, 6, 8.

INSOLVENCY. See FRAUDULENT CONVEYANCES, 6. VOLUNTARY ASSIGNMENT, 1-3.

INSTRUCTIONS TO JURY.

See CRIMINAL LAW, 6-8, 11. DAMAGES, 5. MILLS AND MILL DAMS, 2. SALE OF CHATTELS, 3. SLANDER, 2. STREET RAILWAYS, 1.

1. There being a direct conflict in the evidence as to whether the defendants objected to a bill or account presented by the plaintiff, it was error for the court to ignore or suppress the evidence on the part of the defendants and to charge the jury that where no objections are made to a bill presented it is *prima facie* evidence of the correctness thereof. *Valley Lumber Co. v. Smith,* 304

2. One of the defendants testified that at the time of making a contract he made a memorandum of its terms in a book kept for such purposes. The memorandum was introduced in evidence, and there was no evidence tending to impeach the credibility of the witness in respect thereto. *Held*, that it was error for the court, in charging the jury, to cast suspicion and doubt upon the defendant's testimony and to call special attention to the criticisms of plaintiff's counsel upon the memorandum. *Ibid.*

3. Where a statement made by one of the defendants to the plaintiff was of importance in determining the question of contributory negligence, and the language used, as testified to by the plaintiff,

might have more than one meaning, it was error for the court, in charging the jury, to say what he supposed the defendant meant. *Drevis v. Woods,*   329

4. The trial court, in charging the jury as to the proof of mistake necessary to change the amount of a promissory note, first instructed them that "in order to establish a mistake the proof thereof must be clear, satisfactory, and convincing," but subsequently said that the *burden of proof* was upon the party alleging it to establish the mistake, and by "burden of proof" was simply meant that he must establish the fact "*by a preponderance of the evidence*" that is, his evidence "must be *more weighty, convincing, and satisfactory* than the proof adduced by the other party." *Held*, that the charge was erroneous, the correct rule first stated being afterwards overruled and changed. *Parker v. Hull,*   368

5. In an action against a sheriff for the conversion of plaintiff's goods which had been seized and sold by defendant's deputy as the property of a third person in whose possession they were found, an instruction that if the officer levied upon and sold the property in good faith the plaintiff cannot recover unless, before the sale, he demanded the goods from the officer, is *held* to have been properly refused, the levying officer not being the defendant, upon whom a demand was made, and the evidence not showing that the goods in question were so mingled with those of said third person as not to be readily separated. *Smith v. Welch,* 10 Wis. 91, distinguished. *Norwegian Plow Co. v. Hanthorn,*   529

6. The court having, at the request of the defendant and again in the general charge, instructed the jury that if the sale in question was, with the knowledge of the vendee, made with intent to hinder or delay or defraud the creditors of the vendor it was void, the omission of the words "hinder or delay," in calling attention to it again, and the use of the expression "his creditors generally," without adding "or any of them," are *held* not to have been misleading.   *Ibid.*

7. The question being as to the validity of a sale of goods which were left in the possession of the vendor, the court called attention to the fact that they were so left, and, after reading sec. 2310, R. S., instructed the jury that under that section the presumption was that the sale was fraudulent, but that if the vendee paid full value for the goods that fact would rebut the presumption of fraud. *Held*, that when taken in connection with the other instructions given this instruction was not erroneous as giving the jury to understand that proof of a full consideration paid would conclusively rebut all the evidence of fraud in the case.   *Ibid.*

8. Where the jury has just been told that they must determine what is the truth between the parties "from all the testimony," a charge that they may decide a question as they think "truth and justice between the parties require," is not erroneous as instructing them to determine what is *just* rather than what is according to the contract and the evidence. *Ruege v. Gates,*   634

INSURANCE.

Foreign Insurance Companies.

1. In an action to recover the penalty prescribed by sec. 1920, R. S., for failure by a foreign fire insurance corporation to file the annual statement therein mentioned, if the complaint undertakes to state

the particular facts constituting the cause of action it must state
all the material facts necessary to constitute such cause of action,
including the fact that the defendant company was licensed to do
business in this state. So *held* on appeal from a judgment rendered on default. *State v. Citizens' Ins. Co.* 411

Town Insurance Companies.

2. An incubator building, erected on an acre of ground leased for that
purpose, and used in carrying on the business of hatching chickens
by artificial means and rearing them for the market, is not a "farm
building" within the meaning of sec. 2, ch. 421, Laws of 1885, and
is not insurable by a town insurance company. *O'Neill v. Pleasant Prairie M. F. Ins. Co.* 621

Fire Insurance.

3. A policy covered a "planing-mill building *and addition*" and "machinery. including shafting, gearing, belting, saws, tools, force-pump, and hose therein." The engine-room, from which the entire
motive power was furnished, was situated twenty-two feet from
the mill building, and was connected therewith by a shaft for the
transmission of the power and by a spout through which shavings
were forced into the engine-room. A roadway passed between the
buildings under the shaft and spout. There was no other addition
to the mill building. *Held,* that the policy covered the engine-room and the engine and other machinery therein. *Home Mut.
Ins. Co. v. Roe,* 83

4. Where several concurrent policies of insurance upon real property
have been written with the consent of the respective companies,
and the property is wholly destroyed, the aggregate amount of
such insurance must, under sec. 1943, R. S., "be taken conclusively to be the true value of the property when insured, and the
true amount of loss and measure of damages when destroyed."
Oshkosh G. L. Co. v. Germania F. Ins. Co. 454

5. Where the agent of an insurance company, with knowledge of a forfeiture of the policy, continues to recognize its validity, and enters
into negotiations for a settlement of the loss, whereby the insured
incurs expense or trouble, the forfeiture will be deemed waived.
Ibid.

Life Insurance.

6. Unless a policy of life insurance points out to whom the insurance
money shall be paid in case the beneficiary die before the assured,
the appointment of the beneficiary is revoked by his death. This
rule is not abrogated, where the beneficiary is the wife of the
assured, by sec. 2347, R. S. *Given v. Wis. O. F. M. L. Ins.
Co.* 547

7. The by-laws of a mutual benefit company provided that on the
death of a member "the person designated before death, or his
widow, child or children, mother, sister or sisters," etc., "as the
case may be, *and in the order named,*" should receive the insurance. One G., a member, directed that his insurance be paid
to S., his wife. S. died, and G. thereafter married the plaintiff,
whom on his death he left surviving. *Held,* that the appointment
of S. as beneficiary was revoked by her death, and the insurance
was payable, under the by-laws, to the plaintiff. *Ibid.*

8. It is not probable that sec. 2347, R. S., was intended to affect an
insurance by a purely benevolent association upon the life of a
member for the benefit of those dependent upon him. *Ibid.*

MILLS AND MILL DAMS.

1. Proof of the plaintiff's actual possession and occupancy of land is sufficient *prima facie* proof of title and ownership to enable him to maintain an action to recover damages for negligence in the use of a mill-dam and water-power whereby such land was flowed and injured and the growing crops thereon destroyed — such injury being merely to the possession. *Winchester v. Stevens Point*, 58 Wis. 350, distinguished. *Boyington v. Squires*, 276

2. In such an action it is not error for the court to instruct the jury that the right of the plaintiff to the use and enjoyment of his land is equal to the right of the defendant to the use and enjoyment of his dam and water-power; and that the defendant may pass the whole volume of water running in the stream at any time through his dam, but he may not so increase that volume from his mill-pond as to injure the lands of other owners below, which otherwise would not have been injured. *Ibid.*

MILWAUKEE MUNICIPAL COURT. See CRIMINAL LAW, 3.

MINES AND MINING.

1. A license to work a new and unopened mine, granted by one tenant in common, does not confer any right thus to mine without the concurrent license of the other tenants in common. *Tipping v. Robbins*, 507

2. Sec. 1647, R. S., providing that no license to a miner shall be revocable after a valuable discovery or prospect has been struck, does not apply to a license granted by only one of several joint owners of the land. *Ibid.*

MISTAKE. See EQUITY, 4. INSTRUCTIONS TO JURY, 4. MORTGAGES, 2.

MORTGAGES.

See CHATTEL MORTGAGES. EQUITY, 6, 7.

1. A trust deed of lands, given by a railroad company to secure the payment of bonds and providing that if there should be no default the estate, right, title, and interest of the trustees should cease, determine, and become void, is *held* to be in effect a mortgage and to leave the legal title in the company. *Wis. Cent. R. Co. v. Wis. R. Land Co.* 94

2. The plaintiff owned as her separate property a mortgage of land, executed by her husband. Without any consideration, and for the sole purpose of enabling a subsequent mortgagee to acquire a prior lien, she executed a release of her mortgage, acknowledging full payment and satisfaction. The release was not read or explained to her, and she did not understand that it was a full release. *Held,* that such release, though recorded, did not discharge the lien of mortgage as against the heirs of the mortgagor, or estop the plaintiff from showing that the mortgage had not in fact been paid; and that the release might be reformed so as to make it effective as to the subsequent mortgage only. *Lee v. Wagner,* 191

3. One C., having made a homestead entry of land, assigned the same and conveyed the land by warranty deed to the defendant, who mortgaged the land to one S., and afterwards gave second and third mortgages to the plaintiff. The mortgage to S. was fore-

closed, and the plaintiff, to save her own mortgages, purchased at the foreclosure sale, received the sheriff's deed, and thereafter paid taxes on the land. Subsequently the defendant took the land from the plaintiff to work on shares, and, while so in possession under the plaintiff, made a new homestead entry of the land, commuted the same by payment of the government price, and obtained title from the United States, under sec. 2301, R. S. of U. S. *Held*, that the mortgages given by the defendant were valid, and the title subsequently acquired by him inured to the benefit of the plaintiff. *Spiess v. Neuberg*,   279

4. Some of the facts which make such title inure to the benefit of the plaintiff not being of record, she may maintain an equitable action to establish her right.   *Ibid.*

5. The filing of the notice of the pendency of an action to foreclose a mortgage is inoperative until the complaint is filed; and judgment cannot be rendered, therefore, until twenty days after the filing of the complaint. R. S. sec. 3187. *Dawson v. Mead*,   295

6. The printer's affidavit of the publication of the notice of sale on foreclosure of a mortgage by advertisement, with the notice attached, was in evidence, as was also the affidavit of the deputy sheriff who acted as auctioneer, stating the time and place of the sale, the sum bid, and the name of the purchaser. These affidavits were made and recorded pursuant to secs. 3536, 3537, R. S. The notice of sale stated that it was given by virtue and in pursuance of a power of sale contained in the mortgage. The sheriff's deed was also in evidence, which recited, among other things, that the mortgage contained a power of sale, and that the sale was made pursuant to such power. *Held*, sufficient, in the absence of evidence to the contrary, to prove that the mortgage contained a power of sale and that the proceedings to foreclose it were regular. *Bond v. Carroll*,   347

[7. Whether sec. 4154, R. S., applies to a sheriff's deed given upon the foreclosure of a mortgage by advertisement, not determined.] *Ibid.*

8. In an action to cancel a mortgage which had been assigned to the defendants and which was a lien superior to any claim of the plaintiff, a complaint showing that the mortgage was valid when given, and not showing that it had been paid or anything which should preclude the defendants from purchasing it, is *held* not to state a cause of action. *McMullen v. Mason*,   405

MUNICIPAL BONDS.

1. In this case the refusal of the circuit court to grant a preliminary injunction restraining the holder of municipal bonds from disposing of them pending the action to have them declared void, is *held* not to have been an abuse of discretion, the facts entitling the plaintiff to such relief not being clearly shown. *Verbeck v. Scott*, 59

2. One who buys municipal bonds from a *bona fide* purchaser, is himself a *bona fide* purchaser, notwithstanding any prior knowledge on his part.   *Ibid.*

MUNICIPAL CORPORATIONS.

See BRIDGES. DRAINS. HIGHWAYS, 5. PLEADING, 4. TOWNS.

1. The provision in the charter of the city of Oshkosh (sec. 32, subch. 10, ch. 183, Laws of 1883) that the city shall not be liable for any dam-

ages arising out of any street being in a defective or dangerous condition, unless it be shown that one of the aldermen of the ward had knowledge thereof, etc., does not apply to an obstruction placed in the street by an employee of the city while repairing such street. *Adams v. Oshkosh,* 49

2. Sec. 204 of the Fond du Lac city charter (ch. 240, Laws of 1879), relating to the notice to be given before an action in tort can be maintained against the city, being at variance with sec. 1339, R. S., supersedes that section, and in an action of that nature against said city the complaint must allege the giving of the notice required by the charter. *Plum v. Fond du Lac,* 51 Wis. 393, distinguished. *Hiner v. Fond du Lac,* 74

3. Sec. 206 of said charter provides that in case of injury from the defective or dangerous condition of a sidewalk caused by the negligence of any person, such person shall be primarily liable, and the city shall not be liable until all legal remedies against him have been exhausted. Sec. 207 makes the obligation of lot-owners to keep the sidewalks in repair an absolute one, not dependent on any notice from the city authorities. *Held,* that in an action against the city where the plaintiff has proved the facts which show the primary liability of a lot-owner, the burden is upon him to show further that he has exhausted his legal remedies against such owner. [Whether the latter fact is a condition precedent to the right to maintain the action, performance of which must be averred in the complaint, not determined.] *Amos v. Fond du Lac,* 46 Wis. 695, distinguished. *Ibid.*

4. A sidewalk had been defective for several weeks. On the day of the injury it had been repaired and new planks laid, but the work of spiking the planks down had not been completed. The plaintiff was injured, in the evening, by stepping upon the end of one of such loose planks. The case was tried on the theory that the previous defective condition of the sidewalk was the proximate cause of the injury, and on that theory the jury found that the injury was caused by the negligence of the city. There being no claim or pretense that any city official had anything to do with leaving the new planks loose, or had actual or constructive notice that they were so left, it is *held* that a nonsuit should have been granted. *Ibid.*

5. Where the city authorities are by the charter given "the management and control of the finances and of all property of the city," and are charged with "the government of the city and the exercise of its corporate powers and management of its financial, prudential, and municipal concerns," they may lease a hall owned by the city to be used for concerts, theaters, and other entertainments for which it is adapted. *Bell v. Platteville,* 139

6. *It seems* that an action to restrain a city from exercising powers alleged to be in excess of its corporate authority cannot be maintained by citizens or tax-payers whose private rights are in no way jeopardized, and that such actions should always be in the name of the state and prosecuted by the public authorities. *Ibid.*

7. The common council of a city had, by the charter, "the control and management of the finances of the city and of all other property thereof," and had power to lease the real estate of the city, and to prevent or license and regulate theatrical performances, etc. *Held,* that it might let or use the auditorium of the city hall for theatrical and other entertainments. *Bell v. Platteville,* 71 Wis. 139, followed. *Stone v. Oconomowoc,* 155

injury until after the injured party has exhausted his remedy against the lot-owner. *Held*, that these provisions of the charter are valid, and a person injured by the negligent omission of a lot-owner to keep a sidewalk in repair must first exhaust his remedy against such lot-owner before he can maintain an action against the city. *Henker v. Fond du Lac*,   616

MUNICIPAL COURTS. See CRIMINAL LAW, 3. JURISDICTION.

MURDER. See CRIMINAL LAW, 1, 5-8.

MUTUAL BENEFIT SOCIETIES. See INSURANCE, 6-8.

MUTUALITY. See CONTRACTS, 9.

NAVIGABLE RIVERS. See HIGHWAYS, 3.

NEGLIGENCE.

See APPEAL, 6. BILLS AND NOTES, 5. EQUITY, 4. MASTER AND SERVANT, 1, 3. MILLS AND MILL DAMS. MUNICIPAL CORPORATIONS, 12. NEW TRIAL, 1. RAILROADS, 7, 8. STREET RAILWAYS. TELEGRAPH COMPANIES.

In this action to recover the value of grain alleged to have been burned through defendants' negligence while they were threshing for the plaintiff with a steam-thresher, it is *held* that the evidence does not clearly show that the plaintiff was guilty of contributory negligence in permitting the defendants to continue threshing under the circumstances, and that the question was therefore properly submitted to the jury. *Drevis v. Woods*,   329

NEGOTIABLE INSTRUMENTS. See BILLS AND NOTES.

NEW TRIAL.

See APPEAL, 5, 6, 9, 11. CRIMINAL LAW, 4. SALE OF CHATTELS, 3.

1. Before a case had been placed on the day calendar, the defendant's attorney had twice notified her to call at his office respecting the same. On the day of the trial he telephoned twice to her place of abode that it was important that he should see her, and afterwards called twice at such place of abode, finally finding her there in bed, dead drunk. In her absence a verdict was rendered against her. *Held*, that there was no abuse of discretion in denying a motion to set aside such verdict on the ground of the negligence of her attorney. *Falkenberg v. Gorman*,   8

2. The attorneys in a case stipulated that it should be placed at the foot of the calendar, but with the understanding that if reached in its regular order by a certain day it should then be tried. The stipulation was contrary to the rules of the court. The case was reached on the day mentioned, and in the absence of the defendant a verdict was rendered against her. *Held*, that the making of the stipulation furnished no reason for setting aside the verdict. *Ibid.*

NONSUIT. See MUNICIPAL CORPORATIONS, 4. RAILROADS, 8.

NOTICE.
Of infirmity in note. See BILLS AND NOTES, 3, 4.
Of pendency of action. See EJECTMENT, 4, 5. MORTGAGES, 5.
Of equities in land. See EQUITY, 6.
Of fraud in sale. See EVIDENCE, 12. FRAUDULENT CONVEYANCES, 3.

PARENT AND CHILD.

Where aged parents have been living with a son as members of his
family, having all their wants supplied by him, an agreement to
pay for services rendered by the father during that time should be
clearly shown in order to charge the estate of the son with a claim
for such services. *Bostwick v. Estate of Bostwick*,   273

PARTNERSHIP.

See FRAUDULENT REPRESENTATIONS.

S. and M. owned jointly a distillery. Without the knowledge of S.
M. entered into partnership with the plaintiffs and furnished as
his capital in the firm the said distillery for the use of the firm,
and the agreed value thereof was entered as his capital on the
partnership books. Afterwards S. assented to the agreement so
made by M., and also gave his consent to the United States authorities that the property should be used by the firm for the purposes
of a distillery, and subjected it to all claims of the government
which might grow out of such use. The firm thereafter paid the
taxes and insurance upon the property. S. was refused admittance
to the firm, but M. agreed to divide with him his share of the profits of the partnership business. The business of the firm was unprofitable and was closed up. *Held:*
(1) S. was not a partner in the firm so as to render him personally liable to the members thereof for any part of the losses.
(2) As against S. the entire beneficial ownership of the distillery

property must be deemed to have been in M. when he contributed it for the use of the firm and as his capital therein, and it was therefore firm property and is subject to the payment of the share of the losses chargeable to M. *Riedeburg v. Schmitt*, 644

PATENTS.
Upon inventions. See CONTRACTS, 7,
Of land. See EJECTMENT, 2, 3.

PAYMENT.

See FRAUDULENT CONVEYANCES, 1.

Upon the evidence in this case (stated in the opinion) it is *held* that a certain payment to the plaintiff, claimed to have been made by check payable to him or bearer, was in fact made. *Thorn v. Smith*, 18

PENALTY for failure to file statement, etc. See INSURANCE, 1.

PERSONAL PROPERTY. See BILLS AND NOTES. CHATTEL MORTGAGES. CONTRACTS, 5-7. DEED. EQUITY, 1, 8. EVIDENCE, 12. EXECUTION, 1, 4. FRAUDULENT CONVEYANCES. INSTRUCTIONS TO JURY, 4-7. JUSTICES' COURTS. MUNICIPAL BONDS. NEGLIGENCE. PLEADING, 3. RAILROADS, 1-5. REPLEVIN. SALE OF CHATTELS. VOLUNTARY ASSIGNMENT. 8. WASTE, 1.

PERVERSE VERDICT. See FRAUDULENT CONVEYANCES, 4.

PLACE OF TRIAL. See CHANGE OF VENUE. MANDAMUS, 3.

PLATTEVILLE CITY CHARTER. See MUNICIPAL CORPORATIONS, 5.

PLEADING.

See APPEAL, 7. CRIMINAL LAW, 5, 9, 10. EQUITY, 2. 8. EVIDENCE, 4. INSURANCE, 1. MANDAMUS, 1, 2. MORTGAGES, 8. MUNICIPAL CORPORATIONS, 8, 9. PRACTICE, 1. SALE OF CHATTELS, 1, 2. SLANDER, 1. SUFFRAGE, 4.

1. Where a counterclaim states the main facts which would constitute an affirmative cause of action, but does not definitely state the nature of the damages sustained, the remedy is by motion and not by demurrer. *Schweickhart v. Stuewe*, 1

2. In an action by an attorney to recover for professional services, the defendant denied that a part of the services were performed for him, and omitted to set up a payment which had been made for them. After introducing evidence of such payment he moved to amend his answer so as to allege that if it should be found that the services in question were performed for him then the said payment therefor had been made to and received by the plaintiff. The motion was denied. *Held*, that the defendant should have been allowed to so amend his answer as to obtain credit for the payment, and that the hypothetical form of the proposed amendment was not objectionable. *Thorn v. Smith*, 18

3. In an action upon a contract for the sale and delivery of chattels, where the complaint alleges that the defendant refused to deliver the property, to the damage of the plaintiff in a certain sum, it need not further allege the price or value of the property at the time and place of delivery, or that the plaintiff could have resold the same at a profit. *Conover v. Manke*, 108

RAILROADS.

Carriers.

REFERENCE.

1. Though an order denying a reference is absolute in its terms, the court may at any time during the same term vacate it and grant a reference. *Turner v. Nachtsheim,* · 16

2. An account which contains some twenty charges for different kinds of service, rendered at different times during a period of several months, is a "long account," within the meaning of sec. 2864, R. S. *Ibid.*

3. An action to recover a balance claimed to be due upon a building contract and for extra work and materials, but which, it is alleged, has been fraudulently disallowed by the superintendent — who, by the terms of the contract, was constituted sole arbitrator to determine conclusively all matters pertaining to the contract, including the amount to be allowed for extra work and materials,— is an action *ex contractu,* and if it involves the examination of a long account all the issues therein, including that of fraud, may be referred in the discretion of the trial court. *Littlejohn v. Regents of University,* · 487

REFORMATION of written instrument. See INSTRUCTIONS TO JURY, 4. MORTGAGES, 2.

RELEASE. See EQUITY, 4. FRAUDULENT REPRESENTATIONS, 1 (3). MORTGAGES, 2. SURETYSHIP.

REMOVAL of cause. See JUSTICES' COURTS.

REPLEVIN.

See DEED.

1. The verdict and judgment in replevin must determine the right to the possession of all the property involved, even though a part thereof was not taken from the defendant and the answer did not claim a return of the property. *Carrier v. Carrier,* 111

2. Where the judgment in replevin is for the recovery of five of six horses and one of two wagons claimed, a failure sufficiently to identify those not recovered is probably sufficient ground for a reversal. *Ibid.*

3. Cattle in the possession of a constable under an attachment were replevied by the owner. After the constable had given an undertaking which entitled him to have the cattle returned to him, the replevin suit was dismissed, but the cattle were never actually returned to the possession of the constable, and he afterwards disclaimed such possession and refused to accept the delivery of the cattle upon any condition. *Held,* that the owner could not maintain a second action of replevin against the constable. *McHugh v. Robinson,* 565

RESTRAINT of trade. See CONTRACTS, 7.

RETURN of sheriff. See EXECUTION, 4, 5.

RETURN to alternative writ. See MANDAMUS, 2.

REVOCATION of license. See MINES AND MINING, 2.

REVERSAL OF JUDGMENT. See JUDGMENT, *Reversal.*

RIOT. See CRIMINAL LAW, 10, 11.

RIPON MUNICIPAL COURT. See JURISDICTION.

SERVICE OF SUMMONS.

See JUDGMENT, 8.

1. Where the proof of service by a person other than the. sheriff does not show that a copy of the summons was *left with*, as well as delivered to, the defendant (sec. 2642, R. S.), the court acquires no jurisdiction to render judgment by default. *Wilkinson v. Bayley*, 131

2. Leaving a summons with defendant's foreman and informing him of the contents thereof, where such foreman is not a member of defendant's family nor at his usual place of abode, is not a valid service under subd. 4, sec. 2636, R. S. *McConkey v. McCraney*, 576

SHERIFF. See INSTRUCTIONS TO JURY, 5.

SIDEWALKS. See MUNICIPAL CORPORATIONS, 3, 4, 11, 12, 16. PLEADING, 4.

SLANDER.

1. In an action for slander the complaint alleged that the defendant falsely and maliciously spoke of the plaintiff, an election inspector, the following words: "He counted four votes which were cast for E., for B., for sheriff. . . . It is true; there is no doubt about it. There was a man standing looking right over [plaintiff's] shoulder, and saw him do it. It is a swindle;" and that the defendant thereby falsely and maliciously charged the plaintiff with having knowingly violated the provisions of the law governing the duties of inspectors of election. *Held*, that the language used might fairly be construed as charging a wilful and fraudulent miscount, not a mere mistake, and that the complaint therefore stated a cause of action. *Ellsworth v. Hayes*, 427

2. In such a case, there being no evidence which would justify the jury in finding that the defendant honestly and in good faith made such statements for the purpose of having a recount of the votes under the provisions of ch. 464, Laws of 1885, instructions to the effect that if they were made for such purpose, without malice, the plaintiff cannot recover, were properly refused. *Ibid.*

STATUTE OF FRAUDS. See FRAUDULENT CONVEYANCES. INSTRUCTIONS TO JURY, 7. SALE OF CHATTELS, 3.

STATUTE OF LIMITATIONS. See EJECTMENT, 4. LIMITATION OF ACTIONS.

STATUTES.
Constitutionality. See CRIMINAL LAW, 4. EJECTMENT, 1. HIGHWAYS. RAILROADS, 6. SUFFRAGE. 1.
Construction. See BRIDGES, 1, 3. CHANGE OF VENUE. CRIMINAL LAW, 3, 4, 10. DRAINS, 1, 3. EJECTMENT, 1. 6. EQUITY, 7. ESTATES OF DECEDENTS. EXCISE LAWS. EXECUTION, 1. HIGHWAYS, 1, 4. INSTRUCTIONS TO JURY, 7. INSURANCE, 1, 2, 4, 6, 8. JUDGMENT, 8. JUSTICES' COURTS. LIMITATION OF ACTIONS. MANDAMUS, 3. MINES AND MINING, 2. MORTGAGES, 5-7. MUNICIPAL CORPORATIONS, 1-3, 5, 7, 10, 11, 13, 14, 16. PRACTICE, 2. RAILROADS, 6. REFERENCE, 2, 3. SERVICE OF SUMMONS. SUFFRAGE, 1, 2. SURVIVAL OF ACTIONS. TAXATION, 1, 4. TAX TITLES. TELEGRAPH COMPANIES. VOLUNTARY ASSIGNMENT, 2, 4.

STATUTES CITED, ETC.

STATUTES CITED, ETC.— con.

STIPULATION. See NEW TRIAL, 2.

STOCK, Transfer of. See EQUITY, 8.

STREET RAILWAYS.

1. Plaintiff, in attempting to get on a moving street-car, fell, and was dragged by the car some distance before the car stopped. It was in the winter, snowing, and the car was on a down grade. The testimony of the driver that he set the brakes and held the horses back as soon as he heard the signal to stop, and that the car slid on the track, was contradicted by several witnesses. There was evidence that in winter, when the track was slippery, the cars would slide on the track at that place with the brakes set. *Held*, that a charge that it must be taken as established in the case that cars would, in the winter, on the down grade, slide on the track

with the brakes set, and be beyond the control of the driver, was misleading as making no qualification as to the state of the track, and conveying the idea that the fact was established that the cars did slide on the occasion in question. *Woodard v. West Side St. R. Co.* 625

2. Where plaintiff, in attempting to get on a moving street-car, fell, and was dragged some 160 feet before the car stopped, he would be entitled to recover, even though guilty of negligence in attempting to get on a moving car, if the driver could have avoided the injury by the exercise of reasonable care in stopping the car after he was notified that plaintiff had fallen and was being dragged by the car. *Ibid.*

STREETS. See MUNICIPAL CORPORATIONS, 1, 10–15. RAILROADS, 7.

SUFFRAGE.

See ELECTIONS.

1. Under sec. 1, art. III, Const., the legislature may, by law approved by the people as therein prescribed, extend the right of suffrage to women. *Brown v. Phillips,* 289

2. An "election pertaining to school matters," within the meaning of ch. 211, Laws of 1885 (which gives to women the right to vote at such elections), is an election for the choosing of school officers or school employees. The mere fact that a city, county, or state officer, as incident to his office, is required to do some act which may affect schools (as where a mayor appoints school commissioners), does not make the election of such officer one pertaining to school matters. *Ibid.*

3. *It would seem* that where school officers and other officers are required to be voted for upon the same ballot, the inspectors of election are not authorized to receive the votes of women even for such school officers. *Ibid.*

4. In an action against inspectors of election for refusing to receive the vote of a woman, allegations of the complaint that the plaintiff "was a legally qualified elector . . . and was entitled to vote at such election," are held to be mere conclusions of law and not to be admitted by a demurrer. *Ibid.*

SUMMONS. See SERVICE OF SUMMONS.

SUNDAY. See EXCISE LAWS. VOLUNTARY ASSIGNMENT, 5.

SUPREME COURT. See APPEAL. CRIMINAL LAW, 1, 4.

SURETYSHIP.

The release of the principal debtor without the consent of the surety and without payment of the debt, does not release the surety if he is fully indemnified against loss by reason of having become such. *Jones v. Ward,* 152

SURVIVAL OF ACTIONS.

Whether the words "or other damage to the person" in sec. 4253, R. S., as amended by ch. 280, Laws of 1887 (relating to the survival of actions), should be construed to mean damage resulting from force, not determined. *Hiner v. Fond du Lac,* 74

TAXATION.

See APPEAL, 4. BRIDGES, 2, 3. ESTOPPEL, 1. MUNICIPAL CORPORATIONS, 13, 14. TAX TITLES.

1. By sec. 1, ch. 21, Laws of 1877, the time during which the lands in question were exempted from taxation was "*extended* three years." *Held*, that the three years began to run from the termination of the original exemption, and not from the date when the act of 1877 took effect. *Wis. Cent. R. Co. v. Comstock,*　　88

2. When lands granted to aid in the construction of a railroad have been fully earned, and the company is entitled to a patent therefor, they are taxable by the state although the patent has not in fact been issued.　　　　　.　　　　　*Ibid.*

3. A military bounty land warrant was located on certain lands by one W. in 1857, and the usual certificate of such location was issued. In the same year the commissioner of pensions notified the commissioner of the general land office that said warrant and its assignment to W. were impeached as forgeries, and requested that the patent be withheld. The request was complied with, and no further action was taken until in June, 1868, when the commissioner of pensions assumed to cancel the warrant. The commissioner of the land office acquiesced in such cancellation, and withheld the patent until 1882, when, it having been decided by the secretary of the interior that the cancellation of the warrant was unauthorized, he caused the patent to be issued to W. The lands were sold in May, 1863, for nonpayment of the taxes assessed thereon in 1862. *Held,* that from the location of the warrant in 1857 until the tax sale in 1863 the entire equitable title to, and beneficial interest in, the land was in W., and hence that the land was taxable in 1862. *Calder v. Keegan,* 30 Wis. 127, distinguished. *Farnham v. Sherry,*　　　　　　568

4. Under ch. 105, Laws of 1861, providing that where entries of land had been suspended such lands should not be subject to taxation until such suspension was removed, the filing of a certificate of such suspension, as provided in sec. 8 of the act, was a condition precedent to the right of the owner to claim the benefit of the exemption.　　　　　　*Ibid.*

TAXATION of costs. See APPEAL, 2.

TAX TITLES.

See EJECTMENT, 1, 2, 6. ESTOPPEL, 1. TAXATION.

An affidavit by the county treasurer of the posting of the notices of a tax sale, which states that "he did, in accordance with ch. 1130, R. S., post notices in four public places in said county," etc., but does not state when or where such notices were posted, or that any notice was posted in his office, is insufficient. *Wis. Cent. R. Co. v. Wis. R. Land Co.*　　　94

TELEGRAPH COMPANIES.

1. Ch. 171, Laws of 1885, renders telegraph companies liable for the damages resulting directly from their negligence in the matter of transmitting messages, especially where their agents are acquainted with the contents and significance of such messages. *Cutts v. Western Union Tel. Co.*　　　46

2. In an action to recover damages for the delay in the transmission of a telegram, unless the special injury claimed is shown to have resulted from such delay, only the amount paid for the transmission can be recovered.   *Ibid.*

TENANTS in common. See MINES AND MINING.

TERMS of court. See MANDAMUS, 3.

TITLE to land. See BOUNDARIES. DEED. EJECTMENT. EQUITY, 6, 7. EVIDENCE, 7-9. JUSTICES' COURTS. MILLS AND MILL DAMS, 1. MORTGAGES, 1-4. PARTNERSHIP. TAXATION, 2-4. TAX TITLES.

TORTS. See DAMAGES, 1-3. DEED. EVIDENCE, 7. FRAUDULENT REPRESENTATIONS. INSTRUCTIONS TO JURY, 5. JUSTICES' COURTS. MASTER AND SERVANT, 1-3. MILLS AND MILL DAMS. MUNICIPAL CORPORATIONS, 1-4, 11, 12, 15, 16. NEGLIGENCE. RAILROADS, 6-8. REFERENCE, 3. REPLEVIN. SLANDER. STREET RAILWAYS. SURVIVAL OF ACTIONS. TELEGRAPH COMPANIES. WASTE.

TOWN INSURANCE COMPANIES. See INSURANCE, 2.

TOWNS,

See BRIDGES. DRAINS.

An action upon a demand alleged to be due a town was brought by, and judgment for costs therein was rendered against, "G. W. P., F. R. U., and H. H., supervisors of the" said town. *Held,* that the judgment was not a personal judgment against the persons named, but was against the town and could be enforced only in the manner prescribed by sec. 781, R. S. *Prichard v. Bixby,* 422

TRIAL, Place of. See CHANGE OF VENUE. MANDAMUS, 3.

TRUST DEED. See MORTGAGES, 1.

TRUSTS AND TRUSTEES. See EQUITY, 7. MORTGAGES, 1.

ULTRA VIRES. See MUNICIPAL CORPORATIONS, 5-7.

UNCERTAINTY. See PLEADING, 1. REPLEVIN, 2.

UNCHASTITY. See DAMAGES, 1, 2.

UNLAWFUL ASSEMBLY. See CRIMINAL LAW, 10.

VARIANCE. See MANDAMUS, 1. PRACTICE, 1.

VENDOR AND PURCHASER OF LAND.

See CONTRACTS, 4. DEED. EJECTMENT, 4, 5. WASTE.

1. Though a deed conveying land contains only the usual covenants, a warranty as to the *quality* of the land, which was a part of the prior or contemporaneous agreement of sale, may be shown by parol; and damages for a breach of such warranty may be recouped in an action by the grantor upon a note given for a part of the purchase price. *Green v. Batson,*   54

2. The plaintiff's husband had offered to sell her interest in certain land to the defendant (her brother) for $4,000 if taken at once, but the defendant had refused to give more than $3,500. The plaintiff denied having authorized such offer, and there was no evidence to show that she even knew of it. Afterwards, having made a contract to sell at a large advance, the defendant obtained a quitclaim deed from the plaintiff, paying her $4,000. The plaintiff claims that

when the deed was given the defendant further agreed to pay her whatever he should obtain above $4,000 for her interest. The defendant denies having made such agreement, and claims to have purchased her interest absolutely. It is *held* that, in determining what the terms of the sale were, the trial court gave undue weight to the previous unauthorized offer by the plaintiff's husband, and that, upon the evidence (stated in the opinion), the contract was as claimed by the plaintiff. *Lamar v. Scales,* 159

VENUE. See CHANGE OF VENUE.

VERDICT. See APPEAL, 14. CRIMINAL LAW, 1. DAMAGES, 1-3, 6. EJECTMENT, 6. FRAUDULENT CONVEYANCES, 4. NEW TRIAL. REPLEVIN, 1.

VOLUNTARY ASSIGNMENT.

See EQUITY, 1.

1. An assignment of property, made pursuant to a bankrupt act, the assignee being in effect an officer of the court, and the assigned property being *in custodia legis* and administered by or under the direction of the court, can have no legal operation out of the state in which such proceedings were had. *McClure v. Campbell,* 850

2. The decisions of the supreme court of Minnesota that ch. 148, Gen, Laws Minn. 1881, is a bankrupt act and that the assignee is in effect an officer of the court and the assigned property *in custodia legis,* are *held* binding upon this court. *Ibid.*

[3. Whether a voluntary assignment for the benefit of creditors, executed in Minnesota by a resident of that state pursuant to ch. 41, Gen. Stats. of Minn., would pass to the assignee title to personal property named in such assignment having a *situs* in this state, not determined.] *Ibid.*

4. The sureties upon the bond of an assignee for the benefit of creditors failed to justify as the statute requires, and the court commissioner omitted to indorse upon the bond and copy of the assignment the proper certificates. The bond was not left with the court commissioner, but was filed with the clerk of the circuit court by some other person. Afterwards the bond was withdrawn and redelivered to the assignee, and was then perfected, and the perfected bond, with a copy of the assignment, with the proper indorsements, was again filed with the clerk, three days after the first filing, and before the rights of any creditors had intervened. *Held,* that the failure to comply with the statute in the first instance should not avoid the assignment, notwithstanding sec. 1695, R. S., requires that the bond shall, "*immediately* after its execution," be filed, etc. *Farwell v. Webster,* 485

5. A voluntary assignment duly executed and delivered by one of two partners on a secular day is not invalidated by the fact that the other partner signed it on Sunday. *Ibid.*

WAIVER.
Of right to appeal from judgment. See APPEAL, 4.
Of trial *de novo.* See APPEAL, 14.
Of forfeiture. See INSURANCE, 5.
Of objection that complaint does not state equitable cause of action. See PLEADING, 5.
Of objection to allowance of amendment. See PLEADING, 6.
Of objection to improper remarks of counsel. See PRACTICE, 1.

WARRANTY. See VENDOR, ETC. OF LAND, 1.